REPAIRING THE PAST?

SERIES ON TRANSITIONAL JUSTICE

Background

Countries emerging from long periods of authoritarian rule must often confront a legacy of gross human rights abuses perpetrated over many years. During the past two decades, these age-old issues have been termed "problems of transitional justice", both by academics and policy makers around the world. Given the many experiences and the many issues involved in periods of political transitions and after violent conflicts, it is striking that no book series has taken these issues as their focal point. The new Series on Transitional Justice, published by Intersentia Publishers in Antwerp, Belgium, aims to fill this gap in international research and practice.

Mission

The *Series on Transitional Justice* offers a platform for high-quality research within the rapidly growing field of transitional justice. The research will, of necessity, be inter-disciplinary in nature, drawing from disciplines such as law, political science, history, sociology, criminology, anthropology and psychology, as well as from various specialised fields of study such as human rights, victimology and peace studies. Furthermore, the research will be international in outlook, drawing on the knowledge and experience of academics and other specialists in many different regions of the world.

The series is aimed at a variety of audiences, including senior and junior academic teachers, researchers and students, national and international organisations, policy-makers and practitioners, non-governmental organisations and the media, working in the fields of crime and justice, human rights, humanitarian law and human security, conflict resolution and peace-building.

Structure

The *General Editors* of the new series are Stephan Parmentier, Catholic University of Leuven (sociology of law, criminology, human rights), Jeremy Sarkin, University of the Western Cape (law, human rights, transitional justice) and Elmar G.M. Weitekamp, University of Tübingen (criminology, victimology, restorative justice). All three have substantial experience in the field over many years.

They receive support from an *Editorial Committee* and an *Advisory Board*, consisting of internationally renowned researchers, which strengthens the scientific and international character of the series. There is also a complete review process by national and foreign experts of all manuscripts submitted.

More information can be found on the website: www.intersentia.com.

Contact

- Stephan Parmentier: stephan.parmentier@law.kuleuven.be
- Jeremy Sarkin: jsarkin@global.co.za
- Elmar G.M. Weitekamp: elmar.weitekamp@uni-tuebingen.de

SERIES ON TRANSITIONAL JUSTICE, Volume 1

REPAIRING THE PAST?

International Perspectives on Reparations for Gross Human Rights Abuses

Edited by
Max du Plessis and
Stephen Peté

intersentia
Antwerpen – Oxford

Distribution for the UK:
Hart Publishing Ltd.
16C Worcester Place
Oxford OX1 2JW
UK
Tel: + 44 1865 51 75 30
Fax: + 44 1865 51 07 10

Distribution for Switzerland and Germany:
Schulthess Verlag
Zwingliplatz 2
CH-8022 Zürich
Switzerland
Tel: + 41 1 251 93 36
Fax: + 41 1 261 63 94

Distribution for North America:
Gaunt Inc.
Gaunt Building
3011 Gulf Drive
Holmes Beach
Florida 34217-2199
USA
Tel: + 1 941 778 5211
Fax: + 1 941 778 5252

Distribution for other countries:
Intersentia
Groenstraat 31
BE-2640 Mortsel
Belgium
Tel: + 32 3 680 15 50
Fax: + 32 3 658 71 21

Repairing the Past? International perspectives on reparations for gross human rights abuses
Edited by Max du Plessis and Stephen Peté

Artwork on cover: Author Jan Jordaan, title 'Hurt', medium Linocut, 1999. From the *Universal Declaration of Human Rights – International Print Portfolio, Article 5*, published by Art for Humanity, South Africa, 1999.

ISBN 978-90-5095-492-1
D/2007/7849/19
NUR 828

PREFACE

In our introductory chapter to this work we state that, if this book has a heart, it lies in the recognition of the fact that both ancient and recent human history is littered with examples of widespread and gross violations of human rights. Appalling violations of fundamental human rights continue to be perpetrated in the present day. Despite the enduring and widespread nature of gross human rights violations, however, it is an unfortunate fact that, of the millions of people whose lives have been shattered by torture, rape, the murder of loved ones, or other gross violations of their human rights, only a tiny fraction have any hope of receiving any meaningful form of reparation.

This book may be regarded as a single modest attempt to address the problem outlined above. It is our hope that the individual chapters contained in this book will stimulate debate on the issue of reparations, and that this debate will lead to increased visibility for the many deserving groups striving for some form of meaningful recognition or recompense for past injustices visited upon them.

We do not claim that this book covers the field of reparations in a comprehensive or systematic way. Rather, it is eclectic in nature, due to the diverse areas of interest and expertise of the various contributing authors. Therefore, it should be regarded as a work designed to stimulate debate on a number of themes pertinent to the important topic of reparations, rather than as a text book which sets out to describe an entire field of study. The book is intended for practitioners and other human rights experts who are engaged in the struggle for reparations for gross human rights abuses.

This is a truly international work. As editors we are grateful to have collaborated with a range of outstanding academics and practitioners from around the world, whose individual chapters form the fabric of the book. We have not sought to sensor the, at times robust, political and legal opinions of the various authors, but point out that the views and opinions expressed by the authors are not necessarily those of the editors of this book. Our heartfelt thanks are due to each of the authors. Their hard work and dedication enabled us to meet most of our publication deadlines, producing a book which we hope will contribute to a growing understanding internationally of the importance of reparations for gross human rights abuses.

The management and staff at Intersentia Press have shown unstinting support for this project throughout its long gestation and deserve our sincere thanks. In particular, we wish to thank our managing editor, Kris Moeremans, who steered the project from its inception to final completion, as well as Isabelle Van Dongen, who diligently prepared the final proofs for publication. We also wish to thank Mr Jolyon Ford, of the Human Rights Unit, Commonwealth Secretariat, and Ms Yasmin Sooka, of the Foundation for Human Rights, for peer reviewing the book prior to its publication.

Max du Plessis
Stephen Peté
Durban
December 2006

FOREWORD

YASMIN SOOKA – FORMER COMMISSIONER OF THE SOUTH AFRICAN TRUTH AND RECONCILIATION COMMISSION

'Repairing the Past? International Perspectives on Reparations for Gross Human Rights Abuses', is a timely work which provides a comprehensive overview of the development of reparations, documenting the experiences of victim/ survivor groups in their attempts to secure justice for gross violations of human rights.

In their introductory chapter, entitled 'Reparations for Gross Violations of Human Rights in Context', Max du Plessis and Stephen Peté set out the history of mass killings of civilians and genocide that have taken place in the last century, beginning with the genocide of the Herero people in Namibia by the German Colonial forces and ending with the current genocide that is taking place in Darfur in Sudan. While international law has developed, leading to the recent establishment of the International Criminal Court, which was designed to hold those responsible for gross violations accountable, the international community has been unable to stop the ongoing violence and killing of civilians in Darfur, making a mockery of the notion that 'it should never happen again'.

I believe that the most important components of transitional justice must be the rights of victims, which include the right to the truth, the right to acknowledgement, the right to reparations and the obligation to take steps to ensure that the violations will not occur again. In this way impunity will be addressed, provided that the structural causes of the conflict are comprehensively dealt with. Let us never forget that impunity gives rise to gross violations of human rights.

In theory, the right to reparation is an established right under international law with the earliest examples of reparation arising in the context of wrongs committed by states against states. However, the notion that individuals should be entitled to hold their own governments, corporations or other citizens accountable did not occur to those in power until after the end of the Second World War. The chapter on the history of the holocaust reparations written by Regula Ludi outlines the historical origins of individual reparation mechanisms. Ludi points out that the rights of individuals to redress for state crimes was first recognised in a legal document drafted at the Paris Reparation Conference of 1945. For victims and human rights advocates who had lobbied around this issue, this marked a turning point.

The development of reparation principles and the attempt to establish reparations as a right under international law really came into its own through the appointment by the United Nations of the Special Rapporteurs, Mr Theo van Boven and Mr M. Cherif Bassiouni to work on reparations.

Sadly, the 'Basic Principles' developed by Van Boven and Bassiouni, including the right to reparations, are still an arena of struggle for victims of violations in many countries emerging from conflict, particularly in the last decade.

Often, the development and reconstruction needs of an entire society compete with the rights of victims of gross violations to reparation. In these instances, governments have always found it easy to argue that the needs of the entire society take precedence over a group of victims. A further challenge has been that often successor governments resent the fact that they have to bear the financial burden of dealing with reparations, particularly when the violations were committed by previous rogue regimes.

Ideally, everybody whose rights have been violated should be entitled to reparations. In the opening chapter Max du Plessis and Stephen Peté argue that even if one were to take the word 'reparation' and restrict it to the definition that is widely accepted in international law, it includes diverse measures. They raise the fact that given the broad socio-political context to reparation, debate has raged over whether reparation includes measures such as affirmative action, relief aid provided by developed nations to former colonies, the establishment of truth and reconciliation commissions, as well as whether hearing the 'truth' is sufficient to constitute reparation in itself. Having had first hand experience of working with many diverse victim communities around the world, I am able to attest to the fact that reparations remains a complex issue.

Du Plessis and Peté point out that an even more difficult question to answer is whether or not a particular series of events should qualify as a 'gross abuse of human rights'. They point out that two broad sub-issues present themselves: 'when is 'gross' gross enough' and 'when is 'the past' too long ago'. The first question is difficult to answer and all countries emerging from conflict have had to grapple with it. In South Africa, the mandate of the Truth Commission was limited. The term 'gross violations of human rights' was expressly and narrowly confined to 'killings, abductions, torture and severe ill treatment'. There is no doubt that the Commission interpreted its mandate narrowly giving rise to criticism of its approach by many commentators. Mahmood Mamdani argues that this narrow interpretation of gross violations of human rights led ultimately to a 'diminished truth' which let the beneficiaries of apartheid off the hook. In my work in many countries, I have certainly found Van Boven's proposals on the categories of crimes to which attention should be paid, to be very helpful. His categories include 'genocide, slavery and slavery like practices, summary or arbitrary executions, torture and cruel, inhuman or degrading treatment or punishment, enforced disappearances, arbitrary and prolonged detention, deportation or forcible transfer of population and systematic discrimination, particularly based on race or gender.' One has to adopt a pragmatic view of what is possible in order to avoid raising expectations or making false promises which are often not capable of being fulfilled. Du Plessis and Peté point out that another useful reference-point is the International Criminal Court's codification of what constitutes 'crimes against humanity'. An important point they make is that there is a need to be vigilant about downplaying or diminishing human rights violations; as they assert the right of every victim of an egregious human rights abuse as being worthy of reparation.

Bo Jung Kwon brings a gendered dimension to this debate. She highlights the struggle for justice and redress that has been waged by the 'comfort women' taken by Japanese troops from occupied territories. The situation of the 'comfort women' reveals the complexity of issues concerned with reparations and illustrates the fact that compensation without an official acknowledgement of wrongdoing is inadequate. In her fascinating chapter, Kwon details how the Japanese government's establishment of the 'Asian Women's Fund' in 1995 was harshly critiqued by the women and their governments and was seen as an attempt to evade responsibility for the violations that had been committed against the women. While various ad hoc tribunals and Truth Commissions around the world have advanced the rights of women to deal with crimes such as these, it has not been an easy road to travel to achieve justice. Judge Hideaki's finding in the face of hostile opinion in Japan that the Japanese Diet should have initiated legislation to address the women's suffering, after it admitted in 1993 that it had been involved in the 'comfort women' system, was the first official finding on this issue from any official body in Japan. His finding that an apology by the Japanese government was not necessary as the Constitution did not provide for it was, however, disappointing. Archbishop Desmond Tutu of South Africa has always made the point that one should not underestimate the value of an apology.

Another issue that has given rise to debate is the accountability of non-state actors, particularly trans-national companies, which may be complicit in conflict, or at the very least are shown to benefit financially from conflict. While globalisation has created new opportunities for trans-national corporations to trade anywhere in the world, holding them accountable for violations and obliging them to provide reparations has been difficult. Finding an appropriate forum to deal with these entities has in itself proved to be a major obstacle. Michael Osborne describes the attempt by South African victims to hold multi-nationals accountable under America's Aliens Tort Claims law as one of the most ambitious attempts to use this legislation to obtain justice. Archbishop Tutu, who supported the claims of the South African victims, argued that 'the only way to ensure that business will not support and sustain regimes that are responsible for gross human rights violations in the future is to make it known that such conduct will not ultimately be profitable. This, of course, is one larger purpose, as we understand it, of this litigation'. His message was clear: 'that supporting regimes inflicting gross human rights violations on its people is ultimately unprofitable. We have little doubt that apartheid would not have occurred as it did without the active and knowing support of certain businesses. The continuation of this litigation comports with this greater purpose of South Africa's post-apartheid era, and by giving voice to those harmed by multinational corporations aiding and abetting apartheid it assists the healing and reconciliation process'.

Another issue raised by du Plessis and Peté is: 'Should there be a time limit which prohibits reparations being claimed for violations, however gross, which took place in the distant past?' They ask an important question: 'Are certain past human rights abuses (such as the Slave Trade) so egregious that they will continue to haunt the present unless they are addressed by some sort of reparation?' In recent years, the depredations of slavery, colonialism and the claims by indigenous peoples to ancestral land have demonstrated the hypocrisy of the powerful when confronted by such claims for reparation. Roy L. Brooks and Diane Sammons illustrate the contradictions and legal problems encountered by such claims. They point out that these claims have often been time barred but that they remain a poignant reminder of the suffering of human beings which should be the subject of reparations.

Finally there is always hope, as is demonstrated by the commitment of the Canadian government to pay more than two million Canadian dollars to First Nation children who were abused while in government controlled residential schools. Ken Cooper-Stephenson documents the road that has been walked by the First Nations of Canada in dealing with this bitter aspect of Canadian history. The historic accord reached on November 20, 2005 between the Government of Canada, the Assembly of First Nations and the Churches on reconciliation and compensation, is a victory for victims all over the world. The position of the Canadian government is in direct contrast to the apparent indifference displayed by other governments to the claims of aboriginal peoples and other abused citizens.

There has to be explicit acknowledgement that the marginalisation and dehumanisation of indigenous peoples, which serves to justify the theft of their land, cannot co-exist with respect for human rights.

It is only by looking its own past directly in the eye, acknowledging failings which have resulted in gross violations of human rights, and addressing injustices which have occurred, that a society is able to move forward. Failure to do so will result in the past returning to haunt the present and the future being rooted in a morass of injustice characterised by disputed national narratives.

'Repairing the Past? International Perspectives on Reparations for Gross Human Rights Abuses' is an important guide for lawyers, judges, academics, and human rights practitioners as well as for victims and survivors. It provides a theoretical framework as well as a practical guide based on empirical studies, for dealing with a complex issue that straddles legal and moral boundaries.

TABLE OF CONTENTS

REPARATIONS UNDER INTERNATIONAL CRIMINAL LAW

REPARATIONS FOR GROSS HUMAN RIGHTS VIOLATIONS IN AFRICA – THE GREAT LAKES

PART C: REPARATIONS CLAIMS PURSUED ABROAD

APARTHEID AND THE ALIEN TORTS ACT: GLOBAL JUSTICE MEETS SOVEREIGN EQUALITY

PART D: REPARATIONS CLAIMS PURSUED AT HOME

PART A:
THEORETICAL ISSUES – OF SCALE AND COMPLEXITY

REPARATIONS FOR GROSS VIOLATIONS OF HUMAN RIGHTS IN CONTEXT

STEPHEN PETÉ and MAX DU PLESSIS

1 THE MAGNITUDE AND MULTITUDE OF GROSS HUMAN RIGHTS ABUSES

This book must start with a confession and an apology.

First the confession. A work such as this is not able to do justice to a topic as broad as that set out in the title i.e. reparations for gross human rights abuses. The main focus of this book, the central shocking social fact which gives rise to all the nuanced legal and political debates discussed in this work, is that human beings are capable of treating other human beings with unspeakable cruelty. If this book has a heart, it lies in the recognition of the fact that both ancient and recent human history is littered with examples of widespread and gross violations of human rights. These violations, serious outrages to humanity, continue in places such as Darfur in the Sudan, the Democratic Republic of the Congo, and Iraq, even as this work is being written. The sheer extent of the past and present abuses of human rights makes it impossible for the topic of reparations for such abuses to be dealt with in one short book.

Then the apology. This book is an eclectic mix of perspectives, dealing with a range of specific widespread abuses, which occurred at different times in various parts of the world. Because of the nature of the book, it deals with gross human rights abuses in a highly selective and somewhat arbitrary manner. And because this work deals selectively with only a small fraction of the wide range of gross human rights abuses which have taken place during the relatively recent past it is appropriate that an apology be offered at this early stage of the book. The reader should not lose sight of the broader picture of human suffering captured in the phrase 'gross human rights abuses'. As Michael Osborne (whose chapter on reparations for apartheid is included in this book at pages 231-293) writes: 'Fundamental human rights continue to be violated with impunity almost everywhere. The human rights revolution is not just unfinished. In a sense, it has yet to attain material reality'. For this reason, in order to situate this work within the wider context of human suffering which gives rise to the specific debates raised and analysed in the book, it is important to acknowledge the scale of the more serious violations of human rights that have marked the recent past, starting at the beginning of the twentieth century.

The twentieth century was characterised by industrialised killing and genocide, which occurred on a massive scale and in various parts of the world throughout this period. Apart from the mass killings, totalitarian political regimes subjected their citizens to severe oppression, targeting political opponents and cowing ordinary people into submission, while implementing unjust, racist and/or discriminatory political policies. It is impossible to list all the events which took place during the twentieth century which may be classified as a gross abuse of human rights, but certain of the most serious abuses may be mentioned.

The birth of the twentieth century was marked by what many would call a genocide in the South West part of Africa, now known as Namibia. This was the mass slaughter which took place in 1904-5 of some 60,000 of the Herero people by German colonial forces. This mass killing has all but been forgotten, except by the descendents of those who were killed, and is analysed by Sid Harring in his contribution to this book.

Ten years after the mass killing of the Herero, another genocide took place, this time in Armenia carried out by Turkish forces. Over a million Armenians were killed in what has been described as 'the first of the modern ideologically motivated genocides', but to this day the Turkish state refuses to accept responsibility for what took place.[1]

After the industrialised killing which took place during the First World War further mass killings, this time of civilians, were to follow. Joseph Stalin, who ruled over the Soviet Union from 1924 onward, presided over one of the most genocidal regimes of the twentieth century. Martin Shaw summarises the horrors perpetrated by Joseph Stalin and his regime as follows:

> "The landmark in the development of Stalin's terror was the violent campaign known as the 'liquidation of the kulaks' at the beginning of the 1930s... Through mass killings and deportations, the peasantry was destroyed as a class with a capacity for resistance, and agricultural production declined. At the same time, Stalin exported food from the main agricultural areas, compounding the peasants' defeat with a terrible state-made famine in 1932-3... It is estimated that at least ten million people died. Millions more were forced into the industrializing cities as well as the rapidly enlarged labour camp system... Stalin killed his own citizens on a scale comparable to the Nazis. His camp system and terror swallowed millions of victims. Stalin deported supposed 'enemy' nations, such as the Crimean Tartars, Volga Germans and Chechens, from one end of the Soviet Union to another. As in the deportations of the kulaks, so in the deportation of these nationalities, huge numbers died."[2]

1 Chalk and Jonassohn 1990:249, quoted in Martin Shaw (2003) *War and Genocide* Polity Press: Cambridge at 32-3.

2 Martin Shaw (2003) *War and Genocide* Polity Press: Cambridge at 54-56.

The cruelties of Stalin's rule were more than matched by those of Adolph Hitler and his Nazi regime. It is now well known that the Nazis were responsible for the murder of around six million Jews, in the most heartless and cruel circumstances imaginable.[3]

As if this most infamous of genocides was not enough, Shaw points out that the Nazis were also responsible for 'the genocidal killing of (according to the best estimates available) as many as 10 million Slav civilians (including Poles, Russians, Belorussians and Ukrainians), 3 million Soviet prisoners of war, 250,000 Roma, over 200,000 homosexuals and up to 100,000 people with mental and physical disabilities.'[4]

Together with the horrific crimes of genocide committed by the regimes of Stalin and the Nazis, must rank the genocidal massacres committed during the 1930s and 1940s by Japanese troops in China and the far East. In December 1937, for example, Imperial Japanese troops captured Nanking, the capital of China. What followed has become known as the 'rape of Nanking'. Irish Chang describes the way in which '[t]ens of thousands of young men were rounded up and herded to the outer areas of the city, where they were mowed down by machine guns, used for bayonet practice, or soaked with gasoline and burned alive' and explains that '[f]or months the streets of the city were heaped with corpses and reeked with the stench of rotting human flesh'.[5] Martin Shaw sums up the horror of this and subsequent genocides committed by Japanese troops as follows:

> "Tens of thousands of women were raped and killed. The slaughter repelled even Nazi observers. The International Military Tribunal of the Far East later estimated that more than 260,000 non-combatants were killed on the streets of the city – a greater death toll than at Hiroshima or Dresden... The slaughter at Nanking was only the most prominent episode in a long history of extreme violence against civilians in Japan's wars... As late as 1945, the crimes of Nanking were repeated in Manila, the capital of the Philippines, where an estimated 100,000 were killed out of a population of 700,000."[6]

Apart from these horrors committed by the Axis powers during the Second World War, the mass killings of civilians during Allied bombing campaigns over this period

---

[3] In the early stages of the war, Hitler ordered a 'euthanasia' programme, designed to kill mentally handicapped people in Germany itself, in which gas chambers disguised as showers were first devised. Thereafter, mobile 'gas vans' accompanied the mass killing in the east, and experiments with mass gassing began in camps. By the closing months of 1941 the Nazi leaders had concretised a plan of mass extermination. Jewish ghettos across Europe were cleared and Jews were forcibly transported to concentration camps that became killing centres. The gas chambers and crematoria at the camps were specifically designed for mass extermination. Martin Shaw records that at Auschwitz-Birkenau alone, the largest and most notorious centre, 1.3 million Jews may have been killed from late 1941 to late 1944. See further Martin Shaw (2003) *War and Genocide* Polity Press: Cambridge at 80.

[4] Martin Shaw (2003) *War and Genocide* Polity Press: Cambridge at 78.

[5] Irish Chang 1998:4, quoted in Martin Shaw (2003) *War and Genocide* Polity Press: Cambridge at 98.

[6] Martin Shaw (2003) *War and Genocide* Polity Press: Cambridge at 98.

should not escape notice. The Allied 'fire-bombing' of Hamburg in 1943 is believed to have claimed approximately 45,000 lives, whereas the fire-bombing of Dresden in 1945 is thought to have killed 70,000 or more people. The incendiary attack on Tokyo by the United States air force was estimated by the US Strategic Bombing Survey to have caused 87,793 deaths. This was followed by the systematic destruction of other Japanese cities, culminating in the annihilation of Hiroshima and Nagasaki by atomic bombs.[7]

Mass killing of civilians did not cease in 1945 with the end of the Second World War. The greatest single mass death of civilians in the twentieth century took place between 1959 and 1961 in China. Mao Tse-tung's policy known as the 'Great Leap Forward' caused a state-made famine across rural China, which resulted in an estimated 30-40 million deaths. Shaw points out that: 'While the scale of mass death was hardly intended, it was a direct and foreseeable consequence of Mao's attempt to subordinate the peasantry to his will.'[8]

Barely a decade later in 1971, the world would witness yet another genocide, this time in Bangladesh. In March of that year, what was then known as East Pakistan (the present Bangladesh) was attacked by military forces from West Pakistan (the present Pakistan). The purpose of the attack was to crush the Awami League, which was demanding regional autonomy from West Pakistan. In the genocide which followed it is alleged that between one and three million people were killed. According to A.J. Rummel:

> "The human death toll over only 267 days was incredible. Just to give for five out of the eighteen districts some incomplete statistics published in Bangladesh newspapers or by an Inquiry Committee, the Pakistani army killed 100,000 Bengalis in Dacca, 150,000 in Khulna, 75,000 in Jessore, 95,000 in Comilla, and 100,000 in Chittagong. For eighteen districts the total is 1,247,000 killed. This was an incomplete toll, and to this day no one really knows the final toll. Some estimates of the democide [Rummel's "death by government"] are much lower – one is of 300,000 dead – but most range from 1 million to 3 million. ... The Pakistani army and allied paramilitary groups killed about one out of every sixty-one people in Pakistan overall; one out of every twenty-five Bengalis, Hindus, and others in East Pakistan."[9]

A few years later in Cambodia, the world would witness yet another genocide. In the three years following the ascension to power of Pol Pot and his Khmer Rouge in 1975, approximately one and a half million Cambodians, around one fifth of the total population of seven million, would die in what became known as Cambodia's 'killing fields'.[10]

---

7 See Martin Shaw (2003) *War and Genocide* Polity Press: Cambridge at 127.

8 Martin Shaw (2003) *War and Genocide* Polity Press: Cambridge at 39.

9 A.J. Rummel (1994) *Death by Government* at 331.

10 Philip Short (2004) *Pol Pot – The History of a Nightmare* John Murray (Publishers): London at 10-1.

During this same period, Indonesia was beginning its brutal occupation of East Timor, which was to result in what many would also call genocide.[11] Referring to a 2500 page United Nations report on the occupation of East Timor, a recent article in *The Australian* states as follows:

> "The report blames the Indonesian government and the security forces for the deaths of as many as 183,000 civilians, more than 90 per cent of whom died from hunger and illness. It claims Indonesian police or soldiers were to blame for 70 per cent of the 18,600 unlawful killings or disappearances between 1975 and 1999... It documents a litany of massacres, thousands of summary executions of civilians and the torture of 8500 East Timorese – with horrific details of public beheadings, the mutilation of genitalia, the burying and burning alive of victims, use of cigarettes to burn victims, and ears and genitals being lopped off to display to families. Thousands of East Timorese women were raped and sexually assaulted during the occupation and the report concludes that rape was also used by the Indonesian military as a weapon of war... The deaths amounted to almost a third of East Timor's pre-invasion population. The report found that after taking into account a peacetime baseline mortality rate, the number of East Timorese whose deaths could be directly attributed to Indonesia's deliberate starvation policy was between 84,200 and 183,000 people from 1975 until 1999."[12]

Recent decades have witnessed genocide and mass killing on a scale as horrific as any in the more distant past. The genocidal conflict that erupted in the 1990s following the break up of Yugoslavia 'claimed over a quarter of a million deaths in Bosnia, the overwhelming majority of them civilian, and made two million people refugees.'[13] The most well known of the massacres which occurred during this 'genocidal war', characterised by ethnic cleansing and the use of rape as a weapon of war, took place in 1995 in the town of Srebrenica in Eastern Bosnia. Dutch United Nations troops handed over 7,000 male Muslim refugees to the Bosnian Serb army under the command of Ratko Mladic, following which most of them were slaughtered.

Perhaps the most horrifying of the recent genocides, however, took place in 1994 on the continent of Africa. John Reader sets out the following shocking statistics which reveal the extent of the genocide which occurred in Rwanda:

> "The definitive United Nations report concluded that 500,000 people had been killed, but this could be conservative. An estimate arrived at by deducting the known number of Tutsi survivors (in the refugee centres) from 1991 census figures (adjusted to take account of a 3.2 per cent population growth rate), concludes that between 800,000 and 850,000 Tutsi died in the genocide, plus between 10,000 and 30,000 Hutu. The Tutsi population had been reduced from about

---

11 See, for example, Noam Chomsky and Edward S. Herman (1980) *The Washington Connection and Third World Fascism*, in which it is argued that the Indonesian occupation resulted in the deaths of about one third of the Timorese population, a greater *per capita* death toll than was suffered in any genocide since the Jewish Holocaust.

12 The Australian 19 January 2006.

13 Martin Shaw (2003) *War and Genocide* Polity Press: Cambridge at 192.

> 930,000 to no more than 130,000 in the space of 100 days. For every Tutsi remaining alive, seven had died."[14]

As shocking as these cold statistics may be, they do not capture the true horror of what happened in Rwanda during the genocide. It is worth quoting John Reader once again:

> "A 1,200-page report on the Rwanda genocide contains the testimonies of survivors and helpless onlookers who witnessed some of the killings. The scale and brutality are horrifying: rape, torture, mutilation, unspeakably cruel murder; mothers forced to watch their children die before being killed themselves; children forced to kill their families. Mutilations were common, and macabre ritual was evident: 'Brutality here does not end with murder. At massacre sites, corpses, many of them those of children, have been methodically dismembered and the body parts stacked neatly in separate piles.' Page after page, the reports are numbing to the point of disbelief. Inhuman. How could people do these terrible things?"[15]

And then there is the case of Darfur in the Sudan. This genocide-in-the-making is in the process of unfolding as we type this chapter. According to Ben Kiernan, the A. Whitney Griswold Professor of History and Director of the Genocide Studies Program at Yale University: 'In two years of mass killings and forced population displacements, Sudan and its Arab Janjaweed militias have caused the deaths of over 200,000 Africans in the country's Darfur provinces.'[16]

Of course, the mass killings in Rwanda and Sudan do not represent the sum total of gross human rights abuses on the African continent during the past century. To describe all these abuses is beyond the scope of this book.[17] Some examples which spring to mind, however, are the violations committed between 1974 and 1991 by the repressive Dergue regime of Mengitsu Haile-Mariam in Ethiopia, with over 70,000 killed;[18] the case of Chad under Hissène Habré, with around 40,000 alleged to have been killed and 200,000 tortured;[19] Uganda under Idi Amin, with 73,000 alleged to have been killed, and more recently the genocidal activities of the Lords Resistance Army;[20] the Central African Republic under Bokassa, who was alleged to have been guilty of cannibalism; Zaire (Democratic Republic of Congo) under the rule of Mobutu; Sierra Leone under Foday Sankoh, whose rule led to the limbs of thousands

---

14 John Reader (1998) *Africa – A Biography of the Continent* Penguin Books: London at page 670. See also the chapter in this book by Jeremy Sarkin (at pages 197-228).

15 John Reader (1998) *Africa – A Biography of the Continent* Penguin Books: London at page 671.

16 YaleGlobal 4 February 2005.

17 For detail in relation to the abuses committed in the Great Lakes Area of Africa, see the chapter in this book by Jeremy Sarkin at pages 197-228.

18 Geoffrey Robertson QC (2002) *Crimes Against Humanity – The Struggle for Global Justice – Second Edition* Penguin Books: London at 220.

19 Geoffrey Robertson QC (2002) *Crimes Against Humanity – The Struggle for Global Justice – Second Edition* Penguin Books: London at 219.

20 Geoffrey Robertson QC (2002) *Crimes Against Humanity – The Struggle for Global Justice – Second Edition* Penguin Books: London at 219-220.

of opponents being amputated; Zimbabwe under Robert Mugabe, whose North Korean trained 5th Brigade is alleged to have massacred 20,000 civilians in the province of Matabeleland during the 1980s; and, of course, South Africa under the control of Afrikaner nationalists, whose policy of 'apartheid' was declared a crime against humanity, and resulted in thousands of politically motivated murders and the displacement of millions of people.

The scourge of gross human rights abuses is truly global. South America, for example, has a similar history to Africa of repressive regimes which have been guilty of grossly abusing the human rights of their citizens. For instance, the people of Chile suffered for many years under the regime of General Augusto Pinochet, who assumed power in a coup in 1973, and whose regime was characterised by widespread torture and politically inspired murders, including about 4,000 'disappearances'.[21] The people of Argentina suffered in a similar manner. The country was ruled by a series of military juntas between 1976 and 1983, and the military engaged in a so called 'dirty war' against its left-wing opponents. During the period of military rule, at least 9,000 people suspected of being opposed to the military regime were 'disappeared'. Robertson comments as follows on the cruelty of these 'disappearances':

> "For friends and relations, the continuing horror of not knowing any details of the victim's fate adds a special layer of cruelty, driving them either to despair or to the courage displayed by the Mothers of the Plaza del Mayo, whose weekly demonstrations on behalf of their lost children did more than anything else to expose the wickedness of the Argentinian junta."[22]

In the case of Guatemala, the mass killings were truly horrific in their scale. Victoria Sanford, a Senior Research Fellow at the Institute on Violence and Survival at the Virginia Foundation for the Humanities states as follows:

> "In its final report, the Commission for Historical Clarification (CEH- Guatemalan Truth Commission) concluded that army massacres had destroyed 626 villages, more than 200,000 people were killed or disappeared, 1.5 million were displaced by the violence, and more than 150,000 were driven to seek refuge in Mexico. Further, the Commission found the state responsible for ninety-three percent of the acts of violence and the guerrillas (URNG-Guatemalan Revolutionary Union) responsible for three percent."[23]

---

21 Geoffrey Robertson QC (2002) *Crimes Against Humanity – The Struggle for Global Justice – Second Edition* Penguin Books: London at 285.

22 Geoffrey Robertson QC (2002) *Crimes Against Humanity – The Struggle for Global Justice – Second Edition* Penguin Books: London at 262.

23 See website http://www.cis.yale.edu/gsp/guatemala/charts1.html. Sanford cites the following source in support of her assertions: CEH, Guatemala Memoria del Silencio, vols. 1–12 (Guatemala City: CEH, 1999), vol 5:42.

In El Salvador, it is alleged that there were up to 22,000 disappearances,[24] and in relation to Haiti, Geoffrey Robertson states as follows:

> "The psychopathic cruelty and greed of 'Papa Doc' and 'Baby Doc' and their Tontons Macoutes made Haiti a human rights blackspot from 1957 until 1986, when the US airlifted Jean-Claude Duvalier ('Baby Doc') to luxurious retirement in the south of France. Over this period, 40,000 citizens were senselessly killed."[25]

The brief descriptions set out above are not exhaustive, and do not begin to capture the true horror of gross human rights abuses which have taken place during the last century. Stanley Cohen sums up the suffering of millions of innocent people since the end of the second world war in the following moving terms:

> "In the half-century since the end of the Second World War, some 25 million people have been killed, mostly civilians and by their own governments, in internal conflicts and ethnic, nationalist or religious violence. Civilian fatalities have climbed from 5 per cent of war-related deaths at the turn of the century to more than 90 per cent in the 1990s. About 50 million people were forced to flee their homes. In 1998, more than 2,000 people every month were killed or maimed by land-mine explosions. It is impossible to even estimate the numbers injured and disabled, tortured and raped, during these conflicts. The statistics on poverty, hunger, and children dying from preventable diseases continue to defy the imagination: 17 million people a year die from infectious and parasitic diseases such a measles, diarrhoea and malaria; 600 million are chronically undernourished; 3 million die of TB; if everyone had access to safe water and basic sanitation, 2 million young lives would be saved each year."[26]

It is numbing to extrapolate – as one can – this horror to the centuries before the twentieth. History is replete with genocide; humanity's inhumanity is sadly one of its most recognisable features. As Judge Richard Goldstone, former Chief Prosecutor at The Hague Tribunals has wryly commented: 'The hope of "never again" is eclipsed by the 'reality of again and again'.[27] The precise manner in which the gross abuses which have been mentioned may be categorised as 'genocide' or 'war crimes' or 'crimes against humanity' is perhaps beside the point. What is important is to recognise the massive scale and horrifying regularity with which the human rights of ordinary people all over the world are grossly abused. Indeed, the scale and regularity of the abuses threaten to overwhelm the concept of reparation, particularly where reparation is seen

---

[24] Geoffrey Robertson QC (2002) *Crimes Against Humanity – The Struggle for Global Justice – Second Edition* Penguin Books: London at 286.

[25] Geoffrey Robertson QC (2002) *Crimes Against Humanity – The Struggle for Global Justice – Second Edition* Penguin Books: London at 286-7.

[26] Stanley Cohen, *States of Denial*, at 287.

[27] 'Were They Just Obeying Orders?', *The Guardian*, May 7, 1996, at 10, quoted in Simon Chesterman 'Never Again ... and Again: Law, Order, and the Gender of War Crimes in Bosnia and Beyond', (1997) 22 *Yale J. of Int. Law*, 299 at 316.

as compensation. Any debate on the question of reparations must be situated within this social and political context and must acknowledge that it is an immense task even to describe the true magnitude and scale of human suffering, much less seek to repair the consequences of this suffering.

2 REPARATIONS AS A HUMAN RIGHTS IDEAL

So too, the rise of the concept of reparations must be understood against the development of international law and the body of norms that today we recognise as 'human rights'. Given that international law was a law conceived originally to govern relations between states, the earliest examples of reparations arose in the context of wrongs committed by States against other States. Put another way, reparations were claimed by the recognised subjects of international law – States vis-à-vis States – and not by individuals. Thus, in the aftermath of conflict, victorious states asserted a claim for recompense for military and civilian damage against the vanquished state. Following the First World War, article 231 of the Treaty of Versailles (the so-called 'war guilt' clause) held Germany solely responsible for all 'loss and damage' suffered by the Allies during the war and provided the basis for 'reparations'. The term 'reparations' was used by Woodrow Wilson to denote civilian damages, but when he used that term he understood it to be restricted to a claim made by the Allied States against the conquered Axis States for wrongs committed against civilians. International law's preoccupation with the relations *between* states gave rise to its blind spot: a failure to consider, let alone acknowledge, the harm suffered by individuals *within* states at the hands of their own governments or other citizens.

As Regula Ludi points out in her chapter in this book (*Reflections on Holocaust Reparations*, at pages 119-144), following the end of the Second World War, for the first time an individual right to redress for state crimes (as opposed to the traditional right of states to war reparations) was recognised in a legal document drafted at the Paris Reparation Conference of 1945. That came about due to the efforts of American diplomats who inserted a special clause in the final agreement of January 1946 to allocate a share of war reparations for stateless 'nonrepatriable' victims of Nazi action. This development soon came to be overtaken in Germany by a range of other measures designed to secure victim reparation for Nazi atrocities, measures which continue to this day. But returning to 1945, it is important to recognise that the Paris Reparations Conference marked a turning point. It stood alongside a larger movement that also traces its formal inception to 1945, and which would come to symbolise the importance of *individuals*, including their claims for reparations for gross abuses of human rights, under international law. The aim of this movement was the protection of human rights at the international level, and led to the establishment of the United Nations. The Charter of the United Nations obliges member States to promote 'universal respect for, and observance of human rights and fundamental freedoms for all without distinction as to race, sex, language or religion'. The content of the rights to be protected have been spelt out in a variety of instruments since then. The rise of human rights law had an obvious impact on the idea of reparations. Through human rights law individuals were given a voice to claim reparations for the harm imposed on them by their own States. Of course, it is not only States that violate human rights; there is an increasing number of claims for reparations for the harm imposed on individuals by entities other than States. For example, Michael Osborne's chapter in this book (at pages 231-293) highlights attempts to bring reparations claims against transnational *corporations* for their complicity in the system of apartheid.

The right to bring a claim for a violation of internationally recognised human rights is well established in various human rights treaties. Article 8 of the Universal Declaration of Human Rights[28] states that '[e]veryone has the right to an effective remedy by the competent national tribunals for acts violating the fundamental rights granted him by the constitution or by law'. Similarly, article 2(3)(a) of the International Covenant on Civil and Political Rights,[29] ratified by more than 140 countries, states that '[e]ach State Party to the present Covenant undertakes: (a) To ensure that any person whose rights or freedoms as herein recognized are violated shall have an effective remedy, notwithstanding that the violation has been committed by persons acting in an official capacity...'.[30] Article 6 of the UN Convention on the Elimination of All Forms of Racial Discrimination[31] provides that '[s]tate parties shall assure to everyone within their jurisdiction effective protection and remedies ... against any acts of racial discrimination which violate his human rights ..., as well as the right to seek from such tribunals just and adequate reparation or satisfaction for any damage suffered as a result of such discrimination'. So too, article 14 of the UN Convention Against Torture and Cruel, Inhuman or Degrading Treatment or Punishment[32] requires each state party to 'ensure in its legal system that the victim of an act of torture obtains redress and has an enforceable right to fair and adequate compensations, including the means for as full rehabilitation as possible'.[33]

So, if a State is party to one or more international human rights treaties, such as the International Covenant on Civil and Political Rights of 1966; or the United Nations Convention on the Elimination of All Forms of Racial Discrimination of 1966; or the United Nations Convention Against Torture and Cruel, Inhuman or Degrading

[28] General Assembly Resolution 217A (III).

[29] General Assembly Resolution 2200 A (XXI), annex.

[30] For a review of the jurisprudence of the Human Rights Committee of the ICCPR on the question of reparations, see Jenkins – "After the Dry White Season: The Dilemmas of Reparation and Reconstruction in South Africa" (2000) 16 *South African Journal on Human Rights* 423-9.

[31] ILM (1966) 5 352.

[32] ILM (1985) 24 535.

[33] For a review of the jurisprudence of the UN Committee against Torture on reparations, see Jenkins op cit 429-430.

Treatment or Punishment of 1983, it will be bound by the provisions of the treaty or treaties to which it is a party. And it will be bound too by the provisions providing for remedies and requiring reparation in the event of a breach of the treaty by a State party. The problem, however, is that many of the States in which massive violations of human rights occur or occurred, either are not a party to any international human rights treaties, or were not party to any such treaties when the violations took place. As Catherine Jenkins points out:

> "From the perspective of victims of repressive regimes, a particular difficulty may arise from the fact that their governments were not parties to relevant human rights treaties for part or all of the period during which the acts of state violence or discrimination were committed."[34]

If international human rights treaty law does not provide a solution in situations such as those outlined above, what about international customary law? Not surprisingly, the United Nations Organisation (the founding principle of which was to promote and protect human rights) has paid particular attention to this issue, through the work of a series of Special Rapporteurs.[35] This work led to the production of a set of *Basic Principles and Guidelines on the Right to a Remedy and Reparation for Victims of Gross Violations of International Human Rights Law and Serious Violations of International Humanitarian Law*, which has recently been adopted by the United Nations General Assembly, on 16 December 2005.[36]

According to the Basic Principles there is an obligation on states to respect, ensure respect for, and enforce the norms of both international human rights law and humanitarian law. These norms are contained in customary international law, as well as in the treaties to which a particular state is a party. States are obliged to prevent violations; to investigate any violations which do occur and, where appropriate, take action against the violator in accordance with domestic and international law; to provide victims with equal and effective access to justice; to provide appropriate remedies to victims; and to provide for or facilitate reparation to victims.[37]

Reparation to victims is thus recognised as an integral part of the obligation imposed on states by international human rights law and humanitarian law. In terms

---

34 Catherine Jenkins "After the Dry White Season: The Dilemmas of Reparation and Reconstruction in South Africa" (2000) 16 *South African Journal on Human Rights* 421-2.

35 Mr Theo Van Boven was appointed in 1989 by the UN Sub-Commission on Prevention of Discrimination and Protection of Minorities. The Sub-Commission suggested that international standards needed to be developed and remaining gaps filled to ensure that victims of gross violations in particular would have an enforceable right to restitution, compensation and rehabilitation. See his Final Report on the Right to Restitution, Compensation and Rehabilitation for Victims of Gross Violations of Human Rights and Fundamental Freedoms, Mr Theo van Boven, UN Doc No E/CN 4/Sub 2/1993/8. Van Boven's study was taken forward by the UN through the appointment of Mr M Cherif Bassiouni, an expert on reparations.

36 General Assembly Resolution A/Res/60/147.

37 See Articles 1-3 of the Basic Principles.

of the Basic Principles, a State has the obligation to ensure respect for human rights, which includes the duty to prevent violations, to investigate violations, to take appropriate action against the violators and to afford remedies to victims. Where there has been a violation of internationally recognised human rights, a state has responsibility to make just and adequate reparation to all persons within the jurisdiction of the offending State. Reparation should respond to the needs and wishes of the victims and be proportionate to the gravity of the violations and the resulting harm. It should include restitution, compensation, rehabilitation, satisfaction and guarantees of non-repetition. In addition to providing reparation to individuals, States should make adequate provision for collective reparations for groups of victims and special measures should be taken to afford opportunities for self-development and advancement to groups who, as a result of human rights violations, were denied such opportunities.[38]

As this brief discursis demonstrates, in practice reparations may include an extremely wide range of measures as emphasised by Max du Plessis in his account of the different forms and manifestations of reparations as that term is understood in contemporary international law in this book at pages 147-177. Various chapters in this book describe attempts to secure one or more of these measures of reparations. Each claim relates to a different context and concerns a different type of serious human rights abuse.

The concept of reparations has come of age, with increasing clarity as to what may be claimed as reparations, the wide scale of reparations measures, and the subtleties and nuances attached to a reparations claim. Individuals and groups have been approaching courts and other fora in order to secure reparations. Books such as this one have been[39] and are being written on the topic of reparations and its relevance to those who have suffered gross human rights abuses. The United Nations has adopted resolutions on the issue of reparations. The importance of reparations is recognised in the aims of the newest institutions created within the United Nations fold. Perhaps the best example is provided by the recently created International Criminal Court. Andreas O'Shea's chapter (see pages 179-196) describes the significant advances made in the Rome Statute of the International Criminal Court in relation to victims. Victims are defined broadly and may benefit from various protective measures. Furthermore, in an improvement on the provisions relating to the *ad hoc* Tribunals for Rwanda and the former Yugoslavia, victims may receive reparations for injury. With the establishment of a trust fund for the benefit of victims and their families, the Rome Statute

[38] Basic Principles, articles 15 to 23.

[39] See for example M Bossuyt, P Lemmens, K De Feyter and S Parmentier (eds), *Out of the Ashes: Reparation for Victims of Gross and Systematic Human Rights Violations*, Intersentia, 2006; Pablo de Greiff (ed) *The Handbook of Reparations*, Oxford, 2006, and Alfred Brophy, *Reparations: Pro and Con*, Oxford, 2006.

shows concern for the rights and interests of those whose tragic stories lie at the heart of the International Criminal Court's process.

These promising developments on the ground have not as yet been matched by the development of a fully fledged theory of reparative justice. As Michael Freeman's chapter in this book makes clear, (at pages 29-51) whereas liberal theories of distributive justice (such as that advanced by John Rawls) are fully developed and widely accepted, until recently theories of reparative justice had been relatively neglected. Moreover, liberal theories of distributive justice have not yet been properly integrated or balanced with theories of reparative justice. Freeman describes the potential tension between reparative and distributive justice, *inter alia*, as follows:

> "There can be a tension between reparative and distributive justice, because backward-looking policies may weaken society's capacity to build a more just future. Given limited resources, the demands of distributive justice may place some constraints on reparation. Yet reparative justice may be right in itself, and it might contribute to a more stable and just future."

Despite the theoretical difficulties involved in balancing distributive with reparative justice, it is submitted that Freeman is correct when he calls for reparative justice to be given a more prominent place in liberal political theory. The developments in international human rights law – and the practical steps taken by human rights lawyers to achieve reparations – suggest that the time is right for a renewed interest by theorists in issues of reparative justice.

3 OF DRAWING LINES – 'REPARATIONS FOR WHAT?'

Because of the scale (both temporal and geographic) of human rights abuses, the concept of reparations is complex and contested in nature. The question arises whether it is in fact possible, in theory or in practice, to repair the past. It is for this reason that the main title of this work – 'Repairing the Past?' – has been posed as a question.

There are a wide range of measures which, in practice, may be interpreted as different forms of reparation. Even if the word 'reparation' is restricted to its broadly accepted meaning in terms of international law, it may include measures as diverse as restitution in kind, compensation, satisfaction, and assurances and guarantees of non-repetition. Each of these measures is multi-faceted and subject to much nuanced legal debate. Take the example of 'satisfaction'. It is particularly difficult to draw the contours of 'satisfaction' as a form of reparation. Consider in this regard the international law rules on State-State responsibility. The State that has injured another State is obliged to 'give satisfaction for the injury caused by that act insofar as it cannot be made good by restitution or compensation'.[40] Such measures may take the form of an 'acknowledgment of the breach, an expression of regret, a formal apology or another appropriate modality'.[41] In particular satisfaction provides reparation for moral damage such as emotional injury, mental suffering, injury to reputation and similar damage suffered by nationals of the injured State.[42] Thus it serves a useful role in providing reparation for those injuries, which cannot be assessed in financial terms and which amount to an affront to the State.[43]

Given the broad socio-political context within which the issue of reparation arises, debate rages about whether reparation – as a form of satisfaction – may be taken to include measures such as affirmative action, relief aid provided by developed nations to former colonies, the establishment of truth and reconciliation commissions, and so on. Another topical debate is whether 'truth' is sufficient to constitute reparation. The question is asked whether international criminal trials constitute, in and of themselves, sufficient reparation for the victims of gross human rights abuses. It cannot be denied that international criminal trials have a commemorative potential. They are a mechanism for building an objective and impartial record of events.[44] This was true of Nuremberg, and it is true also in respect of the other international criminal tribunals that have been created since 1990. There is, however, a tension between the production of history and the task of conducting a criminal trial. A criminal trial with its elaborate rules regarding relevance and inadmissibility of evidence, as well as its focus on the accused in court, means that it is never able to provide a definitive and comprehensive record of history. However, such trials are able to provide a coherent account of tragic events, a 'judicial truth' if you will. Acting in concert with local initiatives such as truth commissions which rely on popular participation, such trials may assist in painting the fullest possible picture of history.[45] This is pointed out by Bo Jung Kwon in her chapter (at pages 413-436) on legal redress for Korean comfort women. In her chapter she points out that 'the legal system is capable of punishing wrongdoers, offering healing and closure through listening, and establishing historical veracity to prevent further crimes'. At its simplest then, a criminal trial of those responsible for gross human rights violations may – aside from the justice it metes out to the perpetrator responsible for the abuse of particular victims – contribute to the creation of an objective account of events and play an important role in 'fighting

40 See James Crawford, *The International Law Commission's Articles on State Responsibility: Introduction, Text and Commentaries*, (2002), Article 37(1) at 231.
41 Article 37(2), *ibid.*
42 See the Commentary to Article 37, ILC Articles on State Responsibility in Crawford op cit at 231.
43 See Commentary to Article 37, ILC Articles on State Responsibility, in Crawford op cit at 231.
44 Antonio Cassese, 'On the Current Trends towards Criminal Prosecution and Punishment of Breaches of International Humanitarian Law', (1998) vol. 9, no.1, *EJIL*, 2 at14, available at http://www.ejil.org/journal/vol9/no1,art1-01.html.
45 See Payam Akhavan, 'Justice in The Hague, Peace in the Former Yugoslavia? A Commentary on the United Nations War Crimes Tribunal', (1998), 20, *HRQ*, 737 at 784.

forgetting'. Through the process of memorialising, the trial may render 'satisfaction' to other victims not directly involved in the trial.

Perhaps a prior – but equally difficult question – is the issue of whether a particular series of events should or should not qualify as a 'gross abuse of human rights'. In practice, this issue is central to any discussion relating to reparations, since it deals with the following question: 'Reparations for what?' Two broad sub-issues immediately present themselves, which are discussed in the sections which follow.

3.1 WHEN IS 'GROSS' GROSS ENOUGH?

First, which types of events should qualify as violations that are sufficiently 'gross' to attract reparations? Put differently, is the duty to make reparation practically limited to serious violations, and if so, on what basis? While human rights lawyers have accepted that all victims of violations, however grave, have a right to reparation, it is clear that limited resources and capacity mean that those involved in the struggle for human rights and reparation will inevitably focus their attention on abuses that are more serious. How one decides which specific violations are sufficiently gross to justify pursuing a claim for reparations – thereby excluding less serious violations – is of critical importance to any reparations project, initiative or challenge.

Labelling and categorising is an inevitable and essential means by which to make sense of human rights violations perpetrated against individuals, particularly where (as in apartheid South Africa, to give but one example) such abuses have been widespread, different in nature, have occurred over a long period of time, and been dealt with by a body (such as the South African Truth and Reconciliation Commission) with limited resources and capacity. It is to be expected that each separate response to human rights violations will be filtered through the lens of a particular country's social, political and historical understanding of those human rights violations which most urgently require reparation. In this respect, the human and financial resources of, for example, a truth commission, will loom large. That being said, it seems plain that those involved in any reparative process ought to strive for as expansive and encompassing an understanding of 'gross human rights violations' as is reasonably possible, so as to ensure that the widest range of victims may lay claim to reparations. In this regard it has been proposed by Theo Van Boven that '[p]articular attention must be paid to the gross violations of human rights and fundamental freedoms, which include at least the following: genocide, slavery and slavery-like practices; summary or arbitrary executions; torture and cruel, inhuman or degrading treatment or punishment; enforced disappearance; arbitrary and prolonged detention; deportation or forcible transfer of population; and systematic discrimination, in particular based on race or gender'.[46] The proposal makes sense, as it acknowledges that the scale of human misery is so large relative to what is possible by way of redress, that our efforts as human rights lawyers and activists need to be directed to and focused on the most serious human rights abuses. Indeed, as the chapters in this book make clear, the efforts at achieving reparation for human rights abuses by and large relate to the type of gross human rights abuses included in Van Boven's list.

Perhaps another useful standard against which to measure which human rights violations deserve inclusion on any proposed list of 'gross' infractions is the International Criminal Court's codification of 'crimes against humanity'. Genocide is the ultimate crime against humanity, with its own specific definition and locus within international law.[47] But a further category of conduct has developed over time under the label 'crime against humanity'. The term 'crime against humanity' was first used in its contemporary sense to condemn the atrocities committed by the Turkish forces against their own Greek and Armenian subjects during World War I. Although no prosecutions ultimately took place, the immediate response of the Allied powers to the massacres which took place was for France, the United Kingdom and Russia to proclaim that all members of the Turkish government would be held responsible together with their agents for the 'crimes against humanity and civilization'.[48] At Nuremberg, the idea of a crime against humanity arose once more. The Nuremberg and Tokyo tribunals utilised the technical term 'crime against humanity' to secure, for the first time, the prosecution of individuals for offences that shocked humankind. For those interested in reparations, the importance of the term is that it denotes behaviour or conduct which the international community – by codification in the Rome Statute of the International Criminal Court – today regards as an offence to 'humanness'. The specific acts or classes of offences that make up crimes against humanity under the Rome Statute are those commonly associated with egregious abuses of human rights, when committed on a widespread or systematic scale. The underlying acts include: murder;[49] extermination[50] (involving mass or large-scale killing, or the intentional infliction of conditions inimical to life – *inter alia*, the

46 See his Final Report on the Right to Restitution, Compensation and Rehabilitation for Victims of Gross Violations of Human Rights and Fundamental Freedoms, Mr Theo van Boven, UN Doc No E/CN 4/Sub 2/1993/8, para 137(1).

47 Genocide – the worst of all crimes – has developed an independent existence under international law, starting with the Genocide Convention of 1948 and most recently codified as a self-standing crime under the Rome Statute of the International Criminal Court.

48 The unratified Treaty of Sevres of 1920 (*UK Treaty Series No 11* (1920) provided for the surrender by Turkey of persons 'responsible for the massacres committed during the continuance of the state of war on territory which formed part of the Turkish Empire' (article 230) but in 1923 the Treaty of Lausanne (*UK Treaty Series No 16* (1923), Part VIII) granted amnesty to these persons. See V N Adrian 'Genocide as a Problem of National and International Law: The World War I Armenian Case and its Contemporary Legal Ramifications' (1989) 14 *Yale Journal of International Law* 221.

49 Article 7(1)(a).

50 Article 7(1)(b).

deprivation of food and medicine – calculated to bring about the destruction of part of a population[51]); enslavement;[52] deportation or forcible transfer of population[53] (being the 'forced displacement of the persons concerned by expulsion or other coercive acts from the area in which they are lawfully present, without grounds permitted under international law'[54]); imprisonment or other severe deprivation of physical liberty in violation of fundamental rules of international law;[55] torture[56] (being 'the intentional infliction of severe pain or suffering, whether physical or mental, upon a person in the custody or under the control of the accused'[57]); sexual violence (which includes 'rape, sexual slavery, enforced prostitution, forced pregnancy, enforced sterilisation, or any other form of sexual violence of comparable gravity'[58]); persecution[59] (being 'the intentional and severe deprivation of fundamental rights contrary to international law by reason of the identity of the group or collectivity'[60]); enforced disappearance[61] (being 'the arrest, detention or abduction of persons by, or with the authorization, support or acquiescence of, a State or a political organization, followed by a refusal to acknowledge that deprivation of freedom or to give information on the fate or whereabouts of those persons, with the intention of removing them from the protection of the law for a prolonged period of time'[62]); the crime of apartheid[63] (which includes 'inhumane acts of a character similar to [other crimes against humanity], committed in the context of an institutionalized regime of systematic oppression and domination by one racial group over any other racial group or groups and committed with the intention of maintaining the regime')[64] and other inhumane acts[65] (which are acts 'of a similar character to [other crimes against humanity] intentionally causing great suffering, or serious injury to body or to mental or physical health').[66]

The Rome Statute's list of acts that make up crimes that shock our humanity is notably wide in its spread. We submit that it is a good standard against which to measure the grossness or otherwise of human rights abuses when considering claims

51 Article 7(2)(b).
52 Article 7(1)(c).
53 Article 7(1)(d).
54 Article 7(2)(d)
55 Article 7(1)(e).
56 Article 7(1)(f).
57 Article 7(2)(e).
58 Article 7(1)(g).
59 Article 7(1)(h).
60 Article 7(2)(g).
61 Article 7(1)(i).
62 Article 7(2)(i).
63 Article 7(1)(j).
64 Article 7(2)(h).
65 Article 7(1)(k).
66 Article 7(1)(k).

for reparation. When these underlying acts are committed against victims on a widespread or systematic scale, the victim's entitlement to reparation for the injury suffered should be beyond doubt. In this regard we draw particular attention to the chapter by Mahmood Mamdani entitled 'Amnesty or Impunity? A Preliminary Critique of the Report of the Truth and Reconciliation Commission of South Africa' at pages 83 to 118. In his chapter Mamdani highlights the manner in which the privileging of certain human rights abuses over others may lead to a failure of justice. Mamdani has the following to say in relation to the manner in which the South African Truth and Reconciliation Commission dealt with the question of forced removals under apartheid:

> "A widely distributed and cited investigation by The Surplus People Project estimated that 3.5 million people were forcibly moved by the South African state between 1960 and 1982 in support of the program of developing ethnic homelands. The Commission acknowledged that 3.5 million had indeed been moved forcibly, and that the process involved 'collective expulsions, forced migration, bulldozing, gutting or seizure of homes, the mandatory carrying of passes, forced removals into rural ghettos and increased poverty and desperation.' Not even a generation had passed since these brutalities had ended. Not surprisingly, both surviving victims and their advocates among community organizers and activists had assumed that forced removals would be the core focus of a Truth and Reconciliation Commission."

In our view, both according to Van Boven's list and in terms of the Rome Statute's understanding of crimes against humanity, the acts described by Mamdani in the above quotation amount to serious, gross and inexcusable human rights violations committed on a widespread *and* systematic scale. Yet, as Mamdani points out '...the Commission was not obliging: after noting that 'forced removals' were 'an assault on the rights and dignity of millions of South Africans', the Commission claimed it could not acknowledge them since these violations may not have been 'gross' as defined by the Act.'

The problem illustrated by Mamdani is one that reaches beyond a critique of the South African Truth and Reconciliation Commission. Those committed to human rights must avoid the unnecessary downplaying or diminishing of human rights violations. They would do well to take into account the accepted examples of crimes that are considered to be so gross that they offend against humanity, and to appreciate that all the victims of such egregious human rights abuses are worthy of reparations, in relevant form.

3.2 WHEN IS THE PAST TOO LONG AGO?

When asking the question 'reparations for what?' a second sub-issue arises, namely, should there be a time limit which prohibits reparations being claimed for violations, however gross, which took place in the distant past? In respect of the duty to make reparation, does it matter, for example, that the violations complained of occurred during the North Atlantic Slave Trade? Are certain past human rights abuses (such as the Slave Trade) so egregious that they will continue to haunt the present unless they are addressed by some sort of reparation? As Diane Sammons points out in her chapter on corporate reparations for descendants of enslaved African-Americans (see pages 315-358), one significant practical obstacle to such reparations claims is that they are liable to be dismissed in terms of relevant statutes of limitations. The statute of limitation problem is a manifestation of a larger problem presented by reparations claims: how can or should the law of today respond to events that happened years, sometimes centuries ago, under laws or moral codes that sanctioned such conduct?

During recent times, international lawyers have begun to grapple with the question of whether or not certain States ought to be held accountable at international law for crimes committed as part of the Atlantic Slave Trade. These crimes against humanity are well documented and took place over a period of three centuries, from around 1600 until about 1900. They resulted in the deaths of around two million people in the middle passage and the enslavement of eleven million others. The Atlantic Slave Trade was officially sanctioned by the various 'great powers' which engaged in and benefited from the trade. The harm caused both to the slaves and the countries from which they were abducted, is clearly discernable today in the form of the deep structural inequalities which characterise the relations between the descendants of the slaves and those of their colonial masters, as well as the relations between the former slave-owning states and the countries from which the slaves were taken.

At first glance, one might be forgiven for thinking that it would not be all that difficult for lawyers and courts to attribute legal responsibility for this crime against humanity, and to agree on some form of just reparations which could go some way towards righting the wrong. But that would be to underestimate the extent to which the prevailing legal discourse is able to confuse and obfuscate the issues at stake in this matter. Most involved in the debate accept that a great moral wrong was perpetrated by the 'great powers' against thirteen million enslaved Africans, but very few are willing to risk stating that this moral wrong is also a legal wrong.

The reason put forward for this remarkable disjunction between international law and justice in regard to slavery, is that slavery was not a crime in terms of international law at the time these crimes were perpetrated by the 'great powers'. As late as 1825 therefore, the US Chief Justice was able to show in the *Antelope Case* that slave-trading was lawful, notwithstanding international condemnation of its immorality, since it was then 'sanctioned by the laws of all nations who possess distant colonies'.[67] The conclusion reached is that it is not possible to hold the 'great powers' liable for actions

[67] (1825) 23 US (10 Wheat) 64, cited in Geoffrey Robertson *Crimes Against Humanity: The Struggle for Global Justice* (2000) at 209.

which, however repugnant we find them today, were not considered to be crimes when they were committed. Thus, an unprecedented crime against humanity involving thirteen million Africans is banished from the realm of the law and relegated to the field of morality, as if it were no more than an offence to our sensibilities, a sin perhaps, but not serious enough to deserve the label 'crime'.

It is not difficult to see through the legal fiction by means of which this legal vanishing trick is accomplished. At the time the crime against humanity we now call the Atlantic Slave Trade was being perpetrated, the 'great powers' prosecuting and controlling the slave trade, were the same powers which defined the status and content of international law. Since the perpetrators of the crime of slavery did not regard their crime to be criminal, and since they possessed the power to shape and define the content of international law, they were able to construct a legal fiction which is still strong enough to deter courts from determining a legal claim for reparations for slavery. This fiction has an obfuscatory quality: it hides the power that animates the legal rule against reparations for slavery. In the international law context, this obfuscatory quality is identified by Roling, who states that:

> "[i]n all positive law is hidden the element of power and the element of interest. Law is not the same as power, nor is it the same as interest, but it gives expression to the former power-relation. Law has the inclination to serve primarily the interests of the powerful. 'European' international law, the traditional law of nations, makes no exception to this rule. It served the interest of prosperous nations."[68]

The legal fiction is dressed up in what is known as the doctrine of inter-temporal law. The doctrine is one of the central devices used in constructing and maintaining the notion that there can be no valid legal claim in international law against the great powers for reparations for slavery. Taken at face value, the doctrine seems to be based on sound common sense. The analogy between this doctrine and the presumption against the retrospective application of law in the domestic legal sphere is obvious. One of the first principles that law students are taught is that, except in the most exceptional circumstances, it is unfair for the law, in particular criminal law, to be applied retrospectively. After all, who can deny that it is profoundly unjust for a person to be found guilty and punished for actions which, when they were committed, were not considered or defined as criminal. In the same way, the doctrine of inter-temporal law maintains that it is not permissible at international law to hold States liable for actions which, although they might be contrary to the norms of international law if committed today, were not considered to be contrary to international law as it existed at the time the actions were committed. In simple terms, the doctrine requires that

68 BVA Roling, *International Law in an Expanded World,* (1960) 15.

one judge the legality or otherwise of State action in terms of the norms of international law which were in place at the time the particular action was committed.

Therefore as a legal fiction, the inter-temporal doctrine sounds reasonable enough. As soon as one begins to examine the actions of States in their social and historical context, however, the real injustices which are hidden from view through operation of the doctrine emerge into plain sight. Most would accept that international law as we know it developed as a consequence of the transition from pre-modernity to modernity, which began in Europe around the seventeenth century with the dawning of the Age of Enlightenment. With the emergence and development of the modern nation State in Europe, came the need to regulate relations between these new players on the global stage. As they grew in power and began to expand their spheres of influence to other parts of the globe, it became increasingly apparent that it was in the interests of all members of this exclusive club of 'great powers', to play their game of colonial domination according to an accepted set of rules. Peter Malanczuk makes this point as follows:

> "The notion of European international law was prepared by academic writers who during the formative period of international law provided legal concepts and systematic arguments justifying the interests of the emerging powers, especially with regard to the ambitions of their own respective countries, as may be noted in the development of the law of the sea."[69]

Malanczuk goes on to point out the complicity of international law at this time in the process of colonial conquest and domination carried out by the 'great powers':

> "There is... no doubt that the concepts of international law prevailing at this time served to facilitate the process of colonization. Sovereignty could be acquired over *terrae nullius*, territory allegedly belonging to nobody, a notion applied to areas throughout the world lacking a strong central power able to resist conquest."[70]

Of course, the citizens of the 'great powers' represented only a fraction of the world's population. Yet the tribes and peoples subjected to the colonial domination of the 'great powers' had no say in the rules according to which their domination was planned and executed. This fact contributed to appalling human rights violations inflicted on indigenous peoples in the name of 'colonialism' or 'assimilation'. The examples are legion, and not restricted to early colonial expansion. See for instance the chapter by Mark Harris (at pages 389-409) on Australia's response to claims for reparations arising out of Australian government policy between 1910 and 1970, which

---

69 Malanczuk, P. (1997) *Akehurst's Modern Introduction to International Law – Seventh Revised Edition.* London: Routledge. Page 15.

70 *Ibid.* at page 19.

involved removing Aboriginal children from their parents as part of a grand design to '[wipe] out Indigenous families, communities and cultures'.

International law's rarefied nature meant that, in truth, it consisted of a set of rules that was merely 'inter-national' – reflecting the views and customs of a small number of European states engaged in a common project of global domination by means of a massive programme of colonial expansion. To hold that we must now judge the successors of the 'great powers' in terms of their own mutually agreed rules of domination is ludicrous. Mayo Moran eloquently sums up the problem as follows:

> "The heart of the problem concerns the troubling complicity of law as a tool of massive discrimination and injustice. How ought law now respond to law then? The relationship of contemporary law and legal values to their disconcerting predecessors engages fundamental questions of law's self-identity. These questions we have not generally confronted. So we can expect, and indeed we see, institutional anxiety to augment more general collective anxiety about the scope and implications of historic wrongdoing. We may be tempted... to try to sidestep the confrontation with our past by insisting that any such direct engagement on the wisdom of our legal past is precluded by our legal present. However, it seems both possible and important to craft a better *legal* response, even if all of its contours are not entirely clear. Looking to the nature and meaning of constitutional values and the influence they exert on the court's ability to 'blindly' enforce some other legal act or exercise of sovereignty – be it of the past or elsewhere – may serve as a guide. And perhaps if we acknowledge the undeniable respects in which the past is indeed another country, we may find some legal inspiration to assist us in reconciling the need to respect our own fundamental values and the complexity of judgment across the difficult moral distance of time. This task holds great significance for the very meaning of law. Indeed, it is precisely because reparations cases remind us of the complicity of the legal system in the enforcement of mass injustice that they so pointedly call for law itself to reassert its own moral self-understanding."[71]

Moran's point is echoed in the chapter in this book by Roy Brooks regarding the struggle by African-Americans for redress for slavery (see pages 297-313). Brooks highlights the manner in which litigation aimed at reparations has failed before US Courts, one reason being the Courts' view that the plaintiffs' claims are time-barred. In response, he notes that 'slave redress cases present a normative challenge to the US legal system.' That is because '[i]f the slave descendants' claims are morally compelling [which they obviously are], then they *must* be cognizable under US law; otherwise, the extant law stands as the present incarnation of America's worst atrocity and the corrupt laws that made it possible'.

Whether one adopts a positivist or natural law view, there are further good reasons for rejecting the rigid application of the inter-temporal law doctrine to preclude a

[71] Moran, M. (2003) *The Limits of Influence: Mack and the Influence of the Charter on Private Law.* Unpublished Conference Paper presented at the Commonwealth Legal Education Association Conference held at the University of Windsor, Ontario, Canada between 12 and 14 June 2003.

reparations claim for gross human rights abuses committed during the slave trade. A positivist may argue that it is simply not possible to apply the doctrine of inter-temporal law to the case of reparations for slavery, since there was no proper 'international legal system' (as properly understood) in place during the time these crimes against humanity were being perpetrated. All that existed at the time was a set of rules formulated by those who perpetrated and benefited from these crimes, which should not now be graced with the appellation 'international law', nor be allowed to bind the successors of those who had no say in their formulation and suffered unspeakably as a result of their application. It may also be argued that even if the doctrine of inter-temporal law is to be applied, justice demands the adoption of a greatly expanded definition of 'international law', as it existed at the time of the slave trade. The views of both the 'great powers' as well as those subject to their colonial domination ought to be considered. It is no answer to state that the views of the tribes whose members were being enslaved are irrelevant to the status of international law at the time. They may have been irrelevant to the 'great powers' at the time, but it is surely not tenable to adopt this view today, in our efforts to provide a more balanced definition of 'international law' at that time. The fact that a continent was colonised and its statesmen and leaders silenced, does not mean that we should accept the views of the oppressors as the only source of the content of international law at the time.

So too, a strong argument may be made in terms of natural law theory to override the application of the inter-temporal law doctrine. In an important sense, the present international legal system is founded upon the fiction that every human being possesses human rights. These rights are regarded as being inalienable, eternal and non-culture specific. This fiction is to be found in theories propounded by natural law thinkers from Augustine and Aquinas, to Radbruch and Finnis. Cicero provides the following classic definition of natural law, which emphasises that it is eternal, unchanging, and non-culture specific:

> "Law in the proper sense is right reason in harmony with nature. It is spread through the whole human community, unchanging and eternal, calling people to their duty by its commands and deterring them from wrong-doing by its prohibitions… This law cannot be countermanded, nor can it be in any way rescinded. We cannot be exempted from this law by any decree of the senate or the people… There will not be one such law in Rome and one such law in Athens, one now and another in the future, but all peoples at all times will be embraced by a single and eternal and unchangeable law; and there will be, as it were, one lord and master of us all – the god who is the author, proposer and interpreter of that law."[72]

To attack the idea that human rights are inalienable, eternal and non-culture specific is to threaten the very foundations of the present system of international human rights

72 Cicero (1998) *'The Republic' and 'The Laws'*. Trans. N. Rudd. Oxford: Oxford University Press at pages 68 and 69.

protection. This fiction is, in effect, all that finally stands between us and the horrors of Auschwitz and Belsen, the killing fields of East Timor and Cambodia, and the Rwandan genocide. It is a fiction which has gained increasing acceptance within the international community since the trials of the Nazi war criminals at Nuremberg following World War Two. A leading scholar, Martti Koskenniemi, points to the difficulties encountered in discarding the idea of natural law, particularly in relation to international human rights law:

> "Once the idea of a natural law is discarded, it seems difficult to justify an obligation that is not voluntarily assumed… The matter is particularly important in regard to norms intended to safeguard basic human rights and fundamental freedoms. If the only states bound to respect such rights and freedoms are the states that have formally become parties to the relevant instruments – and even then only within the scope of their often compromised wordings and multiple reservations – then many important political values would seem to lack adequate protection. It is inherently difficult to accept the notion that states are legally bound not to engage in genocide, for example, only if they have ratified and not formally denounced the 1948 Genocide Convention. Some norms seem so basic, so important, that it is more than slightly artificial to argue that states are legally bound to comply with them simply because there exists an agreement between them to that effect, rather than because, in the words of the International Court of Justice (ICJ), non-compliance would 'shock [] the conscience of mankind' and be contrary to 'elementary considerations of humanity.'"[73]

But how do these arguments, linking concepts of natural law to international law, translate into a possible claim for reparations for crimes – like the slave trade – committed centuries ago? Even if we accept that those in power were and are able to shape and define international law in its positive sense, this does not mean that all laws passed by those in power ought necessarily to qualify as 'law' for the purposes of the inter-temporal doctrine. Certain rules of international law, as understood and applied by the 'great powers' in the past, may be so reprehensible in terms of a timeless conception of natural law, as to forfeit the right, both in the past and the present, and specifically in relation to the application of the inter-temporal doctrine, to be termed law at all. For the 'great powers' of today to accept, for the purposes of the application of the inter-temporal doctrine, that the Atlantic Slave Trade was 'legal' at the time it was conducted, is to attack the very foundations of international human rights law. The same point might be made in relation to any other gross human rights abuse committed at a time when the conduct was considered justified. Ken Cooper-Stephenson, writing in this book on the topic of residential school abuse in Canada (see pages 359-388), provides one answer which is attractive. He suggests that a present day claim may be founded on the ground that there was, by the gross abuse, a violation

---

73 Koskenniemi, M. (1990) *The Pull of the Mainstream*. 88 Mich. L. Rev. 1946. in Steiner, H. J. and Alston, P. (2000) *International Human Rights in Context – Law, Politics, Morals – Second Edition*. Oxford University Press: Oxford. Page 78

of existing rights which was not corrected in its immediate aftermath or an event or violation of rights which in retrospect is now considered as wrongful and deserving of correction or readjustment but which was not perceived as such at the time, and as a result of either, there is a present-day harm or maldistribution of rights, which, as a matter of current distributive justice ought to be rectified by the State, because the current State authorities are now the managers of present-day distributive entitlements, which ought to be made fair.

The point may be expressed simply as follows: Justice is a timeless concept. It may be suppressed, it may be denied, and by means of clever legal doctrines it may be made to disappear from sight altogether. Its timelessness, however, is something that all men and women understand. Thomas Jefferson, who himself was conflicted about slavery, acknowledged this. He wrote: 'The whole commerce between master and slave is a perpetual exercise of the more boisterous passions, the most unremitting despotism on the one part, and degrading submission on the other ... indeed I tremble for my country when I reflect that God is just, that his justice cannot sleep for ever'.Therein, perhaps, lies the importance of reparations claims. Reparations claims for gross human rights abuses, even those abuses committed in a long-distant past, are a means, however incomplete, by which to ensure that justice never sleeps.

4 CONCLUSION

Human history is soaked in blood. The mass slaughter, rape and torture of one group of human beings by another in the name of some or other twisted ideology fuelled by racial, religious or political fanaticism, is by no means a rare occurrence. During the last one hundred years alone, instances of widespread and gross violations of human rights, ranging from deliberate mass slaughter to considered policies which knowingly resulted in widespread starvation, have been so common that it is difficult even to construct a proper list of the most serious cases. Many of the most appalling examples of gross and widespread abuse have been neither acknowledged by the perpetrators, nor have the instances of abuse been properly investigated and recorded. It is rare for those responsible to be prosecuted before competent legal tribunals at either a domestic or international level. When prosecutions do take place, they are often highly selective, targeting only a small number of high profile offenders, allowing the great majority of perpetrators to escape any form of liability whatsoever. And then there is the issue of reparations. It is an unfortunate fact that, of the millions of people whose lives have been shattered by torture, rape, the murder of loved ones, or other gross violations of their human rights, only a tiny fraction have any hope of receiving any meaningful form of reparations. Often, it is only those groups with access to some form of political or economic power, which are able to mobilise significant support in favour of their particular claim for reparations, which then results in a successful claim. For the countless millions of powerless and forgotten victims of gross human rights abuses, however, the prospect of receiving any form of reparations remains virtually non-existent. It is hoped that this book will contribute in some way towards strengthening the principle that those who have suffered a gross abuse of their human rights, whatever their political or economic background, are entitled to meaningful reparation.

BACK TO THE FUTURE: THE HISTORICAL DIMENSION OF LIBERAL JUSTICE

Michael Freeman

1 ON JUSTICE

If A wrongfully harms B, then, in the absence of overriding considerations, A should compensate B for the wrong. If I wrongfully (deliberately or negligently) damage your property, then I should repair it, or replace it with its equivalent, or pay you equivalent financial compensation, and perhaps I should pay you some additional compensation for the inconvenience and other non-material harms that my act has caused you. Such wrongful acts damage just relations between the parties, and justice seems to require that the wrongdoer should repair the damage. The obligation to make reparation thus seems to follow from basic ideas of justice, wrongdoing and unjustified harm. Since gross human rights abuses are extreme wrongs, they would seem to give rise to strong obligations of reparation. This conclusion is, however, oversimplified in several ways.

Firstly, gross human rights violations are likely to involve wrongdoers who are not only individuals, but also role-holders in complex organisations (army, security services, police, death squads, etc.); the victims may be numerous and targeted because of group membership (racial, ethnic, religious, political, etc.); and some individuals may belong to both categories: victims may have collaborated in wrongs done to others. This may mean that the simple model of wrongdoer A paying reparations for harm done to victim B may not apply, and the analysis of reparative justice, if applicable at all, will have to be more complex.

Secondly, reparation involves transfers of goods (material and/or non-material), and the justice of such transfers does not depend only on previous wrongdoing for which they are reparations. Suppose, for example, that A stole land from B, who had stolen it from C. A real-life example might be communist expropriation of assets from members of the 'bourgeoisie', who may have acquired them from Nazis, who had in turn expropriated them from Jews. Should post-Communist regimes compensate the expropriated bourgeois or the Jews, or both? What if the victims of these wrongs – the bourgeois and the Jews – are well off while others, not involved in these wrongs, are needy? Put abstractly, even though A has wronged B, it is doubtful whether A should pay reparations to B. It may be that A should pay reparations for any wrongful harm done to B, but the payment of such reparations does not necessarily produce a just outcome, nor even a more just state of affairs than that which would exist if A did not pay the reparations. Reparation (re)distributes goods, and it is therefore only one part of the structure of justice (or injustice) in society.

Thirdly, gross human rights abuses may persist over long periods of time. The long-term consequences of such abuses may be intergenerational, so that the original perpetrators and victims are dead when the question of reparations arises. Individuals who have not themselves committed human rights abuses may be unwilling to contribute to the payment of reparations for them, and yet the abuses may have persisting harmful consequences long after the abuses themselves have ceased. Insofar as the later situation is unjust, it calls for rectification, and yet it is not obvious that 'reparations' are the best way to achieve this, and, even if they are, it is not obvious who should pay reparations to whom. Claims have been made, for example, that 'the West' should pay reparations to 'Africa' for slavery. Yet almost no-one in the West has engaged in slavery; some (for example, indigenous Americans) have been victims of Western injustices; and not all Africans have been victims of slavery (some may even have benefited from it).

Fourthly, the idea of 'reparation' is problematic for reasons that are independent of the concept of justice. The past is past, and cannot, literally, be 'repaired'. *Compensation* can be paid for past wrongs, but it is notoriously difficult to determine adequate compensation for serious wrongs, such as murder or torture. Massive human rights abuses, such as the Holocaust or apartheid, seem to overwhelm the concepts of reparation and compensation. The fact that no reparation could be adequate for some wrongs is, however, no reason to do nothing, for doing nothing may itself be a wrong. The harm done by a past wrong can be mitigated, and there may well be an obligation to make reparations to this end.

Fifthly, notwithstanding the obvious, *prima facie* obligation to make reparation for wrongful harms, Western theories of justice, especially their modern liberal versions, find it difficult to think about historical injustice. From Plato to Rawls, they have given priority to ideal conceptions of the just society.[1] Such theories are analytical, and largely exclude the (non-ideal) world of history. Modern theories of justice sometimes acknowledge, in passing, that many injustices – such as those of colonialism and slavery – were committed in the past, but these theories are mainly synchronic, treating of relations among contemporaries. They emphasise rights and obligations, benefits and burdens, which arise from the interactions (actual or hypothetical) of individuals and/or groups. There is surprisingly little wrongdoing in theories of justice, and consequently little call for reparations.

---

1 J. Rawls, *A Theory of Justice*, (Oxford: Oxford University Press, 1972), 8-9.

Conceptions of justice may be not only ideal but also comprehensive. Justice, Aristotle said, is complete virtue.[2] Alternatively, a society may be considered just when everything is right, and thus is in a state of moral and political equilibrium.[3] Rawls said that justice was the first virtue of social institutions. His conception of social justice, however, was limited to providing a standard whereby the *distributive* aspects of the basic structure of society were to be assessed. This standard was not to be confused with principles defining the other virtues, for social arrangements might be efficient or inefficient, and many other things, as well as just or unjust.[4] Rawls' theory of distributive justice says nothing about reparations for historical injustice. Such reparations might distribute goods more fairly, but just reparation and fair distribution are distinct ideas, and are not necessarily mutually compatible.

Since the concept of justice is deeply controversial – some would say 'essentially contested' – there is a case for distinguishing procedural from substantive justice, and thinking of the former as a mean to resolve disagreements about the latter in a fair manner.[5] Procedural justice may require some form of democracy, since a fair procedure may plausibly be considered to entail giving everyone a voice, indeed, in some sense, an equal voice. Procedural justice and deliberative democracy may nevertheless fail to resolve deep disagreements, including disagreements about substantive justice.[6] Justice may therefore require democracy, but clearly democracies can be unjust by some plausible criteria, such as the meeting of basic needs, or, indeed, the reparation of past wrongs.

An ancient conception of justice requires that everyone be given their due. This may be quite indeterminate, but it suggests that simple majoritarian democracy is insufficient for justice, and must be supplemented by a conception of universal rights.[7] Various criteria of justice have been proposed, such as fairness, desert, need and the fulfilment of reasonable expectations. Conflicts may arise both among and within the criteria: meeting some needs may, for example, mean neglecting others. Whatever the criteria of justice, obligations arising from these criteria are commonly thought to entail rights of those to whom the obligations are owed. Contractual obligations and rights provide a clear example. It is often assumed that human rights entail obligations. Rights therefore entail costs, and thus meeting the demands of justice and rights must depend to some extent on the availability of resources. Insofar as there may be, in some

---

2 Aristotle, *The Nicomachean Ethics*, (Harmonsdworth: Penguin Books, 1955), Book Five, 141.

3 T. Campbell, *Justice*, (Basingstoke: Macmillan, second edition, 2001), 24, 164.

4 Rawls, *A Theory of Justice*, 3-4, 9.

5 Campbell, *Justice*, 250.

6 A. Weale, 'Contractarian Theory, Deliberative Democracy and General Agreement', in K. Dowding, R. E. Goodin and C. Pateman (eds), *Justice and Democracy*, (Cambridge: Cambridge University Press, 2004), 93.

7 Campbell, *Justice*, 12-13, 25, 76, 84.

circumstances, a right to reparation resulting from past human rights abuses, this right may be constrained by the costs of fulfilling it.

The rule of law may be necessary, but not sufficient for justice, in that it creates stable expectations and prevents unfair arbitrariness, although the content of law may, of course, be unjust in various ways. The rule of law provides legitimacy to judicial decision-making, although the power of judges can be controversial, especially when they are interpreting and implementing human-rights standards that are vague and have important social and political implications. There is an unresolved issue about the proper roles of elected legislatures and judiciaries in the implementation of democratic and human rights.[8]

The requirements of justice may conflict with those of liberty, utility and humanity, and we cannot confidently say *a priori* which should prevail. So-called 'libertarians' accord priority to liberty, and do not value conceptions of distributive justice that they consider to be restrictive of liberty.[9] Humanity may prevail over justice, when, for example, punishing wrongdoers according to their desert may seem cruel because of their ill health. Utility might 'trump' justice if the utility is great and the injustice slight. The priority of prudence over justice has been accorded considerable weight when new democracies have had to decide whether or not to prosecute alleged perpetrators of gross human-rights violations under the previous regime, while the stability of the new democratic regime remains uncertain.

Communitarian philosophers have criticised liberal theories of justice on the ground that they employ a concept of the autonomous 'self', which is empty. Real selves, they maintain, are constituted by social beliefs, norms and values. Liberals respond that, insofar as selves are socially constructed, this refutes neither the reality nor the fundamental moral importance of autonomy. The concept of human rights is usually thought to presuppose this liberal line of argument.[10] To connect the concept of human rights to the problem of reparations for historical injustice, however, it is necessary to recognise that individuals have a sense of identity, which is constituted in part by *memory*, and that memory is partly collective insofar as it is shared in community with others. There is a tension between the liberal concept of autonomy and the communitarian conception of identity, for collective identities place constraints on individual autonomy. Insofar as claims for reparations are based on collective identities (for example, reparations for Jews, Japanese-Americans, Africans, African-Americans) they may rest on theoretical grounds inconsistent with those of liberal justice. The claim for reparations requires the recognition that the 'self' is partly constituted by its history. Liberal theory can include reparative justice, therefore, only

---

8 Campbell, *Justice*, 33, 75, 243; M. Freeman, 'Rights', in P.B. Clarke and J. Foweraker (eds), *Encyclopedia of Democratic Thought*, (London: Routledge, 2001), 628-32.

9 Campbell, *Justice*, 13-15, 18.

10 J. Donnelly, *Universal Human Rights in Theory and Practice*, (Ithaca, NY: Cornell University Press, second edition, 2003).

if it recognises this historical nature of the self. Liberalism can, and should, do this, but it requires a more social conception of the self than liberal theory has often employed. The recognition of the historical self is consistent with respect for human rights, but only on the basis of careful analysis of its individual and collective aspects.

The case for reparative justice can, therefore, seem straightforward. If A wrongfully harms B, A should 'repair' the harm so far as possible. Analysis shows, however, that the idea of repairing harm is complex. The idea of making reparations for historical injustice is also problematic for liberal theory, because the liberal conception of justice is ideal and synchronic, and has difficulty in incorporating the rectification of past injustices. Yet reparations for gross human rights abuses and respect for human rights now are both grounded in the idea of human rights, which is widely endorsed by the liberal theory of justice. There is a need, therefore, to reconcile reparative justice with liberal theory. I shall try to show how this can be done.

2 HISTORICAL JUSTICE

Janna Thompson has eloquently made the case for taking historical justice seriously. Many people, she reminds us, have been treated with extreme injustice in the past, and neither they nor their heirs have received any compensation for their suffering. The effects of such historical injustices persist long after the perpetrators and their victims are dead. They haunt the memories of descendants, blight the history of peoples, and poison relations between communities. They are the root cause of many existing inequities. They have motivated some of the bloodiest conflicts of history. There are strong reasons, therefore, both of principle and of practical politics to accord to historical injustice a more important role in political theory.[11]

The recognition of historical injustice is necessary to analyse the contemporary state of justice. To fail to acknowledge historical injustice is to demean, and thus to discriminate against its victims. To treat those suffering from the consequences of past injustice as 'equal citizens' with those who are not suffering in this way is to deny an important form of social inequality. It is to risk misunderstanding the root causes of current conflicts by denying their history. Injustice is historically constructed. Addressing injustice, therefore, requires the concept of historical injustice.

Historical injustices may have contributed to the power, wealth and status of later generations, who have benefited, directly or indirectly, knowingly or unknowingly, from the injustices. They may be hidden supports for the self-esteem of these beneficiaries, while they induce lack of self-esteem and despair in the descendants of

---

11 J. Thompson, *Taking Responsibility for the Past: Reparation and Historical Justice*, (Cambridge, Polity, 2002), vii.

the victims.[12] The perspective of historical injustice views authoritarianism, not simply as a regime-type from which a number of peoples have been liberated in 'transitions', but, rather, as an integral part of the historical development of contemporary liberal democracies.[13] Henry Shue has argued that the theory of human rights requires, but still lacks, a theory of corresponding duties. The idea of historical justice suggests that it requires not only a primary theory of what duties people owe to others, but also a secondary theory of what duties are owed when primary duties have not been fulfilled.[14] The theory of reparations is part of the theory of secondary duties required by the theory of human rights.

The distinction between distributive and historical justice appears to reproduce the dispute between the rival theories of justice proposed by John Rawls and Robert Nozick. Rawls' theory was criticised by Nozick on the ground that it required a 'pattern' of distribution, as many theories of distributive justice have done: for example, the principle of giving everyone their due or that of giving to each according to their need. There are two basic flaws in such theories, according to Nozick. The first is that they assume that there already exist some things to be distributed according to the required pattern, and fail to show that they are justly distributable at all. The second flaw is that, if a just pattern were to be established, it would have to forbid any exercise of freedom that changed the pattern. Instead of 'patterned' principles of justice, Nozick developed a theory of 'just holdings'. These are holdings that have been derived justly (without coercion or deception) from previous just holdings. If holdings are transferred unjustly (for example, by theft), the theory calls for the rectification of this injustice.[15]

Nozick's theory of justice is therefore 'historical' in the sense that the justice of any particular holding depends on the justice of its history: a just holding is a holding that derives from an uncorrupted chain of just holdings and just transfers. It recognises historical injustice in that it requires the rectification of any past unjust transfer. The theory is, however, strictly individualistic. Nozickean individuals have rights, but not identities. Collectivities do not have rights unless individuals freely agree that they should. The theory will not, therefore, support the conclusions of those who believe that memory, identity and community can ground claims to reparations for historical injustice. The individualism of the theory is, however, valuable as a check on the impact that collective claims for reparations might have on individual rights.

---

12 Thompson, *Taking Responsibility*, 9, 66, 106.

13 J. Torpey, 'Introduction: Politics and the Past', in J. Torpey (ed.), *Politics and the Past: On Repairing Historical Injustices*, (Lanham, MD: Rowman & Littlefield, 2003), 9.

14 H. Shue, 'Thickening Convergence: Human Rights and Cultural Diversity', in D. K. Chatterjee (ed.), *The Ethics of Assistance: Morality and the Distant Needy*, (Cambridge: Cambridge University Press, 2004), 217-41; L. E. Lomasky, 'Compensation and the Bounds of Rights', in J. W. Chapman (ed.), *Compensatory Justice*,(New York, NY: New York University Press, 1991), 26.

15 R. Nozick, *Anarchy, State, and Utopia*, (Oxford: Basil Blackwell, 1974).

Nozick's theory has several defects, however. I shall mention only those that relate to reparative justice. The first is that, since just holdings are holdings derived justly from previous just holdings, just holdings must be traceable through an unbroken line of just transfers to an original just holding. There is, however, no uncontroversial way to identify *this* original position. The second problem arises only if the first has been solved. Nozick's theory does not allow us to be selective in the rectification of historical injustices by, for example, according priority to the most serious or the most recent. *Any* historical injustice taints all holdings derived from it – for ever. The justice of all actual holdings would be doubtful, and this uncertainty is incompatible with any conception of justice that could be used in real-world situations. A third problem is that, even if we could identify an original position and an unjust transfer at some point in history, rectification of this injustice would require us to know what would have happened had the injustice not been committed. This counter-factual knowledge may be in principle unobtainable.[16] Finally, the injustice of certain past transfers may be perfectly clear, but the rectification required may be overwhelmingly complex or even impossible to determine. Demands for reparations for slavery are often said to suffer from this defect.[17]

These theoretical difficulties have important practical implications. The failure to rectify the injustices associated with imperialism, and the difficulty that we have in identifying who owes what to whom, underlie many of the current controversies, not only about reparations for slavery and colonialism, but also over the supposed 'right to development', minority rights, multiculturalism, and the rights of indigenous peoples. These topics have been central to recent political philosophy, but it has rarely been recognised that these problems are the product of historical injustice.[18] The literature on the justice of minority rights and that on reparations for historical injustice usually do not refer to each other. If, as theorists of historical injustice commonly claim, historical injustice persists in contemporary inequalities, then the comparison of these two bodies of theory should illuminate both.

Will Kymlicka has criticised the liberal conception of human rights, for example, on the ground that it cannot provide equal citizenship for all. The structure of contemporary liberal societies unjustly disadvantages certain groups, such as indigenous peoples, and, he maintains, certain collective rights are necessary to implement the *liberal* principle of the equal right to justice. Those whose culture is socially dominant can defend their culture without special rights. Those whose culture

---

16 J. Waldron, 'Superseding Historic Injustice', (1992) 103 *Ethics*, 8.

17 G. C. Loury, 'Trans-Generational Justice – Compensatory vs. Interpretative Approaches', paper presented to the international conference on 'Reparations: An Interdisciplinary Examination of Some Philosophical Issues', Department of Philosophy, Queen's University, Kingston, Ontario, Canada, 6-8 February, 2004, 13.

18 P. Kelly (ed.), *Multiculturalism Reconsidered: 'Culture and Equality' and its Critics*, (Cambridge: Polity, 2002).

is subordinate cannot do so. This inequality in the conditions of citizenship is unjust. In this situation equal rights entail special rights.[19] Whereas Kymlicka defends a liberal theory of minority rights, James Tully has criticised the 'monological' character of liberal constitutionalism, and argued that it should be replaced, in a multicultural society, by intercultural dialogue.[20] Liberals fear that multiculturalism is a thin disguise for the defence of illiberal practices.[21] Multiculturalists criticise liberals for defending an authoritarian form of liberalism.[22]

We have, therefore, three theoretical approaches to liberalism, human rights and historical injustice. The first, 'classical' approach says that justice requires full respect for human rights and equal citizenship in a democracy. This approach views collective rights with suspicion, because they may easily threaten individual human rights. It does not rule out reparations, but they are marginal to its concerns. The second approach holds that the 'classical' theory is not genuinely egalitarian, because it fails to recognise structural inequalities based on cultural hierarchies. Although these cultural hierarchies are the products of historical injustice, this approach defends collective rights for subordinate groups on the ground of a group-sensitive, neo-Rawlsian, liberal conception of justice, and not on the ground of the rectification of historical injustice. The third approach argues that 'classical' liberalism bears the marks of its imperial past in its failure to recognise the worth of minority cultures that may not be fully liberal. This approach is more historical and somewhat more communitarian than the other two. Although it seems to be motivated by a concern with historical injustice, this plays little role in its theories, which advance principles of culture-sensitive justice, in which reparations are absent, though not necessarily ruled out. Unjust cultural inequalities have historical origins, but the injustice is said to lie in the contemporary inequality, not in the historical origins. The concern of minority-rights theorists and multiculturalists is with *culture* and current inequalities, not with reparations.

The liberal theory of justice provides a robust defence of human rights, especially those of vulnerable categories of individuals, such as women and children, who have been victims of historical injustice, and remain victims of present injustice.

---

19 W. Kymlicka, *Multicultural Citizenship: A Liberal Theory of Minority Rights*, (Oxford: Clarendon Press, 1995).

20 J. Tully, *Strange Multiplicities: Constitutionalism in an Age of Diversity*, (Cambridge: Cambridge University Press, 1995).

21 B. Barry, *Culture and Equality: An Egalitarian Critique of Multiculturalism*, (Cambridge: Polity, 2001)); J. Cohen (ed.), *Is Multiculturalism Bad for Women?*, (Princeton, NJ: Princeton University Press).

22 J. Chaplin, 'How Much Cultural and Religious Pluralism Can Liberalism Tolerate?', in J. Horton (ed.), *Liberalism, Multiculturalism and Toleration*, (Basingstoke: Macmillan, 1993), 39-46; B. Parekh, *Rethinking Multiculturalism: Cultural Diversity and Political Theory*, (Basingstoke: Macmillan, 2000), and 'Barry and the Dangers of Liberalism', in Kelly (ed.), *Multiculturalism Reconsidered*, 133-50; J. Tully, 'The Illiberal Liberal: Brian Barry's Polemical Attack on Multiculturalism', in Kelly (ed.), *Multiculturalism Reconsidered*, 102-13.

Communitarians and multiculturalists are often at best unclear on these important issues. The 'classical' liberal theory is, however, vulnerable to at least two objections. The first is that it ignores the persisting effects of historical injustice, including its effects on culture and cultural hierarchies. In particular, although liberalism unreservedly condemns racism and racial discrimination, it underestimates the contribution of historical injustices to inequalities of status and self-esteem in contemporary society. Consequently, it underestimates the role of history and culture in the structure of contemporary injustice. The second objection is that contemporary, synchronic justice is given priority over the rectification of historical injustices. Liberal justice suffers from a moral amnesia that overlooks the crimes of the past in designing social policies for the present. Forgetting or denying past injustice makes the theory of contemporary justice incomplete.

The 'classical' liberal theory of justice, therefore, can recognise that wrong ought to be rectified so far as possible, but is reluctant to recognise special rights for minorities that have suffered historical injustice on the ground that this would violate the principle of equal rights. Samuel Freeman has pointed out, however, that the Rawlsian theory of justice is an *ideal* theory. In liberal theory, he argues, some departure from the liberal ideal of fair equal opportunity is permissible in less than ideal circumstances to rectify past and present discrimination, and when it would promote the conditions of equality needed for a just society.[23] The debate over liberalism and multiculturalism suffers from a failure to distinguish between ideal and non-ideal theory. It is precisely in the field of non-ideal theory, which Rawls explicitly set aside, that the theory of reparations for historical injustice must be located.

In the non-ideal (i.e., the actual) world, wrongs stand in need of repair. As liberals readily recognise that sick people need health care that healthy people do not, so, in the transition from repressive to liberal regimes, victims of torture require special treatment *arising from past injustice.* If the victims of negligence have the right to compensation, the victims of human rights abuses have at least a *prima facie* right to reparations. The right is only *prima facie*, because making reparations encounters numerous difficulties: full restitution may be impossible (in the case of political murders, or even of lesser crimes, for example); losses may well be unquantifiable; resources may be scarce; there may be other, just claims on those resources; and there may be resistance to reparations which, though not justified, cannot be overcome, or can be overcome only at enormous cost. Massive human-rights violations overwhelm national and international legal and political institutions, and there are dangers in raising unrealistic expectations. Pablo de Greiff has suggested that, insofar as reparations contribute to the constitution of a new political community, they are

---

23 S. Freeman, 'Liberalism and the Accommodation of Group Claims', in Kelly (ed.), *Multiculturalism Reconsidered*, 27.

political rather than juridical.[24] The rule of law and human rights may, however, fail to create a stable, just society if due recognition and fair reparation are not given to the victims of historical injustice. This recognition and the rectification of historical injustices (so far as possible) may be necessary to equal citizenship and equal justice in the present. They are therefore necessary to liberal justice.

3 REPARATIVE JUSTICE

Reparations were historically claims made by states on other states, which they alleged had wronged them. Sometimes, they were a form of 'victors' justice', by which the winners of war demanded compensation from the losers. The reparations demanded of Germany after the First World War are the best-known example. However, after the Second World War, Germany agreed to pay reparations both to organisations representing victims of Nazism and to the state of Israel. The gradual emergence of the global human-rights movement in the decades following the Second World War raised questions as to whether all victims of gross human rights abuses might have the right to reparations. These questions were raised in connection with the transitions from authoritarianism to democracy that took place at the end of the century, but they were not confined to such contexts: claims for reparations for African slavery were made, for example. These claims gave rise to questions of principle and to practical questions. Who was entitled to reparations? Who had the obligation to pay them? What form should reparations take? If there was a *prima facie* right to reparations, could it be overridden by other considerations, such as social stability and the building of a more just future?[25]

In international law states have obligations to pay reparations for breaches of their legal obligations.[26] The UN Human Rights Commission's special rapporteur on the right to restitution, compensation and rehabilitation for victims of gross violations of human rights, M. Cherif Bassiouni, has proposed that a duty of states to provide for or facilitate reparation to victims of violations of international human rights and

---

24 P. De Greiff, 'Justice and Reparations', paper presented to the international conference on 'Reparations: An Interdisciplinary Examination of Some Philosophical Issues', Department of Philosophy, Queen's University, Kingston, Ontario, Canada, 6-8 February 2004.

25 T. McCarthy, 'Coming to Terms with Our Past, Part II: On the Morality and Politics of Reparations for Slavery', (2004) 32 *Political Theory*, 750-1.

26 M. du Plessis, 'Historical Injustice and International Law: An Exploratory Discussion of Reparation for Slavery', (2003) 25 *Human Rights Quarterly*, 629.

humanitarian law, and a right of victims to reparation for harm suffered, should be recognised.[27]

The first principle of reparative justice is that the wrongdoer pays. Bassiouni has proposed that, if the party responsible for human-rights violations is unable or unwilling to meet their obligations, the state should endeavour to provide reparations to victims, and, if the state or government under whose authority the violation occurred is no longer in existence, the successor state or government should provide reparation to the victims.[28] The move from the obligation of wrongdoers to that of states is not obvious, however, because the ground of these obligations must be different. States represent, and spend the resources of, those who may be not only innocent of the violations, but may have been its victims. State responsibility for reparations when the state is 'innocent' requires supporting argument.

This argument begins with Aristotle's distinction between distributive and corrective justice. The first tells us the right way to distribute whatever is distributable in society, while the second rectifies unfairness in transactions. Locke argued for a right of victims of injustice (that is, rights violations) to reparations, and Kant thought that perpetrators of injustice ought to try to remedy their injustice. Although the distinction between distributive and corrective justice is common, and useful, corrective justice is a sub-type of distributive justice insofar as it specifies rightful (re)distributions. The requirements of distributive and corrective justice may, however, not always be mutually compatible. If A harms B, A may owe reparation to B, even if some reasonable principles of distributive justice (based, say, on need or desert) require the transfer of goods from B to A. All corrective justice refers to injustice committed in the past. The idea of reparative justice, however, has been extended to injustice committed in the distant past, when the direct perpetrators and victims are now dead. This raises questions about the obligations and rights of their heirs.

The simplest form of corrective justice is *restitution*: A steals land from B; A returns the land to B. Restitution may, however, be impossible, if A and B are dead and/or the asset stolen has been destroyed or is not identifiable. Where restitution is impossible, *compensation* is a second-best form of corrective justice. However, if the original wrongdoer and victim are dead, it is not obvious who should pay compensation to whom, nor is the amount of compensation always clear. Also, wrongdoing does not cause only material damage: the victim is *wronged*. Corrective justice may, therefore, require the righting of the wrong, and this may require appropriate symbolic recognition of wrongdoing by the perpetrator (in the form of an apology, for example)

---

27 United Nations Economic and Social Council, Commission on Human Rights, *Civil and Political Rights, Including the Question of: Independence of the Judiciary, Administration of Justice, Impunity: The right to restitution, compensation and rehabilitations for victims of gross violations of human rights and fundamental freedoms*. Final report of the Special Rapporteur, Mr. M. Cherif Bassiouni, submitted in accordance with Commission resolution 1999/33, E/CN.4/2000/62, 18 January 2000, 7, 9.

28 United Nations, *Civil and Political Rights*, 9-10.

and of the harm done to the victim: in the case of massive human-rights violations, some memorialisation of the wrong may be appropriate.

The principle of restitution requires that, if A wrongfully takes x from B, A ought to return x to B. If A and B are dead, the current holders of x ought perhaps to return x to the lawful heirs of B. This may, however, be impracticable, or even wrong, for several reasons: it may not be possible to identify the original owners and/or their heirs; the current holders may have invested effort and skill into improving x, and have a reasonable expectation that they are the rightful owners of x; the current holders may be much needier than those who claim x as the heirs of B; the social utility of the status quo may far outweigh that of restitution, for example if many innocent individuals are dependent on the current holder's retaining use of x. Restitution may be impracticable or inappropriate for rectifying some forms of serious injustice – such as genocide or slavery – although it may form part of a suitable reparations package.[29]

More complex than the idea of restitution is that of *unjust enrichment*. If A steals x from B, and then gives it to C, C ought, *ceteris paribus*, to restore it to A. However, if C has used x to obtain further advantages, and B has suffered further disadvantages as a consequence of having lost x, C may owe reparations to B on the ground of unjust enrichment. This may be true even if we cannot identify precisely what C has gained thereby. If A was a slave-owner, B was A's slave, and C was A's business partner, A and C may have been unjustly enriched by the enslavement of B, but it may be impossible to say by exactly how much. The problem becomes more complicated if A and B are now long dead, and the descendants of B now claim reparations from the descendants of A on the ground of the injustice done by A to B. Unjust enrichment seems to entail an obligation to pay reparations, but implementing this principle raises severe difficulties of principle and practice.

When restitution is impossible or morally undesirable, compensation may be required. Both restitution and compensation may be dubious if they are likely to stimulate injustice, because, for example, the recipients are corrupt or incompetent. Where compensation is the best option, it should 'undo' the injustice so far as possible, but, for some serious injustices, compensation may be impossible to quantify, and may seem morally inappropriate. Compensation may be offensive, but it may also express remorse, respect for the dignity of the victims, and/or a commitment not to repeat the injustice. Compensation does not 'rectify' a wrong, but a compensated wrong is generally preferable to an uncompensated wrong. Even where there is a clear and serious injustice, it may not be clear how much compensation should be paid, who should pay it, and/or to whom it should be paid. This is particularly so when the

[29] Du Plessis, 'Historical Injustice', 648; C. S. Maier, 'Overcoming the Past? Narrative and Negotiations, Remembering, and Reparation: Issues at the Interface of History and the Law', in Torpey (ed.), *Politics and the Past*, 296-7.

injustice was committed in the distant past, as, for example, in the case of African slavery. However, where adequate compensation is impossible because the injustice was too deep and/or too widespread, compensation may be appropriate for those who suffered most.[30]

Charles Maier has pointed out that consideration of corrective justice commonly employs 're' words: recording, remembering, retribution, reparation, reconciliation. But none of these actions can undo the past. 'We repair and remember because we cannot return'. Injustice damages communities, or makes their emergence impossible. All the 're' actions are designed to make the best of a situation, which is what it is and cannot be otherwise. Rectificatory justice seeks to restore, or to create a political community, and in this sense to achieve *political* reconciliation, which must be distinguished from the religious sense of reconciliation, which may be unattainable, and is a matter for individuals rather than for public policy. Symbolic acknowledgement of past injustice, apologies, truth commissions and commemorations, may all contribute to this form of rectificatory justice by delegitimating the previous regime, reaffirming the dignity of those who suffered from it, and affirming a commitment to a more just future.[31]

4 ARE HISTORICAL AND DISTRIBUTIVE JUSTICE COMPATIBLE?

Reparative justice is part of distributive justice, because it (re)distributes goods justly. Reparative justice may seem to differ from distributive justice, however, because the former seeks to rectify wrongs done in the past, whereas the latter seeks to rectify the present and the future. Reparative justice, however, also looks to the future insofar as it 'repairs' injustice (so far as possible) and thereby contributes to a better future. Nevertheless, reparative justice responds to claims from the past, and is thus conceptually distinct from distributive justice, which allocates goods now and for the future. Because the ground of each form of justice is different, there is the possibility that they may not be mutually compatible.

---

30 Du Plessis, 'Historical Injustice', 630, 649, 651; S. Kershnar, *Justice for the Past* (Albany, NY: State University of New York Press, 2004), 40-1; Torpey, 'Introduction', 16; R. E. Howard-Hassmann, 'Moral Integrity and Reparations for Africa', in Torpey (ed.), *Politics and the Past*, ; R. C. Roberts, 'Justice and Rectification: A Taxonomy of Justice', in R. C. Roberts (ed.), *Injustice and Rectification*, (New York: Peter Lang, 2002), 9, 11-12, 15, 18, 169, note 10; Maier, 'Overcoming the Past?', 297; A. Valls, 'Racial Justice as Transitional Justice, (2003) XXXVI *Polity*, 57, 71; G. F. Gaus, 'Does Compensation Restore Equality?', in Chapman (ed.), *Compensatory Justice*, 63-5, 72-3, 77, note 31; Lomasky, 'Compensation', 23, 30; E. F. Paul, 'Set-Asides, Reparations, and Compensatory Justice', in Chapman (ed.), *Compensatory Justice*, 127-8.

31 Maier, 'Overcoming the Past?', 295-8, 302; Valls, 'Racial Justice', 57-8.

Recognition of past injustice, and of the obligation to make reparations for it, may have beneficial practical consequences for distributive justice now. Max du Plessis has suggested that Western demands for human-rights improvements in developing countries might carry more moral and political force if Western nations were more willing to acknowledge the injustice that they had perpetrated in the past, and to take the case for reparations seriously. Denial of the case for reparations can therefore poison the present, and thus undermine prospects for justice in the future.[32]

Loren Lomasky has argued that there is an important difference between distributive and compensatory justice. Distributive justice is impartial: everyone gets the benefits and burdens specified by its principles. Compensatory justice arises from a particular injustice committed by one party against another. Neither the right to compensation nor the obligation to make it is impersonal: on the contrary, it arises from a particular interpersonal relation. This may bring about a conflict between rectificatory and distributive justice when the injustice was committed in the distant past. The more distant the injustice, the more uncertain the rights and obligations to which it gives rise, the more reparative justice should give way to distributive justice. Although this principle yields criteria for deciding the priority between reparative and distributive justice, it leaves open the possibility that each may generate plausible claims that come into conflict. This is particularly clear when land wrongfully taken provides the basis for a relatively just life for many people who did not commit the original wrongful taking.[33]

We saw earlier that Nozick's theory of rectification was unsatisfactory. Even if it were not, however, his theory of entitlements would raise problems about the relation between historical and distributive justice. The proposition that A should have x because it is A's historical entitlement (as in Nozick's theory and the land claims of many indigenous peoples) may conflict with the proposition that A should *not* have x, *whatever the historical relation between A and x*, because A's having x violates a principle of distributive justice: for example, that it leaves B in morally unjustifiable need. The needs of the latter would surely 'trump' the claims of the former. A. John Simmons points out that even Nozick allowed that no theory of just acquisition would be plausible unless it contained the 'Lockean proviso' that 'enough and as good' is left for others. The Lockean proviso is, however, a *pattern* principle that limits the permissibility of Nozickean holdings. Even Nozick himself allowed that the difficulties of determining who is entitled to what now according to his theory were such that something like Rawls' 'difference principle' – distributing primary goods in the way most favourable to the worst-off in society – might be the best approximation to what

32 Du Plessis, 'Historical Injustice', 627-8, 641.

33 Lomasky, 'Compensation', 28; A. J. Simmons, 'Historical Rights and Fair Shares', in *Justification and Legitimacy: Essays on Rights and Obligations* (Cambridge: Cambridge University Press, 2001), 243.

would be the outcome of applying his own theory.[34] Theories of historical entitlement are, therefore, questionable in principle, and very difficult to apply in practice. This suggests that they cannot stand alone, but must be qualified by theories of distributive justice.

5 REMEDIAL RESPONSIBILITY

If an historical injustice has occurred, the question arises as to who owes what to whom now. Who should pay for African slavery, and to whom should payment be made? Some writers argue that, if the historical injustice had not occurred, present claimants would not have been born, and that they cannot therefore claim that the injustice has made them worse off. If there had been no African slavery, there would now be no 'African-Americans', at least not with their present identities, and therefore African-Americans have no valid claims on the ground that they have suffered as a consequence of slavery. This argument seems counter-intuitive, and, if the intuition is morally sound, the case for reparation must not depend on the kinds of argument from biology and identity that are criticised in this way.[35]

Simple models of corrective justice often treat of relations among individuals: A wrongs B; A should pay reparations to B. However, if there is unjust, institutionalised discrimination against a group within society, does society collectively owe compensation to the group as a collectivity, and may this obligation override the rights of individuals? These questions are raised by some affirmative action programmes. Some rights-theorists hold that collectivities may not override individual rights to fulfil their obligations, but collectivities cannot fulfil their obligations without some cost to their members, and so we have to work out what obligations collective responsibilities entail for members of those collectivities.[36]

Collectivities may be obliged to make reparations on the ground that they have been unjustly enriched by the injustice. The amount of the compensation may be the amount of unjust enrichment or the amount of loss, which may not be the same, and both amounts may be difficult to calculate. The argument from unjust enrichment is commonly made for the obligation of 'the West' to make reparations for imperialism. There is a complex debate about the causes of Western wealth, but it seems plausible to believe that the injustices of imperialism, including the slave trade, made a significant contribution to that wealth. The obligation to make reparation for injustice does not depend on unjust enrichment, however. If A wrongs B, but, despite

---

[34] Simmons, 'Historical Rights', 233; R. Nozick, *Anarchy, State, and Utopia*, 231.

[35] J. S. Fishkin, 'Justice Between Generations: Compensation, Identity, and Group Membership', in Chapman (ed.), *Compensatory Justice*, 93.

[36] Kershnar, *Justice for the Past*, 48-9.

this, B flourishes and A plunges into decline, A still has a *prima facie* obligation to make reparation to B for the wrong. This argument, however, leaves open the question as to why Westerners now, who were not responsible for imperialism, should pay reparations for the injustices committed by Westerners in the past.

Rhoda Howard-Hassmann believes that Article 28 of the Universal Declaration of Human Rights grounds such an obligation. This article states that everyone is entitled to a social and international order in which the rights set forth in the Declaration can be fully realised. This implies, Howard-Hassmann says, that 'everyone has an obligation to ensure that such an order exists'.[37] This argument moves too quickly, for it has several flaws: 1) the putative right is questionable on the ground that it cannot be implemented; 2) the inference that 'everyone' has an obligation to implement Article 28 is implausible on the ground that it entails intolerable, or at best, extremely vague duties; 3) the putative obligations are not obligations to make reparations, and therefore leave open the question as to whether such obligations *also* exist.

Stephen Kershnar argues that innocent beneficiaries of unjust acts have no obligation to make reparations, especially when the identification of perpetrators, victims and amount of harm done is uncertain. To make an innocent person pay for the wrongs of others is to violate the rights of that person. A has an obligation to pay compensation to B only if A committed a wrong, and if that wrong was the cause of harm to B. *Benefiting* from an injustice is insufficient to generate an obligation to compensate the victim. The beneficiary is not like the receiver of stolen goods, because knowingly receiving stolen goods is a wrong, whereas merely being a beneficiary of a wrong is not itself a wrong. Beneficiaries of wrongs are liable for compensation only if they consented to receive the benefits of wrongdoing with adequate knowledge of that wrongdoing. Beneficiaries of historical injustice may indeed be descendants of victims. Should native Americans pay reparations to Africans for African slavery?

Similarly, simply being a member of a group that has suffered injustice in the past does not ground a right to reparation. Some members of wronged groups may be beneficiaries of injustice: some African-Americans may be better off than they would have been (had they existed at all) had slavery not happened, because they have benefited from the 'unjust enrichment' of American society as a whole. Compensating groups for historical wrongs may also raise questions of *desert*. To penalise a deserving member of a beneficiary group in favour of an undeserving member of a victim group (say, in university admissions) seems to violate rights of the deserving person. This judgement is complicated by the possibility that an individual from a disadvantaged group may be more deserving than a rival from an advantaged group if their achievement is the same, because that achievement required more effort from the

[37] Howard-Hassmann, 'Moral Integrity', 199.

disadvantaged individual. The identification of a person as 'undeserving' may itself be a harmful consequence of past injustices.[38]

The putative obligation to make reparations for past injustice encounters the objection, not only that it may violate the rights of innocent individuals, but also that it may be undemocratic. A democratic government may claim the right to strike whatever balance it sees fit between reparations (if any) and other demands, including those of justice, on its available resources. It may, for example, give priority to economic development generally, or to helping the worst-off, or to making pragmatic concessions to power-holders for the sake of the common good.

Notwithstanding arguments that collective reparations for historical injustices may violate individual rights or democratic sovereignty, some collective reparations – such as those Germany made for Nazi crimes or the USA made to Japanese-Americans – have been made, and seem to have some moral justification. How can they then be justified? Transgenerational collective rights and obligations are familiar enough. *Pace* Kershnar, collectivities, such as corporations, may have obligations to rectify past wrongs that no current individual has committed. States may have transgenerational obligations *qua* states, and their citizens may consequently have obligations *qua* citizens. This is generally accepted where there is clearly state continuity, but may be problematic where there has been a radical discontinuity in the nature of the state or of the regime: the obligations of a new state or regime to make reparations for the crimes of its predecessor are not obvious, and may seem like punishing the innocent (or the victims) for the crimes of the guilty. New regimes may, however, make reparations precisely to symbolise the discontinuity with the past.

Janna Thompson holds that obligations to repair past wrongs are based on a conception of a society or nation as an intergenerational community. Members of such communities undertake obligations that they believe will bind future generations, and consequently they should accept obligations incurred by earlier generations. Thus, she argues that the help that the people of East Timor gave to Australia during the Second World War generated an obligation on the part of Australia to help the East Timorese in time of need. Transgenerational agreements between nations are a practical and moral necessity. Such agreements entail obligations to repair breaches, and these obligations, like the agreements from which they derive, are transgenerational. Such transgenerational obligations of reparations may override contemporary rights. Thompson identifies her theory as Burkean in its account of transgenerational moral relations, but without any necessary conservative implications for social change. It opposes theories of justice, obligation and rights that ignore the historical dimension of our social existence. The theory of transgenerational obligation does not hold when there is a radical discontinuity between the community of generations. Thus the

[38] Kershnar, *Justice for the Past*, 5, 36-47, 55, 58, 62, 64-5, 71, 76-7, 139 note 24; du Plessis, 'Historical Injustice', 632, 642; McCarthy, 'Coming to Terms', 759.

modern Greek government has no obligation to make reparations to the descendants of ancient Athenian slaves (even if we could identify them). The theory accords better with the common-sense view of responsibility for ancient wrongs than does the Nozickean theory of rights, which denies the obligation to make reparations only on the ground of inadequate knowledge.[39] David Miller places less emphasis than Thompson on the practice of making international agreements, since their bindingness on future generations is the question to be settled, and more on the argument that, insofar as citizens identify with the nation, take pride in the past achievements of their forbears, and enjoy the benefits they have bequeathed, they have an obligation to repair their wrongs. The extent of the obligation depends on the extent of the benefit. Those excluded from the benefits of citizenship may accordingly be exempted from its obligations.[40] In both theories, membership of a nation entails obligations to take responsibility for the nation's past injustices.

States and nations may therefore have collective responsibilities, and citizens and nationals may have obligations, arising not from individual guilt, but from their citizenship or membership of the nation. Some rights and obligations may persist transgenerationally, even though the question as to who owes what to whom has become complicated and/or obscured by the passage of time, if the original injustice adversely affects the identity and self-esteem of later generations. If, for example, land has religious significance for a people, its theft does not simply bequeath a material obligation of compensation to later generations, but an issue of equal citizenship, since, as a result of the original wrongdoing, current descendants of the perpetrators and the victims do not enjoy equal rights to freedom of religion. Where such an injustice persists, members of society may owe reparations to the victim group, not because they are guilty of the original wrong, but because they are citizens with duties to rectify injustices. These duties must be reconciled with other duties of justice. They are generally consistent with, indeed may be required by, respect for the human rights of all.[41]

Kershnar's argument that innocent individuals have no obligation to make reparations for wrongs that they have not caused may also not apply in a straightforward way to the complex structures of gross human rights abuses. In such situations, individuals may, of course, be responsible for particular crimes, such as torture or

---

39 Thompson, *Taking Responsibility*, xviii-xix, 29, 33-40, 89, 148, 153.

40 D. Miller, *National Responsibility and Global Justice*, chapter 6 (draft). I am very grateful to David Miller for allowing me to read a copy of this draft.

41 R. G. Teitel, *Transitional Justice*, (Oxford: Oxford University Press, 2000), 139-40; Simmons, 'Historical Rights', 247; Thompson, *Taking Responsibility*, ix, 30, 36, 60-1, 63, 68-9; B. Hamber, 'Reparation as Symbol: Narratives of Resistance, Reticence and Possibility in South Africa', paper presented to the international conference on 'Reparations: An Interdisciplinary Examination of Some Philosophical Issues', Department of Philosophy, Queen's University, Kingston, Ontario, Canada, 6-8 February 2004, 19; du Plessis, 'Historical Injustice', 633; Waldron, 'Superseding Historic Injustice', 16, 19-20; McCarthy, 'Coming to Terms', 756-7; Paul, 'Set-Asides', 124.

murder. However, where society is structured oppressively – as in Communist systems – responsibility may be diffused very widely. Leaders may be more responsible than followers, but the distinction between persecutors and victims – though clear enough in some cases (for example, in cases of torture) – may become quite blurred to a significant extent. In such cases, the obligation of reparations, and even their desirability, comes into question.

Thompson concedes that the collective obligation to make reparations is conditioned by other considerations of justice. The idea of collective responsibility also carries the danger of collective vengeance, and thus of massive human rights violations.[42] Collective responsibility must therefore be combined with respect for human rights. However, the 'nationalist' theories of Thompson and Miller are vulnerable to the objection that the nation may not itself be a just entity. The fulfilment of a putative national obligation to make reparations may, therefore, aggravate rather than rectify injustice overall. Both Thompson and Miller make the obligation of reparation subject to the requirements of justice, but a tension remains between collective obligations to collectivities and individual rights.

6 OBJECTIONS TO REPARATIONS

There are several objections to the very idea of repairing the past. The first is that the past cannot be changed, still less 'repaired'. A second objection is that history is so full of injustice that adequate reparation is impossible. Attempts to make partial reparation run up against the Nozickean objection that partial reparation may itself be unjust, leaving holdings in the 'wrong' hands. Another kind of objection is that the utilitarian cost of adequate reparations would be intolerable. Those who believe that rights and justice should generally 'trump' utility might, and perhaps should, hesitate if the utilitarian cost were very high. This objection can be reformulated as a requirement of justice based on 'innocent' expectations. Jeremy Waldron argues that the requirements of justice, including the obligation to make reparations, may change with changing circumstances: just indigenous land claims, for example, may differ now from what they were when the land was originally taken, because of large-scale population movements of relatively innocent people. The principles of justice should govern what we do *now*; in this sense, justice is present- and future-, not past-oriented.[43] However, when circumstances have been changed by wrongdoing, for

42 F. Abdel-Nour, 'National Responsibility', (2003) 31 *Political Theory*, 695, 705, 709.
43 Waldron, 'Superseding Historic Injustice'.

example by imperial conquest, changing circumstances provide a weak argument against reparations.[44]

A further objection to reparations is that we cannot 'rectify' historical injustices because we cannot know, counter-factually, how the victims of the injustice would have acted if the injustice had not occurred, if we assume, as we usually do in our moral thinking, that their choices would have manifested freedom of the will and would not have merely been the result of causal laws that we fully understand.[45] Simmons suggests that the problem of counter-factuals is exaggerated, and that counter-factuals play a useful, even necessary, role in common-sense practical reason. If I had not been mugged, I would now feel better (even though something worse might have happened to me).

Thomas McCarthy argues that the counter-factual objection to reparations can be overcome if the following conditions are met: the historical injustice is clear; the victims of the injustice clearly suffered from it; their descendants are clearly worse off now than they would have been if the historical injustice had not occurred; there is a plausible explanatory narrative that connects the original with current injustice. This narrative may include an account of how an injustice incapacitates its victims from recovering from the wrong done to them, or from making claims for reparations 'in good time'. In these circumstances, McCarthy suggests, we cannot calculate the appropriate reparations precisely, because of the problem of counter-factuals, but we can know that we owe reparations, and the allocation of reparations should be guided by the principles of distributive justice. Such narratives may well be contested, but such contestation is precisely how democracies conduct their quest for justice.[46] Cass Sunstein has, however, suggested that the counter-factual problem is so intractable in principle that McCarthy's solution collapses into the problem of distributive justice. The difficulty of offering plausible explanatory narratives over long periods of time supports the common-sense belief that the more ancient the injustice, the weaker the case for reparations now. Nevertheless, one might think that the worse the injustice, the longer the possibility of reparations should remain open.[47]

Thompson and Simmons both believe that 'common-sense counterfactuals' give descendants rights over property wrongfully taken from their ancestors,[48] but this raises several problems: 1) theories of inheritance are controversial; 2) inheritance rights

---

[44] Simmons, 'Historical Rights', 238; J. A. Corlett, 'Wrongdoing, Reparations and Native Americans', in Roberts (ed.), *Injustice and Rectification*, 160-1.

[45] Waldron, 'Superseding Historic Injustice', 9-10; Corlett, 'Wrongdoing', 161; McCarthy, 'Coming to Terms', 755; Howard-Hassmann, 'Moral Integrity', 195.

[46] McCarthy, 'Coming to Terms', 755-6, 759-61; Simmons, 'Historical Rights', 228; du Plessis, 'Historical Injustice', 647, 656; Thompson, *Taking Responsibility*, 82.

[47] C. R. Sunstein, 'The Limits of Compensatory Justice', in Chapman (ed.), *Compensatory Justice*, 294-6; Thompson, *Taking Responsibility*, 80; Teitel, *Transitional Justice*, 62; compare United Nations, *Civil and Political Rights*, 8.

[48] Thompson, *Taking Responsibility*, 111, 122, 128; Simmons, 'Historical Rights', 244-5.

are culturally variable; 3) inheritance would be difficult to trace over long periods of time; and 4) rights of inheritance (if there are any) would have to compete with other claims of justice.

Rights and obligations do not change simply *because* time passes. They can change *over time*, however, because victims and perpetrators die, new rights and obligations emerge, and the problem of counter-factuals makes the determination of appropriate reparation difficult in principle and in practice. These difficulties by no means necessarily annihilate the obligations of reparative justice, both because of the basic principle that injustice should be rectified so far as possible, and because, as Thompson rightly emphasises, historical injustices often poison present social relations. Reparative justice should be combined with distributive justice, and the more difficult it is to achieve reparative justice, the more it should be dominated by distributive justice. Where the duty of reparation is clear, however, it may override some rights (though not basic human rights), insofar as private interests may sometimes legitimately be subordinated to a just collective purpose.

7 RETRIBUTIVE JUSTICE

The question of retributive justice is related to that of reparations because some have argued that the punishment of at least the most serious violators of human rights is a form of *reparation* for their victims and/or for society. Crime redistributes goods wrongfully, and, some say, punishment is thus a form of distributive justice.[49] It is argued that victims have a right to the prosecution of their persecutors, and that amnesties for such perpetrators constitute a second violation of the human rights of their victims.[50] The right of victims to have the violators of their rights prosecuted is, however, not absolute, for it may be overridden by weightier moral or practical considerations. Where prosecutions are not possible, truth commissions, reparations and perhaps non-criminal forms of punishment (such as debarment of at least the worst violators from public office) may be called for.[51] The relations between

49 Roberts, 'Justice and Rectification', 26-7; D. Markel, 'The Justice of Amnesty? Towards a Theory of Retributivism in Recovering States', (1999) 49 *University of Toronto Law Journal*, 421, 427-30; Lomasky, 'Compensation', 33.

50 Teitel, *Transitional Justice*, 64-5, 125; J. E. Méndez, 'Accountability for Past Abuses', (1997) 19 *Human Rights Quarterly*, 255-82; B. Chigara, *Amnesty in International Law: The Legality under International Law of National Amnesty Laws*, (Harlow: Longman, 2002).

51 T. M. Scanlon, 'Punishment and the Rule of Law', in H. H. Koh and R. C. Slye (eds), *Deliberative Democracy and Human Rights*, (New Haven, CT: Yale University Press, 1999), 261-2; Méndez, 'Accountability'.

retributive justice and the construction of stable liberal democracies are complex, and not well understood, so that sweeping generalisations about them are inappropriate.[52]

8 APOLOGY

Apology can also be a form of reparation.[53] Some say that apologies are unimportant, because they are cheap and usually insincere. If apologies are cheap, however, it is hard to explain why they are so rare, although they may have become more common recently. Sincere apologies are possible and may help to 'repair' the damage caused by historical injustice. Victims may reject apologies without material reparations as inadequate, and material reparations without apologies may also seem unsatisfactory. Sincere apologies, appropriately symbolised, redistribute respect and status. They should be combined with credible guarantees that the abuses will not recur in future. Sincere apologies may have a transformative effect insofar as they symbolise a break with a repressive past. Where the apologisers and the addressees of the apology are collective, there may be questions as to who is qualified to offer, and who to accept, apologies. Finally, truth commissions and apologies, though conceptually distinct, are intimately interrelated in that *really* telling the truth about gross human rights abuses implies apology. Apologies are rarely, if ever, enough to rectify gross human rights abuses, but their role in reparation should not for that reason be underestimated.[54]

9 CONCLUSIONS

We have no comprehensive and integrated theory of reparative justice, comparable with Rawls' theory of distributive justice, and, given the diversity of circumstances in which reparations might be claimed, and the contested character of theories of justice, we should not expect consensus on such a theory. There is not even agreement among those committed to human rights and democracy as to whether 'drawing a thick line' under the past or acknowledging it is the better policy: it may be that the former is justifiable in some situations, and the latter is preferable in others. In some situations, however, failure to acknowledge past wrongs is closely associated with the persistence

---

52 E. Kiss, 'Moral Ambition within and beyond Political Constraints: Reflections on Restorative Justice', in R. I. Rotberg and D. Thompson (eds), *Truth v. Justice: The Morality of Truth Commissions*, (Princeton, NJ: Princeton University Press, 2000), 80-4; Markel, 'The Justice of Amnesty?, 413-4.

53 Du Plessis, 'Historical Injustice', 630-1; Thompson, *Taking Responsibility*, 51; M. Gibney, R. E. Howard-Hassmann, J.-M. Coicaud and N. Steiner (eds), *The Age of Apology: The West Confronts Its Past*, (Tokyo: United Nations University Press, forthcoming 2007).

54 L. F. Kort, 'What Is An Apology?', in Roberts (ed.), *Injustice and Rectification*, 105-10; K. A. Gill, 'The Moral Functions of an Apology', in Roberts (ed.), *Injustice and Rectification*, 111-23.

of injustice. There can be a tension between reparative and distributive justice, because backward-looking policies may weaken society's capacity to build a more just future. Given limited resources, the demands of distributive justice may place some constraints on reparation. Yet reparative justice may be right in itself, and it might contribute to a more stable and just future. The case for reparations is grounded in human rights, and respecting human rights now may not exhaust the obligations of reparation. So far as possible, neither reparative justice nor human rights should be allowed to 'trump' the other.

Some see dangers in 'the politics of victimhood', which may keep historical victims in subordinate positions or encourage unjust forms of revenge (or both). Recognition of historical injustice does not necessarily have these consequences, however. Emphasis on 'repair' may mistake politics for therapy. Victims of human rights abuses may need, and have a right to, appropriate therapy, but, *politically*, their right is to equality of respect and citizenship. The politics of reparation should be governed by principles of justice, but it must to some extent be a politics of contestation. Juan Méndez argues that those who advocate the Weberian ethic of responsibility to diminish justice for the victims of gross human rights abuses in the face of political opposition blame the victims and the supporters of human rights rather than the violators for consequent human rights violations. This is, however, only a special case of the conflict between justice and power that pervades all politics. There is an obligation to do justice, but not at any cost. Political decision-makers are responsible for the foreseeable consequences of their choices, and even the politics of human rights has to be pragmatic.[55]

Rawls and other philosophers have made the case for giving ideal theory priority over non-ideal theory: we must have a conception of ideal justice in order to identify and remedy injustice. This idealism has, however, led to a neglect of reparative justice. Recent attention to the need to repair the past (so far as possible) for the sake of justice and for the sake of a better future is therefore very welcome. We now understand, however, that taking historical injustice seriously raises complex empirical questions, and there is no consensus on the applicable principles, partly because there is no consensus on the criteria of justice. The principles of human rights have extraordinary merit, but they are not sufficient to generate an adequate theory of reparative justice. The victims of gross human rights abuses have a strong claim for reparation – stronger than has generally been recognised in theory or in practice – but their rights have to be reconciled with those of others and with the practical demands of building future societies that respect human rights, democracy and the rule of law. There is no guarantee that all desirable objectives are compossible. Reparative justice is a good among other goods. It does, however, deserve a more prominent place in liberal political theory.

---

[55] Méndez, 'Accountability', 271; McCarthy, 'Coming to Terms', 768; Kiss, 'Moral Ambition, 72; A. Schaap, *Political Reconciliation* (London: Routledge, 2005), 21, 151.

TAKING APOLOGY SERIOUSLY

CATHERINE JENKINS

"Reparations cannot be deprived of their great historical meaning, to overcome private revenge and attain public justice. What we witness today, the reductionist approach that tends to assimilate them to mere pecuniary compensation... for damage suffered, in my view constitutes a regrettable distortion of their true meaning."

Judge A. A. Cancado Trindade[1]

1 INTRODUCTION

A Seattle newspaper in 2004 published an editorial headed 'Apology is fine, but justice is better.'[2] In this simple but compelling phrase, it conveyed the notion of a dichotomy between apology and justice and implied that it might be possible to have one or the other, but not both. The editorial, which reflected on the US Government's response to the land claims of Native Americans, epitomised the weary cynicism felt by some observers about the 'age of apology' into which we are now said to have entered.[3] It rightly emphasised the need to be alert to and wary of attempts to conceal or dress up in fine words the perpetration of further injustice against those already wronged. Nevertheless, there is no necessary dichotomy between apology and justice. Indeed, for some victims of injustice, contemporary and historic, individual and collective, apology forms an essential ingredient of the justice sought.

---

1 Inter-American Court of Human Rights, Bulacio v Argentina, 18 September 2003, Separate Opinion, para.34. All judgments of the Inter-American Court of Human Rights referred to in this Chapter are available online at http://www.corteidh.org.

2 Seattle Post – Intelligencer, 11 July 2004, M. Trahant, 'Apology is fine but justice is better', available at http://seattlepi.nwsource.com/opinion/181495_trahant11.html

3 The 'age of apology' expression was coined by Prof. R. L. Brooks. See 'When Sorry Isn't Enough: The Controversy Over Apologies and Reparations for Human Injustice', 1999, p.3. See further the chapter in this book by Professor Brooks in which he develops his 'atonement' (apology plus reparations) model as a form of redress for the harm done to African Americans by the institution of slavery.

In the law of state responsibility, an apology from one state to another for an internationally wrongful act is an established form of reparation. Its capacity to prevent the escalation of conflict between nations and to ensure that wrongs committed by one nation against another do not fester is apparently accepted with little difficulty by international lawyers. The role of apology as a form of reparation for violations of human rights and international humanitarian law, however, is relatively poorly established and receives little attention from international courts and tribunals, practising international lawyers or international law academics. This chapter considers whether more can and should be done to promote apology as a form of reparation for human rights violations and crimes under international law. It argues that it is time for international lawyers to take apology seriously.

In some national legal systems, the importance of apology has long been recognised. In their fascinating and insightful piece of comparative law scholarship published in 1986, Hiroshi Wagatsuma and Arthur Rosett observed that 'a basic assumption in Japanese society' seemed to be 'that apology is an integral part of every resolution of conflict'.[4] They recount the story of what happened to two American servicemen who, on the advice of their Japanese lawyer, had paid $1,000 in compensation to a Japanese woman they were accused of raping and thereafter obtained a letter from her stating that she absolved them completely. In these circumstances, there was a good prospect that the servicemen would not be convicted. In court, however, when asked by the Japanese judge whether they had anything to say, the Americans simply stated that they were not guilty and failed to offer apologies – an omission that had never occurred to their Japanese lawyer. The Americans were sentenced to the maximum term of imprisonment, not suspended. As Wagatsuma and Rosett note, 'Japanese students need only hear what the servicemen said to the judge to react. They know what happened next. Only Americans have to be told.'[5]

In other municipal legal systems, a growing interest in apology as part of a new way of dealing with civil disputes, crime and administrative law matters is already evident, and a process of discussion, reflection and experimentation is well under way. In recent years, for example, a wide range of countries have introduced so-called 'restorative justice' processes into their criminal justice systems.[6] Typically, these processes involve diverting some cases from the formal criminal justice system by agreement between the offender and the offended. By encouraging offenders to face victims, acknowledge their wrongdoing, come to an understanding of the human

4 Wagatsuma and Rosett, 'The Implications of Apology: Law and Culture in Japan and the United States' (1986) 20 Law and Society Review 461, at p.462.

5 *Ibid.*, p.463. This story was first told by John Haley in 'Sheathing the Sword of Justice in Japan: An Essay on Law without Sanctions' (1982) 8 Jo. of Jap. Stud.265.

6 Countries which have introduced such processes include New Zealand, Australia, Canada, the UK, Belgium, Ireland, India, Israel, Jordan, Japan, Korea, East Timor, Thailand, Singapore, South Africa and the USA.

consequences of their actions, feel remorse and make reparation in an agreed form, it is thought that victims' needs will be better met, re-offending deterred, and offenders reintegrated.[7] The jury is still 'out' on the conclusions to be drawn from these experiments.[8] There is, however, already a body of research on the role of apology which in broad terms confirms its importance.[9] The restorative justice movement has served to highlight the full range of concerns and needs of victims of crime and to emphasise that those concerns and needs may well extend beyond a desire for punishment. It has prompted even those who do not favour the introduction of restorative justice processes to think creatively about reforms that might enable the formal criminal justice system to respond more fully to the needs of victims and to benefit society as a whole. Such reforms have included the creation of victims' charters and changes to criminal procedure and the laws of evidence. Amongst the issues receiving attention has been whether the formal criminal justice system should do more to provide victims with an apology, and if so, how this might be achieved.[10]

In civil disputes as in criminal cases, the contemporary interest in apology reflects both the search for more appropriate remedies in the formal legal system and the desire to avert litigation or divert disputes in to less formal channels. This confirms the early insights of Wagatsuma and Rosett, who, noting the different place accorded to apology in Japanese and American legal cultures, suggested that according an increased place to apology would enrich American law, enable it to deal better with the heart of certain types of injury, and relieve it of the 'pressure to convert all damages into dollars'[11] They also argued that 'society at large might be better off and better able to advance social peace if the law...encouraged people to apologise to those they have wronged and to compensate them for their losses. Lawsuits may never be filed in such situations.'[12]

Increased pressure for apology as a remedy has also obliged courts in a number of jurisdictions to consider how they should react to defendants in civil cases who are unwilling to apologise. In a disability discrimination case in Hong Kong, for example, the defendant, a taxi driver who had been successfully sued under the Disability Discrimination Ordinance for harassment of a paraplegic passenger, declined to

---

7 The classic account of this approach is Braithwaite, J., 'Crime, Shame and Reintegration' (1989) Cambridge University Press.

8 See for a review Braithwaite, J., 'Restorative justice: Assessing optimistic and pessimistic accounts' (1999) 25 Crime & Justice 1 and, by the same author, 'Restorative Justice and Responsive Regulation' (2002) Oxford University Press.

9 See e.g. McNamara, M.R. and Dhami, M.K., 'The Role of Apology in Restorative Justice', paper presented at the 6th International Conference on Restorative Justice held at Simon Fraser University, B.C., Canada, 1-4 June 2003, available at http://www.sfu.ca/cfrj/fulltext/mcnamara.pdf for a review of the literature.

10 See e.g. in relation to the US criminal justice system Bibas, S. and Bierschbach, R.A., 'Integrating Remorse and Apology into Criminal Procedure' (2005) 114 Yale L.J. 101. These authors sparked a lively debate on whether an apology should save an offender from jail.

11 Wagatsuma and Rosett, note 4 above, at p. 488.

12 *Ibid.*

apologise and argued that he could not be compelled to do so, as that would amount to an infringement of his human rights under Hong Kong's Basic Law and Bill of Rights. The Hong Kong Court of Final Appeal held that the District Court did have power under the Ordinance to order an apology, even where the defendant was unwilling to apologise, as this would not necessarily constitute an infringement of the defendant's rights.[13] The decision was welcomed by the Hong Kong Equal Opportunities Commission (EOC), whose chairperson stated that it saw an apology in an appropriate case as 'serving a significant education function, as well as being an effective remedy.'[14] The EOC suggested that in cases where the Court decided not to order an unwilling defendant to apologise, it was likely that the Court would substantially increase the amount of damages payable.[15]

The reaction of the Hong Kong EOC to the judgment in the disability case reflects a growing enthusiasm for apology among administrative law bodies. In Australia in 2002, the Human Rights and Equal Opportunities Commission recommended that the Commonwealth of Australia pay compensation and apologise to five asylum seekers who had been detained and mistreated in an Immigration Reception and Processing Centre. It observed:

> "Apologies are important remedies for breaches of human rights. An apology has, at least to some extent, the potential to alleviate the suffering of those who have been wronged."[16]

In Canada, the Ombudsman of British Columbia has recently released a report stressing the importance of an apology when a person has been unfairly treated by a public agency and urging government to enact appropriate legislation to encourage this.[17] 'My experience as Ombudsman has demonstrated to me the power of an apology in settling disputes', he wrote.[18]

The examples given above highlight the increasing attention given in national legal systems to the role of apology in responding to *contemporary* wrongs done both by one individual to another and by the State to one of its citizens. In a number of countries, calls for apology have also been a feature of campaigns for redress by groups of victims for *historical* injustices committed by States, churches, corporations and

---

13 Ma Bik Yung v Ko Chuen, HK Court of Final Appeal, (2002) 2 HKLRD 1. The Court stated that it would only order an insincere apology where this would redress the plaintiff's loss and damage to some extent and it was a reasonable act for the defendant to perform in the circumstances of the case.

14 Hong Kong EOC News Release, 5 October 2001.

15 In South Africa, the High Court in 2002 gave a defendant in a defamation case a choice between publishing a retraction and apology or paying damages of R200,000: see Mineworkers Investment Co. (Pty) Ltd. v Modibane (2002) (6) SA 512 (W).

16 HREOC Report No.24, 2002. The complaint was brought on behalf of the asylum seekers by Amnesty International.

17 Ombudsman of British Columbia, Special Report No. 27, 'The Power of an Apology: Removing the Legal Barriers', 8 Feb 2006, available at http://www.ombud.gov.bc.ca.

18 Office of the Ombudsman, News Release, 8 February 2006, available at the same website.

other institutions, often against groups of victims. Some of these demands have been transnational: former prisoners of war, 'comfort women' and victims of biological warfare seeking an apology from Japan, for example, or groups such as the Maori or Herero peoples seeking apologies from former colonial powers. In other cases, groups have sought, or are still seeking, apologies from their own governments and other institutions in their home countries: examples include Australia's 'stolen generation', Japanese Americans interned during World War II, black South Africans for apartheid, Bosnian Muslims for the Srebrenica massacre, African American survivors of the Tuskegee, Alabama, syphilis experiment, as well as Chinese Canadians and Native Americans. Last, but not least, is the call for an apology for slavery, which is both national and transnational.

What is an apology, and why is it called for? It is to these issues that we now turn.

2 WHAT IS AN APOLOGY?

Apology is not easy to define for the purposes of this Chapter, which deals with both inter-personal apologies and 'collective' apologies by States and other institutions. Goffmann in 1971 described apologetic behaviour as part of the 'remedial work' which serves the crucial function of repairing relationships after injury.[19] This definition of apology by reference to its purpose or function is discussed further below. It constitutes a minimal definition which would undoubtedly command wide acceptance, and is useful in that it seems equally valid in relation to both inter-personal and collective apologies. It is not surprising, however, that what is perceived as constituting appropriate 'remedial work' varies from one society to another, and, as already noted, the precise forms of apologetic behaviour, the circumstances in which an apology is considered appropriate and the exact significance attached to it do vary.[20] Much of the research on apology has focused on its role in Western societies; more wide-ranging comparative research would be valuable in assessing the potential role of apology in relation to violations of international law.

The cultural variations already observed are striking: for example, as Wagatsuma and Rosett noted, in Japan, whilst it is important for the person responsible for harm to express his feeling of deep regret, 'the cultural assumption of social harmony would lead the Japanese to accept the external act of apology at face value and not to disturb the superficial concord by challenging the sincerity of the person apologising. [...] In this context, the external act of apology becomes significant as an act of self-denigration and submission, which of itself is the important message. Then the internal

19 Goffmann, E., 'Relations in Public: Micro-Studies of the Public Order'(1971).

20 See e.g. Wagatsuma and Rosett, note 4 above.

state of mind of the person who tenders the apology is of less concern.'[21] In the USA, in contrast, the internal state of mind of the person apologising assumes greater importance.

Basing his analysis expressly on a Western understanding of apology, Nicholas Tavuchis suggests that, from a sociological perspective, 'the major task of apology is to resolve conflicts and somehow restore an antecedent moral order', through, minimally, 'acknowledgment of the legitimacy of the violated rule, admission of fault and responsibility for its violation, and the expression of genuine regret and remorse for the harm done.'[22] Apology strives to counter the 'risks of retaliation and the progressive escalation of conflict' that result from transgression.[23] In Tavuchis' view, it does so not by offering a justification or excuse for the offending behaviour, but by acknowledging that one has no excuse or justification for it:

> "An apology... requires...acknowledgment and painful embracement of our deeds, coupled with a declaration of regret...In its purest expression, an apology clearly announces that 'I have no excuses for what I did or did not do or say. I am sorry and regretful. I care. Forgive me.'"[24]

Salman Akhtar offers the following assessment of the psychological significance of such a process to victims of political violence:

> "Acknowledgement by the perpetrator that he has indeed harmed the victim is an important factor in the latter's recovery from the trauma (Akhtar, 1995, 1999). It undoes the profoundly deleterious effects of "gaslighting" (i.e. denying that anything destructive is being done to someone). To harm someone and then to question his or her perception of it is a double jeopardy, tantamount to "soul murder" (Shengold, 1989). Note in this connection the pain those who deny the Holocaust cause Jews and, in a clinical parallel, the anguish induced in a sexually abused child whose 'non-abusive' parent refused to believe the occurrence of such an event. Recognising the Holocaust and the sexual abuse, in contrast, improves reality testing, and facilitates mourning. Such a move is given further impetus if the perpetrator shows signs of remorse, apologises and offers emotional reparation, material reparation, or both. This testifies to the verity of one's grievance and functions as a graft over one's psychic wounds. A secondary increase in self-esteem

---

21 Wagatsuma and Rosett, note 4 above, at p.473.

22 Tavuchis, N., 'Mea Culpa: A Sociology of Apology and Reconciliation' (Stanford U.P. 1991), pp.3 and 5.

23 *Ibid.*, p.17.

24 *Ibid.*, p.19. This understanding of the nature of apology illustrates the fact that the concept of apology also varies across time: in ancient Greece, it connoted primarily a defence or justification of one's actions, sometimes by reference to the influence of the gods. Commenting on Agamemnon's famous 'apology' in The Iliad, E.R. Dodds remarked: "By impatient modern readers these words of Agamemnon's have sometimes been dismissed as a weak excuse or evasion of responsibility." ('The Greeks and the Irrational', University of California Press, 1951, p.3.). Tavuchis is careful to note that his analysis of apology is based on modern Western culture. Rosalind Shaw has argued, based on her anthropological research in West Africa, that apologies which do not amount to the 'ideal type' described by Tavuchis may nevertheless be accepted and considered important in the context of transitional justice in Sierra Leone: see note 86 below.

follows that permits further mourning. A dialectic relationship gradually develops between such enhanced healthy narcissism and the emerging capacity to let go of the grief."[25]

The sociological and psychological analyses offered by Tavuchis and Akhtar suggest that apology should be regarded in international law terms as an important measure of satisfaction to victims. Beyond this, a meaningful apology implicitly promises that the harmful act will not happen again: in international law terms, a guarantee of non-repetition. This often neglected aspect of apology is important, and may take on particular significance in societies emerging from a period of conflict, in which individuals or groups may have been oppressed and abused or people with violent recent pasts are being reintegrated into their communities.

Apologies may, of course, be rejected, acknowledged or accepted. What moves the offended party to accept an apology is intriguing, given the obvious inability of the apology, on one level, to right the wrong done. The precise content of the apology, the demeanour of the apologiser and the extent to which the apology conforms to cultural expectations may all be important. Ultimately, the explanation for our willingness to accept apologies must lie in our socialisation as children, when, as Tavuchis points out, we find ourselves alternately cast in the roles of offender and offended. Through repeated instruction in the intricacies of apologetic behaviour, the 'foundations for more durable moral orientations towards deviance, apology, and forgiveness' may be laid.[26]

Tavuchis argues that, beyond the benefits it confers on those who have been wronged, an apology has civilising and humanising effects on wider society; 'it is quintessentially social, that is, a *relational* symbolic gesture occurring in a complex interpersonal field, with enormous reverberatory potential that encapsulates, recapitulates and pays homage to a moral order rendered problematic by the very act that calls it forth.'[27]

The emphasis, especially in Western literature on apology, on the importance of sincere feelings (e.g. of sorrow or caring) have led some to question whether meaningful apologies can be given by States, corporations, churches and other institutions that are inherently incapable of having feelings. The concept of a meaningful apology by such bodies is not something that can be rejected out of hand in the light of the persistent demands for such apologies in recent years by victims, in relation to both contemporary and historic injustices, and the readiness of a number of such bodies to offer apologies. Clearly, States, corporations and other bodies are capable of taking collective decisions to engage in 'remedial work' aimed at repairing relationships between themselves and others to whom they have caused harm.

25 Akhtar, S., 'The Psychodynamic Dimension of Terrorism', Ch.6 in 'Terrorism and War: Unconscious Dynamics of Political Violence' (2002), p.95.

26 Tavuchis, note 22 above, at p. 66.

27 *Ibid.*, p. 14.

Acknowledging the violation, accepting responsibility for the harm caused and promising not to repeat the act in future – all important ingredients of apology – may be a valuable part of this remedial work and actions of this type are perfectly within the capacities of such bodies. Expressions of sorrow and regret made in a representative capacity by individuals at the helm of governments, corporations and other bodies may also be highly valued by those injured or wronged. In contra-distinction to inter-personal apologies, it seems generally to be an important aspect of collective apologies that they should be made publicly and/or publicly recorded.[28] Apologies from these bodies therefore involve a combination of actions taken publicly with the authority of and on behalf of the body concerned.

In the light of this discussion of the concept of apology, it is easy to see why legal proceedings (or the threat of them) may be perceived as a barrier to apology. If apology involves an acknowledgment of wrongdoing and an acceptance of political or moral responsibility for it, does apology also imply, for example, an admission of criminal liability, or of legal liability to pay financial compensation? It seems to this author that an apology normally implies a *willingness* to do whatever is appropriate to repair the harm caused. The *legal* implications of apology, however, vary from one legal system to another, as we have seen, and in some cases are currently under discussion and review.

3 WHY HAVE INTERNATIONAL LAWYERS SHOWN LITTLE INTEREST IN APOLOGY?

The literature on apology produced by international lawyers is, to date, minimal.[29] Even in one of the rare publications edited by an international law scholar, Roy Brooks, dealing with 'the controversy over apologies and reparations for human injustice', the vast majority of the contributions are by authors from other disciplines, such as history, philosophy, sociology and religion. Of the legal contributors to the volume, the majority claim no particular interest or expertise in international law. One of the very few writings on the subject of apology by an international and comparative law specialist, Hilary Josephs. was inspired by the work of Arthur Rosett and written to

[28] *Ibid.*, p. 109.

[29] The author is referring to literature published in the English language.

honour him on his retirement.[30] The focus of her article is on State apologies.[31] The small number of other writings that touch on the subject include two interesting articles prompted by the 2003 sentencing judgment of the ICTY in the *Plavsic* case.[32] Passing references to apology may occasionally be found in the work of other international law scholars.[33] Apology as a form of reparation receives several pages of discussion in Martha Minow's well-known work on the ways in which societies respond to mass atrocities.[34]

It is fascinating but difficult to assess why the subject of apology seems to have so little appeal. Indeed, the lack of apparent interest might lead one to suppose that the very concepts of law and apology are regarded by some as oxymoronic. A number of factors may be at play here; in the absence of any empirical research, the following must be treated as intelligent speculation.

3.1 THE FOCUS ON RETRIBUTION THROUGH INTERNATIONAL CRIMINAL JUSTICE

One factor may be the intense focus by human rights lawyers, during the last 15-20 years, on retributive justice and the campaign against impunity. Huge effort has been expended in promoting accountability through formal legal processes: primarily in pressing for prosecutions in national courts and for the establishment of internationally funded criminal tribunals. During the very period when domestic lawyers have begun to show more interest in averting litigation and finding solutions outside the formal justice system, through ADR mechanisms and experiments in restorative justice, international lawyers have been battling to set up new courts and to ensure that more people are prosecuted and imprisoned. During this period, the issue of reparation (other than in the form of investigation and prosecution) has been largely neglected.

---

30 Josephs, Hilary K., 'The Remedy of Apology in Comparative and International Law: Self-Healing and Reconciliation' (2004) 18 Emory Int'l L.Rev. 53.

31 The same focus is shared by two pieces co-authored by Mark Gibney, a professor of political science with expertise in international law: see Gibney, M. and Warner, D., 'What Does It Mean to Say "I'm Sorry"?' (2000) 28 Denver Jo. of Int'l Law and Politics 223; and Gibney, M. and Roxstrom, E., 'The Status of State Apologies' (2001) 23 HRQ 911. More recently, Prof. Gibney and colleagues have attempted to stimulate wider interest in the subject of apology by coordinating a project, 'The Age of Apology: The West Confronts Its Past', leading to a forthcoming book of the same name.

32 Combs, Nancy A., 'The Prosecutor v Plavsic' (2003) 97 AJIL 929 and Tieger, A., 'Remorse and Mitigation in the International Criminal Tribunal for the former Yugoslavia' (2003) 16 Leiden Jo. of Int'l Law 777.

33 See e.g. Sadat, Leila, 'Exile, Amnesty and International Law' (2006) 81 Notre Dame L. Rev. 955.

34 'Between Vengeance and Forgiveness: Facing History After Genocide and Mass Violence' (1998) Beacon Press. See p. 112-117.

The worrying absence of criminological research from the field of international criminal law has been noted.[35] The British NGO 'Redress' has commented upon the absence of research in to what forms of reparation are wanted by and most beneficial to survivors of torture, and has stressed the importance of this.[36] In the campaign against impunity, the importance of retributive justice to some victims and survivors of human rights abuses has been rightly emphasised. This tight focus, no doubt very necessary for campaigning purposes, is only now beginning to give way to recognition of the importance to victims of other forms of reparation. The new, wider focus encompasses material forms of redress, such as restitution and financial compensation – the Rome Statute of the International Criminal Court is a significant improvement on the mandates of the *ad hoc* international criminal tribunals in this respect – but there are still scant signs of recognition of the importance of 'symbolic' forms of reparation such as apology.[37] One positive development is the adoption in 2005 (after some 15 years of delay) by the UN Human Rights Commission of the UN Basic Principles on Reparation for Victims of Gross Human Rights Abuses and Serious Violations of International Humanitarian Law, which formally recognise a 'public apology, including acknowledgment of the facts and acceptance of responsibility', as a form of reparation.[38]

---

[35] Roberts, P., 'For Criminology in International Criminal Justice' (2003) 1 Jo. of Int'l Crim. Justice 315. Roberts observes, for example, that criminological research on municipal criminal law has 'consistently queried the effectiveness of deterrence as a penal strategy', but that 'the international criminal justice paradigm of individual responsibility is often premised on a presumption that criminal prohibitions effectively deter crime': see Section 4(A). He argues that insights gathered from criminological research on municipal law may 'contribute valuable raw material for reworking' in the international criminal justice context. Arguably such insights have played a role in the drafting of the Rome Statute of the International Criminal Court. See in this respect William Schabas 'Penalties' in Antonio Cassese, *The Rome Statute of the International Criminal Court: A Commentary Vol II* (2003) 1533, who asserts that if there is an overall picture to emerge from the Statute on sentencing, '... it is of a relatively humane and enlightened sentencing scheme' to which penal reformers, judges and lawyers, parliamentarians and journalists will turn 'as a model in debates on sentencing policy before national courts'.

[36] The Redress Trust, 'Torture Survivors' Perceptions of Reparation: Preliminary Survey' (2001).

[37] The Rome Statute of the International Criminal Court, Art. 75(2), allows the Court to 'make an order directly against a convicted person specifying appropriate reparations to, or in respect of, victims, including restitution, compensation and rehabilitation.' It does not specifically mention symbolic reparation of any kind, and the establishment of the Trust Fund pursuant to Art.79 suggests the most likely form of reparation is financial compensation. Victims should have an opportunity to make representations to the Court before any such order is made [Art.75(3)]. See further on reparations under international criminal law the chapter in this book by Andreas O'Shea at pages 179-196.

[38] Basic Principles on the Right to a Remedy and Reparation for Victims of Gross Violations of International Human Rights Law and Serious Violations of International Humanitarian Law, Human Rights Resolution 2005/35, UN Commission on Human Rights. 19 April 2005, para.22 (e). Public apology is categorised in the Basic Principles as a measure of satisfaction; it is not listed as a guarantee of non-repetition. In its Resolution adopting the text of the Basic Principles, the Commission on Human Rights recommended 'that States take the Basic Principles and Guidelines into account, promote respect thereof and bring them to the attention of members of the executive bodies of Government, in particular law enforcement officials and military and security forces, legislative

The issue of apology indirectly raises the question of the purpose of criminal prosecutions and highlights the different perspectives of international lawyers on this. In one recent paper, for example, Leila Sadat suggests that public trials for international crimes should be seen as valuable for the purposes of punishing a defendant, allowing victims to be heard and recording an 'official' version of the truth. Other authors emphasise the putative deterrent value of prosecutions. Few mention the issue of reparation to victims. Sadat, however, comments that 'in the best case scenario, victims and survivors might even receive an apology from their tormentors'.[39] Her perspective does not deny the value of apology – indeed, she describes apology as 'leading not only to the reestablishment of social order but also to individual healing' – but implies that the best international lawyers can do is simply to get on with prosecutions and hope that apologies will follow as an incidental benefit.[40] In some cases, apology may indeed follow a prosecution; yet if apology is accepted as important, is 'prosecuting and hoping' really the best that can be done?

3.2 THE CONCEPT OF AN APOLOGETIC THRESHOLD

Some international lawyers may instinctively share Tavuchis' view that

> "...too heinous an offence would go beyond the purview of apology and be unforgivable. In this instance, an apology would sound as if it were only making light of the enormity of the transgression and, effectively, offend further."[41]

---

bodies, the judiciary, victims and their representatives, human rights defenders and lawyers, the media and the public in general'. It also recommended adoption of the Principles by other organs of the UN, including the General Assembly.

39 Sadat, L.N., 'Exile, Amnesty and International Law', note 33 above, at p. 983/4.

40 *Ibid.* Sadat argues – mistakenly in my view – that it was a conviction by the ICTY which finally succeeded in securing a State apology for the Srebrenica massacre. Gen. Krstic was convicted by the ICTY in 2001. Although this may have had some indirect effect, the more proximate cause of the apology by the Bosnian Serb government in 2004 was the report of its own commission, published a month before the apology was tendered.

41 Tavuchis, note 22 above, at p.21. He cites Albert Speer as an example of someone whose complicities 'so violated human sensibilities that no apology could possibly mollify feelings of violation, outrage and revulsion in order to call forth the cleansing spirit of forgiveness' and argues that Speer himself recognised this in his memoirs. [Tavuchis, p.21]. Speer's comment, often repeated, is usually translated as 'No apologies are possible.' Taken in context, however, Speer's comment seems to have been that no *justifications* were possible. He refers to the fact that he had been repeatedly asked what he 'actually knew of the persecution, the deportation and the annihilation of the Jews.' He lists the answers he had previously given to his questioners, but states that he no longer gives them, because they are 'efforts at legalistic exculpation', adding that he believes his questioners posed the question wrongly. 'Whether I knew or did not know, or how much or how little I knew, is totally unimportant when I consider what horrors I ought to have known about...Those who ask me are fundamentally expecting me to offer justifications. But I have none.' Speer, A., 'Inside the Third Reich' (Phoenix edition), p. 171.

On this view, apology would be seen as irrelevant and inappropriate in cases of gross human rights violations and serious violations of humanitarian law, or 'radical evil'.[42] Tavuchis' concern about the risk of an apology causing further offence is an important one. The content of an apology for serious wrongdoing would certainly need to be carefully considered and to reflect the gravity of the wrong done and harm caused. For many victims, apologies alone would not be an adequate response in cases of serious wrongdoing, and would need to be accompanied by other measures. Yet Tavuchis does not offer any solid basis for his personal view that some offences are inherently beyond the purview of apology, and the current prevalence of demands for apology even for very serious human rights abuses militates against his position.

3.3 INTERNATIONAL LAW CULTURE

Two possible factors could be the current Eurocentricity and still male-dominated nature of the international law world. Based on the work of Wagatsuma and Rosett, for example, it is easy to imagine that apology might appear higher on the agenda if the international law world were dominated by Japanese-educated lawyers, rather than Americans and Europeans. Equally, topics such as apology seem to be regarded by some Western-educated lawyers as the 'soft' or 'touch-feely' end of international law, or even 'not really law', in contrast to black-letter law subjects or the machismo of retributive justice.[43] Most of today's leading international lawyers would not have been exposed to human rights and international criminal law issues in their legal education; nor would they be likely to have experienced a socio-legal or 'law in context' approach to legal studies. Even today, the subject of reparation is a neglected part of the international law curriculum, and discussion of symbolic reparation, including apology, is likely to be altogether absent from the syllabus of most law schools.

These aspects of legal education and culture may contribute to a feeling that calls for apology are not properly the province of international lawyers and of international courts and tribunals, but rather of politicians, psychologists, churchmen and philosophers. This attitude is perhaps more understandable in relation to calls for apology for historical injustices. Nevertheless, it is an approach that cannot be justified,

---

42 The concept of apology as appropriate reparation only for minor transgressions of international law may at first sight appear to be reinforced by the comments of the International Court of Justice in the *LaGrand* (*Germany v USA*) case on state responsibility: judgment of 27 June 2001, available at the Court's website http://www.icj-cij.org. On closer analysis, however, the ICJ 's comments reflect the position that apology *alone* would not be adequate in cases of breach involving very serious consequences – such as, in that case, the execution of two individuals.

43 It is impossible to establish other than through anecdotal evidence that these sorts of topics are viewed by some international lawyers as 'women's work', or as part of the 'feminisation' of international law. As indicated above, the work that is currently being done on apology is not by any means the exclusive province of women.

since even calls for apology for historical injustices may be made in the shadow of the law, if not in actual legal proceedings; and many contemporary calls for apology do arise in the context of legal proceedings in international criminal tribunals and regional human rights courts. Victims of serious human rights abuses in various Latin American countries, for example, have for more than 10 years been asking the Inter-American Court of Human Rights to order a public apology in addition to other forms of reparation.[44]

Another aspect of legal culture generally (and this is not peculiar to international law) is that much academic writing is reactive, especially to developments in case law. Since apology has been so little discussed in the case law of international courts and tribunals, it is perhaps not surprising that the literature remains small. It is striking that two of the few relevant journal articles were prompted by the sentencing judgment of the International Criminal Tribunal for the former Yugoslavia in the *Plavsic* case.[45]

3.4 STATE SOVEREIGNTY

State sovereignty may be in decline, but the extent to which regional and international courts may impinge on it in attempting to remedy injustice is still a live issue. International lawyers will be familiar with the consistent jurisprudence of the European Court of Human Rights, allowing States considerable latitude in deciding how to provide redress for breaches of the European Convention on Human Rights. Even in extreme cases, the Court has apparently never considered requiring a State to make a public apology to the victims. Its jurisprudence and that of the increasingly 'victim-friendly' Inter-American Court of Human Rights is discussed further below.

The idea of a court-ordered apology is difficult conceptually for many lawyers and probably for none more so than international lawyers. We have seen that in municipal legal systems, courts have begun to consider the issue of how to deal with individual defendants who are reluctant or unwilling to apologise. This question assumes even greater difficulty in the case of States, in the light of the deference traditionally accorded to them.

The process of critical reflection about law and apology that has been under way for some years in municipal legal systems has barely begun in the field of international law. Important assumptions about the relevance of apology in cases of serious wrongdoing and the role of lawyers in relation to it have therefore remained largely unchallenged. Reparation, insofar as it has been a focus of attention at all, has tended to be conceived of largely in terms of punishment and financial compensation. There

---

44 See e.g. Caballero Delgado and Santana v Colombia, Reparations Judgment of 29 January 1997, at paras. 21 and 58.

45 See note 32 above.

is no doubt that the value of apology for human rights abuses is now recognised in theory, as in the UN Basic Principles on Reparation referred to above, but formal recognition alone is of limited value. The important and difficult question remains as to how apology may best be promoted and secured for those victims who desire it.

It follows from the discussion in this section that a necessary first step is to stimulate greater discussion about international law and apology. In the experience of this author, international lawyers and law students are generally responsive to the issue when it is raised. This should not be surprising, given that apology is both a very familiar concept – there are few who have not called for or offered an apology – and one which has the added attraction of being somewhat mysterious in its operation. But in addition to raising the profile of apology on the international law agenda, we must also explore in more detail the ways in which international lawyers and international courts and tribunals might do more to promote apology, and the challenges and difficulties associated with doing so. The next section offers some preliminary reflections on the promotion of apology through three different mechanisms: regional human rights organs; international criminal tribunals; and truth commissions. In relation to the first, we shall be concerned with the question of apologies from States; in relation to the other two, primarily – though not exclusively – with apologies from individuals.

4. PROMOTING APOLOGY

4.1 REGIONAL HUMAN RIGHTS CONVENTIONS AND ORGANS

Both the European and American regional human rights conventions contain provisions relating to remedies and reparation for victims of human rights violations.[46] Both Conventions require States parties to 'secure' or 'ensure' the Convention rights to all those within their jurisdiction and to provide effective recourse at national level for violations of human rights. Both systems include a regional human rights court to which States and individuals may, either directly or indirectly, bring complaints of violations. Both Conventions also contain provisions for the 'friendly settlement' of disputes. Under the European Convention, the European Court of Human Rights is (since the demise of the Commission) required to place itself at the disposal of the parties for this purpose; in the American system, the same role is fulfilled by the Inter-

[46] See The European Convention for the Protection of Human Rights and Fundamental Freedoms, 1953, arts.1, 13 and 41, and the American Convention on Human Rights, 1969, arts.1, 25 and 63.

American Commission on Human Rights.[47] Neither Convention contains any express mention of apology.

Given the observations of Tavuchis, Wagatsuma and Rosett discussed above about the potential of apology to avert litigation, it seems obvious that apology should be taken seriously by the European Court and Inter-American Commission in the friendly settlement process. Some States do offer an apology as part of a settlement, which may also contain an agreement to undertake other measures, such as the payment of financial compensation. Whether consistent and systematic attention is given by the regional bodies under these Conventions to the possible negotiation of an apology is not known, though it seems likely that this aspect of friendly settlement is given more attention by the Inter-American Commission than by the European Court.[48] Further research is required here to establish current practice and explore possible improvements to it. The ways in which the European Court and Inter-American Commission view their role in the friendly settlement process is likely to affect their approach to apology. The Conventions' requirement that each of these bodies 'place itself at the disposal of the parties' suggests a rather passive role, in which apology might only be considered if placed on the negotiating table by one or other of the parties; if, on the other hand, a more pro-active view of the role is taken, apology could be suggested for consideration even where the parties themselves had overlooked its possible value.

It is clear that defendant States sometimes offer an apology as part of an effort to have a claim against them struck out, where friendly settlement has not been possible. In 2005, for example, the European Court struck out the case of *Meriakri v Republic of Moldova* after Moldova offered an official apology, financial compensation in the sum of 890 Euros and other undertakings.[49] The victim, who was unhappy with the amount of compensation offered and had concerns about continuing violations of the right in question, had asked the Court not to strike out the case. Interestingly, the Court, in reaching its decision to strike out, seems to have paid little or no attention to the apology; it does no more than record it without comment. If the Court should decide as a matter of policy to encourage apology in the European system, noting it with appreciation when it is offered would clearly be desirable.

Given the heavy case loads in both regional human rights systems, encouraging friendly settlement and/or attractive offers which could justify striking out cases might be expected to have some appeal for the regional bodies. Encouraging apology could therefore be in their own self-interest as well as in that of the victim, though it should never, of course, be encouraged at the expense of victims.

---

47 *Ibid.*, arts.38 and 48 respectively.

48 This tentative conclusion is drawn largely by inference from the jurisprudence of the Inter-American Court.

49 Case no.53487/99, judgment of 1 March 2005, (2005) ECHR 148.

The vast majority of cases of human rights violations never reach the regional mechanisms. This means that a critical role to be played by the European and Inter-American Courts of Human Rights is that of defining what States must do in order to redress human rights violations at the national level. The two Courts have taken different approaches to this issue, with the Inter-American Court – after a hesitant start – taking a more interventionist and creative approach. There is potential for both Courts to do more to promote apology.

The European Court of Human Rights has consistently interpreted its powers narrowly, refusing to direct States to take specific action other than the payment of damages to remedy human rights violations. It has repeatedly stated that 'it is for the State to choose the means to be used in its domestic legal system in order to comply with the provisions of the Convention or to redress the situation that has given rise to the violation of the Convention'.[50] In the late 1990s, however, the Court held that the 'nature and gravity of the violations complained of' had implications for the nature of the 'effective remedy' to be provided by States under Article13 of the Convention. For example, where an individual had an arguable claim that his or her home and possessions had been purposely destroyed by agents of the State, the notion of an 'effective remedy' entailed, according to the Court, 'in addition to the payment of compensation, where appropriate and without prejudice to any other remedy available in the domestic system, an obligation on the respondent state to carry out a thorough and effective investigation capable of leading to the identification and punishment of those responsible…'.[51] The Court has been very reluctant to extend this jurisprudence and to specify other measures as part of the obligation to provide an 'effective remedy'. It would, however, be possible for the Court to do so and to specify that an effective remedy includes – at least in certain cases – an obligation on the respondent State publicly to apologise to the victim for the violation.

The European Court has made limited use of its own power to afford 'just satisfaction' to the injured party in cases where the internal law of the respondent State allows only partial reparation to be made for the consequences of a violation.[52] The Court has regularly held that its judgment of State wrongdoing itself constitutes adequate satisfaction. This has led the Court in numerous cases to grant only a declaratory judgment with no pecuniary damages, to say nothing of any other form of relief sought by victims.[53]

---

50 Guerra and Others v Italy, 1998-1 (No.64), Reports 210, at 230, para. 74.

51 Selcuk and Asker v Turkey, judgment of 24 April 1998, para. 96.

52 European Convention, art. 41.

53 These cases are too numerous to list, but see e.g. Silver v UK (1983) 5 E.H.R.R. 347. For general comment on and criticism of this practice of the Court see Shelton, D., 'Remedies in International Human Rights Law', (1999) 201-213. Criticism of the Court's practice under this article is not new: see e.g. Higgins, R., 'Damages for Violation of One's Human Rights', in Sims, N. (ed.) 'Explorations in Ethics and International Relations, Essays in Honour of Sydney D. Bailey' (1981).

It would be timely now for the European Court to reconsider its policy on reparation, taking into account the UN Basic Principles. Although the Court has, no doubt in part through its deference to State sovereignty, succeeded in securing a high level of compliance with its judgments, its reluctance to do more to ensure that the needs and wishes of victims are met and to take a 'victim-centred' approach to reparation is at variance with the over-arching theme of the Basic Principles.

In rethinking its approach to apology, the European Court of Human Rights may take some inspiration from the recent efforts of the Inter-American Court of Human Rights to recognise and respond to the needs and wishes of victims. The approach of the Inter-American Court to its wide remedial power under the Convention has been driven forward by the humanity and critical reflection of its President, Judge Cancado Trindade. In 2003, he described the area of reparations due to victims as an area 'where the law still seems to be in its early childhood, and it still has much to learn from other branches of human knowledge (psychology, philosophy, humanities in general).'[54] He criticised what he called the reductionist approach that tends to equate reparations with financial compensation, and emphasised what he saw as the 'great historical meaning' of reparations: to 'overcome private revenge and attain public justice.'[55]

Though he was not referring directly to the question of apology, Judge Cancado Trindade's focus on the attainment of 'public justice' and on the need for the law to learn lessons from other disciplines is entirely consistent with according greater importance to apologies for human rights abuses. It is clear from the case law of the Inter-American Court that some victims or groups of victims do want a public apology. The Inter-American Commission has pursued this on their behalf, including it in the relief sought from the Inter-American Court. In the early cases in which a call for a public apology was made, the Inter-American Court, in its usually very brief consideration of the matter, tended to say that the judgment of the Court in favour of the victims was in itself a form of 'moral satisfaction', a matter of public record, and that no further measures of satisfaction, such as an apology, were necessary.[56] Indeed, in the *Caballero Delgado* case, the ordering of further reparations was described by the Court as 'improper'.[57] It may be that this failure to respond fully to the needs of the victims for 'public justice' stemmed from a general approach to reparations that was simply narrow and ill-considered, as Judge Cancado Trindade has argued. The fact that in some recent cases the Inter-American Court has been willing to include apology in the order made by it does appear to herald a more open-minded approach and a greater willingness to meet victims' needs for forms of reparation other than money. In the case of *Moiwana Village v. Suriname*, for example the court order contained

[54] Inter-American Court of Human Rights, Bulacio v Argentina, 2003, separate opinion, para. 21.

[55] See the quotation at the head of this chapter.

[56] See e.g. Caballero Delgado and Santana, note 44 above, para. 58.

[57] *Ibid.* In that case, the Agent for Colombia had recognised Colombia's responsibility at the public hearing, but the Commission had asked that the state apologise to the victims' relatives and to society.

inter alia a provision requiring the respondent State to make 'an act of public apology and recognition of its international responsibility' for the violations committed ('un acto de disculpa publica y reconocimiento de responsabilidad internacional').[58] The Inter-American Court has expressly characterised public apology as both a measure of satisfaction for victims and a guarantee of non-repetition.[59]

It must be noted, however, that at least some of the cases in which the Inter-American Court has made an order for apology have been cases in which the State concerned has apparently not objected to making a public apology.[60] There is obviously a serious question as to whether defendants who are unwilling to apologise should be ordered to do so. Some take the view that apology is by definition something that must be done voluntarily if it is to have any value as a form of reparation. In some recent cases, the Inter-American Court has stopped short of making an order for public apology but has ordered the making of 'a public act of recognition of responsibility' ('un acto publico de reconocimiento de su responsibilidad').[61] This is a creative development, requiring an important element of apology – an acknowledgment of responsibility. It may in some cases be a good compromise which is sufficient to satisfy victims and encourage compliance by the State concerned. It is clearly, however, not the same as requiring an apology – though the distinction is usually lost on the media reporting the Court's judgments, and public pressure has sometimes resulted in an apology being tendered at the public ceremonies at which the 'acknowledgment of responsibility' ordered by the Court is made.

---

58 Moiwana Village v Suriname, judgment of 15 June 2005. Public apology seems to be becoming a more regular feature of the Court's judgments and orders: see, for example, the recent cases of The Massacre of Pueblo Bello v Colombia, judgment of 31 January 2006, para. 277; and Baldeon Garcia v Peru, judgment of 6 April 2006, para. 204. In the latter case the Court ordered the apology to be given by the state to the family of the dead man for having concealed the truth about their loved one's detention, torture and extra-judicial execution for 15 years. The state was also ordered to make other non-pecuniary forms of reparation, such as naming a street, a square or a school after the dead man.

59 See e.g. the Moiwana Village case, note 58 above, para.216 and the Baldeon Garcia case, note 58 above, para. 204.

60 In the Moiwana Village case referred to above, the Court noted with appreciation Suriname's statement that it had 'no objections to issuing a public apology to the whole nation with regard to the occurrences that took place in the Village of Moiwana and to the survivors and family members in particular.' (para.216). It is not clear whether the same was true of Peru in the Baldeon Garcia case; there is no reference to such a concession by Peru in the relevant paragraph of the judgment.

61 See e.g. Yakye Axa Indigenous Community v Paraguay, Judgment of 17 June 2005 and Yatama v. Nicaragua, Judgment of 23 June 2005. In the latter case, the Court specified that parts of the Order should be published in national newspapers and on national radio and that the recognition of responsibility should be made in the three indigenous languages of the region.

4.2 INTERNATIONAL CRIMINAL TRIBUNALS

With few exceptions, public apologies have been largely conspicuous by their absence from proceedings in the *ad hoc* International Criminal Tribunals for the former Yugoslavia and for Rwanda, as well as in the Special Court for Sierra Leone.[62]

There are at least two possible reasons for the absence of apologies. One obvious explanation is that those responsible for crimes within the jurisdiction of the Tribunals do not feel remorseful about their actions and see no need to apologise. The other is that the consequences of apologising for such crimes are potentially very serious for the person apologising. This is, of course, particularly true of apologies offered *before* conviction.

The Tribunals have shown limited interest in apology, and where they have done so, they have not always made clear why. In the International Criminal Tribunal for Rwanda (ICTR), for example, the Tribunal specifically gave Jean Kambanda, the former Prime Minister of Rwanda, the opportunity at his sentencing hearing to explain his voluntary participation in the genocide and to express 'contrition, regret or sympathy for the victims in Rwanda'.[63] Kambanda's failure to take this opportunity was noted by the Tribunal, which sentenced him to life imprisonment, despite his guilty plea. But the ICTR did not explain the relevance and importance of an expression of contrition, regret or sympathy; no mention was made of its possible significance to victims as a form of reparation. From the judgment, the presence or absence of Kambanda's remorse and his willingness or otherwise to express it appears to have been used simply as a means of establishing his character, for the purpose of individualising his sentence. Much turns here on the ICTR's analysis of its own role and of the purposes of its proceedings. The relevant jurisprudence of the International Criminal Tribunal for the former Yugoslavia (ICTY) is considered further below.

Kambanda's case starkly illustrates the difficulty of promoting apology for political crimes. The former Prime Minister had pleaded guilty pursuant to a plea agreement in which he had made 'full admissions of all the relevant facts alleged in the indictment'.[64] These included acknowledgments of responsibility for some horrifying decisions, statements, actions and omissions. Yet the plea agreement contained no word of remorse or regret, and Kambanda failed to take the opportunity to apologise

---

62 Exceptions include, at the ICTY, apologies from Momir Nikolic and Dragan Obrenovic (2003) and from Milan Babic (2004). The latter committed suicide in his cell in 2006. Mrs. Biljana Plavsic, a former member of the Bosnian Serb leadership, is often said to have apologised when pleading guilty in 2002, but it is not clear that she did in fact do so, though she certainly acknowledged responsibility. See further below. In the ICTR, Omar Serushago apologised publicly when pleading guilty in [1999]; Georges Ruggiu expressed remorse; a few other accused variously expressed 'sympathy' [Akayesu], 'sorrow' [Rutaganda], 'distress' [Musema]. The latter, insofar as they fail to acknowledge personal responsibility, lack an important element of apology.

63 P. v Kambanda, ICTR 97-23-S, Judgment and Sentence, 4 Sept. 1998, para. 51.

64 Kambanda judgment, para. 39.

at the Tribunal when it could only have been to his advantage to do so. In its judgment, the ICTR alluded to Kambanda's fears for the safety of his family, but it is hard to see these as an explanation for his failure to apologise. A considerable amount of time is devoted in the literature on apology, and in some of the decisions of the ICTY, to the risk that people may shed crocodile tears for their crimes. Yet the Kambanda case and many others like it suggest that the main problem is not a propensity to apologise insincerely, but the extreme reluctance of authors of political crimes to apologise in any shape or form. This experience is so widespread that it would be naïve to attribute the phenomenon simply to some shortcomings in legal policy or practice. For those who have committed crimes out of political conviction, and perhaps especially crimes involving the demonising or dehumanising of victims, 'sorry' may indeed be the hardest word.[65] At least in the relatively short time frame of a criminal prosecution in the immediate aftermath of the events in question, remorse and apology will be out of the question for some.

Nevertheless, given the need of some victims and survivors to hear an apology, international criminal tribunals should do what they can to encourage this. It is difficult for the tribunals to generate remorse where none exists, but 'mainstreaming' the importance of reparation and especially of apology requires all those participating in the international criminal justice process to be alive to the issue at all stages. The provision of counselling services or pastoral support to awaiting trial detainees may assist some to begin to reflect critically on their past actions, or to build on any existing pangs of conscience. The Office of the Prosecutor, in negotiating plea agreements, can ask the accused to consider including not just admissions of fact but also an apology; it is not clear whether this was done in the Kambanda case, for example. Lawyers advising those accused may also be able to raise the issue of apology with their clients. The judges must give clear and consistent signals that they recognise the value of apology; so far, the signals have been mixed, as discussed below. The issue of apology should not be regarded as closed even after an accused has been convicted and sentenced. It remains possible, and there are a number of ways in which it could be encouraged. Finally, 'mainstreaming' apologies also means recognising the importance of communicating apologies to the wider communities affected, so that those who have suffered are made aware that this form of reparation has been offered.[66] This is

65 Benjamin Ferencz, one of the prosecutors at Nuremberg, has criticised the accused in that trial for showing no remorse whatsoever: 'I never heard a defendant say "I'm sorry". I have waited many years in vain for such a statement.' See also below on apology in the amnesty process of the South African Truth and Reconciliation Commission.

66 Concentration so far seems to have centred on bringing apologies home to the 'perpetrator' community, with the aim of forcing them to face up to the past. However important this may be, it is essential from a victim-centred perspective not to neglect communication of the apology to the audience to whom the apology is primarily and properly directed: those who have been wronged.

especially important since tribunal proceedings often take place a very long way from the home of those most closely affected.

Encouraging apology means giving the accused every opportunity to apologise. At present, unless the accused pleads guilty, there is in practice little opportunity for him to apologise; but even those who have pleaded 'not guilty' at trial should be explicitly afforded a further opportunity to apologise if they are convicted. The emotions of both victims and perpetrators are dynamic, not static. The experience of the trial, including the testimony of survivors and those who have lost loved ones, will have some impact on some defendants. In the same way that victim impact statements have come to be widely regarded as important in domestic criminal law, supporting and encouraging witnesses in international criminal trials to testify about the impact of the crimes on them, either at trial or before sentence, may help to promote apology. A more radical version of international criminal justice could involve bringing (willing) victims and survivors together with (willing) accused or convicted persons in private meetings.[67] Judges should ask direct questions that attempt to stimulate self-examination and empathy. In the *Nikolic* case, for example, Judge Carmen Maria Argibay asked the accused (who had pleaded guilty pursuant to a plea agreement) some basic but searching questions: 'Why did you do it?' 'Can you think of the youngest son of all those killed in the Srebrenica massacre?'[68]

The simplest way in which apology may be encouraged in international criminal justice is by taking it into account as a mitigating factor in sentencing. The difficulty with this approach is, of course, that it is something of a blunt instrument, and raises concerns about insincere apologies being in effect traded for sentence reductions. This issue has troubled the ICTY in particular. In general, the Tribunal has attempted to 'test' the sincerity of professed remorse by reference to 'objective' factors such as the accused's actions and demeanour, sometimes with the assistance of testimony from the Office of the Prosecutor. Where the remorse has been accepted by the ICTY as sincere, it has been taken into account as a mitigating factor in sentencing, despite the fact that remorse is not expressly mentioned as a possible mitigating factor in the Rules. An early precedent for this was set in the *Erdemovic* case.[69] Drazen Erdemovic, a soldier

---

67 A sensible and properly funded scheme for such meetings would not have to begin and end within the relatively short time frame of the trial and sentencing process; it could continue, or even begin, during the term of any prison sentence. One of the problems with the existing international criminal justice system is that it is seen as concluded once the accused person is 'put away'. Even at national level, restorative justice programs rarely involve work with convicted prisoners, but there are exceptions: see e.g. Operation Phoenix, a Quaker initiative which works with offenders in Eshowe Prison, South Africa.

68 See the report of the Coalition for International Justice, 29 October 2003, 'Bosnian Serb Expresses Sincere Remorse for Srebrenica Crimes', available at http://www.cij.org. The first question is described in the CIJ report as 'the question that haunts so many'.

69 Prosecutor v Erdemovic, Case No. IT-96-22-Tbis, Sentencing Judgment, 5 March 1998, para. 16. See also Prosecutor v Sikirica et al, Case No.IT-95-8-S, Sentencing Judgment, 13 November 2001, paras. 152, 194, 230.

in the Bosnian Serb army, admitted having participated in the summary execution of Bosnian Muslim men in connection with the Srebrenica massacre. Erdemovic, who had come forward voluntarily, apparently as a result of his remorse, estimated that he had personally killed 70 men. He expressed his remorse in a brief statement to the Tribunal, discussed further below. Taking into account his voluntary surrender, guilty plea and the evidence of an investigator from the Office of the Prosecutor, the trial chamber accepted that his remorse was genuine and took it into account as a mitigating factor in sentencing him to ten years' imprisonment.

The most high-profile case in which the ICTY was required to consider remorse as a mitigating factor was that of Mrs. Biljana Plavsic. Mrs. Plavsic, then aged 72, a former member of the Bosnian Serb leadership, initially pleaded not guilty to all the charges in the indictment. Before trial, however, she asked to change her plea to one of guilty to a charge of persecution, a crime against humanity, pursuant to a plea agreement under which a charge of genocide was dropped. Her lawyer, Eugene O'Sullivan, said her main motive in making the change had been to express remorse. Both prosecution and defence lawyers insisted that no deals had been made regarding her sentence. In support of her motion for change of plea, Mrs. Plavsic filed a Statement in which she stated that by 'accepting responsibility and expressing her remorse fully and unconditionally', she hoped to 'offer some consolation to the innocent victims – Muslim, Croat and Serb – of the war in Bosnia and Herzegovina'.[70] She invited others, especially leaders, to examine themselves and their own conduct'.[71] Her change of plea was accepted.

At her sentencing hearing in December 2002, Mrs. Plavsic read a long statement to the Tribunal, in which she accepted that the Serb leadership, of which she was part, 'led an effort which victimised countless innocent people' and accepted responsibility for her part in the 'litany of suffering that this produced'. She accepted that she had been repeatedly informed of allegations of cruel and inhuman conduct against non-Serbs, but had 'refused to accept them or even to investigate'. Mrs. Plavsic conceded that explanations of self-defence and survival offered no justification: 'By the end, it was said, even among our own people, that in this war we had lost our nobility of character.' She expressed her hope that by having come to the truth, spoken it and accepted responsibility, she would 'help the Muslim, Croat and even Serb innocent victims not to be overtaken with bitterness, which often becomes hatred and is in the end self-destructive'. Nowhere in her long statement did Mrs. Plavsic formally apologise to the victims; the word 'sorry' did not appear in her text, nor did she express remorse, sorrow or regret in so many words. Although clearly an acknowledgement of facts and responsibility, it is not self-evident that her statement can properly be

---

70 Plavsic Written Statement, 30 September 2002, cited in the Sentencing Judgment of 27 Feb. 2003, para. 19.

71 *Ibid.*

regarded as an apology, though it has sometimes been described as such.[72] A large part of her statement appeared to be directed towards protecting the Bosnian Serb people and contained numerous references to 'us', 'my own people', 'our people' – a disturbing continuation of ethnic differentiation. It also extolled the character of the Serbian people and ended with an appeal to the Tribunal to do all within its power 'to bring justice to both sides'. According to one reporter, her statement was read 'in a flat voice', and did not placate a Bosnian Muslim survivor of the Srebrenica massacre, who is recorded as having said afterwards:

> "I feel like crying. There was nothing human in her words, not a note of apology. She didn't do it for me. She did it for the Serbian cause."[73]

The ICTY accepted Mrs. Plavsic's statement at the sentencing hearing 'together with expressions in her earlier statement in support of the motion to change her plea' as 'an expression of remorse to be considered as part of the mitigating circumstances connected with a guilty plea.'[74] The ICTY added: 'Indeed, it may be argued that by her guilty plea, Mrs. Plavsic had already demonstrated remorse.'[75] Overall, the Trial Chamber found that the following were the 'relevant, substantial, mitigating circumstances' in the case: the 'guilty plea (together with remorse and reconciliation); voluntary surrender; post-conflict conduct; and age.'[76] Whilst it attached weight to each of these circumstances, the Tribunal stated that it attached 'great weight' to Mrs. Plavsic's guilty plea and post-conflict conduct, which, together, made 'a formidable body of mitigation'. Mrs. Plavsic was sentenced to 11 years' imprisonment – only a year more than Erdemovic, a common soldier, and 29 years less than the 40 years meted out to General Krstic for Srebrenica.

It is clear from the *Erdemovic* and *Plavsic* cases that, although the ICTY has been willing to take into account remorse as a mitigating factor in connection with a guilty plea, it does not pay particular attention to the words used by an accused and does not attempt to assess whether they amount to an apology.[77] The Tribunal's willingness to accept the argument that a guilty plea is itself evidence of remorse, when it is of course capable of many other interpretations, demonstrates that in the Tribunal's view, remorse may be expressed with no words of apology at all. Interestingly, the ICTY rarely uses the word 'apology'; in the *Plavsic* case, it used the word only when

---

72 See e.g. Boraine, A., 'War Criminal's Remorse Could Help Bosnia Heal', Int'l Herald Trib., 18 Dec. 2002.

73 Marlise Simons, New York Times report, 18 December 2002. The survivor whose comments were reported was Emir Suljagic.

74 Prosecutor v Biljana Plavsic, IT-00-39&40/1-S, Sentencing Judgment of 27 February 2003, para. 73.

75 *Ibid.*

76 *Ibid.*, para. 110.

77 In fact, in the Obrenovic Sentencing Judgment, the Trial Chamber specifically stated that the deeds of the accused were more important than his words: para. 146.

summarising testimony given by a witness, Alex Boraine, who had himself used the word 'apology' to describe Plavsic's statement. Both the Erdemovic and Plavsic statements could be regarded as falling short of a genuine apology. Both came perilously close to being a political statement. Erdemovic's statement could probably more aptly be described as an expression of sympathy, using a passive form which did not acknowledge his personal responsibility. Moreover, he, like Plavsic, could not confine himself to referring to the Bosniak victims he had wronged, but insisted on pointing out that there were Serb victims in the war, too. 'I only wish to say that I feel sorry for all the victims, not only for the ones who were killed then at that farm. I feel sorry for all the victims in the former Bosnia and Herzegovina regardless of their nationality.' These kind of 'moral equivalence' statements – to the effect that there were wrongs on all sides – are out of place in authentic apologies. Whilst the Tribunal is right in saying that actions matter, it is mistaken if it believes that words do not.[78]

If sentence discounts are to be given in international criminal tribunals partly on the basis that guilty pleas and expressions of remorse provide solace to victims and assist in processes of reconciliation and the maintenance of peace and security, the tribunals should pay more attention to ensuring that the words and behaviour of defendants are genuinely likely to contribute to those ends.[79] Anything less than a clear and unqualified apology should not be accepted. Milan Babic, another Serb leader, who also pleaded guilty under a plea agreement, seems to have had a better sense of what was appropriate and necessary: 'I allowed myself to participate in the persecution of the worst kind against people only because they were Croats, not Serbs. I ask my brother Croats to forgive us, their brother Serbs,' he told the ICTY in January 2004. 'I stand before this Tribunal with a deep sense of shame and remorse.' In his case, however, despite this unequivocal apology and the fact that he had – unlike Plavsic – testified against Milosevic, the ICTY imposed a sentence of 13 years' imprisonment.[80] Dragan Obrenovic, a 32 year old army major, was another of the small number of defendants who chose to apologise to the victims and their families. His statement of remorse and apology was simple and powerful.[81] The ICTY accepted that he had taken 'few direct actions ... to further the murder operations' at Srebrenica; he had pleaded guilty, again pursuant to a plea agreement, and had cooperated fully with the

[78] Apologies are speech acts, in which considerable sensitivity is required if the apology is to work its magic – see generally Tavuchis, note 22 above.

[79] See the Plavsic Sentencing Judgment, paras. 66-81. The ICTY accepted testimony about the importance of acknowledgement and acceptance of responsibility for grave crimes in furthering reconciliation, the maintenance of peace in the former Yugoslavia and international peace and security. It also noted Alex Boraine's view that 'genuine and voluntary expressions of remorse often provide a degree of closure for victims' [para. 77].

[80] The Prosecution had asked only for an 11 year sentence for Babic. He appealed unsuccessfully against sentence in 2005 and committed suicide in March 2006, aged 50.

[81] The relevant parts of the Statement are reproduced in the Sentencing Judgment of 10 December 2003, at para. 120.

Prosecution. The ICTY had accepted testimony about his character, including evidence from a Bosnian Muslim whose life he had saved, and his remorse was accepted as sincere. Despite this, he was sentenced to 17 years' imprisonment in December 2003.[82]

Whilst these judgments, especially the *Plavsic* judgment, show some recognition that international criminal justice has objectives beyond retribution and deterrence, the idea of apology as a form of reparation to victims that is valuable for that reason alone, as well as for its possible contribution to peace, is not clearly and consistently recognised and articulated. Apologies contain, but go beyond, an acknowledgment of facts and responsibility. Whilst the ICTY seems in recent years to have grasped the importance of acknowledgment, it has not adequately distinguished between acknowledgment and apology and recognised the value of the latter. This may be driven partly by the fact that, whilst admissions and acknowledgments are valuable to international tribunals in terms of completing their case-loads expeditiously and cost-effectively, apologies have no 'added value' for the tribunals themselves. It must be hoped that the ICC, which has a stronger, albeit still limited, mandate in relation to reparation and rehabilitation, will take apology more seriously.

There are, of course, pressures on international tribunals to 'get results' in the short-term sense of disposing of their case-load as quickly and cost-effectively as possible. It has been suggested that the ICTY's willingness to accept the Plavsic plea bargain and statement rather uncritically was motivated by such considerations.[83] The ICTY has tried, somewhat unconvincingly, to stress the benefits of plea bargains for victims. At the very least, such agreements should not be allowed to prejudice victims' interests; and reconsidering plea bargaining as a tool for encouraging not merely admissions but also apologies could help to ensure that they do genuinely provide benefits for all concerned. This is not to suggest that perfunctory, insincere apologies should be encouraged; it would be for the tribunal to decide how much weight to attach to any apology offered, in the light of all the circumstances and evidence.

Both the ICTR and the ICTY have been accused at various times of neglecting victims or treating them poorly, and it is clear that the International Criminal Court hopes to learn from their mistakes. Taking apology seriously is one way in which it could do so.

---

82 Based on the Nikolic case, however, what can probably be said is that if an apology is made but not completely accepted by the ICTY as genuine, based on the accused's conduct, the accused will pay a price. Nikolic, whose statement of remorse and apology was described at the time as 'one of the most moving, tragic and hopeful moments in the Tribunal's history', was sentenced to 27 years' imprisonment. See the Nikolic Sentencing Judgment of 2 December 2003.

83 Combs, note 32 above.

4.3 TRUTH COMMISSIONS

Since the evolution of truth commissions in the 1990s as a regular feature of attempts by transitional and post-conflict societies to deal with past human rights abuses, the whole issue of reparation has often been delegated to them.[84] In Sierra Leone, where for the first time a truth commission ran alongside an internationally funded Special Court, this division of labour was entrenched: Amnesty International noted in 2005 that when it had raised the issue of reparations with officials and staff of the Special Court for Sierra Leone, 'the response has been that the Special Court has neither the mandate nor the resources to consider reparations and that they fall within the remit of the TRC, rather than the Special Court.'[85]

Truth commissions are generally staffed by people from a range of professional backgrounds, including human rights lawyers, but also doctors and mental health professionals, writers, clergy, academics and others. Perhaps because of this combined expertise, some truth commissions have shown awareness of the importance of symbolism, both in the proceedings of the commission and in terms of its recommendations. This is most famously true of the South African Truth and Reconciliation Commission, headed by Archbishop Desmond Tutu. Tim Kelsall and Rosalind Shaw have commented on the importance of ritual and symbolism in the Sierra Leone TRC.[86] Shaw notes that 'people turned out in large numbers to listen to perpetrators' apologies in the TRC's district hearings'.[87]

The Report of the Sierra Leone TRC advocates – in addition to material reparation – symbolic reparation, in the form of public apologies, memorials, commemoration ceremonies, and symbolic reburials for victims. Under the heading 'Public Apology', the Commission

---

84 The first 'truth commission' to draw the world's attention was the Argentine Commission on the Disappeared in 1983. It was not, however, until the 1990s that truth commissions became a regular feature of the landscape. A useful collection of materials on truth commissions can be found at http://www.usip.org.

85 Amnesty International, Statement to the National Victims Commemoration Conference, Freetown, 1 March 2005, AI Index: AFR51/002/2005.

86 Kelsall, T., 'Truth, Lies, Ritual: Preliminary Reflections on the Truth and Reconciliation Commission in Sierra Leone' (2005) 26 HRQ 361; Shaw, R., 'Transitional Subjectivities: Reconciling Ex-Combatants in Northern Sierra Leone', conference paper, Carr Centre for Human Rights, 2004-05. Interestingly, Shaw argues that even some apologies which did not fit the Western liberal model or 'ideal type' described by Tavuchis (involving unequivocal acceptance of responsibility for wrongdoing) were popularly accepted by the audience at TRC hearings in Northern Sierra Leone, in her view because they were performances of moral transformation representing signs that the speakers' 'hearts' had changed and were now 'cool'. This suggests a view of apology that places emphasis on its potential value as a guarantee of non-repetition – naturally important to a community into which ex-combatants with very violent recent pasts are being re-integrated.

87 Shaw, R., 'Rethinking Truth and Reconciliation Commissions – Lessons from Sierra Leone' (2005) United States Institute of Peace, Special Report No. 130.

"...recommends that individuals, groups, bodies and organisations who bear any responsibility for the abuses and violations committed during the war, be encouraged to apologise publicly. The Commission further recommends that the government acknowledge the suffering Sierra Leoneans went through during the conflict and unreservedly apologise to the people for all actions and inactions of all governments since 1961."[88]

The Sierra Leone TRC also specifically identified apology as important in fostering the process of national reconciliation.[89]

An important aspect of symbolic reparation, including apology, is that it can be provided to all victims, even where, because the number of victims is very large and/or the country very poor, the provision of substantial financial reparation may be very difficult.

Truth commissions face many of the same difficulties as courts and tribunals in encouraging apology. The risk of criminal prosecutions resulting from their proceedings may discourage some individuals from apologising, and even where, as in South Africa, a conditional amnesty was offered, perpetrators of human rights abuses did not generally rush to apologise. Despite these difficulties, truth commissions can encourage a national and individual focus and reflection on issues of acknowledgment, apology, forgiveness and reconciliation, and do constitute valuable fora in which apology, both from individuals and from governments and other institutions, may be offered. Truth and reconciliation commissions are usually staffed wholly or partly by nationals, which should facilitate – though does not guarantee – sensitivity to local culture and expectations.

The main disadvantage of leaving reparation issues to truth commissions is the fact that they are invariably able only to make non-binding recommendations, and, sadly, the notorious weakness of truth commissions has been the failure of governments to implement their recommendations. In South Africa, for example, the refusal of the government to accept and implement the TRC's recommendations on reparation and prosecution has disappointed victims and the human rights community. In Sierra Leone, Amnesty International has lamented the fact that more has not been done by the government to make the TRC's detailed recommendations on reparation known.[90] Given the historical record of governments in relation to TRC recommendations, it is not surprising that Amnesty International urged the Special Court of Sierra Leone to do more on reparations and made some creative suggestions:

"The assumption has been that reparations will be dealt with by the TRC. It is unfortunate, however, that the Special Court has not pursued this issue further. It could, for example, consider:

---

88 Final Report of the Sierra Leone TRC, 2005, Vol. 2, Ch. 4, para. 197. The TRC also recommended measures in the areas of health, pensions, education, skills training and micro-credit, as well as community reparations.

89 Final Report, Vol. 2, Ch. 3, para. 518.

90 Amnesty International Statement, note 83 above.

> establishing a programme to provide restitution of property...; working with the government to establish effective mechanisms for victims to make claims for compensation against those convicted by the Special Court in the national courts under the Criminal Procedure Act, 1965; and consulting with civil society and international actors in Sierra Leone to examine how other forms of reparation should be awarded, such as a judicial decision restoring the dignity, reputation and legal and social rights of the victim and of people closely associated with the victim, or an apology including public acknowledgment of the facts and acceptance of responsibility."[91]

This statement from a leading international human rights NGO is a clear indication that international civil society is increasingly alive to the importance of reparation, including symbolic reparation, such as apology, and that – consistent with the UN Basic Principles – it wishes to see reparation treated as a right of victims, rather than an act of largesse by government.

5 CONCLUSION

The subject of reparation has attracted increasing attention as other battles, such as the battle for the International Criminal Court, have been won. The UN Basic Principles on Reparation have finally been approved. Civil society is beginning to apply greater pressure for reparation, including symbolic reparation, to be provided to victims.[92] The work of truth commissions, especially that of the South African Truth and Reconciliation Commission, has contributed to greater interest in the relationship between truth, reparation, forgiveness and reconciliation. The Inter-American Court of Human Rights has become more creative in addressing reparation issues, and has taken a lead in recognising that reparation is more than a question of money.[93] International criminal tribunals, too, have taken some initial steps towards acknowledging the needs and wishes of victims.

Most depressing is perhaps the persistent absence of these subjects from law school curricula. A new cadre of international lawyers, including international criminal lawyers, with a greater openness to insights from other disciplines and cultures, is sorely needed.

---

[91] Amnesty International, 1 March 2005. AI Index: AFR 51/002/2005.

[92] The example of the work of AI in relation to Sierra Leone is mentioned above. The human rights NGO Interights, based in London, which (inter alia) assists victims with communications to the UN Human Rights Committee under the International Covenant on Civil and Political Rights, has also recognised apology as an 'effective remedy': see Interights letter dated 29 August 2005 to the President of Angola in the case of Rafael Marques de Morais [HRC1128/2002], in which various remedies including a public apology to the victim were urged.

[93] Judge Cancado Trindade has emphasised the importance of reparation as a necessary display of human solidarity in the face of the fragility of the human condition and of man's cruelty. See Bulacio v Argentina, note 1 above.

The lack of empirical research on the needs and wishes of victims has already been noted. It is not the purpose of this article to argue that apology is always wanted, or always enough. It is, however, clearly sometimes wanted, either as a measure of satisfaction, or as a guarantee of non-repetition, or both. As the preliminary reflections above indicate, there is more that international lawyers, courts and tribunals can do to promote it. As to whether it is enough, symbolic reparation alone will often not be sufficient to satisfy the very real needs of victims, who may well need and want compensation, medical care and other forms of material reparation.[94] Apology should never be degraded to the status of a cheap 'get-out'. There is, of course, always a risk that apologies may be offered disingenuously, either by States or individuals, to generous and unsuspecting people. They may be offered dismissively, to obtain personal advantage, such as sentence reductions, either in international criminal justice processes or in national fora, such as the *gacaca* courts in post-genocide Rwanda. Intelligent and aware lawyers should be well-placed to recognise and protect victims from such abuses. Humanity and wisdom, not sentimentality, about apology is required.

94 In South Africa, during the period of debate about what form reparation should take for the human rights violations dealt with by the TRC, a memorable cartoon was published in which a victim was shown saying to the government, 'I'll accept symbolic reparations when you give me symbolic bills.'

AMNESTY OR IMPUNITY? A PRELIMINARY CRITIQUE OF THE REPORT OF THE TRUTH AND RECONCILIATION COMMISSION OF SOUTH AFRICA (TRC)[1]

Mahmood Mamdani

The Truth and Reconciliation Commission of South Africa was the fruit of a political compromise. The terms of the compromise both made possible the Commission and set the limits within which it would work. These limits, in turn, defined the space available to the Commission to interpret its terms of reference and define its agenda. This paper takes the compromise legislation that set up the TRC as a historical given and focuses attention on the TRC's interpretation of its terms of reference.

The TRC claimed to be different from its predecessors, whether in Latin America or Eastern Europe. It would practice neither impunity nor vengeance. It was determined to avoid not one but two pitfalls: on the one hand reconciliation turned into an unprincipled embrace of political evil and, on the other hand, a pursuit of justice so relentless as to turn into revenge. To do so, the Commission was determined to address *both* 'victims' and 'perpetrators', not just one of them.

This double determination was first written into South Africa's *Interim* Constitution that paved the way for the legislation that set up the TRC. First, there would be no *blanket* amnesty. Amnesty would be *conditional.* It would not be a group amnesty. Every perpetrator would have to be identified individually, and would have to own up to his or her guilt – *the truth* – before receiving amnesty from legal prosecution. Second, the victim who is so *acknowledged* would give up the right to prosecute perpetrators in courts of law. Justice for the victim would thus not be criminal but restorative: acknowledgement would be followed by reparations. In sum, individual amnesty for the perpetrator, truth for the society and acknowledgement and

[1] An earlier version of this paper appeared in Seyla Benhabib, Ian Shapiro and Danilo Petranovich, eds., *Identities, Affiliations, and Allegiances* (Cambridge University Press, 2007), and is reproduced with permission from Cambridge University Press.

reparations for the victim – this was the pact built into the legislation that set up the TRC.

The Act, however, did not clearly define the 'victim,' and therefore, the 'perpetrator'. The Commission would have to do it. This paper argues that the single most important decision that determined the scope and depth of the Commission's work was its definition of 'victim,' and thus, 'perpetrator'. Without a *comprehensive* acknowledgement of victims of apartheid, there would only be a *limited* identification of perpetrators and only a *partial* understanding of the legal regime that made possible the 'crime against humanity' – and unfortunately there was. From this perspective, the paper identifies *two* key limitations in the Commission's Report.

First, the TRC *individualised* the victims of apartheid. Though it acknowledged apartheid as a 'crime against humanity' which targeted entire communities for ethnic and racial policing and cleansing, the Commission majority was reluctant to go beyond the formal acknowledgement. The Commission's analysis reduced apartheid from a relationship between the state and entire communities to one between the state and individuals. Where entire communities were victims of gross violations of rights, the Commission acknowledged only individual victims. If the 'crime against humanity' involved a targeting of entire communities for racial and ethnic cleansing and policing, individualising the victim obliterated this particular – many would argue *central* – truth of apartheid. Limiting the definition of harm and remedy to individuals only centre-staged political activists as victims of apartheid, as indeed happened with the victim hearings. The consequence was to narrow the TRC perspective to a *political* reconciliation between state agents and political activists, individual members of a fractured political elite, rather than the 'national unity and reconciliation' mandated by the legislation that set it up. To pursue its actual mandate, the TRC needed to broaden its perspective, for to work for a *social* reconciliation between perpetrators and victims required addressing the relationship between the state and the entire South African people.

Second, by focusing on individuals and obscuring the victimisation of communities, the TRC was unable to highlight the bifurcated nature of apartheid as a form of power that governed natives differently from non-natives. If the apartheid state spoke the language of *rights* to the white population, it disaggregated the native population into tribal groups – each to be administered under a separate set of laws – in the name of enforcing *custom*. Rights and custom were two different and contradictory languages: the former claimed to circumscribe power, the latter to enable it. Whereas the former claimed to be a rule of law, the latter claimed the legitimacy of custom and tradition. The TRC's failure lay in focusing exclusively on the 'civil' regime and in totally ignoring the 'customary' regime. No wonder, it failed even to recommend reforms that would put in place a single unitary regime – rule of law understood as formal equality before the law – for all South Africans in a post-apartheid South Africa.

Finally, the TRC extended *impunity* to most perpetrators of apartheid. In the absence of a full acknowledgement of victims of apartheid, there could not be a complete identification of its perpetrators. To the extent the TRC did not acknowledge the full truth, to that extent the amnesty intended to be *individual* turned into a *group* amnesty. For the simple fact is that the perpetrator who was not so identified was a perpetrator who enjoyed impunity.

The chapter is organised in four parts. Parts One and Two deal with the findings of the Commission and the definitions that paved the way for these findings. The last two parts offer an alternative reading of the Commission's Report, and suggest the lines along which the Report could have been re-written if the TRC had defined its terms consistently with the acknowledgement that apartheid was indeed 'a crime against humanity'. The conclusion argues that the Commission's method of analysis – one that dehistoricised and decontextualized social processes, and at the same time individualised outcomes – provided the meeting point for two otherwise radically different perspectives and projects: the religious perspective dominant in the TRC and the secular perspective of the human rights community that reinforced it internationally.

1 FINDINGS

When the TRC issued its report in 1999, it was sharply critiqued by leaders of major parties to the constitutional pact – the National Party and the African National Congress. For the TRC, this was proof enough that its report was not only non-partisan but also non-political. If anything, the critique from yesterday's main adversaries seemed to vindicate the Commission's work and affirm the credibility of its report.

More interesting than the criticism from political parties was their shared silence. It was not just that the TRC's critique focused on the findings that implicated major parties and their leaders in violations of human rights; these same findings also rewrote the story of apartheid in a rather fundamental way, a fact about which the same parties remained curiously silent. This larger fact never did become the subject of a public discussion. Let me turn to some of the findings in the Commission's Report to illustrate my point.

The big finding, one that led to a public split in the Commission and appeared as a minority view penned to the Report, was that apartheid was indeed 'a crime against humanity'.[2] At the same time, the Commission acknowledged 20,000+ 'victims' of apartheid for whom it recommended reparations.[3] Could a 'crime against humanity'

---

[2] Truth and Reconciliation Commission of South Africa, ***Report***, vol. 1, pp. 70-71, Para 78.

[3] Truth and Reconciliation Commission of South Africa, ***Report***, vol. 5, chapter 2.

that involved a racial and ethnic cleansing of the bulk of its population have only 20,000+ victims?

Who were the victims, and who the perpetrators, of apartheid? The Commission's answer is worked out in the Report through a statistical analysis of victims and perpetrators of this 'crime against humanity'. It highlights two related conclusions. The *first* follows a historical overview of the Commission's mandate from 1960 to 1994. The mandate began with the banning of parties following the Sharpeville massacre in 1960, and closed with the first democratic elections in 1994. The Commission's research staff compiled a list of violations over the full mandate, and then divided this into four periods:

- from 1960 (Sharpeville) to 1976 (the Soweto Uprising)
- from 1976 to 1983 (beginning of the state of emergency)
- from 1983 to 1990 (the unbanning of political parties), and
- from 1990 to 1994 (the first democratic elections)

This is how the Commission concluded its statistical analysis of violations: 'The graph below shows that most violations reported by deponents took place in the period after the unbanning of political parties (1990-1994) followed closely by the years in which states of emergency were in force (1983-1989)'.[4] Roughly half of all violations recorded by the Commission are said to have occurred during the period of transition from apartheid, and another 35% at the height of the popular struggle against apartheid, also the years of emergency rule in townships. Conversely, only 15% of the violations are said to have been committed in the heyday of apartheid. If these statistics are to be believed, then the 'crime against humanity' took place not when the grand design of apartheid was *implemented*, but when it was *challenged*. If so, would it make sense to speak of apartheid, as and when implemented, as a 'crime against humanity'?

The *second* conclusion concerns the killings. The Report identifies the organisations of the persons killed as '*victim organizations*' and those of perpetrators as '*perpetrator organizations*'. The list of 'victim organizations' places the ANC at the head, followed by the IFP, with South African Police [SAP] in 7th place, *followed* by the Azanian Peoples Organisation [AZAPO].[5] The IFP was said to be the *primary* 'perpetrator organization': 'The number of violations allegedly committed by the IFP dominates the graph, with the SAP and the ANC showing the second and third highest numbers of alleged violations.'[6] The accompanying graph lists the South African Defense Forces [SADF] as the fourth 'perpetrator organization', trailing the Inkatha Freedom Party [IFP], the South African Police [SAP] and the African National Congress [ANC]. The

4 Truth and Reconciliation Commission of South Africa, ***Report***, vol. 1, p. 172, Para 25.

5 Truth and Reconciliation Commission of South Africa, ***Report***, vol. 3, p. 7, Table D2A.1-1.

6 Truth and Reconciliation Commission of South Africa, ***Report***, vol. 3, p. 3, Para 33.

Report then clarifies the context in which the IFP emerged as the leading – and ANC the third – 'perpetrator organization' in the country: 'The majority of reports of human rights violations in the region [Natal and Kwazulu] refer to the conflict between supporters of the IFP and the ANC-aligned supporters of the UDF.'[7]

A leading researcher for the Commission once remarked to me in a private conversation: 'I could not believe that most perpetrators of apartheid were black.' The observation raises a question the Commission never posed. If not only most victims, but also most perpetrators, were black people, was this 'crime against humanity' primarily a 'black-on-black' affair, whose principal perpetrator was the IFP, and third major perpetrator the ANC? Were the apologists of apartheid right in claiming that the order was a necessary check on 'black-on-black' violence, or was the violence produced by the order called apartheid? I suspect the Commission never posed the question because it was in no position to answer it.

In this chapter, I argue that the Commission's conclusions followed from the way it defined its own mandate, particularly from how it defined 'victim' and 'perpetrator'. Not only are these definitions inconsistent with the Commission's own acknowledgement that apartheid was 'a crime against humanity', they came in the way of the Commission acknowledging the evidence of this very crime – not because this evidence was not available, but because the Commission was unable or unwilling to underline the meaning of the evidence compiled by its own research staff and found in its own Report. To validate this evidence requires understanding apartheid as a form of the state, an organised power whose 'victims' were not individuals but groups classified and administered by the same power.

2 A MATTER OF DEFINITION

The Commission Report acknowledges two major debates that concerned the interpretation of the Commission's terms of reference. Both debates raged within and outside the Commission. The first debate focused on the understanding of 'gross violations', the second on the meaning of 'severe ill-treatment'.

2.1 GROSS VIOLATIONS

'There had been an expectation,' notes the opening chapter of the final volume of the Commission's 5-volume Report, 'that the Commission would investigate many of the human rights violations which were caused, for example, by the denial of freedom of movement through the pass laws, by forced removals of peoples from their land, by

7 Truth and Reconciliation Commission of South Africa, ***Report***, vol. 3, p. 162, Para 24.

the denial of the franchise to citizens, by the treatment of farm workers and other labour disputes, and by discrimination in such areas as education and work opportunities. Many organisations lobbied the Commission to insist that these issues should farm part of its investigations. Commission members, too, felt that these were important areas that could not be ignored. Nevertheless, they could not be interpreted as falling directly within the Commission's mandate.'[8]

The argument that prevailed in the Commission is outlined in 'the mandate' chapter of the Report, and is anchored in section 1(1)(ix) of the Act that set up the TRC:

> "… 'gross violation of human rights' means the violation of human rights through – (a) the killing, abduction, torture or severe ill treatment of any person; or (b) any attempt, conspiracy, incitement, instigation, command or procurement to commit an act referred to in paragraph (a), *which emanated from conflicts of the past* and which was committed *during the period 1 March 1960 to 10 May 1994* within or outside the Republic, and the commission of which was advised, planned, directed, commanded or ordered, by any person *acting with a political motive* (section 1(1)(ix)."[9] (*italics* mine)

The paragraph contains three limitations, which I have italicised in the above quote. The first and the most obvious is the time limitation: it limits the mandate of the Commission to investigating 'gross violation of human rights' during the period from 1 March 1960 to 10 May 1994. The next two are limitations of scope: that these violations have 'emanated from conflicts of the past,' and that they be committed 'with a political motive.' The limitation in time was unambiguous. But the limitations in scope were not: they would have to be interpreted by the Commission.

The matter of definitions is discussed in two chapters in the five-volume Report: chapter four on 'the mandate' in the first volume, and chapter one on 'analysis of gross violations of human rights' in the final volume. The Report acknowledges that the scope of the Commission's inquiry was defined so ambiguously that it required an interpretation: 'Before findings could be made, clarity was required on definitions and criteria.'[10]

Conflicts of the Past. The Commission majority distinguished 'conflicts of the past' from 'policies of apartheid.' It went on to argue that 'conflicts of the past' excluded 'policies of apartheid,' thus driving home its conviction that the Commission's mandate included violations emanating from 'conflicts of the past', but not from 'policies of apartheid'. In the words of the Report: 'This definition limited the attention

---

8 Truth and Reconciliation Commission of South Africa, ***Report***, vol. 5, p. 11, Para 48.
9 Truth and Reconciliation Commission of South Africa, ***Report***, vol. 1, p. 60, Para 42.
10 Truth and Reconciliation Commission of South Africa, ***Report***, vol. 5, pps. 10-11, Para 46-47.

of the Commission to events which emanated from conflicts of the past, rather than from the policies of apartheid.'[11]

But nowhere did the Act contrast and distinguish 'conflicts of the past' from 'policies of apartheid'. Section 3. (1), which set out 'the objectives of the Commission', required the Commission to establish 'as complete a picture as possible of the causes, nature and extent of the gross violations of human rights which were committed during the period from 1 March 1960 to the cut-off date, including the antecedents, circumstances, factors and contexts of such violations, ...'. The section that followed required the Commission to 'facilitate, and where necessary initiate or coordinate inquiries into- (i) gross violations of human rights, including violations which were part of a systematic pattern of abuse ...'.[12]

Notwithstanding the emphasis on establishing 'as complete a picture as possible' and highlighting 'systematic patterns of abuse,' the Commission turned the distinction between two kinds of violations, those emanating from 'policies of apartheid' and those from 'conflicts of the past', to relegate the former to *context* and to acknowledge only the latter as *violations* that would merit reparations. The result was to narrow the scope of the Commission's hearings so extraordinarily that the first phase of hearings were confined to *individual* victims. When disaffection with this narrow interpretation fed criticism both within and outside the Commission, the TRC responded with a series of *institutional* hearings. Instead of broadening the definition of victims from individuals to groups, institutionally defined and targeted, the institutional hearings were said to be of only *background* use, providing a backdrop that would further highlight individual stories provided in victim hearings. In other words, the institutional hearings were said to be about context rather than conflict, policies rather than violations. Referring to these hearings, the Commission wrote: 'These submissions made a valuable contribution to the section of the final report dealing with the broad context within which the gross violations of human rights took place, although they could not be considered as victim hearings. They gave depth to the larger picture, but they still excluded individuals from recognition and from access to reparations, and many people remained aggrieved.'[13] After mapping the nature of apartheid in three eloquent but summary pages, 'the mandate' section of the Report dismissed it in a single sentence as background to its real work: 'It is this systematic and all-pervading character of apartheid that provides the background for the present investigation.'[14] Reduced to 'the context' or 'the background' of gross human rights violations, apartheid was effectively written out of the report of the TRC.

---

[11] Truth and Reconciliation Commission of South Africa, ***Report***, vol. 5, p. 11, Para 48.

[12] Truth and Reconciliation Commission of South Africa, ***Report***, vol. 1, pp. 55-56, Para 31.

[13] Truth and Reconciliation Commission of South Africa, ***Report***, vol. 5, p. 11, Para 49.

[14] Truth and Reconciliation Commission of South Africa, ***Report***, vol. 1, p. 62, para 51; the summary is in pages 25-28 of the same volume.

Political Motive. The second qualification on acknowledging a violation was that it had to be carried out by a person 'acting with a political motive'. To qualify for amnesty, a perpetrator had not only to make a 'full disclosure of relevant facts' but had also to establish that the violations in question were carried out 'with a political objective'.[15]

For the TRC's machinery to swing into action, a person had to file a complaint that s/he had suffered a 'gross violation'. The Commission then made a finding on the claim. One of the reasons for a negative finding was that 'there appeared to be no political motive'.[16] To meet the Commission's criterion that a violation be shown as the outcome of a political motive, the violation had *either* to be committed by 'any member or supporter of a publicly known political organization or liberation movement on behalf of or in support of that organization or movement, *in furtherance of a political struggle* waged by that organization or movement (section 20(2)(a))' or it had to be committed by 'any employee of the state (or any former state) or any member of the security forces of the state (or any former state) in the course of his or her duties ... *with the objective of countering or otherwise resisting the said struggle* (section 20(2)(b)).'[17]

Whether an act could be considered as political or not depended on the answer to a larger question: What was a political act and what a legal act? Was apartheid itself a political project or a legal project? We shall see that this question was central to the legal hearings: Was apartheid a rule of law or not? What happens when the state resorts to law to violate rights? Five top judges at the legal systems hearing urged the Commission to acknowledge 'that apartheid was in and of itself a gross violation of human rights'.[18]

Whereas the legal hearings concluded that apartheid was *not* a rule of law, the victim hearings proceeded on the narrow assumption that the project of apartheid – its policies – was *not* political. If the Commission had fully accepted the outcome of the legal hearings, it would have defined the very agenda of apartheid – and not just its defence – as political. But the Commission did not. At the same time, the legal hearings were unable to provide more than a one-eyed glimpse of the bifurcated legal regime that we know as apartheid.

Had the victim hearings been driven by the broader interpretation, they would have addressed all gross violations suffered – within the time limitation specified by the legislation – by the people of South Africa under apartheid. By championing a narrow interpretation, however, the Commission acknowledged only those violations suffered by political activists or state agents. It consequently ignored apartheid as experienced by the broad masses of the people of South Africa.

---

15 Truth and Reconciliation Commission of South Africa, ***Report***, vol. 1, p. 57, Para 32 (d).
16 Truth and Reconciliation Commission of South Africa, ***Report***, vol. 5, p. 14, Para 62.
17 Truth and Reconciliation Commission of South Africa, ***Report***, vol. 1, p. 82-83, Para 123.
18 Truth and Reconciliation Commission of South Africa, ***Report***, vol. 4, p. 288, Para 18.

2.2 SEVERE ILL-TREATMENT

The Act defined 'gross violations of human rights' as including 'the killing, abduction, torture or severe ill-treatment of any person ...'.[19] This provision gave those who did not succeed in getting the Commission to bring under scrutiny the entire project of apartheid, including its policies, an opportunity to organise for a second round of battle. Strong pressure was brought on the Commission to include the grossest forms of violations perpetrated through apartheid law under the rubric of 'severe ill-treatment.' The Report noted the pressure from a strong civil society organisation: 'The CALS submission argued that the definition of 'severe ill-treatment' should be interpreted to include apartheid abuses such as forced removals, pass law arrests, alienation of land and breaking up of families.'[20]

The debate around the interpretation of 'severe ill-treatment' is particularly illuminating. It went through several rounds. Each time, the Commission majority endeavoured to justify a narrow definition of 'victim.' Every successive attempt attests to the failure of the previous attempt. At the outset, the Commission majority acknowledged that 'the ordinary meaning' of severe ill-treatment 'suggests that all those whose rights had been violated during conflicts of the past were covered by this definition and fell, therefore, within the mandate of the Commission.' But it still resolved to set this ordinary meaning aside, and restated its original position: that 'the focus of its work was not on the effects of laws passed by the apartheid government, nor on general policies of that government or of other organizations, however morally offensive these may be.'[21] But a mere restatement of this narrow definition of the political could not justify the refusal to acknowledge what obviously appeared as instances of 'severe ill-treatment'. To make it convincing, the Commission majority made three further distinctions between rights – between 'bodily integrity rights' and 'subsistence rights', individual and group rights and, finally, between political and non-political motivations behind each violation – and ruled that only politically motivated violations of bodily integrity (but not subsistence) rights of individuals (but not groups) fell within its legislative purview. But this too was difficult to maintain consistently in the face of mounting evidence that often showed the irrelevance of these distinctions in the specific context of apartheid.

'Bodily integrity rights' vs. 'subsistence rights.' 'Severe ill-treatment,' the Commission acknowledged at the outset, is 'cruel, inhuman or degrading treatment' under international law and 'ill treatment' under South African law. The Commission then resolved that only 'bodily integrity rights' fell within its terms of reference. 'Bodily

---

19 Truth and Reconciliation Commission of South Africa, ***Report***, vol. 1, p. 60, Para 42.
20 Truth and Reconciliation Commission of South Africa, ***Report***, vol. 4, p. 288, Para 18.
21 Truth and Reconciliation Commission of South Africa, ***Report***, vol. 1, p. 64, Para 55.

integrity rights' were in turn defined as: 'Acts or omissions that deliberately and directly inflict severe mental or physical suffering on a victim.'[22]

The distinction between 'bodily integrity rights' and 'subsistence rights' echoes a familiar distinction in social theory between the realm of the political and that of the economic, that of the state and that of the market, the former the source of oppressive practices that directly deny rights, and the latter the source of inequalities that indirectly limit the exercise of rights and thereby diminish the potential of life. But practices such as coerced labour and forced removals could also not be classified either as just economic or as just political; they were both. Where a command economy obtained, the familiar distinction between the political and the economic simply could not illuminate those practices where political power directly intervened in the sphere of economic relations. Like slavery, coerced labour and forced removals required the direct and continued use of force. They could not be dismissed as structural outcomes lacking in agency and, therefore, not signifying a *violation*. Rather than an outcome of 'the dull compulsion of market forces', to use a formulation of Marx, these practices were characteristic of extra-economic forms of coercion. Rather than illuminate the divide between the economic and the political, they tended to bridge that divide.

The Commission, too, developed doubts about the familiar and rigid distinction between the economic and political, and voiced this in the final volume of its Report. The doubt surfaced when the Commission dealt with 'arson' and at first dismissed it as a violation of 'subsistence rights' but not 'bodily integrity rights.' In time, however, the Commission wondered whether the loss of home and possessions may also not result in displacement and great mental anguish – precisely why arson may be employed for political purposes.

> "Arson was a frequent allegation, and at first it did not seem to constitute a gross violation in terms of the Act. The more it was discussed, the more it was seen as a deliberate tool used by political groupings to devastate an area and force people to move away, the more it became necessary to consider it seriously. Eventually, a decision was taken: arson would be considered as "severe ill treatment" if it resulted in the destruction of a person's dwelling to the extent that the person could no longer live there. The motivation for this decision lay partly in the result – the displacement of the person – and partly in the psychological suffering of a person experiencing the total loss of home and possessions."[23]

In the end, the Commission found it necessary to stretch the meaning of 'bodily integrity rights' to include rights over both person *and* property. Even if belatedly, the Commission came to acknowledge that 'the destruction of a person's house through arson or other attacks' constituted 'severe ill-treatment' and qualified as a gross

[22] Truth and Reconciliation Commission of South Africa, ***Report***, vol. 1, p. 80, Para 116.
[23] Truth and Reconciliation Commission of South Africa, ***Report***, vol. 5, p. 12, Para 53.

violation.[24] The Commission thus came to distinguish between those who lost a home and those who lost only 'cattle or vehicles', and thus not 'their entire livelihood' – acknowledging the former but not the latter as victims of gross violations. But the concession, we shall see, only landed the Commission in deeper contradictions.

Individual vs. Group rights. Following the above shift, the Commission went on to compile a list of acts 'regarded as constituting severe ill treatment.' The list included 'banning or banishment'; banning referred to 'the restriction of a person by house arrest,' banishment to 'the enforced transfer of a person from one area to another.'[25] The list gives rise to more questions than it settles. Why was the 'enforced transfer of a person from one area to another' a violation of a right over one's person, but not the migrant labour system that involved both coerced movement and coerced labour? If 'the destruction of a person's house through arson or other attacks' was a gross violation of a right, then why did not a similar destruction through bulldozing, a practice characteristic of forced removals? Could it be that the former involved *identified* individuals, whereas the latter usually involved the implementation of state policy by *unidentified* individuals or groups?

In a discussion on why it decided to close the list of victims towards the end of its deliberations, the Commission gave a pragmatic reason: 'it became increasingly clear that there would be no value in simply handing the government a list which included a broad category of unidentified persons for consideration as victims deserving of reparations.'[26] The Commission 'resolved, therefore, to confine the number of victims eligible for reparations to three areas.' These included 'victims who personally made statements to the Commission,' 'victims named in a statement by a relative or other interested person,' and 'victims identified through the amnesty process.'[27] The result was a list of individuals, with no reference to groups. But if the violence of apartheid targeted groups more than specific individuals, it would not be surprising if most victims of apartheid turned out to be unidentified individuals. This, in turn, would be an argument for giving reparations to communities rather than individuals.

Political vs. Non-Political Motives. It is the Commission's narrow interpretation of 'political motive' which decisively ruled out gross violations of rights suffered by the ordinary people, and limited the Commission's concern to gross violations that occurred in the course of the political conflict between state agents and political activists. We have seen that the Commission was willing to stretch its early emphasis on 'bodily integrity rights' to include the violation of property rights. In rare instances,

---

24 Truth and Reconciliation Commission of South Africa, ***Report***, vol. 1, p. 81, Para 119.

25 Truth and Reconciliation Commission of South Africa, ***Report***, vol. 1, p. 81, Para 119.

26 Truth and Reconciliation Commission of South Africa, ***Report***, vol. 1, p. 86, Para 134.

27 Truth and Reconciliation Commission of South Africa, ***Report***, vol. 1, p. 86, Para 136.

it was even willing to put aside its determination to focus exclusively on the violation of rights of individuals to include injury to groups. One such rare instance was its finding on the *Seven Day War* in Natal and Kwazulu:

> "The Commission finds that from 25-31 March 1990, the communities in the lower Vulindlela and Edendale valleys, south of Pietermaritzburg, were subjected to an armed invasion by thousands of unknown Inkatha supporters, and that during this week over 200 residents of these areas were killed, hundreds of homes looted and burnt down and as many as 20,000 people were forced to flee from their homes. These acts constitute gross human rights violations, and unknown members of Inkatha are held accountable. …"[28]

Yet, if the final list of victims acknowledged and published by the Commission for its entire mandate was 20,000+, it is doubtful that these victims of a single event – numbering 'as many as 20,000 people' – found their way in the list of acknowledged victims entitled to reparations. In other words, 'unknown members of Inkatha' were held accountable as perpetrators, but their victims – 'as many as 20,000 people' who 'were forced to flee from their homes' – were not acknowledged. Had they been, the community would have been entitled to reparations.

The Commission was only loosely bound by the legislation that created it. Reflecting on its willingness to stretch otherwise rigid qualifications, the Commission recognised that it was indeed not tightly bound by legislation: 'the Act did not provide clear guidelines for the interpretation of the definition of 'gross violations of human rights.' This was no less than an admission that it had considerable latitude in interpreting terms, such as defining the meaning of victim. When it made use of this latitude, the Commission argued that 'the underlying objective of the legislators was to make it possible for the Commission to recognize and acknowledge as many people as possible as victims of the past political conflict', claiming that 'this objective, in turn, was central to the Commission's overall task to promote national unity and reconciliation.' The seven-page deliberation on 'defining gross violations of human rights' ended with the claim that 'the Commission made a conscious decision to err on the side of inclusivity.'[29]

But the commitment to being inclusive is precisely what the Commission set aside when it defined its terms of reference to exclude the project of apartheid, determined that the project itself should not be defined as political. As a result, it turned a blind eye to gross violations that occurred in the course of the implementation of apartheid. In the end, the Commission was forced to concede that it had really ignored a substantial part of 'gross violations of human rights' under apartheid. To justify this exclusion, it pointed to the same legislation that it otherwise complained 'did not provide clear guidelines.' The result was often a hopeless muddle as in the following

---

28 Truth and Reconciliation Commission of South Africa, ***Report***, vol. 3, p. 267, Para 292.

29 Truth and Reconciliation Commission of South Africa, ***Report***, vol. 1, pps. 70-71, 78, Para 82, 108.

instance, where the Report speaks of the Commission in the third person: 'Hence, the Commission fully recognized that large-scale human rights violations were committed through legislation designed to enforce apartheid, through security legislation designed to criminalize resistance to the state, and through similar legislation passed by governments in the homelands. Its task, however, was limited to examining those 'gross violations of human rights' as defined in the Act. This should not be taken to mean, however, that those 'gross violations of human rights' (killing, torture, abduction and severe ill-treatment) were the only very serious human rights violations that occurred.'[30]

3 THE BIG PICTURE THE COMMISSION OBSCURED: THE CRIME AGAINST HUMANITY

In an appendix to the chapter on 'the mandate', the Commission argued thus: 'The recognition of apartheid as a crime against humanity remains a fundamental starting point for reconciliation in South Africa.'[31] To explain why apartheid was a crime against humanity, the appendix goes to cite the 1996 Draft Code of Crimes against the Peace and Security of Mankind proposed by the International Law Commission: 'A crime against humanity means any of the following acts, when committed in a systematic manner or on a large scale and instigated or directed by a government or by any organization or group: ... (f) institutionalized discrimination on racial, ethnic or religious grounds involving the violation of fundamental human rights and freedoms and resulting in seriously disadvantaging a part of the population.'[32] The ground for declaring apartheid a 'crime against humanity' were not individual violations – killing, arson, etc. – that the Commission acknowledged but the racial and ethnic cleansing – 'institutionalized discrimination' – that the Commission refused to acknowledge. This, surely, was why this is the last the Commission Report speaks of apartheid as a 'crime against humanity,' instead of considering it as the promised 'fundamental starting point' for reconciliation in South Africa.

In this section of the chapter, I intend to pursue a line of inquiry that uses some of the evidence scattered through the pages of the Commission's Report to sketch the outlines for the kind of report the Commission could have written had it considered apartheid – and not just the attempt to defend it – as the political project whose implementation led to gross violations of rights in South Africa.

30 Truth and Reconciliation Commission of South Africa, ***Report***, vol. 1, p. 65, Para 59.
31 Truth and Reconciliation Commission of South Africa, ***Report***, vol. 1, p. 94, Para 1.
32 Truth and Reconciliation Commission of South Africa, ***Report***, vol. 1, p. 96, Para 13.

4 FORCED REMOVALS

The legal basis of apartheid was a system of law that distinguished between 'natives' and 'non-natives.' Those indigenous to the land were defined as 'natives' and immigrants – including those alleged to be so (Coloureds) – were defined as 'non-natives.' The law ethnicised natives and racialised non-natives. Non-natives were further distinguished between the master race (whites) and subject races (Indians, Coloureds), all governed through civil law. In contrast natives were divided into so many 'tribes', each to be governed by its own 'customary law'. The earliest tribe to be subjugated to a colonial customary law was the Zulu in colonial Natal.

The 1891 Natal Native Code conferred on the British governor general the title of the Supreme Chief of the Zulus. His powers included the power to move natives from one location to another. The 1927 Native Administration Act transferred that power to the Minister of Bantu Administration and Development, then in charge of all natives in South Africa. The TRC recognised that the 1927 Act:

> "empowered the Minister of Bantu Administration and Development (acting through the Governor General) to order "any tribe or native" to proceed forthwith to any designated place and not to leave it again without permission "whenever [the Minister deemed] it expedient in the general public interest." No specific reason for the banishment was needed; the "removal" of the individual was in the interest of "maintaining peace and good order in the tribe". Banished people were not charged in a court of law and had no opportunity to defend themselves."[33]

The Commission's Report acknowledges the 1927 Act, but only when it comes to the banishment of *individual* 'natives'. It notes that up to 97 persons – mostly chiefs and headmen who had opposed government policy – had been banished up to 1960, and that over 40 remained banished in 1986. It then goes on to give their circumstances of banishment.[34] What the Report does not do is link the provisions of the 1927 Native Administration Act to the forced removal of entire communities, defined ethnically and removed on those grounds, a practice that reached truly inhuman proportions in the period of its mandate, 1960 to 1994.

In 1959, the apartheid government passed the Promotion of Bantu Self-Government Act. The Act was to provide the legal umbrella for a far-reaching ethnic and racial cleansing of 87% of the land that was defined as 'white' South Africa. The racial cleansing of areas declared 'white' was followed by a reorganisation of the majority black population into fragmented ethnic homelands – a result of a subsidiary ethnic cleansing. This twin process was at the heart of the contention that apartheid was indeed a 'crime against humanity'. At the same time, the distinction between the

33 Truth and Reconciliation Commission of South Africa, ***Report***, vol. 2, pp. 165-66, Para 4.

34 Truth and Reconciliation Commission of South Africa, ***Report***, vol. 2, pp. 166-67, Para 5-12.

banishment of individuals and groups did not neatly coincide with a distinction between punishment and policy. Just like the forcible relocation of individuals (banishment) – which the Commission considered a gross violation of human rights – the forced relocation of communities (which the Commission did *not* consider a gross violation) could also be meted out as a punishment to resistant communities. It was, after all, characteristic of colonial power to punish entire communities for actions of individual residents. To illustrate my point, I will cite below several instances of 'forced removals' – all taken from the Commission Report, but all dismissed as not meeting the Commission's definition of a 'gross' violation of rights.

Transkei and the Pondoland Revolt. Transkei was the first homeland to be granted independence, in 1963. This declaration was preceded by the Pondoland Revolt, a peasant revolt against homeland authorities, a development that took place in the Pondoland region of the Transkei in 1960-61 – during the mandate of the Commission – and was memorialised by Govan Mbeki's book on the subject.[35] The Revolt was also followed by the first phase of 'forced removals'. 'The forced removal of hundreds of thousands of people from their homes,' the Commission acknowledged, 'generated a climate of fear which resulted in a period of relative quiescence in political resistance until the 1970s.'[36] Its findings stated:

> "The Commission finds that the state used several chiefs in the Transkei region to silence political opposition to the policy of apartheid, using methods including banishment, forced removal of political opponents and destruction of their property."[37]

The focus of the ethnic cleansing of these 'hundreds of thousands of peoples' was the Eastern Cape; yet, the Commission acknowledged a paltry 324 cases of 'severe ill treatment' over this period in Eastern Cape.[38]

Ciskei and Opposition to home Rule. The Ciskei became self-governing in 1972. The Commission recorded 'several occasions during the 1980s' when the government of Ciskei 'targeted entire communities opposed to homeland rule.' The punishment was 'forced removals or incorporation into the homeland.' In the mid-1980s, for example, 'the Kuni community was evicted from Ciskei en masse and dumped at the roadside in South Africa, where they later found a home at Needs Camp outside East London.' Even harsher treatment was meted out to another community that was tossed back

---

35 Govan Mbeki, *The Peasants' Revolt*, London: Penguin, 1964.

36 Truth and Reconciliation Commission of South Africa, ***Report***, vol. 3, pp. 36-7, Para 9.

37 Truth and Reconciliation Commission of South Africa, ***Report***, vol. 3, p. 55, Para 84.

38 Truth and Reconciliation Commission of South Africa, ***Report***, vol. 3, p. 37, Para 10; also see, same page, Figure B2B3 – 3: "Percentage of human rights violations in the region, by period: 1960-1975". The text gives 42% as the share of "cases of severe ill treatment" for 1960-75, and the accompanying graph gives the total number of violations as 770. 42% of 770 is 323.4!

and forth through the 1980s. At first 'forcibly removed across the border into Ciskei' in the early 1980s, this 'large group of residents fled at least twice from Potsdam outside Mdantsane following assaults by police and vigilantes.' Each time, 'South African security forces forcibly loaded the group onto trucks and drove them back to Potsdam.' Finally, they were granted permanent residence at Eluxolweni in South Africa.[39] The Commission's report gives no figures of how large or small was this community, nor of gross violations for the period. Yet, one thing is clear: the Commission did not acknowledge this community as a victim of 'severe ill treatment' by the apartheid state.

Bophutatswana and Opposition to Home Rule. When they refused to accept the citizenship of the newly created Bophutatswana homeland, the non-Tswana were forcibly evicted from the Kromdraai squatter area where they had hitherto lived. Their children were 'barred from attending schools in Bophutatswana.' The Commission noted that 'an estimated fifteen to twenty thousand non-Tswanas' were resettled on a farm called 'Onverwacht'. Here is the Commission's description of the farm:

> "The farm, later renamed Botshabelo, had been acquired by the South African government for the purpose of 'relocating' people from white farms and from the deproclaimed townships of the Orange Free State. The terrain consisted of rocky, barren veld on which plots were marked out by tin toilets. Employment opportunities were few. Residents were forced to travel the ten kilometers to Thaba'Nchuor or the sixty kilometers to Bloemfontein if they were lucky enough to have a job. Schooling and health facilities remained totally inadequate."[40]

Batshebelo 'became the largest single relocation area in the country.'[41] Though the Commission estimated that 'fifteen to twenty thousand' non-Tswana were forcibly moved to this location between May 1979 and January 1980, it said 'comparatively few statements were received from the Orange Free State' where Batshebelo was located, and it acknowledged less than 20 cases of 'severe ill treatment' for 1979-80 for the whole of Orange Free State.[42]

Western Cape. The region known as Western Cape comprises the provinces of Western Cape and Northern Cape. Marked by the physical elimination (genocide) of the indigenous Khoisan population, the large-scale kidnapping of Khoisan children into forced labour, and the importation of thousands of Indonesian, Indian and East African slaves, the peculiar pre-apartheid history of this region was exaggerated by

---

39 Truth and Reconciliation Commission of South Africa, ***Report***, vol. 2, pp. 433-34, Para 126-129.

40 Truth and Reconciliation Commission of South Africa, ***Report***, vol. 3, pp. 332-33, Para 15.

41 Truth and Reconciliation Commission of South Africa, ***Report***, vol. 3, p. 333, Para 16.

42 Truth and Reconciliation Commission of South Africa, ***Report***, vol. 3, pp. 334-35, Para 23; also see Figure C2-1: Number of Gross Human Rights Violations in the Orange Free State, by year.

its declaration as a 'coloured labour preference area' which gradually turned it into a region with a majority branded as 'Coloured'.

The Commission found that 'the Northern Cape has a long history of land dispossession and forced removals.' Referring to the 1960s, the opening phase of its own mandate, the Commission acknowledged that 'Africans were removed mainly to Bophuthatswana, often making way for South African Defence Force (SADF) military camps.' In the 1980s, forced removals led to the privatisation of 'independent communal farming settlements.' But its Report gives no numbers for those forcibly removed from communities. When it comes to identifying victims of gross human rights violations in the region, the Commission records that 52% were victims of 'severe ill treatment' and notes: 'The most common form of severe ill treatment reported was beating, followed closely by incarceration and shooting injuries.'[43] There is no mention of 'forced removals.'

Transvaal. Transvaal is the industrial hub of South Africa. At its heart is Southwest Township (Soweto). During the 1960s, 'the government worked systematically to reverse the flow of Africans to the urban areas and to restructure the industrial workforce into one composed primarily of migrant labor.' The Commission cited estimates that 'over a million labor tenants and farm squatters and 400,000 city dwellers were resettled in the homelands, the population of which increased by 70% in the 1960s.'[44] This single word – 'resettlement' – summed up a series of actions, from bulldozing of homes to destruction of fixed property to relocation of movable property and persons, all involving the direct use of force and brutality in different degrees. It was a period of great repression, even if there was little overt resistance – why it is supremely ironic that the Commission recorded 'the lowest number of violations (473) for this period', ascribing these low figures to 'factors such as the distance of the events that have been overshadowed by more recent political conflict, the death of potential deponents and the fading memory of deponents.'[45] The one thing the Commission did not consider was its own responsibility: could it be that certain knowledge that the Commission did not consider 'forced removals' as gross violations of human rights – rather than 'the fading memory of deponents' – kept 'deponents' from filing grievances with the Commission. Could it be that the Commission's own decision to interpret its own terms narrowly blotted from the official record the most repressive practices affecting large numbers of ordinary people in South Africa?

Not only were black homeland residents who resisted its independence – such as by refusing homeland citizenship –forcibly removed, black residents in 'white' South Africa who were defined as 'black spots' were also targeted for forced removal. A widely

---

43 Truth and Reconciliation Commission of South Africa, ***Report***, vol. 3, pp. 391, 393, Para 8, 18.

44 Truth and Reconciliation Commission of South Africa, ***Report***, vol. 3, pp. 529-30, Para 8.

45 Truth and Reconciliation Commission of South Africa, ***Report***, vol. 3, p. 531, Para 15.

distributed and cited investigation by The Surplus People Project estimated that 3.5 million people were forcibly moved by the South African state between 1960 and 1982 in support of the program of developing ethnic homelands. The Commission acknowledged that 3.5 million had indeed been moved forcibly,[46] and that the process involved 'collective expulsions, forced migration, bulldozing, gutting or seizure of homes, the mandatory carrying of passes, forced removals into rural ghettos and increased poverty and desperation.'[47] Not even a generation had passed since these brutalities had ended. Not surprisingly, both surviving victims and their advocates among community organisers and activists had assumed that forced removals would be the core focus of a Truth and Reconciliation Commission. But the Commission was not obliging: after noting that 'forced removals' were 'an assault on the rights and dignity of millions of South Africans,' the Commission claimed it could not acknowledge them since these violations 'may not have been 'gross' as defined by the Act.'[48]

The phenomenon of 'forced removals' puts in doubt all three binaries around which the Commission had constructed its extremely narrow interpretation of what constituted a 'gross' violation: the distinction between 'bodily integrity rights' and 'subsistence rights,' between individual and group rights, and between 'political' and non-political motives. Forced removals violated *both* person and property of those targeted. They violated rights of *both* groups and individuals, *in that order*, since those targeted were first and foremost defined as groups – racialised in white South Africa as 'black spots' and ethnicised in demarcated Homelands as 'ethnic strangers' – and only then as individual members of these groups. Finally, though some were removed from Homelands for direct opposition to the project of apartheid, *all* forced removals were a direct result of state implementation of the political project that was grand apartheid, a project whose sum and substance was to *racialise* space and communities in *white* South Africa and *ethnicise* space and communities in *black* South Africa.

5 PASS LAWS AND COERCED LABOUR

Pass laws involved racial and ethnic monitoring of the black population and racial targeting of suspected political opponents. The year with which the mandate of the Commission began, 1960, was the year the National party government extended pass laws to 'native' women. The Sharpeville demonstrations of 21 March 1960 were the culmination of mass protests against this development.

After 1960, every 'native' adult in South Africa, male or female, was required to carry a passbook. Correspondingly, the movement of every 'native' in the country was

46 Truth and Reconciliation Commission of South Africa, ***Report***, vol. 2, p. 409, Para 34.
47 Truth and Reconciliation Commission of South Africa, ***Report***, vol. 1, p. 34, Para 45.
48 Truth and Reconciliation Commission of South Africa, ***Report***, vol. 1, p. 34, Para 43.

monitored through administrative regulations enforced by the police. According to estimates made by the South African Institute of Race Relations, over a million people had been administratively ordered to leave urban areas by 1972.[49] Besides monitoring the 'native' population, pass laws were also put to a very specific political purpose. 'From the early sixties,' the Commission noted, 'the pass laws were the primary instrument used by the state to arrest and charge its political opponents.'[50]

Pass law offenders formed a large proportion of the prison population for as long as pass laws were in force – which they were for most of the Commission's mandate. Indeed, the Commission found that the proportion of pass law offenders was 'as high as one in every four inmates during the 1960s and 1970s.'[51] Pass law offenders were sent to prison for only one reason: that they did not meet the administrative requirement that the racialised and ethnicised black majority of the population carry a pass book and conform to administrative restrictions on their day-to-day movement. The Commission accepted that 'the treatment of pass law offenders could well be interpreted as a human rights violation' but still refused to include the category of pass law prisoners in the institutional hearings on prisons. In spite of the fact that 'a strong argument was made for the inclusion of this category of common law prisoners in the hearings,' the Commission refused on the grounds that these were common law prisoners and not 'political prisoners'. Yet, the only 'common law' these prisoners had violated was the pass law, the law that criminalised the exercise of a basic human right, the right of free movement. To consider those imprisoned for the transgression of *only* the pass law as common law prisoners – and explicitly to deny them the status of political prisoners – was to uphold the legal framework of apartheid. In the words of the Commission: 'it was decided that the pass laws and their effects fell outside the Commission's mandate, especially given the requirement that every violation had to originate within a political context.'[52]

When a State brands its entire population racially, then tags every member of the racialised majority with documents that allow administrative officials to monitor their every movement – and utilises the plethora of racially-focused administrative regulations at its command to target suspected political opponents – from which point of view can it be said that the motive behind this set of practices was not political?

---

49 Truth and Reconciliation Commission of South Africa, ***Report***, vol. 3, p. 528, Para 3.
50 Truth and Reconciliation Commission of South Africa, ***Report***, vol. 3, p. 163, Para 28.
51 Truth and Reconciliation Commission of South Africa, ***Report***, vol. 4, p. 200, Para 8.
52 Truth and Reconciliation Commission of South Africa, ***Report***, vol. 4, p. 200, Para 6-8, 10.

6 FARM PRISON SYSTEM

The category of pass law prisoners were not the only ones excluded from the Commission's institutional hearings on prisons and denied acknowledgement as having suffered 'gross violations of human rights' in the period 1960-1994. At least two other important categories were also excluded.

The first of these was the category of *farm prisoners*. The notorious farm prisons system was directly connected to the pass law system. Failure by a black person to produce a pass resulted in an arrest. As the number of arrests grew, so did the financial burden on the state. The Department of Native Affairs proposed a solution to this problem in General Circular 23 of 1954:

> "It is common knowledge that large numbers of natives are daily being arrested for contraventions of a purely technical nature. These arrests cost the state large sums of money and serve no useful purpose. The Department of Justice, the South African Police and this Department have therefore held consultations on the problem and have evolved a scheme, the object of which is to induce unemployed natives roaming about the streets in the various urban areas to accept employment outside such urban areas."[53]

When 'natives' henceforth failed to produce a pass, they 'were not taken to court but to labour bureaux where they would be induced or forced to volunteer.' In theory, they were to be told that if they 'volunteered' for farm labour, charges against them would be dropped as an exchange. The result, the Commission noted, was that 'arrests for failure to produce a pass became a rich source of labour for the farms,' ensuring the farmers 'a cheap supply of labour.' The kind of abuse that could be visited on such a 'volunteer' was brought to public knowledge by an affidavit of one such labourer, Robert Ncube, signed in the late 1950s:

> "After I had been there [on a farm] for about four months, I noticed one day a boss boy, Tumela, who was only about sixteen years old, beating one of the workers who was cutting firewood. After the assault I noticed this man's nose was bleeding a lot. The man sat down and his nose continued to bleed and he was left there until we were locked up at six o'clock. The following morning he was unable to get up and work. He was shivering all the time. He did not work for three days and on that Saturday morning he died. The boss boy, Philip, told four of the workers to carry him into the room where the dead are kept and the body was left there until Monday morning. On Monday afternoon about half past four, I and seven others, including Philip, carried the body and buried it on the farm. There were other graves where we buried him. I never saw a doctor or the police come to see the body before it was buried."[54]

---

53 Cited in Truth and Reconciliation Commission of South Africa, ***Report***, vol. 4, p. 202, Para 16.

54 Cited in Truth and Reconciliation Commission of South Africa, ***Report***, vol. 4, p. 203, Para 17.

The Commission took note of these facts, but the category of farm prisoners did not feature in the prison hearings. Why not? Because, said the Commission, 'nobody came forward to give evidence.'[55] Nobody, in this instance, presumably refers to the victims of the farm labour system; it could not possibly refer to its institutional managers since the Commission had the legal right to subpoena reluctant or even unwilling witnesses, and had done so in other instances but, obviously, not in this.

7 DETENTION WITHOUT TRIAL

The second category of prisoners excluded from prison hearings was that of *prisoners detained without trial.* The number so detained between 1960 and 1990 were estimated at 'some 80,000 South Africans' by the Human Rights Committee, whose reports were made available to the Commission. The Committee pointed out that detention was frequently accompanied by torture and, at times, by death. Indeed, individuals were often detained so they could be interrogated and intimidated with impunity. In the words of the Human Rights Committee, as cited by the Commission:

> "There can be little doubt that the security police regard their ability to torture detainees with total impunity as the cornerstone of the detention system. It put the detainee at complete mercy for the purpose of extracting information, statements and confessions, often regardless of whether true or not, in order to secure a successful prosecution and neutralization of yet another opponent of the apartheid system. Sometimes torture is used on detainees before they have ever been asked their first question to soften them up. Other times, torture is used late in the interrogation process when the detainee is being stubborn and difficult."[56]

The most notorious instance of death in detention was that of Steve Biko. But the numbers of those detained, of those tortured, and even of those killed, were not small. The Commission cited without comment the estimates of the Human Rights Committee that some 80,000 had been detained between 1960 and 1990 – and that 'up to 80 per cent of whom were eventually released without charge and barely 4 per cent of whom were ever convicted of any crime'[57]. It then cited an estimate of those tortured – 'As many as 20,000 detainees are thought to have been tortured in detention'[58] – without citing any source. As regards deaths in detention, the Commis-

55 Truth and Reconciliation Commission of South Africa, ***Report***, vol. 4, p. 202, Para 16.

56 This from a march 1983 paper by the Committee, cited in Human Rights Committee, ***A Crime Against Humanity***, ed. By Max Coleman, 1998; quoted in Truth and Reconciliation Commission of South Africa, ***Report***, vol. 4, p. 201, Para 13.

57 Truth and Reconciliation Commission of South Africa, ***Report***, vol. 4, p. 201, Para 12.

58 Truth and Reconciliation Commission of South Africa, ***Report***, vol. 4, p, 201, Para 14.

sion noted 73 deaths of detainees held under security legislation but could not give estimates of how many held under common law may have died in detention.[59]

The Commission gave no legal reasons for excluding the category of detainees from prison hearings. It said its reasons were practical rather than legal. It simply did not have the time: 'There were practical rather than legal reasons for excluding detention from the prison hearings. The working group had to take into account the fact that only two days could be allocated to the hearing, putting immense strain on an already overloaded program.'[60] To consider the consequence for a Commission charged with 'establishing as complete a picture as possible of the causes, nature and extent of the gross violations of human rights' from 1960 to 1994, let us simply keep in mind the numbers involved: an estimated 80,000 detained, of whom 20,000 were said to have been tortured in detention, against some 20,000+ acknowledged by the Commission as victims of gross violations of human rights. If the Commission could acknowledge the detention, torture and death of Steve Biko as a gross violation of human rights, why could it not extend the same acknowledgement to others who met a similar fate?

8 RULE OF LAW

Robert A. Williams has recently argued that 'a distinctive feature of the West's colonizing discourses of conquest' has been a 'central vision of a universal order established through law and lawgiving.'[61] Hannah Arendt, too, remarked on the Nazi claim that their rule was consonant with the rule of law.[62] Similarly, anyone who has studied apartheid's state discourse cannot but be struck by its claim to being a rule of law.

Let me illustrate the point with two examples. I have already discussed above the case of the farm labour system, whereby pass law offenders were given the choice between a jail term and 'volunteering' to work on a farm. When the (earlier cited) affidavit which testified to death from beatings in one farm brought the abuse of conscripted labour to public attention, the state suspended the farm labour system and followed with a legal reform within weeks. The amended Prisons Act of 1959 plugged two loop-holes: first, it introduced a procedure whereby 'short-term offenders' could be quickly processed by the courts and dispatched to farms; second, it put any inquiry into farm life beyond the pale of freedom of the press, by providing both 'that

59 Truth and Reconciliation Commission of South Africa, ***Report***, vol. 4, p. 201-2, Para 14.

60 Truth and Reconciliation Commission of South Africa, ***Report***, vol. 4, p. 201, Para 11.

61 Robert A. Williams, Jr., ***The American Indian in Western Legal Thought: The Discourses of Conquest***, New York: Oxford University Press, 1990, p. 18-19.

62 Hannah Artendt, ***The Origins of Totalitarianism***, New York: Harcourt Brace & Co., 1973.

the farms be considered prisons and that it was a criminal offence to publish anything about prison conditions without the prior consent of the Commissioner of Prisons.'[63]

Another example from the same period further illuminates how the apartheid regime both fetishised and brandished legality. Before 1956, the courts sometimes ruled against the Department of Native Affairs when it summarily evicted and expelled 'natives' from urban areas. To put a stop to the meddling of the courts, Verwoerd passed the Native Prohibition of Interdict Act through Parliament in 1956. The Act prohibited any court of law from interfering with removal orders against 'natives' anywhere in the country. And the courts obliged, presumably because they upheld the rule of law. Verwoerd celebrated in parliament: 'The courts have nothing more to do than to accept and explain the laws.'[64] Today, it would seem that Verwoerd's statute not only limited the agenda of apartheid's courts, but also of the post-apartheid TRC.

If a crime against humanity was perpetrated under the cloak of a rule of law, then how are we to understand the very notion of a rule of law? As part of its mandate, the TRC was asked to 'make recommendations to the President with regard to the creation of institutions conducive to a stable and fair society and the institutional, administrative and legislative measures which should be taken or introduced in order to prevent the commission of violations of human rights.'[65] To respond to this part of its mandate, the Commission organised institutional hearings on the judiciary. David Dyzenhaus framed the debate in his opening submission to the hearings in the following manner. Does the law 'primarily consist of rules which owe their existence to positive enactment by a legislature or explicit recognition by a court,' or does it consist of 'the principles which make sense of the idea of government under the rule of law, the idea that such government is subject to the constraint of principles such as fairness, reasonableness and equality of treatment'? He sketched two alternative interpretations of the rule of law: one, a wholly procedural and positivist 'plain fact approach' that informed the apartheid legal project, and the other 'an anti-positivist theory of law' concerned with both procedure and substance of the law. In contrast to the plain fact approach which reduces the law to 'the content of the commands of the powerful,' and 'requires judges to ignore in their interpretation of the law their substantive convictions about what the law should be,' Dyzenhaus called for an understanding of law 'as the expression of a relationship of reciprocity between ruler

[63] Truth and Reconciliation Commission of South Africa, ***Report***, vol. 4, p. 201-03.
Truth and Reconciliation Commission of South Africa, ***Report***, vol. 4, p. 203, Para 18.

[64] Ivan Thomas Evans, *Bureaucracy and race: Native Authorities in South Africa*, Berkeley, California: UC Press, 1997, p. 116.

[65] Truth and Reconciliation Commission of South Africa, ***Report***, vol. 1, p. 57, Para 31.

and ruled, one in which the rulers commit themselves not only to being accountable to law, but to making law before which all subjects are equal.'[66]

In the Dyzenhaus submission, adherence to the rule of law means both that the law sets a limit to the exercise of state power – so that rulers are 'accountable to law' – and that the law treats all subjects as equals. But the Commission found itself in a dilemma. *If it repudiated 'the plain fact' approach in favor of 'an anti-positivist theory of law'* – if it indeed made a distinction between what was legal and what was legitimate, between law and right – it would have to broaden the terms of its own interpretation and acknowledge that whenever apartheid law treated subjects unequally, as when it created racially or ethnically discriminatory legislation, that piece of legislation could not be taken as the dividing line between what was legal and what was political. Thus, for example, the Commission would have to consider pass law offenders as not just common law prisoners but also as political prisoners. Similarly, 'forced removals' would have to be considered not as an expression of rule of law – however immoral – but as an integral part of a racialised and ethnicised political project that was antithetical to a rule of law. *At the same time*, the Commission could not afford to uphold the legality of apartheid as a form or rule of law lest it be seen as embracing the legal fetishism of apartheid. The Commission resolved this dilemma by an embrace of the anti-positivist theory of law in its *institutional* hearing but an adherence to the plain fact approach in its *victim* hearings. In the institutional hearings, it denied that apartheid represented a rule of law; but in its victim hearings, it continued to take apartheid law as providing the dividing line between what was legal and what was political – even where the law obviously treated its subjects unequally, as when it discriminated against the majority on racial and/or ethnic grounds.

The Dyzenhaus submission was deeply flawed. The legal machinery that it held up for analysis was limited to the set of laws, the court system and the legal practices that governed the non-native population of South Africa. This, indeed, was the legal system that spoke the language of rights and claimed the mantle of a rule of law. When it came to the native population, the problem was not simply that they were excluded from the promise of a rights-based rule of law, thus compromising its formal claims. The fact was that natives were ruled by a different set of laws, system of courts, and practices which together made an entirely different claim to legitimacy, that it enforced 'tradition' and 'custom.' This flaw was shared by the Commission. It is no accident that the 'customary' regime remains almost invisible in the Commission's report. Anyone reading the 5-volume report is unlikely to be particularly enlightened as to how apartheid ruled its native subjects.

This is why, when the Commission came to narrating the history of the legal regime in South Africa, its account was confined to the history of the 'civil' regime that ruled

66 David Dyzenhaus, ***Judging the Judges, Judging Ourselves: Truth, Reconciliation and the Apartheid Legal Order,*** Oxford: Hart Publishing, 1998, pp. 183, 152.

non-natives; it had nothing to say of the process by which the multiple 'customary' regimes that ruled natives came into place. This is how the Commission summed up the history of rule of law in its 'findings in respect of the state and its allies' in the final volume of the Report:

> "At the beginning of the mandate period, the system of government in the country was undoubtedly an unjust and discriminatory one, but it was still essentially a system of laws, albeit unjust laws. In the course of the first two decades of the mandate period, the rule of law was steadily eroded and the system of public administration purged of its remaining democratic substance. By the time President Botha took power, the system was characterized by severe repression. It had not yet, however, adopted a policy of killing its opponents. ... The period during which the South African state ventured into the realm of criminal misconduct stretches from P W Botha's accession to power in 1978 into the early 1990s, including a part of the period in which his successor held office."[67] (*italics* mine)

Though the lines of demarcation between the periods are blurred, the Commission identified *three* developments as key to eroding the rule of law. The *first* was the restructuring of the judiciary with the support of a parliamentary majority, a development the Commission considered as 'equivalent to a constitutional fraud'. The chapter on institutional hearings on 'the legal community' speaks of the beginning of 'superficial adherence of 'rule of law' by the National Party' from the mid-1950s with 'the restructuring of judicial personnel and the Appellate Division,' when 'the white electorate lent its support to the constitutional fraud resorted to by the Government to circumvent the entrenched clauses of the South Africa Act.'[68] The *second* development that led to the erosion of the rule of law was the use of methods of torture against political opponents and detainees. The chapter on 'the State inside South Africa between 1960 and 1990' cites no less an authority than Joe Slovo that 'up to 1960/61, the underground struggle was fought on a gentlemanly terrain' and that 'there was still a rule of law' with 'a fair trial in their courts'. Slovo then added: 'Up to 1963, I know of no incident of any political prisoner being tortured.' The Commission went on to qualify Slovo's statement: 'While torture does not appear to have been used on urban-based, ANC political detainees until 1963, the Commission received information about the extensive use of *all* forms of torture on rural insurgents involved in the Pondoland Revolt in 1960 and against members and supporters of the *Poqo* movement of the PAC.' This shift in the use of torture from criminal to political cases also coincided with the availability of foreign assistance in the technology of torture: 'It was widely believed by many political activists of the time that, in the early 1960s, a special squad of security policemen received special training in torture techniques in France and Algeria and that this accounted for a sudden and dramatic increase in

---

67 Truth and Reconciliation Commission of South Africa, ***Report***, vol. 5, p. 213, Para 81, 80.

68 Truth and Reconciliation Commission of South Africa, ***Report***, vol. 4, p. 101, Para 32.

torture.'[69] The *third* development the Commission identified as key to undermining the rule of law was the shift of 'real rule-making power ... from Parliament and the cabinet to a non-elected administrative body, the State Security Council (SSC) which operated beyond public scrutiny.' With this shift in the 1980s, 'it became clear that the rule of law had run its course.' Initially, the SSC 'targeted members of 'terrorist' groups operating outside of South Africa.' Then, 'from the mid-1980s, it began focusing on opponents inside South Africa.'[70]

It is this narrative of the breakdown of rule of law in South Africa, beginning with the circumventing of the South Africa Act in the mid-1950s and culminating in 'state-sanctioned murder' in the mid-1980s, that makes sense of why the Commission interpreted its otherwise broad mandate so narrowly – why it focused wholly on the removal of constitutional limits to the exercise of state power, and not at all on the creation of a judicial structure that racialised and ethnicised the population into fundamentally *unequal* population groups. Whereas the *former* development was internal to the history of apartheid, it is the *latter* development that really defined apartheid as a legal form of the state and provided the true benchmark for its legal birth and illuminated the real contours of its legal personality.

9 A RACIALISED/ETHNICISED LEGAL STRUCTURE

Apartheid did not spring full-blown, like Athena from the head of Zeus, in 1951. The prehistory of apartheid as a form of the state is marked by four legal enactments: the Natal Code of Native Law in 1891, the South Africa Act of 1910, the Native Administration Act of 1927, and the Bantu Authorities Act of 1951.[71] True, none of these were enacted during the mandate of the Commission, but together they provide the legal *context* in which 'gross violations of human rights' unfolded in the mandate period. To make better sense of the violations the Commission did acknowledge, and to grasp fully the significance of those it chose to ignore, it is useful to begin with a brief summary of these four pieces of legislation.

Even by the standards of its times, the Natal Code of Native Law (1891) was a draconian piece of legislation. For the first time in the history of South Africa, it employed the law as an instrument of despotism. The 1891 law aimed to reorganise not only relations between the state and natives, but also relations within native society. The law employed the language of native *tradition* to enforce a wholly new

69 Truth and Reconciliation Commission of South Africa, ***Report***, vol. 2, p. 195, Para 121-123.
70 Truth and Reconciliation Commission of South Africa, ***Report***, vol. 1, pp. 42-3, Para 76, 79.
71 For an elaboration of the argument in this section, see, Mahmood Mamdani, ***Citizen and Subject: Contemporary Africa and the Legacy of Late Colonialism***, Princeton: Princeton University Press, 1996.

tradition, that of colonial despotism. It recognised 'the officer for the time being administering the Government of the Colony of Natal' as 'Supreme Chief' (S. 5). The powers of the Supreme Chief far exceeded those of any precolonial despot: he could fix 'the least number of houses which shall compose a kraal' (S. 42), forcibly move 'any tribe, portion thereof,' to any part of the colony (S. 37), 'amalgamate or divide any tribe(s)' (S. 33), 'appoint all chiefs' (S. 33), or remove any for 'political offence, or for incompetency, or other just cause' (S. 34). He had 'absolute power' to call upon all 'natives' to 'supply armed men or levies' to defend the colony from external aggression or internal rebellion (S. 35) and 'to supply labour for public works and the general needs of the colony.' (S. 36)

In addition to providing the legal basis for absolute authority over natives, the 1891 law also laid out the legal basis for patriarchal control over all minors and women in each kraal. As a 'general rule,' it decreed, 'all the inmates of a kraal are minors in law,' the exception being married males or widowers, or 'adult males not related to the kraal head.' (S. 72) The section on 'personal status' ordained that unless exempted by the High Court, 'females are always considered minors and without independent power.' (S. 94) They can 'neither inherit nor bequeath.' (S. 143) All income may be controlled by the head of the kraal (S. 138), who was recognised as 'the absolute owner of all property belonging to his kraal' (S. 68) and who was given powers to disinherit any son who may disobey him (S. 140). It was his duty 'to settle all disputes within the kraal' (S. 68). In addition, kraal heads were to 'rank as constables within the precincts of their own kraals and are authorized to arrest summarily any person therein.' (S. 74). They were also given powers to 'inflict corporal punishment upon inmates of their kraals' for 'any just cause'.

The Supreme Chief possessed not only rule-making but also judicial powers. Effectively, he stood above the law. He ruled by decree, without judicial or parliamentary restraint: 'The Supreme Chief is not subject to the Supreme Court or to any other court of law' for any action 'done either personally or in Council.' (S. 40). This bit of absolutism was reproduced in the South Africa Act when South Africa was unified and declared a democracy for whites. Section 147 of the South Africa Act vested control and administration of native affairs throughout the union in the Governor-General who was to act with the advice of the Executive Council, not Parliament. This union of English and Afrikaners that followed the Boer War was forged around one single agreement: democracy for whites and rule by decree over natives.

During the next four decades, a debate raged over the form of rule by decree over natives. Three questions were at issue: the unit of rule, its mediating authority, and its legal form. Should the *unit* of the rule be territorial or ethnic, the village or the tribe? Should the *mediating authority* be the village headman supervised by white officials under a High Commissioner (the Cape model) or a full-fledged – even if subordinate – state apparatus organised around the institution of chiefship and supervised by the Supreme Chief (the Natal model)? Finally, should the legal form be of modern Western law stressing the *exclusion* of natives from civil rights on racial grounds, or should it be one of 'customary' law calling for the *incorporation* of natives by different tribal authorities, administering multiple *ethnically specific* despotisms as so many exercises in enforcing custom on members of different tribes? The choice between the Cape and the Natal model was between two radically different forms of colonial despotism, the former territorial, the latter ethnic.

The choice was made in two steps, the first in 1927, then in 1951. The Native Administration Act of 1927 generalised the Natal model whereby the Governor ruled as the Supreme Chief through native chiefs administering a 'customary' law, but with one exception, the Cape, where white commissioners supervised native headmen, and were in turn supervised by the Governor as the High Commissioner. The Bantu Authorities Act of 1951 brought this exception to an end, for the first time generalising the Natal model over the entire country.

The rule of apartheid was bifurcated in nature. As I have said before, the law simultaneously racialised and ethnicised the population. *Races* were defined as those not native, not indigenous; whether they were accorded full civil rights (whites) or only residual rights (Coloureds, Indians), races were governed through civil law. In contrast, *tribes* were defined as those indigenous, those native to the land; set apart ethnically, each tribe was ruled through its own patriarchal authority claiming to enforce its version of colonially-sanctioned patriarchy as 'customary law'. The bifurcated nature of law and of the law-enforcing authority was the main – but not the only – reason every effort to impose law and order in the face of resistance more often than not pit black perpetrators against black victims, why both the violence of apartheid and the repression that it unleashed primarily took the form that the press dubbed 'black-on-black violence'. Where the black population was fragmented into so many ethnicized native authorities, 'black-on-black violence' included both the violence of the native authority on its ethnic subjects and the resistance of these same subjects. Ethnicity was forged as a political identity through contradictory but related processes that included both top-down forms of rule and bottom-up forms of resistance.

The Commission's Report had little to say about either 'customary law' or the authority that enforced it. The section titled 'courts of chiefs and headmen' is a half page long and begins with the following illuminating observation: 'Many civil legal matters in South Africa are decided by bodies outside the formal court structure, namely tribunals administered by chiefs in the former homeland areas, under laws dating from the colonial period.'[72]

The Commission made no recommendation affecting the bifurcated nature of the legal system. Its focus was on ensuring the legal accountability of rulers, not the legal equality of the ruled. Even if all recommendations made by the Commission are to

72 Truth and Reconciliation Commission of South Africa, ***Report***, vol. 5, p. 327, Para 59.

be implemented, it will leave in place the bifurcated division between civil and customary law. Its reforms will help *de-racialise* civil law and civil power, but will not really promote a process tending to *de-ethnicise* customary law and customary authority. This is why we must ask: if the legal project of apartheid was to link racial exclusion to ethnic incorporation through fragmentation, through a bifurcated legal structure that comprised both civil and customary courts, then will not a legal reform that focuses on civil law but leaves customary law and customary legal authority in place tend to reproduce that same bifurcated legal structure, albeit in a de-racialised form? Will not the outcome of a partial reform as this, be a non-racial apartheid?

10 AMNESTY – BUT NO REPARATIONS – FOR A 'CRIME AGAINST HUMANITY'

The mandate chapter of the Commission's Report has an appendix titled 'A Crime against Humanity.' *In the first paragraph*, the Commission 'affirms its judgment that apartheid, as a system of enforced racial discrimination and separation, was a crime against humanity.' It then adds: 'The recognition of apartheid as a crime against humanity remains a fundamental starting point for reconciliation in South Africa.'[73]

There follows a discussion of 'a crime against humanity.' To locate the specific way in which apartheid constituted 'a crime against humanity,' the Report cites the 1996 Draft Code of Crimes against the Peace and Security of Mankind, a code that lists a set of acts, any of which may specifically constitute a crime against humanity. According to Article 18(f), these include 'institutionalized discrimination on racial, ethnic, or religious grounds involving the violation of fundamental human rights and freedoms and resulting in seriously disadvantaging a part of the population.'[74] The irony was that, whereas the Commission recognised this 'system of enforced racial discrimination and separation' as a crime against humanity, it did not acknowledge any victims of this crime. As a consequence, it also recognised no perpetrators. We thus have a crime against humanity without either victims or perpetrators.

In the second paragraph, the Commission addresses the foreign audience likely to take seriously the finding of a 'crime against humanity': 'This sharing of the international community's basic moral and legal position on apartheid should not be understood as a call for international criminal prosecution of those who formulated and implemented apartheid policies. Indeed, such a course would militate against the

73 Truth and Reconciliation Commission of South Africa, ***Report***, vol. 1, p. 94, Para 1; also see, vol. 5, p. 222, Para 101.

74 Truth and Reconciliation Commission of South Africa, ***Report***, vol. 1, p. 96, Para 13.

very principles on which this Commission was established.'[75] At another point, the Commission says the culpability for this crime is more moral than legal.[76] Let us recall that the principles on which the Commission was established not only ruled out a blanket amnesty, they also involved an exchange: *amnesty* for perpetrators, *truth* for the society (and not just for victims) and *reparations* for victims.

The core victims of the crime against humanity, of this 'system of enforced racial discrimination and separation,' could not have been individuals; they had to be *entire communities* marked out on grounds of race and ethnicity. Their injuries included forced relocation, forced disruption of community and family life, coerced labor through administrative and statutory regulation of movement and location, etc. To address their grievances required reparations for communities, not for individuals. From this point of view, one can see the extreme inadequacy of the Commission's main recommendation that victims receive 'individual reparation grants in the form of money' since a monetary package 'gives freedom of choice to the recipient.'[77]

11 A DISSENTING VIEW

There were many debates inside the Commission, but only one led to a formal expression of dissent appended as a minority view to the Commission's report. This was penned under the name of Commissioner Wynand Malan. The minority position highlighted three issues: an inconsistent interpretation of the Act, an absolutist approach to historical questions and, as a consequence, an inadequate ethics of responsibility and reconciliation. I would like to elaborate on each before concluding the chapter.

Interpretation. Commissioner Malan was keenly aware of the internal tension in the Commission's Report: *on the one hand*, a bold but formal rejection of the claim that apartheid's legality represented legitimacy (a rule of law) alongside a formal acknowledgement of apartheid as a crime against humanity; *on the other hand*, a refusal to follow through on all the implications of this bold first move, instead interpreting its mandate narrowly and conservatively. Malan called for a consistent point of view that

[75] Truth and Reconciliation Commission of South Africa, ***Report***, vol. 1, p. 94, Para 2; also see, vol. 5, p. 349, Para 114.

[76] Truth and Reconciliation Commission of South Africa, ***Report***, vol. 1, p. 132, Para 104.

[77] Truth and Reconciliation Commission of South Africa, ***Report***, vol. 5, p. 179, Para 45 and 43. The full recommendation read: "It is recommended that the recipients of urgent interim reparation and individual reparation grants should be victims as found by the Commission, as well as their relatives and dependents who are found to be in urgent need, after the consideration of a completed prescribed application form, according to the proposed urgency criteria." Truth and Reconciliation Commission of South Africa, ***Report***, vol. 5, p. 176, Para 33.

would set aside the question of apartheid and its legitimacy and legality. This is how he put his 'main reservation': 'The Act does not put apartheid on trial. It accepts that apartheid has been convicted by the negotiations at Kempton Park and executed by the adoption of our new Constitution. The Act charges the Commission to deal with gross human rights violations, with crimes both *under apartheid law and present law*'[78] (*italics* mine). At the same time, Malan was clear that the Commission stay away from any reference to international law: 'international law does not provide for the granting of amnesty for a crime against humanity.'[79]

Malan was right that the Commission was inconsistent and contradictory in interpreting its own mandate. But was the Commission's mandate really to hold accountable those state officials who had committed crimes under apartheid law but were let go by apartheid courts? Or was it to go beyond the question of power – a question settled at Kempton Park – to address the question of how apartheid power had impacted on society?

Moral/Ethical vs. Historical Approach. Why would the Commission acknowledge apartheid as 'a crime against humanity' but not take full responsibility for such a finding? For Malan, this highlighted a broader tendency in the Commission to view its subject matter through the lenses of a morality play, whose 'dogmatic and absolutist' text was drawn from 'religious thought' for 'the juxtaposition of forces of light and forces of darkness, good and evil is inherent to religious thought.'[80] Instead of this 'moral-ethical approach,' Malan called for 'a real historical evaluation of roles played by various actors,' so as to 'reframe and shift from good versus evil to good versus bad, where clearly even good has different meanings.'[81] Instead of the 'religious conversion model of confession, repentance and forgiveness' which 'is by the very dogma of religion at the level of the very personal, of the individual against his or her God or offended neighbour', he called for a focus on communities.[82]

Whereas Malan was concerned to reclaim the agency of Afrikaners as that of an oppressed people – and thereby redefine Afrikaner Nationalism as 'a reactive phenomenon' against the larger canvass of British imperialism[83] – my concern is that the Commission tended to dehistoricise the phenomenon of apartheid by seeing it as just another version of a political dictatorship that carried out gross violations of human rights. In trying to locate South African history on a universal plane of rights violations, it dislocated both apartheid and its victims from a larger history of colonialism and its victims. This dislocation was established through an analogy with

78 Truth and Reconciliation Commission of South Africa, ***Report***, vol. 5, p. 440, Para 18.
79 Truth and Reconciliation Commission of South Africa, ***Report***, vol. 5, p. 449, Para 63.
80 Truth and Reconciliation Commission of South Africa, ***Report***, vol. 5, p. 440, Para 17.
81 Truth and Reconciliation Commission of South Africa, ***Report***, vol. 5, pp. 440-41, Para 21, 22.
82 Truth and Reconciliation Commission of South Africa, ***Report***, vol. 5, pp. 442-43, Para 30.
83 Truth and Reconciliation Commission of South Africa, ***Report***, vol. 5, p. 445, Para 40.

particular Latin American dictatorships, such as the Chilean and the Argentinean. The analogy was enthusiastically embraced in two conferences organised by Alex Borraine – who later became the Vice Chair of the Commission – through two NGOs: the Institute for a Democratic Alternative in South Africa (IDASA) and Justice in Transition. Had it been made with full regard to the difference in historical contexts, the analogy would have illuminated much. But the analogy was established on the basis of a series of resemblances: Didn't both situations give rise to a context where political adversaries tended to get mutually exhausted in a protracted, endless, struggle? Didn't the adversaries in both cases attain a kind of political wisdom in the absence of outright victory, a mutual recognition that the waste of life and resources need not continue? Weren't both situations constrained by a global context that simultaneously underlined the need for compromise and facilitate it? Didn't both societies have to face a common question: how would past perpetrators and their victims live together in a new society?

The TRC pursued the analogy without regard to what was distinctive about the context of apartheid. In its eagerness to assert the general and universal relevance of the South African experience – not as much of apartheid as of the reconciliation that followed – the Commission rewrote the history of apartheid as one of a drama played out within a fractured political elite: state agents against political activists. The particular Latin analogy obscured what was distinctive about apartheid. It obscured the fact that the violence of apartheid was aimed mainly at entire communities and not individuals, and, as a consequence, reconciliation too would need to be between communities and not just individuals. Finally, it obscured the fact that, unlike political dictatorships that could look back to a time in history when today's adversaries were members of a single political community – and could thus speak of reconciling, and thereby restoring that political community – South Africa was confronted with a unique challenge: how to bring erstwhile colonisers and colonised into a single political community *for the first time ever in history*? For the simple fact was that whereas white South Africans had lived under a rule of law, the people of South Africa – white and black – had yet to live under a single rule of law, the basis of a single political community.

Reconciliation and Responsibility. Malan called for a double shift, from the plane of morality to that of history, and from a focus on the personal and the individual to one on community. But if morality evolves historically, how does this affect responsibility? In Malan's words: 'Slavery is a crime against humanity. Yet Paul, in his letters to the Ephesians and Colossians, is uncritical of the institution and discusses the duties of slaves and their masters. Given a different international balance of power, colonialism too might have been found a crime against humanity.'[84] In other words, the consciousness of right and wrong, of good and bad, does not predate history; it is a part of

[84] Truth and Reconciliation Commission of South Africa, ***Report***, vol. 5, p. 448, Para 58.

history. The point is to go beyond recognising 'perpetrators and victims of gross human rights violations.' This is how Malan summed up his point: 'If we can reframe our history to include both perpetrators and victims as victims of the ultimate perpetrator – namely the conflict of the past, we will have fully achieved unity and reconciliation and an awareness of the real threat to our future – which is a dogmatic or ideological division that polarizes the nation instead of promoting genuine political activity.'[85] From this perspective, the ultimate perpetrator is history. Rephrased, recognising victims and perpetrators of apartheid can only be the first step to reconciliation. The next step is to recognise both as *survivors* who must together shape a *common* future.

From this point of view, reconciliation cannot be between victims and perpetrators; it can only be between survivors. Restorative justice is the precondition for integrating perpetrators and victims in a single community, a community of survivors. To do so, restorative justice needs to reach out *both* to the perpetrator *and* to the victim in a double move. The first requires disassociating the perpetrator from his/her action in Gandhian fashion: 'seeing both the deed and the doer and severing them from each other.' The second 'involves the state acknowledging violations against victims.'[86] The shift of focus from the agency of the perpetrator to the nature of the act and of the harm done does not lead to a focus away from the victim, provided the state steps in between the victim and the perpetrator, and takes over responsibility for both acknowledging and redressing all violations.

Malan was sceptical of the Commission's boast that, unlike previous offers of a blanket amnesty, it had offered an amnesty with a difference: since individual perpetrators received amnesty only in return for telling the truth about crimes they had committed under apartheid. How complete was this truth, Malan asked, when 'all too often deceased individuals were implicated'?[87] Could it be that in making truth the prerequisite for an amnesty that had been agreed upon as part of a prior political compromise, the Commission really turned truth into a casualty?

The Commission did not have to tailor the truth for political objectives. The Act that set up the Commission had already distinguished between the Amnesty Committee and the rest of the Commission. The Amnesty Committee differed from the rest of the Commission both in the manner of its appointment and in its powers. Whereas the rest of the Commission was appointed through a transparent process, the amnesty committee was not: also, whereas decisions of the rest of the Commission were as recommendations to government, those of the amnesty committee were final. They were subject neither to the overall Commission majority nor to a governmental

---

85 Truth and Reconciliation Commission of South Africa, ***Report***, vol. 5, p. 443, Para 34; it is for survivors to "succeed in integrating, through political engagement, all our histories, in order to discontinue the battles of the past."

86 Truth and Reconciliation Commission of South Africa, ***Report***, vol. 5, pp. 443-44, Para 35, 36.

87 Truth and Reconciliation Commission of South Africa, ***Report***, vol. 5, p. 441, Para 25.

veto. Ironically, this difference gave the Commission (which I speak of as excluding the amnesty committee) considerable freedom in pursuing its overall objective: national unity and reconciliation.

That freedom, and that responsibility, lay in exploring the link between the political reconciliation at Kempton Park and a larger social reconciliation that was the Commission's core mandate. It lay in seeing truth not as an alternative but as a pre-requisite to justice. Rather than exploring alternatives to justice, the Commission's challenge lay in exploring alternative forms of justice. For the state to integrate both victims and perpetrators – as survivors – into a single post-apartheid political community, it would have to acknowledge the majority as victims and take responsibility for reparations.

The Act defined the overall objective of the Commission as promoting national unity and reconciliation. In limiting the definition of victims to political activists whose rights had been grossly violated, the Commission narrowed its overall objective to promoting unity and reconciliation within South Africa's fractured political elite. From the quest of social reconciliation, it narrowed its mandate to that of a political reconciliation. In an attempt to reinforce the political compromise achieved at Kempton Park, it crafted a moral and intellectual compromise. Whereas the morality of the political compromise may be defended, that of the moral and intellectual compromise – the diminished truth as told by the Commission – is difficult to defend.

12 CONCLUSION

From the outset, there was a strong tendency in the TRC not only to *dehistoricise* and *decontextualise* the story of apartheid but also to individualise the wrongs done by apartheid. Wynand Malan's minority report blamed this tendency on the religious messianism of the leadership in the Commission. This religious mode of thought received powerful international support from secular quarters. If the religious discourse was located in the churches that provided the leadership of the TRC, a parallel secular discourse was characteristic of the human rights community that provided the bulk of the technical assistance for the TRC, both as preparatory support before its constitution and as research and organisational support during its operation.

If the leadership of the TRC was eager to make the story of apartheid – especially the lessons of reconciliation – universally available, its ambitions were easy to reconcile with equally universalist aspirations of those in the human rights community who looked forward to framing the problem of apartheid as one of a violation of individual rights, albeit on a wide scale. Both shared the tendency to dehistoricise and decontextualise social processes, and to individualise their outcomes. For this reason, the confluence of two modes of thought – one religious, the other secular – around the project of the TRC should be of more than just historical interest. It is also of theoretical interest.

The Commission's Report did not just downplay apartheid, the 'crime against humanity.' It also showed little understanding of the legal machinery through which this crime against humanity was perpetrated in the guise of a rule of law. The Commission's limitations were not only reflected in its prognosis of the past, the story of apartheid, but also its prescriptions of the – particularly legal – reform that is needed to dismantle the institutional legacy of apartheid in the legal domain.

I have argued that apartheid promoted two related political identities through its legal project: race and ethnicity. These bifurcations presume and reinforce two related presumptions: that race was about a hierarchy of civilisation, and ethnicity about its absence, i.e., barbarism. This presumption is reproduced in the Report of the Commission in two related ways. *First*, the Commission appears blind to the legal and administrative apparatus that apartheid created to govern the domain of barbarism, i.e., the native population classified into so-called tribes. Through this apparatus, which it called 'customary,' apartheid regulated the day-to-day lives of most of its victims. *Second*, the Commission took its stand on the domain of civilisation. It had eyes for only the apparatus of civil law that governed white civil society and excluded black society, and that was at the heart of the claim that apartheid was indeed a rule of law. This identification seems to have been so unthought that the Commission was often prone to think of the South African legal system as part of a larger entity it called 'the Western world'! In the chapter on the 'institutional hearings: the legal community', the Commission indicted the judiciary 'which willingly participated in producing the highest capital punishment rate *in the 'Western' world* by the mid-1980s ...'[88] (*italics* mine). The same statement is repeated in the final volume, in the findings on the judiciary which indict 'the participation of judges in producing the highest capital punishment rate *in the 'western' world*'[89] (*italics* mine). From whose point of view, one may ask, is South Africa a part of the 'western' world?

If the Commission did not focus on the bifurcated nature of South African law and legal authority, it could only be because the Commission paid little attention to gross violations suffered by the vast majority of the South African population, violations that took the form of pass laws, forced removals, convict labour for farms, detentions without trial, etc. Any systematic examination of these violations would have brought the Commission face to face with the entire phalanx of laws and authorities – which used the language of custom rather than rights – and without which there would have been no apartheid (separate development) in South Africa. At the same time, an understanding of Native Authorities as integral to apartheid would have given the Commission an insight into how 'black-on-black violence' was

88 Truth and Reconciliation Commission of South Africa, ***Report***, vol. 4, p. 103, Para 34(i).
89 Truth and Reconciliation Commission of South Africa, ***Report***, vol. 5, p. 254, Para 158(d).

integral to the state-organised violence that fuelled apartheid as a crime against humanity.

HISTORICAL REFLECTIONS ON HOLOCAUST REPARATIONS: UNFINISHED BUSINESS OR AN EXAMPLE FOR OTHER REPARATIONS CAMPAIGNS?

REGULA LUDI

1 INTRODUCTION

In Western thinking, the Nazi Holocaust has become the symbol of absolute evil, a moral universal that serves as a standard against which to measure gross human rights violations.[1] The struggle to comprehend the origins of the 'Final Solution', the Nazi decision to destroy European Jewry, and cope with its legacies has troubled the minds of generations of scholars, policy planners and individuals who were directly or indirectly affected by these events.[2] Many measures currently under discussion as possible responses to suffering caused by administrative massacres were first devised and tested in reaction to the crimes of the Nazi regime. However, as their evaluation illustrates, there is no easy answer to the question of how to cope with legacies of such widespread abuse.[3] Recent literature on transitional justice stresses the many dilemmas associated with establishing accountability and restoring legal order in the aftermath of systemic violence. Criminal prosecution of the main perpetrators, for instance, inevitably focuses on selected individuals and, with regard to representations of a

---

1 J. C. ALEXANDER, 'On the Social Construction of Moral Universals. The 'Holocaust' from War Crime to Trauma Drama,' (2002) 5:1 *European Journal of Social Theory*, 5–58.

2 The literature on Holocaust historiography is a fast growing area. For overviews with references to the older publications see D. STONE (ed.), *The Historiography of the Holocaust* (Basingstoke: Palgrave Macmillan, 2004); G. NE'EMAN ARAD (ed), 'Passing into History: Nazism and the Holocaust beyond Memory. In Honor of Saul Friedländer on His Sixty-Fifth Birthday', (1997) 9:1/2 *History & Memory* (Special Issue). On recent controversies over interpretations of the Holocaust: G. D. ROSENFELD, 'The Politics of Uniqueness: Reflections on the Recent Polemical Turn in Holocaust and Genocide Scholarship,' (1999) 13:1 *Holocaust and Genocide Studies,* 28-61.

3 See for instance R. T. TEITEL, *Transitional Justice* (Oxford: Oxford University Press, 2000) and H. KÖNIG, M. KOHLSTRUCK and A. WÖLL (eds.), *Vergangenheitsbewältigung am Ende des 20. Jahrhunderts* (Wiesbaden: Westdeutscher Verlag, 1998).

contested past, risks eclipsing the fact of widespread public and bureaucratic involvement in the abuses.[4] At times, trials and lustration also fail to satisfy the victims' expectation that they will be vindicated, especially when high-profile perpetrators, against whom there is overwhelming evidence, are acquitted for technical reasons. Against this backdrop, authors have suggested victim-based approaches as an alternative to criminal prosecution. Many also see efforts at reconciliation and restorative justice, including reparations, as complementary measures embodying the promise of both vindicating the victims and avoiding the aforementioned problems.[5]

But with regard to victim reparations, the legal situation is sketchy. Absent an internationally recognised right to redress for human rights violations, the case of Holocaust reparations serves as a precedent, since it remains 'unequalled' in its scale, as Jon Elster emphasises in his recent book on transitional justice.[6] When gauged only by the sum of money involved, the record is indeed remarkable: By the end of 2004, German expenditure for the rehabilitation of Nazi victims amounted to more than 62 billion euros.[7] Accordingly, Holocaust reparations have come to represent, for some, Germany's exemplary efforts to redress the wrongs of the Nazi regime.[8] This positive assessment is supported by the recent success of Holocaust-era litigation in American courts. Acclaimed for being 'a template for a new era of financial relief and recognition for the victims of crimes against humanity,' these lawsuits, with their international publicity, have turned Holocaust reparations into a model for the mushrooming restitution movement and fostered the idea of victim reparations as a panacea for all sorts of evils.[9] The historian Elazar Barkan, for instance, considers the appearance of reparations movements on a global scale as an indicator of a new morality emerging in international relations – a morality that is based on mutual

---

4 Dealing with these problems in regard to trials against Nazi perpetrators: D. BLOXHAM, *Genocide on Trial. War Crimes Trials and the Formation of Holocaust History and Memory* (Oxford: Oxford University Press, 2003); L. DOUGLAS, *The Memory of Judgment. Making Law and History in the Trials of the Holocaust* (New Haven: Yale University Press, 2001).

5 M. MINOW, *Between Vengeance and Forgiveness. Facing History after Genocide and Mass Violence* (Boston: Beacon Press, 1998).

6 J. ELSTER, *Closing the Books: Transitional Justice in Historical Perspective* (Cambridge: Cambridge University Press, 2004), xi.

7 Leistungen der öffentlichen Hand auf dem Gebiet der Wiedergutmachung, Stand 31. Dezember 2004', ed. BUNDESMINISTERIUM DER FINANZEN, www.bundesfinanzministerium.de.

8 For an example see R. ROBINSON, *The Debt. What America Owes to Blacks* (New York: Plume, 2001) who repeatedly refers to the German model to make a case for slavery reparations to African-Americans.

9 M. J. BAZYLER, *Holocaust Justice. The Battle for Restitution in America's Courts* (New York – London: New York University Press, 2003), 330. On legal questions see D. SHELTON, 'Righting Wrongs: Reparations in the Articles of State Responsibility,' (2002) 96:4 *The American Journal of International Law,* 833-856; R. PISILLO-MAZZESCHI, 'International Obligations to Provide for Reparation Claims,' in A. RANDELZHOFER and C. TOMUSCHAT (eds.), *State Responsibility and the Individual- Reparation in Instances of Grave Violations of Human Rights* (The Hague – London – Boston: Martinus Nijhoff Publishers, 1999), 149-172.

willingness of victims and perpetrators (or their descendants) to engage in negotiations over the interpretation of the past and reach compromises as to the obligations this entails.[10]

This optimistic conclusion is based upon the fact that States and transnational corporations have been ready to make settlements with Holocaust survivors involving high compensation payments. But this is a recent phenomenon. In the 1990s, Holocaust-era litigation benefited from the collapse of communism and global integration, which made companies more vulnerable to international naming and shaming. In addition, a changing interpretation of the Holocaust engendered new public sensitivity toward the victims and growing interest in their stories.[11] It may be, therefore, that the success of the plaintiffs in relation to Holocaust restitution claims was closely linked to specific historical circumstances, making it the exception rather than the rule in such matters. So we have to ask whether Holocaust reparations are a suitable model for today's and tomorrow's restitution campaigns. Does the Holocaust reparations model really testify to the appearance of a new global morality, as some authors have suggested? Did German reparations accomplish what – according to current theory – this type of redress is expected to fulfil, that is, recognition of State responsibility by the perpetrator nation, social rehabilitation of the victims and their reinstatement as full citizens? To find answers to these questions, recent developments need to be examined in a wider historical context. For an overall assessment, we cannot judge Holocaust reparations simply according to the amount of money transferred to survivors. We also need to look at the winding road taken by reparations' politics since the end of the Second World War. What were the purpose and rationale of reparations? Who were the beneficiaries of restitution and compensation mechanisms, and for what types of abuses did claimants receive redress? Who financed compensation payments, and did such payments entail acknowledgement of legal responsibility by the State?

I shall try to find answers to these questions by addressing four dimensions of Holocaust reparations: First I shall discuss the emergence of victim reparations in the context of international law in the course of the post-war 'Juridical Revolution,' the

---

10 E. Barkan, *The Guilt of Nations. Restitution and Negotiating Historical Injustices* (Baltimore – London: The Johns Hopkins University Press, 2000); see also the contributions in R. L. Brooks (ed.), *When Sorry Isn't Enough. The Controversy over Apologies and Reparations for Human Injustice* (New York – London: New York University Press, 1999).

11 D. Levy and N. Sznaider, *Erinnerung im globalen Zeitalter: Der Holocaust* (Frankfurt: Fischer Taschenbuch Verlag, 2001). Some authors criticise the fact that victimisation has become a 'growing industry' with past victimisation, rather than progressive visions of the future, serving as the basis for claims to social justice. See E. Barkan, 'Restitution and Amending Historical Injustices in International Morality,' in J. Torpey (ed.), *Politics and the Past. On Repairing Historical Injustices* (Lanham: Rowman & Littlefield, 2003), 92, citing Ian Buruma; also J. Torpey, '"Making Whole What Has Been Smashed": Reflections on Reparations,' (2001) 73:2 *Journal of Modern History*, 333–358, and the critical reflections by C. S. Maier, 'A Surfeit of memory? Reflections on History, Melancholy and Denial,' (1993) 5:2 *History & Memory*, 136-152.

bundle of legal responses to Nazi atrocities.[12] The second and third aspects to be examined relate to German diplomatic and domestic policies in response to victims' claims, including lump-sum payments to Israel and various European countries as well as domestic legislation regarding property restitution, compensation payments for the violation of basic rights and the repeal of abusive judgments.[13] Finally, the fourth issue concerns recognition of victimhood and allocation of benefits in compensation practice.

In the following, I shall focus attention on the West German State (1949–1990). Of the three States that followed the Third Reich – the Federal Republic of Germany (FRG); the German Democratic Republic (GDR); and Austria – West Germany was the only one to adopt a comprehensive program of victim reparations and to acknowledge international obligations towards survivors of Nazi crimes. Austria and East Germany, in contrast, did not ignore the problem, but they both refused to endorse legal obligations arising from Nazi crimes, and only introduced special welfare programs for Nazi victims that did not include acknowledgement of State responsibility.[14] For this reason the West German example serves as the model in most current debates.

Occasionally I use the term 'Holocaust reparations' as a short form for restitution and compensation measures that covered a whole variety of Nazi abuses. This could be misleading since the very meaning of the Holocaust is the subject of intense debate. Nonetheless I use 'Holocaust reparations' as a synonym for the more accurate expression 'reparations for the victims of Nazi persecution' because it is the term that most readers are familiar with in the context of current debates.

2 VICTIM REPARATIONS: A POST-WAR INNOVATION

Holocaust reparations encompass all measures aimed at undoing and redressing the consequences of Nazi persecution, as incomplete as this project inevitably remains in the face of Nazi genocide and mass murder. Apart from the fact that aid came too late for millions who had died, post-war efforts at dealing with the consequences of

---

12 M. IGNATIEFF, *Human Rights as Politics and Idolatry* (Princeton: Princeton University Press, 2001), 5.

13 Of all the measures of victim reparations, the repeal of abusive judgements has attracted little scholarly attention. For an exception see R. VOGL, *Stückwerk und Verdrängung. Wiedergutmachung nationalsozialistischen Strafjustizunrechts in Deutschland* (Berlin: Verlag Arno Spitz, 1997).

14 On Austria see B. BAILER-GALANDA, *Die Entstehung der Rückstellungs- und Entschädigungsgesetzgebung: Die Republik Österreich und das in der NS-Zeit entzogene Vermögen* (Vienna: Oldenbourg, 2003); on East-Germany C. HÖLSCHER, *NS-Verfolgte im "antifaschistischen Staat": Vereinnahmung und Ausgrenzung in der ostdeutschen Wiedergutmachung (1945-1989)* (Berlin: Metropol, 2002).

Nazi abuses also faced numerous conceptual obstacles. A striking example is the problem of displaced persons. As a consequence of Nazi occupation, huge populations from all over Europe lost their homes. In 1945, millions were stranded in Germany, millions more still on the move, with no place to which they could return. Among them were liberated concentration camp survivors, POWs, ethnic Germans who were expelled from Eastern Europe and refugees of all types. With ties to their former homes severed and survival in their countries of origin no longer guaranteed, repatriation was out of the question for many. As stateless (or 'non-repatriable') persons they depended on resettlement programs, failing which they faced the dire prospect of staying in camps for an indefinite time.[15] Furthermore, Nazi policies of expropriation and plunder had transformed property relations beyond recognition: Looted assets had crossed borders and changed hands so many times, often with the help of neutral intermediaries, that it was almost impossible to trace their origins or identify their rightful owners. Moreover, mass murder had extinguished whole families, leaving their property 'heirless'.[16]

In short, the transnational character of Nazi policies of persecution and extermination posed a major challenge to a legal system relying on the nation state as its basic unit. Mitigating and disentangling the consequences of Nazi rule thus confronted the victorious powers with a myriad technical, financial and legal dilemmas, with no examples to rely on. According to the existing body of international law at the time, a future German State was only obligated to redress rights violations committed by the Nazis against foreigners and inhabitants of occupied territories. Following the precedent of the Versailles treaty, this category of abuses was covered largely by the war reparation claim that the Allies imposed on defeated Germany in 1945.[17] But this did not establish individual entitlement to compensation payments. According to the classical doctrine of international law, individual complaints against foreign States had to be mediated through the claimants' government. Also, domestic allocation of war reparations was left entirely within the discretion of recipient States which mostly followed national traditions of dealing with war-related damages. This birthed an inconsistent practice in post-war Europe. Often, distribution relied on existing welfare schemes for veterans and war victims, which were devised after the Great War, and was dictated by national requirements and domestic priorities in relation to post-war reconstruction. Some States, for instance, recognised claims by foreign residents, while others restricted compensation to their own nationals exclusively. Some treated

[15] M. Wyman, *DPs. Europe's Displaced Persons, 1945-1951* (Ithaca – London: Cornell University Press, 1998).

[16] M. Dean, C. Goschler and P. Ther (eds.), *Robbery and Restitution: the Conflict over Jewish Property in Europe*, (New York – Oxford: Berghahn, 2006).

[17] P. d'Argent, *Les réparations de guerre en droit public. La responsabilité internationale des Etats à l'épreuve de la guerre* (Brussels – Paris: Bruylant, 2002) and J. Fisch, *Reparationen nach dem Zweiten Weltkrieg* (Munich: C.H. Beck, 1992).

damages resulting from Nazi persecution on the same footing as war damages, others passed special legislation.[18]

In default of uniform patterns, compensation practice reflected deficiencies within international law: Whether a person would receive compensation depended on her nationality and not on the affliction she suffered. Moreover, there existed no obligation requiring Germany to redress Nazi crimes against German citizens or stateless persons as it was sheltered from international intervention regarding domestic treatment of its own nationals by the principles of national sovereignty and domestic jurisdiction. Jewish organisations had pointed out this unacceptable legal situation as early as the 1930s, when the Nazi regime began targeting its own citizens.[19] During the war the Jewish organisations repeatedly reminded the Allies of the unparalleled nature of Nazi race persecution and insisted that the exceptional situation created by Nazi genocidal policies required special responses to tackle its consequences and save the remnants of Jewish life in Europe.[20]

During the last phase of the war, as more information about the Holocaust emerged, restitution schemes and claims for collective reparations in favour of the Jewish people proliferated.[21] Some of these arguments resonated with Allied postwar planners. At the Paris Reparation Conference of 1945, American diplomats successfully inserted a special clause in the final agreement of January 1946 to earmark a share of war reparations for stateless and so-called non-repatriable victims of Nazi action. This was in 'recognition of the fact that large numbers of persons have suffered heavily at the hands of the Nazis and now stand in dire need of aid to promote their rehabilitation but will be unable to claim the assistance of any Government receiving reparation from Germany.' The Paris document also required neutral States to contribute to this special reparations pool by liquidating German assets and identifying and liquidating heirless assets of Nazi victims in their territories, and transferring the resulting proceeds to an international organisation tasked with the resettlement of Nazi victims.[22]

These provisions were remarkable. The Paris Reparation Agreement was the first legal document to recognise an individual right to redress for state crimes (as distinct

18 For Western Europe see P. Lagrou, *The Legacy of Nazi Occupation. Patriotic Memory and National Recovery in Western Europe, 1945-1965* (Cambridge: Cambridge University Press, 2000); F. Cochet, *Les exclus de la victoire. Histoire des prisonniers de guerre, déportés et S.T.O (1945-1985)* (Paris : Kronos, 1992).

19 P. G. Lauren, *The Evolution of International Human Rights. Visions Seen* (Philadelphia: University of Pennsylvania Press, 1998), 105-138.

20 D. S. Wyman, *The Abandonment of the Jews: America and the Holocaust 1941-1945* (New York: Pantheon Books, 1985).

21 N. Robinson, *Indemnification and Reparations. Jewish Aspects* (New York, World Jewish Congress, 1944), S. Moses, *Jewish Post-War Claims* (Tel Aviv 1944) ed. W.-D. Barz (Münster: LIT Verlag, 2001).

22 Centre Historique des Archives Nationales (CHAN), AJ34, Vol. 5 : Agreement on Reparation from Germany, on the Establishment of an Interallied Reparation Agency and on the Restitution of Monetary Gold, Paris, 14 January, 1946.

from the established right of States to war reparations).[23] Moreover, it required non-belligerents to participate in the general settlement of war-related problems. This may be understood as a response to the transnational character of Nazi crimes. But the Paris Reparation Conference was the only international event directly addressing the problems of persecution victims. In the end, it failed to create a new international standard incorporating an individual right to reparations, irrespective of the injured person's origin or nationality.

Only a comprehensive practice in Germany could correct such omission, by becoming an international precedent. As a principle, it was beyond question that a future German State would be obligated to redress Nazi crimes. In dealing with defeated Germany, however, the victorious powers hesitated to establish binding obligations. This reflected their preoccupation with the perpetrators and corresponding disinterest in the victims. But it was also a consequence of the rapidly deteriorating political climate. Fundamental disagreement between the Allies on the question of war reparations soon overshadowed occupation policy and prevented coordination. The Soviets prioritised high reparation deliveries from their occupation zone and continued dismantling production units until the early 1950s. In their eyes, individual reparations were subordinated to their overall reparation claim. The Western Allies, in contrast, were worried about rising occupation costs and soon reduced their reparation demands in favour of economic recovery.[24]

Diverging approaches to reconstruction, therefore, determined the concretisation of victim reparations in Germany. In the West, occupation authorities implemented property restitution first, while according less urgency to compensation measures, which they delegated to local German bureaucracies. Due to a lack of uniform principles and Allied supervision, special welfare programs for the victims became the targets of German power struggles. In this manner, Allied neglect contributed to a confusing legal situation that became a lasting predicament of 'Wiedergutmachung' (the official German term for victim reparations, literally 'making good for'). The German-Jewish expert Walter Schwarz would later use the expression 'legal jungle' to characterise German legislation and highlight the fact that it lacked logic and method.[25] In many respects, this verdict may even be extended to the international situation of Holocaust reparations where victim categories would soon multiply with different legal entitlements and different criteria of eligibility. Against this backdrop,

---

23 R. PISILLO-MAZZESCHI, 'International Obligations to Provide for Reparation Claims," in *State Responsibility and the Individual. Reparation in Instances of Grave Violations of Human Rights*, ed. A. RANDELZHOFER and C. TOMUSCHAT (The Hague – London – Boston: Martinus Nijhoff Publishers 1999), 149-172.

24 J. FISCH, *Reparationen nach dem Zweiten Weltkrieg* (Munich: C.H. Beck, 1992).

25 In the German original: 'legislativer Wildwuchs', see W. SCHWARZ, 'Die Wiedergutmachung nationalsozialistischen Unrechts durch die Bundesrepublik Deutschland. Ein Überblick', in L. HERBST and C. GOSCHLER (eds.), *Wiedergutmachung in der Bundesrepublik Deutschland* (Munich: Oldenbourg, Verlag 1989), 33. The German term 'Wiedergutmachung' refers to the full range of victim reparations.

many efforts at redress remained disappointingly incomplete or came decades after the events.

The fragmentary and disparate nature of victim reparations contrasted in a striking manner with the legal innovations adopted by the Nuremberg trials. Nuremberg had a lasting impact on the development of international law beyond putting leading members of the Nazi regime on trial. With reliance on the idea of 'crimes against humanity', the London Charter of the International Military Tribunal extended international liability to a wide variety of State-committed and -condoned cruelties inflicted on innocent civilians. In so doing, the Allies transcended the limitations of the law of war at the time and set an important precedent for future human rights legislation.[26] But they failed to do the same with regard to repairing past injustice.

3 THE INTERNATIONAL CONTEXT: THE LUXEMBOURG TREATY AND ITS HISTORICAL SIGNIFICANCE

In the spring of 1952, official delegates of the Israeli government, the newly founded *Conference on Jewish Material Claims against Germany* (a Jewish umbrella organisation, commonly referred to as the Claims Conference) and the Adenauer administration came together in the Dutch town of Wassenaar to enter into negotiations over collective Jewish reparation claims. Not only is the history of these proceedings rich in anecdotes and legends, but the event itself – taking place just a few years after the demise of the Third Reich – was obviously fraught with emotion. A difficult process of mutual rapprochement had preceded the official talks, with clandestine meetings taking place and secret notes being exchanged. This process came to a head in Adenauer's famous acknowledgment of State responsibility for Nazi crimes, which the Chancellor pronounced in the German parliament in September 1951.[27] Although much criticised for its evasive wording, Adenauer's statement broke the deadlock, opening the door for direct talks between representatives of the victimised and the former perpetrators. The resulting Luxembourg agreements of 1952 consisted of a treaty between the FRG and the Jewish State, with Germany promising the payment of three billion Deutsche Marks to reimburse Israel for the resettlement of 500,000 surviving Holocaust victims. Attached to this treaty were two protocols, one expressing Germany's commitment to amending domestic compensation legislation, the other

---

[26] G.R. UEBERSCHÄR (ed.), *Der Nationalsozialismus vor Gericht. Die alliierten Prozesse gegen Kriegsverbrecher und Soldaten 1943-1952* (Frankfurt: Fischer Taschenbuch Verlag, 1999), S. POWER, *'A Problem from Hell. America and the Age of Genocide* (New York: Perennial, 2003).

[27] C. GOSCHLER, *Schuld und Schulden. Die Politik der Wiedergutmachung für NS-Verfolgte seit 1945* (Göttingen: Wallstein Verlag, 2005), 159-163.

relating to the sum of 450 million Marks that the FRG pledged to pay to the Claims Conference as compensation for heirless Jewish assets in Germany.[28] The wording of these documents diligently avoided any reference to expiation for the Holocaust.

The Luxembourg Treaty, often called the 'Magna Carta' of German compensation policy, is commonly understood as the beginning of Holocaust reparations. Authors regard it as a watershed in international law and consider it 'the gauge for future restitution claims.'[29] But is this interpretation justified? Certainly not, if popular approval at the time serves as the yardstick. In both countries, public opinion was markedly hostile to the negotiations. Many Jews opposed efforts at reconciliation with the perpetrators in principle, and rejected German payments as 'blood money'. Israel's deep financial crisis shortly after national independence eventually helped turn the tide in the Knesset.[30] Still, Israeli negotiators carefully avoided phrasing the agreement in such a way that it would leave the impression of atonement and redemption. The treaty was also extremely unpopular in Germany. Just 11 percent of the German public supported payments to the Jews without reservations, and an overwhelming majority did not consider victim reparations a necessity or obligation. Only the unwavering support of the social-democratic opposition guaranteed ratification of the treaty.[31]

Its unpopularity at the time notwithstanding, the Luxembourg agreement is historically significant for three reasons. For the first time in modern history, representatives of former perpetrators and victims engaged in direct talks, without external constraints or pressure on the part of the victorious powers.[32] Secondly, the treaty was linked to West German acknowledgment of State responsibility for Nazi crimes. East Germany and Austria, in contrast, disclaimed all liability; the former

28 For a comprehensive overview of the negotiations see N. SAGI, *German Reparations: A History of the Negotiations* (New York: St. Martin's Press, 1986). R. W. ZWEIG, *German Reparations and the Jewish World. A History of the Claims Conference*, 2nd revised edition (London: Frank Cass, 2001) highlights the position of the Jewish organisations involved; see also S. SHAFIR, *Ambiguous Relations. The American Jewish Community and Germany since 1945* (Detroit: Wayne State University Press, 1999) and the relevant essays in L. HERBST and C. GOSCHLER (eds.), *Wiedergutmachung in der Bundesrepublik Deutschland* (Munich: Oldenbourg Verlag, 1989).

29 E. BARKAN, *The Guilt of Nations. Restitution and Negotiating Historical Injustices* (Baltimore and London: The Johns Hopkins University Press), xxiii f.; H. G. HOCKERTS, 'Wiedergutmachung in Deutschland. Eine historische Bilanz 1945-2000,' (2001) 49:2 *Vierteljahrshefte für Zeitgeschichte*, 181.

30 Y. WEITZ, 'The Road to Wassenaar: How the Decision and Direct Negotiations between Israel and Germany Was Approved,' (2000) 27 *Yad Vashem Studies*, 311-350; N. BARZEL, 'Dignity, Hatred and Memory – Reparations from Germany: The Debates in the 1950s,' (1994) 24 *Yad Vashem Studies*, 245-280; T. SEGEV, *The Seventh Million. The Israelis and the Holocaust* (New York. Hill and Wang, 1993).

31 M. WOLFFSOHN, 'Globalentschädigung für Israel und die Juden? Adenauer und die Opposition in der Bundesregierung,' in L. HERBST and C. GOSCHLER (eds.), *Wiedergutmachung in der Bundesrepublik Deutschland* (Munich: Oldenbourg Verlag, 1989), 161-190.

32 M. WOLFFSOHN, 'Das deutsch-israelische Wiedergutmachungsabkommen von 1952 im internationalen Zusammenhang,' (1988) 36:4 *Vierteljahrshefte für Zeitgeschichte*, 691-731; Y.A. JELINEK, 'Die Krise der Shilumim/Wiedergutmachungs-Verhandlungen im Sommer 1952,' (1990) 38:1 *Vierteljahrshefte für Zeitgeschichte*, 113-139.

claimed to represent the antifascist tradition in Germany and the latter invoked the notorious 'victim myth', the contention that Austria was the first victim of Nazi aggression.[33] Thirdly, West Germany's acknowledgment that it owed legal obligations toward the victims set a precedent in international law by recognising the legitimacy of collective claims to reparation. Until that time Jews had been denied collective claims and were not officially represented in the negotiations dealing with defeated Germany and the post-war order. Legally, neither the State of Israel nor Jewish organisations were entitled to raise claims on behalf of Holocaust victims, since the State of Israel did not exist at the time of the events, and Jewish organisations were not bodies recognised under international law. The Luxembourg treaty, however, transcended such restrictions and, through the normative power of the factual, inscribed legitimacy upon collective reparations claims of a community without a State of its own. This was unparalleled and would become a precedent for the reparations movement.[34]

By improving West Germany's international reputation, the Luxembourg Treaty was an important trump card for the Adenauer government in the systemic conflict of the Cold War. However, it is one of history's ironies that this newly won respectability allowed the FRG to shelve its obligations towards other victim categories. An international conference of West Germany's Western creditors that took place in London at the same time as the Wassenaar negotiations, led to a favourable resolution of Germany's financial liabilities. The resulting London Debt Agreement of 1953 alleviated a large portion of German pre-war and post-war debts while postponing the resolution of all remaining wartime liabilities to the day on which a future peace agreement would be signed. At a crucial moment in the Cold War, this settlement helped restore Germany's international credit and support the country's integration into the Western alliance. But this came at the expense of Nazi victims from formerly

---

33 M. R. Lespius, 'Das Erbe des Nationalsozialismus und die politische Kultur der Nachfolgestaaten des 'Großdeutschen Reiches',' in M. Haller (ed.), *Kultur und Gesellschaft* (Frankfurt – New York: Campus, 1989), 247–265; J. Danyel (ed.), *Die geteilte Vergangenheit. Zum Umgang mit Nationalsozialismus und Widerstand in den beiden deutschen Staaten* (Berlin: Akademie Verlag, 1995); Historikerkommission der Republik Österreich, *Schlussbericht der Historikerkommission der Republik Österreich. Vermögensentzug während der NS-Zeit sowie Rückstellungen und Entschädigungen seit 1945 in Österreich. Zusammenfassungen und Einschätzungen* (Vienna – Munich: Oldenbourg Verlag, 2003).

34 Most explicit is the interpretation by E. Barkan, *The Guilt of Nations. Restitution and Negotiating Historical Injustices* (Baltimore and London: The Johns Hopkins University Press, 2000), p. 3-29.

occupied territories, since their claims, being considered wartime liabilities, were adjourned indefinitely.[35]

Under pressure from national victim associations, the governments of several Western European countries insisted on separate resolution of their citizens' compensation claims. They argued that Nazi abuses, because of their unprecedented scale, required additional redress in excess of the usual damages covered by war reparations. It took almost ten years, however, for these demands to be settled. Only in the late 1950s did the West German government demonstrate its readiness to negotiate special compensation agreements with West European countries, including both former belligerents and neutrals. In the early 1960s it made lump-sum payments to Belgium, Denmark, France, Great Britain, Greece, Italy, Luxembourg, The Netherlands, Norway, Sweden and Switzerland.[36]

Survivors living in Eastern Europe, in contrast, remained excluded from German compensation payments until the fall of the Iron Curtain. According to what was called the 'diplomatic clause', the FRG refused to negotiate with governments with which it had no diplomatic relations, and consequently declined compensation payments to their citizens. Basically this included all allies of the East German State. The only exception were victims of pseudo-medical experiments living in Poland. International sympathy for this small group of survivors, who had suffered extraordinary cruelties at the hands of Nazi doctors, eventually compelled the West German government to yield to the demands of victims' advocates, by awarding compensation payments to this group of survivors.[37] After the collapse of Communism, a unified German State

---

35 C. Pawlita, *'Wiedergutmachung' als Rechtsfrage? Die politische und juristische Auseinandersetzung um Entschädigung für die Opfer nationalsozialistischer Verfolgung (1945 bis 1990)* (Frankfurt – Bern: Peter Lang, 1993), 238-254. U. Herbert, 'Nicht entschädigungsfähig? Die Wiedergutmachungs-ansprüche der Ausländer,' in L. Herbst and C. Goschler (eds.), *Wiedergutmachung in der Bundesrepublik Deutschland* (Munich: Oldenbourg Verlag, 1989), 272-302; U. Herbert, 'Zwangsarbeiter im 'Dritten Reich' und das Problem der Entschädigung,' in D. Stiefel (ed.), *Die politische Ökonomie des Holocaust. Zur wirtschaftlichen Logik von Verfolgung und 'Wiedergutmachung'* (Vienna: Verlag für Geschichte und Politik, 2001) 220–224; on the agreement's significance for victim reparations H. G. Hockerts, 'Wiedergutmachung in Deutschland. Eine historische Bilanz 1945-2000,' (2001) 49:2 *Vierteljahrshefte für Zeitgeschichte,* 191f.

36 E. Féaux de la Croix and H. Rumpf, *Der Werdegang des Entschädigungsrechts unter national- und völkerrechtlichem und politologischem Aspekt* (Die Wiedergutmachung nationalsozialistischen Unrechts durch die Bundesrepublik Deutschland, Vol. 3) (Munich: C. H. Beck, 1985), 201-287; S. Schrafstetter, 'The Diplomacy of *Wiedergutmachung*: Memory, the Cold War, and the Western European Victims of Nazism, 1956-1964' (Winter 2003) 17:3 *Holocaust and Genocide Studies,* 459-479; U. Lappenküper, 'Die Bundesrepublik Deutschland und die „Wiedergutmachung" für französische Opfer nationalsozialistischen Unrechts,' (2001) 28:3 *Francia,* 75-101; R. Ludi and A.-A. Speck, 'Swiss Victims of National Socialism: An Example of how Switzerland Came to Terms with the Past,' in J.K. Roth and E. Maxwell (eds) *Remembering for the Future: The Holocaust in an Age of Genocide,* vol. 2, (London: Palgrave, 2001), 907-922; R. Ludi, ‚Die Parzellierung der Vergangenheit: Schweizer NS-Opfer und die Grenzen der Wiedergutmachung,' 29 (2003) *Studien und Quellen,* 101-128.

37 H. G. Hockerts, 'Wiedergutmachung in Deutschland. Eine historische Bilanz 1945-2000,' (2001) 49:2 *Vierteljahrshefte für Zeitgeschichte,* 194f.

eventually settled claims raised by citizens from Eastern Europe, the Baltic States, Russia, Belarus and Ukraine. It paid considerable funds to these countries, which were earmarked for victim reparations. Almost half a century after the events, however, these payments came too late for the majority of Nazi victims, who had died.[38]

4 CHRONOLOGY OF VICTIM REPARATIONS IN THE FEDERAL REPUBLIC OF GERMANY

The Luxembourg treaty has become the symbol of German Holocaust reparations. But such equation is problematic. It promotes a narrow focus on what is really a much wider issue. The agreement only covered a fraction of the entire German debt, and made victim reparations appear as if they were an exclusively German-Jewish affair. There was a risk that the massive atrocities committed by the Nazis beyond the Jewish genocide would be obscured, an interpretation that has led to complaints by excluded groups and promoted rivalries among different survivor communities over the 'moral capital' (to use a term of the French sociologist Pierre Bourdieu) enshrined in narratives of victimisation and suffering.[39] Such controversies remind us that victim reparations cannot be separated from the underlying historical narratives and their significance for current constructions of group identities, which are open to contention and exposed to shifting interpretations of the past. It is these processes – cycles of political opportunity rather than abstract principles or lofty ideas about restorative justice – which determine the mechanisms of integration and exclusion at work in victim reparations. An overview of domestic compensation policies in Germany demonstrates that, in reality, victim reparations were fragmentary, exclusionary, and at times barely testified to German willingness to 'make good for' Nazi abuses.

The chronology of victim reparations in Germany may be broken down roughly into four phases: The immediate post-war years (1945-1949) were the formative period setting in place principles and structures. The first decade and a half that followed the establishment of the two German States (1949-1965), the period of the German miracle in the West, witnessed the emergence of a West German reparations regime characterised by intensive federal legislation and gradual extension of benefits. The

---

38 C. GOSCHLER, *Schuld und Schulden. Die Politik der Wiedergutmachung für NS-Verfolgte seit 1945* (Göttingen: Wallstein Verlag, 2005), 429-437.

39 Emblematic are the debates over the creation of a Holocaust Memorial Museum in the United States and the appropriate figure of murdered victims to commemorate (on the one hand 6 million representing the Jewish victims, while on the other hand 11 million being a figure that includes other groups, for instance Roma and Sinti, Russian POWs and disabled Germans killed by the Nazis for racial reasons). See E. T. LINENTHAL, *Preserving Memory. The Struggle to Create America's Holocaust Museum* (new York, Columbia University Press, 1995) For critical reflections see also I. BURUMA, 'The Joys and Perils of Victimhood,' *The New York Review of Books*, 8 April 1999; J.-M. CHAUMONT, *La concurrence des victims. Génocide, identité, reconnaissance* (Paris: La Découverte & Syros, 1997).

1970s and 1980s were characterised by growing public sensitivity toward the Nazi victims epitomised by public scandals over the 'forgotten victims.' The 1990s, finally, marked a new era in the field of Holocaust reparations, with accelerated transnationalisation of restitution campaigns on the one hand, and the suggestion of a closure on the other hand, symbolised by the successful settlement of Holocaust-era litigation.

4.1 THE OCCUPATION PERIOD (1945–1949)

In the years following its defeat, Germany was divided into four occupation zones. Each zone was under the control of Allied military authorities appointed by one of the four victorious powers (United States, Soviet Union, United Kingdom and France). To coordinate occupation policy, the Allies established a Control Council in Berlin, but its capacities were soon paralysed by the onset of Cold War tensions. The occupation period lasted until the fall of 1949, when the newly founded Federal Republic of Germany (West Germany) and the German Democratic Republic (East Germany) each became semi-sovereign States.

During military occupation, the victorious powers in each of their zones claimed decision-making power over transitional justice measures: for instance, criminal prosecution of Nazi perpetrators, denazification, re-education programs and rehabilitation of victims. Allied post-war planning set the course and in many respects turned Germany into a laboratory for testing measures designed to respond to the enormity of Nazi destruction. Most of the programs employed therefore had no precedent. As a result, the outcome of transitional policies was often ambiguous at best. Instead of encouraging self-examination and instilling a sense of responsibility in the German public, programs directed at eradicating the social, political and cultural impacts of Nazism provoked resistance. Denazification in particular proved a failure, as it bred feelings of victimisation among former party members and fellow travellers. Also, with growing international tensions on the horizon, Allied efforts faltered before many programs could be completed successfully.[40]

As a result, inconsistency and lack of unity became characteristic of the transitional justice project in general. This applied especially to early efforts at victim reparations. The Allies, for instance, treated property restitution and compensation procedures as two different issues, which resulted in an artificial line being drawn between

---

40 W. Benz, *Potsdam 1945. Besatzungsherrschaft und Neuaufbau im Vier-Zonen-Deutschland* (Munich: Deutscher Taschenbuch Verlag, 2005); on denazification: C. Vollnhals, 'Denazification in the Western Zones. The Failed Experiment,' in S. U. Larsen (ed.), *Modern Europe after Fascism* (New York: Columbia University Press, 1998), 149-195; L. Niethammer, *Die Mitläuferfabrik. Die Entnazifizierung am Beispiel Bayerns* (Berlin – Bonn: J. H. W. Dietz, 1982).

categories of injustice that often overlapped in practice. The Western Allies also gave priority to property restitution and paid much less attention to other forms of redress. In 1947 the American occupation authorities were the first to enact legislation dealing with property restitution, which established a special procedure under the supervision of U.S. military authorities to protect victims' rights and guarantee speedy reversal of expropriation measures. The French and British soon followed suit. The Soviet military administration, however, not only prioritised war reparation payments over individual redress, but also considered property restitution at odds with the ongoing collectivisation of private ownership.[41]

Policy planners had no clear vision as to the correct manner in which to redress intangible damages: how to compensate someone for time spent in detention – under the dreadful conditions that prevailed in concentration camps or ghettos, for instance – or for years of terror. At first, compensation measures were regarded as a form of public assistance for needy survivors rather than as part of a reparations program. The occupying powers left decision-making to the German authorities. These local and regional actors often resorted to bureaucratic welfare routine and devised compensation procedures in accordance with conventional methods of public assistance. Some local authorities adopted the initiatives proposed by victim associations. In many places, solidarity networks consisting of concentration camp survivors were the first to take the necessary action to care for ill and impoverished survivors. But far from representing all Nazi victims, these associations attracted mostly well-organised political prisoners, many of whom had selective ideas about the purpose of victim reparations.[42] In their eyes, the primary goal of compensation was a symbolic one, consisting of rewards for antifascist accomplishments and decorating those who opposed Nazism. A German communist made this clear when declaring in 1947 that 'redress is not restitution of material and immaterial rights but a question of political education.'[43]

As a consequence, early compensation legislation often mirrored power relations among different victim categories. It also testified to the moral authority that former political prisoners claimed on the basis of their antifascist accomplishments under the Nazi regime. Early compensation programs, as the other side of the coin, were often

41 See C. Goschler and J. Lillteicher, *'Arisierung" und Restitution. Die Rückerstattung jüdischen Eigentums in Deutschland und Österreich nach 1945 und 1989,* (Göttingen: Wallstein Verlag, 2002), D. Stiefel, *Die politische Ökonomie des Holocaust. Zur wirtschaftlichen Logik von Verfolgung und Wiedergutmachung* (Vienna: Verlag für Geschichte und Politik, 2001).

42 S. zur Nieden, *Unwürdige Opfer: Die Aberkennung von NS-Verfolgten in Berlin 1945 bis 1949* (Berlin: Metropol, 2003).

43 Statement by Franz Heitges, cited in C. Goschler, *Schuld und Schulden. Die Politik der Wiedergutmachung für NS-Verfolgte seit 1945* (Göttingen: Wallstein Verlag, 2005), 85.

characterised by obvious discrimination against victims of racial persecution.[44] Similar patterns emerged in other European countries, for instance in France, where former Resistance fighters and political prisoners succeeded in securing privileged access to pensions and other benefits at the expense of Jewish victims, who often faced public contempt because they were considered 'passive victims' by many, a status associated with weakness and shame.[45] In West Germany, occupation authorities generally corrected the aforementioned prejudices and sometimes even reversed victim hierarchies established by German legislation. Gradually, victim associations and their antifascist rhetoric lost influence on reparations policy. Increasingly in the deteriorating climate of the Cold War, they were suspected of subversive activity. In the early 1950s, both German states banned the only umbrella organisation that united victims from all occupation zones.[46]

By the end of the 1940s, the achievements of compensation policy were rather discouraging. Property restitution, in contrast to monetary compensation, attracted much more attention on the part of the Western occupation authorities, each creating special procedures to return property to its rightful owners. A number of reasons explain the speedy legislation in this area. Standing in a Lockean tradition of legal thinking that stressed ownership as being at the core of human rights, property restitution appeared as the most tangible expression of an individual's restoration to the status of a full citizen. This was particularly important for the Jews who represented up to 80% of expropriation victims in Germany and suffered from the lasting impact of vicious Nazi propaganda and anti-Semitic legislation that made them second-class citizens.[47] Apart from that, property restitution promised a number of political, social and economic advantages for reconstruction policy. It came at almost no additional cost, unlike other forms of victim reparations that required public expenditure. It enabled impoverished refugees to rebuild their lives, thereby reducing the expense of caring for them in asylum countries as well as in Germany. It also restored stability to property relations and contributed to a more favourable climate for investment and economic recovery in war-damaged Germany. Finally, in the context of the ideological battles of the cold war, the commitment to private ownership by the Western powers sent a clear signal of opposition to those who called for collectivisation and nationalisation as alternative approaches to European reconstruction.[48]

---

44 C. Goschler, *Schuld und Schulden. Die Politik der Wiedergutmachung für NS-Verfolgte seit 1945* (Göttingen: Wallstein Verlag, 2005), 47-99, S. zur Nieden, *Unwürdige Opfer: Die Aberkennung von NS-Verfolgten in Berlin 1945 bis 1949* (Berlin: Metropol, 2003).

45 A. Wieviorka, *Déportation et génocide. Entre la mémoire et l'oubli* (Paris : Plon, 1992).

46 E. Reuter and D. Hansel, Das *kurze Leben der VVN von 1947 bis 1953* (Berlin: Edition Ost, 1997).

47 C. Goschler, *Schuld und Schulden. Die Politik der Wiedergutmachung für NS-Verfolgte seit 1945* (Göttingen: Wallstein Verlag, 2005), 100.

48 J. Killick, *The United States and European Reconstruction, 1945–1960* (Keele: Keele University Press, 1997).

However, property restitution raised some thorny issues. The question of so-called 'heirless assets' eventually motivated American legislators to abandon legal traditions and comply with the demands of Jewish organisations. Under normal circumstances, the inheritance of a person who had died without heirs would devolve upon the State. But since whole Jewish families had perished in the Holocaust, it was out of the question for a German successor State to become the beneficiary of the Nazi genocide. Therefore Jewish organisations lobbied occupation authorities to assign heirless assets to special agencies working for Jewish reconstruction. In all Western zones, military governments eventually introduced special procedures for the handling of heirless assets by restitution organisations.[49]

Unlike compensation measures, property restitution was innovative in addressing the consequences of Nazi destruction and extermination. The special attention paid by the Western Allies to these issues guaranteed speedy procedures, although the resolution of more complicated restitution cases often occupied courts for many years. Nevertheless, when compared to other transitional justice measures, property restitution in the West was relatively successful. In East Germany and most of Eastern Europe, however, the new authorities quickly abandoned restitution in the late 1940s, when they came increasingly under Soviet influence. The question of ownership rights, however, would resurface in the 1990s to become the catalyst for grappling with several layers of past injustice hypostasised in property relations.[50]

4.2 PERPETRATOR INTEGRATION AND VICTIM REPARATIONS IN THE EARLY FEDERAL REPUBLIC

Anticipating a German inclination to avoid obligations arising from the Nazi era, the Western Allies considered victim reparations as a precondition for German statehood. Before transferring sovereignty rights, they required a commitment by the new authorities of the West German State that they would maintain and improve existing provisions related to property restitution and compensation for other rights violations.[51] As a consequence, federal legislation of the 1950s was aimed primarily at assimilating local and regional practices. The compensation laws of 1953 and 1956

---

49 N. SAGI, 'Die Rolle der jüdischen Organisationen in den USA und die Claims Conference,' in L. HERBST and C. GOSCHLER, *Wiedergutmachung in der Bundesrepublik Deutschland* (Munich: R. Oldenbourg, 1989), 99-118.

50 C. HOREL, *La restitution des biens juifs et le renouveau juif en Europe centrale: Hongrie, Slovaquie, République Tchèque* (Frankfurt: Peter Lang, 2002) and M. DEAN, C. GOSCHLER and P. THER (eds.), *Robbery and Restitution: the Conflict over Jewish Property in Europe*, (New York – Oxford: Berghahn, 2006).

51 K. DOEHRING, B. J. FEHN and H. G. HOCKERTS, *Jahrhundertschuld – Jahrhundertsühne. Reparationen, Wiedergutmachung, Entschädigung für nationalsozialistisches Kriegs- und Verfolgungsunrecht* (Munich: Olzog Verlag, 2001), 18.

respectively provided for different categories of benefits. On the one hand, they introduced pensions for those who had suffered severe health damage or lost their breadwinner. Mostly this was modelled on the existing social security system. On the other hand, legislation provided for one-time payments for the death of close kin, detention and other severe restrictions of personal freedom rights – for example, confinement in ghettos, Jews being obligated to wear the yellow star in public, or living in hiding for years. Ideally, compensation payments should have contributed to the legal and social rehabilitation of victims. By enabling survivors to complete their education, re-establish their business and reclaim their former jobs, these payments in the best case allowed them to live a decent life without being constrained by the material consequences of the persecution they had suffered.[52]

With Allied influence in decline however, German authorities repeatedly sacrificed victims' rights in favour of other political priorities: for instance, compensation claims made by German refugees and expellees from Eastern Europe, as well as demands by war victims and veterans. Recipients of these special welfare measures often included former members of the Nazi party, beneficiaries of Nazi policies as well as perpetrators of Nazi abuse. In West Germany, legislation to promote the rehabilitation of former Nazis often preceded measures in favour of their victims.[53] Thus the early 1950s turned out to be a period of smooth reintegration of compromised elites, not only in West Germany but also in East Germany, Austria and many formerly occupied countries.[54] Under these circumstances, reparations simply appeared to amount to an unavoidable concession to prevent international outrage over conspicuous leniency towards the perpetrators.

Silence about Nazi crimes and widespread neglect of Nazi victims contrasted strikingly with omnipresent concern about German victimisation. The new authorities, for instance, established a Federal ministry for German expellees and refugees. No such institution existed for the victims of Nazi persecution.[55] Therefore, complaints by Nazi victims mostly failed to resonate with the wider German public or with the majority of lawmakers. Only a handful of actors who worked behind the scenes and were shielded from public scrutiny prevented victim reparations from sinking into oblivion.

---

52 For the most comprehensive survey of German legislation see the six volumes BUNDESMINISTERIUM DER FINANZEN (ed), *Die Wiedergutmachung nationalsozialistischen Unrechts durch die BundesrepublikDeutschland* (Munich: C. H. Beck, 1974-1987).

53 N. FREI, *Adenauer's Germany and the Nazi Past: The Politics of Amnesty and Integration* (New York: Columbia University Press, 2002), J. HERF, *Divided Memory. The Nazi Past in the Two Germanys* (Cambridge: Harvard University Press, 1997).

54 I. DEÁK, J. T. GROSS and T. JUDT (eds.), *The Politics of Retribution in Europe. World War II and its Aftermath* (Princeton: Princeton University Press, 2000).

55 R. G. MOELLER, *War Stories. The Search for a Usable Past in the Federal Republic of Germany* (Berkeley: University of California Press, 2001); See also W. BENZ, *Die Gründung der Bundesrepublik. Von der Bizone zum souveränen Staat* (München: Deutscher Taschenbuch Verlag, 1999); K. SONTHEIMER, *Die Adenauer Ära. Grundlegung der Bundesrepublik* (Munich: Deutscher Taschenbuch Verlag, 2003).

Mostly, legal improvements were achieved by a small network of German officials, individual members of parliament and a handful of victims' advocates.[56]

Beginning in the late 1950s, the political climate slowly changed, accompanied by a shift in the perception of the Holocaust. Renewed international efforts at criminal prosecution of leading Nazi perpetrators led to spectacular and highly publicised trials in the early 1960s. In 1961, for the first time in post-war history, the Eichmann trial in Jerusalem drew attention to the Holocaust as the epitome of Nazi perversity. It changed perceptions of Nazi crimes and of their perpetrators and victims as well. A few years after this, former staff of the Auschwitz camp system were tried in Frankfurt.[57] These events encouraged Germans to grapple afresh with questions of guilt and responsibility, public debates that coalesced with political efforts to extend and eventually lift statutes of limitation for the most severe Nazi crimes.[58] These developments, however, did not necessarily include public commitments to redressing the wrongs. Instead, lawmakers when passing the so-called 'Schlussgesetz', the final compensation legislation, in 1965, considered victim reparations to be a closed chapter. This was in line with a general desire to rule out remaining liabilities which originated during the Nazi era.[59] But compared to the intensified efforts to put perpetrators on trial, corresponding endeavours in the realm of victim reparations appear rather weak. This testifies to the ambiguous and sometimes paradoxical nature of policies dealing with the Nazi past during the early period of the Federal Republic.[60]

4.3 DISCOVERING THE 'SURVIVOR SYNDROME' AND THE 'FORGOTTEN VICTIMS'

During the 1980s, victim reparations underwent major revisions after a paradigm shift in medical diagnostics exposed previous expert opinions as no longer sustainable, and changing cultural values discredited earlier practices. Ground-breaking research by the American psychiatrist William G. Niederland who specialised in the treatment of Nazi victims revealed the existence of long-term consequences of persecution, which became known as the 'survivor syndrome.' This term referred to Niederland's

---

56 C. Goschler, *Wiedergutmachung. Westdeutschland und die Verfolgten des Nationalsozialismus 1945-1954* (Munich: C. H. Beck, 1992), 203ff.

57 P. Krause, *Der Eichmann-Prozess in der deutschen Presse* (Frankfurt: Campus, 2002); I. Wojak (ed.) *Auschwitz-Prozess 4 Ks 2/63 Frankfurt am Main* (Frankfurt: Fritz Bauer Institut, 2004).

58 P. Reichel, *Vergangenheitsbewältigung in Deutschland. Die Auseinandersetzung mit der NS-Diktatur von 1945 bis heute* (Munich: C. H. Beck, 2001), 158-198.

59 C. Goschler, *Schuld und Schulden. Die Politik der Wiedergutmachung für NS-Verfolgte seit 1945* (Göttingen: Wallstein Verlag, 2005), 219ff., 254-288.

60 J. Herf, *Divided Memory. The Nazi Past in the Two Germanys* (Cambridge: Harvard University Press, 1997).

observation that many of his patients who had shown no symptoms over an extended period of time, suddenly suffered deterioration in their mental or physical condition. In his eyes a direct link existed between the traumatic experiences suffered by victims of Nazi persecution and these symptoms. Though long rejected by German medical experts, Niederland's hypothesis eventually prevailed, to the relief of Nazi victims who had not been able to obtain compensation.[61]

Shifting cultural values from the late 1960s onwards also brought about a growing tolerance towards previously stigmatised groups. As the stark fault lines which characterised the early Cold War began to erode, political choices made in these years became questionable. This led to intensified public scrutiny of compensation practice. At the same time, the mass media popularised Holocaust memory in a way that sensitised the public to the suffering of the victims.[62] Growing public sympathy with the victims also arose out of generational conflicts, with younger people accusing their parents of denying the Nazi past. Against this backdrop, scandals during the 1980s exposed shortfalls and prejudices inherent in compensation practice. Hearings before parliamentary commissions eventually corroborated allegations of post-war discrimination against Roma and Sinti, homosexuals, and various other victim groups, who had not been previously recognised as victims of Nazi persecution.[63] This altered public opinion of victim reparations eventually led to some legal changes, although these were belated and half-hearted. But this new view of victim reparations impacted historiography and inspired investigations into the various dimensions of Nazi racial policies, even more so since this was a period of heated debates over the significance of the Nazi period, and in particular the Holocaust, in German history.[64]

---

61 W. Focke, *William G. Niederland. Psychiater der Verfolgten* (Würzburg: Königshausen und Neumann, 1992); W. G. Niederland, 'Die verkannten Opfer. Späte Entschädigung für seelische Schäden,' L. Herbst and C. Goschler, *Wiedergutmachung in der Bundesrepublik Deutschland* (Munich: Oldenbourg Verlag, 1989), 351-360; on the role of medical experts see also C. Pross, *Paying for the Past. The Struggle over Reparations for Surviving Victims of the Nazi Terror* (Baltimore: Johns Hopkins University Press, 1998).

62 A. Assmann and U. Frevert, *Geschichtsvergessenheit – Geschichtsversessenheit. Vom Umgang mit deutschen Vergangenheiten nach 1945* (Stuttgart: Deutsche Verlagsanstalt, 1999), 266-271

63 See C. Pross, *Paying for the Past. The Struggle over Reparations for Surviving Victims of the Nazi Terror* (Baltimore: Johns Hopkins University Press, 1998); W. Benz, 'Homosexuelle und 'Gemeinschaftsfremde". Zur Diskriminierung von Opfergruppen nach der nationalsozialistischen Verfolgung,' (1998) 14 *Dachauer Hefte*, 3-16, G. Margalit, 'The Representation of the Nazi Persecution of the Gypsies in German Discourse after 1945,' (1999) 17:2 *German History* , 221-240; S. Milton, 'Persecuting the Survivors: The Continuity of 'Anti-Gypsyism" in Post-War Germany and Austria,' in S. Tebbutt (ed.), *Sinti and Roma: Gypsies in German-Speaking Society and Literature* (Oxford: Berghahn Books, 1998), 35-48; A. Pretzel (ed.), *NS-Opfer unter Vorbehalt. Homosexuelle Männer in Berlin nach 1945* (Münster – Hamburg – London: LIT Verlag, 2002).

64 C. S. Maier, *The Unmasterable Past: History, Holocaust and German National Identity* (Cambridge: Harvard University Press, 1988).

4.4 HOLOCAUST RESTITUTION CAMPAIGNS AFTER THE COLLAPSE OF COMMUNISM

It took the restitution campaigns of the 1990s to finally address many long suppressed and neglected issues. One of them was the role of big business under the Nazi regime. Major German and international corporations had been involved in and benefited from the organised robbery of the Nazi period, and the exploitation of forced labour. When sued by former slave labourers in the 1950s and 1960s, these corporations denied liability by pretending that they had acted under constraint by Nazi authorities. Historical evidence, however, reveals that this was not the case. Instead, companies competed for the allocation of slave labourers. For a long time, the London Debt Agreement of 1953 provided another line of defence. During the 1950s and 60s German courts consistently referred to this document to immunise the corporate world against victims' claims. Thus former slave labourers generally missed out on compensation payments.[65]

Then Swiss banks became the target of Holocaust restitution campaigns in the mid-1990s. Victim organisations accused the banks of obstructing restitution, denying the existence of heirless assets in their vaults and thwarting survivors' attempts to reclaim their property. Having appeared detached from such allegations for most of the Cold War era, Swiss banks suddenly became a symbol of companies which had profiteered from the Holocaust. This impression was reinforced by their initial refusal to face up to their past. But with changing international circumstances and intensified global competition, they could no longer hide behind Swiss neutrality and special banking legislation. When Holocaust survivors sued major Swiss banks in American courts and launched a well-orchestrated media campaign, not only Switzerland's banking industry but the whole nation slid into a deep crisis, which soon affected other European countries. In the course of these events, former slave labourers took their cue and filed class-action lawsuits against major German corporations.[66] Victim organisations conducted the litigation together with a highly effective media campaign. This exposed the affected corporations to possible boycott and the risk of permanent damage to their reputations. Under these circumstances, most corporations eventually decided to settle with the plaintiffs. In 1998, Swiss banks agreed to pay $1.25 billion for unreturned assets. In 2000, the German parliament passed legislation to establish a foundation called 'Remembrance, Responsibility and the Future', with an endowment of 5.11 billion Euros, half of which amount was provided by the German

65 K. R. GROSSMANN, *Die Ehrenschuld. Kurzgeschichte der Wiedergutmachung* (Frankfurt – Berlin: Ullstein, 1967), 93 ff..

66 J. AUTHERS and R. WOLFFE, *The Victim's Fortune. Inside the Epic Battle over the Debts of the Holocaust* (New York: Harper Collins, 2002).

government, and half of which was to be raised among German corporations. This money was dedicated to the compensation of former forced labourers.[67]

These events left a lasting imprint. Reparations movements all over the world modelled their claims on the successful strategies followed during the Holocaust litigation, with its combination of class-action suits in US courts and international media campaigns.[68] The 'naming and shaming' strategy of survivors proved highly effective, as it obligated powerful corporations and States to negotiate and re-evaluate their history.[69] However, more recent Holocaust-era litigation, benefiting from a unique opportunity in the 1990s, appears to be more of an exception than the rule in the long and protracted history of reparations for Nazi victims. On the one hand, this history can be read as one of progressive growth, of a gradual increase in compensation payments and an extension of the circle of recipients. By itself, however, this conclusion is misleading. The image of a linear development is just one side of the story, while the other side is one of denial and deliberate obstruction by lawmakers and those responsible for the implementation of victim reparations. This dark side of reparations practice came to the fore during the debates of the 1990s when survivors testified time and again of demoralisation and frustration in their efforts to get redress. This draws attention to a final dimension of victim reparations that requires discussion: the fact that legislation and its enforcement inevitably create distinctions that reflect power relations.

5 THE DIALECTICS OF VICTIMHOOD: DEFINITIONS, VICTIM HIERARCHIES AND MECHANISMS OF EXCLUSION

The definition of Nazi victims has been exposed over the years to changing interpretations of Nazism and its criminal nature. Reparations practice, in turn, consolidated existing ideas of Nazi crimes and helped draw the line between tolerable and illicit forms of repression. The resulting construction of victimhood and its recognition shaped normative ideas of the victim, which, in turn, moulded legal terms and their

---

67 S. Spiliotis, *Verantwortung und Rechtsfrieden: die Stiftung der deutschen Wirtschaft* (Frankfurt: Fischer, 2003); G. Saathoff, 'Entschädigung für Zwangsarbeiter? Entstehung und Leistungen der Bundesstiftung' Erinnerung, Verantwortung und Zukunft im Kontext der Debatte um die "vergessenen Oper",' in H. G. Hockerts and C. Kuller (eds.), *Nach der Verfolgung. Wiedergutmachung nationalsozialistischen Unrechts in Deutschland* (Göttingen: Wallstein, 2003), 241-273. Also: C. Thonke, *Hitlers langer Schatten. Der mühevolle Weg zur Entschädigung der NS-Opfer* (Vienna: Böhlau, 2004).

68 M. J. Bazyler, *Holocaust Justice. The Battle for Restitution in America's Courts* (New York, London: New York University Press, 2003), 307-334.

69 S. E. Eizenstat, *Imperfect Justice. Looted Assets, Slave Labor, and the Unfinished Business of World War II* (New York, Public Affairs, 2003).

interpretation in practice. By mutually reinforcing each other, these developments produced a dialectic of integration and exclusion. Compensation practice created new realities: The event of recognition as a victim or denial of that status decided the life chances of an individual. Officially recognised victimhood attested to a person's undeserved victimisation, while denial conversely implied that the affliction suffered had been due to a legitimate act of crime prevention, for instance, or justified by the exigencies of war. In other words, denial conveyed a message to a claimant that she had brought the affliction upon herself and, consequently, deserved it. The post-war history of communists who had been victimised by the Nazis illustrates this process. Immediately after the Second World War, these victims often belonged to political prisoner associations which were successful in securing a high position in the victim hierarchy for their members. In 1956, however, the FRG banned the communist party. The German Constitutional Court followed suit. It confirmed a tendency among compensation agencies to reject claims by communist victims of Nazi persecution. Following this decision, these victims lost their entitlement to redress, even for claims relating to torture and detention in concentration camps. The judgment of the Constitutional Court was based on a legal clause stating that claimants who opposed the existing political order forfeited their right to reparations, a provision meant to exclude former Nazis from special benefits dedicated to the victims. But under Cold War conditions, and growing anti-communism in the West, this provision became the trap for a group of survivors which had been among the first to suffer severe abuses at the hands of the Nazis.[70]

The exclusion of communists not only implied that they had provoked and therefore deserved repression, but at the same time also conferred legitimacy on a specific category of Nazi human rights violations. Such decisions defined the scope of defensible Nazi acts and also the circumstances under which State authorities in general were justified in restricting a person's fundamental rights. Often, they merely echoed existing prejudice against marginalised social groups. In so doing, they conveyed the impression that human rights were conditional, in particular for those who suffered from stigmatisation and enjoyed little public esteem – Roma and Sinti, the homeless, beggars, alcoholics, prostitutes, homosexuals, and the mentally ill, all had little chance of success in their claims for compensation.[71]

In sum, the category of legally recognised victims barely overlapped with the social group of those who had actually suffered persecution by the Nazis. Discriminatory practices had various origins. Some reflected entrenched prejudice among compensa-

---

[70] G. Jaspers, 'Die disqualifizierten Opfer. Der Kalte Krieg und die Entschädigung für Kommunisten,' L. Herbst and C. Goschler (eds.), *Wiedergutmachung in der Bundesrepublik Deutschland* (Munich: Oldenbourg Verlag, 1989), 361-384.

[71] C. Reimesch, *Vergessene Opfer des Nationalsozialismus? Zur Entschädigung von Homosexuellen, Kriegsdienstverweigerern, Sinti und Roma und Kommunisten in der Bundesrepublik Deutschland* (Berlin: Verlag für Wissenschaft und Kultur, 2003).

tion agencies and their staff, others resulted from competition over limited funding and the varying degrees of influence specific victim groups were able to mobilise or a combination of all three factors. But even the legal definition of a Nazi victim was exclusive. From the very beginning, it did not cover all acts of Nazi persecution. Instead it limited entitlement to redress to those who were victimised for *political* and *racial* reasons or for their *religion* or *world-view*. This definition – which would become the standard, the canonical formula, throughout German legislation – first appeared in Allied documents around 1943, placing its main emphasis on the rationale and motives of Nazi persecution rather than the plain fact of a human rights violation. Early on, authors complained about its limits. Some German lawmakers, for instance, included nationality as an additional reason for persecution which should fall within the definition.[72] But federal authorities feared that this would open the floodgates and obligate the German State to offer compensation to all foreign nationals victimised by the Nazis. Thus the courts consistently rejected claims by foreigners (apart from some very narrowly defined exceptions depending on the claimants' residency) and they even argued that foreign resistance fighters and political opponents of the Nazi regime had acted only for patriotic (in other words non-political) motives, meaning that their claims could be dismissed.[73]

Unlike many other countries, where special commissions consisting of victims' representatives and State officials decided claims, German legislation assigned the allocation of compensation payments to State agencies – many of which employed officials who had started their careers under the Nazi regime. Thus compensation procedures became a highly ambiguous if not frustrating experience for the claimants. Even if victims found recognition they were still required to undergo embarrassing examinations, overcome many obstacles in order to provide evidence, and withstand emotionally stressful questioning that reminded them of previous encounters with the Nazi State apparatus. It was even possible for victims to face the same officials and experts who had been involved in their persecution.[74]

Political circumstances further limited the beneficial effects of redress. Funds were limited in the early years of the FRG, and competition over scarce resources raged among different victim groups – including the German refugees from the East, veterans and war victims with their powerful pressure groups and important constituencies.

---

72 C. GOSCHLER, *Schuld und Schulden. Die Politik der Wiedergutmachung für NS-Verfolgte seit 1945* (Göttingen: Wallstein Verlag, 2005), 48. For a comprehensive collection of early German legislation on victim reparations see U.S. Holocaust Memorial Museum Archives, RG 67.005 M (The World Jewish Congress New York Office Records. Series C, Box C251, file 4).

73 C. PAWLITA, 'Der Beitrag der Rechtssprechung zur Entschädigung von NS-Unrecht und der Begriff der politischen Verfolgung,' in H. G. HOCKERTS and C. KULLERS (eds.) *Nach der Verfolgung. Wiedergutmachung nationalsozialistischen Unrechts in Deutschland* (Göttingen: Wallstein Verlag, 2003), 79-101.

74 C. PROSS, *Paying for the Past. The Struggle over Reparations for Surviving Victims of the Nazi Terror* (Baltimore: Johns Hopkins University Press, 1998).

Often, the ensuing rhetoric exposed survivors to public hostility and entrenched prejudice.[75] Rivalries also occurred between different categories of Nazi victims trying to monopolise the moral authority associated with recognised victimhood and exclude from recognition all those they declared to be morally unfit. The selection criteria used to decide whether or not a particular group should be recognised as victims often testified to the lasting impact of Nazi propaganda, even on its opponents.[76] In short, those who would later become the 'forgotten victims' did not simply fade into oblivion; their exclusion was the result of deliberate political choices.[77]

In sum, decisions about integration or exclusion had different origins, some resulting from political constraints or preferences, others having their roots in the activity of victim groups or efforts at constructing specific memories of the past. This was not a German particularity but may be observed in other European countries. Almost everywhere competition over scarce financial resources turned recognised victimhood into a desired good, and resulted in victims' striving for the restrictive allocation of this desirable status. In a very specific way this struggle linked the welfare benefits with the symbolic dimensions of reparations. This process promoted the emergence of victim hierarchies following active-passive dichotomies, and involved judgments as to what was appropriate conduct in the face of Nazi oppression and brutality.[78] Such hierarchies have been reversed fundamentally since their original construction. More and more, ideal victimhood is being identified with undeserved affliction, which means that children are regarded as the paradigmatic victims, in contrast to the earlier, masculinised and militant ideal of survivors of Nazi persecution. In more recent debates, Jews who suffered only for being Jews, have come to replace the political victims and resistance fighters as epitomising the Nazi victim. As demonstrated above, the practice and outcome of German victim reparations were determined by many factors unrelated to the actual purpose of redress.

---

75 L. WIEGAND, 'Kriegsfolgengesetzgebung in der Bundesrepublik Deutschland,' (1995) 35 *Archiv für Sozialgeschichte*, 71-90; R. G. MOELLER, *War Stories. The Search for a Usable Past in the Federal Republic of Germany* (Berkeley: University of California Press, 2001); referring to similar conflicts in Western Europe: P. LAGROU, *The Legacy of Nazi Occupation. Patriotic Memory and National Recovery in Western Europe, 1945-1965* (Cambridge: Cambridge University Press, 2000).

76 C. REIMESCH, *Vergessene Opfer des Nationalsozialismus? Zur Entschädigung von Homosexuellen, Kriegsdienstverweigerern, Sinti und Roma und Kommunisten in der Bundesrepublik Deutschland* (Berlin: Verlag für Wissenschaft und Kultur, 2003).

77 S. ZUR NIEDEN, *Unwürdige Opfer. Die Aberkennung von NS-Verfolgten in Berlin 1945 bis 1949* (Berlin: Metropol, 2003).

78 A. WIEVIORKA, *Déportation et Génocide. Entre la Mémoire et l'oubli* (Paris: Plon, 1992).

6 CONCLUSION: WHAT DID HOLOCAUST REPARATIONS ACHIEVE?

Did Holocaust reparations accomplish the goal of redress? Did they endorse State responsibility? Did they achieve social rehabilitation of the victims? Finally, did they restore victims to their status of full citizens and liberate them from the repercussions of vicious propaganda and racial persecution?

Reparations cannot undo abuses, cannot wake the dead or reverse traumatising experience. Even in the best of all worlds they remain severely limited in comparison to the injuries caused by gross human rights violations. Even with these reservations in mind, the conclusions about Holocaust reparations are ambivalent.

First, West Germany did recognise political responsibility, most explicitly in the Luxembourg Agreement. It did so in contrast to the other two successor States of the Third Reich. But in reality German endorsement of obligations towards the victims was often dictated by political circumstances and opportunistic motives. Consequently a large number of Nazi victims, mostly for reasons of their nationality, never, or only at a very late date, received compensation payments. Germany also expressed State responsibility by using public funds for reparations payments. This signalled that the German society as a whole bore some degree of responsibility for the legacies of the Nazi era. Various other models for financing compensation payments had been under discussion directly after the Second World War: for instance, using heirless assets, denazification fees, or imposing special taxes on former members of the Nazi party for reparations purposes were proposed. All of these alternatives were discarded – using heirless assets because it was hardly justifiable that reparations should be paid from Jewish wealth instead of German contributions, and special taxes because they were seen as a political hazard that would alienate a large portion of the German population from the new political order. Nevertheless, some of the most ardent advocates of victim reparations complained that general taxes would also punish those who opposed the Nazi regime, and thereby blur individual and collective responsibility. Moreover, they argued that equity required that those who had benefited from the Nazi regime should return some of the wealth they had acquired unjustly.[79] The problem of responsibility obviously was not an easy one to solve, and no conclusive answer could be found.

Secondly, compensation payments actually contributed to the social rehabilitation of the victims by alleviating their situation. Compensation legislation covered many different forms of damage resulting from persecution. It followed the principles of social security since it was meant to relieve Nazi victims of the humiliating conse-

79 See on these debates H.-D. KREIKAMP, 'Zur Entstehung des Entschädigungsgesetzes der amerikanischen Besatzungszone, in Wiedergutmachung in der Bundesrepublik Deutschland,' in L. HERBST and C. GOSCHLER (eds.), *Wiedergutmachung in der Bundesrepublik Deutschland* (Munich: Oldenbourg Verlag, 1989).

quences of having to apply for public assistance. As a result, compensation enabled many to rebuild their lives, complete the education they missed, or receive pensions if they suffered from permanent disabilities. But all this applied only to those who found recognition for their claims. For those who were left out in the cold, it possibly even aggravated their situation. Once their claims were rejected, they could no longer blame their misery on Nazi injustice. In this respect, compensation practice produced social distinctions between those who were granted the moral capital of recognised victimhood, and those who were denied it, in the initially amorphous group of persecution victims.

Thirdly, moral restoration was closely linked to social rehabilitation, since the latter relied on official recognition of victimhood. Its denial, in contrast, made universal human rights appear conditional. This had a lasting impact on the culture of human rights.

The historical example of redress for the Holocaust and other Nazi atrocities shows that individual victim reparations were fraught with many pitfalls and resulted in unintended, often paradoxical outcomes. Furthermore, it needs to be assessed in the wider context of transitional policies which have impacted victim reparations from the very beginning. Considering the uniqueness of the historical events to which these policies of redress have responded and the specific historical circumstances of their emergence, Holocaust reparations serve as a poor example for future reparations campaigns, other than to warn of the dilemmas and difficult decisions attached to the almost impossible project of redressing past wrongs.

PART B: REPARATIONS AND INTERNATIONAL LAW

REPARATIONS AND INTERNATIONAL LAW: HOW ARE REPARATIONS TO BE DETERMINED (PAST WRONG OR CURRENT EFFECTS), AGAINST WHOM, AND WHAT FORM SHOULD THEY TAKE?

MAX DU PLESSIS*

1 INTRODUCTION

Around two centuries ago the anti-slavery movement of the 19th century campaigned to abolish the slave trade that had become a part of 'civilised' European and American life.[1] While the anti-slavers and their movement achieved victory in their campaign to outlaw slavery and the trade, a new campaign is currently underway. That crusade – driven by a group that I shall term 'reparationists' – is for compensatory justice for the acts of slavery committed in previous centuries.[2] The stakes in this crusade are high, and the issues are controversial.[3]

---

* *This chapter draws extensively from an article written by the same author and published as "Reparations and International Law: How are Reparations to be Determined (Past Wrong or Current Effects), Against Whom, and What Form Should They Take?" The Windsor Yearbook of Access to Justice, 2003, 4 pp 41-69* and before that, "Historical Injustice and International Law: An Exploratory Discussion of Reparation for Slavery" (2003) 25 (3) Hum. Rts. Q. 625.

1 See in general Louis Henkin "International Law: Politics, Values and Functions" 216 *Collected Courses of Hague Academy of International Law* 13 (vol. IV, 1989) at 208, cited in Henry Steiner and Philip Alston, *International Human Rights in Context: Law, Politics, Morals* (2nd Ed) (2000) at 127.

2 As an example of the campaigning, see the website of the Africa Reparations Movement at http://www.arm.arc.ac.uk. For an example of collected material and relevant web links see the Social Science Information Gateway hosted by the British Library of Political and Economic Science, London School of Economics, at http://www.sosig.ac.uk/roads/subject-listing/World/slavery.html.

3 The recent events in Durban at the United Nations World Conference against Racism, Discrimination, Xenophobia and Related Intolerance, to which South Africa played host in 2001, illustrate the level and intensity of debate. One of the most divisive issues at the Durban Conference, an issue which threatened at first to prevent the Conference from taking place, and then nearly derailed the Conference once it got underway, is that of reparation for slavery. The United States, for instance, insisted that it would not attend the Conference if the agenda included the item of reparation for

This chapter discusses reparation for slavery[4] as a vehicle for broader discussion about reparation claims for past injustices. The perspective is that of an international lawyer. In the context of slavery reparation, as is the case with many other contexts involving reparation claims for mass atrocities, international law principles are engaged and often expressly relied upon. As we shall see in the slavery context, for instance, African States are claiming reparation against Western States, and are casting their claims in the language of international law – State responsibility, crimes against humanity, genocide – and calling for reparation in the form of restitution, compensation, and/or satisfaction, terms that are reflected in the international law rules on State responsibility.[5]

---

slavery. See Duncan Campbell "America may boycott racism summit", *The Guardian*, July 28 2001, available at www.guardian.co.uk/unracism/story/0,1099,541530,00.html. The US eventually capitulated and chose to attend, but then, along with Israel, walked out of the Conference over the issue of Israel's treatment of the Palestinians. After their walk out, talks between African and European Union countries on the subject of slavery and reparations moved higher up on the Conference agenda. However, these talks soon ran into deep difficulties after African nations hardened their position with the result that European diplomats at the Conference expressed doubts about whether an agreement could be reached on the topic. See *BBC News*, "Conference split on slavery issue", Wednesday, 5 September 2001, available at http://.bbc.co.uk/hi/English/world.africa/newsid_1526000/1526511.stm.

Hereinafter the Conference will be referred to as the "Durban Conference". The text of the Declaration that emanated from the Conference is available at http://www.un.org/WCAR/, and will hereinafter be referred to as "the Durban Declaration".

4 Claims made by reparationists are loosely referred to as claims for reparation for "slavery" but it is clear that reparationists are using that expression to refer to an umbrella concept which encompasses the policy of slave-trading, acts committed during the execution of that policy (such as the horrors of the Middle Passage), the continuing deprivation of liberty and treatment of slaves after arrival in the West, and the effects of slavery on succeeding generations in the form of social and economic inequality. For ease of reference I will be referring to reparation for "slavery" and the "slave trade" interchangeably in this paper.

5 Some short disclaimers before I begin. The issue of reparation for slavery is at once overwhelming and complex. It is overwhelming because of the scale on which slavery was practised. During the Atlantic slave trade period alone (1440 – 1870), it is estimated that at least 13 million Africans were illegally transported from the shores of West Africa to the Western Hemisphere. Of those thirteen million, only an approximate number of 11,328,000 were delivered to the New World, with the result that around 1,672,000 persons died en route (See Hugh Thomas, *The Slave Trade: The Story of the Atlantic Slave Trade, 1440-1870* (1997) 804-805). It is complex because of the number of different scenarios in which claims could ostensibly arise in the African context. Africa, for instance, has experienced a triple heritage of slavery – indigenous, Islamic and Western, giving rise to the possibility of multifarious inter-state claims (see Ali Mazrui "Global Africa: From abolitionists to reparationists" (1994) 37 (3) *Africa Studies Review* 1 at 1).

As a result, rather than attempting a comprehensive trawl of all the historical scenarios that might found reparation claims, my aim here is somewhat more modest. My focus is limited to those claims for reparation which arise out of the Atlantic slave trade, a historical period which spans some four centuries from 1440-1870. And, as I have said, my concern is the call for reparation made by Africa against those Western states that historically perpetrated acts of slavery.

This is one of the main contexts in which the issue of reparation for slavery was debated at the UN World Conference in Durban and accordingly attracts my attention. Aside from the international context, various domestic claims by nationals of States against their governments for participation

Although I express my doubts about the viability of a claim for reparation for slavery from within the current international law paradigm of State responsibility, a brief discussion of the international law on responsibility remains relevant. The paradigm provides the frame of reference for any slavery reparation claim, and indeed, the forms of reparation that exist in the legal paradigm are the forms of retributive and compensatory justice which reparationists argue for when pursuing their claims. Because of the weaknesses identified in respect of legal claims for slavery reparation, as an alternative I have considered ways in which political strategies might be employed to achieve reparation. In so doing, I have considered the difficulties that face slavery reparationists in their attempts to secure reparation (in its various forms). While there are no firm answers, the suggestion here is that the topic of reparations requires creative and strategic thinking. And in discussing the various problems attendant to reparation for slavery, I hope to have given some idea of the complexities involved in answering the questions facing those that claim reparations for past gross human rights abuses – how reparations might be determined, against whom, and what form they should take.

---

in slavery can likewise be envisaged. A good example of such a claim is that of the African-Americans who claim reparation for slavery from the United States government. Similar claims can be envisaged by Africans against their governments/rulers for slavery perpetrated against them by predecessor governments/rulers. As a South African, for instance, I am aware that calls for reparation for slavery might be made by South African slave descendants against the South African government for the slavery that was practised there during the early years of the nation's existence (for an historical account of slavery practised within South Africa, see the Reader's Digest, *Illustrated History of South Africa*,(3rd Edition) (1994) 48-53; Paul Lovemore, *Transformations in Slavery: A History of Slavery in Africa*, (1983) 232-234); and Frank Welsh, *A History of South Africa*, (revised Edition) (2000) 59-61. However, I am not concerned here with such domestic claims directly except in so far as they provide examples and guidance for a discussion of international claims for reparation on behalf of Africa as against the West.

One last point. There is a measure of definitional generalisation in the paper. Reparationists loosely use the term "the West" to denote a collective of largely developed entities that as colonial powers involved themselves in slavery. But it should be immediately apparent that not all "Western" entities were guilty of slavery. Some powers in the West did not partake in the activity and the measure of guilt between those that did is by no means uniform; likewise, not all African regions were subjected to slavery, and some lost more than others to the trade (for a detailed work setting out facts and figures as regards participation in the slave trade and data as to slave exports per African region, see Lovemore (above) chapter 3). I do not even begin to consider the fact that some African groups during the Atlantic slave trade period assisted the Westerners in procuring fellow Africans for slavery. In this regard, see Lovemore *ibid.* 66-87.

The practice of slavery, which stretches back so far into the past, implicates so many groups of people, and touched the lives of so many millions, defies neat definitions and descriptions for those interested in pursuing reparation. My ultimate concern is to investigate the feasibility of claims for reparation made by one group (African) against another (the West). To do so in a workable fashion, I have, along with reparationists, been forced to resort to labels.

2 REPARATION FOR SLAVERY

2.1 CALLS FOR REPARATION FOR SLAVERY AND INTERNATIONAL LAW

The strength of the moral argument for reparation for slavery appears to be unassailable. Historical evidence confirms – as delegates at the Durban Conference put it – that 'slavery and the slave trade, including the transatlantic slave trade, were appalling tragedies in the history of humanity not only because of their abhorrent barbarism but also in terms of their magnitude, organized nature and especially their negation of the essence of the victims, and … that slavery and the slave trade are a crime against humanity and should always have been so, especially the transatlantic slave trade'.[6]

This section focuses on the argument of reparationists who suggest that there is a *legal* channel which must be pursued in order to achieve reparation for slavery. Various legal routes to reparation are envisaged by reparationists. In the domestic context, for instance, African Americans have brought actions against surviving businesses within the United States that profited from slavery.[7] At the international level, claims are envisaged by States (or international organisations on their behalf) against other States for their practice or endorsement of slavery during the Atlantic slave trade.[8] The latter is of primary interest to me in this paper, given that the call by Africa for reparation from the West is situated at the international level. This context, involving claims of guilt being levelled at States, ostensibly triggers issues of State responsibility in international law.

---

6 See Article 13 of the Durban Declaration. See too Tuneen Chisolm who, in the African American context, describes the Atlantic slave trade as follows: "The enslavement of Africans in America from 1619 to 1865 is one of the most callous, vexatious, near-genocidal violations of human rights in world history". (Tuneen Chisolm "Sweep Around Your Own Front Door: Examining the Argument for Legislative African American Reparations" (1999) 147 *University of Pennsylvania LR* 677 678).

7 See for instance, the recent class-action lawsuits filed against US companies that benefited from the slave trade. In March 2002 Aetna Inc., CSX Corp. and FleetBoston Financial Corp. were named in a lawsuit filed in the Brooklyn Federal Court on behalf of a black activist. In May a second lawsuit was filed in federal court in Newark, N.J., on behalf of a former director of the National Association for the Advancement of Colored People, against New York Life Insurance Co., Wall Street investment firm Brown Brothers Harriman & Co. and Norfolk Southern Corp. (Deborah Kong, "2nd Lawsuit filed asking reparations", *The Washington Times*, 2 May 2002, www.washtimes.com). See also the chapters in this book by Roy Brooks and Diane Sammons which deal with reparations claims by African-Americans for slavery.

8 Lord Anthony Gifford, for instance, a leading advocate of reparation for slavery, writes that the enslavement of Africans was a crime against humanity such that reparation, a concept which "is firmly established and actively pursued by states, on behalf of their injured nationals, against other wrongdoing states", is due under international law principles. See Gifford, "The Legal Basis of the Claim for Reparations", (1993), p. 6, available at www.arm.arc.co.uk/legalBasis.html, hereinafter referred to as Gifford "Legal Basis".

International responsibility is commonly considered in relation to States which are viewed as the normal subjects of international law.[9] Responsibility today is regarded as a general principle of international law and has formed the basis of an extensive study, lasting nearly 40 years, by the International Law Commission (ILC). Under the guidance of Professor James Crawford, the project has come to a close in the adoption by the ILC of its Articles on State Responsibility (2001).[10] Generally speaking, the principle of responsibility is a natural concomitant of the substantive rules of international law, and the law of responsibility is concerned with the happenings and consequences of illegal acts and the reparation which such illegal acts entail. As the Permanent Court of International Justice famously noted in the *Chorzow Factory (Jurisdiction) Case*: 'It is a principle of international law that the breach of an engagement involves an obligation to make reparation in an adequate form.'[11]

Reparationists worldwide intuitively cleave to this idea of responsibility in their drive for slavery reparation and, as we shall see later, many of the forms of reparation for which they argue mirror those which are found in the international area of State-State responsibility.[12]

2.2 INTERNATIONAL LAW AND THE SOBERING DOCTRINE OF INTER-TEMPORAL LAW

Assume that African States (loosely defined) intend to claim reparations from Western States (loosely defined) for the centuries of slavery and slave trading perpetrated against the people of Africa.[13] And assume that they are attempting to bring the claim on the basis of international law principles of State responsibility; that is, that certain Western governments remain responsible for the acts committed by their predecessors against African people.

---

9 Brownlie *Principles of Public International Law* (1982) 3rd Ed. 431.

10 See James Crawford, *The International Law Commission's Articles on State Responsibility: Introduction, Text and Commentaries*, (2002).

11 *Case concerning the Factory at Chorzow*, (1927) PCIJ Series A No 9, 21

12 See for instance, Gifford, "Legal Basis" op cit at 6 where he cites the *Chorzow Factory Case* and employs its description of reparation (as encompassing restitution and compensation) as relevant to his argument for slavery reparation.

13 The example is not unduly hypothetical. The African call for reparation in the past few years has been made by the OAU (now the AU) on behalf of African States. This strategy reflects a suggestion, made by Lord Anthony Gifford at the First Pan African Conference on Reparations, that "some form of appropriate, representative and trustworthy body" be identified that can process the claim on behalf of "all Africans, on the continent of Africa ... who suffer the consequences of the crime of mass kidnap and enslavement". As regards the defendants, Gifford suggests that the claim should be brought against the governments of those countries that promoted and were enriched by the African slave trade and the institution of slavery. See Gifford "Legal Basis" op cit at 4.

Leaving aside for the moment the problems associated with the immensity of such a claim,[14] the most striking hurdle facing reparationists is one that prefigures any practical difficulties associated with its enforcement. In the language of State responsibility, reparationists face the task of proving that present-day Western States are 'responsible' for the slavery practised during the Atlantic slave trade. Any attempt to pin responsibility on today's governments for the slavery committed by their predecessors runs into obvious difficulties involving complex questions of State succession, continuity and identity.[15] Perhaps more fundamentally, reparationists face the hurdle of showing that the conduct complained of was unlawful at the time it was committed. It is here that we need to pause and consider the ILC Articles on State Responsibility (2001).

In Chapter II of the Articles[16] the International Law Commission stipulates that one of the essential conditions for the international responsibility of a State is that the conduct in question is attributable to the State under international law. The general rule is that the only conduct attributable to the State at an international level is that of its organs of government, or of others who have acted under the direction, instigation or control of those organs. Without more, this general rule would serve to catch the conduct of all nations who through their agencies involved themselves in the slave trade, making such conduct attributable to the nation in question. However, such attribution is only the first step in the process of imputing international responsibility. As a normative question, attribution must be clearly distinguished from the characterisation of conduct as internationally wrongful.[17] In order to establish whether such conduct amounts to a breach of an international obligation of the State concerned one is obliged to consider the general conditions of State responsibility set out in Chapter III of the Articles. And it is at this point that reparationists have to confront the sobering doctrine of inter-temporal law. Article 13 of Chapter III provides as follows:

> "An act of a State does not constitute a breach of an international obligation unless the State is bound by the obligation in question at the time the act occurs."

---

[14] Lord Gifford himself concedes that "hundreds of millions of people, in different continents of the world, have an interest in this claim. Their losses seem almost impossible to quantify." (*Ibid.*).

[15] Many of the Western States singled out for reparation claims are a mere shadow of their former colonial selves. In any event, the dominant theory of rights would frustrate claims being brought against existing States for conduct committed by predecessor governments and over which they had no control. See the discussion further below.

[16] The Articles deal with responsibility in a logical sequence, starting with a definition in Chapter I of the basic principles of responsibility, and moving on in Chapter II to define the conditions under which conduct is attributable to the State. Chapter III spells out in general terms the conditions under which such conduct amounts to a breach of an international obligation of the State concerned.

[17] See the Commentary to ILC Articles (2001), Chapter II, Attribution of Conduct to a State, in Crawford op cit at 92.

Article 13 states the basic principle that, for international responsibility to exist, the breach must take place at a time when the State is bound by the obligation, and is a guarantee for States against the retrospective application of international law in matters of State responsibility.[18] International human rights law adopts the same view.[19] Moreover, an examination of international practice and jurisprudence shows that this principle has hitherto been constantly applied, being either explicitly mentioned or implicitly followed.[20]

It is therefore clear that the lawfulness or wrongfulness of an act in international law must be established on the basis of obligations in force at the time when the act was performed.

---

18 The most common use of this doctrine is in relation to the question of title to territory. Many States acquired title to territory through conquest which was an accepted method of acquiring territory until after World War I. The inter-temporal law doctrine insists that these titles are to be judged by the law in force at the time the title was first asserted and not by the law of today. As stated by Judge Huber in the *Island of Palmas* case:
"A juridical fact must be appreciated in the light of the law contemporary with it, and not the law in force at the time when a dispute in regard to it arises or falls to be settled." (United Nations, Reports of International Arbitral Awards, vol. II, 829 (1949) at 845).
See in general Rosalyn Higgins, "Time and the Law: International Perspectives on an Old Problem", (1997), 46, *ICLQ* 501.

19 See Article 11(2), of the Universal Declaration of Human Rights (1948); Article 7(1), of the European Convention for the Protection of Human Rights and Fundamental Freedoms (1950); and Article 15(1), of the International Covenant on Civil and Political Rights (1966). All three Conventions provide that "No one shall be held guilty of any penal offence on account of any act or omission which did not constitute a penal offence, under national or international law, at the time when it was committed."

20 The European Commission of Human Rights provides a clear statement on the subject in its decision on application 1151/61. A Belgian national, relying on article 5(5) of the European Convention on Human Rights, claimed compensation from the German Government for the damage caused him by the detention and death of his father in a German concentration camp in 1945. The Commission rejected his claim, pointing out that:
"While it is true that article 5, paragraph 5, of the Convention, relied on by the applicant, provides that "Everyone who has been the victim of arrest or detention in contravention of the provisions of this Article shall have an enforceable right to compensation", the Commission has nevertheless found, on a number of occasions, that only a deprivation of liberty subsequent to the entry into force of the Convention for the respondent State can be effected "in contravention of" the aforesaid article 5 ...; and that the arrest and detention of the applicant's father, however blameworthy they may have been from the standpoint of morality and fairness, took place at a time when the Convention did not yet exist and to which the Contracting States have not made it retroactively applicable". (Council of Europe, European Commission of Human Rights Recueil des décisions de la Commission européenne des droits de l'homme (Strasbourg) No. 7 (March 1962) at 119 (translation by the United Nations Secretariat).

What then of slavery and slave-trading?[21] It appears clear that those who argue for reparation will be met with the refrain that these practices were not outlawed in international law during the period of the Atlantic slave trade. Principles of morality are not by themselves a sufficient condition for the emergence of an international law rule – there must be evidence of a wide State practice before a rule crystallises – and as late as 1825 therefore, the US Chief Justice was able to show in the *Antelope Case* that slave trading was lawful, notwithstanding international condemnation of its immorality, since it was then 'sanctioned by the laws of all nations who possess distant colonies.'[22] The general conclusion in the *Antelope Case* is echoed by Sirs Robert Jennings and Arthur Watts who, in one of the leading English works on public international law, indicate that in the early years of the nineteenth century customary international law did not condemn the institution of slavery and the traffic in slaves.[23] The United Kingdom abolished slave trafficking throughout its colonies in 1807, signed the Treaty of Paris in 1814 with France which led to cooperation in the drive towards the abolition of slavery, and in Vienna in 1815 succeeded in obtaining from the Powers a solemn condemnation of the slave trade in principal.[24] However, Jennings and Watts state that this was not enough to make the traffic in slaves a crime *jure gentium* at the time, and accordingly a number of treaties were entered into, beginning with the Treaty of London in 1841 (between the UK, Austria, France, Prussia and

---

21 I am focusing here on claims for the acts associated with slavery and slave trading. However, some reparationists argue that the reparation should be sought for the crime of genocide committed against the African people by way of slavery and the slave trade, on the grounds that "the numbers involved, their inhumane handling during transhipment, and their resultant deaths ... establish a prima facie case of genocide." (See Ricardo Laremont, "Political versus Legal Strategies for the African Slaverly [sic] Reparations Movement", (1999), 2, *Africa Studies Quarterly*, issue 4, at 2 and 3 (available at http://web.africa.ufl.edu/asq/v2/v2i4.htm.); see also Gifford "Legal Basis" op cit at 4). Besides the fact that the crime of genocide which has developed in international criminal law would in all likelihood not be proved (genocide requires special intent to physically destroy a group in whole or in part and it seems clear that, while treatment of slaves was callous in the extreme, this special intent would be difficult to establish, not least of all because slaves were of economic value to slave traders and owners), a further problem is that genocide itself only became outlawed in international law after the Second World War (see in this regard Nina Jorgensen, *The Responsibility of States for International Crimes*, (2000) at 32-35).
A more powerful argument which deserves consideration by reparationists is that presented by Geraldine Van Bueren. She argues that in 1823 Britain and the US agreed to classify the slave trade as a form of piracy. Van Bueren suggests that because piracy had been illegal under international law well before the 17th century, the agreement by the US and Britain to regard the slave trade as a form of piracy shows that at least from the early 19th century amounts to an expression of legal guilt (see Geraldine Van Bueren "It's Britain's guilty secret", *The Guardian*, May 25, 2001). This argument needs to be explored more fully by reparationists as it ostensibly allows reparation claims to be brought in international law for acts of slavery committed after 1823 by association with the crime of piracy.

22 (1825) 23 US (10 Wheat) 64 cited in Geoffrey Robertson, *Crimes Against Humanity: The Struggle for Global Justice*, (2000) 209.

23 Jennings and Watts, *Oppenheim's International Law, Vol. 1 Peace* (1996), 9th edition, 979.

24 *Ibid.*

Russia) which aimed to ensure international cooperation in the suppression of the trade.[25]

So while it is undoubtedly clear that slavery and traffic in slaves are today prohibited in customary and conventional international law, the precise point at which these policies and practices became outlawed in international law is impossible to fix. In the words of Geoffrey Robertson,

> "[T]here was no defining moment like the Nuremberg judgment, but rather an accumulation of treaties throughout the nineteenth century and a gradual abandonment by the Great Powers of their toleration of the practice, marked in turn by military offensives against traders ... and by domestic court declarations that freed any slave brought within the jurisdiction. The point came somewhere between 1885 (the Treaty of Berlin forbidding slave-trading) and 1926, when the Slavery Convention confirmed that states had jurisdiction to punish slavers wherever they were apprehended."[26]

Any claims in international law for reparation for the Atlantic slave trade, be they from States against other States or citizens against their own States, will therefore have to overcome the doctrine of inter-temporal law.[27]

One argument put forward by reparationists in an attempt to overcome the problem of the inter-temporal law principle is that the acts of slavery committed *then* amount to a violation of fundamental norms of international law *now*. Put differently, reparationists point out that the prohibition against slavery has attained the force of a *jus cogens* norm in contemporary international law with the result that there is some

---

25 *Ibid.*

26 Robertson op cit at 209.

27 Of course, there are numerous arguments that might be made against the application of the doctrine of inter-temporal law (see for instance the chapter by Stephen Pete and Max du Plessis in this book at p. 3). The most obvious is that the inter-temporal law doctrine fails to register the fact that international law has traditionally served the interests of the powerful. Thus, while Western States would be eager to rely on the fact that slavery was lawful in international law at the time it was practised, it is clear that the lawfulness of that practice was determined by Western States themselves. As the critical legal studies movement has shown, law has an obfuscatory quality, always hiding the power that animates any legal rule. In the international law context, this obfuscatory quality is identified by Roling, who says that:
"In all positive law is hidden the element of power and the element of interest. Law is not the same as power, nor is it the same as interest, but it gives expression to the former power-relation. Law has the inclination to serve primarily the interests of the powerful. 'European' international law, the traditional law of nations, makes no exception to this rule. It served the interest of prosperous nations." (BVA Roling, *International Law in an Expanded World*, (1960) 15).
It thus becomes plain that the notion of European international law provided legal concepts and systemic arguments justifying the interests of the emerging Western powers, one such interest being the procurement of slaves. Nonetheless, while one strategy of slavery reparationists might aim at subverting the doctrine of inter-temporal law along these lines, the radical nature of this strategy will meet with fierce opposition. A more plausible strategy therefore appears to be an argument based on justice and morality which seeks to achieve reparations by working outside of the existing legal framework. See below *infra* for detail.

form of retrospective responsibility for the States who perpetrated slavery in the past. It is likely that this argument will remain attractive to reparationists in light of the decision of the delegates at the Durban Conference to define the slavery committed during the Atlantic slave trade as a 'crime against humanity'.[28] However, the ILC Articles on State Responsibility make it clear that such retrospective blaming is not possible. The Commentary to Article 13 provides as follows:

> "(5) State responsibility can extend to acts of the utmost seriousness, and the regime of responsibility in such cases will be correspondingly stringent. But even when a new peremptory norm of general international law comes into existence ... this does not entail any retrospective assumption of responsibility. ...
> (6) Accordingly it is appropriate to apply the intertemporal principle to all international obligations, and article 13 is general in its application."

It should be mentioned that Article 13 does not rule out the possibility of a State agreeing to make reparation for damage caused as a result of conduct which was not, at the time committed, a breach of any international obligation in force for that State.[29] However, retrospective assumption of responsibility is rare in international law,[30] and is unimaginable in the context of reparation for slavery. The position of Western States was made clear at the Durban Conference, and their delegates ensured that the wording of the final Declaration would form no basis for legal claims by African States for reparation from the West.[31]

---

28 Lord Gifford's paper pre-empts the Conference in its insistence that historians can show "without difficulty how the invasion of African territories, the mass capture of Africans, the horrors of the middle passage, the chattelisation of Africans in the Americas, the extermination of the language and culture of the transported Africans, constitute violations of [the international laws prohibiting crimes against humanity and genocide]". (See Gifford "Legal Basis" op cit at 4).

29 See paragraph 6, Commentary to Article 13 of the ILC Articles on State Responsibility (2001), in Crawford op cit at 132-133.

30 *Ibid.*

31 At best the Declaration declares a "moral" obligation on Western States to respond to the practice of slavery. In Article 102 of the Declaration the delegates affirm that "[w]e are aware of the moral obligation on the part of all concerned States and call upon these States to take appropriate and effective measures to halt and reverse the lasting consequences of those practices".
See also Anthony Sebok "The hidden legal issues behind the U.N. racism conference", *FindLaw Forum*, CNN.com, at www.cnn.com/2001/Law/09/columns/fl.sebok.racismconference.0910/. Sebok argues that due to the spectre of current and future reparation demands, the nations of the EU and the US were very concerned, going into the Conference, about the tenor and content of any discussion of the legacy of the trans-Atlantic slave trade. "They wanted to avoid a scenario where such discussion could be used to fuel more Holocaust-style litigation, leading to more multibillion dollar settlements". After the US walked out, the EU was left to protect its interests alone, but, Sebok points out, the eventual draft offers no apology at all: "It 'acknowledges' that slavery, 'including the trans-Atlantic slave trade' were 'appalling tragedies.' Yet it does not say who was responsible for these tragedies – thus refraining from offering any confession of responsibility or blame that future plaintiffs seeking reparations could use in negotiation, court proceedings, or public statements."

In conclusion then, while human rights lawyers and reparationists may be eager to cast claims in legal language because of the currency of 'rights talk', the legal path, at least insofar as international law is concerned, is likely to continue to attract significant opposition from States.

2.3 THINKING OUTSIDE THE LEGAL BOX – POLITICAL STRATEGIES AND ARGUMENTS FROM MORALITY AND AFRICAN-CENTRED CONSCIOUSNESS

Given the strictures of the legal paradigm, it appears that any feasible strategy for reparation for slavery must draw on moral argument to secure political settlement of reparation claims.[32] Political strategies for the pursuit of domestic and international justice are, of course, familiar tools in the hands of human rights lawyers. Such a strategy is discernible, for instance, in the OAU's decision to pursue a political, as opposed to purely legal, course to obtain reparation. In 1992, under the leadership of Chief Mashood Abiola, the OAU instigated the creation of the OAU Group of Eminent Persons for Reparations. The Group was charged with pressing the *political* agenda for reparation for the African slave trade and in 1993 convened the First Pan-African Conference on Reparations in Abuja, Nigeria, where it adopted the Abuja Declaration that officially committed the OAU to obtain reparation for slavery from the West.[33]

In considering these political, or moral, arguments for reparation, we begin to focus on the intricacies of how reparations are to be determined, against whom, and what form they should take.

2.3.1 A moral global economy as incentive for reparation

Slavery presents the West with a peculiar dilemma. As a loose confederation of states emphasising the need for international relations grounded upon democracy and human rights,[34] the West has to face the problem of how to deal with its own past and

---

32 As Graham Hughes concludes (using the offensive language of the day) in the context of the African American claims, "[i]t is not possible to set up a viable argument for compensation payments to Negroes within the confines of existing legal theory, but there remains the question of the strength of the moral case for instituting both political and private schemes of compensatory nature". (Graham Hughes "Reparations for Blacks" (1968) 43 *N.Y.U. L. Rev.*1063 1064, cited in Vincene Verdun "If the Shoe Fits, Wear It: An Analysis of Reparations to African Americans", (1993), 67, no 3, *Tulane LR*, 629 fn 96).

33 See Ricardo Laremont op cit at 1.

34 There is a wide literature on the emerging right to democracy in international law. In particular see Thomas Franck "The Emerging Right to Democratic Governance" (1992) 86 *AJIL* 46 and James Crawford "Democracy in International Law" (1992) 64 *Brit. Ybk Int.L* 539. See too the recent and

the historical injustices of the slavery and colonialism it practised.[35] This dilemma allows reparationists their first opening to argue that reparation for slavery is a prerequisite of a moral global economy, and they have done so by pointing to a growing trend in the international community for governments to provide reparation to victims of historical human rights abuses.[36] The examples are well known and include Germany's enactment since World War II of several measures to pay victims more than US $50 billion in post-war reparation.[37] More recently, the Japanese government announced a US $1 billion programme to undertake cultural and vocational projects as a token of apology for wrongs committed against former 'comfort women'.[38] In 1990 Austria made payments to the total of $25 million to Jewish survivors of the Holocaust.[39] And it is not only the original Axis powers that have begun to provide reparation. Within the United States itself, the Civil Liberties Act of 1988[40] provides reparation for the World War II internment of Japanese Americans.[41] The Act provides for an acknowledgment and apology for the grave injustices done, and grants: (1) compensation in the amount of $20,000 to individuals of Japanese ancestry who were interned, and living on the date of the enactment of

---

excellent work by Susan Marks, *The Riddle of all Constitutions: International Law, Democracy and the Critique of Ideology* (2000), Oxford University Press, Oxford, United Kingdom.

35 See in this regard Elazar Barkan, "Payback Time: Restitution and the Moral Economy of Nations" (Sept. – Oct. 1996), *TIKKUN*, 52 58. Barkan writes about the moral economy incentive in the context of African American calls for reparation for slavery but this idea is reflected in much of the thinking of African reparationists in their struggle for reparation from the West.

36 See, for instance, David Love "US needs to pay reparations for slavery", *The Progressive Media Project*, Jan. 26, 2000, available at http://www.progressive.org/mpbvlo00.htm. This argument is most evident in the claims made by African Americans against the US government. As an example see the websites of the African American Reparation Action Network (http://www.angelfire.com/super/freedom/) and the National Coalition of Blacks for Reparations in America (http://www.ncobra.com/), both of which list all the past claims for reparation which have been settled as an attempt to exert moral pressure for reparation for slavery. Of course, this strategy of the African Americans in their pursuit of reparation from the US government is equally appropriate to the claims made by African States as against the West.

37 Tong Yu "Reparations for Former Comfort Women of World War II", (1995), 36, *Harvard International Law Journal*, 528, 537 – see further the chapter in this book by Regula Ludi at pp. 119-144.

38 See Yu *ibid.* 528. Beginning in 1932 and continuing through World War II, Japan established a system of military brothels called "comfort stations" throughout Asia. These comfort stations were staffed by comfort women – taken from Korea, China, the Philippines and other Asian countries by force or deceit – who provided sexual services to Japanese soldiers. See further the chapter by Bo Jung Kwon in this book at p. 413.

39 Gifford "Legal Basis" op cit at 2.

40 50 U.S.C. app. § 1989-1989d (1994).

41 During World War II, all individuals of Japanese ancestry living in the United States were excluded from military zones and subject to forced relocation to detention centres pursuant to Executive Order 9066. In the 1980's a Commission was established to study the effects of Executive Order 9066 on Japanese American citizens. As a result of the Commission's finding that there were "fundamental violations of the basic civil liberties and constitutional rights" of the internees, Congress passed the Civil Liberties Act. The Act also provided reparation to the Aleuts, a group of civilian residents of the Pribilof and Aleutian Islands who were relocated to temporary camps in isolated regions of Alaska.

the Act (or to their living heirs); and (2) a public education fund to facilitate public awareness of the internment and prevent a recurrence.[42]

According to reparationists, in a moral economy of nations, reparation is essential to achieves two goals. First, and most obviously, it provides a means to rectify historical injustices.[43] Secondly, it serves to facilitate higher awareness of public morality through

---

42 See Chisolm op cit at 713-715. African Americans who call for reparations for slavery draw heavily on the Civil Liberties Act in support of their claim, arguing that the Act "established a precedent for legislative compensation to a particular racial group that suffered unique injuries due to racially motivated law enforcement" (Chisolm *ibid.* 716).

43 Another way of putting the moral global economy argument is in terms of justice principles. It is clear that the moral global economy is premised on the idea of righting past injustices. For reparationists to point out the hypocrisy of Western efforts to promote human rights and democracy without contemporaneous Western acknowledgment of past injustices, is to force the West into the justice cul-de-sac, be it the libertarian theory of Robert Nozick, or the liberal theory of John Rawls. As is well known, in terms of Robert Nozick's libertarian "entitlement theory of justice" the justice of any distribution of goods depends on the history of the transaction. In other words, the justice of distributing goods is assessed not by where they end up but by how the distribution itself came about. We are to, therefore, look at the history of the acquisition and transfer of the goods in question: if the transactions of acquisition and transfer were freely entered into without force or fraud, then a just distribution of goods has taken place. Nozick's entitlement theory of justice thus works from a hypothetical assumption that everyone in a given society at point T is entitled to the goods they currently possess. However, writes Nozick, "not all actual situations are generated in accordance with the two principles of justice in holdings: the principle of justice in acquisition and the principle of justice in transfer. Some people steal from others, or defraud them, or enslave them, seizing their product and preventing them from living as they choose." (Robert Nozick, *Anarchy, State, and Utopia*, (1974) at 152). When this occurs, Nozick accepts that the State may intervene in the rights of others to provide distributive justice. This is done in accordance with Nozick's principle of "justice in rectification". He does not elaborate on this principle, but accepts that "past injustices might be so great as to make necessary in the short run a more extensive state in order to rectify them." (Nozick *ibid.* 231).

The liberal theory of justice advanced by John Rawls would arguably also support a claim for reparation. Unlike Nozick's theory which suggests a focus on correcting the injustices of the past, Rawls' theory is concerned with correcting existing inequalities in pursuit of what Rawls calls "justice as fairness". The inequality between the West and Africa, a legacy (whatever the measure) of slavery, places Africa and Africans in the position of "disadvantaged" members of global society. In accordance with Rawls' difference principle, such disadvantage needs to be redressed:

"[W]e may observe that the difference principle gives some weight to the principle of redress. That is the principle that undeserved inequalities call for redress; and since inequalities of birth and natural endowment are underserved, these inequalities are to be somehow compensated for. Thus the principle holds that in order to treat all persons equally, to provide genuine equality of opportunity, society must give more attention to those with fewer native assets and to those born into the less favourable social positions ...Those who have been favoured by nature, whoever they are, may gain from their good fortune only on terms that improve the situation of those who have lost out." (John Rawls, *A Theory of Justice*, (1972) at 100-101).

The existing Western States that deny responsibility for the slavery committed by their predecessors find themselves nonetheless favoured by the inheritance of enviably stable and prosperous economies. These States are thus held to Rawls' principle of redress: having been so favoured, they may only continue to gain from their good fortune on terms that improve the situation of those who have lost out. Such terms must include reparation for the Africans who have been born into the less favourable positions in the world, and who have, moreover, contributed historically to the prosperity of the

the use of market mechanisms, and in the process both parties' histories are given recognition, ultimately leading to a transfer of economic resources.[44] Such a transfer occurs through the conclusion of agreements that are entered into voluntarily between the parties, although this willingness to enter into such agreements often results from political pressure which draws on moral argument.[45] While this political approach is not without its problems,[46] reparationists draw inspiration from the examples mentioned above and others to argue that there is a moral obligation to provide reparation for slavery. To them such reparation is an integral part of any moral global economy, for without it, the injustices of slavery are not dealt with and the history of Africa not legitimised.[47] But the political arm-twist comes from the argument that the West cannot endorse the notion of a just world order while simultaneously avoiding the issue of reparation for past injustices. For if it does not commit to reparation for slavery with the same zeal it has demonstrated in advancing human rights abroad, it runs the risk of being labelled hypocritical.[48]

Western economies through the institution of slavery. In this regard see also David Johnson, Steve Pete, Max du Plessis, *Jurisprudence – A South African Perspective*, (2001- Butterworths, Durban) at 187.

44 Barkan argues that if "the success of the moral economy of restitution is measured 'by the degree to which it enables the victims to claim a share of the economic pie … and legitimize their side of history', then America cannot hope to achieve an equal society without granting reparations to African Americans." (see Barkan op cit at 57).

45 *Ibid.* at 54.

46 For example, some argue that it is facile to lump claims for reparation for slavery together with claims for compensation for the Holocaust. It is true that in the 1990s the issue of historical reparation gained momentum with a series of lawsuits related to the Holocaust, but among the reasons for settlement of these claims is that Swiss banks and German businesses wanted to prevent themselves from being frozen out of the most lucrative markets in the world (notably that of the US) if they didn't settle. (See Jon Silberman, "Compensation for slavery", *BBC News, World:Americas*, Tuesday, 4 September 2001, available at http://news.bbc.co.uk//hi/english/world/americas/newsid_1523000/1523669.stm). While one could speculate that the financial muscle of the black community in the US might provide similar leverage in relation to the slave trade, it is not obvious that African States have similar clout vis-à-vis the West when it comes to the issue of slavery reparations. This much is apparent from the outcome of the Durban Conference.

47 The idea of legitimising a party's history – of breaking the history of silence – is a powerful theme in human rights initiatives. This theme is apparent, for instance, in the creation of The Women's International War Crimes Tribunal 2000 for the trial of Japanese Military Sexual Slavery, established in response to Japan's continuing failure to prosecute, apologise and provide reparation for Japan's military institutionalisation of rape, sexual slavery, trafficking, torture and other forms of sexual violence against Asian "comfort women". One of the reasons for constituting the Tribunal was "out of the conviction that these failures must not be allowed to silence the voices of the survivors", its power, "like so many human rights initiatives, [lying] in its capacity to examine the evidence and develop an enduring historical record". See the summary of findings of the Tribunal on 12 December 2000 in the matter of *The Prosecutors and the Peoples of the Asia-Pacific Region v Emperor Hirohito et a*l. *and the Government of Japan*, para 5 (available at www1.jca.apc.org/vaww-net-japan/e_new/judgement.html).

48 It is significant that the Durban Declaration registers, albeit obliquely, the "moral" obligation on Western States to respond to the practices of the past. See Article 102 of the Declaration quoted above at fn 31.

2.3.2 *Past wrong, current effect, against whom? Looking towards a collective conscience*

While reparationists might wish to pursue the argument for a moral global economy through the provision of reparation, the details of such a claim will invariably have to confront two difficult questions: first, *are reparations to be determined by focusing on the past wrong as opposed to the current and ongoing effects of that wrong*?; and secondly, *against whom should the claim be directed*?

One of the central obstacles to establishing a right – be it legal or moral – to reparation, is that of causation. That is true of any reparation claim that spans vast periods of time, and the obstacle is well illustrated by the problems that confront those who argue for reparation for slavery. In order to found liability for past wrongs in relation to slavery, reparationists need to show that current Western States bear responsibility for the actions of their predecessors during the period of the Atlantic slave trade. It is one thing to be able to show that the acts of Western powers at a certain point in history caused injury to the innocent victims of the slave-trade; it is quite another to insist that the breach perpetrated *then* carries through to found responsibility for Western States *now*.

In the national context this issue of 'historical' causation has proven insurmountable to African-American legal attempts to claim compensation from the present-day US government for the acts of slavery perpetrated in the early years of the nation's existence. As yet, they have not successfully been able to sue for reparation in domestic US courts. For instance, in the first federal appellate court case to be heard on African-American reparations – *Cato v United States* – the plaintiffs sued the United States for damages for past and present injustices related to ancestral slavery. The court dismissed their claim for lack of an arguable basis in law, in particular, lack of causation and standing.[49]

Tuneen Chisolm, an American academic, writes that the standing doctrine and causation doctrine are barriers to African American reparation suits in tort, largely because of a dominant theory of rights.[50] Within this paradigm, each individual is responsible for his or her behaviour only. Thus vicarious liability for the actions of others is only applicable where the defendant has control over the offender; if no such control relationship exists, then there is no legal (or moral) responsibility for the actions of others. In keeping with the dominant perspective that the individual wrongdoer must pay for the wrong, the law accepts the corollary principle that a non-wrongdoer should not be required to pay for the wrong.[51] The death of the last slave and slaveholder, therefore, puts paid to reparations for slavery through judicial relief.

---

[49] 70 F.3d 1103 (9th Cir. 1995) at 1110-11, cited in Chisolm op cit 709.

[50] Chisolm op cit 710, drawing on the work of Vincene Verdun op cit at 597.

[51] See Verdun *ibid.* 622 fn 61.

As Chisolm concedes, 'cases based in tort necessarily fail for lack of standing and/or causation. Therefore, the tort suit as a vehicle for African American reparations is not a viable option.'[52]

There is no reason to believe that the position is different at the international level. The international law rules on State responsibility (both in the inter-State context and the international human rights context) presuppose that there is a connection between a past wrong and a present claim.[53] Similarly, any legal claim for reparation for slavery at the international level faces the seemingly insurmountable hurdle of proving that the present day Western States caused the injury complained of.

It is important to stress that the dominant theory of rights presents an obstacle not only to legal attempts to claim reparation, but also to political claims, and opponents of reparation to Africans (and African Americans) analyse the merits of the remedy from this dominant perspective. With their insistence that an actor should pay only for harm that is actually caused by that actor, and that only those victims that actually suffered should receive justice, such opponents conclude that the idea of reparation for slavery is 'absurd, frivolous, or unworthy of serious consideration.'[54]

Is there any way around this problem in the political pursuit of reparation for slavery? To reparationists, an answer lies in the idea of solidarity. In stark contrast with the dominant perspective, African Americans, for instance, frame their claims for reparation in terms of group identity.[55] This community is constituted through the experience of common struggle. Mari Matsuda describes the kinship wrought of common struggles in the following terms:

> "Victims necessarily think of themselves as a group, because they are treated and survive as a group. The wealthy black person still comes up against the color line. The educated Japanese still comes up against the assumption of Asian inferiority. The wrongs of the past cut into the heart of the privileged as well as the suffering."[56]

A similar strategy is evident in the political agenda of the OAU and its commitment to seeking reparation through some form of 'appropriate, representative and trustworthy body' that represents the claims of all Africans.[57] At the level of community

---

52 Chisolm op cit 712. But see the criticisms of such conservative judicial thinking in Diane Sammons' chapter in this book at page 315.

53 See for instance Brownlie, *Principles of Public International Law*, (1979) 436.

54 Verdun op cit 625.

55 Verdun *ibid.* 631.

56 Mari Matsuda "Looking to the Bottom: Critical Legal Studies and Reparations" (1987) 22 *Harvard C.R.-C.L. Law Review*, 323 376.

57 For instance, see Lord Gifford who argues that "[t]he details of reparations settlement would have to be negotiated with an appropriate body of representatives of African people around the world" (Lord Gifford, House of Lords debate on reparations for slavery, 14th March 1996 (Hansard), (hereinafter referred to as Gifford "House of Lords", available at http://www.arm.arc.co.uk [no page numbers]).

of African States, the OAU is able to advance what might be termed an 'African consciousness'. This African consciousness is reflected in the Preamble to the Draft Declaration of the African Preparatory Regional Meeting for the World Conference Against Racism:

> "[T]he African peoples attach great importance to their values of brotherhood, solidarity, tolerance and multiculturalism, which constitute the moral ground and the inspiring source for our struggle."[58]

From this perspective group identity allows all Africans to perceive the call for reparation through the lens of communalism and collectivism, and to identify a continuing and uncompensated wrong to a corpus of Africans throughout the world. The result is that the same factor that would inhibit a claim for reparation from the dominant perspective becomes, instead, an empowering means for achieving reparation when viewed from the perspective of an African consciousness.

What about the perpetrators of slavery? Against whom should the reparation claims be directed? From the standpoint of the African consciousness, the wrongdoer is similarly not limited to some prescribed set of individuals such as slave owners, or one guilty State in particular.[59] Rather, the more appropriate description of the wrongdoer is also to be drawn from an understanding of the collective: the West, through governments, laws, courts, consumers, producers, economic ideology and institutions perpetrated and perpetuated the institution of slavery. Thus the logic goes that the West as a collective must be held responsible for reparation. Furthermore, the West, unlike individuals, does not have a natural life. As a result, the African consciousness perspective becomes a vehicle for arguing against the dominant perspective of rights which seals off claims for reparation along with the death of the last slave-holder. To do so, argue reparationists, is to ignore the fact that the countries that practised slavery are doing well and still reaping the benefits of slave labour.[60]

---

58 See the Reports of Preparatory Meetings and Activities at the International , Regional and National Levels, Report of the Regional Conference for Africa (Dakar, 22-24 January 2001), available at http://www.un.org/WCAR/.

59 Verdun op cit 636.

60 See in this regard Verdun *ibid.* 638-9. Similar thinking is evidenced in a Human Rights Watch Report, prepared in anticipation of the Durban Conference and in connection with African American claims for reparation. The relevant passage reads:
"We recognize that to hold [governments] responsible for past crimes is, as a practical matter, to hold today's citizens or taxpayers responsible. We believe this attribution of responsibility can be justified by reference to the economic benefits that these countries derived from, say, slavery or abusive colonialism – benefits that presumably helped to jumpstart their industrialization and thus continue to the present. We note that this rationale would apply even to immigrants who arrived in a beneficiary country after these abusive practices ended, since they, too, presumably have benefited from the advanced economy they joined". (See *Human Rights Watch*, "An Approach to Reparations" July 19, 2001, available at http://www. hrwatch.org, at 6).

Having identified a collective victim and wrongdoer as part of an overall political strategy, reparationists are still faced with the question: what is the uncompensated wrong? This brings into sharp focus the issue of whether reparations are to be determined in accordance with past wrongs or current effects, and the slavery reparationists provide some useful cues for other reparation contexts.

In respect of the slavery context, various wrongs are identified as being un-repaired, but broadly they can be classed under three heads. *First*: the mass kidnap and enslavement of Africans. *Second*: the contribution made by slaves to the prosperity of the slave-owning nations. *Third*: the consequences of slavery which manifest themselves in continuing systemic discrimination.

The first injury is readily apparent from the historical evidence that documents the Atlantic slave trade. The injury is easily identified by historians and other experts who can reliably prove 'the invasion of African territories, the mass capture of Africans, the horrors of the middle passage, the chattelisation of Africans in the Americas, the extermination of the language and culture of the transported Africans'.[61]

The second injury would require historical, sociological, and economic evidence. Some experts argue, for example, that the slave trade was a principal factor which contributed towards the generation of wealth by Western nations. For instance, Marketti, who developed a mathematical formula to determine the value of slave labour exploited from African Americans, writes:

> "I am convinced that [the United States'] present day wealth, rather than a result of how economic activity was organized or of access to natural resources, is more attributable to the fact that at a crucial point in the development of the industrial United States, large amounts of free labor were deployed, from which surplus was extracted and filtered through various exchange mechanisms to nearly every budding industrial enterprise in the nation".[62]

While there is obvious disagreement about the extent to which slavery boosted economic development in the West, it is equally clear that an argument can be made that the use of slave labour was a significant contributing factor.[63]

---

61 Gifford "House of Lords" op cit.

62 See Jim Marketti "Black Equity in the Slave Industry", (1972), 2, *Rev. Black. Pol. Econ*, 43 at 43-44 and the other sources quoted in Verdun (op cit) 630 fn. 99.

63 Note the comments of Gifford "Legal Basis" op cit at 11 where he takes for granted that "[h]istorians will advise as to which countries have profited most from slavery and the slave trade. The major European maritime trading nations and the colonisers can be easily identified. So can the United States, as a country which grew rich on slave labour and the exploitation of African Americans". In the African American context, see Randall Robinson, *The Debt: What America owes Blacks*, (2001), and the other sources referred to in Tara Mack, "Payback time", *The Guardian* 11 August 2001.

The third injury is perhaps the most contentious, and the one most difficult to prove.[64] Essentially, the argument runs that slavery has a continuing effect which is manifested in racial inequalities which exist not only as between individuals, but also as between nation blocs.[65] For instance, in the African American context Oliver and Shapiro argue as follows:

> "Disparities in wealth between blacks and whites are not the product of haphazard events, inborn traits, isolated incidents or solely contemporary individual accomplishment. Rather, wealth inequality has been structured over many generations through the same systemic barriers that have hampered blacks throughout their history in American society: slavery, Jim Crow, so-called de jure discrimination, and institutionalized racism."[66]

Lord Gifford makes the same argument more generally:

> "[T]here is a further element in the legacy of the slave trade which is the damage done within Britain, within the United States and other Western societies. The inhuman philosophy of white supremacy and black inferiority was inculcated into European peoples to justify the atrocities which were being committed by a Christian people upon fellow human beings. That philosophy continues to poison our society today."[67]

---

64 As is conceded by Chisolm, "[t]he inequalities between blacks and whites ... often manifest themselves, and are therefore expressed, in terms that do not clearly relate back to slavery and the ensuing discrimination". See Chisolm op cit at 687.

65 The Durban Declaration tentatively suggests as much in Article 13. After acknowledging that slavery and the slave trade "were appalling tragedies" the Article states that these acts "are among the major sources and manifestations of [existing] racism ... and that Africans and people of African descent, Asians and people of Asian descent and indigenous peoples were victims of these acts and continue to be victims of their consequences."

66 Melvin Oliver and Thomas Shapiro, *Black Wealth/White Wealth: A New Perspective on Racial Inequality* (1995) 12-13, quoted in Chisolm op cit 687. See also the charged assertion by Mazrui that "[t]he consequences of slavery in the United States did not end with the Emancipation Proclamation of 1863, but continue today in the disproportionate black presence in American jails, the disproportionate black infant mortality rates, the disproportionate self-destructive juvenile black violence. The damage of the past is in the present. The black community is chained to the bondage of its own tragic history." (Mazrui op cit at 9). The same premise is evident in the report by Human Rights Watch, prepared in anticipation of the Durban Conference in connection with African American claims for reparation. The report states that "we would accept that most African-Americans continue to suffer the effects of slavery in the United States ..." and accordingly proposes that studies be undertaken to "reveal the extent to which a government's past practices contribute to contemporary economic and social deprivation, educate the public about this continuing effect, acknowledge responsibility for it, and propose methods for rectifying these effects and making amends." (See Human Rights Watch Report op cit at 2).

67 Gifford "House of Lords" op cit. In different words, Verdun writes that the injury amounts to a "presumption of inferiority, devaluation of self-esteem, and other emotional injuries, pain, and suffering, that resulted from the institution of slavery". (See Verdun op cit 631-2)

Such racism, practised between people, is also perceived to be at work between nations. The following plea by Mazrui is indicative of a belief that Africa as a whole is being sidelined in global affairs:

> "And why should all the permanent seats of the United Nations Security Council be given to countries which are already powerful outside the UN? Is there not a case for giving Africa a permanent seat with a veto[68] – not because Africa is powerful but because it has been rendered powerless across generations? ... There is a primordial debt to be paid to black peoples for hundreds of years of enslavement and degradation. Some of the causes of global apartheid lie deep in that history."[69]

While the connection between slavery and continuing patterns of racism needs to be examined in more detail, one cannot discount the fact that current social and economic inequalities between whites and blacks, and between the West and Africa, have some relation to past patterns of discrimination, foremost of which must be slavery.[70] Slavery, an institution supported by the belief that people were inferior and appropriately subordinated because of their race, is a practice that is inexorably linked with the ideology of racism.[71] To assume that the statistics reflecting inequities between the West and Africa have no relation to such past patterns of discrimination is to accept the argument that these statistics correctly reflect the inherent abilities or disabilities of Africa and its people. While it is plainly obvious that there are innumerable social and political factors which contributed towards these inequities, it is equally as clear that the practice of slavery deserves inclusion high up on that list.

---

68 How the permanent African seat would be occupied on the Security Council is something that Mazrui suggests will have to be worked out between the UN and the OAU. For instance, the seat could rotate between East, West, Southern, Northern and Central Africa over a period to be agreed upon. See Mazrui op cit 8. As it turns out, today there are continuing and increasing calls by developing states for an overhaul of the Security Council's composition.

69 Mazrui *ibid.* 16.

70 In the African American context, see Chisolm op cit 689–702 for an analysis of the link between slavery in the United States and existing manifestations of racial discrimination. In the international context, the delegates at the Durban Conference have acknowledged this link obliquely. Article 158 of the Durban Declaration provides that States recognise "that these historical injustices [slavery, colonialism, genocide, apartheid] have undeniably contributed to the poverty, underdevelopment, marginalization, social exclusion, economic disparities, instability and insecurity that affect many people in different parts of the world, in particular in developing countries".

71 In this regard see Verdun op cit 633-4, who draws on the work of Charles Lawrence to argue that the origins of racism were in rational and premeditated acts such as slavery. Lawrence writes that: "Racism is in large part a product of the unconscious. It is a set of beliefs whereby we irrationally attach significance to something we called race. I do not mean to imply that racism does not have its origins in the rational and premeditated acts of those who sought and seek property and power... It is a part of our common historical experience and, therefore, part of our culture. It arises from the assumptions we have learned to make about the world, ourselves, and others as well as from the patterns of our fundamental social activities ... It is a malady that we all share, because we have all been scarred by a common history." (Charles Lawrence, "The Id, the Ego, and Equal Protection: Reckoning with Unconscious Racism", (1987), 39, *Stan. L. Rev.*, 317, 330-31).

2.4 THE REPARATIONS ENVISAGED – WHAT FORM SHOULD THEY TAKE?

On the assumption that the political strategies for slavery reparation prove morally compelling, the next real difficulty lies in determining the exact nature of reparation which ought to be claimed and the mechanics of how such reparation is to be provided. It is at this stage that the context of slavery reparations might helpfully suggest answers to the question of what form reparations should take.

As stated earlier, reparationists appear to have taken their cue from the current paradigm of State responsibility and consider that there are three forms of reparation to be entertained in the context of slavery – restitution, compensation, and satisfaction – either singly or in combination.[72] I have explained that any legal claim for reparation will face difficulties, perhaps insurmountable difficulties, were it to be premised on the rules of State responsibility in international law. Nonetheless, the State responsibility paradigm provides a common frame of reference for the parties involved and is useful in the political context in which the claims are advanced by Africa as against the West, or for that matter, any other context involving claims for reparation arising out of mass atrocity.

The ILC Articles on State Responsibility provide in Article 34, under the heading 'Forms of reparation', that '[f]ull reparation for the injury caused by the internationally wrongful act shall take the form of restitution, compensation and satisfaction, either singly or in combination …'.

Restitution in kind ('to re-establish the situation which existed before the wrongful act was committed'[73]) is the first form of reparation available to a State injured by an internationally wrongful act. It was granted for instance in the *Temple* case[74] where Thailand was ordered to return to Cambodia religious objects which it had taken illegally from a temple in Cambodia.[75]

Restitution in kind is granted only in exceptional cases and monetary *compensation* as a form of reparation is far more commonly used as a means of 'wiping out the consequences of the illegal act'.[76] In this regard the ILC Articles provide that the State

---

72 While the assertion of these reparation claims would take place outside of the legal context of the ILC Articles, reparationists can nonetheless profit from the Articles' suggestion that the different forms of reparation are to be pursued with the goal of achieving "full reparation" for the wrong committed.

73 ILC Articles on State Responsibility, Article 35, in Crawford op cit at 213.

74 ICJ Reports 1962, 6.

75 It is clear that the obligation to make restitution is not unlimited, and the ILC Articles provide the following qualifications with respect to the grant of restitution. Restitution will not be granted where it is "materially impossible" (Article 35(a), in Crawford op cit), and it may not be granted where it would "involve a burden out of all proportion to the benefit deriving from restitution instead of compensation" (Article 35(b), in Crawford *ibid.*).

76 DJ Harris, *Cases and Materials on International Law* (1998), 5th edition, at 518.

responsible for an internationally wrongful act is 'under an obligation to compensate for the damage caused thereby, insofar as such damage is not made good by restitution'.[77] Compensation in this context is granted for any 'financially assessable damage including loss of profits insofar as it is established'.[78] For instance, in the *Chorzow Factory Case* compensation was awarded to Germany for the wrongful dispossession by Poland of the Chorzow Factory – then owned by German companies – in breach of a treaty concluded between the two States. The PCIJ held that where restitution in kind was not possible, payment must be made of a 'sum corresponding to the value which restitution in kind would bear'.[79]

The third form of reparation to be found in the ILC Articles on State Responsibility and which bears relevance for reparationists, is that of *satisfaction*. The State responsible for an internationally wrongful act is obliged to 'give satisfaction for the injury caused by that act insofar as it cannot be made good by restitution or compensation'.[80] Such measures may take the form of an 'acknowledgment of the breach, an expression of regret, a formal apology or another appropriate modality'.[81] Satisfaction provides reparation in particular for moral damage such as emotional injury, mental suffering, injury to reputation and similar damage suffered by nationals of the injured State.[82] It is not a standard form of reparation, in the sense that the injury to a State may be fully repaired by restitution and/or compensation, but its place is well-established in international law and it serves a useful role in providing reparation for those injuries, not financially assessable, which amount to an affront to the State.[83]

These three forms of reparation are called into service singly or in combination by reparationists in their arguments against the West. It is worthwhile noting that the ILC Articles themselves treat these forms of reparation as part of a coherent package aimed at providing 'full reparation' for international wrongs. Article 31 of the Articles reads that '[t]he responsible State is under an obligation to make full reparation for the injury caused by the internationally wrongful act'. Accordingly, the pursuit of 'full reparation' involves the flexible use of each of the types of reparation mentioned,

---

77 Article 36(1), in Crawford op cit at 218.

78 Article 36(2), *ibid.*

79 *Chorzow Factory Case* op cit 29

80 Article 37(1), in Crawford op cit at 231.

81 Article 37(2), *ibid.*

82 See the Commentary to Article 37, ILC Articles on State Responsibility in Crawford op cit at 231. An illustration of satisfaction as a form of reparation is provided in the *Borchgrave case* (PCIJ) Rep. Series A/B No 72 (1937). In that case a Belgian national working at the Belgian Embassy in Madrid was found dead on the roadside in Spain in 1936. The court listed the reparation sought by Belgium in diplomatic proceedings with Spain as follows: "In consequence, proceeding on the principles of international law relating to the responsibility of States, the Belgian Government demanded as reparation: (1) an expression of the Spanish Government's excuses and regrets; (2) transfer of the corpse to the port of embarcation with military honours; … (4) just punishment of the guilty" (at 165).

83 See Commentary to Article 37, ILC Articles on State Responsibility, in Crawford op cit at 231.

and to the extent that one form of reparation is dispensed with or is unavailable in the circumstances, others become correspondingly more important.[84]

2.4.1 Restitution

As a form of reparation, restitution will have limited application, particularly in the slavery context, given the scale of slavery and the extent of time over which it took place. At best then, restitution might be possible in relation to acts which were committed generally as part of the policy of slavery perpetrated by the West. For instance, it is not inconceivable that various treasures and works of art that were taken by colonial powers in the process of enslaving African people might be restored to African States. Gifford mentions as an example the Benin Bronzes, which are to be found in the British museum. This form of reparation was recognised by the delegates at Durban who, in the final Declaration, recorded 'the need to develop programmes for the social and economic development of [developing countries]' in various areas, one of which is the '[r]estitution of art objects, historical artefacts and documents to their countries of origin'.[85] Another example of restitution as a relevant form of reparation in this context is the granting of assistance to persons who wish to return to Africa, even though their numbers may be small. In this regard the Durban Declaration calls for programmes aimed at the 'facilitation of welcomed return and resettlement of the descendants of enslaved Africans'.[86]

2.4.2 Compensation

Compensation for slavery – or any other mass atrocity – presents arguably the most difficulties as a form of reparation, and is politically the most controversial. What appears to drive reparationists – whatever their cause – in claiming monetary payment, is the belief, as Martha Minow puts it, that the core idea behind reparation stems from the compensatory theory of justice: '[i]njuries can and must be compensated. Wrongdoers should pay victims for losses. Afterwards the slate can be wiped clean.'[87] This notion of justice is commonplace in the context of bankruptcy, contract, and personal injury law. International law rules of State responsibility endorse the same notion of justice and provide that compensation is available as legal recompense for 'any financially assessable damage'. However, the problem, as Minow points out, is that there is a sense of 'inappropriateness of putting a value on losses from mass

84 See Articles 31 and 34 and Commentary to Article 34, ILC Articles on State Responsibility, in Crawford op cit at 212.

85 Article 158 of the Durban Declaration.

86 *Ibid.*

87 Martha Minow *Between Vengeance and Forgiveness* (1998), at 104.

atrocity'.[88] This is particularly true in respect of reparation for slavery where one is confronted with a variety of problems, the first of which is how to assess the damage.

Gifford argues that the damage might be classified and researched under different headings: economic damage, cultural damage, social damage and psychological damage. However, to put monetary figures on any of the elements raises questions to which Gifford himself has no answers:

> "[H]ow do you assess the value of the loss to an African people of a young person, kidnapped and transported over 200 years ago? What figure can be placed on the psychological damage inflicted by a system that is still deeply racist?[89] Can it be proved that the slave system destroyed old and flourishing African civilisations, and if so, how is their value to be measured? What level of restitution is appropriate for the African peoples of the Diaspora?"[90]

Gifford's rhetorical questions do not pose the only problems besetting compensation awards. Even if a meaningful assessment of damage can be performed, how, for instance, will justice be done as between the claimants? Not all Africans (individuals or States) suffered equally, and some may not have suffered at all.[91] Opponents of reparation for slavery therefore insist that any meaningful compensation requires that the various classes of injured victims be segregated to avoid some being over-compensated and others under-compensated.[92]

One plausible solution to this problem appears to lie in the idea of the African consciousness. Reparationists, perceiving issues from a communitarian point of view, would find a uniform award consistent with group injury.[93] Such uniform awards of compensation have already been made in other contexts. For instance, reparation paid to Japanese Americans for their internment during the Second World War were uniform and did not conform to the dominant view that damages should be consistent with the relative injuries of the parties.[94] And the South African Truth and Reconciliation Commission's Reparations Committee recommended a one-off payment for the victims of apartheid human rights abuses. Through a reliance on the African

---

88 *Ibid.*

89 As Chisolm notes: "It is simply unrealistic to think that relief from the effects of deep-rooted iniquities and discrimination can be resolved by a lump sum payment." (Chisolm op cit at 723). Jay Parker, Founder and President of the Lincoln Institute for Research and Education expresses similar sentiments, arguing that no amount of restitution can make up for slavery or somehow cure imperfect race relations in America. (See Julie Foster, "Slavery reparations lawsuit brewing" *WorldNetDaily*, 23 January 2001).

90 Gifford "Legal Basis" op cit 5.

91 South Africa is a prime example. While South Africa may feasibly have a legitimate call for reparation for colonisation, it is difficult to see how it could make a similar claim in respect of slavery. Few, if any, of its people were exploited during the Atlantic slave trade.

92 Verdun op cit 658.

93 Verdun *ibid.*

94 A uniform amount of $20,000 was paid to individuals of Japanese ancestry who were interned.

consciousness, the idea of collective justice would be one way to overcome problems of distributive justice on an individual level.

Such a collective perspective would, in any event, need to be adopted to overcome problems of distributing blame as between wrongdoers. Opponents of reparation insist that only those who were to blame for slavery ought to pay compensation, and then only such an amount as is commensurate with their blame. Those advocating reparation have examined the possibility of forcing payments from companies and individuals that benefited from slavery, but Gifford concedes that 'such an approach would create more problems than it solved':

> "Enormous research would be needed to identify the companies and the families, to determine how much money was made by their ancestors, and to calculate how much should be forfeited by the present shareholders or family members. The process would inevitably be somewhat arbitrary, and potentially oppressive, and it would be rejected both by the targets themselves and their governments."[95]

A collective approach again presents itself as the only viable alternative. Gifford suggests quite reasonably that it is more appropriate to concentrate on the governments of the countries which fostered and supported the slave trade, which legitimised the institution of slavery, and which profited as a result.

However, even if the African consciousness method makes uniform compensation by a collective of States a viable option, there are more significant problems to be faced. One of the most difficult to deal with is this: in assessing compensation claims, how far back should one go? As Human Rights Watch has pointed out in this regard, '[b]ecause human history is filled with wrongs, many of which amount to severe human rights abuse, significant practical problems arise once a certain time has elapsed in building a theory of reparations on claims of descendancy alone.'[96] By going back too far, 'most everyone could make a case of some sort for reparations, trivializing the concept', and of course, 'the older a wrong, the less the residents of countries called on to provide reparations will feel an obligation to make amends'.[97]

A focus on past wrongs and attempts to make amends by payments to living victims means that the total amount of any monetary award (be it to specific States or groups or individuals within those States) would quickly approach excessive sums which would serve only to scare Western governments away from the bargaining table.[98] The

---

95 Gifford "Legal Basis" op cit 5.

96 Human Rights Watch Report op cit at 1.

97 *Ibid.*

98 See, for example, the excessive and arbitrary amount called for by a group describing themselves as 'The African World Reparations and Repatriation Truth Commission' which recently demanded $777 thousand billion to be paid within 5 years by Western governments as compensation for slavery. The figure was reportedly arrived at on the basis of the number of lives lost to Africa during the slave-trade, as well as an assessment of the worth of the gold, diamonds and other minerals

number of claimants it is meant to serve (States directly, and their citizens indirectly) renders compensation, already riddled with the internal difficulties I have identified, unworkable.

Is compensation, therefore, to be cast aside as a form of reparation for slavery? I believe not. So long as calls by reparationists for compensation for slavery are pragmatic there is no reason why they cannot be aligned with existing calls by developing States for assistance under the rubric of the emerging right to development in international law.[99] The call for compensation ought thus to shift away from attempts to compensate for racial injustices against victims of the past (whereby States and their descendants hope to benefit in some way or another), and focus instead on correcting contemporary effects of past wrongs as they continue to present themselves in the here and now. Put differently, reparationists should focus less on demands for money to *redress* the historical wrongs of slavery and concentrate instead on demands for compensation to *address* the current effects of slavery which manifest themselves in the continuing racial inequality that pervades our world, in the form of social and economic discrimination.[100]

The drive for compensation for slavery therefore needs to be more carefully focused and more purposively applied for it to draw any support from the developed world. In this regard the call for compensation should be informed by the eventual goals for which reparationists strive. To my mind such goals would best be achieved not through an impossible attempt to compensate the descendants of the victims of slavery in the

taken from the continent during colonial rule. (See *BBC News, World: Africa* "Trillions demanded in slavery reparations", Friday, August 20, 1999, available at http://news.bbc.co.uk/hi/English/world/Africa/newsid_424000/424984.stm).

It is quite clear that such risible claims do the reparation movement far more damage than good, and simply fuel an unfortunate but understandable reticence on the part of governments to address the issue of compensatory reparation.

99 A right to development has been identified in international law as a controversial, but important example of a claimed "solidarity" human right. Crawford suggests that the following assessment of the right to development by Umozurike appears to be the most balanced:

"The right to development ... appears not to have attained the definitive status of rule of law despite its powerful advocates. Its inclusion in the African Charter will be as effective as the Charter itself. The negative duty not to impede the development of States may go down well; the positive duty to aid such development, in the absence of specific accords, is a higher level of commitment that still rests on non legal considerations". (Umozurike *AJIL* (1983) 77 902 907 quoted in Crawford (ed) *The Rights of Peoples* (1988) 65-66).

See also Bedjaoui "Some Unorthodox Reflections on the Right to Development" in Snyder and Slinn (eds) *International Law of Development: Comparative Perspectives* (1987) 87.

100 It is of course not impossible to imagine that compensation which is paid with the aim of correcting a past injustice committed against someone's ancestor, at the same time achieves economic justice for that person because she continues to suffer the effects of the slavery perpetrated against her ancestor, perhaps through lack of means or poor schooling etc. However, this overlap of achievements is not guaranteed. A focus exclusively on righting past wrongs could all too easily "deliver what might look like windfalls to people who assert vicarious claims to reparations but have suffered no harm themselves". (Human Rights Watch Report op cit at 2). It is for this reason that I propose an approach that focuses on contemporary effects of slavery as manifested in inequality between States.

past – which Western States will consistently balk at – but by empowering the people and States of Africa in relation to their situation in the present. This empowerment ought surely to be the purpose behind Africa's call for reparation? As Mazrui points out, '[e]mpowering the African people in relation to [their] ... states is the challenge of democratization. Empowering the ... African states in relation to the world system is the challenge of international centering.'[101] The details of how compensation can be used to democratise and internationally centre need to be worked out, but some tentative suggestions are advanced here.[102]

As regards democratisation, the West may continue to increase material support to democratic trends in Africa. International lawyers have since the early 1990s been arguing that the empowerment of the people within States is best advanced through the creation of democratic governments that represent them. As President Thabo Mbeki has said, '[t]he new wave of democracy sweeping the African continent is a ... sign that the conditions are emerging for the African people to realise a life of prosperity and to achieve the rebirth of our continent.'[103]

As regards international centring, programmes of development are essential for the reconstruction of Africa and many such programmes are already underway, giving credence to the idea of a right to development in international law. The advantage of such development programmes would be a discussion of reparation claims in terms of the impact of past slavery practices on contemporary respect for economic and social rights in the world order.[104] This focus would make it more likely for a Western public to accept the need to end a contemporary wrong connected to a historical injustice than to provide compensation for past wrongs *per se*. An approach thus based on economic and social rights would allow for an alignment of compensation schemes with the world's most acute development challenges – instead of doling out money on the principle that past victims deserve justice, the compensation becomes a vehicle for rectifying the social and economic problems that underpin today's victims' continuing marginalisation.[105] Accordingly, compensation payments would be used for investment in education, housing, health care, job training, and skills transfer –

---

101 Mazrui op cit 5.

102 The Senegalese President Abdoulaye Wade has articulated the ideas I mention here by reference to what he considers to be a "Marshall Plan" for Africa, or what President Mbeki sees as "The New Africa Initiative". Such a plan is intended to mitigate the scourge of slavery and its devastating and lingering effect on the continent. (See Qfeibea Quist-Arcton, "Slavery Issue Struggles to Get a Hearing in Durban", *AllAfrica.Com*, September 4, 2001, available at http://allafrica.com/stories/200109040564.html); See also the views of Abe Ajayi "Unfinished Business: Confronting the Legacies of Slavery and Colonialism in Africa" available at www.african-century.com/acphp/ac_list_articles.php).

103 In an address at the National Summit of Unity and Reconciliation, Rwanda, 18 October 2000, available at www.sapa.org.za.

104 See the Report of Human Rights Watch op cit at 4. As the report points out, a focus on economic and social rights provides greater urgency than traditional reparation claims because it asks us to "rectify today's injustices rather than yesterday's." (*Ibid.*).

105 Human Rights Watch Report *ibid.*

portfolios which would assist African states to centre themselves internationally through an improvement of the infrastructure of Africa as a whole. International scholarships and exchange programmes for Africans would be a small part of this effort.[106] As a last point, it is trite that another development initiative by the West would be a continuation of measures to cancel the intolerable burden of debt which has become an impediment to sustainable development in many African countries.[107]

To conclude, it is fitting to observe the eventual agreement of the delegates at the Durban Conference on this controversial form of reparation. The Durban Declaration shows an abandonment, no doubt due to sustained pressure from Western governments that remained at the Conference, of the original position put forward by African ministers in their preparatory meeting in Dakar in January 2001. There the ministers had committed themselves to a position in anticipation of the Durban Conference which would focus on the provision of compensation to a group unsatisfactorily described as the 'victims of the slave trade'.[108] Besides the difficulty of identification of such victims, it is clear that the inclination of African States was to focus on righting the historical injustices of the past. In happy contradistinction to that position, the Durban Declaration has adopted a development-based vision of compensatory justice, a vision that while not providing a guaranteed buy-in from Western States, will at least avoid their overt opposition. Article 158 of the Declaration provides as follows:

> "[T]hat these historical injustices have undeniably contributed to the poverty, underdevelopment, marginalization, social exclusion, economic disparities, instability and insecurity that affect many people in different parts of the world, in particular in developing countries. The Conference recognizes the need to develop programmes for the social and economic development of these societies and the Diaspora, within the framework of a new partnership based on the spirit of solidarity and mutual respect, in the ... areas [of, *inter alia*] debt relief; poverty eradication; building or strengthening democratic institutions; transfer of technology; infrastructure development; education ...".

2.4.3 Satisfaction

I come now to a consideration of *satisfaction* as a form of reparation for slavery. There is little doubt that the logical starting point for repair by the West would be a formal apology for the acts of slavery perpetrated in the past. Bill Clinton and Pope John Paul have set an example in this regard by apologising informally to distinct African

---

106 Mazrui op cit 7.

107 *Ibid.*

108 See the Reports of Preparatory Meetings and Activities at the International , Regional and National Levels, Report of the Regional Conference for Africa (Dakar, 22-24 January 2001), available at http://www.un.org/WCAR/. Article 2 of the Declaration provided that: "An International Compensation Scheme should be set up for victims of the slave trade, as well as victims of any other transnational racist policies and acts, in addition to the national funds or any equivalent national mechanisms aimed at fulfilling the right to compensation".

communities for slavery. On a visit to various sub-Saharan nations, Clinton made an informal apology in Uganda for America's part in the slave trade.[109] The Pope set a similar example on a visit to the slave dungeons of Goree in Senegal in February 1992, asking forgiveness for slavery.[110]

A formal apology would be a measure of satisfaction, a recognised form of reparation in international law. In anticipation of the Durban Conference, African ministers called for such an apology in their Draft Declaration in the following terms:

> "[T]he first logical and credible step to be taken at this juncture of our collective struggle is for the World Conference against racism to declare solemnly that the international community as a whole fully recognises the historical injustices of slave trade and colonialism as the most massive human rights violations in the history of mankind; ...
> [T]his recognition would be meaningless without the explicit apology by ex-colonial powers or their successors for those violations, and ... this apology should be duly reflected in the final Declaration of the World conference against racism, racial discrimination, xenophobia and related intolerance."[111]

This stance was echoed, albeit in weakened form, by the South African Foreign Minister, Nkosozana Dlamini Zuma who opined that one of the methods of dealing with slavery 'would be to acknowledge and recognise there was a historic injustice'.[112] Martha Minow considers that official apologies can correct a public record, afford public acknowledgement of a violation, assign responsibility, but that they 'are less good at warranting any promise about the future, given the shifts in officeholders'.[113] As a result, unless the apology is 'accompanied by direct and immediate actions ... that manifest responsibility for the violation, the official apology may seem superficial, insincere, or meaningless'.[114] It is with this point in mind that other measures of satisfaction become increasingly important – for instance, measures aimed at raising public awareness of slavery. These measures would focus on 'legitimising' the victims' side of history, and would be consistent with providing the moral global economy that reparationists strive for. The Durban Declaration reflects such thinking in urging the United Nations, other appropriate international and regional organisations and States to 'redress the marginalization of Africa's contribution to world history and civilization

---

109 Nancy Mathis, "President Acknowledges U.S. 'Sins' Against Africa", *Houston Chronicle*, March 25 1998 cited in Chisolm op cit 704 fn 160.

110 Gifford "House of Lords" op cit.

111 Draft Declaration of the African preparatory meeting for the World Conference Against Racism, Racial Discrimination, Xenophobia and related Intolerance, as adopted by the Ambassadorial meeting on 8th December 2000, Articles 21 and 22.

112 *Reuters*, "Countries should be ready to discuss compensation for slavery – Dlamini-Zuma", March 23 2001. The Durban Declaration however equivocates on the "apology" which the States' delegates offer.

113 Minow op cit at 116.

114 Minow *ibid.*

by developing and implementing a specific and comprehensive programme of research, education and mass communication to disseminate widely a balanced and objective presentation of Africa's seminal and valuable contribution to humanity.'[115] In this regard, one thinks of public education funds to facilitate public awareness of slavery and systemic discrimination. Chinweizu speaks, for instance, of the creation of a 'Black Heritage Education Curriculum', to teach Africans their true history and to restore their sense of self-worth.[116] Similar measures include the institution of monuments and memorial days. In so doing, Africans as a group will eventually benefit as fallacies of inferiority are replaced by a true understanding of how integral the African presence has been to the success of Western economies.[117]

3 CONCLUSION

Reparation for slavery – or any other form of mass-atrocity – is a multifaceted issue that requires realistic political debate. In the context of slavery, the seemingly intractable legal problems associated with a claim for reparation, means that other, more overtly political strategies, may have to be turned to for success.

However, within the political realm the success of any strategy will be weakened by unrealistic demands for unworkable forms of reparation. In respect of slavery, return of stolen artefacts, expressions of regret for the slave trade, and programmes to raise public awareness of slavery are examples of legitimate and feasible forms of reparation which African States, either corporately or singly, are entitled to on any moral account. But if Africans are to secure a moral global economy through the device of an African consciousness, African States have to adopt a purposive approach to their calls for compensatory justice which will draw the support of Western States. An approach which focuses on contemporary development problems has the advantage of being aligned with existing international human rights struggles under the banner of socio-economic advancement and the right to development. By translating the duty

115 Article 118 of the Durban Declaration. See too Article 119 which "Invites States and relevant international organizations and non-governmental organizations to build upon the efforts of the Slave Route Project of the United Nations Educational Scientific and Cultural Organization and its theme of "Breaking the silence" by developing texts and testimony, slavery multi-media centres and/or programmes that will collect, record, organize, exhibit and publish the existing data relevant to the history of slavery and the trans-Atlantic, Mediterranean and Indian Ocean slave trades, paying particular attention to the thoughts and actions of the victims of slavery and the slave trade, in their quest for freedom and justice."

116 Chinweizu, "Reparations and A New Global Order: A Comparative Overview", paper read at the second Plenary Session of the First Pan-African Conference on Reparations, Abuja, Nigeria, April 27, 1993 (available at www.arm.arc.co.uk).

117 Chisolm makes a similar point with regard to the African Americans and their presence as a driving force behind the success of the capitalist foundation of the United States (Chisolm op cit 723).

to make compensatory reparation for past racist practices into a duty to speed up development of third world States, reparationists 'provide another reason for doing the right thing'.[118]

As a whole, each of the forms of reparation discussed in this chapter present their own promises and problems as responses to the history of slavery, and will no doubt hold different promises and problems as responses to other mass atrocities. This much is clear, whatever the reparation context, be it slavery, colonialism, genocide, or any other mass atrocity. While many Western States are understandably concerned about the implications of reparation claims, it is only through reasoned and appropriately goal-directed argument that reparationists will be able to convince them of an alternative that is worse. That alternative, in the words of Geraldine Van Bueren, is 'that the passage of time has made Western states cosy with injustice'.[119]

118 See Human Rights Watch Report op cit at 5.

119 Geraldine Van Bueren op cit.

REPARATIONS UNDER INTERNATIONAL CRIMINAL LAW

Andreas O'Shea

1 INTRODUCTION

International criminal law by its very nature focuses on punishment of serious international offences as its main objective. It differs from national criminal law by the attention it pays to offences which not only wrong a State or a particular community but offend the international community as a whole. However, its *raison d'etre* is intricately connected to the pursuit of international peace and security. It is but one solution to the general problem of how to address past human rights violations in order to restore the damaged society and ensure no repetition of these undesirable events in that society or elsewhere in the world. It sits side by side with, complements and competes with other mechanisms for the restoration of international peace and security including amnesties, truth commissions, exclusionary measures against those responsible for past wrongs (in particular lustration laws) and reparations to the victims.

Not unsurprisingly international criminal law finds its roots in the development of norms designed to limit the effects of war. These are nearly as old as war itself. Evidence of such norms can be found in the historical records of for instance the Chinese, the Mayas and the ancient Greeks.[1] Later in history, principles on the regulation of war were codified in national military manuals,[2] but ultimately being a matter of universal concern, the laws of war have developed internationally through the practice and customs of States[3] and collective codification in international treaties designed for this specific purpose.[4] In modern history the laws of war were most recently extensively codified in the four Geneva Conventions on the Laws of War of

---

1 See Sun Tzu, *The Art of War* (L. Giles trans. 1944); M. Cherif Bassiouni, 'International Law and the Holocaust' (1979) 9 *Cal West Int'l LJ* 202, at 203; A Aymard and J. Auboyer, *L'Orient et la Grece Antique*, 1953, at 293-99.

2 Like the *Oxford Manual* of 1880 and the *Lieber Instructions* of 1863, in Schindler and Toman, *The Laws of Armed Conflicts*, 1981 at 35 and 3 respectively.

3 See Theodor Meron, *Human Rights and Humanitarian Norms as Customary Law*, 1989.

4 See Schindler and Toman, note 2 *supra*.

1949.[5] It is in the last fifty years that international criminal laws have expanded their frontiers to other internationally reprehensible offences such as genocide,[6] crimes against humanity,[7] apartheid[8] and offences against diplomats and UN personnel.[9]

The Geneva Conventions provide for a general obligation on States to prosecute grave breaches of these conventions before their own courts.[10] The substance of international criminal law has been refined on the international level, and its enforcement has in the past generally been left to individual States. While there are isolated examples of the collective enforcement of international criminal law in the sense of courts representing the interests of a plurality of States,[11] this development has really only taken serious strides in the last 15 years, with the establishment of *ad hoc* tribunals like the International Criminal Tribunal for the former Yugoslavia,[12] the International Criminal Tribunal for Rwanda[13] and the Special Court for Sierra Leone,[14] and finally with the birth of the International Criminal Court, a permanent institution.[15]

Developments in international criminal law, mainly on the international plane, have taken place quite independently from developments in other aspects of transitional justice, particularly those taking place on the national level. Thus, one sees

---

5 Geneva Convention for the Amelioration of the Condition of the Wounded and Sick in Armed Forces in the Field of August 12, 1949 (1950) 75 UNTS 31-83; Geneva Convention for the Amelioration of the Condition of the Wounded, Sick and Shipwrecked Members of Armed Forces at Sea of August 12, 1949 (1950) 75 UNTS 85-133; Geneva Convention Relative to the Treatment of Prisoners of War of August 12, 1949 (1950) 75 UNTS 135-285; Geneva Convention Relative to the Protection of Civilian Persons in Time of War of August 12, 1949 (1950) 75 UNTS 287-417: also found in International Committee of the Red Cross, *The Geneva Conventions of August 12 1949*.

6 By virtue of the Convention for the Prevention and Punishment of the Crime of Genocide of 1948: see generally William Schabas, *Genocide in International Law*, 2000.

7 See Cherif M. Bassiouni, *Crimes Against Humanity in International Law*, 1992.

8 Pursuant to the International Convention on the Suppression and Punishment of the Crime of Apartheid of 1973.

9 Pursuant to the Convention on the Prevention and Punishment of Crimes against Internationally Protected and Persons including Diplomatic Agents of 1973.

10 See articles 49, 50, 129 and 146 respectively of the four Geneva Conventions, note 5 *supra*.

11 The earliest recorded being in 1474 with the prosecution of Peter Von Hagenbach in Breisach, Germany: see Bassiouni, 'The Prosecution of International Crimes and the Establishment of an International Criminal Court', in M. Cherif Bassiouni (ed.) *International Criminal Law*, 1986, vol. 3: Enforcement, citing George Schwarzenberger, *International Law as Applied by the International Courts and Tribunals*, 1968, vol. II, *The Law of Armed Conflict*, at 462-6. Following the Second World War, the Nuremburg and Tokyo Tribunals were established.

12 Established by Security Council resolution 827 (1993) on Establishing an International Tribunal for the Prosecution of Persons Responsible for Serious Violations of International Humanitarian Law Committed in the Territory of the Former Yugoslavia (1993) 32 ILM 1203.

13 Established by Security Council resolution 955 establishing the International Tribunal for Rwanda (1994) 33 ILM 1598.

14 Established by the Agreement Between the United Nations and the Government of Sierra Leone on the Establishment of a Special Court for Sierra Leone of 16 January 2002, UN Doc. S/2000/915.

15 Established by the Statute of the International Criminal Court (1998) 37 ILM 999.

very little account being taken of international criminal law in national processes of amnesty, truth commissions and reparations, while in the international arena, very little credence or understanding has been directed at the need for national reconciliation through alternatives to punishment.[16] Yet, all these mechanisms are aimed at the same general objective – establishing peace and ensuring the respect of human rights. So, in principle attempts to look at international criminal law and its processes in a more holistic fashion which takes into account the requirements of reconciliation and the needs of victims should be welcomed.

Such thinking goes against the instincts of many criminal lawyers trained in the context of national systems where criminal trials have been carefully separated from the pursuit of civil claims and generally detached from the broader objectives of stabilising society, which lies at the root of criminal law. The idea that a criminal court should concern itself with questions of reparations just does not feel right for many lawyers. We as lawyers need to take a step back though and examine what exactly prevents us from embracing such concepts. If it is down to the way things have been done in our own national jurisdictions, then we must resist our instincts and examine with an open mind the purpose and advantages of international criminal processes incorporating some reference to the other pillars of transitional justice. Apart from any questions over the legitimacy of the national separation of civil and criminal law, it must be remembered that on the international level there is no adequate system of jurisdiction for civil claims by individuals to replace the often ineffective or inappropriate national mechanisms in time of conflict.[17]

Reparations in any form, as one of these pillars of the general process of transitional justice, has not traditionally been the concern of international criminal courts or the national criminal courts in many national jurisdictions. It has only recently become a recognised element of the international process, through mechanisms envisaged for the International Criminal Court. This results from pressure from victims groups and support from lawyers whose own legal systems embrace some form of victim participation and reparation.[18]

So, how and in what manner can reparations become the concern of an international criminal court? This relatively new aspect of international criminal law has not yet received a great deal of academic attention.[19] Further, the discussion on this subject

---

16 See Andreas O'Shea, *Amnesty for Crime in International Law and Practice*, 2002.

17 Claims to the Human Rights Committee under the International Covenant on Civil and Political Rights of 1966 and it Second Optional Protocol and under regional instruments depend on state consent to this process, state responsibility and exhaustion of local remedies.

18 Generally being civil law jurisdictions.

19 See however Christian P J Muttukumaru, 'Reparations for Victims', in Flavia Lattanzi and William A Schabas, *Essays on the Rome Statute of the International Criminal Court*, 1999, at 303-310; David Donat-Cattin, 'Article 75: Reparations to Victims', in Otto Triffterer (ed), *Commentary on the Rome Statute of the International Criminal Court*, 1999, at 965-978; Gilbert Bitti and Håkan Friman, 'Participation of Victims in the Proceedings', in Roy Lee, *International Criminal Court: Elements of Crimes and Rules of Procedure and Evidence*, 2001, at 456-491.

to date has focused on the position of victims in the limited sense of those who have suffered the consequences of crimes alleged against the accused. However, perhaps the least controversial aspect of reparations in an international criminal court is that of reparation to an accused who is unlawfully arrested or detained, had a conviction reversed having served part of his sentence, or who is ultimately found to be innocent following a fair trial. Such a person may also in one sense be viewed as a victim of the conflict.

The last scenario of a finding of not guilty at first glance has less immediate consequences for a person than an accused unlawfully treated or wrongly serving a sentence. However, there are particularly harsh examples of pre-trial and post-trial circumstances which may not reach the threshold of unlawfulness simply because they are explicable in terms of procedures, but are nonetheless strenuous for the accused. Experience has shown that a person accused before an international tribunal may spend a significant period of time, usually years, in detention, before the final resolution of his or her case. For instance, Dr Andre Rwamakuba, the former Minister of Primary and Secondary Education in Rwanda, was arrested in 1995 by the Namibian authorities on behalf of the International Criminal Tribunal for Rwanda, released in 1996 on the request of the Prosecutor at the Rwanda Tribunal, re-arrested and taken to Arusha to be detained at the same Tribunal in 1998, tried in November 2003, and then, following the trial being declared a mistrial, tried a second time in July 2005. This constituted a total experience of more than nine years of detention. An application for dismissal of the charges for abuse of process failed on the basis that the delays could be explained by legitimate reasons and the procedures had continued without significant interruption.[20]

Further, unlike on the national level, even once the accused has been acquitted of all charges, it may not be possible to secure his actual freedom where he cannot safely return to his own country and requires some other State to grant him asylum. The granting of asylum to acquitted persons has proved extraordinarily difficult as political pressures and a presumption of guilt in the political arena militate against States accepting to host such persons, who are then held in 'safe houses' pending the resolution of their predicament.

It would seem perfectly natural that the international tribunal responsible for authorising the person's continued detention and subsequent restraint of freedom should be in a position to order some form of reparation for the years lost in a person's life while facing false allegations. The main obstacle if there is one to this form of reparations is the financial limitations of the process, but if hundreds of thousands of dollars can be spent on pursuing a case against an innocent person, then the expense must be justified in fairness.

---

[20] *Prosecutor v Andre Rwamakuba*, Decision on Defence Motion for Stay of Proceedings on Grounds of Undue Delay, 2005.

The other equally important but more difficult and legally controversial aspect of reparations is the major question of reparations to the victims of the crimes forming the subject matter of the trials. The legal controversy being referred to here arises not from the principle of reparations for victims, which is well established in international law,[21] but from the question whether this should form part of the function of a criminal court, and the implications in terms of victims representation in the proceedings themselves. On the one side it is said that dealing with reparations would distract an international criminal court from its main function of bringing those most responsible to justice and create a practical difficulty for judges from different legal traditions determining the nature and extent of reparations.[22] Some States have also apparently expressed concern over the implications for their own national legal systems which do not recognise the idea of provision of reparations in the criminal legal context.[23] On the other side, and this is the concern which ultimately prevailed in the negotiations leading up to the conclusion of the Statute of the International Criminal Court, it is felt that an international criminal process partially designed to achieve reconciliation should give expression not only to retributive justice but also to restorative justice.[24]

2 REPARATIONS FOR ACCUSED AND RELEASED PERSONS

The current structure of international criminal law enforcement, on the international collective as opposed to the national state level, involves the use of international tribunals as courts of criminal law which apply international law and employ judges and lawyers from different nations. Until 1 July 2003,[25] these were temporary institutions for specific conflicts, including the International Criminal Tribunal for the former Yugoslavia, the International Criminal Tribunal for Rwanda and the Special Court for Sierra Leone.

---

21 See Study Concerning the Right to Restitution, Compensation and Rehabilitation for Victims of Gross Violations of Human Rights and Fundamental Freedoms: Final Report submitted by Theo van Boven, Special Rapporteur to the Sub-Commission on the Prevention of Discrimination and Protection of Minorities, conclusions and recommendations: reproduced in (1996) 59 *Law and Contemporary Problems* 283; See further the chapter by Max du Plessis on the right to reparations under international law in this work.

22 See Muttukumaru, 'Reparations for Victims', *ibid.*, 303-4.

23 *Ibid.*, 304.

24 *Ibid.*, 304.

25 When the International Criminal Court Statute entered into force: in terms of Article 126(1) of the Statute of the International Criminal Court.

The Statutes[26] and Rules[27] which govern the International Criminal Tribunals for Rwanda and for the former Yugoslavia, as well as those of the Special Court for Sierra Leone, contain no express provisions for the compensation of acquitted persons for the time spent in detention or indeed any abuses which they might have suffered. However, the Trial Chambers, that is the bench's of judges designated for trials, have a general power to make such orders as are necessary for the fair conduct of the trial.[28] Arguably, this power must include the whole trial process to its very conclusion and may form the basis of an order for reparations.

The Appeals Chamber of the International Criminal Tribunal for Rwanda, in its decision in *Barayagwiza* of review of its prior decision for dismissal on grounds of abuse of process, provided in its disposition for the compensation of the accused in the event that he was ultimately acquitted, or in the alternative for years off sentence if convicted.[29] However, this novel aspect of the decision is oddly unreasoned and it can be inferred from the circumstances that the decision was based on a finding of a violation of the rights of the accused quite apart from the question of guilt or innocence.

The difficulty which arises is that no budget has been envisaged for compensation of accused. Budgetary matters (and all other administrative matters) are managed by an organ of the Tribunal known as the Registry.[30] Although such considerations should not influence the making of judicial orders, the reality is that the judges cooperate quite closely with the Registry before making orders with financial consequences. This is done through the legal officers and court coordinators designated to judges and chambers. Furthermore, while there is a general provision to make necessary orders, judges would normally be reluctant to do so unless persuaded that their order is enforceable and backed up by sufficient resources and logistical support from the Registry.

Victims groups might very well ask the question why, if a court can offer compensation to those acquitted, it cannot also offer compensation to the victims of crimes? The simple answer to this would be that the court holds a special responsibility towards the accused arrested and detained at its request, and it is a question of the

---

26 Statute of the International Criminal Tribunal for Rwanda; Statute of the International Criminal Tribunal for the former Yugoslavia; Statute of the Special Court for Sierra Leone.

27 Rules of Procedure and Evidence of the International Criminal Tribunal for Rwanda; Rules of Procedure and Evidence of the International Criminal Tribunal for the former Yugoslavia; Rules of Procedure and Evidence of the Special Court for Sierra Leone.

28 See Rule 54 of the Rules of Procedure and Evidence of the International Criminal Tribunal for Rwanda; Rule 54 of the Rules of Procedure and Evidence of the International Criminal Tribunal for the former Yugoslavia and Rule 54 of the Rules of Procedure and Evidence of the Special Court for Sierra Leone.

29 Decision on Review and/or Reconsideration, 14 September 2000.

30 See Article 17 of the Statute of the International Criminal Tribunal for the former Yugoslavia; Article 16 of the Statute of the International Criminal Tribunal for Rwanda; Article 16 of the Statute of the Special Court for Sierra Leone.

limits of the powers and the budget. One could nonetheless expect some loud political noises considering the already subjective reactions of governments and victims groups to acquittals of those charged with serious international crimes.[31]

In July 2003, the International Criminal Court came into existence. The Court was created by a treaty adopted in 1998 between a number of States.[32] It differs from the other international criminal tribunals in that it is a permanent institution designed to cover different conflicts and is not confined to any specific conflict situation. It is limited in the exercise of its jurisdiction in that it may only apply to crimes committed after 1 July 2003[33] and pertaining to perpetrators who are nationals of State parties,[34] crimes committed within the territory of State parties[35] or on referral from the Security Council of the United Nations.[36] The Court is a new institution and no trial has yet run its course before it.

Article 85 of the Statute of this court, being its governing instrument, provides for three instances where an accused person might claim compensation. First, it foresees this where there has been an unlawful arrest or detention.[37] Second, compensation is possible when a conviction is reversed for a miscarriage of justice and the accused has already undergone part of his or her sentence.[38] Finally, it is envisaged that in exceptional circumstances the Court might order compensation for an acquitted person.[39]

The provision for compensation in circumstances of an acquittal are fairly circumscribed since it is provided that:

> "In exceptional circumstances, where the Court finds conclusive facts showing that there has been a grave and manifest miscarriage of justice, it may in its discretion award compensation, according to the criteria provided in the Rules of Procedure and Evidence, to a person who has been released from detention following a final decision of acquittal or a termination of proceedings for that reason."

In one sense, if a person is acquitted of a serious crime and the presumption of innocence is taken seriously, there is of necessity a grave and manifest miscarriage of justice by wrongly detaining and putting through a trial an innocent person. However, the clause is clearly designed to limit the circumstances in which compensation may

---

31 See Mucyo, Procureur General of Rwanda, reaction to Appeal Chamber's confirmation of the acquittal of Ntagarura and Bagambiki.

32 The Statute of the International Criminal Court, note 15 *supra*.

33 See Article 11(1) in association with Article 126(1) of the Statute of the International Criminal Court.

34 Article 12(2)(b) of the Statute of the International Criminal Court.

35 Article 12(2)(a) of the Statute of the International Criminal Court.

36 Article 13(b) of the Statute of the International Criminal Court.

37 Article 85(1) of the Statute of the International Criminal Court.

38 Article 85(2) of the Statute of the International Criminal Court.

39 Article 85(3) of the Statute of the International Criminal Court.

be awarded to acquitted persons. The Rules of Procedure and Evidence (rules governing the manner in which criminal proceedings are conducted by the parties and the judges) give no further guidance on the scope of these limitations but confine themselves to setting out the procedure. It will therefore be left to the judges to develop the appropriate meaning to be derived from the notions of exceptional circumstances and grave and manifest miscarriage of justice. Factors which might come into play are irregularities in the detention of the accused, long detention before trial, and evidence of foul play in the bringing of a prosecution.

The procedure for claiming compensation in one of the approved situations is outlined in Rules 173 to 175. The person seeking compensation makes an application in writing to the Presidency of the Court.[40] This application must be submitted within six months of the relevant decision giving rise to the potential right to compensation, that is the decision concerning the unlawfulness of arrest or detention, the decision reversing conviction or the judgment of acquittal, as the case may be.[41] A bench of judges is then designated to hear the matter, which must not include any of the judges involved in the previous judgment or judgments in relation to the accused.[42] The application is served on the prosecution which has the opportunity to respond.[43] A hearing will be held unless both parties consent to the matter being decided on the papers.[44]

In relation to the compensation to be awarded, Rule 175 simply provides that the judges shall take into account the consequences of the grave and manifest miscarriage of justice on the personal, family, social and professional situation of the person filing the request.[45]

3 REPARATIONS FOR VICTIMS OF CRIMES

3.1 PRINCIPLE OF REPARATIONS FOR VICTIMS

The question of reparation for victims is traditionally separated from that of criminal proceedings in international tribunals and many national jurisdictions. The separation is manifest in the Rules of Procedure and Evidence of the International Criminal Tribunals for Rwanda and for the former Yugoslavia, as well as that for the Special Court for Sierra Leone, where it is provided that the victims may make claims before

40 Rule 173(1) of the Rules of Procedure and Evidence of the International Criminal Court.
41 Rule 173(2) of the Rules of Procedure and Evidence of the International Criminal Court.
42 Rule 173(1) of the Rules of Procedure and Evidence of the International Criminal Court.
43 Rule 174(1) of the Rules of Procedure and Evidence of the International Criminal Court.
44 Rule 174(2) of the Rules of Procedure and Evidence of the International Criminal Court.
45 Rule 175 of the Rules of Procedure and Evidence of the International Criminal Court.

their national jurisdictions.[46] While disowning the task, these Tribunals, oddly, expressly provide for a right for victims to seek compensation before their national jurisdictions. Does this impose an obligation on States to ensure the ability for victims to introduce such claims domestically? Since the Rules of Procedure and Evidence derive from the Statute, which, being a Security Council document is binding on all states, they are capable of creating obligations for States. However, this can only occur to the extent that the Statute envisages the power to create such extra obligations. Powers may only reasonably be said to have been envisaged in the Statute when they clearly derive as a foreseeable consequence of the power to create rules. It is suggested that this is not in fact the case here, since it is not necessary for the functioning of the Tribunal that it have the ability to direct States on matters not directly related to the conduct of the criminal proceedings.

It is in the International Criminal Court (hereinafter ICC) process that the question of reparations for victims of crimes is confronted head on for the first time in the history of international criminal tribunals. Both the power of the Court to award reparations and the representation of victims before it have been given considerable thought in the drafting of the Statute and the Rules of Procedure and Evidence.

3.2 INSTITUTIONAL FRAMEWORK FOR THE PROVISION OF REPARATIONS IN INTERNATIONAL CRIMINAL PROCESS

In addition to the role of the Trial Chamber of the ICC, the Registry of the Court will form an important part of the structure for the issue of reparations. Within the Registry is established a Victims and Witnesses Unit.[47] This unit will be able to assist in the execution of court orders, advise the court on victim and witness issues, as well as assist the victims on the question of representation in order to make their views and observations known to the court or otherwise participate in the proceedings.

Also within the institutional framework for victims, it is envisaged that a 'Trust Fund' will be created by the Assembly of State Parties.[48] It is for the Assembly of State Parties to determine the 'criteria' by which the Trust Fund will operate.[49] The existence of such a fund makes it possible for the court's new if incidental role of ensuring reparation for victims, to have a measure of meaning, as such an objective could not

---

46 Rule 106 of the Rules of Procedure and Evidence of the International Criminal Tribunal for the former Yugoslavia; Rule 106 of the Rules of Procedure and Evidence of the International Criminal Tribunal for Rwanda; Rule 105 of the Rules of Procedure and Evidence of the Special Court for Sierra Leone.

47 Article 43(6) of the ICC Statute.

48 Article 79 of the ICC Statute.

49 Article 79(3) of the ICC Statute.

realistically depend on orders against accused only, who are frequently by misfortune or ruse, indigent by the time of their arrest, if not before. It is not entirely clear from the terms of the Statute itself how the budget of the Trust Fund will be developed. For instance, no specific provision is made as to contributions from States. There is merely reference to a power accorded to the judges to order the transfer of moneys raised from fines and forfeiture to the Fund.[50]

3.3 THE ESTABLISHMENT OF PRINCIPLES ON REPARATIONS

The ICC Statute goes far in promoting a recognised goal of securing reparations for victims, by not confining its provisions merely to establishing the institutional mechanisms for the execution of this endeavour, but additionally by giving direct indications as to the measures to be taken with regard to reparations. Under Article 75 of the Statute, the judges are directed to establish principles for the reparation of victims and are given the power to make orders and invite representations.

In establishing principles, the learned judges will be able to draw on experience from national jurisdictions, including criminal proceedings and reparation processes. There is little to draw upon from the international plane save for certain general declarations[51] and pronouncements made by tribunals in the inter-State context or in the enforcement of treaties for the protection of human rights. No direct experience can be drawn upon in the context of international criminal proceedings.

One basic principle of interest here is that reparations may take different forms which need not necessarily be monetary. The judges may permit themselves to order or recommend different forms of reparation. Thus, reparations may take the form of apology, commemoration (erection of a monument, naming public places after a victim or the designation of a day of rest), or public insurance such as access to social and health care.[52] A court may be limited in its ability to order some forms of reparation without the consent or cooperation of States or the accused in certain instances.

---

50 Article 79(2) of the ICC Statute.

51 *Declaration of Basic Principles of Justice for Victims of Crime and Abuse of Power,* and *Draft Principles and Guidelines and Guidelines on the Right to Reparation for Victims of Violations of Human Rights and International Humanitarian Law.*

52 See *UN Handbook on Justice of Victims of Crime*; referred to in David Donat-Cattin, note 1 *supra*, at 971-2.

3.4 THE SOURCE OF REPARATIONS

In the ICC, an order may be made against a convicted person for reparations to the victim. It is not clear whether this must be treated as a completely separate issue from that of sentencing or whether sentencing should be dealt with in conjunction with the question of reparations. Although the matter of reparations is not expressly treated as a sentencing issue, it would seem fair and appropriate to measure the proposed sentence against any reparations the judges are thinking of awarding. After all, ordering the accused to pay compensation is a punitive measure and it would not be right for an accused to be in a better position simply because he has disposed of all his financial resources or successfully hidden them from public view. The provision on orders of reparation against the accused might even afford a means of broadening the options available to the judges. A prison sentence could be combined with an order to undertake some form of community service for the benefit of victims.

Otherwise, the Court may make an order for reparations which employs the funds available in the Trust Fund.[53] It is clear that this is not viewed under the Statute as an absolute right for victims, but rather as a matter of judicial discretion to be exercised 'where appropriate'.[54] How this discretion ought to be exercised will depend on what criteria have been created by the Assembly of State Parties for the use of the operation of the Trust Fund in association with any principles determined by the judges with respect to reparations in accordance with their basic obligation to determine such principles.

The International Criminal Court Statute does not recognise a power to award reparations to victims against a State. Such a power would have changed the essential nature of the court as a court addressing the responsibility of individuals.[55] Neither is there any legal basis upon which a recommendation could be made to the State except in respect of the exercise of the Court's own power to provide reparations.

3.5 THE ENFORCEMENT OF ORDERS OF REPARATIONS

Since the assets of a convicted person will be located within the national jurisdiction of States, the enforcement of any order for reparations made against that person necessarily depends on the cooperation of States. Accordingly, specific provision is made to ensure that such cooperation is secured. Unlike the *ad hoc* tribunals, the ICC is established by treaty, rather than Security Council resolution which is binding on

53 Article 75 (2).

54 *Ibid.*

55 See Article 25 of the ICC Statute.

all States.[56] Thus, only those States which are party to the Statute are under an obligation to cooperate and then only to the extent specifically set out in the treaty. The general obligation on State parties to cooperate is set out in Article 86 of the Statute. In terms of this article, 'States Parties shall in accordance with the provisions of this Statute, cooperate fully with the Court with the investigation and prosecution of crimes within the jurisdiction of the Court.' Arguably, this provision excludes matters outside the investigation and prosecution process. However, the specific forms of cooperation under Article 93(1) are made directly applicable to the enforcement of orders of reparation by virtue of Article 75 (4). Notably, such measures include the identification and whereabouts of persons or location of items;[57] the service of documents including judicial documents;[58] the execution of searches and seizures;[59] the provision of records and documents, including official records and documents;[60] the identification, tracing and freezing or seizure of proceeds, property and assets and instrumentalities of crimes for the purpose of eventual forfeiture, without prejudice to the *bone fide* rights of third parties.[61]

Apart from these general mechanisms for the facilitation of the work of the Court in relation to reparations, there is further a concrete obligation upon States to enforce orders for reparations in so far as the recovery of monies and property are concerned. This derives from the application of enforcement measures for fines and forfeiture[62] to orders for reparations.[63]

4 VICTIM PARTICIPATION

To the extent that the final outcome of criminal proceedings may impact upon reparations for victims, as well as the fact that the conviction of those most responsible is a form of catharsis for the victim, the question of participation in those proceedings is a matter of great relevance to victims seeking reparations. The participation of victims in international criminal court proceedings is a new phenomenon. None of the *ad hoc* tribunals expressly provided for such a possibility. There was one instance where the lawyer of a prosecution witness was permitted to sit in on the proceedings.[64] There have also been instances where Tribunals have permitted monitoring of

56 Under Article 25 of the UN Charter.
57 Article 93 (1)(a) of the Statute of the International Criminal Court.
58 Article 93 (1)(d) of the Statute of the International Criminal Court.
59 Article 93 (1)(h) of the Statute of the International Criminal Court.
60 Article 93 (1)(i) of the Statute of the International Criminal Court.
61 Article 93 (1)(k) of the Statute of the International Criminal Court.
62 Article 109 of the Statute of the International Criminal Court.
63 Article 95 (5) of the Statute of the International Criminal Court.
64 In the case of *Prosecutor v Bagosora et al*, the lawyer for General Dallair was permitted to sit in court.

proceedings by international and national NGOs,[65] and participation in the form of *amicus curiae* in proceedings of organisations representing the interests of certain classes of victims.[66]

The ICC Statute directly envisages the participation of victims in international criminal proceedings before the International Criminal Court, with limitations. Understandably, victims are permitted to make representations before an order for reparations is made in terms of Article 75. However, the proposed victim participation potentially goes much further than that, encompassing even the trial process itself. In terms of Article 68 (3) of the Statute:

> "Where the personal interests of the victims are affected, the Court shall permit their views and concerns to be presented and considered at stages of the proceedings determined to be appropriate by the Court and in a manner which is not prejudicial to or inconsistent with the rights of the accused and a fair and impartial trial."

This gives a very wide scope to the judges on this question and it remains to be seen to what extent the right to a fair trial will constitute an obstacle to meaningful participation. To give effect to this entitlement, it will be necessary to consider the logistics of victim representation in terms of the provision of legal advice and assistance as well as how to prevent interference and delay in the proceedings from too much input into proceedings while preserving some equality between the rights of victims. These issues have been pre-empted to some extent in the Rules of Procedure and Evidence of the Court.

The question of victim representation rests upon the same basic principle as that applicable to accused. That is to say that victims are free to have the legal representation of their choice.[67] Moreover, the Registry will provide assistance in terms of the choice of legal representation[68] as well as payment of that representative in appropriate cases.[69]

However, the choice of legal representative is subject to certain limitations. First, a legal representative of a victim must be appropriately qualified. To be appropriately qualified the lawyer needs to possess 'established competence in international or criminal law and procedure, as well as the necessary relevant experience, whether as judge, prosecutor, advocate or in other similar capacity, in criminal proceedings'.[70] It is further required that he or she have excellent knowledge of one of the working

65 See e.g. Order on Trial Monitoring in Closed Session, 27 October 2004, Special Court for Sierra Leone (TC1); Order on Trial Monitoring in Closed Session, 5 November 2004, Special Court for Sierra Leone (TC1).

66 See *Prosecutor v Sesay*, Decision on Amnesty; *Prosecutor v Norman*, Decision on Child Soldiers.

67 See Rule 90(1) of the Rules of Procedure and Evidence of the International Criminal Court.

68 See Rule 90(2) of the Rules of Procedure and Evidence of the International Criminal Court.

69 See Rule 90(6) of the Rules of Procedure and Evidence of the International Criminal Court.

70 Rule 22(1).

languages of the Court.[71] The Registry maintains a list of counsel appropriately qualified and available for assignment to cases.[72]

Secondly, there is the obvious problem of not derailing the proceedings by allowing the participation of too many actors. This problem has been anticipated in the rules of Procedure and Evidence in providing the Chamber with the power to request victims or groups of victims to choose a common legal representative,[73] and in the event of them being unwilling or unable to do so, to request the Registry to do so.[74]

Finally, as with accused persons, it is possible that the Chamber may exercise a degree of control over the removal of counsel to the extent that the rights of the accused or victims might be affected by such decisions. In the case of accused persons this control is expressly envisaged in the rules and it is undoubtedly the case that there is less reason to interfere with freedom of choice where the rights of the accused and consequently a fair trial are not directly at stake. Nonetheless, the Chamber will have a residual authority to exercise some continuing control over the removal or replacement of counsel to the extent that it may have any impact on the proceedings.[75]

With regard to the question of financial assistance, the position is that the rules only expressly provide for the possibility of such assistance in the case of the appointment of a common legal representative.[76] In practice this is unlikely to create any difficulty since it is hard to envisage any situation likely to be the subject of proceedings before the International Criminal Court which would not involve the necessity of a common legal representative. The serious, widespread or systematic nature of the crimes likely to come before the Court will usually involve the interest of a variety of victims' groups.

In considering the question of reparations the views of victims will automatically be heard and taken into account by the Chamber.[77] As far as the criminal proceedings generally are concerned, a victim or group of victims who wishes/wish to participate in the proceedings must make an application to the court.[78] The application is in writing and made in the initial instance to the Registry which then transmits it to the relevant Chamber.[79] Although the Chamber has discretion in the matter, it would appear that in the case of victims possessing an interest in the matter such discretion

---

71 Idem.

72 Rules 21 and 22.

73 Rule 90(2).

74 Rule 90(3).

75 See e.g. *Prosecutor v Sesay, Kallon and Gbao*, Decision on Application by Counsel for the Third Accused to Withdraw from the Case, 5 April 2006 (Trial Chamber of Special Court for Sierra Leone), and Written Reasons for the Decision on Application by Counsel for the Third Accused to Withdraw from the Case, 19 June 2006.

76 See Rule 90(2).

77 See Article 68(3) of the Statute and generally Rule 94 and 95, as well as Rule 97(2) (on quantifying reparations).

78 Rule 89(1).

79 Idem.

is confined to directing in which stages of the proceedings they may participate and the manner of such participation.[80] It is only when a person or group does not qualify as victim with a proper interest in the proceedings that the application may be rejected entirely.[81] This is likely to be a matter of considerable concern to the principle parties and in particular the defence. Accordingly when an application is made for victim participation, both the prosecution and defence are afforded the opportunity to respond to such application.[82]

In the event that participation is permitted, such participation may but need not include direct participation in the hearings.[83] It might equally be confined to written representations where the Chamber so orders.[84] It is clear that the form of participation is capable of being potentially quite meaningful since Rule 89(1) specifies that it may include the making of opening and closing statements and Rule 91(3) envisages the possibility of questions being put to witnesses. Beyond that, since it is for the Chamber to determine the manner and stages of participation, it remains to be seen how extensively the Chambers will permit victim participation and how the jurisprudence on the parameters of such participation will develop.

Specific provision is made in the rules for the possibility of putting questions to witnesses to anticipate the problem of potential prejudice to the accused and a fair trial. A legal representative of a victim would require the Chamber's permission to question a witness and the Chamber may require intended questions to be put in writing. It will in such cases communicate them to the prosecution and 'if appropriate' the defence, and allow observations from the parties within a specified time limit.[85] The Chamber will make a ruling on such requests having regard to the stage of the proceedings, the rights of the accused, the interests of the witnesses, and the need for a fair, impartial and expeditious trial.[86]

The idea that the victim's representative may put questions raises potentially serious difficulties for the defence and arguably the right to a fair trial. One issue which will need to be explored is the impact upon equality of arms. The interests of the victims and that of the prosecution will generally coincide. The interests of the victims and that of the accused may often conflict.

80 Idem.
81 See Rule 89(2).
82 Rule 89(1).
83 Rule 91(2).
84 Idem.
85 Rule 91(3)(a).
86 Rule 91(3)(b).

5 AN INTERNATIONAL REPARATIONS FUND

While it is progressive and inspiring that the International Criminal Court might provide a right for victims to participate in the international criminal process and receive reparations through an order of the court, reparations undoubtedly does not serve as the main objective of an international criminal court.

There is perhaps room for some consideration of the possibility of establishing an international reparations fund independently of any international criminal court or tribunal but which could give meaningful reparations in response to the factual findings of an international criminal trial. The advantage of such an initiative would be that it would have as its sole purpose the provision of reparations in a manner that does not depend upon the blessing of any court whose frame of reference is primarily punitive.

Such an international body could be established through the conclusion of a treaty between States, which might even be a protocol to the International Criminal Court Statute. There are obviously a number of ways in which such an institution might be organised. The organs of such a body could for instance consist of a council to manage the budget and relations with States and other institutions, a reparations panel with a decision making power on specific questions of reparations, and an administrative organ to manage the internal needs of the organisation. Like the International Criminal Court itself,[87] if it is an international organisation with member States it might benefit from an international legal personality enabling it to interact on the international political plane and enter into negotiations and dealings with States, the International Criminal Court and other international organisations on an equal international legal footing.

6 RELATIONSHIP BETWEEN REPARATIONS AND THE DUTY TO PROSECUTE INTERNATIONAL CRIMES

Some assert an absolute duty to prosecute international crimes under international law.[88] The clearest and most widely adopted statement of the *opinio juris* of States to this effect is the declaration in the preamble to the Statute of the International Criminal Court that States have a duty to prosecute international crimes.[89] State practice generally would tend to refute that this is an absolute duty and certainly a failure to

87 See Article 4(1) of the ICC Statute granting the ICC international legal personality.

88 See Cherif M. Bassiouni, *International Criminal Law Conventions and their Penal Provisions*, 2nd ed., 2000, at 50.

89 See note 15 *supra*.

prosecute was the practice prior to the entry into force of the International Criminal Court Statute.[90]

The duty to prosecute international crimes may be derived from a number of treaty provisions in human rights treaties and international humanitarian law treaties. This duty can be sub-divided into the duty with respect to certain specific crimes which are classified as the most serious international crimes, and the duty with respect to international crimes generally. With respect to the former, there would appear to be an unmitigated duty to prosecute and such category includes, in particular, grave breaches of the laws and customs of war as set out in the Geneva Conventions[91] as well as the crimes of genocide[92] and torture.[93] International crimes generally must be prevented as part of the State's duty to promote and secure human rights and ensure respect for the provisions of the Geneva Conventions on the laws of war.[94]

Some States have found it appropriate to find innovative solutions to the problem of how to address the wrongs of the past which do not necessarily involve the prosecution of all alleged international crimes. So, mechanisms have been put in place[95] such as truth commissions,[96] amnesty for crimes[97] and reparations for victims,[98] perhaps in combination with some instances of punishment. Such mechanisms may be viewed as genuine attempts to address the State's duty to secure human rights and respect for the rules of humanitarian law and therefore do not necessarily violate any duty of the State. There may be a direct correlation between the efforts of a State to provide reparations to victims and its ability to justify the non-prosecution of offences. Where crimes are not prosecuted the State may to a degree compensate this failure by nonetheless investigating such crimes and attempting to provide some form of reparations to the victims. Some would argue that this is a more direct and meaningful way of providing justice to victims of crimes in a transitional society where moving

---

90 See Andreas O'Shea, *Amnesty for Crime in International Law and Practice*, note 16 *supra*, at 228-266.

91 See note 10 *supra*.

92 See note 6 *supra*.

93 Pursuant to the customary international law and the Convention against Torture and Other Cruel Inhuman or Degrading Treatment of 1984; see generally Burger, Herman J. and Hans Danelius, *The United Nations Convention Against Torture: a Handbook on the Convention Against Torture and Other Cruel, Inhuman and Degrading Treatment or Punishment*, 1988.

94 See Article 56 of the United Nations Charter; Article 2(1) of the International Covenant on Civil and Political Rights; Article 1 of the African Charter on Human and Peoples' Rights; Article 1 of the European Convention for the Protection of Human Rights and Fundamental Freedoms of 1950; Article 1 respectively of the four Geneva Conventions of 1949: see note 5 *supra*.

95 See Andreas O'Shea, 'Transitional Justice for the Victims of Past Human Rights Violations: The Global Context', in John C Mubangizi, *The Protection of Human Rights in South Africa: A Legal and Practical Analysis*, 2004.

96 See Priscilla B Hayner, 'Fifteen Truth Commissions-1974-1994: A Comparative Study' (1994) 16 *HRQ* 597.

97 See Andreas O'Shea, *Amnesty for Crimes in International Law and Practice*, note 16 *supra*.

98 See for instance Catherine Jenkins, 'After the Dry White Season: the dilemmas of Reparations and Reconstruction in South Africa' (2000) 3 *SAJHR* 415; and generally the other chapters of this work.

forward and quashing resentment between groups is essential to the well-being of the society damaged by conflict.[99]

7 CONCLUSION

The idea of transitional justice for a society following conflict in the national arena has long moved away from the idea that punishment is the ultimate and exclusive solution to addressing the wrongs of the past or that it should not be viewed in combination with other processes such as that of reparations. From Nuremberg and the Tokyo Tribunals through to the more recent ICTY, ICTR and Special Court for Sierra Leone, there has been little real reflection of this reality on the international level when establishing international processes of justice. We have not observed the establishment of international truth commissions or international processes of reparations in conjunction or cooperation with the formation of international courts. Prior to the inception of the International Criminal Court, even in the context of the planning and operation of international tribunals there had been no serious effort to approach transitional justice from a broader perspective than its punitive aspect.

This has changed significantly with the creation of the International Criminal Court, where reparations for victims featured prominently in the thinking behind the operation of the court. It still remains to be seen how the specific provisions on this area will be applied but a major step forward has been taken in terms of viewing justice in a broader perspective in international mechanisms of justice. Strangely, the most direct issue of reparations in international criminal proceedings, that of reparations to accused persons ultimately found to be innocent, received no attention in the Rules of any of the *ad hoc* tribunals. Similarly, in the International Criminal Court Statute, it appears that very limited recognition has been accorded to this right. Firmer commitments have been made to those subject to illegal treatment and the recipients of punishment following a conviction subsequently overturned.

Nonetheless, that the development in relation to reparations has taken place in the building of an international criminal law culture after only 13 years of serious international commitment to the field, is a reflection of just how fast moving this new area of jurisprudence has become.

---

99 See for instance John Dugard, 'Reconciliation and Justice: The South African Experience' (1998) 8 *Transnational Law and Contemporary Problems* 227.

REPARATIONS FOR GROSS HUMAN RIGHTS VIOLATIONS IN AFRICA – THE GREAT LAKES

JEREMY SARKIN

1 INTRODUCTION

In the recent past securing reparations for the victims of harm caused by gross human rights violations has become more of a priority due to major developments internationally,[1] regionally, and locally.[2] These developments have occurred at an institutional level with the formation of bodies such as the International Criminal Court[3] as well as the international criminal tribunals for Yugoslavia and Rwanda.[4] Also, there has been development in the jurisprudence and standards relating to when reparations are due.[5] These developments and advances, however, have not often translated into specific reparations for victims; especially in Africa where gross human rights abuses have been part of the landscape within pre-colonial, colonial, and post-colonial societies and countries.

---

1 R.P. MAZZESCHI, 'International Obligations to Provide for Reparation Claims', in A. RANDELZHOFER and C. TOMUSCHAT (eds.), *State Responsibility and the Individual: Reparation in Instances of Grave Violations of Human Rights*, (The Hague – London – Boston:Kluwer, 1999), 149.

2 J. SARKIN, 'Holding Multinational Corporations Accountable for Human Rights and Humanitarian Law Violations Committed During Colonialism and Apartheid: An Evaluation of the Prospects of Such Cases in Light of the Herero of Namibia's Genocide Case and South African Apartheid Cases Being Brought in The United States under the Alien Torts Claims Act', in E. BREMS AND P.VAN DER HEEDE (eds.), *Bedrijven en Mensenrechten*, (Antwerp: Maklu, 2003), 174.

3 C.P.J. MUTTUKUMARU, 'Reparations to Victims', in R.Y. LEE (ed.), *The International Criminal Court The Making of the Rome Statute,* (The Hague – London – Boston: Kluwer Law International, 1999), 262.

4 See further, J. SARKIN, 'Reparation for Past Wrongs: Using Domestic Courts Around the World, Especially the United States, to Pursue African Human Rights Claims', (2004) 32(2) *IJLI (International Journal of Legal Information)*, 339.

5 See, for example, *The 1992 UN Declaration on the Protection of All Persons from Enforced Disappearances*, Article 19 (UN Doc. A/47/49, 18 December 1992); *The 2005 Basic Principles and Guidelines on the Right to a Remedy and Reparation for Victims of Violations of International Human Rights and Humanitarian Law* (UN Doc. A/C.3/60/L.24, 24 October 2005); and *The Articles on the Responsibility of States for Internationally Wrongful Acts adopted by the International Law Commission in* 2001, Articles 31 to 34.

Any discussion of reparations due for those who have suffered gross human rights abuses in the Great Lakes area of central Africa has to begin within an analysis of events during the nineteenth century, when the European powers carved up Africa into different areas of exploitation. This is not to say that no abuses occurred before the colonial period, but reparations for those abuses would be practicably impossible to secure because identifying specific perpetrators would be extraordinarily difficult. However, claims against colonial powers, could be brought, although numerous legal difficulties would have to be surmounted. Claims relating to events before 1885 are not likely to be successful. It was in this year that the scramble for Africa culminated and saw the colonial powers meeting at the Berlin Conference to draft a Treaty which would determine which colonial power would take control in which area of Africa. The treaty that was drafted provided that the local population would be well treated by the colonisers. As a result of the agreements reached and set out in the treaty, borders were established which took no interest in where different tribes were situated. Groups were divided up regardless of language, culture, ethnicity or other affinity. To this day the colonial borders remain sacrosanct, not because they are deemed acceptable, but because to open up the issue to debate would lead inevitably to conflict. Rivalries over these borders, already a problem, would become an even greater issue within Africa and would lead to further wars and loss of life.

The arbitrary colonial borders coupled with policies of rigid ethnic identity and a pervasive environment of underdevelopment have resulted in the sad fact that 20 of the 48 genocides and 'politicides' that occurred worldwide between 1945 and 1995 have taken place in Africa.[6] Much blame for what occurs today on the African continent is rooted in the past. Much conflict is created by competition for scarce resources in an environment of poverty and underdevelopment, which is a result of colonisation. It is, however, not correct to blame only colonisation for the continent's woes. At least part of the blame must be laid at the door of African leaders, who have done little to promote democracy, good governance, the rule of law and human rights, since the 1960s when many of their countries gained independence from the colonial powers. Problems of poverty and scarce resources have been compounded by rampant corruption, cronyism and nepotism. Hopefully, as the African Union develops, mechanisms such as the New Partnership for African Development (NEPAD) and the African Peer Review mechanism will be in a position to deal with such problems more directly.

The issue of reparations will be examined on two fronts: first historical claims going back to colonial times will be examined, and second, those claims related to events

[6] See H. Solomon, '*"Analysing Conflicts" in The European Platform for Conflict Prevention and Transformation-Searching for Peace in Africa: An overview of Conflict Prevention and Management Activities*', (Amsterdam, 1999), 34. See further P. Brogan, *World Conflicts-Why and Where They are Happening.* (London: Bloomsburg Publishing Ltd, 1992).

that have occurred in the more recent past will be discussed. This chapter will focus on three countries in the Great Lakes region: Burundi, Rwanda and the Democratic Republic of the Congo (DRC). Other countries in the region will be touched upon in passing partly because issues relevant to these countries directly affect the States which are the main focus of this chapter. In the domestic context, what has occurred in these countries will be examined to determine what has been done to provide reparations, and what types of reparations are under discussion, recommended or legislated. The role of the International Court of Justice (ICJ) as well as the International Criminal Tribunal for Rwanda (ICTR) will also be discussed, with a focus on their ability to provide restitution both to countries and victims in light of two recent decisions of the ICJ and decisions emanating from the ICTR.

2 REPARATIONS FOR ABUSES COMMITTED DURING THE COLONIAL ERA

In the past claiming reparations for historical violations has proved extremely difficult. Part of the reason for this is that, until recently, within the international legal system, individuals were supposedly not accorded many rights, nor the specific means with which to obtain damages or reparations for human rights or humanitarian law violations.[7] While opportunities for redress were quite limited in the past, this situation has changed in recent years. The last decade of the twentieth century saw 'a remarkable, and in some respects revolutionary, attempt to restructure the classical approach to peacemaking and the resolution of matters relating to the international consequences of war.'[8] Thus, human rights, human rights protections, reparations for human rights, and humanitarian law abuses, have never received more attention than at the present. In spite of this, it is difficult for individual victims to find fora at the international or regional levels within which to bring their claims for reparations. At the same time the opportunities available to victims of gross human rights violations to bring these cases before courts within their own States, are strictly limited for a variety of reasons. This too has been changing.

---

7 See L. Sohn, 'The New International Law: Protection of the Rights of Individuals Rather than States', (1982) 32 *Am. U. Int'l L. Rev* 1.

8 Rudolf Dolzer, 'The Settlement of War-Related Claims: Does International Law Recognize a Victim's Private Right of Action? Lessons after 1945',(2002) *Berkeley Journal of International Law* 296, 302.

Human rights agendas have changed dramatically, with issues of apology[9] and reparation for abuses committed during colonialism,[10] the Atlantic Slave Trade, and the apartheid period coming to the fore. This shift may be attributed to the fact that there is a realisation that what occurred during the years of colonialism and apartheid, for example, during which time people and resources were exploited, cannot be ignored. There is a consciousness that the numerous human rights abuses which occurred, including, *inter alia*, crimes against humanity, war crimes, genocide,[11] extermination, disappearances, torture, forced removals, slavery, racial discrimination, and other cruel, inhuman, or degrading treatment,[12] need somehow to be dealt with appropriately.

This realisation has led to a greater focus on human rights issues as many former colonised states investigate the past in order to learn precisely what occurred. Truth commissions have been set up in a number of countries to deal with gross human rights abuses committed in the past. Thus, in Africa alone, truth commissions have been, or are being held in South Africa, Nigeria, Ghana, Chad, Uganda, the DRC, Liberia, Burundi, and Morocco amongst others. Partly this is so because the legacy of colonialism has left a lasting imprint on the landscape of the colonised countries in the form of underdevelopment. Because of the legacy of the past, life for many people in these countries is one of extreme hardship. Some, however, blame the major economic, social, and cultural problems experienced in many African countries on the effects of mismanagement post independence. Whatever the cause, it is contended by the former colonial powers that what occurred in the past must be understood in the context of the time, when the type of conduct complained of was legitimate and lawful. It is argued that concepts that are defined as international crimes today, such as genocide, crimes against humanity, and others, were not known then, and were not considered to be crimes during colonial times. It is argued that there cannot be liability for events which were not crimes when they were 'committed' and which were only later defined as human rights violations. It is also argued that, in any case, the former colonial powers provide reparations for past conduct in the form of development aid.

---

9 R. Brooks, (Ed.) *When Sorry Isn't Enough: The Controversy over Apologies and Reparations for Human Injustice*, (London – New York: New York University Press, 1999).

10 Most countries in Africa, for example, went through a colonial period under the domination of countries such as France, Germany, Great Britain, Italy, Belgium, and Portugal.

11 Before the term but not the crime had even been conceived.

12 For international crimes, see D.L. Shelton, 'Reparations for Victims of International Crimes', in D.L. Shelton (ed.), *International Crimes, Peace and Human Rights: The Role of the International Criminal Court* (Ardsley: Transnational Publishers, 2000), 137. On domestic crimes, see J. Sarkin and W. Binchy (eds.), *Human Rights, the Citizen and the State*, (Dublin: Round Hall, Sweet and Maxwell, 2001). See also J. Sarkin, J. Van De Lanotte and Y. Haeck (eds.), *Resolving the Tensions between Crime and Human Rights: European and South African Perspectives*, (Antwerp: Maklu, 2001).

In spite of these claims, many in the former colonised States argue that the former colonial powers owe their former colonies, and often certain groups within those former colonies, compensation for the ill effects of the colonial years, as the implications are still felt in the former colonies, often by specific communities. The argument made by former colonial powers, that development aid is given to alleviate these problems, is seen by many in the colonised States as a complete misunderstanding of the problem. Former colonisers are often accused of misstating the amount and type of aid given. It is also argued that aid is not given to the most deserving recipients, and that those directly affected by the past receive little or no assistance at all.

An important issue to formerly colonised peoples concerns their dignity. Those abused in the past often believe that some degree of assistance to reclaim their dignity ought to be offered. For these and many other related reasons, it is of critical importance to the former colonies, and many of the groups and individuals who live in those countries, that they receive compensation or some other type of reparation for past human rights violations. While it was believed previously that compensation or redress for past abuses would never be offered, and that the only way to secure any sort of redress was via foreign aid and investment by the previous colonial powers, developments in the theoretical and practical field of reparations worldwide have begun to change this perception.

In some countries, certain communities maintain that the way in which they were exploited in the past is the reason they now suffer economic as well as other hardships. This was recognised, for example, at the World Conference against Racism, Racial Discrimination, Xenophobia and Related Intolerance (WCAR), held in Durban, South Africa, from 31 August, until 8 September, 2001. Three prime examples of this attitude are Articles 13, 14 and 158 of the declaration of the conference. Article 13 reads:

> "We acknowledge that slavery and the slave trade, including the transatlantic slave trade, were appalling tragedies in the history of humanity not only because of their abhorrent barbarism but also in terms of their magnitude, organized nature and especially their negation of the essence of the victims, and further acknowledge that slavery and the slave trade are a crime against humanity and should always have been so, especially the transatlantic slave trade, and are among the major sources and manifestations of racism, racial discrimination, xenophobia and related intolerance, and that Africans and people of African descent, Asians and people of Asian descent and indigenous peoples were victims of these acts and continue to be victims of their consequences".

Article 14 reads:

> "We recognize that colonialism has led to racism, racial discrimination, xenophobia and related intolerance, and that Africans and people of African descent, and people of Asian descent and indigenous peoples were victims of colonialism and continue to be victims of its consequences. We acknowledge the suffering caused by colonialism and affirm that, wherever and whenever it occurred, it must be condemned and its reoccurrence prevented. We further regret that the

effects and persistence of these structures and practices have been among the factors contributing to lasting social and economic inequalities in many parts of the world today."

Article 158 notes in part:

"... that these historical injustices have undeniably contributed to the poverty, underdevelopment, marginalization, social exclusion, economic disparities, instability and insecurity that affect many people in different parts of the world, in particular developing countries. The Conference recognizes the need to develop programmes for the social and economic development of these societies and the Diaspora, within the framework of a new partnership based on the spirit of solidarity and mutual respect".

3 COLONIAL ABUSE AND ITS EFFECTS

Colonial racist ideology used ethnicity as a means of political manipulation for strategic purposes. This is a major cause of ongoing tension in the region.[13] Racist policies eroded the pre-colonial flexibility on issues of ethnic identity, and established rigid boundaries between people based on ethnicity.[14] When the King of Belgium became interested in central Africa in the 1870s, for example, he established a Survey Committee for the Upper Congo that was later replaced by the International Congo Association in 1879.[15] At the Berlin Conference of 1884/5, the borders of the Congo were fixed without regard to settlement patterns or what was best for those living in the region. The Belgian Parliament endorsed Belgian King Leopold's personal right to the territory.[16] As a result of the ransacking and destruction which followed, international indignation forced the government of Belgium to take over control.[17] During this time, cultural organisations based on ethnic identity were permitted, but all political movements were banned. This resulted in ethnic membership becoming the main form of identification,[18] a situation that was further exacerbated by the paternalistic style of rule over the Belgian Congo.[19]

---

13 O.C. Eze, *Human Rights in Africa: Some Selected Problems*, (Lagos: Nigerian Institute of International Affairs,1984).

14 R. Lemarchand, *Burundi, Ethnocide as Discourse and Practice*, (Cambridge: Cambridge University Press, 1994), 6-16.

15 J. Stengers, 'The Congo Free State and the Belgian Congo', in L.H. Gann and P. Duignan (eds.), *Colonialism in Africa 1870-1960*, (Cambridge: Cambridge University Press, 1969), Volume 1.

16 A.P. Merriam, *Congo, Background of Conflict*, (Evanston, Ill: Northwestern University Press, 1961), 4. K. Nkrumah, *Challenge of the Congo: A case study of the Foreign Pressure in an Independent State.* (London: Panaf, 1974), 3.

17 C. Kabemba, *Whither the DRC?, Causes of the conflict in the Democratic Republic of Congo, and the Way Forward*, (Johannesburg: Centre for Policy Studies, March 1999), 6.

18 *Ibid.*

19 R. Slade, *The Belgian Congo*, (London: Oxford University Press, 1961), 4.

Mamdani and Jordan note that the Belgians also developed a system of indirect rule, the legacy of which is important to understand the origins of the problems in the DRC.[20] This system saw the colony divided into two separate legal systems, one civic and the other ethnic. Civil law was under the control of the central State, while local authorities oversaw customary law that enforced ethnic power.[21] This led to a kind of 'dual citizenship' in terms of which specific rights were tied explicitly to membership of particular indigenous ethnic groups.[22] Dividing ethnic groups in this way has resulted in serious conflict between groups. A good example of this is the history of slaughter which characterises the relationship between the Hutus and Tutsis in Burundi and Rwanda. Conflict in one country has tended to stoke fears and hatred in another.[23]

Burundi and Rwanda were colonised by Germany which used the existing tribal structures and operated through a system of 'indirect' rule. This system preserved the concentration of political power in the hands of the Tutsis, who were given easier access to education, economic resources and employment. When the Belgians took over in 1916, administering the region as part of the League of Nations Mandate Territory and thereafter the United Nations Trust Territory of Ruanda-Urundi, they continued to use the 'indirect rule' system introduced by the Germans.[24] It was Belgian colonisers in Rwanda who, in the 1930s, conducted a census, formally classifying Rwandans as Tutsi, Hutu or Twa,[25] and issued ethnic identity cards to all Rwandans based on these classifications.[26] The 'racial' distinction was based on height and skin-colour differences and may have been an attempt to identify and give preference to those Rwandans perceived as having a 'more European' look. The shorter, darker Hutu were classified as 'Bantu', analogous to the 'serfs' of medieval European feudalism. The lighter-skinned Tutsis were earmarked for leadership positions because the Belgians ascribed to them a greater intelligence and ability for leadership. Under

---

20 M. Mamdani and A. Jordan, *Preliminary Thoughts on the Congo Crisis*, (Cape Town: Centre for African Studies, University of Cape Town, 1998). See further M. Mamdani, 'The Social Basis of Constitutionalism in Africa', (1990) 28 *Journal of Modern African Studies*, 359-374.

21 W. Breytenbach, D. Chilemba, T.A. Brown, and C. Plantive, 'Conflicts in the Congo: From Kivu to Kabila', (1999) 8(5) *African Security Review*, 34.

22 *Ibid.*

23 Human Rights Watch, *Proxy Targets:- Civilians in the War in Burundi*, 1998.

24 F. Reyntjens, *Burundi. Breaking the Cycle of Violence*, (London:Minority Rights Group International, 1995), 7.

25 See generally, A. Destexhe, *Rwanda and Genocide in the Twentieth Century*, (London: Pluto, 1995), 2-3.

26 See A. De Waal and R. Amber, *Rwanda: Death, Despair and Defiance*, (United Kingdon: African Rights, 1994).

Belgian rule, the Tutsis were awarded educational, social, and economic advantages while the Hutus were denied privileges and relegated to peasant status.[27]

This experience of ethnic oppression, combined with 60 years of colonial rule, as well as a series of massacres perpetrated against them by Tutsis in Rwanda and in neighbouring Burundi, all acted to embitter the Hutu group. Du Preez describes the genocide against the Tutsis in Rwanda during 1963 and 1964 as a vengeful response to the political, social and cultural domination by Tutsis that preceded the 1959 Hutu revolution.[28] Newbury understands Hutu identity as being created out of Hutu peasants' common experience of oppression during the colonial era.[29] Additionally, some see the genocide of 1994 perpetrated by Hutus against Tutsis in Rwanda as part of a struggle to recreate Hutu identity, giving Hutu peasants, who were previously excluded from power and privilege, a common experience of being powerful. A long history of Hutu repression may help to explain why many Hutus still refuse to regard the mass killings of Tutsis in 1994 as a genocide, perceiving the events either as part of an ongoing civil war or as self-defence. Recognising the pivotal influence of the colonial period on contemporary Rwanda, one scholar has characterised the genocide and ongoing violence in the following way:

> "Large scale violence in Rwanda was brought on by a blend of enforced ethnic intolerance, constructed hierarchies, social inequalities, and material scarcity. For many generations common language, culture and religion kept categorizations of Hutu, Tutsi, and Twa mutable. Political construction of divisive ethnic identities helped create the environment which allowed for the surge of human atrocity."[30]

Another example of colonial abuse, the repercussions of which are still being felt today, is to be found in Kenya, and involves injuries inflicted over the years by British soldiers. A total of 228 Samburu and Maasai farmers in Kenya launched a successful case in the British courts, and received £4.5m in damages from the UK's Ministry of Defence (MoD) because their family members were killed or maimed over the past 50 years by British Army explosives left behind on military ranges in that country. The claim, launched in 2000 before the High Court, accused the UK Ministry of Defence of failing

---

27 See AFRICA WATCH COMMITTEE (NOW HUMAN RIGHTS WATCH/AFRICA), *Rwanda Talking Peace and Waging War: Human Rights since the October 1990 Invasion*, (27 Jan. 1992) Vol. IV, Issue No. 3. Rwanda, a German colony from 1890 to 1916, was mandated, along with Burundi, to Belgium by the League of Nations after World War I. Under Belgian rule, the Tutsi held all of the nation's forty-three chiefdoms, 549 out of 559 subchiefdoms, and over 80 percent of government positions in fields such as the judiciary, agriculture, and veterinary sciences.

28 In 1963 the minority Tutsi were attacked by the majority Hutu. See P. DU PREEZ, *Genocide: The Psychology of Mass Murder*, (London – New York: Boyars/Bowerdean, 1994).

29 See C. NEWBURY, *The Cohesion of Oppression Clientship And Ethnicity in Rwanda, 1860-1960*, (New York: Columbia University Press, 1988).

30 C.J. FERSTMAN, 'Rwanda's Domestic Trials for Genocide and Crimes Against Humanity', (1997) 5 *Human Rights Brief*,1.

to remove all potentially dangerous devices from their bases in Kenya, with the same degree of care that they exercised at their bases in Cyprus and Canada. While this claim was settled, another claim is still pending, which relates to a second group of 1044 claimants. These claimants were offered about half a million pounds in November 2003 to settle the matter, but turned the settlement offer down. A number of other cases have been launched, including claims of rape filed against British army soldiers.[31] About 650 Kenyan women are to receive British legal aid to prosecute various claims relating to incidents of rape allegedly committed by British soldiers in Kenya between 1972 and 2002. The MoD is being sued for negligence, in that it failed to take steps to prevent the rapes.[32]

Another important case relating to abuses committed during the colonial period, which has the potential to establish an important legal precedent, involves a claim by the Maasai community. The case challenges a British court decision handed down in 1913, which forced some 10,000 Maasai off their land in Laikipia and into a new area on the Tanzanian border, where they were affected by malaria.[33] If successful, this claim would have major implications for issues related to land dispossession around the world, particularly in the case of land dispossession during colonialism. Such claims by individuals against the State have been addressed in Australia, New Zealand, South Africa, and the United States. Claims by one country against another have not been successful. Britain, however, was willing to provide some compensation to Zimbabwe in the 1990s for land in possession of white farmers.

The Maasai claim is not the only such case involving Britain. For example, the Nandi people of Uganda are preparing to sue Britain for killing their prophet Koitalel arap Samoei in 1905 during a military campaign to suppress Nandi resistance. Allied to claims such as this is a request by the Pan-African Reparations Movement to set up a Commission to investigate how many Kenyans were killed and maimed during the colonial rule. The group argues that the 'British should compensate our freedom fighters, particularly the Mau Mau who gallantly resisted colonial oppression and exploitation.'[34]

Britain was also sued by the Kabaka of Buganda, Ronald Muwenda Mutebi, the government of Uganda, the Electoral Commission (EC), the Uganda Land Board, and 366 absentee landlords in Buyaga and Bugangaizi counties in Kibaale, for plundering resources and killing people in the Bunyoro-Kitara Kingdom of Uganda during the

---

31 M. Day and J. Patterson, 'The Mass Rape of Kenyan Women by British Soldiers', (2003) *LGD (Law, Social Justice & Global Development Journal)*, available at: http://elj.warwick.ac.uk/global/2003-2/day.html.

32 United Nations Office for the Coordination of Humanitarian Affairs Integrated Regional Information Network IRIN Africa English reports, 7/2/2003.

33 Paul Redfern, 'Colonialism: Britain faces lawsuits', (Nairobi, 26 January 2004) *The East African Standard.*

34 'Amadi Mugasia group seeks probe on colonialists', (24 November 2003) *The East African Standard.*

1890s. The plaintiffs sought compensation in the amount of $250 million for genocide and dispossessing Bunyoro's indigenous people. However, in August 2005 the Ugandan High Court cleared Britain of plundering resources and killing people in Bunyoro-Kitara Kingdom, and ordered that the case be sent to the land division of the High Court.[35]

Thus, the number of cases rooted in transgressions committed during colonial times is growing. Such cases include claims of the Herero of Namibia against various multi-national companies that has been brought in the USA.[36] Additionally, other cases such as the *Abebe-Jira v. Negewo*[37] case relating to more recent events in Africa have also been filed in the USA. In that case, Ethiopian victims filed suit against a former official of the government in that country charging torture. Each plaintiff was awarded $200,000 in compensatory damages and $300,000 in punitive damages.

4 THE DEMOCRATIC REPUBLIC OF THE CONGO

Historically, the DRC has been a highly polarised, divided and conflict-ridden society. This is a result of divide and rule tactics, combined with a continued policy of relying on and entrenching ethnic identity, together with a practice of excluding certain groups from power. It is the second largest country in sub-Saharan Africa and shares borders with nine countries: Burundi, Uganda, Angola, Sudan, Congo-Brazzaville, Central African Republic, Zambia, and Tanzania. Its artificially defined colonial borders[38] include more than 200 separate ethnic groups.[39] The origins of the conflict in the DRC must be understood as having both domestic as well as regional dimensions.

In the late 1950s as other countries in the region began moving towards independence, the Belgians began to take steps towards greater autonomy for the DRC. In May 1960 general elections took place, and the first national government was formed with Patrice Lumumba of the Mouvement National Congolais (MNC) as Prime Minister. The first cabinet comprised leaders from many different parties with ethnicity at the core of their political support. Immediately after independence the mineral-rich

---

35 Lydia Mukisa, 'Court Clears UK On Bunyoro Killings', (24 August 2005) *The Monitor*.

36 J. Sarkin, 'Reparation for Past Wrongs: Using Domestic Courts around the World, especially the United States, to Pursue African Human Rights Claims', (2004) 32(2) *IJLI* (*International Journal of Legal Information*), 339.

37 72 F.3d 844 (11th Cir. 1996).

38 M. Mamdani, 'Preliminary Thoughts on the Congo Crisis', *Conference of experts, officials and interested parties from Eastern and Southern Africa on the crisis in the DRC*, (Harare, 23 September 1998), 1.

39 F. Reyntjens, 'Briefing, The Second Congo War: More than a Remake', (1999) *African Affairs*, 241-250. H. Weiss, 'War and Peace in the Democratic Republic of the Congo', (2000) *Nordiska Afrikainstitut*, Current African Issues No. 22, 13.

province of Katanga declared itself independent.[40] Lumumba called on the UN to intercede, shortly before he was killed at the beginning of 1961. Between 1960 and 1963 the Congo was a UN protectorate. After several years of conflict in various parts of the country, in 1965 Mobutu Sese Seko came to power in a *coup d'état* and changed the name of the country to Zaire.

Mobutu remained in power for 32 years, plundering the country without implementing any reforms beneficial to the population as a whole. As Mobutu's political power decreased, he ruled increasingly through his army.[41] Mobutu continued to focus on ethnic identity as a method of 'divide and rule'. In 1981, he enacted a law granting citizenship to those with an ancestor born before 1885 within the area of the Congo. This decree deprived the Banyamulenge (ethnic Tutsis), who had resided in the South Kivu region for generations, and the Banyarwanda, a Rwandan speaking population of North Kivu composed of 25 percent Tutsis and 75 percent Hutus, of their citizenship.[42] The Banyamulenge were prohibited from owning land and could be dispossessed of land they had lived on for many years. This policy towards the Banyamulenge saw other groups beginning to pursue land claims against the Tutsis. There were increased social pressures due to food shortages which were the result of a population growth of over 3 per cent per annum, together with only 3 per cent of land being arable. Not surprisingly, in1993 tribal clashes began to occur in the Kivu province.[43] In response to the militarisation of ordinary life, many of the Native Authorities within the Kivu province created their own military units, drawing on Hunde, Nande and Nyanga militias, known as the Mai-Mai.[44] Encouraged and supported by the Zairian military, the Mai-Mai attacked communities, killing thousands and displacing about 300,000 civilians.[45]

Mobutu collaborated with the Forces Armées Rwandaises, (the former Rwandan Armed Forces known as the ex-FAR), and helped them to rearm. The alliance between Mobutu and the Hutu regime in Rwanda, as well as the events following the Tutsi genocide in Rwanda, put further pressure on the Banyamulenge. Between 1993 and 1996 they drew closer to the Tutsis of Rwanda. In December 1995, a new law was passed stating that the Banyamulenge were no longer allowed to acquire homes or

---

[40] H. WEISS, 'War and Peace in the Democratic Republic of the Congo', (2000) *Nordiska Afrikainstitut*, Current African Issues No. 22, 21. C. KABEMBA, *Whither the DRC?, Causes of the conflict in the Democratic Republic of Congo, and the Way Forward*, (Johannesburg: Centre for Policy Studies, March 1999), 7.

[41] C. KABEMBA, Whither the DRC?, Causes of the conflict in the Democratic Republic of Congo, and the Way Forward, (Johannesburg: Centre for Policy Studies, March 1999), 9.

[42] H. SOLOMON, 'Some Reflections on the Crisis in Zaire', (15 February 1997) *ISS Occasional Papers (Institute for Security Studies)*, 1.

[43] *Ibid.*

[44] M. MAMDANI, 'Preliminary Thoughts on the Congo Crisis', *Conference of experts, officials and interested parties from Eastern and Southern Africa on the crisis in the DRC*, (Harare, 23 September 1998), 6-7.

[45] HUMAN RIGHTS WATCH, *Summary of the 1997 Report*, 7.

land. Furthermore, the Zairian army chief General Aundu announced that the local Hunde, Nyanga and Tembo people had the right to expel 'foreigners'[46] from the land.[47] The Banyamulenge found themselves in conflict not only with people who had lived around them for many years, but also with the Interahamwe from Rwanda, and the Zairian Army which enforced unjust laws against them.

In May 1996 about 100 Tutsis were killed at Mokoto church, and in September Zairian soldiers killed about 35 Banyamulenge. Between September and October 1996, about 2,000 Banyamulenge were killed by the Interahamwe and the Zairian army. In October 1996 the situation deteriorated further when the Deputy Director of South Kivu province stated that the 300,000 Banyamulenge had to leave Zaire for Rwanda within a week or they would be seen to be rebels and hunted down. Three days later the Banyamulenge retaliated by attacking the Lemera Hospital in Bukavu.

The uprising by the Banyamulenge was joined by Laurent Kabila and his rebel troops which formed the Alliance de Forces Démocratiques pour la Libération du Congo-Zaire (ADFL). Kabila was supported by Rwanda, Angola, Uganda and Burundi.[48] The Mai-Mai also joined the rebellion against Mobutu in order to target other groups such as the Interahamwe of Rwanda.[49] In addition, the Katanga Tigers or Katanga Gendarmes, a group mainly made up of Katangese soldiers who had fled to Angola after the secession of Katanga failed in 1962, joined the alliance.

The effect of the Rwandan genocide was critical for the DRC, as the shift from a Hutu government to a Tutsi one in 1994 had precipitated a mass exodus of Hutus from the north-west region of Rwanda into the DRC to escape Tutsi vengeance for the Hutu-led genocide. Thus, the Congo became an unwilling host to an estimated one million refugees. Along with these refugees came defeated soldiers, administrators and political leaders, as well as the Interahamwe,[50] which was made up of remnants of the Rwandan militia, the members of which were directly responsible for the genocide in Rwanda.[51] In the refugee camps established by the UN High Commissioner for Refugees close to the Rwandan border, the former political and military structures re-established themselves and began launching attacks on the Tutsi population in the

---

46 After the victory of Kabila resentments against the Tutsis, now being seen as foreigners from all the Congolese, grew even further. H. Weiss, 'War and Peace in the Democratic Republic of the Congo', (2000) *Nordiska Afrikainstitut*, Current African Issues No. 22, 8.

47 H. Solomon, 'Some Reflections on the Crisis in Zaire', (15 February 1997) *ISS Occasional Papers (Institute for Security Studies)*, 2.

48 F. Reyntjens, 'Briefing: The Second Congo War: More than a Remake', (1999) *African Affairs* 241.

49 M. Mamdani, 'Preliminary Thoughts on the Congo Crisis', *Conference of experts, officials and interested parties from Eastern and Southern Africa on the crisis in the DRC*, (Harare, 23 September 1998), 7.

50 Interahamwe means "those who work together", J. Havermans, 'Rwandan Crisis Lingers On', in *Searching for Peace in Africa: An Overview of Conflict Prevention and Management Activities*, (Utrecht, 2000), 247-257.

51 Human Rights Watch, *Democratic Republic of the Congo, Report 1997*, 8.

Kivus. In northern Kivu, hundreds of Tutsis were killed and about 18,000 were driven into exile in Uganda and Rwanda.[52]

In September 1996, the Banyamulenge of South Kivu, faced with the danger of ethnic cleansing after an estimated 2,000 Banyamulenge were massacred and an unknown number of women were raped,[53] together with militias, the ex-FAR and Zairian troops attacked the Zairian Armed Forces (FAZ), as well as the Interahamwe. As soon as these attacks began, Rwandan troops entered the Congo and the first Congo war began.[54] Zimbabwe, Namibia, and Angola fought in support of the DRC government, while other groups were supported by Rwanda, Uganda and Burundi.[55]

It was in this context that Laurent Kabila came to power on 17 May 1997. Initially, Kabila was seen as supportive of the views and aspirations of various ethnic groups, but he soon started to exclude the Banyamulenge and other Tutsis from power. Kabila actively sought to gain the support of the Congolese by fermenting hatred of the Banyamulenge.[56] Ethnic persecution, especially directed at the Tutsi population, took place. Even after Laurent Kabila was assassinated and his son Joseph Kabila took over, many gross human rights violations were reported, and the region remains unstable to this day.

5 THE DEMOCRATIC REPUBLIC OF THE CONGO'S TRANSITION AND DEALING WITH THE PAST

Peace talks aimed at reaching a settlement in the DRC took place at Sun City in South Africa over a number of months in 2002. The process was known as the 'Inter-Congolese Dialogue' (ICD). An agreement was concluded on 17 December 2002, a transitional constitution came into force in April 2003, and the transitional government assumed power during July 2003. A law establishing a Truth and Reconciliation Commission was promulgated by the President on 30 July 2004. The TRC law directed that the commission was to take measures to compensate the victims of the DRC's violent past and 'completely restore their dignity.' Article 41 of the TRC law states:

---

52 HUMAN RIGHTS WATCH, *Summary of the 1997 Report,* 7.

53 *Ibid.*

54 H. WEISS, 'War and Peace in the Democratic Republic of the Congo', (2000) *Nordiska Afrikainstitut,* Current African Issues No. 22, 2.

55 C. KABEMBA, *Whither the DRC?, Causes of the conflict in the Democratic Republic of Congo, and the Way Forward,* (Johannesburg: Centre for Policy Studies, March 1999), 16.

56 W. BREYTENBACH, D. CHILEMBA, T.A. BROWN, and C. PLANTIVE, 'Conflicts in the Congo: From Kivu to Kabila', (1999) 8(5) *African Security Review,* 34.

> "At every time and in every circumstance, reparations are decided by agreement between the parties. The agreements concluded under the aegis of the TRC on reparation or restitution have the value of a contract and, as such, the value of *res judicata.*"[57]

Thus, the commission is given additional responsibilities, including a role in achieving agreements between the factions. To ensure that agreements between parties are implemented, the TRC is going to have to ensure that the resources are found for this purpose. Crucially, the commission is given authority to compensate victims directly, which has not been the case with other such commissions. Usually, TRCs are directed to recommend reparations to other State organs, which then determine what should be awarded in practice. The additional responsibilities placed on the TRC in the DRC were criticised by some who argued that this could 'paralyze the commission and divert attention and resources from other important issues.'[58] It has also been argued that Article 55 of the TRC law which states that the 'final report will include recommendations on reparations due to victims and on their rehabilitation', contradicts Article 41.[59]

Although the TRC has been given powers to award reparations, the really critical question is whether or not sufficient resources will be found to cover these reparations.

6 RWANDA

Rwanda gained full independence in 1962, and even though a new Constitution was enacted in which considerable weight was accorded to civil and human rights, including the notion of equality, the tension between Hutus and Tutsis escalated. In 1973, Juvenal Habyarimana, a Hutu who was the army Chief of Staff, staged a successful coup, usurping the democratically-elected President Kayibanda, also a Hutu. Once in power, Habyarimana's party, the National Revolutionary Movement for Development (MRND), entrenched Hutu domination and encouraged anti-Tutsi sentiment. Finally, Hutu extremists set up their own radio and television station, Radio Television Libre des Milles Collines, to broadcast their messages of hatred against Tutsis. Habyarimana attempted to entrench his political power among the Hutu majority, not only by encouraging a common hatred for Tutsis, but also by reversing Rwanda's progress towards democracy in favour of a one-party dictatorship. To these ends, Habyarimana dissolved the National Assembly, endowed the presidency with its former draconian powers, and abolished all political parties except for the MRND. He revised the Rwandan Constitution so that all political activity was organised by

---

57 Federico Borello, 'A First Few Steps: The Long Road to a Just Peace in the Democratic Republic of the Congo', (October 2004) *ICTJ (International Centre for Transitional Justice)*, 44.

58 *Ibid.*

59 *Ibid.*

the MRND, including nominations for presidential candidates. The president of the MRND was the only eligible candidate for the Rwandan presidency. Habyarimana's manipulation of political power and ethnic stereotyping was successful because of underlying anxiety among the Hutus, which stemmed from a national economic crisis, diminishing access to land (especially troublesome in a predominantly agricultural society like Rwanda), and an ever-increasing problem of overpopulation.[60]

In reaction to the anti-Tutsi sentiment generated by Habyarimana's regime, many Tutsis fled and sought refuge in neighbouring countries. In 1990, 4,000 Tutsis who had previously fled to Uganda formed the Rwandese Patriotic Front (RPF) and returned to Rwanda to seek revenge. The invasion fuelled the ethnic conflict between the Tutsis and the Hutus in Rwanda and a civil war erupted. Hutus suspected that Tutsis who had remained in Rwanda were sympathetic to the RPF invaders. These civilian Tutsis became the primary targets of Hutu attacks. Between October 1990 and January 1994, over 2,000 Tutsis, as well as Hutus who were in opposition to the government, were killed. In addition, militias were formed, allegedly independent of the government, to continue violence against Tutsis and anyone else who opposed the government.

Before the Rwandan genocide of 1994, the Hutu government capitalised on Hutu peasant fears by scapegoating the Tutsi minority through propaganda designed to incite hatred against them. This involved spreading fear by means of rumours, threats, and lies, including the claim that the RPF was planning an invasion from Burundi, and was plotting to murder the Hutu president. Competition for scarce resources also played a part in creating an explosive situation. Prior to April 1994, Rwanda was experiencing desperate land pressure.[61] The landlocked, overpopulated country could not allocate its land resources fairly to its inhabitants[62] and population density placed chronic pressure on arable land.[63] Moreover, a collapse in the international coffee price crippled many small landholders and co-operatives involved in producing coffee, one

---

60 See M. Monshipouri, *Democratization, Liberalization and Human Rights in the Third World*, (Boulder: L. Rienner Publishers, 1995), 25-26. Here the author identifies types of constraints to the full realization of human rights conditions and democratization and noting environmental, ecological, and geographical limitations as a barrier, particularly when combined with internal sources of poverty such as population pressure, low agricultural production, underutilisation of labor, land, and capital.

61 According to Prunier: "at least part of the reason why it was carried out so thoroughly by the ordinary rank-and-file peasants...was the feeling that there were too many people on too little land, and that with a few less there would be more for the survivors." See G. Prunier, *The Rwandan Crisis: History of a Genocide*, (New York – Hong Kong: Colubmia University Press, 1995).

62 See generally, A. Destexhe, *Rwanda and Genocide in the Twentieth Century*, (London: Pluto, 1995).

63 Rwanda has a total area of 26,340 sq. km with 24,950 sq. km of land and 1,390 sq km of water. Its land boundaries are 893 km and it borders on Burundi, Democratic Republic of the Congo, Tanzania, and Uganda. 35 percent of the land is arable. Its population was estimated in July 1997 to be 7,737,537 with a population growth rate of 8.24 per cent. Agriculture dominates with coffee and tea being 80-90 per cent of exports. See *World Factbook*, 1997.

of the principle exports[64] of the once-booming economy. On the political level, life in Rwanda was permanently tense. A situation of low-level civil war existed prior to the genocide, which placed the RPF at the heart of the extremist Hutu fear of the Tutsi. The RPF view was that the ethnic labels of Hutu and Tutsi were colonial constructions that should be discarded: Tutsi and Hutu were, in reality, one people, speaking the same language and sharing the same physical appearance, political institutions, and territory.

The RPF gained increasing international support during the 1990s and President Juvenal Habyarimana, bowing to international pressure, began negotiations aimed at including Tutsis in the government and in other institutions. The prospect of multi-party elections and power-sharing was on the political agenda, creating anxiety for extremist Hutus within the army and the government. These extremists Hutus supported the Hamitic-Bantu idea of ethnic separation.[65] It was this clique of extremist Hutus who sought to derail the negotiation process in order to retain their positions of power and financial privileges.

Together with the political and socio-economic problems prevailing in Rwanda, psychological factors also played a role in creating the conditions within which genocide could take place. Simmering hatred and anger could be manipulated by politicians, and the fears of individuals and groups could be exploited for political ends.[66] Situational stresses such as poverty, political conflict, decline in power, and threats to prestige, combined with an explosive emotional brew deliberately stirred up by means of political manipulation, resulted in a tendency amongst certain individuals to scapegoat and persecute those perceived as different to themselves.[67]

The Hutu massacre of the Tutsis may be understood as an extreme form of scapegoating, whereby the dominant group (or individual) shores up its threatened concept-of-self by devaluing those perceived as outsiders. The situation in which the Tutsi minority found itself was ripe for this kind of scapegoating. Not only was there a history of extreme ethnic conflict, but the very existence of the RPF was a threat to the Hutu ideology. Moreover, historically Tutsis had enjoyed wealth and positions that leaders of the dominant Hutu group would have liked for themselves.

The genocide that took place in Rwanda, in which about a million people were killed, was a result of all these factors.[68] The Tutsi were systematically killed in order to destroy the group to which they belonged. Some moderate Hutus were killed too.

---

64 Coffee accounted for 79 percent of exports in 1988. *Ibid.*

65 See A. De Waal and R. Amber, *Rwanda: Death, Despair and Defiance*, (United Kingdon: African Rights, 1994).

66 See generally R.L. Atikinson, *et al.*, *Introduction to Psychology*, (10th ed. 1990).

67 See E. Staub, 'Genocide and Mass Killings: Cultural, Societal and Psychological Origins', in H.T. Himmelweit and G. Gaskel (eds), *Societal Psychology*, (Newbury Park, California: Sage, 1990), 230.

68 See further Philipp Gourevitch, *We wish to inform you that tomorrow we will be killed with our families*, (London: Macmillan, 2000).

The genocide lasted for less than three months, after which time the RPF was able to take control of the country and install a new mainly Tutsi-led government.

7 REPARATIONS IN RWANDA

After the genocide, the new government in Rwanda began by focusing on prosecutions.[69] The idea of a truth commission was rejected,[70] as was, at least initially, the notion of achieving reconciliation.[71]

As for reparations, the Rwandan Parliament passed the *Organic Law no. 08/96* on the Organization of Prosecutions for Offenses Constituting Genocide or Crimes Against Humanity Committed since October 1, 1990. This law provides for compensation and reparation for victims from those found guilty, but no system of general compensation exists for victims. The law also makes reference to an indemnification fund.

The use of traditional courts, known as gacaca, was introduced after it was realised that the normal courts would not be able to cope with all the trials that Rwanda intended to hold. While these courts were to have begun operations in 2002, most are not yet in operation. In January 2006 Human Rights Watch reported that while these courts were supposed to be legitimate because of their popular participation, many Rwandans did not trust them and even boycotted them. Human Rights Watch also described how some judges ignored the rules of these courts and jailed hundreds in preventive detention or because they gave false or incomplete evidence. Human Rights Watch also reported that about 10,000 people fled to neighbouring countries fearing false accusations and unfair trials, and that many of the courts failed to win public confidence for reasons such as the fact that hundreds of the judges themselves were accused of crimes, some witnesses were unwilling to testify, and the courts were barred from dealing with cases where RPF soldiers were involved. Human Rights Watch stated that there were perceptions that the courts were delivering one-sided justice.[72]

Under the gacaca system, those found guilty of offences concerning the confiscation of property are liable to pay reparations and the property must be returned to the victim. If the property cannot be returned there must be payment or work performed to make up the value of the property. Additionally, community service punishments,

---

69 See CARLA J. FERSTMAN, 'Domestic Trials for Genocide and Crimes against Humanity: The Example of Rwanda', in *N Passas: International Crimes*, (London: Dartmouth, 2003), 515.

70 JEREMY SARKIN, 'The Necessity and Challenges of Establishing a Truth and Reconciliation Commission in Rwanda', (1999) *Human Rights Quarterly 21*, 767.

71 JEREMY SARKIN, 'The Tension between Justice and Reconciliation in Rwanda: Politics, Human Rights, Due Process and the Role of the Gacaca courts in dealing with the Genocide', (2001) *Journal of African Law* 45, 2, 143.

72 HUMAN RIGHTS WATCH, *World Report: Rwanda,* (January 2006).

which may be classified as a type of reparation, have been imposed. Almost 900 people have been sentenced to community service since September 2005. It is known as 'TIG', which is short for 'Travaux D'interet General' ('works of general interest'), and those in the programme are known as 'Tigistes'. Rwandan Justice Minister Edda Mukabagwiza notes that the 'programme allows the tigistes to acquire new professional skills that will help facilitate their reintegration into society.' The programme is not without controversy and survivors argue that sentences such as building a house, or other types of work are insignificant and that the punishment ought to be more in concert with the crime.[73]

While the 2001 Gacaca Law made provision for a compensation fund in the Act itself, the Assistance Fund for Genocide Survivors (*Fonds d'assistance aux rescapés du génocide*), also known as the FARG fund, provides funding to victims of the genocide for education, health needs, and housing. For people to claim from the FARG fund they must be needy and have escaped from the genocide or massacres between 1 October 1990 and 31 December 1994. Needy persons are defined in the law as including orphans, widows and the handicapped, but the definition does not limit itself to these groups.[74] The funds for the FARG come from the State, NGOs and individuals. All Rwandans over 18 are required to pay at least 100 Rwandese francs to the fund per year, while salaried individuals are required to contribute 1 percent of their annual salary to the fund, and 2 percent of payments awarded by tribunals dealing with the genocide or massacres must go to the FARG. The Rwandan State is required to contribute 5 percent of its budget to FARG. The United States and the Netherlands have also contributed to FARG. In 1999, USAID contributed US 2 million dollars while in 2000 Holland gave 1.3 million dollars. The US supplemented its amount with a further 2 million in 2002. Rombouts notes that the 'most general criticism levelled at FARG is that it is a 'Tutsi' fund.'

Since 1996, there have been several drafts of a law aimed at creating a Fonds d'Indemnisation (FIND). This is to be an indemnification fund for victims of genocide. Controversy has arisen over whether or not such a law will be passed after Justice Minister Edda Mukabagwiza stated controversially on 13 December 2005 that it was going to be impractical to provide reparations to the survivors of the 1994 genocide. Initially, the minister provided little justification for his statements, but later he revealed that a previous bill had not made much progress in Parliament. According to the minister, the bill had failed because of the difficulties inherent in valuing human life for purposes of compensation; in identifying the appropriate beneficiaries for

73 Aimable Twahirwa, 'Community Service Offends Across the Board', (12 January 2006) *Inter press news agency*, available at http://www.ipsnews.net/africa/nota.asp?idnews=31703.

74 Heidy Rombouts, *Victim Organisations and the Politics of Reparations: a case study on Rwanda*, (Antwerp: Intersentia, 2004), 375.

compensation; and in adequately compensating the many thousands of victims with very limited resources.[75]

In January 2006 the minister announced that the State had proposals to establish a comprehensive assistance plan for the survivors. The minister added that a draft bill was being sent to various stakeholders so as to obtain their input on the proposed law. It was hoped that the law would take effect sometime in 2006. The minister stated that the idea was to create a fund into which 'well wishers' could contribute in order to assist survivors. The minister added that the government was considering increasing its five per cent contribution to the Fund for Assistance of Genocide Survivors (FARG) and stated that potential donors had been identified, including the United Nations, private institutions and members of the international community. Further funding was expected by way of a percentage of the proceeds from the Travaux D'interet General (TIG), which requires those released from custody to take on income-generating communal work. Funding would also be derived from the proceeds of the properties of those convicted of genocide crimes (even those convicted in absentia) which would be auctioned. As for the type of assistance that the Fund would provide, the draft law provides that survivors' needs in areas such as education, health, and shelter, will be met. Specifically, the needs of the elderly will be catered for.[76]

Reparations have also been stated as being owed by various States that played a role in the Rwandan genocide, even by omission. Thus, a panel established by the Organization of African Unity (OAU), entitled the 'International Panel of Eminent Personalities', was created in order to 'investigate the 1994 genocide in Rwanda and the surrounding events in the Great Lakes.' In 2000 the panel presented its report entitled *Rwanda: The Preventable Genocide.* The report concluded that States that failed to stop the genocide were liable to Rwanda and the victims for reparations. While a number of States have been accused, France has borne the brunt of the criticism. While a French Parliamentary inquiry held in 1998 exonerated French troops of guilt in relation to the genocide, in 2005 an inquiry by a group of French individuals, including historians, lawyers, and human rights workers, alleged that French troops had helped those doing the attacking more than those that were being attacked. Rwanda also established a commission of inquiry into France's role in the genocide. A Rwandan prosecutor has opened a formal inquiry into allegations that the French security forces, with about 2,500 members deployed in the country at the time of Opération Turquoise, actively conspired in the genocide. This is the result of a case brought by six Rwandans, some of whom have claimed that they personally saw French troops participating in the killings that occurred. It is interesting to note that in 2000, the OAU's International Panel of Eminent Personalities, in their report *Rwanda: The*

---

75 James Munyaneza, 'Rwanda Plan for Survivors Fund On As UN Moves to Assist', (Kigali, 18 January 2006), *The New Times.*

76 *Ibid.*

Preventable Genocide, found that there were countries that had played a role in the genocide and owed reparations. The report did not name these countries, but stated:

> "Apologies alone are not adequate. In the name of both justice and accountability, reparations are owed to Rwanda by actors in the international community for their roles before, during, and since the genocide. The case of Germany after World War II is pertinent here. We call on the UN secretary-general to establish a commission to determine a formula for reparations and to identify which countries should be obligated to pay, based on the principles set out in the report, titled The Right to Restitution, Compensation and Rehabilitation for Victims of Gross Violations of Human Rights and Fundamental Freedoms, submitted January 18, 2000, to the UN Economic and Social Council."[77]

8 BURUNDI

Ethnic rivalries, which existed in the period before Burundi gained independence, continued and in fact increased after independence. During this period there were two main political parties in Burundi. The Union pour le Progrès National (UPRONA) was led by Prince Rwagasore, the eldest son of the *mwami* (king). UPRONA was a nationalist movement, the aim of which was to unite all groups and interests. The Parti Démocrate Chretien (PDC) was more politically conservative.[78] Rwagasore, being a *ganwa*, and therefore a Tutsi, but having the appearance of a Hutu, was able to operate beyond the strictures of ethnic politics to a certain extent, and played a unifying role.[79] His political party was triumphant, receiving about 80 percent of the vote in the first elections held in 1961. His assassination two weeks later in a PDC plot[80] marks a crucial point in Burundian history, as open conflict between Hutus and Tutsis erupted. Without the unifying influence of Rwagasore, ethnic tensions could not be contained. UPRONA, the governing party, experienced a leadership crisis. As a result a bitter struggle for control took place between Hutu and Tutsi factions.[81]

After independence in 1962, the *mwami* attempted to maintain a balance of power by making certain that equal numbers of Hutus and Tutsis were in government. However, the continuing ethnic violence in Rwanda coupled with the fact that tens

---

77 OAU Report, *Rwanda: The Preventable Genocide*, page 266, para. 12, available at http://www.oau-oua.org/Document/ipep/ipep.htm.

78 F. Reyntjens, *Burundi. Breaking the Cycle of Violence*, (London:Minority Rights Group International, 1995), 7. R. Lemarchand, *Burundi, Ethnocide as Discourse and Practice*, (Cambridge: Cambridge University Press, 1994), 52.

79 R. Lemarchand, *Burundi, Ethnocide as Discourse and Practice*, (Cambridge: Cambridge University Press, 1994), 52-53.

80 *Ibid.*

81 F. Reyntjens, *Burundi. Breaking the Cycle of Violence*, (London:Minority Rights Group International, 1995), 7. R. Lemarchand, *Burundi, Ethnocide as Discourse and Practice*, (Cambridge: Cambridge University Press, 1994), 59.

of thousands of Rwandan Tutsi refugees had entered Burundi, destabilised the political situation. In 1965 the political instability was exacerbated by the assassination of the Hutu Prime Minister Pierre Ngendandwe by a Rwandan refugee.[82] Despite elections a few months later that saw Hutu politicians gain the majority in Parliament, the *mwami* refused to appoint a Hutu prime minister, and appointed a Tutsi instead. This led to a failed coup staged by the Hutu-dominated *gendarmerie* in October 1965, during which about 500 Tutsis were killed. Resulting violence perpetrated by Tutsis led to the deaths of between 2,500 and 5,000 Hutus, including several prominent politicians.[83]

In 1966, the monarchy was overthrown in a coup led by Tutsi members of the army. The new President, Colonel Michel Micombero, declared Burundi a republic and political power shifted to the army, dominated by Tutsis from the south of the country.[84] Without the monarchy to act as a stabilising influence, the polarisation between the ethnic groups increased.[85] Over time, the Parliament and the civil service were torn apart by major ethnic rivalries[86] and many Hutus were removed from the army. Various Hutu officers were charged with plotting to overthrow the government of President Micombero.

In 1972, Hutu militants slaughtered Tutsis in southern Burundi. While the Tutsi-dominated military resisted the uprising, the perception amongst the Tutsi elite was that this could be the start of a Hutu inspired revolution. The Tutsi army and Tutsi mobs began massacring Hutu civilians, killing up to 150,000 of them, including many Hutu intellectuals. This violence allowed a kill-or-be-killed mentality to take root among the general population.[87]

While little inter-ethnic violence took place between 1972 and 1986, leadership battles were fought between Tutsi factions. Colonel Jean Baptiste Bagaza seized power in a bloodless coup in 1976 but was overthrown in 1987, by Major Pierre Buyoya.[88]

Inter-ethnic violence resurfaced in 1988 when Hutus living in northern Burundi, believing that they were about to be attacked, killed several thousand neighbouring Tutsis. To avenge the Tutsi deaths, the army responded by killing as many as 20,000

82 F. Reyntjens, *Burundi. Breaking the Cycle of Violence*, (London:Minority Rights Group International, 1995), 7.

83 R. Lemarchand, *Burundi, Ethnocide as Discourse and Practice*, (Cambridge: Cambridge University Press, 1994), 59-60 and 71-74.

84 F. Reyntjens, *Burundi. Breaking the Cycle of Violence*, (London:Minority Rights Group International, 1995), 4.

85 R. Lemarchand, *Burundi, Ethnocide as Discourse and Practice*, (Cambridge: Cambridge University Press, 1994), 59-60.

86 R. Lemarchand, *Burundi, Ethnocide as Discourse and Practice*, (Cambridge: Cambridge University Press, 1994), 66.

87 F. Reyntjens, *Burundi. Breaking the Cycle of Violence*, (London:Minority Rights Group International, 1995), 7.

88 *Ibid.*, 8-9.

Hutus, many of whom had not been involved in the fighting.[89] Realising that he needed to include all groups in the government, President Buyoya dismissed various Tutsi hardliners from the cabinet, doubled the number of Hutu ministers, and appointed a Hutu prime minister. In 1992, a new constitution was adopted that permitted a pluralist party system.[90] In spite of these reforms, ethnic tensions continued as the military and the judiciary remained almost entirely Tutsi.

In July 1993, Melchior Ndadaye, a Hutu, was elected President of Burundi in the first democratic presidential election. He received nearly two-thirds of the votes. The election result filled Tutsis with apprehension as they believed Hutus had voted *en bloc* for Ndadaye.[91] Attempts to reassure the Tutsi population seem to have been unsuccessful. Ndadaye was assassinated on 21 October 1993 during a coup led by a Tutsi faction within the army. Hutus, believing that they had been deprived of the right to govern Burundi, resorted to violence against Tutsis. Even though a Hutu president was appointed eventually in February of 1994, Tutsi political parties negotiated greater power for themselves. This led to another coup in July 1996, during which Hutu President Ntibantunganya was ousted and replaced by former Tutsi president Buyoya.[92]

After years of conflict, Burundi inaugurated a new Constitution which reserved a certain proportion of seats for different ethnic groups and held elections in 2005. In March 2005, the Secretary-General of the United Nations, Kofi Annan, recommended the establishment of a truth commission for Burundi, as well as a special court to hold accountable those accused of genocide, crimes against humanity and war crimes committed in Burundi after 1962. In an effort to enhance objectivity, impartiality, and credibility, Annan suggested that the Truth Commission include a substantial international component.[93] In June 2005, the Security Council adopted a resolution creating a mixed truth commission and a special court.[94] In November 2005, a commission established in order to identify all Burundian political prisoners being held in captivity, began its work. In January 2006, a total of 673 prisoners were released on the basis of a report from the commission.

---

89 *See* R. Lemarchand, *Burundi, Ethnocide as Discourse and Practice*, (Cambridge: Cambridge University Press, 1994), 118-130.

90 See Art. 53 of the 1992 Constitution; *Ibid.*, 131-159.

91 F. Reyntjens, *Burundi. Breaking the Cycle of Violence*, (London:Minority Rights Group International, 1995), 10-11.

92 F. Reyntjens, *Burundi. Breaking the Cycle of Violence*, (London:Minority Rights Group International, 1995), 16-19.

93 UN Office for the Coordination of Humanitarian Affairs, 'Burundi: Annan recommends dual inquiries on genocide', (29 March 2005), available at: http://www.irinnews.org/print.asp?ReportID=46349.

94 IRIN news, 'Burundi: Government pleased with UN resolution on truth commission', (22 June 2005) *IRIN (Integrated Regional Information Networks)*, available at http://www.irinnews.org/report.asp?ReportID=47763&SelectRegion=Great_Lakes&SelectCountry=BURUNDI.

At the end of 2005, the Burundian President signed a decree creating a 25-member National Truth and Reconciliation Commission (TRC). Over a two-year period the TRC is to investigate acts of genocide, crimes against humanity, and war crimes committed between 1962 and the present. The commission will also deal with questions of restitution and appropriate compensation for stolen or destroyed property.

With a quarter of a million people returning to the country, the question of land restitution is of particular significance. Local commissions are to decide cases where there are disputes. According to the law, the Truth Commission must decide issues relating to the return of property to those from whom it was stolen, as well as the payment of compensation for property that has been destroyed. It must also decide on what other types and amounts of compensation ought to be paid by perpetrators.[95]

To facilitate the process of resolving disputes relating to land and other types of property, the Arusha Peace and Reconciliation Agreement (APRA) established a number of principles, including the principle that everyone has the right to own property, and that fair and equitable compensation should be provided to victims whose rights to property had been interfered with. The law provides that every refugee or war victim is entitled to recover his or her property and, if this is not possible, he or she is entitled to fair compensation. Even those who do not return to Burundi are entitled to just compensation if their land was expropriated without compensation. To assist the process of restoration, an inventory of destroyed property in urban areas is to be drawn up. Other measures to be taken include a registry of rural lands, the enactment of an inheritance law, and a survey of rural lands. A Sub-Commission is to deal with land issues and will examine all cases involving land belonging to refugees who have lived outside the country for long periods, as well as those cases involving the State. The Sub-Commission will also examine all contentious cases where it is alleged that there has been an abuse of the redistribution process.[96]

9 THE AFRICAN COMMISSION ON HUMAN AND PEOPLES' RIGHTS

Article 21(2) of the African Charter on Human and Peoples' Rights, refers to adequate compensation in respect of spoliation of resources. The African Charter has been supervised and enforced until now by the African Commission on Human and

95 Tracy Dexter and Philippe Ntahombaye, 'The Role of Informal Justice Systems in Fostering the Rule of Law in Post-Conflict Situations The Case of Burundi', (July 2005) *The Centre for Humanitarian Dialogue*, 37.

96 International Human Rights Law Group, 'Transitional Justice And Human Rights Provisions In The Arusha Peace And Reconciliation Agreement For Burundi', 19-20, available at http://www.globalrights.org/site/DocServer/BurundiTJGuide_Eng.pdf?docID=205.

Peoples' Rights. Generally speaking, however, the African Commission, unlike many other human rights supervisory and enforcement organs, has been very reluctant to award damages or reparations even in cases where it determines that there have been violations of the Charter. In *Henry Kalenga v. Zambia*,[97] even though the complainant was detained and held without a trial by order of the President, the Commission closed the file on this matter after the person was released. The fact that he was released and no further correspondence was received in relation to the case was deemed sufficient to justify the closing of the file by the Commission. In the case of *Louis Mega Mekongo v. Cameroon*,[98] the Commission found that the complainant was entitled to reparations for prejudice he had suffered, but that the amount of such reparations should be determined in accordance with the laws of Cameroon.[99]

In the *Malawi Africa Association and Others v. Mauritania* case, the Commission made an elaborate recommendation in its findings against the respondent, the State of Mauritania.[100] The Commission ordered the Mauritanian government, *inter alia*, to take appropriate measures to ensure the payment of compensatory benefits to widows and beneficiaries of the victims of the alleged violations.[101]

These cases are, however, exceptions to the rule, as in the majority of cases the African Commission has not awarded reparations. Therefore, it has not always been regarded as an effective institution to enable victims to achieve redress. Furthermore, the fact that until recently (with the creation of the African Court of Human and Peoples' Rights) there was no regional court structure, limited the options open to victims who wish to obtain reparations.

The creation of an African Court of Human Rights,[102] after the requisite 15 countries ratified the Protocol for the Court's establishment,[103] took five years to achieve.[104] The Court's important role in the field of human rights is made clear by the fact that it will be able to issue binding and enforceable decisions. The Court came into being on 25 February 2004. The Court was established because it was not

---

97 Henry Kalenga v. Zambia, African Commission on Human and Peoples' Rights, Comm. No. 11/88 (1994).

98 Embga Mekongo Louis v. Cameroon, African Commission on Human and Peoples' Rights, Comm. No. 59/91 (1995).

99 *Ibid.*

100 Malawi Africa Association and Others v. Mauritania, African Commission on Human and Peoples' Rights, Comm. No. 54/91, 61/91, 98/93, 164/97 to 196/97, and 210/98 (2000). S. Gumedze, 'Bringing communications before the African Commission on Human Rights and People's Rights', (2005) *African Human Rights Law Journal Volume 3 No. 1.*

101 Organisation Mondiale Contre La Torture v. Rwanda, African Commission on Human and Peoples' Rights, Comm. Nos. 27/89, 46/91, 49/91, 99/93 (1996).

102 *The Protocol to the African Charter on Human and Peoples' Rights Establishing an African Court on Human and Peoples' Rights.*

103 These countries are Algeria, Burkina Faso, Burundi, Gambia, Libya, Lesotho, Mali, Mauritania, Rwanda, South Africa, Senegal, Togo, Uganda, Ivory Coast, and the Comoros.

104 It was adopted by the Assembly of Heads of State and Government of the Organization of African Unity (OAU), at its 34th Ordinary Session, June 1998, in Ouagadougou, Burkina-Faso.

considered wise to have two courts under the auspices of the African Union: the African Court of Human and Peoples' Rights and the African Court of Justice. In July 2004, the African Union merged the two Courts in order to circumvent any problems which might arise. The combined Court will hear human rights cases referred to it by the African Commission on Human and Peoples' Rights, as well as by States that are parties to the Protocol establishing the Court. It will not, however, allow individuals or NGOs to initiate cases, unless the State in respect of which the case is being brought consents to such jurisdiction. The Court is, however, authorised to order appropriate remedies when there is a violation of rights.

Judges of the court were elected in January 2006 at the African Heads of State and Government summit in Khartoum, Sudan. The Court should begin its work in the not too distant future.

10 THE INTERNATIONAL CRIMINAL TRIBUNAL FOR RWANDA

The establishment of the war crimes tribunals for Rwanda[105] and Yugoslavia provided little assistance to victims in the way of reparations.[106] In fact, the statutes for both of these tribunals are silent on the issue of reparations for victims.[107] While both statutes provide that the trial chamber may order the return of any property or proceeds acquired by criminal conduct, including by means of duress, to their rightful owners,[108] this process does not amount to reparations in the strict sense, but is simply a process of restitution. As far as restitution is concerned, Rule 105 of the Rules of Procedure and Evidence of both tribunals provides that:

> "(B) Pursuant to the relevant national legislation, a victim or persons claiming through him may bring an action in a national court or other competent body to obtain compensation.
> (C) For the purposes of a claim made under Sub-Rule (B) the judgment of the Tribunal shall be final and binding as to the criminal responsibility of the convicted person for such injury."

The International Federation for Human Rights (FIDH) reported, in a study relating to victims who appeared before the International Criminal Tribunal for Rwanda

---

105 Daniel J. Rearick, 'Innocent until Alleged Guilty: Provisional Release at the ICTR', (Summer 2003) *Harvard International Law Journal* 44, 577.

106 See further on sentencing: W.A. Schabas, 'Sentencing by International Tribunals: A Human Rights Approach', (1997) 7 *Duke J Comp & Int'l L (Duke Journal of Comparative and International Law)* 2, at 461.

107 S.Vandeginste, 'Victims of Genocide, Crimes against Humanity and War Crimes in Rwanda: The Legal and Institutional Framework of their Right to Reparation', in J. Torpey (ed), Politics and the Past: On Repairing Historical Injustices, (Lanham, MD: Rowman & Littlefield, 2003).

108 ICTR, Article 23(3) and ICTY, Article 24(3).

(ICTR), that these victims have had difficulties in relation to a range of issues. These difficulties ranged from a lack of protective measures when they returned home and being unaware of the consequences of testifying anonymously, to a high level of frustration experienced due to the absence of a *partie civile* system and having no right to reparations.[109] Victims have received little assistance from the two tribunals and have not been able to play a meaningful rule in the proceedings.[110]

11 CLAIMS BETWEEN STATES IN THE GREAT LAKES FOR REPARATIONS

The war that took place in the DRC in the 1990s involved a number of countries. Soldiers from Zimbabwe, Namibia and Angola fought in support of the then DRC government, while Rwanda, Uganda and Burundi supported groups opposing the government. Rwanda supported Kabila out of fear that groups such as the Interahamwe had re-established themselves in refugee camps on Congolese soil. Uganda supported Kabila because the DRC had been used as a springboard for attacks on Uganda by anti-Museveni forces. Burundi supported Kabila because The Forces for the Defence of Democracy (FDD), a military wing of the Conseil National pour la Défence de la Démocratie (CNDD), a Hutu militia, used the DRC to mount attacks on Burundi.

Angola joined through the means of Uniao Nacional para a Independencia Total de Angola (Unita). Mobutu supported Unita despite the 1994 Lusaka Peace Accord, and used the DRC for supplies.

Critically, as discussed above, many of the reasons for the conflict are rooted in the legacy of colonialism. Some have argued, however, that the true reasons for the involvement in the war by these countries, was their hope of access to the DRC's resources, especially diamonds. As a result of the conflict it is estimated that 4 million people have been killed.

The DRC instituted proceedings before the International Court of Justice (ICJ) in 1999, complaining that Uganda, Burundi and Rwanda had violated international law by invading the DRC and demanding that these countries withdraw. The ICJ ruled in favour of the DRC in 2000, but actual withdrawal did not happen until 2003. As such the DRC filed three further cases to be decided by the ICJ. In respect of the DRC's claim against Rwanda, the Court dismissed the case as being outside its jurisdiction.

---

109 The International Federation for Human Rights (FIDH) Report, 'Victims in the balance,' available at: http://www.fidh.org/afriq/rapport/2002/rw343f.pdf.

110 C. Jorda and J. De Hemptinne, 'The Status and Role of the Victim', in A. Cassese, P. Gaeta, and J.R.W.D. Jones (eds.), *The Rome Statute of the International Criminal Court: A Commentary*, (USA – Oxford University Press, 2002), vol. II, 1387-8.

The DRC withdrew its claims against Burundi after an out-of-court settlement was reached. In respect of its claim against Uganda, the ICJ[111] upheld the claims brought by the DRC against Uganda, and ruled that Uganda was responsible for the looting, plundering and exploitation of the DRC's natural resources, including timber and gold. The court found that these acts were committed by members of the Ugandan military in the territory of the DRC. Uganda's self-defence claims were dismissed by the court, which also censured Uganda for using child soldiers and inciting ethnic violence. While the court found Uganda responsible for the violations it had committed, it nonetheless observed that the actions of the various parties to the conflict contributed to the immense suffering endured by the population of the DRC.[112] As far as reparations were concerned, the Court held that:

> "... it is well established in general international law that a State which bears responsibility for an internationally wrongful act is under an obligation to make full reparation for the injury caused by that act ... Upon examination of the case file, given the character of the internationally wrongful acts for which Uganda has been found responsible (illegal use of force, violation of sovereignty and territorial integrity, military intervention, occupation of Ituri, violations of international human rights law and of international humanitarian law, looting, plunder and exploitation of the DRC's natural resources), the Court considers that those acts resulted in injury to the DRC and to persons on its territory. Having satisfied itself that this injury was caused to the DRC by Uganda, the Court finds that Uganda has an obligation to make reparation accordingly."[113]

The Court, however, also found that the DRC's armed forces attacked the Ugandan Embassy in Kinshasa, maltreated Ugandan diplomats and others at the Embassy, and failed to provide the Embassy and the Ugandan diplomats with effective protection, which violated obligations owed under the Vienna Convention on Diplomatic Relations of 1961. Accordingly, so found the Court, the DRC owed reparations too. The Court did not award specific reparations, but noted that it was up to the parties themselves to determine the amount of reparations that would be paid between themselves. If the parties could not agree on an amount, the Court reserved for itself the right to settle the issue.[114]

The DRC initially filed a claim for six to ten billion US dollars, but said that it would review those numbers after the case was decided.[115] However, any amount, even a fraction of these amounts, would cripple Uganda even further as it has a debt of $4

---

111 ICJ 19 December 2005 Case Concerning Armed Activities On The Territory Of The Congo, Democratic Republic Of The Congo v. Uganda.

112 *Ibid.*, para. 221.

113 *Ibid.*, para. 259.

114 *Ibid.*, Finding 14.

115 Anjan Sundaram, 'Congo Reconsiders Damages Owed by Uganda', (20 December 2005) *Associated Press.*

billion which costs about $200 million to service annually. It has an annual revenue of only about US$700 million after expenditure. Additionally donor aid has recently been halted by a number of international donors over concerns about the way the country is being governed.[116]

At the beginning of February 2006, the ICJ ruled 15 to 2 that it could not hear the case between the DRC and Rwanda[117] as it did not have the jurisdiction to hear the matter in which the DRC accused Rwanda of 'massive, serious and flagrant violations of human rights and of international humanitarian law' including aggression, mass killings, rape, arbitrary detentions, systematic looting, and assassinations.[118] The ICJ found that Rwanda was not subject to the jurisdiction of the Court even though the DRC claimed that for many reasons Rwanda had submitted to jurisdiction. These bases of jurisdiction included the Convention against Torture, the fact that Rwanda had participated in the proceedings already, the Convention on the Prevention and Punishment of the Crime of Genocide, the Convention on the Elimination of All Forms of Racial Discrimination, the Convention on the Elimination of All Forms of Discrimination Against Women, the Constitution of the World Health Organization, the UNESCO Constitution, the Montreal Convention for the Suppression of Unlawful Acts against the Safety of Civil Aviation, and the Vienna Convention on the Law of Treaties. The Court, however, determined that none of these instruments gave jurisdiction to the Court, as Rwanda was either not a party to the treaty concerned, such as the Convention Against Torture, or had made a reservation in adopting a particular treaty to the acceptance of the ICJ jurisdiction's in a matter relating to that treaty. While the DRC attempted to show that by various statements the Government of Rwanda indicated that it was revoking its reservations, the Court found that this had not been done or that if such an indication had been given the correct lodging of such a withdrawal had not occurred.

The most interesting treaty dealt with, in the context of Rwanda's recent past, was the Convention on the Prevention and Punishment of the Crime of Genocide. While it was found that both Rwanda and the DRC were Parties to the Convention, Rwanda had entered a reservation to exclude the jurisdiction of the Court under Article IX of the Convention. This article provides that disputes between contracting State parties regarding the interpretation, application, or fulfilment of the Convention shall be submitted to the ICJ for determination. Thus, Rwanda argued that although it was a party to the treaty, it had made an explicit reservation thereto, the result of which was that the ICJ could not exercise jurisdiction in cases where Rwanda was brought

---

116 Michael A. Weinstein, 'Uganda: Museveni on the Ropes, Instability Ahead', (4 January 2006) *PINR (The Power and Interest News Report).*

117 ICJ 20 September 2002, Armed Activities on the Territory of the Congo (New Application: 2002) (Democratic Republic of the Congo v. Rwanda).

118 Frank Nyakairu, 'Rwanda wins Congo case in World Court', (Kampala, Uganda, 4 February 2006) *Daily Monitor.*

before it as a party. The DRC alleged that the validity of the reservation made by Rwanda was questionable, as the Convention contains *jus cogens* norms in respect of which no reservations are permissible. The Court, however, held that the issue was not about a reservation on the substantive questions on genocide, but rather on procedural questions, namely jurisdiction. The Court held that consent was a necessary basis for it to hear cases before it. On the question of whether Rwanda had withdrawn this reservation, the Court ruled that statements made by Rwandan officials that were alleged to indicate such a withdrawal were not specific enough to uphold the argument. Thus, the Court found that the Genocide Convention could not constitute a basis of jurisdiction in the case. The Court went to great lengths to indicate, on a number of occasions, including at the beginning and at the conclusion of its judgment, that the questions of the merits of the case were not dealt with by the Court. At the beginning the Court states:

> "The Court notes first of all that at the present stage of the proceedings it cannot consider any matter relating to the merits of this dispute between the DRC and Rwanda. In accordance with the decision taken in its Order of 18 September 2002 (see paragraph 6 above), the Court is required to address only the questions of whether it is competent to hear the dispute and whether the DRC's Application is admissible."

A more forceful and direct statement about the inability of the Court to deal with the merits of the case is found right at the end of the ruling:

> "While the Court has come to the conclusion that it cannot accept any of the grounds put forward by the DRC to establish its jurisdiction in the present case, and cannot therefore entertain the latter's Application, it stresses that it has reached this conclusion solely in the context of the preliminary question of whether it has jurisdiction in this case the issue to be determined at this stage of the proceedings (see paragraph 14 above). The Court is precluded by its Statute from taking any position on the merits of the claims made by the DRC. However, as the Court has stated on numerous previous occasions, there is a fundamental distinction between the question of the acceptance by States of the Court's jurisdiction and the conformity of their acts with international law. Whether or not States have accepted the jurisdiction of the Court, they are required to fulfil their obligations under the United Nations Charter and the other rules of international law, including international humanitarian and human rights law, and they remain responsible for acts attributable to them which are contrary to international law."[119]

In the last line, the Court emphasises the need for States to live up to their international obligations, even if it did not have jurisdiction to hear the specific claims raised by the DRC.

---

[119] ICJ 20 September 2002, Armed Activities on the Territory of the Congo (New Application: 2002) (Democratic Republic of the Congo v. Rwanda), para. 127.

While the ICJ was giving its ruling, a ministerial session of the UN Security Council on security in the Great Lakes region agreed to a resolution urging States to enforce the arms embargo in the DRC and to deal with the trafficking of arms and natural resources across the borders of the countries concerned. Uganda, Rwanda, the DRC, and Burundi were also ordered to take measures to prevent their territories from being used by armed groups. Additionally, a panel of UN experts, in a confidential report that was leaked to the press, proposed a new system to track the DRC's mineral exports so as to limit the looting by illegal armed groups that are suspected of collaborating with Uganda and Rwanda. The panel noted that as 'long as no enhanced security of the precious mineral assets of the DRC is found, they represent to any armed group, warlord or criminal organization a ready catalyst for violence.'[120] The panel also accused Uganda and Rwanda of refusing to give straight answers about the role they played in the illegal mineral trade in the DRC.[121]

12 DEBT RELIEF, DEVELOPMENT AID AND REPARATIONS

There is a realisation that Africa and especially the Great Lakes region needs assistance to deal with its problems. Debt relief is an opportunity to provide this assistance and is currently being championed in respect of Africa. Some argue that debt relief ought to be discussed as a means to attain reparations for what was done in Africa and to Africans during the colonial period. Thus, a group of organisations meeting in Zambia stated in a declaration emanating from the conference that they 'will make reasonable, rational demands for reparations to compensate for the economic, social and environmental damage incurred by our people.'[122]

Regardless of the motivations and the reason for the programme, some type of debt relief system has been in operation since 1996. It was, however, the 2005 initiative, under the Multilateral Debt Relief Initiative (MDRI) by the G8, that moved the programme forward for heavily indebted poor countries (HIPCs).

The HIPC initiative, for countries with annual income per head of $825 or less, was established in 1996 by the World Bank and the International Monetary Fund (IMF), to reduce poor countries' debts. The IMF only accepted $380 per capita by the end of 2005. Even if countries have per capita incomes that fall within the HIPC system, they must meet certain conditions, including requirements that their economic

---

120 'UN experts want to better trace DR Congo's mineral exports', available at: http://www.monuc.org/news.aspx?newsID=9826.

121 Irwin Arieff, 'Africa's Great Lakes governments renew peace vows', (Reuters, 27 Jan 2006), available at: http://www.alertnet.org/thenews/newsdesk/N2711051.htm.

122 The Lusaka Declaration: Towards an 'Africa Consensus' on Sustainable Solutions to the Debt Problem 19-21 May 1999, available at: http://www.aidc.org.za/?q=book/view/44.

policies reduce poverty. Thus, these countries must take steps to reduce public spending, privatise basic services, and liberalise their trade mechanisms, to be eligible for debt relief.

At this time, 18 countries have met the requirements of the HIPC including Rwanda, Tanzania, and Uganda. Another 10 countries are at the first stage of the HIPC eligibility process and receive some relief on their debt repayments. These countries include Burundi and the Democratic Republic of Congo. The HIPC list will be finalised by the end of 2006 and countries that may make the list include Central African Republic and the Republic of the Congo. On successfully entering the HIPC programme, a country will receive some debt payment relief and, on completing HIPC, it will enjoy complete cancellation of debt incurred by it.

The HIPC programme is extensively criticised for only delivering 48 billion US dollars in debt cancellation over a 10-year period and because no country in the HIPC has achieved debt sustainability. In fact, poor countries worldwide owe US$523 billion in debt, Africa's share being US$330 billion. African countries spend US$15 billion each year simply servicing their debt load. While the revised programme is meant to address some of the programme's short-comings, critics still argue that the programme will take too long to achieve its intended purposes, and even then not all countries will be able to attain all the programme goals.[123] Jubilee 2000, a network of NGOs, which subsequently changed its name to Jubilee Debt Coalition, has argued that:

> "Debt cancellation is a matter of justice, not aid; we need to end the perpetual indebtedness of poor countries and the damage this continues to cause, as well as improve relations between North and South. Debt relief must not count towards the pre-existing target that aid should reach 0.7% of national income. In any case, both debt cancellation and aid levels of at least this proportion are needed to eradicate poverty."[124]

Another plan on the table to assist poor African countries is the proposal for an African Marshall Plan. To this end, Ibrahima Fall, the UN secretary general representative in the Great Lakes region, called on the international community to create 'a second Marshall Plan' to salvage countries in the region.[125] He argues that such a plan is necessary to 'help countries of the region rediscover the path to stability and development'. This is not the first time a Marshall Plan has been proposed. In January 2005, for example, British Chancellor of the Exchequer, Gordon Brown, proposed such

123 See generally Jubilee Debt Coalition Heavily Indebted Poor Countries Initiative, available at: http://www.jubileedebtcampaign.org.uk/.

124 JUBILEE DEBT COALITION, 'How Jubilee Debt Campaign demands differ from UK government proposals', available at: http://www.jubileedebtcampaign.org.uk/.

125 'Top UN official moots `Marshall Plan` for Great Lakes', (Bangui, 21 February 2006), *Angola Press*, available at: http://www.angolapress-angop.ao/noticia-e.asp?ID=418594.

a course of action for African countries. He did note, however, that the days of the UK apologising for colonialism were over.[126]

While not technically reparations, the effect of debt relief is to act as a form of redress, which would undoubtedly draw the support of African States.

13 CONCLUSION

While there have been tremendous theoretical advances for victim reparation over the last few years, these have not often become the practical reality, especially for victims in Africa. Even victims, such as those in South Africa who have had lawyers and funding necessary to gain access to the institutions that could hear their cases, including the courts of the USA, have not been successful. Unfortunately many victims in Africa have not had the resources or access to lawyers to pursue their claims. Even African countries have not been able to pursue their claims against each other successfully, that is, until the ICJ decision in 2006 between the DRC and Uganda. That decision may prove instrumental in increasing both the number of cases brought and their success rates. As far as individuals are concerned, there is a greater tendency to bring such cases, even in the courts of other countries, and a trend towards bringing such cases may develop as individuals learn from previous examples.

The establishment and existence of the African Court on Human and Peoples' Rights may also mean that we see more victims being compensated for harm that they have suffered. The fact that the International Criminal Court is looking to prosecute people responsible for crimes in the DRC and Uganda may, if there is a conviction, see victims being able to claim from the ICC Victims Trust Fund.[127] Undoubtedly, the issue of reparations for gross human rights violations has been advanced over the last few years. However, the practical reality falls far short and few victims in the Great Lakes are now benefiting or in the future will benefit from these initiatives. It is more likely that debt relief and development aid – a form of redress –will have a greater and more lasting impact. The most important question is whether the effects of such initiatives will in fact be felt by those who need and deserve reparations most.

---

126 ''No UK apology' for colonial past' (25 January 2005), *BBC News*, available at: http://news.bbc.co.uk/1/hi/uk_politics/4176805.stm.

127 C. Jorda and J. De Hemptinne, 'The Status and Role of the Victim', in A. Cassese, P. Gaeta, and J.R.W.D. Jones (eds.), *The Rome Statute of the International Criminal Court: A Commentary*, (USA – Oxford University Press, 2002), vol. II, 1387-8. See further the chapter in this book by Andreas O'Shea (at pages 179-196).

PART C: REPARATIONS CLAIMS PURSUED ABROAD

APARTHEID AND THE ALIEN TORTS ACT: GLOBAL JUSTICE MEETS SOVEREIGN EQUALITY

MICHAEL OSBORNE[1]

1 INTRODUCTION

The lawsuits filed in the United States by victims of apartheid represent perhaps the most ambitious attempt thus far to use the Alien Torts Claims Act (the *ATS*), to obtain compensation for the human rights violations of transnational corporations. The dismissal by a New York Court of a consolidated action against corporations active in South Africa during apartheid therefore came as a blow to human rights activists, who had hoped that the ATS was emerging perhaps as the only effective means available anywhere of holding corporations legally accountable for international human rights violations. (The matter is, at time of writing, on appeal.)

It is said that the Universal Declaration of Human Rights of 1948 inaugurated a human rights revolution. Over the next half-century, the broad promises of the Declaration were fleshed out in a series of conventions and multilateral treaties, addressing areas ranging from civil rights, to social and economic rights, to environmental rights. But for the most part, these documents embody unrealised ideals. Human rights have continued to be violated with impunity almost everywhere. The human rights revolution is not just unfinished. For many, it has yet to attain material reality.

One of the gaps in human rights enforcement has been in its failure to address violations perpetrated by non-state actors. Both individuals and corporations have largely escaped responsibility. That has begun to change. The *Pinochet* case undermined one of the redoubts of individual impunity; the immunity historically enjoyed by heads of state. But the problem of holding corporations to account for their international misdeeds has remained intractable.

It is now generally accepted that corporations can be both criminally and civilly liable under international law. Yet, it has proven very difficult to find a forum to which

[1] He thanks Diane Sammons, Alisa Valderrama and Susannah Cowen for their valuable comments.

they can be summoned. Home-country courts are seldom receptive to suits alleging human rights abuses by their corporate citizens committed in distant lands. Tribunals of host countries, ever hungry for foreign investment, are likewise often closed to suits against foreign corporations. (The apartheid case teaches that, just as individual perpetrators are often immunised by post-transition amnesty programs, transnational corporations may benefit from the protection of a new government.) Finally, corporations do not generally fall under the jurisdiction of international criminal tribunals.

Human rights activists hope the ATS may help fill this gap. In recent years, the statute, enacted more than 200 years ago by the first Congress of the United States, has been invoked to hold corporations civilly liable in U.S. federal courts for international human rights violations around the globe. Although very few victims have actually received compensation, the symbolic importance of the suits is inestimable. The ATS offers significant advantages to human rights plaintiffs. For one thing, an ATS suit has an extraordinarily broad jurisdictional reach. U.S. federal courts are open not only to action against transnationals incorporated in the United States; they will also hear actions lodged against non-U.S. corporations which merely 'do business' within America's borders. Moreover, the U.S. federal court system offers plaintiffs unmatched procedural advantages, including lenient pleading standards, the availability of class actions, and extensive discovery opportunities. What is more, U.S. courts, sitting as they do at the hub of an economic system in which transnational corporations are conjoined in an increasingly dense network of commercial relationships, have become accustomed, perhaps more than any other domestic tribunals, to adjudicating disputes arising from distant corners of the earth.

That having been said, human rights victims invoking the ATS face formidable hurdles that have seen many suits thrown out of court at inception. Only a narrow class of international law violations is actionable under the ATS, and the Supreme Court's first modern ATS judgment, *Sosa v Alvarez-Machain* (2004), handed down shortly before the apartheid decision, offered only limited guidance in identifying precisely which violations fall into this category. Nor did *Sosa* shed much light on another question that has vexed ATS actions – i.e. can corporations be liable for aiding and abetting violations by states? The Supreme Court also did not take the opportunity to clarify the parameters of possibly the most serious impediment to ATS petitioners: judicial deference to pronouncements from the U.S. State Department in cases implicating foreign policy.

In the *Apartheid* case, each of these issues was decided against Plaintiffs. First, the district court held that Plaintiffs had not alleged conduct by the corporate Defendants, all of which were present in one form or another in South Africa during the apartheid era, that fell within the scope of actionable ATS violations. Second, the corporations could not be held liable as aiders and abettors of violations by the apartheid regime. Third, the Court invoked representations by Washington and the South African government, claiming that adjudication of the case in New York would prejudice U.S./South Africa relations, undermine international commerce, and affront South Africa's sovereignty.

This contribution, using the apartheid suit as an exemplar, explores both the opportunities offered by and the limitations of the ATS. The first section reviews the history invoked by Plaintiffs in support of their charge that international corporations were complicit in the system of apartheid. In that context I consider the findings of the Truth and Reconciliation Commission, the limitations and findings of which laid the foundations for the New York suit. The second section reviews ATS case law, as a means of understanding the scope and limits of the statute. Third, I explore the problems encountered in finding a forum for cases against transnational corporations, and the extent to which the ATS may serve as a surrogate in that regard. Next, is an examination of the judgment of the New York court, and criticism of that decision. And finally, I analyse the court's treatment of the objections by the U.S. and the South African governments to the suits. That will afford the opportunity to consider some of the most vexing questions raised by the ATS, including the scope of extraterritorial jurisdiction of American courts, arguments regarding the issue of foreign policy deference, the merits of privatised foreign policy pursued by the civil suits, and the implications of the ATS for sovereign equality and world order. We will see that, for all its inadequacies, the Supreme Court's *Sosa* decision may assist in securing the legitimacy of the ATS as a means to challenging the worst human rights violations of the modern corporate giants.

2 APARTHEID AND THE TRC

After the first Dutch settlers arrived in what is now Cape Town in 1652, and as colonial expansion into South Africa continued through the 18th and 19th centuries, black South Africans were subjected to slavery, subjugation, exclusion and separation by successive colonial governments.[2] The discovery of diamonds and gold in the interior during the latter part of the 19th century laid the foundation for the modern South African industrial state. Its economy was built on the back of exploited black labour, the indigenous agricultural economy having been destroyed when blacks were forced off the country's scarce arable land to make way for white farmers. The labour requirements of the mines and burgeoning urban industry came to be serviced by a migratory labour system. That system evolved by the mid 20th century into the system of

---

2 The history referred to in this introduction is traversed in L. THOMPSON, *A History of South Africa*, (Jonathan Ball, 2006); N. WORDEN, *The Making of Modern South Africa* (Blackwell Publishers Ltd, 2000); D. O'MEARA, *Forty Lost Years: the Apartheid State and the Politics of the National Party 1948-1994* (Athens: Ohio University Press, 1996).

geographic separation and political repression, known as apartheid. A raft of legislation created a regime under which Africans were confined to 'Bantustans', to be shipped into white South Africa to labour in the mines and factories. They were housed in squalid compounds, then sent back to the impoverished Bantustans when their labour was no longer required. The National Party, which assumed power in 1948, formalised and consolidated the system, classifying South Africans into four races – white, 'Coloured', Asiatic (Indian), and Native (African). Only whites enjoyed the franchise. In the years that followed, African rebellions against apartheid were brutally crushed, with thousands imprisoned, tortured or killed.[3]

But that part of the story is well known. The particular historical backdrop to the apartheid reparations cases is less familiar. The central premise of the suits is that big business, having participated in the design of the system, was a full and willing partner in the implementation of apartheid. Big business profited enormously from the employment of Africans in slave-like conditions. Thus, far from being merely innocent bystanders, South Africa's big corporations were active participants in the apartheid system. Foreign corporations were important economic actors from the beginning. In some cases, they constituted the monopolies that controlled gold and diamond mining. These massive corporations later came to dominate either directly or through their subsidiaries, the rest of South Africa's industrial economy. They also provided indispensable assistance to the government and its military, furnishing oil, capital and armaments.[4]

International condemnation of apartheid began to mount in the 1960s. Trade sanctions and embargoes were imposed by many countries. International condemnation of apartheid culminated in 1968 with a declaration by the General Assembly of the United Nations that apartheid was a crime against humanity.[5] Oil and capital embargoes followed,[6] and the Security Council imposed a mandatory arms embargo

---

3 The statutory foundations of apartheid and its legal history are ably rendered in J. DUGARD, *Human Rights and the South Africa Legal Order* (Juta, 1979). Amongst key apartheid statutes: *The Prohibition of Mixed Marriages Act* of 1949 (outlawing marriages between whites and blacks); *Population Registration Act* of 1950 (classifying population into "white," "Bantu" (black African), and "Coloured" (mixed race)); *Group Areas Act* of 1950 (dividing land into separate residential zones, and reserving the most desirable land for whites); *Pass Laws Act* of 1952 (requiring all Africans over sixteen to carry an identification document, and allowing the government or employers to expel a worker from an area for any reason and at any time); *Bantu Education Act* of 1953 (relegating blacks to schools expressly designed to prepare black children for menial labour in service of the white economy); *Riotous Assemblies Act* of 1953 (allowing the Justice Minister to prohibit any gathering); *Public Safety Act* of 1953 (allowing for the declaration of a state of emergency at any time); *Industrial Conciliation Act* of 1956 (excluding blacks from virtually all non-menial jobs in the public and private sectors).

4 A full account of the relevant economic history summarised here is to be found in a work by S. TERREBLANCHE, *A History of Inequality in South Africa* (U.N.P. 2002), Ch. 4.

5 General Assembly Resolution, *The Policies of apartheid of the Government of South Africa* A/RES/2396 (XXIII), 2 December 1968.

6 U.N.G.A. Res. 35/206 (Dec. 1980).

in 1977.[7] In 1984, the Security Council described apartheid as a crime against humanity.[8] Subsequently, the role of transnational corporations came under the spotlight. A 1976 General Assembly resolution, the first of many, declared that companies that failed to divest from South Africa had become accomplices to the crimes of the apartheid regime.[9]

Questions of historical responsibility and reparations were on the table after South Africans began to negotiate the transition from apartheid to democracy in the early 1990s. There were demands for a great reckoning. But there was also a pragmatic recognition that the apartheid government would not voluntarily surrender power to a regime committed to vengeance. It was also recognised that an attempt to remedy the inequities of history through wholesale expropriation would provoke capital flight and the departure of vital skilled white labour. Accordingly, retribution and redistribution were sacrificed for reconciliation and reconstruction. Under the Truth and Reconciliation Commission (the *TRC*), perpetrators of apartheid atrocities were promised full amnesty – provided they came forward with a full account of their depredations. The guilty would escape punishment, once they had shown where the bodies were buried.

The TRC process was subject to a number of crucial limitations, which, as we shall see, prompted the filing of the apartheid reparations suits in the U.S. Those granted amnesty were immunised from both criminal and civil liability.[10] The TRC interpreted

---

7 Security Council Resolution, the *Question of South Africa*, S/RES/418, 4 November 1977.

8 Security Council Resolution, S/RES/556, 23 October 1984.

9 General Assembly Resolution, *Policies of Apartheid of the Government of South Africa: Economic Collaboration with South Africa*, A/RES/31/6 H, 9 November 1976. General Assembly Resolution, *Adverse consequences for the enjoyment of human rights of political, military, economic and other forms of assistance given to colonial and racist regimes in Southern Africa*, A/RES/31/33, 30 November 1976; General Assembly Resolution, *Policies of Apartheid of the Government of South Africa: Comprehensive and Mandatory Sanctions Against the Racist Regime of South Africa and Imposition, Co*-ordination *and Strict Monitoring of Measures Against Racist South Africa* A/RES/44/27 C&D, 22 November 1989.

10 The constitutionality of the TRC was challenged in the newly created Constitutional Court, as violating the right to access to justice under both domestic and international law. In *Azanian Peoples Org. (AZAPO) v. President of South Africa*, 1996 (4) SALR 671 (CC), the Court dismissed the challenge, holding that the Constitution itself authorised the granting of both criminal and civil amnesty and that such amnesty was not inconsistent with international law. See J. DUGARD, 'Is the Truth and Reconciliation Process Compatible with International Law? An Unanswered Question,' (1997) *SAJHR* 258; C. JENKINS, 'After the Dry White Season: The Dilemmas of Reparation and Reconstruction in South Africa,' 16 *SAJHR*. 415 (2000); S. L. RUSSEL-BROWN, 'Out of the Crooked Timber of Humanity: The Conflict Between South Africa's Truth and Reconciliation Commission and International Human Rights Norms Regarding Effective Remedies,' 26 *Hast. Int'l & Comp.* L. Rev. 227 (2003).

its mandate as allowing it to address only individual violations; systemic and global offences were not deemed to be within its ambit:[11]

> "[There was] no attempt to bring within the ambit of the amnesty enquiry acts that constituted a crime under international law but were not criminal under the law of apartheid. Death and suffering caused by forcible population removals, inhuman influx control laws and arbitrary detention-without-trial laws permitting merciless interrogation in solitary confinement, that qualified as crimes against humanity, [were] excluded from the amnesty process."[12]

As a consequence of the TRC's narrow focus, little attention was given to private blameworthiness in general, or to corporate responsibility in particular.[13] No amnesty was sought or given arising out of the corporations' participation in apartheid. The *Final TRC Report* did, however, note that business failed to take responsibility for its 'involvement in state security initiatives specifically designed to sustain apartheid rule',[14] and alleged that the mining industry had been intimately involved both in designing and in implementing apartheid policies.[15] Private corporations, moreover, were said to be 'willing collaborators in the creation of [the apartheid] war machine'.[16] Significantly, the report envisages a possible civil claim against the Anglo American Corporation (one of the Defendants in the apartheid litigation), grounded on the

---

11 See P. ANDREWS, 'Reparations for Apartheid's Victims: The Path to Reconciliation?', 53 *DePaul L. Rev.* 1155 (2004), 1166 (although "apartheid was deemed a crime against humanity under international law, the TRC in its methodology and operation reduced apartheid's crimes to individual acts of gross violations of human rights") (also noting (at 1174), government's stalling on paying limited reparations to victims of apartheid). See further the chapter in this book by Mahmood Mamdani at pages 83-118).

12 DUGARD, *Ibid.* 262. Regarding the *Azapo* decision, Dugard concludes as follows: "at the outset Mahomed DP should have enquired more thoroughly into the compatibility of the epilogue with both conventional and customary international law. The latter enquiry would probably have revealed that state practice is too unsettled to support a rule obliging states to prosecute those alleged to have committed crimes against humanity in all circumstances." (At 267.) Compare *Prosecutor v. Furundzija*, Case No. IT-95-17/1-T, Judgment, n.172 (Dec. 10, 1998) (citing *Compilation of General Comments and General Recommendations Adopted by Human Rights Treaty Bodies*, U.N. Doc. HRI/GEN/1 Rev. 1 at 30 (1994)). ("Amnesties are generally incompatible with the duty of States to investigate torture ... States may not deprive individuals of the right to an effective remedy, including compensation and such full rehabilitation as may be possible.")

13 See S. TERREBLANCHE, *supra* at 125.

14 Final Report of the Truth and Reconciliation Commission of South Africa ("*Final TRC Report*") Vol 4, Ch. 2, para 166. The *Final TRC Report* was issued in two parts: Volumes 1-5 in 1998 (available at *http://www.goshen.edu/library/EMBARGO/*) and Volume 6 in 2003 (available at *http://www.info.gov.za/otherdocs/2003/trc.*) Of particular relevance for present purposes are Vol. 4, Ch. 2, 'Institutional Hearing: Business and Labour,' and Vol. 6, § 2, Chap. 5, 'Reparations and the Business Sector' A937-51.

15 *Final TRC Report*, Vol. 4, Ch. 2, paras. 23, 63, 161; Vol. 5, Ch. 6, para 156.

16 *Final TRC Report*, Vol. 4, Ch. 2, para. 126.

'extent to which decades of profits were based on systemic violations of human rights.'[17]

3 THE ALIEN TORT STATUTE

Some of the Plaintiffs who filed ATS suits in U.S. courts in 2002 were apartheid victims disappointed by the outcome of the TRC process. Before examining those suits in detail, we review the coming to life of the ATS in 1980, and its subsequent development into a tool for use against transnational corporations in U.S. federal courts.

3.1 THE ATS AS LATE-BLOOMER

The ATS reads as follows:

> "The district courts shall have original jurisdiction of any civil action by an alien for a tort only, committed in violation of the law of nations or a treaty of the United States."[18]

The ATS lay dormant on the statute books for the first two centuries of its existence. In 1980 it sprang to life. A man whose brother had been tortured to death by a Paraguayan policeman filed suit in a New York federal court after the policeman had been found in the U.S. In a celebrated decision, the court read the ATS to allow claims for gross human rights violations, irrespective of the nationality of the victim or the

---

17 *Final TRC Report*, Vol. 6, s. 2, Ch. 5, para. 60; see also *Final TRC Report*, Vol. 6 s. 5, Ch. 1, para. 25. (Victims' "right to reparation is acknowledged and can be enforced in terms of international law.") While it cannot seriously be contested that many corporations participated to a greater or lesser extent in apartheid, the broader claim that South African apartheid can properly be treated as "racial capitalism", in the sense that apartheid represented the interests of the South African capitalist class, has been the subject of much academic debate. (See *Final TRC Report* Vol. 4, Ch. 2, paras. 6, 8.) See D. POSEL, et al, 'Debating "Race" in South African Scholarship,' *Transformation* 47 (2001). (*http://www.transformation.und.ac.za/issue%2047/47%20editorial.pdf*) (while Marxist scholars see cheap black labour power as "the linchpin of apartheid, the point of effective fusion of political and economic interests," other scholars viewed apartheid as economically irrational because it guaranteed skills shortages, coupled with artificially constricted domestic markets for locally produced goods, both of which were antithetical to the interest of big business).

18 28 U.S.C. s. 1350 (2005). Closely related to the ATS is the *Torture Victim Protection Act* (*TVPA*), which provides that "an individual who under actual or apparent authority, or color of law, of any foreign nation" subjects another to torture or extrajudicial killing is liable for damages in a civil action. 28 U.S.C. § 1350(2)(a)(1)-(2) (2000). Unlike the ATS, the TVPA offers a remedy both to "aliens" and to US citizens. However, as apparent from its text, the TVPA is narrower in scope. The Digwamaje plaintiffs in *Apartheid Litigation*, 346 F. Supp. 2d 538 (S.D.N.Y. 2004), brought suit under both the ATS and the TVPA, but the latter suit was dismissed along with the former. (At 555).

perpetrator, and irrespective of where the alleged violation had taken place.[19] It is difficult to overstate the importance of the court's finding to the effect that:

> "In the twentieth century the international community has come to recognize the common danger posed by the flagrant disregard of basic human rights and particularly the right to be free of torture. . . . Indeed, for purposes of civil liability, the torturer has become – like the pirate and slave trader before him – *hostis humani generis*, an enemy of all mankind. Our holding today, giving effect to a jurisdictional provision enacted by our First Congress, is a small but important step in the fulfillment of the ageless dream to free all people from brutal violence."[20]

The court found that cases holding that violations committed by a state against its own citizens did not violate international law were 'out of tune with the current usage and practice of international law.'[21] International law had to be interpreted 'not as it was in 1789, but as it has evolved and exists among the nations of the world today.'[22]

In the years that followed, torture, war crimes, summary execution, disappearance, crimes against humanity, and slavery were held actionable under the ATS. But until 2004 none of these cases reached the Supreme Court, leaving open the question whether the highest court would give its blessing to *Filartiga's* expansive reading of the ATS. Finally in 2004, the Supreme Court did pronounce on the ATS, in *Sosa v Alvarez-Machain.*[23] But before turning to that decision, let us survey the development of the ATS in the quarter-century following *Filartiga*. Three milestone cases, two decided in New York, one in California, both confirmed *Filartiga* and significantly broadened the reach of the ATS.

The first of these is *Karadzic,*[24] in which a group of Bosnian refugees sued Radovan Karadzic, leader of the unrecognised Bosnian Serb Republic, alleging that he was responsible for rape, forced prostitution, forced impregnation, torture, assault, battery and summary execution perpetrated by forces under his command against Croat and Muslim citizens of Bosnia-Herzegovina during the course of the civil war. A New York federal court found that Karadzic could not avoid liability on the basis that he acted in a private capacity. Genocide and war crimes were actionable under international law – even if not committed by states, or individuals acting in concert with states.[25]

From *Karadzic's* determination that individuals may, under certain circumstances, be liable under the ATS, it was a short step to holding that corporations could also be liable under the ATS, either by virtue of their conduct in complicity with a state, or because their conduct constituted one of the few international crimes for which

19 *Filartiga v. Pena-Irala,* 630 F.2d 876 (2d Cir. 1980).
20 *Ibid.* 890.
21 *Ibid.* 884.
22 *Ibid.* 881.
23 542 U.S. 692 (2004).
24 *Kadic v Karadzic,* 70 F. 3d 232 (2d Cir. 1995).
25 *Ibid.* 239 – 40.

no state involvement is required. That was affirmed in the second post-*Filartiga* milestone in which the issue was whether a U.S. oil company, Unocal Inc. had, by hiring the army, and providing food, money and logistical support, been complicit in human rights violations committed by the Myanmar army in the course of defending Unocal's oil pipeline.[26] The court held that Unocal could be liable under the ATS for knowing 'practical assistance' to the Myanmar military.[27] The evidence against Unocal was especially compelling: a security consulting company had warned Unocal that the Myanmar government used forced labour to construct roads, and that expected returns would need to be high to justify the political risk.[28] In 2005, while a fresh appeal was pending, *Unocal* settled the matter for an estimated $30 million, the first case in which ATS claimants received any cash compensation.[29]

Wiwa[30] a case against two transnational oil companies operating in Nigeria, may be regarded as a third ATS milestone, for its affirmation of the jurisdiction of U.S. courts to hear properly pleaded ATS claims, even where there exist only attenuated links between the forum and the defendants. Members of an organisation resisting forced removals from the Niger Delta (including relatives of Ken Saro-Wiwa, the writer and activist executed by the Nigerian military regime), sued Royal Dutch Shell and British Petroleum, alleging that, through their wholly-owned subsidiaries, they had used the police and military to suppress resistance.[31] (Plaintiffs also alleged that defendants' corporations had bribed witnesses to testify against Saro-Wiwa at his trial.)[32] The court rejected defendants' *forum non conveniens* plea that the case should be dismissed and referred to England. The court reasoned that it was in the interests of the United States to furnish a forum in which to litigate human rights violations,[33] and plaintiffs, who had limited resources, should not be required to restart their case in a foreign jurisdiction employing new counsel, at considerable expense and delay.[34]

---

26 *Doe v. Unocal Corp*, 395 F.3d 932, 951 (9th Cir. 2002).

27 *Ibid.* 952.

28 Quoted in P. L. HOFFMAN & D. A. ZAHEER, 'The Rules of the Road: Federal Common Law and Aiding and Abetting Under the Alien Tort Claims Act,' 26 *Loy. L.A. Int'l* and *Comp. L. Rev.* 101 (2004), 101. Notably, *Unocal* was only a minority investor in the joint venture alleged to have committed the violations; another participant, Total S.A., a company owned by the French government, was dismissed from the suit for want of personal jurisdiction. 'The Alien Problem', *Economist*, June 9, 2003.

29 See ALLEN, 'Unocal Pays Out in Burma Abuse Case,' *Financial Times*, Dec. 14, 2004, 12. Prior to settlement, the Ninth Circuit vacated its earlier decision.

30 *Wiwa v. Royal Dutch Petroleum Co.*, 226 F.3d 88, 101-03 (2d Cir. 2000).

31 See generally 'Big Oil's Dirty Secrets,' *Economist*, May 8, 2003 (noting bad human rights, environmental, and human rights records of transnational oil companies).

32 *Wiwa, supra* 93.

33 *Ibid.* 100.

34 *Ibid.* 106-07.

3.2 THE ATS AS A RESPONSE TO SYSTEMIC FAILURE

It is because the ATS offers a means of invoking human rights law against trans national corporations (*TNC's*), that the statute may be considered a revolution in the field. As we have seen, the *Wiwa* court recognised the mismatch in the respective resources of plaintiffs and the defendant TNC's. Almost as dramatic is the inequality between TNC's and the governments of the countries in which many do business. (Exxon-Mobil's reported annual revenues exceed the GDP's of all but ten or so of the world's richest states.[35])

The size, power and wealth of TNC's, as well as their extraordinary reach, makes it essential that they be held accountable for their human rights abuses and simultaneously almost impossible so to do. The TNC is a protean creature. It may be incorporated in 50 different jurisdictions and run operations on every continent. Its stockholders – who may themselves be distributed across every country on the planet – are insulated from personal liability. By incorporating subsidiaries remotely, TNC's position themselves to take maximal advantage of lax regulations and lenient corporate governance rules wherever they may be found. Many engage in regulatory arbitrage, distributing risk across national boundaries, as well as amongst their subsidiaries, protected by the virtual immunity offered by the regulatory vacuum in the interstices of national legal regimes.[36]

That vacuum is symptomatic of institutional failure at several levels. TNC's could, in principle, be regulated by the legal regime of the state in which the parent company is headquartered or incorporated.[37] But home state regulation of TNC's foreign conduct is often half-hearted. (Although hesitant to recognise that corporations that

---

35 R. BROOKS, 72 *U.Chi. L. Rev.* 1159 (2005), 1165 (quoting A. GIDDENS, *Runaway World: The Reith Lectures Revisited,* The Director's Lectures (London School of Economics Nov 10, 1999) (*http://www.polity.co.uk/giddens/pdfs/Globalisation.pdf*); see also L.M. BREED, 'Regulating Our 21st Century Ambassadors: A New Approach to Corporate Liability for Human Rights Violations Abroad,' 42 *Va. J. Int'l L.* 1005 (2002) 1007 (revenues of the 100 largest transnational enterprises larger than economies of most states).

36 *Lubbe and others v. Cape Plc.*, [2000] 4 All E.R. 268 (H.L), offers an example of a corporation seeking to insulate itself from liability by taking advantage of lower regulatory standards abroad. Refusing to countenance that, the court imputed direct responsibility upon the U.K. parent company, because of its failure to utilise available scientific knowledge regarding the dangers of asbestos, notwithstanding that its South African subsidiary had complied with local safety regulations. See B. SAHNI, 'The Interpretation of the Corporate Personality of Transnational Corporations,' 15 *Widener L.J.* 1 (2005), 42; N. MENDELSON, 'A Control-Based Approach to Shareholder Liability for Corporate Torts' (2002) 102 *Columbia Law Review,* 1203, 1205, 1239–47; S. PICCIOTTO, 'Rights, Responsibilities and Regulation of International Business,' 42 *Columbia Journal of Transnational Law* 131 (2003), 148. Emerging theories of "enterprise liability" aspire to align the legal formalities of corporate structure with the economic and political realities of modern corporate structure. See P.I. BLUMBERG, '*The Multinational Challenge to Corporation Law: The Search for a New Corporate Personality,*' (1993), 121-50.

37 *Barcelona Traction , Light and Power Company Ltd. (Belg. v. Spain)*, 1970 1.C.J.3 (Feb 1970), 33.

do business abroad may be subject to liability for human rights abuses, countries in the developed world have not been slow to take up their own corporations' rights against expropriation).[38] The democratic imperatives that would ordinarily incline a government to rein in a rogue corporation are diminished where those harmed by its depredations can cast no votes in home state elections. Municipal legal regimes are ill-suited to deal with international human rights infractions.[39] Finally, corporate law regimes make it difficult to 'pierce the veil' between the domestic parent and its foreign subsidiary, as may be necessary to address the misconduct of the foreign entity. The fiction of corporate personality facilitates elaborate shell games, permitting responsibility to be deferred, displaced and diffused across globe-spanning commercial empires.

Regulation of TNC's in host states may be even less effective. Where it is TNC's collaboration with repressive host states that forms the basis of the lawsuit, host state courts are, for obvious reasons, unlikely to be receptive to suits against those entities. But even if not themselves complicit in abuse, host governments and their courts may be readily manipulated or corrupted.[40] Poor countries may be threatened with divestiture when they enforce labour or environmental regulation, or resist pressures

---

38 Usually via diplomatic protection. See generally. I BROWNLIE, *Principles of Public International Law* 465-95 (2d ed. 1972); *Barcelona Traction, Light and Power Company Ltd. (Belg. v. Spain)*, 1970 I.C.J.3 (Feb 1970), 33.

39 See *Presbyterian Church of Sudan v. Talisman Energy, Inc.*, 244 F.Supp.2d 289, 337 (S.D.N.Y. 2003) ("While plaintiffs may be able to obtain the same relief in Canadian courts that they seek in this jurisdiction ... Canadian courts will only be able to treat plaintiffs' allegations as violations of Canadian, rather than international law."); see also G. BASS, *Stay the Hand of Vengeance: the Politics of War Crimes Tribunals* (2000), 12 ("application of municipal law to war crimes is in many ways the legal equivalent of a bad analogy.") In *Presbyterian Church*, it had been alleged that Talisman, a Canadian oil company, collaborated with the Sudanese government in ethnic cleansing to facilitate oil exploration. Although the court had rejected Talisman's motion to dismiss, holding that the complaint sufficiently alleged that it had aided and abetted or conspired with Sudan to commit violations of the law of nations, on September 12, 2006, Judge Cote granted defendants' motion for summary judgment, ruling that plaintiffs had failed to come forward with evidence that Talisman itself had engaged in conduct violating international law. See *Presbyterian Church of Sudan v. Talisman Engergy, Inc.*, 2006 U.S. Dist. LEXIS 64579 (S.D.N.Y. 2006).

40 But see R. VERNON, *Sovereignty at Bay* 46-59 (1971) (arguing that contracts initially favourable to foreign companies tend to be renegotiated as host countries take sunk costs hostage). President Morales' partial appropriation of natural gas facilities ('Crude Politics' *Prospect*, June 2006, 16), in Bolivia comes to mind.

to privatise.[41] The thirst for foreign direct investment may spark the proverbial 'race to the bottom', when TNC's exploit gaps in unsophisticated legal systems, play one country off against the other, and reward the most compliant.[42]

What of regulation at the international level? There has long existed a legal system, largely enforced by arbitration, that adjudicates commercial disputes by applying *lex mercatoria.*[43] But there exists no equivalent public law system to enforce what might be characterised as the human rights duties of TNC's. The International Criminal Court has no jurisdiction over corporations,[44] and traditional international tribunals have long been too hobbled by underfunding and politicisation to monitor the conduct of TNC's[45] effectively. The pressing need to find ways to render TNC's internationally

---

41 See T. FRIEDMAN, *The Lexus and the Olive Tree: Understanding Globalization (N.Y. 2000)* (under globalisation, power of international investors "narrows the political and economic choices of those in power to relatively tight parameters... [P]olitical choices get reduced to ... slight nuances of policy, slight alterations in design to account for local traditions, some loosening here or there."); see contra 'A Crisis of Legitimacy,' *Economist*, Sept 27, 2001 ("the global capital market makes it easier to run big budget deficits, because there is an infinitely larger pool of funds to tap. As for public ownership, on balance, global capital doesn't much care. Investors lending to publicly owned enterprises may see advantages, in fact, notably if government guarantees the debt.") The phenomenon of globalisation is not, of course, unique to our age. See N. FERGUSON, 'Sinking Globalization,' 84 *Foreign Aff.* 2, 66-69 (2005) (discussing the pre-WWI 'first age' globalisation).

42 C. BARNARD, 'Social Dumping and the Race to the Bottom: Some Lessons for the European Union from Delaware?', 25 *Eur. L. Rev.* 57 (2000); M. BARENBERG, '*Law and Labor in the New Global Economy: Through the Lens of United States Federalism*,' 33 *Colum. J. Transnat'l L.* 445 (1995), 448. Indeed, host country governments may go so far as to oppose home state efforts to regulate corporations active in the host country, on the basis that such regulation may costs them jobs. See B. STEPHENS, 'The Amorality of Profit: Transnational Corporations and Human Rights,' 20 *Berkeley J. Int'l L.* 45 (2002), 82.

43 See G. MALYNES, *Consuetudo vel Lex Mercatoria* (1981.) The phrase *lex petrolea* was used in an arbitration award involving an American oil company and the government of Kuwait. See *Government of the State of Kuwait v. The American Independent Oil Company (Aminoil)*, May 24, 1982, Int'l Council for Commercial Arbitration, *Yearbook of Commercial Arbitration* Vol. IX 81 (Pieter Sanders ed., 1984) (cited by L.E. CUERVO, 'The Alien Tort Statute, Corporate Accountability, And The New Lex Petrolea,' 19 *Tul. Envtl. L.J.*. 151 (2006), 209.

44 See A. CLAPHAM, '*Human Rights Obligations of Non-State Actors*' (O.U.P. 2006) 246 (proposed language creating jurisdiction over *juridical persons* was dropped during ICC statute drafting because "time was running out.").

45 L. HENKIN, 'Lexical Priority or Political Question: A Response,' 101 *Harv. L. Rev.* 524 (1987), 529-31 (undercapitalisation of international tribunals support the hearing of claims in national tribunals). It is not within the scope of this contribution to consider the burgeoning field of corporate social responsibility ("CSR"), as opposed to corporate accountability. A set of norms (the *Human Rights Responsibilities of Transnational Corporations and Other Business Enterprises*), was adopted on August 14, 2003, by the UN Sub-Commission for the Promotion and Protection of Human Rights (the "UN Norms"), UN doc. E/CN.4/Sub.2/2003/12/Rev.2 (2003.) Although the efficacy of CSR is inherently difficult to measure, writers have pointed to the limits thereof. See J. RICHTER '*Holding Corporations Accountable: Corporate Conduct, International Codes, and Citizen Action*' (London: Zed Books, 2001), 210; see also A. CLAPHAM '*Human Rights Obligations of Non-State Actors*' (OUP, 2006) 195.

accountable was recognised by a U.S. court in an ATS case seeking to hold accountable corporations that supplied herbicides used by the U.S. military in Vietnam:

> "Our vital private activities are conducted primarily under corporate auspices, [and] only corporations have the wherewithal to respond to massive toxic tort suits... Changing personnel means that those individuals who acted on behalf of the corporation and for its profit are often gone or deceased before they or the corporation can be brought to justice."[46]

Against that background, ATS litigation against TNC's may be seen as animated by an overall institutional failure. As Anne-Marie Slaughter puts it, plaintiffs 'compensat[e] for the weakness of international tribunals by turning to effective national courts.'[47] If that is so, the ATS may be thought of as the analogue to the institution of the 'private attorneys general', which, in United States domestic law, play a vital role in the enforcement of regulation that prosecutors lack the capacity or the will to enforce.[48] ATS plaintiffs take advantage of features that make American courts attractive to foreigners in other contexts, including the facility of class actions, lenient pleading standards, the availability of extensive discovery, the principle that parties pay their own costs, and generous damages awards.[49] Moreover, U.S. federal courts, in the course of applying antitrust, securities and other law extraterritorially, have developed a self-consciously global jurisprudence probably unique amongst municipal systems.[50] Thus, the trend towards extraterritorial application of U.S. law associated with TNC's global projection of their vast economic power has rendered them vulnerable to being hauled into U.S. Courts for human rights abuses on the other side of the world.[51]

---

46 *In re "Agent Orange" Product Liability Litigation*, 373 F.Supp.2d 7, 58 (E.D.N.Y. 2005).

47 A.M. SLAUGHTER & D. BOSCO, 'Plaintiff's Diplomacy', 79, *Foreign Affairs, 102* (2000), 107.

48 Private citizens, attracted by the promise of triple damage awards, are responsible for much of the enforcement of U.S. Antitrust and Securities Law. See I.T. BUSCHKIN, 'The Viability of Class Action Lawsuits in a Globalised Economy – Permitting Foreign Claimants to be Members of Class Action Lawsuits in the U.S. Federal Courts,' 90 *Cornell L. Rev.* 1563 (2005).

49 See J. CRAIG & S. LYNK, *Globalisation and the Future of Labour Law* (C.U.P. 2006), 145 – 46 (if advocates have the opportunity to "choose law applied by US Courts, with US procedure and real monetary remedies," using the ATS, it is "hard to explain why they should instead explore transnational regimes with vaguer remedies ... or international standards with no remedies at all.") See also *Smith Kline & French Labs v. Bloch*, 2 All E.R. 72, 74 (Eng. 1983). ("As a moth is drawn to light, so is a litigant drawn to the United States") (Denning MR).

50 A.M. SLAUGHTER, 'A New World Order', (P.U.P. 2004), 3 ("judges in transnational commercial disputes have begun to see themselves as part of a global judicial system").

51 Under the Foreign Corrupt Practices Act (*FCPA*), for example, U.S. corporations are exposed to criminal charges in federal courts for their participation in corruption anywhere in the world. See *SEC v. Montedison, S.p.A.*, Lit. Release No. 15164, 1996 WL 673757 (D.D.C. 1996); KRISCH, 'International Law in Times of Hegemony: Unequal Power and the Shaping of the International Legal Order,' 16 *Eur. J. Int'l L.* 369 (2005), 403. See also DE LISTLE 'Human Rights, Civil Wrongs and Foreign Relations: A "Sinical" Look at the use of U.S. Litigation to Address Human Rights Abuses Abroad,' 52 *De Paul L. Rev.* (2002), 550 (globalisation has "helped to make U.S.-PRC relations more complicated and more important, and thus has made U.S. litigation over Chinese human rights

TNC's potential exposure to litigation arising from their foreign activity has been heightened by a number of trends in the distribution of foreign investment. First, there has been a shift away from the kind of passive off-shore positioning least likely to generate exposure to liability for human rights abuses.[52] More and more western corporations employ large numbers of workers on the ground in massive infrastructural projects,[53] which frequently take the form of joint venture enterprises between foreign corporations and local public corporations.[54] Second, the outsourcing of production to low-wage developing countries fosters links between western-based TNC's and foreign industrial activities that render it difficult for the corporations to distance themselves from foreign abuses.[55] A third development is the privatisation of traditional state functions in the developing world, some of which are taken up by TNC's. At the extreme, this trend may see states effectively abdicating the running of significant parts of their economies to foreign private actors.[56] For example, Royal Dutch Shell has built roads, hospitals and schools near its facilities in the Niger Delta, filling gaps left by the collapse of effective government.[57] In other African countries, even military functions have been outsourced.[58]

3.3 LIMITS OF THE ATS

Although the trends I have been considering might seem to offer no shortage of opportunities for the use of the ATS, there have been relatively few successful suits, and it appears that no final judgment against a corporation has yet been issued.

---

practices seem both more feasible and more threatening to the conduct of U.S. foreign relations in recent years.").

52 See DE LISTLE 'Human Rights, Civil Wrongs and Foreign Relations: A "Sinical" Look at the use of U.S. Litigation to Address Human Rights Abuses Abroad,' 52 *De Paul L. Rev.* (2002), 493.

53 RATNER, 'Corporations And Human Rights: A Theory Of Legal Responsibility', 111 *Yale L.J.* 443 (2001), 459.

54 M. LIKOSKY, 'Human Rights Risk, 'Infrastructure Projects and Developing Countries,' *Global Jurist Advances*, Volume 2, Issue 1 (2002) Article 2; L. LONDIS 'The Corporate Face of the Alien Tort Claims Act,' *Maine L. Rev.* 141 (2005), n. 255.

55 See *Agent Orange, supra* 58 ("While the legal effects of outsourcing to private contractors is unclear, it cannot be ignored under international or United States law.") One critic of globalisation characterises outsourcing as the exporting of the "dark side of production – disciplined, hierarchical labour, ecological pollution," the ultimate objective being to "export the entire working class to invisible Third World sweat shops." S. ZIZEK, 'Nobody has to be Vile,' Vol. 28 *London Review of Books*, No 7 (April 6, 2006).

56 L.A. TAVIS, 'Corporate Governance and the Global Social Void', 35 *Vand. J. Transnat'l L.* 487 (2002).

57 KINLEY, 'From Talk to Walk: The Emergence of Human Rights Responsibilities for Corporations at International Law', 44 VA. J. Int'l L. 931 (2004) n. 193 (citing N. HERTZ, *The Silent Takeover: Global Capitalism and the Death of Democracy* 220-21 (2001)).

58 See L. DICKINSON, 'Government For Hire: Privatizing Foreign Affairs and the Problem of Accountability under International Law', 47 *Wm. & Mary L. Rev.* 135 (2005), 182ff.

That is largely attributable to substantive and procedural hurdles to which we now turn.

- First, save in the cases of genocide and war crimes (for which, as has been seen, an individual may be liable purely on his own account), the unlawful conduct alleged must involve 'state action.'[59] Generally speaking, only a private individual who acts together with state officials, or with 'significant state aid', will be deemed a 'state actor',[60] and thus be potentially subject to the ATS.[61] That said, entities which assume privatised state functions may be vulnerable, since a private actor which performs traditionally state functions may be deemed a state actor for the purposes of the suit.[62]
- Second, a sovereign state (and head of a state), will ordinarily be protected by sovereign immunity.[63] However, such immunity is usually confined to the sovereign or public acts of a foreign state, not to its commercial or private acts.[64] It has also been held that sovereign immunity will not protect acts that violate *jus cogens* (conduct violating the most fundamental principles of international law including racial discrimination)[65] and may not apply to covert acts.[66]
- Third, a court must decline to exercise jurisdiction where to do so would raise a 'political question.'[67] That defence is frequently raised where, as in many ATS

59 *Bigio v. Coca-Cola Co.*, 239 F.3d 440, 449 (2d Cir.2001).

60 *Ibid.* 448 (quoting *Kadic v. Karadzic*, 70 F.3d 232, 245 (2d Cir.1995)).

61 L. LONDIS, *supra* at n. 255.

62 See *Jama v. INS*, 22 F. Supp. 2d 353, 371-72 (D.N.J. 1998) (correctional facility and its officers, directors and guards deemed to be state actors because they were performing government services under contract with the INS). In *Saleh v. Titan*, No. 04 CV 1143 (S.D. Cal. 2004), a corporation contracted by the U.S. military to work at a detention facility in Iraq faced an ATS suit.

63 Foreign States Immunities Act 28 U.S.C. 1605 (1976).

64 *Restatement (Third) of Foreign Relations Law*, 451. See, e.g., *Mwani v. Bin Laden*, No. 04-5266 (D.C.D.C) (2005) (Afghanistan's alleged conduct in providing safe haven for terrorists and terrorist organisations in exchange for compensation did not constitute "commercial activity" sufficient to meet the commercial activity exception to sovereign immunity); *Bao Ge v. Li Peng, 201 F.Supp. 2d, 14, 24 (D.D.C. 2000)* ("allegedly unlawful incarceration and mistreatment of plaintiffs in prison by the Chinese government" arose out of "an alleged abuse of China's police power", which is a sovereign and not a commercial function; fact that soccer balls produced by prison labour were exported to the United States not enough to render operation of Chinese judicial and penal systems "commercial activity.").

65 Sarei v. Rio Tinto, PLC, 456 F. 3d 1069 (9th Cir 2006) 1085; *Trajano v. Marcos*, 978 F.2d 493, 499 (9th Cir. 1992).

66 *Doe v. Li Qiu*, 349. F.Supp.2d 1258, 1285 (N.D. Cal. 2004) (acts by an official which "violate the official laws of his or her nation but which are authorized by covert unofficial policy of the state" not immunized by the FSIA).

67 A related doctrine is "act of state", which applies "when a court must decide – that is, when the outcome of the case turns upon – the effect of official action by a foreign sovereign." *Kirkpatrick & Co. v Env'l Tectonics,* 493 U.S. 400, 406 (1990).

matters, the foreign policy prerogatives of the executive are said to be implicated.[68] This principle led to dismissal of several WWII reparations cases in which it was held that to decide the case would interfere with international settlements entered into by the executive.[69] ATS cases against the Chinese and the Indonesian governments have likewise been dismissed on political question grounds.[70] As we shall see, a political question defence is frequently bolstered by a Statement of Interest (*SOI*) filed by the U.S. State Department.

- Fourth, under the doctrine of comity, if the interest of a foreign sovereign in the conduct at issue outweighs the U.S. interest in vindicating human rights violations, a court may decline to exercise jurisdiction.[71]
- Fifth, under the *forum non conveniens* doctrine (which has already been considered in relation to the *Wiwa* case), a court evaluates whether it would be more practical for the matter to be heard in another jurisdiction, taking into account factors like access to evidence and the cost of obtaining witnesses.[72] Courts generally resist dismissing ATS matters on *forum non conveniens* grounds.[73] In two notable cases where they have done so, the dismissal was subject to the matter being heard in the 'host' country.[74]

---

68 *Chicago & So. Air Lines, Inc. v. Waterman Steamship Corp.*, 333 U.S. 103, 111 (1948) (foreign policy issues are "of a kind for which the Judiciary has neither aptitude, facilities nor responsibility."); *Baker v. Carr*, 369 U.S. 186, 217 (1962) (political question doctrine applies, where "there exists potential embarrassment from multifarious pronouncements" from different branches of the U.S. government).

69 *In re Nazi Era Cases Against German Defendants' Litigation*, 129 F. Supp.2d 370, 377-78 (D.N.J. 2001). See also *Burger-Fischer v. De Gussa AG*, 65 F. Supp.2d 248 (D.N.J. 1999); *Iwanowa v. Ford Motor Co.*, 67 F. Supp.2d 424 (D.N.J. 1999).

70 The political question doctrine – which involves a mandatory justiciability determination – must be distinguished from its cousin, the doctrine of prudential abstention, which is discretionary. See *Whiteman v. Dorotheum GMBH & Co. KG*, 431 F.3d 57, n. 14 (2d Cir. 2005). It would appear that the *Sosa* court, the decision of which is considered below, addressed the doctrine of abstention, not mandatory justiciability.

71 See e.g. *Jota v Texaco*, 157 F. 3d 153 (2d Cir. 1998), (dismissal on comity grounds is warranted if "an adequate forum exists in the objecting nation" and "the defendant sought to be sued in the United States forum is subject to or has consented to the assertion of jurisdiction against it in the foreign forum."); *Sosa supra*, 2782 ("Since enforcement of an international norm by one nation's courts implies that other nations' courts may do the same, I would ask whether the exercise of jurisdiction under the ATS is consistent with those notions of comity that lead each nation to respect the sovereign rights of other nations by limiting the reach of its laws and their enforcement.... Such consideration is necessary to ensure that ATS litigation does not undermine the very harmony that it was intended to promote) (Breyer J, concurring in part).

72 *Gulf Oil Corp. v. Gilbert*, 330 U.S. 501 (1947).

73 See, e.g., *Wiwa v. Royal Dutch Petroleum Co.*, 226 F.3d 88, 101-03 (2d Cir. 2000).

74 *Aguinda v. Texaco, Inc.*, 303 F. 3d 470 (2d Cir. 2002) (requiring defendants to agree to submit to jurisdiction of Ecuadorian courts); *Adamu v. Pfizer*, Inc., 399 F.Supp.2d 495 (S.D.N.Y. 2005) (dismissing suit by Nigerian children alleging that American pharmaceutical company administered experimental antibiotic without informed consent, subject to defendants consenting to accept process in Nigeria and to produce evidence in Nigeria).

3.4 THE ATS REACHES THE SUPREME COURT

In 2004 the U.S. Supreme Court seized the opportunity to resolve some of the differences that had emerged in the ATS jurisprudence of lower federal courts since *Filartiga*. The case arose out of the kidnapping of one Alvarez-Machain, a Mexican physician who had been indicted in the United States as a participant in the murder of a Drug Enforcement Agency agent in Mexico.[75] He had been seized in Mexico by Jose Francisco Sosa, acting at the behest of U.S. authorities, after an unsuccessful attempt to secure his extradition to face trial. Having been acquitted in a U.S. court, Alvarez filed an ATS suit against Sosa.[76]

In dismissing Alvarez's claim, the Supreme Court addressed the vexed question of what international law violations were actionable under the ATS. The Court also commented, with specific reference to the apartheid cases, on the political question doctrine – the principle that courts should avoid hearing matters that would involve it treading on the toes of the executive or legislative branches of government. As we shall see, these observations were to come back to haunt the apartheid plaintiffs.

3.4.1 *The scope of the ATS*

Pre-*Sosa* cases held violations of a variety of international law norms, ranging from genocide,[77] to forced labour,[78] to the right to associate in trade unions,[79] to be actionable under the ATS. The Supreme Court in *Sosa* did not quarrel with these findings, but emphasised that it was only a 'narrow set of violations' – those threatening 'serious consequences in international affairs' – that could be invoked.'[80] Did that mean that *Filartiga* erred in holding that, as the scope of international law had expanded since 1789, so too had the range of actionable violations? The Supreme Court's answer was a cautious 'No'.[81] The norms actionable under the ATS today were only those 'of international character accepted by the civilized world and defined with a specificity comparable to the features of the 18th-century paradigms.'[82] *Sosa* thus

---

75 *Sosa, supra*, 697-98.

76 *Ibid.* (The suit against U.S. agents was dismissed on the basis of sovereign immunity).

77 *Karadzic, supra.*

78 *Unocal, supra.*

79 *Estate of Rodriguez v. Drummond*, 256 F. Supp. 2d 1250, 1264 (N.D. Ala. 2003).

80 *Sosa, supra* 715.

81 The affirmative answer to this questions had been offered by Judge Bork in *Tel-Oren v. Libyan Arab Republic*, 726 F.2d 774, 813 (D.C. Cir. 1984) (because the ATS must be interpreted as incorporating the law of nations as it stood in 1789, the only crimes that could violate the law of nations and thus serve as a basis for an ATS suit would be violations of safe conduct, infringements on the rights of ambassadors, and piracy).

82 *Sosa, supra* 2761-62.

limited the scope of the ATS to 'a handful of heinous actions – each of which violates definable, universal and obligatory norms.'[83] While 'the door [was] still ajar' to novel ATS claims, it was 'subject to vigilant doorkeeping'; and courts should be slow to create new causes of action not specifically authorised by Congress.[84] Despite its cautious approach, the Supreme Court did not discard the standards developed in ATS litigation over the prior 24 years,[85] but said its approach was 'consistent with' the reasoning of many of the courts and judges who faced the issue before it reached this Court.[86]

While there is an ongoing debate about the impact of *Sosa* upon *Filartiga's* expansive interpretation, *Sosa* must clearly be read subject to its (somewhat unusual) facts. The ultimate decision, that Alvarez's 'single illegal detention of less than a day, followed by [his] transfer of custody to lawful authorities and a prompt arraignment, violates no norm of customary international law so well defined as to support the creation of a federal remedy', is not especially far-reaching.[87] Not without reason, a chagrined Justice Scalia, writing in partial concurrence (he agreed with the result, but not with the majority's reasons), complained that the majority opinion represented 'victory for its 'Never Say Never Jurisprudence'' in which the majority 'wags a finger

---

83 *Ibid.* 2765) (citing *Tel-Oren v. Libyan Arab Republic,* 726 F.2d 781 (C.A.D.C.1984), 781 (Edwards, J., concurring.)).

84 *Ibid.* 2764. *Sosa* reflected deep divisions within the Court regarding what judicial conservatives view as the illegitimate domestication of international law via the courts without congressional approval. Justice Souter responded to such concerns both by emphasising that courts should exercise caution in recognising new ACTA causes of action, and by noting that Congress could "modify or cancel any judicial decision so far as it rests on recognizing an international norm as such." (At 2765.) Justice Scalia was not mollified. (He complained that for "over two decades now, unelected federal judges have been usurping [Congress'] lawmaking power by converting what they regard as norms of international law into American law.") (At 2776).

85 However, one little-noticed aspect of *Sosa* could spell trouble for proponents of the expansive interpretation of the ATS. It had been widely assumed that it was settled that individuals and corporations were subject to liability under the ATS. A dictum in *Sosa* can be read as leaving the question open. *Ibid.* n. 20. In 2005, a court sitting in Washington D.C. dismissed an ATS suit brought by Iraqis against two private government contractors who provided interrogators and interpreters to the United States military in Iraq, holding that, under law applicable in the D.C. Circuit, the ATS was not applicable to private parties. *Ibrahim v. Titan Corp.*, 391 F.Supp.2d 10 (D.C.D.C. 2005).

86 *Ibid.* 2765. *Sosa* offered the definition of piracy adopted in *United States v. Smith,* 5 Wheat. 153, 163-180, as an example of a violation of the law of nations that was "under the 18th century paradigm" actionable under the ATS. In *Smith,* a defendant accused of piracy challenged the constitutionality of a statute that punished "the crime of piracy, as defined by the law of nations", arguing that the law of nations did not provide a sufficiently clear definition. The Court rejected that argument. "Whatever may be the diversity of definitions, in other respects, all writers concur in holding, that robbery, or forcible depredations upon the sea, animo furandi, is piracy".

87 *Sosa* at 2769. See KU & YOO, 'Beyond Formalism In Foreign Affairs: A Functional Approach To The Alien Tort Statute,' 2004 *Sup. Ct. Rev.* 153, 170) ("Alvarez-Machain's fault was not that he sought a remedy under the ATS, but that he failed to show that a right against arbitrary detention had truly become a rule of CIL.").

at the lower courts for going too far, and then – repeating the same formula the ambitious lower courts themselves have used – invites them to try again.'[88]

The lower federal courts have accepted that invitation, and in so doing have developed a jurisprudence that is more casuistic than principled. Two post-*Sosa* decisions confirm that the *Filartiga* approach to the ATS has not lost its vitality, while at the same time offering some hints as to how future courts may interpret *Sosa*. In one, a New Jersey federal court considered a complaint alleging that a private German company had participated in genocide against the Herero people during Germany's colonisation of Namibia between 1890 and 1915.[89] The court was willing to find that the atrocities described in the complaint constituted crimes against humanity for ATS purposes.[90] In another case, a Columbian exile alleged that a U.S. oil company was complicit in the Columbian military operations forcibly removing a community to secure a pipeline.[91] This allegation was not 'impermissibly broad', since such violent displacement of persons did 'not occur as often' as the abuse deemed non-actionable in *Sosa*.[92]

Several cases in which ATS actions have been dismissed because the international norm invoked did not rise to the level set by *Sosa* have involved environmental matters. In a case already mentioned, Judge Weinstein ruled that the use in Vietnam of herbicide manufactured by defendants could not form the basis for an ATS claim,

---

88 *Sosa supra* 2776. Justice Scalia's opinion relied in part upon the argument that, because when the ATS was enacted, the "law of nations" was applied by federal courts as part of the "federal common law", there was in principle no scope for the application of the "law of nations", in light of *Erie Railroad v. Tompkins*, which established the federal common law. 304 U.S. 64 (1938). Justice Souter's response to that argument was that it would be "unreasonable to assume that the First Congress would have expected federal courts to lose all capacity to recognize enforceable international norms simply because the common law might lose some metaphysical cachet on the road to modern realism." *Sosa* at 730. See P.L. Hoffman & D.A. Zaheer, 'The Rules of the Road: Federal Common Law and Aiding and Abetting Under the Alien Tort Claims Act,' 26 *Loy. L.A. Int'l & Comp. L. Rev.* 47, 60 (2003) (federal courts have continued to construct a "new" federal common law post-*Erie* in a few particularised categories).

89 *Hereros v. Deutsche Afrika-Linien Gmblt & Co* (No. Civ.A.05-1872 (KSH) (D.C.N.J. Jan. 24, 2006).

90 However, the court ruled that the "amount of time that has passed since these acts occurred, the difficulty of identifying through witnesses who exactly committed them, which persons suffered them, how plaintiffs have the right to assert those victims' rights, and even how damages might be apportioned", rendered the ATS claim too "ill-defined and unsuitable to support the creation of a federal remedy under the restrictions set down in *Sosa*." *Ibid.*

91 *Mujica, et al. v. Occidental Petroleum Corp.*, 381 F. Supp 1164, 1183 (C.D. Cal. 2005).

92 *Ibid.* 1183. By contrast, another *Mujica* allegation, relating to "cruel, inhuman, and degrading treatment", resulting in "gross humiliation, fear, and anguish" could not, said the court, practicably be recognised as constituting an ATS claim, because it "would allow foreign plaintiffs to litigate claims in U.S. courts that bear a strong resemblance to intentional infliction of emotional distress." *Ibid.* 1181. While this rather mechanical comparative analysis appears somewhat facile, the decision does offer an example of a practical way of assuaging *Sosa's* concern that the ATS would open the doors of federal courts to a deluge of suits from the four corners of the globe.

finding that international law 'tended to treat protection of the environment on an ad-hoc, situation-by-situation and case-by-case basis.'[93]

The limits of ATS actionability were starkly illustrated by two cases decided shortly after *Sosa*. In the first, a court held that plaintiffs could not maintain a claim for 'sexual violence', because that norm was not sufficiently recognised under international law, and was not 'specific, universal, and obligatory'.[94] In a second suit, the court dismissed a claim by Nigerian children against Pfizer Inc. for administering an experimental antibiotic without informed consent. Here too, no clear and unambiguous violation of customary international law had been pleaded.[95]

3.4.2 The ATS and the political question doctrine

The most enduring impact of the *Sosa* decision may lie in the Court's *dicta* regarding circumstances under which a Court should abstain from hearing an ATS matter because of its foreign policy implications. Justice Souter, singling out the pending *Apartheid Litigation* matter, observed that where, as in that case, the U.S. and the foreign government concerned had submitted statements opposing the suits, there was a 'strong argument that federal courts should give serious weight to the Executive Branch's view.'[96] Justice Souter acknowledged that the government's views on issues of statutory construction 'merit no special deference' – but held that should the State Department choose to express an opinion regarding a particular case, such opinion might be entitled to deference 'as the considered judgment of the Executive on a particular question of foreign policy.'[97] (I turn below to consider the manner in which this dictum was applied by the district court in the apartheid litigation.)

---

93 *Agent Orange, supra* 129. Moreover, the herbicide use that formed the basis of the suit ended years before 1975; the ratification by the Senate in that year of the 1925 Geneva Protocol and the Biological Weapons Convention in April 1975 did not retroactively render illegal the use of Agent Orange. (At 105-06).

94 *Doe v. Exxon,* 393 F.Supp.2d 20, 24 (D.C.D.C. 2005).

95 *Adamu v. Pfizer, Inc,* 399 F.Supp.2d 495 (S.D.N.Y. 2005).

96 *Sosa supra* 2766, n. 21. See S.M. SCHNEEBAUM, 'The Paquete Habana Sails On: International Law in U.S. Courts after Sosa', 19 *Emory Int'l L. Rev.* 81 (2005), 100 (noting that "[i]t is highly unusual for the Supreme Court, in rendering a decision in a case before it, to opine on another case raising related issues", and questioning whether the Court should be "expressing a view on the ultimate disposition of a case in the very early stages of its development, and as to which the Court most assuredly did not have the views of both sides.") (also noting at 100, Justice Souter's references to the apartheid case "does not display the rigor of much of the rest of the opinion.").

97 Quoting *Republic of Austria v. Altmann*, 541 U.S. 677, 701-02 (2004). Beth Stephens writes that the Supreme Court "invited the executive branch to express its views not about the interpretation of the statutory scheme, but rather about the foreign policy issues implicated by a particular case", and that "the examples *Altmann* cited in support of this invitation all addressed issues on which the law governing sovereign immunity was unclear." '*Sosa v Alvaraz-Machain*: "The Door is Still Ajar for Human Rights Litigation in U.S. Courts", 70 *Brooklyn L. Rev.* 533, (2004), 562.

4 THE APARTHEID LITIGATION

Having reviewed the parameters of the ATS, consideration is now given to the *Apartheid Litigation* decision, beginning with a survey of the parties, the complaints, and the jurisdictional basis for filing the suits in the United States.

4.1 PARTIES AND ALLEGATIONS

In 2002, three groups of plaintiffs, one led by Lungisile Ntsebeza,[98] another by Hermina Digwamaje,[99] and a third sponsored by the Khulumani Support Group,[100] filed ATS actions in eight federal district courts against a slew of transnational corporations, including the world's biggest banks, oil companies and motor manufacturers, that did business in apartheid South Africa. Many of the plaintiffs alleged either having personally been victims of conduct of the South African state during the apartheid era, or that they were relatives of deceased victims.[101] The complaints classed the Defendants into a number of categories, according to the manner and degree in which they were alleged to have participated in the apartheid system.

First, some of the Defendants were said to be directly implicated in the design of government policy. Plaintiffs pointed, for example, to evidence of joint military/business conferences, where representatives of corporations met with political and military leaders to suppress political unrest.[102]

---

98 In the Ntsebeza Complaint ("*N. Compl.*"), Plaintiffs demanded compensatory and punitive damages, and production of Defendants' documents, creation of an international historical commission, and creation of affirmative action and educational programs. (N. Comp. 265, 276). They sought also an order restraining Defendants from destroying documents relating to their investment in apartheid South Africa (N. Compl. 276). The Ntsebeza Plaintiffs were originally represented by a consortium of attorneys, including Ed Fagan, who became well known when he represented victims of the Holocaust in a successful action against Swiss banks. See G. PERDUE, 'The Victim's Fortune: The Struggle for Restitution for Holocaust Victims,' 7 *N.C. Banking Inst.* 423 (2003), 326. Fagan later fell out with other attorneys representing the Ntsebeza Plaintiffs, and was not active in the litigation at the time of the hearing of the motion to dismiss or thereafter.

99 The Digwamaje Complaint ("*D. Compl.*"), was filed on August 2, 2002, on behalf of plaintiffs grouped into putative sub-classes numbering in the hundreds of thousands, seeking $200 billion in compensatory and $200 billion in punitive damages. See D. Compl. 481 & part VI.

100 The Khulumani Complaint (*K. Compl.*), was filed on November 11, 2002, on behalf of the Khulumani Support Group and its 32,700 members, as well as individual plaintiffs who suffered from the crimes of the apartheid regime. See K. Compl. 12. They demanded, amongst other things, disclosure of documents, and compensatory and punitive damages. See K. Comp 690.

101 See e.g., N. Compl. 26 (plaintiff mother of Hector Peterson, 13-year-old shot during peaceful march in Soweto uprising of 1976); D. Compl. 13 (plaintiff severely injured when police attacked train); K. Compl. 47 (plaintiff tortured in prison).

102 N. Compl. 168-69 (purpose of first conference, in 1977, was to deal with violence following Soweto riots of 1976).

Second, there were allegations of collaboration between defendants and the military. For example, defendant General Motors of South Africa (Pty) Limited ('GMSA'), a subsidiary of General Motors Inc., was said to have recruited employees to join a commando force involved in vigilante killings.[103] Defendants, it was said, had assisted in the establishment of local militias and provided them with arms storage facilities effectively outsourcing certain functions and costs of national security to Defendants.[104]

Third, it was alleged that mining company defendants were liable for using lethal force against striking workers.[105] It was also alleged, relying upon the *TRC Final Report*, that corporations cooperated with state security agencies in targeting union leaders.[106]

Fourth, Plaintiffs pointed to the labour conditions endured by employees of the Defendants, invoking in that regard the TRC's finding regarding the mining industry's conduct.[107] Plaintiffs pointed also to racial discrimination suffered at workplaces.[108]

Fifth, it was alleged that Defendants violated UN sanctions by selling arms and other products for military use.[109] For example, the complaints alleged that the German company Rheinmetall A.G. had shipped an ammunition factory to South Africa, using fraudulent export declarations.[110] Daimler Chrysler, it was said, manufactured vehicles designed for use by the military.[111] Oil embargos were routinely violated by Defendants.[112] Defendant ExxonMobil Inc. allegedly supplied oil to the police and military, despite having obtained legal advice that this was in violation of the arms embargo.[113] British Petroleum is quoted as admitting that it 'intentionally set out to thwart' oil embargoes.[114] IBM was said to have developed, marketed, and provided a law enforcement system, specifically designed with the apartheid system's needs and goals in mind.[115]

Finally, it was alleged that foreign banks advanced credit to the apartheid government, knowing that the funds would be used to finance repression.[116] A

---

103 K. Compl. 552 (General Motors envisioned that "plant personnel could be engaged in a composite function, i.e. part normal work and part guard duty", during times of national emergency).

104 E.g., D. Compl. 401 (describing designation of Defendants' installations under National Keypoints Act).

105 E.g., D. Compl. 302 (in 1986 defendant Gencor allegedly dismissed 25,000 striking workers and summoned riot police to attack them).

106 *Final TRC Report*, Vol. 6, s.2, Ch. 5, para 3c, 49, 50; Vol. 4, Ch. 2, para 164.

107 *Final TRC Report*, Vol. 6, s.2, Ch. 5, para 47, 54; Vol. 4, Ch. 2, para 66, 165.

108 E.g. N. Compl. 34.

109 N. Compl. 112-114.

110 K. Compl. 377-83.

111 K. Comp. 529.

112 D. Compl. 207 (citing UN report concluding that almost all oil shipped to South Africa "originates from countries that forbid their oil to be sold to the apartheid regime.").

113 K. Compl. 300.

114 K. Compl. 344; see also N. Compl. 106-108.

115 N. Compl. 82-102.

116 N. Compl. 148-151.

consortium led by defendant banks UBS A.E. and Credit Suisse is said to have rolled over existing government debt at a time when the regime was faltering under the pressure of trade sanctions and internal resistance.[117]

4.2 PERSONAL JURISDICTION OVER THE APARTHEID DEFENDANTS

The *Karadzic* court observed that '[m]ost Americans would probably be surprised to learn that victims of atrocities committed in Bosnia are suing the leader of the insurgent Bosnian-Serb forces' in a Manhattan courthouse.[118] One might say that many South Africans (and, for that matter, Britons), would be surprised that a British-incorporated bank was hauled before a New York court for alleged complicity of one of its subsidiaries in apartheid.[119] While the exercise of jurisdiction over companies incorporated in the United States, or which have their principal places of business in New York, is commonplace,[120] on what basis may a New York federal court exercise jurisdiction over corporations, such as Barclays Bank plc, which are neither incorporated in nor keep their principal places of business in the U.S. for the conduct in distant South Africa?[121]

The 'minimum contacts requirement' of federal personal jurisdiction mandates that a defendant have some link with the United States. But, it need only be a relatively attenuated connection.[122] ATS suits against individuals has been based upon service on persons while in federal custody awaiting extradition,[123] in transit after a visit to the United Nations,[124] and while in Boston for a Harvard graduation.[125] But the

117 N. Compl. 178, 182-183. See *Final TRC Report*, Vol. 6, s.2, Ch. 5, para. 26. ("Banks that gave financial support to the apartheid state were accomplices to a criminal government that consistently violated international law.").

118 *Kadic supra* at 236.

119 See N. Compl. 34, 50 (describing Plaintiff Ntsebeza as a former employee of Barclays Bank PLC headquartered in London).

120 E.g. *Citicorp Inc.* (N Compl. 42; D. Comp. 24); IBM Corp (D. Comp. 37); (K. Compl. 123).

121 E.g. UBS AG, a Swiss Bank (N. Comp. 44); Fujitsu, a Japanese computer company (D. Comp. 36).

122 The necessary jurisdictional contact may be deemed to exist if a defendant has "purposefully directed" his relevant activities against persons within the United States. Thus, in *Mwani v Bin- Laden (No 04-5266) (D.C.D.C. 2005)*, jurisdiction was exercised over Osama Bin-Laden, in an ATS suit brought by Kenyan victims with respect to the bombing of the U.S. embassy in Nairobi, notwithstanding the failure to serve upon him, both because, as the court put it, his address was "not known or easily ascertainable", (at 8), and because, in bombing the embassy, Bin-Laden had "purposefully directed his activities at residents of the United States", the diplomats who were temporarily stationed in Nairobi (at 12).

123 *Forti v. Suarez-Mason*, 672 F. Supp. 1531 (N.D. Cal. 1987).

124 *Kadic v. Karadzic*, 70 F.3d 232, 236 (2d Cir. 1995).

125 *Xuncax v Gramajo, 886 F.Supp. 162 (D. Mass. 1995)*. See 'Thugs Brought to Book', *Economist*, May 20, 1997 (Gramajo was Guatemala's defense minister from 1986 to 1990).

jurisdictional test applicable to corporations is somewhat more stringent. A company need not be incorporated in the United States. But it must 'do business' there,[126] meaning that it conducts 'continuous, permanent, and substantial activity within the forum.'[127] In *Wiwa*, the court assumed jurisdiction over a Dutch corporation on the basis that it maintained agents in New York which worked on investor relations.[128] On that principle, coupled with the fact that New York City still remains in some respects the commercial capital of the world, home to the most important capital markets, places virtually every large TNC in jeopardy of being brought before a U.S. Court.[129] While the *Apartheid Litigation* court did not frontally address the question of personal jurisdiction,[130] it appears that even those Defendants with only limited contacts with the United States would probably not succeed in avoiding jurisdiction in a U.S. Court.[131]

The related question of whether a TNC may be liable under the ATS for the conduct of its foreign subsidiary has also not thus far been canvassed in the apartheid litigation. The issue certainly would arise if the matter were to go forward; in many instances it was a subsidiary of, rather than the named defendant itself, that was active in South Africa.[132] When the issue arises, guidance may be sought from ATS cases lodged against oil companies for human rights abuses allegedly committed in association with Nigerian forces in the Niger delta. In one such case, a court found that Chevron Inc., a U.S. company, could be liable for the acts of its Nigerian

---

126 See *Federal Rule of Civil Procedure* R. 4(k)(2). Some commentators are wrongly under the impression that only companies incorporated in the U.S. are subject to jurisdiction there. See, e.g., S. DEVA, 'Acting Extraterritorially To Tame Multinational Corporations for Human Rights Violations: Who Should 'Bell The Cat'?' 5 *Melb. J. Int'l L.* 37 (2004), 48 ("the extraterritorial regulation of TNCs is actually far less extraterritorial in nature than first impressions indicate", because "such regulation affects only the parent corporation incorporated within the territory but operating abroad through its corporate hands.").

127 *Landoil Resources Corp. v. Alexander & Alexander Servs., Inc.*, 918 F.2d 1039, 1043 (2d Cir. 1990).

128 See *Wiwa v. Royal Dutch Petroleum Co.*, 226 F.3d 88, 96 (2d Cir. 2000) (rejecting defendants' argument that their investor relations office in New York was only indirectly related to its core business, since they had a "need for access to capital markets.").

129 See M. HERMAN, 'British PLCs risk human rights litigation in U.S., *Times Online law*, June 13, 2006 (quoting City lawyer as saying that uncertainty regarding the ATS "is not just discouraging investment in less developed countries, but it is making UK companies think twice about their US listings because they can potentially be sued for what they are doing on the other side of the world.").

130 *Apartheid Litigation supra* 542, n. 3 (motion to dismiss limited to those Defendants as to whom the Court's personal jurisdiction was not contested).

131 An interesting case is presented by two Defendants, Anglo-American PLC and De Beers Corporation, which, having dominated the mining industry in South Africa for over a century, are now listed in London. See N. Compl. 57, 58; D. Compl. 49. See also SAUNDERS 'Rich and Rare are the Gems they War: Holding De Beers Accountable for Trading Conflict Diamonds', 24 *Fordham Int'l L.J.* 1402 (2001) (Considering whether De Beers could be subject to jurisdiction in U.S. court for alleged complicity in the trade in "blood diamonds").

132 See e.g., K. Compl. 117, 470 ("Dresdner Bank AG . . . operated in South Africa utilizing a variety of subsidiaries and associated companies."); D. Compl. 18 (plaintiff subject to racial discrimination by Anglo American plc's subsidiary).

subsidiary, because it was a significant part of Chevron's worldwide operations, and because its earnings were used to fund other Chevron subsidiaries.[133]

Accordingly, the quality and scope of the links between each of the parent company Defendants and its South African subsidiaries would need to be analysed.[134]

4.3 JUDGE SPRIZZO'S DECISION

Defendants moved to dismiss the various apartheid suits, that were consolidated in the Southern District of New York for this purpose,[135] and the matter was heard on November 6, 2003.[136] On November 29, 2004, Judge Sprizzo rendered his decision dismissing all of plaintiff's claims. (It is well accepted that a court should not dismiss a claim if the complaint properly pleads any allegations that, if proven at trial, could support liability.[137]).

The judgment opens by acknowledging the evils of apartheid, a system characterised by 'hatred, racism, and inhuman treatment.'[138] In the Bantustans, said the Judge, '[d]isease and malnourishment were prevalent' and 'economic opportunities, suitable housing, and basic amenities were non-existent.'[139] Africans represented 'nothing more than a 'reserve army of unemployed', whose sole purpose was to wait for its call to duty for the sake of the white economy.'[140] The court went further. Defendants had:

---

133 *Bowoto v. Chevron*, 312 F. Supp. 2d 1229 (N.D. Cal. 2004). But see *Sinaltrainal v. Coca-Cola, Inc.*, 256 F. Supp. 2d 1345, 1354-55 (2003) (dismissing ATS claim because there was no showing that Coca-Cola Inc. exercised "total control" over its subsidiary in Colombia).

134 In some cases the complaints go further, by suggesting that a foreign parent company could incur liability through the activities of its licensee in South Africa, even absent ownership. See, e.g. K. Comp. n. 147 (quoting Dennis Kneale, 'GM, IBM and others Departing South Africa are Faulted for Plans to Continue Sales There,' *Wall St. J.*, Oct 24, 1986 (describing criticism of "increasingly common exit arrangements that typically let departing U.S. companies continue to sell goods and services to newly independent units they leave behind.")). There is an ongoing debate as to whether foreign corporations can incur vicarious liability when they exercise *de facto* control. See generally KINLEY & TADAKI, (2004) 'From Talk To Walk: The Emergence Of Human Rights Responsibilities For Corporations At International Law,' 44 *Va. J. Int'l L.* 931 (2004).

135 *In re South African Apartheid Litigation*, 238 F.Supp. 2d 1379 (J.P.M.L. 2002).

136 The transcript of the hearing is designated herein as "*Hearing Transcript.*"

137 To put it more formally, dismissal is appropriate at this pre-trial stage only "if it appears beyond doubt that the plaintiff can prove no set of facts which would entitle it to relief." On a motion to dismiss, the Court must accordingly accept all facts alleged in the Complaint as true and draw all reasonable inferences in favour of the plaintiff. See e.g., *Jaghory v. New York State Dep't of Educ.*, 131 F.3d 326, 329 (2d Cir.1997.) Once a claim has survived a motion to dismiss, plaintiffs may commence discovery. Given the sensitive nature of the subject matter, it is not difficult to appreciate why Defendants might be anxious to avoid discovery concerning their activities in South Africa. See K. Compl. 690(c) (demanding that Defendants make available "all documents or records related to their operations in and/or cooperation with the Apartheid regime.").

138 *Apartheid Litigation,* 346 F. Supp. 2d 538, 543 (S.D.N.Y. 2004).

139 *Ibid.*

140 *Ibid.* 544 (quoting D. Compl at 81, 84).

> "Benefited from a system that provided a glut of cheap labor. . . and frequently . . . supplied resources, such as technology, money, and oil, to the South African government or to entities controlled by the government. [M]any of those resources were used by the apartheid regime to further its policies of oppression and persecution of the African majority. For example, the South African police shot demonstrators from cars driven by Daimler-Benz engines [and] tracked the whereabouts of African individuals on IBM computers. Defendants ... were required to provide high levels of security so as to protect against civil unrest and African uprisings. The owners of the sites were required to provide storage facilities for arms and to cooperate with the South African Defense Force to provide local defense of the area."[141]

Nonetheless, the Court decided that the suit fell to be dismissed, for four reasons:

First, while Defendants had been advantaged by the system, they had not themselves engaged in behaviour that 'could be fairly treated as that of the State itself.'[142] In that respect, Defendants were no more implicated in apartheid than Coca-Cola had been implicated in official anti-Semitism when it purchased property that it knew the Egyptian government had seized from Jewish owners.[143]

Second, the court rejected Plaintiffs' allegations that, even to the extent that they had not engaged in 'state action' Defendants should be held responsible for collaborating with the regime. Liability for aiding and abetting was, Judge Sprizzo held, not an international norm 'defined with a specificity comparable to the features of the 18th-century paradigms' referred to in *Sosa*.[144] Moreover, under domestic law where Congress has not explicitly provided for a private course of action, it should not be inferred.[145]

Third, there being no state action, or scope for secondary liability under the ATS, Defendants could also not be held liable simply for having 'done business' in apartheid South Africa.[146] The various international instruments upon which Plaintiffs relied, were intended to govern the actions of states only.[147] As for the UN Charter and the International Declaration of Human Rights, these spoke in 'broad aspirational

141 *Ibid.* 545-55 (internal citations and quotes omitted).

142 *Ibid.* 549.

143 *Ibid.* 548 (citing *Bigio v. Coca-Cola Co.*, 239 F.3d 440, 449 (2d Cir.2001.)) The Court (at 549) rejected Plaintiff's reliance upon Judge Wood's decision in *Wiwa v. Royal Dutch Petroleum Co.*, 2002 WL 319 887 (S.D.N.Y. 2002), because in that case, plaintiffs had alleged that defendants "actively cooperated with Nigerian officials in the suppression of a group that was in opposition to the defendants' activities in the region".

144 *Ibid.* 548 (quoting *Sosa*, 2761-762).

145 *Ibid.* 550 (Citing *Cent. Bank of Denv. v. First Interstate Bank of Denv.*, 511 U.S. 164 (1994)).

146 *Ibid.* 551-52.

147 *Ibid.* 551-52. Sprizzo J acknowledged that these instruments punish complicity. But because they were "criminal in nature, and neither was self-executing," they could not generate private liability. *Ibid.* 552.

language that did not meet the specificity required' under the ATS.[148] The Apartheid Convention did not meet the *Sosa* standard because, it was 'not ratified by a number of major world powers' and as such could not be binding international law.[149] The UN embargo prohibited states, not private parties, from exporting arms to the apartheid regime.[150] Finally, the series of General Assembly resolutions condemning corporations that collaborated with the regime were also addressed only to states recommending that nations enact laws to cut off the apartheid regime from the rest of the world.[151]

Fourth, the suit also fell to be dismissed in light of the fact that the South African government had indicated that it believed that allowing the action to proceed would 'pre-empt the ability of the government to handle domestic matters', and would discourage investment in South Africa.[152] Washington, for its part, had said that the action would engender bilateral tension.[153]

4.4 EVALUATING JUDGE SPRIZZO'S JUDGMENT

As will be demonstrated in this section, the first three rationales for the court's decision seem clearly at odds with well-established doctrine and precedent. The fourth rationale, based upon deference to the views of the executive regarding the political implications of the suit, will be discussed in the next section.

4.4.1 State action

Judge Sprizzo's conclusion that the complaints did not allege that Defendants engaged in joint action with the state is difficult to reconcile with the plain language of the complaints. Plaintiffs' allegations regarding Defendants' mustering of commando units at the plant level, for example,[154] clearly meet the requirements for state action.[155]

---

148 *Ibid.* 552-53 ("International agreements often set patently unattainable goals that cannot reasonably be considered legal obligations of those countries to one day fulfill those aspirations.").

149 *Ibid.* 550.

150 *Ibid.* 553. (Citing S.C. Res. 418, U.N. SCOR, 32d Sess., U.N. Doc. S/INF/33 (1977)).

151 *Ibid.* 553.

152 *Ibid.* 553. (Citing Declaration of Minister Penuell Mpapa Maduna, dated July 11, 2003 at 10, 12).

153 *Ibid.* 553. (Citing *Sosa*, at 2766 n. 21). Aside from the independent weight Judge Sprizzo afforded this executive input, it fortified his conclusion to find that aiding and abetting was not actionable under the ATS "given the possible foreign relations repercussions that would result from allowing courts in this country to hear civil suits for the aiding and abetting of violations of international norms across the globe." (*Ibid.* 551).

154 See K. Compl. 552.

155 Notably, Judge Sprizzo did not follow authorities suggesting that, given the difficulty of producing evidence as to state action before discovery, the proper time for addressing the state action requirement was on summary judgment rather than at the motion to dismiss stage. See *Estate of Rodriquez v. Drummond Co., Inc.* v. 256 F. Supp.2d 1250, 1262 (N.D. Ala. 2003; *National Coalition*

Moreover, Judge Sprizzo appeared to have attached no weight to allegations that Defendants engaged in conduct that did not require state action, forced labour being an example,[156] which, if proven at trial, would go well beyond merely 'doing business' in (or with) South Africa.[157]

4.4.2 Sources of international law

Judge Sprizzo's sweeping rejection of Plaintiff's use of international law sources is not easy to square with well-established doctrine. It is trite that many, if not most, general provisions to be found in treaties and declarations do not in and of themselves create international law. But it is beyond doubt that treaties and declarations may constitute *evidence* of international norms.[158] (In *Sosa* itself the Supreme Court explained that the sources of international law are 'the customs and usages of civilized nations', and,

---

Government of the Union of Burma v. Unocal, Inc., 176 F.R.D. 329, 346 (C.D. Cal. 1997.) Judge Sprizzo cited the case of *Atkinson v. B.C.C. Assocs.*, 829 F. Supp. 637, 646-47 (S.D.N.Y.1993), for the proposition that, "even if the relationship between a private actor and the government would create state action with regard to certain activities, it would not mean that everything done by the private actor would be deemed state action." But Plaintiffs did not need to allege that once a given defendant participated in the system under which the commando units were formed everything else that defendant did would count as "joint action." There is no reason that proof that a defendant mobilised what effectively were their own militias (albeit with state support), which were used in violently repressing opposition to apartheid, might suffice to establish a violation of the law of nations.

156 See *Unocal, supra* 946 (describing forced labour as a modern form of slavery, giving rise to responsibility under international law even in the absence of state action).

157 A subsequent decision distinguished *Apartheid Litigation* on the basis of Judge Sprizzo's characterisation of plaintiff's allegations. See *Presbyterian Church*, No. 01 Civ. 9882 (DLC) (S.D.N.Y.) (Aug. 30, 2005) (S.D.N.Y. 2005) ("*South African Apartheid* ... does not apply to the facts of this case, because the plaintiffs allege that [defendant] knowingly assisted Sudan in perpetrating a campaign of genocide and crimes against humanity, not that [defendant] merely transacted business."). Commentators have adopted Judge Sprizzo's reading of the complaints as alleging no direct action by defendants. See, e.g., R. CHAMBERS, 'The Unocal Settlement: Implications for the Developing Law on Corporate Complicity In Human Rights Abuses,' *Human Rights Brief* (2005) 14, 15 (in *Unocal* "the corporate defendant provided direct support and assistance to those who committed the human rights violations, [while] the apartheid allegations extended to 'mere' beneficial or indirect complicity in the state's wrongdoing"); A. SEBOK, 'Enforcing Human Rights in American Courts When the Injury is Indirect,' *Findlaw's Legal Commentary* (2002).
(*www.http//writ.news.findlaw.com/sebok/20020515.html*) (asserting that the South African suits "include no claim that the defendant corporations directly violated the human rights of the plaintiffs").

158 See *Roper v. Simmons*, 125 S. Ct. 1183, 1199 – 1200 (2005) (UN Convention on the Rights of the Child, although unratified by the United States, constitutes evidence of universal opinion re juvenile capital punishment to which the United States should pay heed.); *Flores v. Southern Peru Copper Co.*, 343 F. 3d 88-89 (2nd Cir. 2003) ("[a]ll treaties that have been ratified by at least two States provide some evidence of the custom and practice of nations."); *Sarei supra* at 1161 (violations of provisions of U.N. Convention deemed actionable despite absence of U.S. ratification).

as evidence thereof, 'the works of jurists and commentators').[159] Moreover, the Court's brushing aside of the jurisprudence of the International Criminal Tribunals for the Former Yugoslavia and Rwanda is out of step with other ATS decisions.[160]

4.4.3 *Aiding and abetting liability*

Judge Sprizzo's determination that aiding and abetting liability was not actionable under the ATS is also inconsistent with authority. As a brother judge of the same court had noted only a few months earlier, federal courts 'almost unanimously' allowed ATS actions premised on a theory of aiding and abetting.[161] Observing that the *Presbyterian Church* case had been decided before *Sosa*,[162] Judge Sprizzo held that aiding and abetting a state's infraction 'was not itself an international law violation that is universally accepted as a legal obligation.'[163] A good argument can be made that the court conflated two independent questions. Aiding and abetting is a matter of how far liability extends – quite a distinct question from what constitutes an ATS violation.

If the court had considered international law secondary liability standards, it would have found authorities regarding the elements of various forms of secondary liability

159 Sosa *supra* at 2766-67. Indeed, Judge Sprizzo's approach would reverse *Filartiga*, which relied extensively on unratified and non-self-executing treaties, U.N. resolutions and declarations (630 F. 2d at 882-83), decisions of various international courts or tribunals (630 F.2d at 884), and the works of scholars as a basis of its conclusion that torture was a violation of the "law of nations." (630 F.2d at 880-84).

160 See e.g., *Presbyterian Church*, 226 F.R.D. 456, 478 (S.D.N.Y. 2005).

161 *Agent Orange, supra* at 53 ("There is simply no question that the ATS provides for aiding and abetting liability."). See also *Mehinovic v. Vuckovic,* 198 F.Supp.2d 1322, 1355-1356 (N.D. Ga. 2002) (former Serb soldier liable for aiding and abetting war crimes and other human rights violations in Bosnia-Herzegovina); *Hilao v. Estate of Marcos,* 103 F.3d 767, 776 (9th Cir.1996) (foreign leader could be held liable upon finding that he "directed, ordered, conspired with, or aided the military in torture, summary execution, and disappearance"); *Burnett v. Al Baraka Investment,* 274 F.Supp.2d 86, 100 (D.D.C.2003) (allegations by victims of the September 11 attacks that various entities aided and abetted the perpetrators stated a claim); *Bowoto v. Chevron Texaco Corp.,* 312 F.Supp.2d 1229, 1247 (N.D. Cal. 2004) (plaintiffs could proceed on their claims against an oil company for aiding and abetting military killings in Nigeria); *Bodner v. Banque Paribas,* 114 F.Supp.2d 117, 128 (E.D.N.Y. 2000) (claims that defendant banks aided and abetted the Vichy and Nazi regimes in plundering plaintiffs' assets actionable under the ATS).

162 However, in response to a motion for reconsideration based on *Sosa*, the District Court confirmed that aiding and abetting liability existed under the ATS. *Presbyterian Church of Sudan v. Talisman Energy, Inc.*, 374 F. Supp. 2d 331 (S.D.N.Y. 2005). Moreover, two post-*Sosa* appellate courts subsequently decided similarly. See *Cabello v. Fernandez-Larios*, 402 F.3d 1148 (11th Cir. 2005); *Aldana v. Del Monte Fresh Produce, N.A., Inc.*, No. 04-10234, 2005 WL 1587302 (11th Cir. Jul. 8, 2005).

163 346 F. Supp. 2d at 549. However, Judge Sprizzo's interpretation has found some support, in a subsequent district court decision. See *Corrie v. Caterpillar, Inc*, 403 F. Supp.2d 1019, 1026, (W.D. Wa.) (2005) (dismissing claim of family of peace activist killed by an Israeli military bulldozer in the Gaza Strip, lodged against U.S. manufacturer of bulldozer; "While international law may recognize accomplice liability in some instances, the conduct alleged must first rise to the level of a claim under *Sosa*.").

for international criminal law violations.[164] Most notably, the celebrated *Furundzjia* decision of the International Criminal Tribunal for the Former Yugoslavia, provided a roadmap of secondary liability under international law.[165] *Furundzija* has been cited in a number of ATS judgments.[166]

4.4.4 The conduct of the defendant

The *Unocal* court, following *Furundzija*, held that the defendant could be liable for affording 'practical assistance' to the Myanmar military, insofar as it had hired the army to protect its pipeline from insurgent attacks, and furnished maps and photographs to guide deployment.[167] That test for *actus reus* (the 'culpable act'), was confirmed in *Agent Orange*, in which it was held that private corporations which had manufactured herbicides could in principle be held secondarily liable on that basis under the ATS.[168] Another court adopted the *Furundzija* test when it found that a Chilean military officer could be deemed liable for the death of a political prisoner if he 'substantially assisted some person or persons who personally committed or caused one or more of the wrongful acts that comprise the claim, while knowing that his actions would assist in the illegal or wrongful activity at the time he provided the assistance.'[169]

---

164 Judge Sprizzo held that, if he did apply municipal (U.S.) law that would not assist Plaintiffs because it did not provide for aiding and abetting liability. *Apartheid Litigation* 550. He cited *Central Bank of Denver v. First Interstate Bank of Denver*, 511 U.S. 164, 181-82 (1994) (where Congress has not explicitly provided for aider and abettor liability in civil causes of action, it should not be inferred.) See HOFFMAN & ZAHEER, 'The Rules of the Road: Federal Common Law and Aiding and Abetting Under the Alien Tort Claims Act,' 26 *Loyola-L.A. Int'l & Compl. L.R.* 47, 52 (2003) (nothing turns on the question of whether ATS courts look to international or domestic law, because the standard for aiding and abetting under domestic federal common law and international law are the same in all substantive respects.) Compare D. CHRISTENSEN, 'Corporate liability for overseas human rights abuses: the Alien Tort Statute after Sosa v Alvaraz-Machain,' 62 *Wash. & Lee L. Rev.* 1219 (2005), 1223 ("federal courts have a broad and well developed body of law addressing tort liability that is applicable to human rights offenses".)

165 In *Prosecutor v. Furundzija*, IT-95-17/1 T (Dec. 10, 1998) (reprinted in 38 I.L.M. 317 (1999)), a special police force commander was convicted for violating laws of war and prohibitions against rape and torture. The defendant did not engage in any of the acts of rape or torture that were the subject of the case, but interrogated the victims before, during, and after others committed the violations. The tribunal (at 371) concluded that the defendant had substantially contributed to the crimes by his presence and in interrogating witnesses in conjunction with the crimes.

166 See e.g. *Sosa, supra*, 2783 (Breyer J) (concurring in part); *Agent Orange, supra* 54; *Presbyterian Church, supra* at 340.

167 Unocal, supra 951.

168 *Agent Orange, supra* 54 ("United States courts applying … liability under the ATS have correctly held that under international law, the *actus reas* of aiding and abetting consists of 'practical assistance, encouragement, or moral support which has a substantial effect on the perpetration of the crime'") (citing *Mehinovic*, 198 F.Supp.2d at 1356 (quoting *Furundzija*, 192-249.))

169 *Cabello-Barrueto et al. v Armando Fernandez-Larios*, 402 F. 3d 1148, 1158 (11th Cir. 2005).

How would these tests apply to the allegations in the apartheid case? It is hardly a stretch to say that a given defendant who actively plotted the implementation of violent acts in defence of apartheid furnished 'substantial assistance' to a foreseeable human rights violation.[170] But it is appropriate to emphasise the word *actively* in this context. To attach liability merely for attending a meeting with apartheid's architects comes perilously close to condemning mere association.[171] By the same token, to attach liability for 'acceptance of benefits of a system of exploitation',[172] sweeps too broadly for ATS purposes. The *Furundzija* court emphasised that 'silent approval' of a crime against humanity is ordinarily not a punishable offence.[173] That dictum is a salutary corrective to an overbroad standard that might cast the net so widely as to render the ATS unenforceable.[174] While Judge Sprizzo's characterisation of the allegations in apartheid litigation is open to serious question, he was probably right to insist that it would not suffice to allege simply that Defendants passively accepted the benefits of apartheid exploitation.[175]

---

170 E.g. N. Compl. 168-69 (Business and military leaders met in series of conferences to strategise responses to violent resistance to apartheid.); K. Compl. 283 (Prime Minister Botha announcing that "I want to unite the business leaders of South Africa, representative as they are, behind the South African Defense Force. I think I have succeeded in doing so.").

171 But see *Prosecutor v. Musema*, ICTR-96-13-T, para 126 (Jan. 27, 2000) (*http://www.ictr.org/)* (describing *actus reas* of aiding and abetting as "all acts of assistance in the form of either physical *or moral support*" that "substantially contribute to the commission of the crime" (emphasis added); compare *Unocal, supra,* 951 (leaving open the question whether aiding and abetting such liability should also be imposed for moral support).

172 See Amnesty Int'l & Pax Christi Int'l, *Multinational Enterprises and Human Rights,* 17-18 (2000) ("To accept the benefits of measures by governments or local authorities to improve the business climate which themselves constitute violations of human rights, makes a company a party to those violations."); *Report of the United Nations High Commissioner on Human Rights on the responsibilities of transnational corporations and related business enterprises with regard to human rights,* 15 February 2005, UN doc. E/CN.4/2005/91, para. 34 (suggesting that a private corporation may be deemed complicit "when the company benefits from human rights violations even if it does not positively assist or cause them; and, when the company is silent or inactive in the face of violations.").

173 *Prosecutor v. Furundzija,* IT-95-17/1 T (Dec. 10, 1998), para 208 (citing *The Pig-cart Parade* case, Strafsenat. Urteil vom 10. August 1948 gegen L.u.a. StS 37/48 (*Entscheidungen,* Vol. I at 229 & 234)).

174 But see D.M. AMANN 'Capital Punishment: Corporate Criminal Liability for Gross Violations of Human Rights,' 24 *Hastings Int'l & Comp. L. Rev.* 327 (2001), 336 (although "criminal conviction for what approaches a crime of association ought to be avoided", different considerations may apply to civil litigation against corporations).

175 Granting defendants' summary judgment motion in *Presbyterian Church,* 2006 (*supra*), the Court observed that an ATS plaintiff faced a "demanding burden" when "otherwise lawful acts are designated as the acts which provide substantial assistance, and there is no direct evidence of improper intent and no direct participation in the criminal act." That analysis led Judge Cote to reject plaintiff's argument that the defendant oil company "understood that the Government had cleared and would continue to clear the land of the local population if oil companies were willing to come to the Sudan and explore for oil, and that understanding that to be so, Talisman should not have come." Id at 99-100. It did not, the Court held, suffice that Talisman had "been informed that Government forces forcibly displaced civilian populations to create a buffer zone around oil development sites." Id at 94.

4.4.5 *Intention of the defendant*

What of the subjective element (the *mens rea*), required for secondary liability? Although few ATS cases have considered the issue, a good argument can be made that plaintiff need show only that the defendant had knowledge of the principal's wrongful act. Again, *Furundzija* (in which a policeman was held to have the requisite *mens rea* for aiding and abetting, where he had been present at, but had not personally committed, rape and torture by other offices, is instructive.[176] That case followed in the footsteps of a Nuremberg matter, in which a German manufacturer who furnished Zyklon-B gas, knowing it would be used to commit mass murder, was held liable,[177] notwithstanding that there was no evidence that he actually willed mass murder.[178] Judge Weinstein adopted a similar standard in his encyclopaedic *Agent Orange* decision. He quoted an amicus brief stating that the *mens rea* required for the ATS is 'the knowledge that [the] acts assist the commission of the offence.'[179] Interestingly, a number of early U.S. cases applying international law also demand only knowledge of the principal's wrongful act – as opposed to specific intent that it be carried out.[180] Finally, the fact that the ATS is a civil, not a criminal statute might be said to support

---

176 See also *Prosecutor v. Akayesu*, Judgment, Case No. ICTR-96-4-T, (Sept. 2, 1998), para. 545 (accused need not share specific intent, but need only have "aided, abetted, or instigated one or more persons in the commission of genocide, while knowing that such a person or persons were committing genocide."). See M. DRUMBL. 'Prosecutor v Radislav Kristic: ICTY Authenticates Genocide at Srebernica and Convicts for Aiding and Abetting' (2004) 52 *Melbourne Journal of International Law*, 444 (defendant acquitted of genocide because he lacked the specific intent to destroy the Bosnian Muslims, but convicted of aiding and abetting genocide because he provided assistance to others knowing of genocidal plan).

177 *Trial of Bruno Tesch and Two Others,*1 *Law Reports of Trials of War Crim.* 93, 101 (1947) (Brit. Military Ct., Hamburg, March 1-8, 1946); see also *U.S. v. Krauch*, 8 Trials of War Criminals Before the Nuremberg Military Tribunals Under Control Council Law No. 10, 1081, 1169-72 (1952) (pharmaceutical executives liable for selling experimental vaccines to SS knowing they would be tested on concentration camp inmates).

178 *Ibid.* 155. See Hearing Transcript at 112 (those "tried in Nuremberg were people who were in much more active collaboration with the Nazi government than your facts alleged these people to be.").

179 *Agent Orange supra* 54 (quoting Br. Amici Curiae of the Center for Constitutional Rights, Earthrights International and the International Human Rights Law Clinic at the University of Virginia School of Law, Jan. 18, 2005).

180 See P. HOFFMAN & D.A. ZAHEER, 'The *Rules of the Road: Federal Common Law and Aiding and Abetting Under the Alien Tort Claims Act,' 26 Loy. L.A. Int'l & Comp. L. Rev.* 47, 50 (2003), 130. See also DISKIN, 'The Historical and Modern Foundations for Aiding and Abetting Liability under the Alien Tort Statute,' 47 *Ariz. L. Rev.* (2005*)*, 832 ("reckless conduct must evidence a corporate defendant's awareness that its behavior would likely lead to violations of international law.") In October 2005 Senator Feinstein introduced an amendment to the ATS that would require both "specific intent" and "direct participation" by an ATS defendant, but it was subsequently withdrawn. *See* A.J. Sebok, 'Senator Feinstein's Now-Withdrawn Statute Limiting Non-Citizens' Tort Claims,' *Findlaw Commentaries*, October 2005 (*http://writ.news.findlaw.com/sebok /20051031. html.).*

use of the knowledge test, one less rigorous than that ordinarily applied in criminal cases.[181] Indeed, given that the ATS is, after all, a civil statute, it might even be argued that the negligence standard would be appropriate.[182]

Because it rejected from the start the plaintiff's averral that aiding and abetting could form the basis for ATS liability, the court did not reach the question of what *mens rea* test should be applied to the apartheid Defendants. Suffice to say that had it applied a specific intent test (requiring Defendants actually to have willed the particular harmful conduct in each case), it may have proven difficult for plaintiffs to demonstrate aiding and abetting liability. Especially without discovery, demonstrating specific intent on the part of a corporation can be extraordinarily difficult.[183] If, on the other hand, a court were to apply the 'knowledge' test (which, as we have seen, is supported by the weight of what little authority exists), the widespread international condemnations of apartheid would probably make it impossible for Defendants credibly to deny that they were aware of the wrongs their conduct was facilitating.[184]

4.4.6 *Just doing business?*

As we have seen, application of the standard tests would readily allow those Defendants who participated in the planning and implementation of apartheid to be treated as aiders and abettors. A more difficult question is presented by the cases of those Defendants who furnished 'dual use' goods, or injected capital. Suppose an American tourist visits South Africa in the 1980s.[185] Being a reader of the *New York Times,* he knows that the dollars he spends help to prop up a government engaged in universally condemned human right abuses. Nonetheless, intuition rebels against the notion that

---

181 A. CLAPHAM, *Human Rights Obligations of Non-State Actors* (O.U.P. 2006) 241-44, noting the dearth of international cases treating civil complicity standards, suggests that guidance be sought in rules regarding international civil responsibility for non-state actors, as elaborated in the ILC's Articles on State Responsibility. Under Article 16 of the Articles "a state which aids or assists another state in the commission of an internationally wrongful act by the latter is internationally responsible for so doing if: (a) That state does so with knowledge of the circumstances of the internationally wrongful act and (b) The act would be internationally wrongful if committed by that State".

182 See E. RICE, '*Doe v. Unocal Corporation*: Corporate Liability for International Human Rights Violations,' 33 *U.S.F. L. Rev.* 153 (1998), 167 (future plaintiffs may argue that a "knew or should have known" standard should apply to corporations in light of extensive "political risk" analysis customarily engaged in the course of due diligence).

183 See A.J. SEEBOK, 'Senator Feinstein's Now-Withdrawn Statute Limiting Non-citizen's Tort Claims,' *Findlaw's Legal Commentary*, Oct. 31, 2005 (corporate decisions are often "made by groups of managers, not by single individuals who plan a course of action from beginning to end."). But see *Presbyterian Church* 2006 (*supra*) at 87 (plaintiff must show defendant "specifically directed his acts to assist in the specific violation").

184 See e.g., K. Compl. 517 (Mercedes Benz stockholders were informed during 1988 meeting of conversion of its vehicles for military use).

185 See A. J. SEBOK, 'Enforcing Human Rights in American Courts When the Injury is Indirect,' *Findlaw Legal Commentary* (2002), 2-3.

such a traveller would incur ATS liability. Does it make any difference that a foreign bank injects not thousands, but ten of millions of dollars in the same period – in the face of widespread international criticism that the loans are effectively financing apartheid?[186] (Plaintiffs alleged that certain banks were aware that the capital they supplied directly financed the military).[187]

The law provides no clear answer to these questions. On the one hand, a U.S. federal court has held that merely providing funds to finance foreign terrorist bombings can be the basis for aiding and abetting liability, if such use of the money is reasonably foreseeable.[188] On the other hand, in the *Karl Rasche* case, the chairman of a private bank (Dresdner, also a defendant in *Apartheid Litigation*), was acquitted of financing Nazi industries that used slave labour:

> "Does [defendant] stand in any different position than one who sells supplies or raw materials to a builder building a house, unknowing that the structure will be used for an unlawful purpose? ... [A bank] does not become a partner in enterprise, and the interest charged is merely the gross profit, which the bank realizes from the transaction, out of which it must deduct its business costs."[189]

A similar argument could be made with respect to computers.[190] In 2005, a court, citing *Apartheid Litigation*, dismissed a claim against an American bulldozer manufacturer

186 K. Compl. 397 (UN Special Committee Against Apartheid noting that "[a]t a time when the international community through the General Assembly has repeatedly condemned collaboration with South Africa... we learn today that more than $55.4 billion has been loaned in a six year period to bolster [the] regime"). A report concerning the relationship between Swiss banks and Nazi Germany speculated that the banks may have prolonged the war by providing finance. See S.E. EIZENSTAT & W.Z. SLANY, 'U.S. and Allied Efforts to Recover and Restore Gold and Other Assets Stolen or Hidden by Germany During World War II, A Preliminary Study' (1997). (*www.state.gov/www/regions/eur/holocausthp.html; www.guissani.com./holocaust-assets/welcom.html.*).

187 K. Compl. 431 (alleging that Barclays Bank acquired the R10 million of South Africa Defence Bonds, constituting the largest single purchase).

188 See *Boim v. Quranic Literacy Inst. & Holy Land Found. for Relief and Dev.*, 291 F.3d 1000, 1023 (7th Cir. 2002) (denying motion to dismiss case against U.S. organisation that raised money for Hamas, alleged to have been responsible for terrorist activities in Israel; defendant could be liable under principle of aiding and abetting, "if funding was provided with knowledge of and intent to further violent acts", which must be a reasonably foreseeable result of the funding).

189 *United States v. Von Weizsaecker* (*Ministries* Case) XIV *Trials of War Criminals Before the Nuremberg Military Tribunals* (1952), 854. But see *U.S. v. Friedrich Flick*, 6 Trials of War Criminals Before the Nuremberg Military Tribunals Under Control Council Law No. 10, 1216-1223 (1952) (civilian industrialist convicted for contributing money to the Nazi regime while aware of mass murder).

190 N. Compl. 80-102. See S.R. RATNER, 'Corporations and Human Rights: A Theory of Legal Responsibility,' 111 *Yale L.J.* 443 (2001), 502-03 (international law would not require paper company to stop selling to governmental bureaucracy insofar as such sales do not "directly and substantially" contribute to violations).

lodged by the family of an American peace activist who was killed by an Israeli military bulldozer, a product with both military and non-military uses.[191]

Even assuming a vendor knows the goods he sold to the regime would be used in a manner directly linked to apartheid, the vendor might argue that the product could counterfactually have been obtained from a different source. IBM, which was alleged to have furnished an information processing system specifically designed with the apartheid system's needs and goals in mind, could conceivably raise such a defence. The charge echoes one made regarding IBM's supply of data-processing systems to the Nazi regimes, allegedly used to facilitate the murderous bureaucracy of the Third Reich.[192] One commentator has suggested that, however immoral IBM's behaviour may have been, its technology was probably not indispensable to the Nazi regime.[193]

By the same token, it might be open to Barclays Bank to defend its capital injections by arguing that, had it not purchased bonds earmarked for financing the South African military, another means of raising the necessary capital would have been found.[194] (Comments made at the hearing suggest that Judge Sprizzo may have been receptive to a parallel causation argument from arms dealers who violated the embargo.)[195]

But such a crude 'but for' defence should not succeed.[196] A dictator should no more be able to escape guilt for genocide by showing that his conduct was not a *sine qua non* of a massacre – because his equally ruthless deputy stood ready to step into his shoes – than a cigarette manufacturer should escape liability by showing that the plaintiff

---

191 *Corrie v. Caterpillar, Inc*, 403 F. Supp.2d 1019, 1027 (W.D. Wa.) (2005) ("'a supplier joins a venture only if his fortunes rise or fall with the venture's, so that he gains by its success.").

192 See E. BLACK, *IBM and the Holocaust: The Strategic Alliance between Nazi Germany and America's Most Powerful Corporation* (2001).

193 R. BERNSTEIN, 'I.B.M.'s Sales to the Nazis: Assessing the Culpability,' *N.Y. Times*, March 7, 2001, E8 (without I.B.M.'s technology, "which consisted mainly of punch cards and the machines to tabulate them, the Germans [would have] figured out a way to do what they did anyway.") (cited in B. STEPHENS, 'The Amorality of Profit: Transnational Corporations and Human Rights,' 20 *Berkeley J. Int'l L.* 45, n. 3 (2002).

194 See A. RAMASASTRY, Banks and Human Rights, *Findlaw's Legal Commentary* (2002), 6 ("what appeared to be missing in Apartheid Litigation was any direct connection between the banks' loans and the apartheid regime – any connection, that is, more direct than that, without the loans, the violence could not have continued.").

195 See Hearing Transcript, at 32-33 ("South Africa was buying arms from other people. So was Iraq. .... I don't think anybody abides by [arms embargoes] ... because obviously there is a self-interest in selling your weapons wherever you can.").

196 *Anderson v. Minneapolis, St. Paul & Sault Ste. Marie Ry. Co.*, 179 N.W. 45, 45-46 (Minn. 1920) (defendant liable for damaged caused by fire notwithstanding that damage to plaintiff's property would have been caused by second fire even if he had not started first fire); *Restatement (Second) Of Torts*, §§ 431, 432 (1965) (defendant's misconduct may be deemed a "substantial factor" in bringing about the plaintiff's injury, if two forces are actively operating, one because of the actor's [conduct], the other not because of any misconduct on his part, and each of itself is sufficient to bring about harm to another").

would have smoked another brand had defendant's brand not been on the shelves.[197] In *Unocal* the Ninth Circuit applied a variety of the Restatement's 'substantial factor' test with regard to the forced labour dragooned by the Myanmar military, at the instance of Unocal, to build a pipeline. Unocal was liable because its conduct had a 'substantial effect' on the perpetration of the violation; the abuse 'most probably would not have occurred in the same way' without the military providing security.[198]

4.5 EXPLAINING JUDGE SPRIZZO'S DECISION

It is true that the Second Circuit in the *Karadzic* case[199] held that a 'more searching review' is appropriate with respect to the jurisdictional inquiry into whether a plaintiff has alleged a specific violation of international law.[200] But even given that, it is difficult to avoid the inference that Judge Sprizzo's strict scrutiny of the complaints (in stark contrast with the approach of other courts declining to dismiss ACTA claims they confessed to finding doubtful)[201] evidences a certain antipathy to the expansive reading of the ATS.[202]

---

197 *Burton v. Reynolds Tobacco Co.*, 181 F. Supp. 2d 1256 (D. Kan. 2002) (defendant liable despite evidence that the plaintiff had primarily smoked Camel cigarettes, and had only smoked Lucky Strikes (the defendant's product) when Camel cigarettes were not available).

198 *Unocal supra* at 949-50 (quoting *Prosecutor v. Tadic,* ICTY-94-1, 688 (May 7, 1997), *http://www.un.org/icty/tadic/trials2/judgement/index.htm.*) See also *Presbyterian Church, supra*, 324 (prosecution must prove that the violation "most probably would not have occurred in the same way had not someone acted in the role that the accused in fact assumed.") (quoting *Prosecutor v. Tadic*, Case No. IT-94-1-T, 688 (Int'l Crim. Trib. for Former Yugoslavia Trial Chamber, May 7, 1997). Compare M.J. OSIEL, 'Modes Of Participation In Mass Atrocity,' 8 *Cornell Int'l L.J.* 793, (2005), 798 (under theory of joint criminal enterprise, "factfinders no longer have to try to imagine what subordinates would have done differently had their superior behaved differently... we can look simply at what a particular participant actually did – rather than what he did not do, but hypothetically might have done).

199 70 F.3d 232, 238 (2d Cir. 1995).

200 It is arguable, however, that this aspect of *Karadzic* does not survive *Swierkiewicz v. Sorema N.A.*, 534 U.S. 506, 515 (2002). See *Presbyterian Church, supra* at 308.

201 See, e.g. *Kodak Co. v. Kavlin*. 978 F. Supp. 1078, 1094 (S.D. Fla. 1997) (holding that the plaintiff's complaint of 10-day detention stated cause of action under the ATS sufficient to survive motion to dismiss, notwithstanding court's "deep reservations"); *Estate of Rodriquez v. Drummond Co., Inc.* 256 F. Supp. 2d 1250, 1264 (N.D. Ala. 2003) (accepting "reluctantly" that plaintiffs' allegations with respect to right to organise union was actionable under the ATS at preliminary stage of proceedings) (citing *Aquamar, S.A. v. Del Monte Fresh Produce*, N.A., 179 F.3d 1279, 1295 (11th Cir. 1999).

202 There are indications that Judge Sprizzo sympathised somewhat more with Justice Scalia's sentiments in *Sosa* than with Justice Souter's opinion for the majority. Judge Sprizzo cited with evident approval Justice Scalia's complaint that the *Sosa* majority had "relegated to the lower federal courts the task of grappling with and determining what offenses against international law fit within that narrow class of offenses." *Apartheid Litigation* at 547 (quoting *Sosa* at 2772). Judge Sprizzo added that "it would have been preferable if the Supreme Court "[had] limited the ATS to those violations of international law clearly recognized at the time of its enactment." *Apartheid Litigation* at 547.

All the same, it may have been a tactical error for Plaintiffs to package their claims in voluminous 'shotgun' complaints. Particularised allegations are lost in a sea of more generalised averrals. The court was confronted with three complaints, (comprising nearly 1600 paragraphs), two class actions, each with a potentially vast number of Plaintiffs,[203] numerous named Defendants (including more than one hundred of the largest transnational companies), and a demand for hundreds of billions of dollars in compensation,[204] plus various forms of equitable relief (including the creation of an 'independent historical commission').[205] The manageability of an action is not, strictly speaking, a factor at the motion to dismiss stage. And a court is at liberty to dismiss a complaint in part only.[206] But when plaintiff's cause of action is relatively novel, and the court is for ideological or other reasons not well-disposed towards the suit, the fact that the case as presented appears massively unwieldy may tip the balance decisively in favour of dismissal.[207]

5 THE ATS AS AN IRRITANT TO FOREIGN RELATIONS

While Judge Sprizzo's treatment of customary international law sources is open to serious doubt, and his summary dismissal of the aiding and abetting liability cannot be reconciled with the decisions of several other courts,[208] his treatment of the inputs from Washington and from the South African government was in line with the way some other courts have dealt with such submissions.[209] In this section I critically

---

203 See N. Compl. 196 ("Plaintiff estimates that the individual sub-classes includes hundreds of thousands, if not millions"). The Khulumani complaint was not filed as a class action. But see Hearing Transcript, 33 ("The Khulumani plaintiff says, well, ours is not a class action, but if you look at their list of parties it includes the Khulumani group which has, they say in their papers, 32, 700 members.").

204 See D. Compl. part VI (demanding $200 billion in compensatory damages and $200 billion in punitive damages).

205 Ntsebeza Comp., 30(a). Plaintiffs however suggested on appeal that they might not persist with their demand for such relief. See Brief for Plaintiffs-Appellants, June 14, 2005, n. 13 ("Plaintiffs acknowledge that some of the relief requested in the complaints may raise issues of feasibility, or present potential conflict with the positions taken by the South African government.").

206 E.g. *Laborer Local Health and Benefit Fund v Phillip Morris, Inc.,* 191 F. 3d 229 (2d Cir. 1999).

207 See Hearing Transcript, 94 ("The trouble is you have lumped [your claims] all together in one massive complaint going back over a period of 20 or 30 years with all different types of injuries all lumped together").

208 Hearing Transcript, 116 ("I don't really care what other district judges do because they have the same size commission I have and I don't have to follow them . . . I have no . . . reluctance to disagree with Judge Wood or anybody else in a case of this sort because I know as least as much as she does").

209 In *Sarei v. Rio Tinto, PLC,* 221 F. Supp. 2d 1116 (C.D. Cal. 2002), 1192, the court wrote that "[P]laintiffs have not cited, and the court has not found, a single case in which a court permitted a lawsuit to proceed in the face of an expression of concern such as that communicated by the State Department here". The SOI had stated that "in our judgment, continued adjudication of the claims ... would risk a potentially serious adverse impact on [a] peace process, and hence on the conduct

analyse these inputs. It will be suggested that the supine posture of courts in the face of considerations articulated in some of these documents threatens to politicise and thus delegitimate the ATS. That being said, there are no easy answers to the challenge of enforcing international human rights with the necessary executive prerogatives in foreign affairs.

5.1 THE GOVERNMENT INTERVENTIONS

South African President Mbeki initially adopted a neutral position regarding the apartheid suits.[210] However, in an address to Parliament on 15 April 2003, on the tabling of the *Final TRC Report*, Mbeki remarked that:

> "[W]e consider it completely unacceptable that matters that are central to the future of our country should be adjudicated in foreign courts which bear no responsibility for the well-being of our country and the observance of the perspective contained in our constitution of the promotion of national reconciliation."[211]

Accordingly, in his sworn declaration submitted to the court on July 11, 2003, South African Minister of Justice Penuell Maduna urged that the proceedings be dismissed because they interfered with South Africa's sovereignty. The litigation 'in effect, sought to set up the claimants as a surrogate government.'[212] Maduna added that 'permitting

---

of our foreign relations." See *Sarei v Rio Tinto, PLC,* 456 F. 3d 1069 (9th Cir. August 7, 2006). However, in the latter decision, the Ninth Circuit reversed the decision of the district court, noting that the SOI "explicitly did *not* request that we dismiss this suit on political question grounds", and finding that the proceedings did "not express any disrespect for the executive, even if it would prefer that the suit disappear." (At 1082) (Emphasis in original). See also *Mujica et al. v. Occidental Petroleum Corp.*, 381 F. Supp 1164, 1177 (C.D. Cal. 2005) (some courts have taken the position that, once a plaintiff has pled an ATS claim, the court does not have to address the "practical consequences" of recognising such claims [citing *Doe v. Liu Qi*, 349 F.Supp.2d 1258, 1320-28 (N.D. Cal. 2004); *Sarei*, 348 F. Supp.2d at 1144)], while other courts "have more closely followed the approach provided by the *Sosa* Court" [citing *In re Apartheid Litigation*, 346 F. Supp.2d at 553-54; *Jama v. United States Immigration and Naturalization Service*, 343 F. Supp.2d 338, 360-61 (D.N.J. 2004)].

210 See P. BOND, Book Review: M. DARROW, 'Between Light and Shadow: The World bank, International Monetary Fund and International Human Rights Law,' Centre for Civil Society, UKZN (2005), 6 (*http://www.nu.ac.za/ccs/default.asp?3,28,10,790.*).

211 Quoted in Declaration of P.M. Maduna, July 11, 2003, para 3.2.3 ("*Maduna Declaration*") *(http://www.nftc.org/default/ussabc/south%20african% 20apartheid%20litigation.pdf.)* Minister of Trade and Industries Alex Erwin added in the same debate that "the government rejects the actions of legal practitioners in the USA to exploit our history and will not allow any judgment made [sic] in the USA or elsewhere to be carried out in South Africa." President Mbeki's statement to Parliament was quoted also in a letter addressed by Foreign Minister Zuma to U.S. Secretary of State Powell, dated May 16, 2002 (on file with author).

212 Maduna Declaration, para 7.

this litigation to go forward will, in the government's view, discourage much needed foreign direct investment in South Africa.'[213]

In a letter endorsing these sentiments, the U.S. State Department told the court that adjudication of the apartheid suits 'risk potentially serious adverse consequences for significant interests of the United States.'[214] The letter referred to the input of the South African government, which had:

> "[M]ade clear its view that these cases do not belong in U.S. courts and that they threaten to disrupt and contradict its own laws, policies and processes aimed at dealing with the aftermath of apartheid as an institution... [T]he current Government of South Africa has taken extensive steps to promote reconciliation and redress for apartheid-era injustices. We note that the government pursuing these policies is broadly representative of the victims of apartheid."[215]

The Taft Letter added that it could be anticipated that the suit would be an 'irritant' in U.S.-South African relations;[216] that the litigation might be 'detrimental to U.S. foreign policy interests in promoting sustained economic growth in South Africa';[217] and that the US government was concerned that adjudication of the apartheid cases might deter foreign investment 'where it is most needed.'[218]

We have already seen that Judge Sprizzo relied heavily upon Justice Souter's suggestion that the Apartheid case could be subject to dismissal under the doctrine of 'case-specific deference.'[219] The court offered five rationales under that general heading. First, the action posed 'serious impediments to the flow of international commerce.'[220] Second, it would (in the words of the South African government), 'preempt the ability of the [South African] government to handle domestic matters.'[221] Third (again according to the South African government), the litigation stood to

---

213 Maduna Declaration para 12. The South African government filed an amicus brief when Plaintiffs took Judge Sprizzo's decision on appeal to the Second Circuit in 2005. See Brief *of Amicus Curiae Republic of South Africa in Support of Affirmance*, at 1-2 ("These foreign litigations fundamentally interfere with South Africa's independence and sovereignty and intervene in its internal affairs, including its right under international law to address its apartheid past and to develop policies for its future in the manner it deems most appropriate, subject to the support and approval of the democratic electorate." See also Statement of Bridgette Sylvia Mabandla, Minister of Justice and Constitutional Development, on behalf of the Republic of South Africa, concerning the apartheid-related litigations in the United States Court, October 13, 2005 (reiterating Maduna Declaration).

214 Letter from William H. Taft, IV, Legal Adviser, U.S. Department of State, Washington, Oct 27, 2003 ("Taft letters"), attached to Statement of Interest of the United States, Oct. 30, 2003, p. 2, para 2.

215 Taft Letter, p. 2, para 2.

216 Taft Letter, p. 2, para 3.

217 Taft Letter p. 2, para 3.

218 Taft Letter p. 3, para 2.

219 *Sosa, supra* 2766, n.21 (2004).

220 *Apartheid Litigation, supra*, 553.

221 *Ibid.* See Hearing Transcript at 88 ("I take from [Maduna's letter] that I should mind my own judicial business. That's what I took away from that communication, regardless of all the details set forth therein. They were telling me keep your nose out of our business.").

'discourage needed investment in the South African economy.'[222] Fourth, it would (according to the State Department) 'cause tension between the United States and South Africa.'[223] Fifth (again according the State Department), it would 'hamper the [U.S.] policy of encouraging positive change in developing countries via economic investment.'[224]

Although a number of ATS cases have been dismissed based upon SOIs,[225] the recurring theme is that while such inputs are entitled to respectful deference, they are not binding.[226] Independent judicial assessment is especially indicated where a case touches upon human rights, the vindication of which is quintessentially the province of the judicial branch.[227] Rejecting defendant's political question argument (which was based upon the fact that the alleged violations occurred during a war prosecuted by Washington), the court in the *Agent Orange* decision observed that, were the defendants' position accepted, 'it is difficult to imagine how the law of nations could be enforced in our courts at any time in any controversy.'[228]

The separation of powers principle itself mandates that whether or not a court adjudicates any particular ATS claim should not be dependent upon the vicissitudes of changing administrations.[229] That being so, courts cannot avoid critically assessing

---

222 *Ibid.*

223 *Ibid.* Compare *Presbyterian Church, supra* (it was "telling that the United States has not advised this Court that the continuation of this lawsuit will adversely affect the Government's relations with Canada.").

224 *Apartheid Litigation supra* 553.

225 See *Doe 1 v. Exxon Mobil Corporation*, 393 F. Supp. 2d 20 (D.C.D.C. 2005); *Joo v. Japan* No. 01-7169 (D.C.D.C) (June 28, 2005) (dismissing ATS claim against Japan of Asian "comfort women" where SOI had "demonstrated that adjudication of ATS claim would undo settled foreign policy of state-to-state negotiation with Japan).

226 This was reiterated by the Supreme Court. *Altmann*, 541 U.S. 677 at 702 n. 23 (2004) ("We do not hold ... that executive intervention could or would trump considered application of the FSIA's more neutral principles"). See also *Kadic supra* 250 ("assertion of the political question doctrine by the Executive Branch [through a SOI] [would be] entitled to respectful consideration, [but] would not necessarily preclude adjudication."); *Ungaro-Benages v. Dresdner Bank AG*, 379 F.3d 1227, 1236 (11th Cir. 2004) ("SOI is entitled to deference," but does not alone "take the present litigation outside of the competence of the judiciary."); *Unocal, supra* (SOI not conclusive); *In re Nazi Era Cases Against German Defendants Lit.*, 129 F. Supp.2d 370, 380 (D.N.J. 2001) (SOI "non-binding."). As already noted, in *Sarei, supra,* a decision handed down on August 7, 2006, the Ninth Circuit reversed the dismissal of a suit by inhabitants of Bougainville island who had been forcibly removed by Papua New Guinea army to make way for defendant's mining operations, noting that there was no "unusual need for unquestioning adherence" to the SOI's "nonspecific" invocations of risks to the peace process. The Court added that "given the guarded nature of the SOI, we see no "embarrassment" that would follow from fulfilling our independent duty to determine whether the case should proceed.

227 See Jide Nzelibe, 'The Uniqueness of Foreign Affairs', 89 *Iowa L. Rev.* 941, 1001 (2004).

228 *Supra* at 75. Judge Weinstein cited *Rasul v. Bush*, 124 S.Ct. 2686, 2698 (2004) (ATS claim challenging acts in war against al Qaeda and the Taliban regime deemed justiciable).

229 *Tel-Oren v. Libyan Arab Republic*, 726 F.2d 774, 789 (D.C. Cir. 1982) ("if Congress determined that aliens should be permitted to bring actions in federal courts, only Congress is authorized to decide that those actions 'exacerbate tensions' and should not be heard.") (Edwards J, concurring.) See B. STEPHENS, 'Upsetting Checks And Balances: The Bush Administration's Efforts To Limit Human

a SOI and attempting at least a preliminary assessment of the facts upon which it is based, as well as of the credibility of the risks of which it cautions. We turn to consider such assessments, first in general, then in the apartheid case.

5.2 RISKING RELATIONSHIPS

In recent years, SOIs, often couched in boilerplate language, have offered dire warning about the effects upon relations between the U.S. and the state in which the alleged violation took place. For example, in a case brought by the Falun Gong in 2000, the Chinese Government asserted that the suit would 'seriously interfere' with relations between China (the *PRC*), and the United States.[230] The U.S. State Department followed up with a confirmatory SOI.[231] But taking such assertions at face value implicitly assumes that Beijing is so unsophisticated as not to understand that, by virtue of the separation of powers, U.S. courts may act contrary to the wishes of the executive.[232] Moreover, if Beijing is as acutely sensitive as suggested, one would have expected its relationship with Washington already to be frayed beyond repair: federal courts routinely comment harshly on the human rights policies of many countries (including that of the PRC), in political asylum cases.[233] (As one court has pointed out: '[T]o accept the claim of someone to qualify for refugee status is publicly to accuse some other state of engaging in persecution.')[234]

The State Department's professed sensitivity to Beijing's reaction to ATS cases seems especially disingenuous given its own condemnation of the treatment of Falun Gong,[235] and the fact that it went so far as implicitly to condemn Beijing's human rights records in a SOI submitted in connection with an Indonesian-related ATS suit.[236]

Rights Litigation,' 17 *Harv. Hum. Rts. J.* 169 (2001), 200 ("Review of private tort suits falls within the constitutionally delegated powers of the judicial branch.").

230 *Doe v. Liu Qi*, 349 F. Supp. 2d 1258, 1297-98 (N.D. Cal 2004).

231 Statement of Interest of the United States, *Doe v. Liu Qi*, No. C 02-0672 CW (EMC) (Sept. 26, 2002), 7. Such inputs from the U.S. executive have become routine in ATS claims against the Chinese government. See SOI filed in *Zhou v. Li Peng*, 00 Civ. 6446 (S.D.N.Y.) (WHP), 2-3. (SOI alleging that Tiananmen Square litigation "severely hampers the ability of the United States to implement a robust foreign policy at a time when matters of war and peace are in the balance.").

232 See J. DELISLE, *supra*, 491-92.

233 See *Gao v Ashcroft*, 299 F. 3d 266, 268 (3d Cir. 2002) (citing State Department and Amnesty International reports of beatings, torture and deaths of Falun Gong practitioners by Chinese officials).

234 *M.A. v U.S.I.N.S.* 899 F.2d 304, 313 (4th Cir. 1990).

235 See *Doe v Li Qiu*, 349 F. Supp. 2d 1258, 1297 (N.D. Cal. 2004); U.S. Department of State, Country Reports on Human Rights Practices, 2002: *China* (Mar. 31, 2003), at 23 (*http:// www.state.gov/g/drl/ ls/ rrpt/2002/18239pf.htm.)*

236 See SOI submitted in *Doe, et al v. ExxonMobil, et al.* No. 01-CV-1357 (DDC) (*http://www.usaengage.org/legislative/2003/alientort/ilrf.html*)) (suggesting that Chinese entities, such as the state-owned PRC oil company, "would be far less concerned about human right abuses" than would Exxon Mobil).

While such criticism may grate on the sensibilities of Beijing bureaucrats, there does not appear to be any evidence that bi-lateral relations have suffered as a result.[237] Insofar as the State Department's input is reliant upon Beijing's fulminations, which have a ring of opportunistic affectation, the credibility of the SOI itself is undermined. (Over-use of barely credible SOIs may ultimately prove self-defeating if they lead courts to suspect that the administration is prone to crying wolf).[238]

These considerations suggest that it may be time for a re-examination of one rationale for judicial deference to SOIs: the familiar 'one voice' metaphor.[239] Congress has determined that a principal goal of the foreign policy of the United States is 'to promote the increased observance of internationally recognized human rights by all countries.'[240] The Bush Administration has described the 'central tenet' of American foreign policy as that it will 'speak out honestly about violations of the nonnegotiable demands of human dignity.'[241] When it comes to consider whether to accord 'case-specific' deference to a particular SOI, a court should read such a statement alongside such professed commitments.[242] It might even be said that, in acknowledging that an ATS defendant was complicit in repression in a state that has been the subject of ongoing criticism from Washington, a court is vindicating, rather than undermining, U.S. foreign policy. Certainly, for the judiciary to allow itself to be buffeted by shifting gusts emanating from the State Department is hardly consistent with the principle of separation of power, the very basis for the doctrine of deference upon which the SOI's

237 See *Presbyterian Church, supra,* 346 (in light of the long-standing U.S. condemnation of Sudan, "any criticism ... that would arise as a result of the adjudication of this case would be a mere drop in the bucket."); *Doe v. Unocal Corp.*, 963 F. Supp. 880, 893 (C.D. Cal. 1997) (foreseeing little likelihood of hostile confrontation with the government of Myanmar as a result of the court's forced labour finding, because the executive and legislative branches had previously condemned such practices). This analysis was, however, rejected in the *Li Qiu* case, the matter in which the SOI discussed above was submitted. The court held that while the fact that the executive had already publicly criticised Beijing "might mitigate the potential conflict between coordinate branches of government, it does not eliminate them entirely." 349 F. Supp. 2d at 1297.

238 See B. STEPHENS, 'Sosa v Alvaraz-Machain: "The Door is Still Ajar for Human Rights Litigation in U.S. Courts,"' *70 Brooklyn L. Rev.* 533 (2004), 567 (noting that in terrorism cases decided in 2004 term, the Supreme Court failed to follow executive inputs couched in "super-heated" national security terms).

239 *United States v. Pink*, 315 U.S. 203, 242 (1942) (Frankfurter, J., concurring) ("In our dealings with the outside world, the United States speaks with one voice and acts as one."); see KU & YOO, 'Beyond Formalism In Foreign Affairs: A Functional Approach To The Alien Tort Statute,' *Sup. Ct. Rev.* (2004) 153, 187-88.

240 22 U.S.C. § 2304(a)(1) (1994).

241 'National Security Strategy of the United States of America' (September 2002) (*http://www.whitehouse.gov/nsc/nss.html*). See also G.W. BUSH, 'Securing Freedom's Triumph,' *N.Y. Times*, Sept. 11, 2002, A33 ("We believe that freedom and respect for human rights are owed to every human being, in every culture.").

242 *Trajano v. Marcos*, 978 F.2d 493, 500 (9th Cir. 1992) (government's conflicting positions "in different cases and by different administrations is not a definitive statement by which we are bound.").

proponents rely.[243] Deference to an *ad hoc* assertion, in the face of undisputed evidence to the contrary, is not deference, but obeisance.

Moreover, a large scale, high profile lawsuit involving two countries, even if innocent of direct political connotations, has the potential to become a foreign affairs 'irritant.' It is probably for that reason that judicial abstention in the face of executive opposition has been deemed appropriate only where judicial action would 'seriously interfere with important governmental interests,'[244] and that a speculative threat to the conduct of foreign affairs has been seen as an inadequate basis for abstention.[245]

How do these considerations apply to *Apartheid Litigation?* Judge Sprizzo found consistency in the U.S.'s position *vis-à-vis* South Africa, pointing out that Congress had encouraged investment in apartheid South Africa, under the policy of 'constructive engagement.'[246] But that is a somewhat selective reading of the relevant history. The U.S. at no point imposed comprehensive sanctions upon South Africa. The Reagan Administration's policy of 'constructive engagement' in South Africa was rejected by Congress when it enacted disinvestment legislation in 1986.[247] All of this renders a 'one voice' rationale for deference to the position set out in the Taft letter difficult to sustain.[248]

Moreover, 'chicken-little' warnings of prejudice to U.S./South African relations arising out of the apartheid litigation are difficult to square with a communiqué by the U.S. State Department, issued in May 2006, in which the pending apartheid suit finds no mention, and the two countries are described as enjoying an 'excellent

---

243 See *First Nat'l City Bank v. Banco Nacional de Cuba*, 406 U.S. 759, 773 (1972) (Douglas J) (concurring) (blind adherence to the State Department's stances relegated Court to "a mere errand boy for the executive branch which may choose to pick some people's chestnuts from the fire, but not others."); B.C. FREE, Awaiting *Doe v. Exxon Mobil Corp.*: Advocating The Cautious Use Of Executive Opinions In Alien Tort Claims Act Litigation,' 12 *Pac. Rim L. & Pol'y* 467 2003, 481.

244 *Karadzic*, 70 F.3d at 249 (emphasis added).

245 See *Environmental Tectonics*, 847 F.2d 1052, 1061 (3d Cir. 1988), aff'd, 493 U.S. 400 (1990) ("minor irritant" insufficient to invoke political question doctrine); *Marcos v. Republic of Philippines*, 818 F. 2d 1473, 1488 n. 20 (9th Cir. 1987) (foreign relations embarrassment relatively minor consideration); *Flynn v. Schultz*, 748 F.2d 1186, 1190 (7th Cir. 1984) ("diplomatic repercussions" do not transform issue into political question).

246 *Apartheid Litigation* at 554.

247 The Comprehensive Anti-Apartheid Act ("CAAA") of 1986, 22 U.S.C. 5001 *et seq.*, imposed substantial sanctions on South Africa, and instituted civil and criminal liability for violations of the Act. See *United States v Van den Berg*, 5 F.3d 439, 440 (9th Cir.1993) (discussing the CAAA and its termination by Executive Order in 1991 after South Africa took steps toward democracy.) See also W.B. GOULD, 'South African Sanctions, Carefully Calibrated,' *San Jose Mercury News*, Aug. 3, 1986, C1; W.B. GOULD, 'Black Unions in South Africa: Labor and Apartheid,' 17 *Stan. J. Int'l L.*, 99 (1981).

248 Compare *Presbyterian Church of Sudan v Talisman Energy, Inc.*, 2005 WL 2082846 (S.D.N.Y. 2005) (because plaintiff had not founded its allegations on the fact merely that Talisman did business in Sudan, the matter did not "require a judgment that Canada's executive policy of constructive engagement was or caused a violation of the law of nations.").

bilateral relationship.'[249] Even a 1990s criminal indictment in the U.S. of ARMSCOR, a South African state-owned arms company, gave rise to no more than 'minor strains' in the Washington/Pretoria relationship.[250] Certainly, South Africa's claims that its sovereignty was impugned by a suit[251] brought by the U.S. government against a corporation controlled by the South African government should have carried more weight than a parallel objection to the apartheid suit – in which the South African government is not a defendant, nor has any interest whatsoever in any named defendant.[252]

Ultimately, both the Taft Letter and the Maduna declaration are premised upon an implicit assumption that it is the conduct of the current South African government that is under attack. (Minister Maduna went so far as to caution that if South Africa allowed the suit to go forward it would be 'proclaiming to the world at large that [it was] subservient to the countries in which those courts are located').[253] That is difficult to square with the fact that all the conduct complained of occurred before the transition to democracy.[254] As pointed out by Judge Weinstein in *Agent Orange*, 'this is not a case about reparations between nations, but rather a case about individuals

---

249 U.S. Department of State, Bureau of African Affairs, *Background Note: South Africa* (*http://www.state.gov/r/pa/ei/bgn/2898.htm*) ("since the abolition of apartheid and democratic elections of April 1994, the United States has enjoyed an excellent bilateral relationship with South Africa.").

250 See Federal Research Division of the Library of Congress, *Country Study: South Africa* (*http://countrystudies.us/south-africa*) (describing 1991 indictment alleging that Armscor was part of conspiracy to violate arms embargo). According to the study, the South Africa government requested that the indictment be dropped, "noting that the target of sanctions – the apartheid regime – had been removed from power." Under a settlement reached in 1996, Armscor paid a fine of $1 million. See 'South African Firms Settle Arms Smuggling Case,' *The Risk Report*, Volume 3 Number 3 (May-June 1997), noting that President Mandela unsuccessfully requested President Clinton to drop the case). See also *U.S. v. Jasin* (No. 00-4185) (3d Cir. 2002) (describing an "11-year conspiracy" to evade international arms embargo against South Africa).

251 See Risk Report, op cit. (noting that South African government had refused to facilitate service of U.S. court papers upon Armscor, citing national sovereignty).

252 See L. DHOOGE, 'The Alien Tort Claims Act and the Modern Transnational Enterprise: Deconstructing the Myth of Judicial Activism,' 35 *Geo, J. Int'l L.* 3 (2003), 80 (ATS critics have not named a "single instance of foreign retaliation or significant harm to bilateral relations resulting from ATS lawsuits against transnational enterprises"); see also *Koohi v. United States*, 976 F.2d 1328, 1332 n.3 (9th Cir. 1992) ("we have found no Supreme Court or Court of Appeals decisions which have dismissed a suit brought against a private party on the basis of the political question doctrine") Whatever one might say about other ATS suits, in no sense can the apartheid suits be said to be an attempt to "control a sovereign's treatment of its own citizens within its own territory." See *Sosa*, 542 U.S. at 750 (Scalia J concurring in part and dissenting in part).

253 Press Release, Sept 10, 2003, 9 (attached to September 11, 2003 letter of Minister Maduna addressed to court).

254 See S. Terreblanche, Declaration in Opposition to Defendants' Joint Motion to Dismiss, Sept. 15, 2003 (filed in the Southern District of New York in *Apartheid Litigation)*, para 6 ("there is no allegation that the current government, which represents a fundamentally new political order, is responsible, either indirectly or directly, for [any] violations").

suing other individuals for damages.'[255] It is true that the post-apartheid government may in principle be civilly liable for the conduct of its apartheid predecessors.[256] But the present government can obviously not be deemed responsible for the conduct of private corporations active in South Africa before it assumed power. It is instructive that a number of U.S. courts have held that considerations of foreign sovereignty are muted in cases where the alleged violations occurred under the aegis of a government no longer in power.[257]

It might be argued that even given the fact that the apartheid government no longer rules South Africa, insofar as the suit is based upon allegations that Defendants acted jointly with the state in the design and implementation of a grand scheme that formed the basis of the South African political order for half a century, it touches upon subject matter going to the heart of state sovereignty. But that in itself would hardly justify the dismissal of the apartheid suit *tout court*. As we have seen, Plaintiffs also allege violations committed by Defendants in their own right, quite independently of the apartheid state.[258] A civil suit against a multinational alleging the intentional infliction of harm upon a worker need not offend South Africa's sovereignty, even were the apartheid government still in power.[259] One can also imagine a carefully crafted SOI

---

255 *Agent Orange supra* at 79.

256 See Azapo *supra* at 694-97.

257 See *Banco Nacional de Cuba v. Sabbatino, 376 U.S. 398,* 428 (1964); *Republic of Philippines v. Marcos,* 806 F.2d 344, 359 (2d Cir. 1986); *Wiwa v. Dutch Royal Petroleum Co.*, 2002 WL 319887 at 828 (military regime responsible for alleged torts replaced by democracy); *Bigio v. Coca-Cola Co.*, 239 F.3d 440, 453 (2d Cir. 2001) (new government in power). In *Sarei*, supra, the appellate court overturned a decision in which it was held that the fact that the allegedly culpable government was still in power weighed in favour of dismissal, but noted that plaintiffs had submitted recent letters (the authentication of which was in dispute), purportedly from the Papua New Guinea government stating that the suit would not harm the ongoing peace process on the island of Bougainville – and that in fact "the only way the litigation will impact U.S./PNG foreign relations is if the lititgation is discontinued." *Sarei*, at 1083, n. 13.

258 See, e.g., D. Comp. 302 (Gencor allegedly dismissed 25,000 striking workers and summoned riot police to attack them); N. Compl. 34 (named plaintiff Lungisile Ntsebeza subjected to racial discrimination by defendant Standard Bank plc and/or its subsidiary or affiliate in South Africa); D. Compl. 19 (named plaintiff William Ngobeni paid "slave wages" by Anglo American plc's subsidiary). Of course, it might be argued that, precisely because they were purely "private" in nature, some or all of these allegations do not meet the state action requirement. See *Sarei supra* at 1153-55 (given well-settled status of racial discrimination as a violation of the law of nations, sole issue for resolution was whether the plaintiffs alleged sufficient facts to hold defendants liable as state actors; *in casu* defendants could be deemed state actors, in light of their co-ownership and participation in the mining operation and the Defendants' encouragement and assistance in the military effort to suppress violence. In the *Apartheid Litigation* case, the Court's broad-brush rejection of virtually all of Plaintiffs' argument pre-empted the testing of the complaints at this level of analysis.

259 *Doe v. Exxon,* 393 F.Supp.2d 20, (D.C.D.C. 2005), a case arising out of human rights abuses allegedly perpetuated by the Indonesian government troops upon secessionists, offers a salutary example of an appropriately nuanced SOI. Plaintiffs alleged that U.S. oil companies contracted a unit of the military to use brutal force to protect its installations. The SOI filed (*http://www.usaengage.org /legislative/2003/alientort/ilrf.html),* said the suit would "risk a potentially serious adverse impact on significant interests of the United States", yet acknowledged that this assessment was "necessarily

making such distinctions, and going on separately to consider the different forms of relief sought by the Plaintiffs. The State Department could quite credibly urge that the demand for the establishment of 'educational and training programs' for members of the Plaintiff class[260] should be dismissed, because it directly implicated South African sovereignty.[261] But the same could not be said of the claim for compensatory damages – especially against non-South African corporations, and which would likely be enforced against Defendants' assets in New York.[262] Unfortunately, the sweeping SOI submitted in *Apartheid Litigation* offered the court no such guidance.

5.3 DISRUPTING THE DEAL

Could it be said that even if the suit does not point a finger at the present government for the sins of apartheid, it does represent a collateral assault upon the policy of the post-transition government with regard to domestic reparations? Judge Sprizzo implied as much when he spoke of the potential of adjudication to 'preempt the ability of the government to handle domestic matters.'[263] But that argument is difficult to sustain. There is in truth no conflict between the TRC process in South Africa and ATS

predictive and contingent" on how the case proceeded. The court responded by recognising that the extent to which a suit will be vulnerable to dismissal on the basis that it may tread upon foreign affairs concerns should depend upon the nature of the allegations therein. *Doe 1 v. Exxon Mobil Corporation*, 393 F. Supp. 2d 20 (D.C.D.C. 2005). The Court held that genocide and crimes against humanity "by definition … require adjudication on whether the Indonesian military was engaged in a plan allegedly to eliminate segments of the population," a question treading directly on Indonesia's internal affairs. (At 27). On the other hand, "resolving claims of complicity in arbitrary detention, torture, and extrajudicial killing" posed less of a threat to Indonesia's sovereignty, because "these allegations are more targeted to actions by individuals, rather than a plan of mass killing or mayhem." (At 25).

260 N. Compl. 30(a). No mention of this relief appears in the Prayer for Relief section of the complaint.

261 *Agent Orange, supra* at 46 (abatement and remediation of ongoing health hazards allegedly caused by military's contamination of countryside by herbicides during Vietnam War would require court oversight in areas over which the court had no jurisdiction, and would compromise Vietnam's sovereignty).

262 Minister Maduna singled out these demands as a particularly unacceptable intrusion upon South African sovereignty. (Maduna declaration, para 10).

263 This was a concern of at least one justice in the hearing of the *Sosa* matter. Justice Beyer commented: "Apartheid is a terrible thing, but according to the government . . . the President of South Africa, has told the United States that the judicial efforts to give compensation to victims are interfering with his efforts to build a democratic South Africa. Now, if I have to choose between these two I'd say democratic South Africa, protective of human rights has it all over compensating the victims even though that's terrible." (Transcript of Oral Argument before the U.S. Supreme Court, Mar. 30, 2004, *Sosa v. Alvarez-Machain*, 542 U.S. 692 (2004) (Nos. 03-339, 03- 485) 54). See also *Sarei* supra at 1117, n. 15 (referring to SOI in apartheid case as stating that litigation "interfered with" "domestic development").

litigation in New York.[264] Had the TRC in fact been designed to, or in fact granted, amnesty to the Defendants it might indeed have been 'presumptuous' for U.S. courts to foreclose the 'capacity of South Africa to innovate in this area.'[265] But as we have seen, the TRC expressly contemplated the possibility of litigation to obtain compensation from corporations for their alleged complicity in apartheid.[266] The suggestion that an ATS lawsuit would undermine the TRC process is a *non-sequitur.*[267] It is worth noting that the South African government has never before expressed opposition to foreign civil actions seeking compensation from private parties. The South African government lent its support to asbestos litigation in London against British companies that had interests in South African asbestos mines, a claim that might have been construed as an implicit attack on the limitation of the South African legal process.[268]

It may further be relevant that President Mbeki initially adopted a neutral posture regarding the apartheid suits. In fact, it appears that the decision to oppose the suits

---

264 In a decision handed down late in 2005 (*Chavez v. Carranza* (D.C. W. Tenn) No. 03-2932 M1/P, (Oct. 26, 2005)), a federal court declined an ATS claim for torture lodged against a former El Salvador minister. It was held that because the country's domestic amnesty regime did not prohibit legal claims filed outside of El Salvador, the application of the ATS or TVPA in U.S. federal court did not interfere with the application of the Salvadoran amnesty law. See B. ZAGARIS, 'U.S. Jury Finds Carranza Liable For Crimes Against Humanity,' 22 *Int'l Enforcement L. Rep.* 82 (Feb. 2006) See also M. DEL CARMEN MÁRQUEZ CARRASCO & J.A. FERNÁNDEZ, 'Case Report: In re Pinochet,' in 93 *AJIL* 690 (1999), 694 (discussing Spanish court holding that Chilean amnesty law did not preclude exercise of universal criminal jurisdiction over jus cogens crimes committed by Gen. Augusto Pinochet); *Bano v. Union Carbide Corp.* 273 F. 3d 120, 128 (2d Cir. 2001) ("the right retained by the Bhopal victims to pursue restitution under Indian criminal procedure law can hardly be said to encompass a right to pursue civil remedies under the ATS for violations of international law"); *Ibrahim v. Titan Corp.*, 391 F.Supp.2d 10, 16 (D.C.D.C. 2005) (rejecting political question argument in suit brought by Iraqis against U.S. civilian contractors used at detention facilities, noting that, "unlike in many other reparations cases entangled with political questions, there is no state-negotiated reparations agreement competing for legitimacy with this court's rulings.").

265 M.O. CHIBUNDU, 'Making Customary International Law Through Municipal Adjudication: A Structural Inquiry,' 39 *VA. J. Int'l L.* 1069, 1144 (1999).

266 See D. Tutu, Supplemental Declaration in Opposition to Defendants' Joint Motion to Dismiss, Dec. 15, 2003 (Exh. A to Ntsebeza and Digwamaje Response to Statement of Interest of U.S. Government), para 10 (adding that, far from threatening reconciliation, "the obtaining of compensation for victims of apartheid, to supplement the very modest amount per victim to be awarded as reparations under the TRC process, could promote reconciliation, by addressing the needs of those apartheid victims dissatisfied with the small monetary value of TRC reparations.").

267 Compare *Presbyterian Church of Sudan v. Talisman Energy, Inc.*, 2005 WL 2082846 (S.D.N.Y. 2005) (where the contents of SOI "suggest a lack of understanding about the nature of the claims in the ATS litigation, a court may take that into account in assessing the concerns expressed in the letter.").

268 *Lubbe and others v. Cape Plc.*, [2000] 4 All E.R. 268 (H.L). Minister Maduna attempted to explain the apparent inconsistency between the government's support of plaintiffs in the *Lubbe* matter and its opposition to the apartheid suits on the basis that the former "relates to a damages claim for injuries (diseases) sustained by the plaintiffs and their families . . . whereas the New York Claim is based on the general supposition that all of business actively supported apartheid." (Ministerial Press Release, Sept 10, 2003, 10) (attached to September 11, 2003 letter of Minister Maduna to Hon. J. Sprizzo).

may have been formulated *ad hoc* in response to the very litigation at issue.[269] It is one thing to accord decisive weight to credibly articulated concerns that reconciliation may be jeopardised by a lengthy trial in a foreign court raking over atrocities that have been fully dealt with domestically. It is quite another to defer to conclusory statements from Pretoria, as endorsed by Washington, that are exhaustively rebutted, as we shall soon see, in declarations submitted by persons who are amongst the most eminent authorities in the field. A good argument can be made that, just as courts should not defer to the politically based preferences of the incumbent administration in Washington, they should not be swayed by the unsupported claims of a foreign government.

Beth Stephens comments that the fact that the post-Apartheid government opposes the litigation provides support for the Court's suggestion that the executive branch view was entitled to what Justice Souter called 'serious weight.'[270] She adds, however, that an 'exhaustion of domestic remedies might be a more appropriate doctrine on which to challenge the litigation' in light of the fact that South Africa has a functioning judicial system.[271] Stephens' point is well made. While it is true that the ATS, (unlike the TVPA), apparently does not require exhaustion of domestic remedies,[272] an

---

269 It has been suggested in the ATS context that "any intervention, no matter how skilful or tactful, is invariably disliked." *Supra*, 1115 (Bybee J.) (dissenting) (quoting D. MUMMERY, 'The Content of the Duty to Exhaust Local Judicial Remedies,' 58 *Am. J. Int'l L.* 389, 390 (1964)). Beyond that, it has been suggested that the South African government succumbed to pressure from big business. See C. TERREBLANCHE, *Sunday Independent*, June 29, 2003 (Minister Maduna said that business was "willing to work with [the government] to convince American courts that as South Africans we can find workable and less destructive solutions.") One may speculate that the government's intervention in the suit reflects the same "symbiotic" relationship between ANC leaders and the corporate sector that, according to Sampie Terreblanche (*supra* at 125), made it expedient for the new government "not to pressure the TRC into uncovering the truth about systematic exploitation, or to delegitimise the corporate sector for its part in the design and utilisation of repressive labour systems".

270 Sosa, *supra* 733, n. 21.

271 See also W. GOULD, 'Fundamental Rights at Work and the Law of Nations: An American Lawyer's Perspective' 23 *Hofstra Lab. & Emp. L.J.* 1 (2005), 38 ('South Africa's own courts provide a forum for redress which may be exhausted, a feature that distinguishes it from many other countries where human rights violations are present.").

272 Until recently, neither the Supreme Court nor any appellate Court had resolved the issue whether the ATS requires exhaustion of local remedies. The Ninth Circuit in *Sarei*, supra, after an exhaustive consideration of applicable law, concluded that it did not. While there did exist an "international norm of exhaustion," that norm "does not speak to the hybrid situation ... where a domestic court in a sovereign country, rather than an international tribunal, is charged with adjudicating violations of customary international law through the vehicle of a civil suit." *Supra* at 1096. However, Judge Bybee, in a scholarly dissent, differed in this regard:

> "If we respect the international norm requiring exhaustion, we will minimize the number of cases that involve potential meddling in other country's affairs. In fact, we will intervene only where governments are so inadequate as not to provide adequate remedies. With exhaustion, we get the best of both worlds. We retain a commitment to the principle of international comity, while stepping in to render justice where required – and only where required. While adjudicating the exhaustion requirement requires occasional inquiries into the internal affairs of other nations

objection based upon sovereignty would undoubtedly be reinforced if courts in the foreign state where the violations occurred were open to substantially the same suit. Be that as it may, the exhaustion argument would probably not assist Defendants in this instance, since it appears that South African courts would not enjoy personal jurisdiction over Defendants in the apartheid case.[273]

5.4 THE ECONOMIC COSTS OF JUSTICE

It is difficult to discern the basis of Judge Sprizzo's (twice-stated) conclusion that the suit raises 'the prospect of serious impediments to the flow of international commerce.'[274] That consequence is not contemplated in either the Taft letter or the Maduna Declaration. (In the former there appears only the more modest claim that suits of this general nature might discourage investment in 'many areas of the developing world.') For a court to speculate about future patterns of international investment seems at odds with the rationale most often used to justify judicial deference – that judges lack the expertise, and the institutional capacity to deal with such imponderables.

Plaintiffs attempted to rebut the Taft letter and the Maduna Declaration by submitting a declaration by former World Bank Chief Economist Joseph Stiglitz, who told the court that Maduna's concern that investment in South Africa would be undermined by the suit was without foundation. In fact, Stiglitz urged that holding accountable those who contributed to apartheid abuses would create a 'more favourable business climate', thereby contributing to South Africa's development.[275] Plaintiffs also submitted declarations by Professor Terreblanche, a leading South

(in cases where the adequacy of remedies is not readily apparent) ... this infrequent inquiry is preferable to offering international intervention on behalf of every foreign plaintiff who shops a claim in American courts." (*supra* 1115, n. 14).

273 See Dec. of Charles Forsyth, filed in support of Ntsebeza plaintiffs' opposition to plaintiffs' motion to dismiss, *Tachiona v. Mugabe*, 216 F. Supp. 2d 262, 275 (S.D.N.Y 2002) (TVPA exhaustion requirement satisfied where Zimbabwean judicial system was controlled by defendant); *Xuncax v. Gramajo*, 886 F.Supp. 162, 178 (D. Mass. 1995) (TVPA exhaustion not required when foreign remedies are "'unobtainable, ineffective, inadequate, or obviously futile"'). An English court's rejection of a *forum non conveniens* argument in *Lubbe v. Cape PLC Afrika*, [1999] 10 I.L. Pr. 113, 127ff (C.A.) (Eng.)), on the grounds, inter alia, that plaintiffs would likely not be able to obtain legal aid in South Africa, provides an interesting comparative perspective. Compare *Sarei, supra*, 221 F. Supp. 2d at 1170. (Papua New Guinea not adequate forum owing to the unavailability of class actions and contingency fee representation).

274 *Apartheid Litigation* at 553. Compare *Presbyterian Church of Sudan v Talisman Energy, Inc.* 2005 WL 2082846 (S.D.N.Y. 2005) (rejecting argument that "Canadian firms will likely absent themselves from Sudan and therefore not contribute to its economic revitalization out of fear of U.S. courts.").

275 Khulumani Support Group, 'Joseph Stiglitz Endorses Khulumani Lawsuit,' August 10, 2003 (*http://www.khulumani.net/content/view/242/27/).*

African economist,[276] and Desmond Tutu.[277] Both affirmed that South Africa, as a country with an exemplary human rights record compared to that of many other developing nations competing for foreign direct investment,[278] actually stood to benefit from the shift in the diversion of global direct investment away from persistent human rights abusers likely to be triggered by vigorous ATS enforcement.[279]

It does not appear that Judge Sprizzo accorded any weight to these attempts to rebut the Taft Letter and the Maduna Declaration.[280] It is quite understandable that a court would shrink from adjudicating competing views of foreign statements, Washington bureaucrats, and independent experts regarding the possible fallout of high profile international litigation.[281] On the other hand, it places plaintiffs in an invidious position to be precluded from responding to inputs that may well lead to the dismissal of their complaints – especially where, as in the apartheid suits, those inputs expressly adopt vigorously contested factual claims made by the Defendants.[282]

---

276 S. Terreblanche, Declaration in Opposition to Defendants' Joint Motion to Dismiss, Sept. 15, 2003 (filed in the Southern District of New York in *Apartheid Litigation).*

277 D. Tutu, Supplemental Declaration in Opposition to Defendants' Joint Motion to Dismiss, Dec. 15, 2003 (Exh. A to Ntsebeza and Digwamaje Response to Statement of Interest of U.S. Government).

278 Compare U.S. Department of State, 2005 Country Reports on Human Rights Practices: *http://www.state.gov/g/drl/rls/hrrpt/2005/61593.htm* (South African government "generally respected the human rights of its citizens"), with *http://www.state.gov/g/drl/rls/hrrpt/2005/61605.htm* (Chinese government's "human rights record remained poor, and the government continued to commit numerous and serious abuses.").

279 See Tutu Declaration, para 12; Terreblanche Declaration. para 19. Indeed, pressure from foreign investors in the wake of the *Unocal* decision appears to have resulted in the re-allocation of capital from persistent violators to less repressive states. When the California Employee Retirement System, which controls $176 billion in investment capital, announced that it would suspend investment in several countries with poor human rights records, including Indonesia, Thailand, Malaysia, and the Philippines, and simultaneously announced that it would consider new investment in Poland and Hungary, owing to improvements in those countries, Asian markets were hit, and the Asian countries sought negotiations to win back investment. See S.F. DIAMOND, 'The PetroChina Syndrome: Regulating Capital Markets in the Anti-globalization Era,' 29 *J. Corp. L.* 39 (2003), 71. See C. BRAUNSCHWEIG, 'LPs Carry Their Weight Beyond Venture Capital,' *Buyouts*, Sept. 9, 2002. It is also notable that, the *Presbyterian Church* case, *supra* was pending. Talisman shares were discounted based on perceived political risk because stockholders became "tired of continually having to monitor and analyze events relating to Sudan." See Press Release, 'Talisman Energy, Inc., Talisman to Sell Sudan Assets for C$1.2 Billion' (Oct. 30, 2002) (http://www2.ccnmatthews.com/scripts/ccn-release.pl/2002/10/30/1030131n.html/cp-tlm.).

280 See Judge Sprizzo, Transcript, 88 ("So you want me to make a finding that the South African government lied to me? I'm not going to do that.").

281 See *Atlee v. Laird*, 347 F. Supp. 689, 702 (D.C. Pa. 1972) ("major element [of the political question doctrine] concerns the inherent inability of a court to predict the international consequences flowing from a decision on the merits."). See also KU & YOO, '*Beyond Formalism In Foreign Affairs: A Functional Approach To The Alien Tort Statute*,' 2004 *Sup. Ct. Rev.* 153, at 75 (ATS cases "often involve multipolar disputes in which multiple potential parties raise legal claims, and chains of events are complex and multifaceted.").

282 See, e.g. Press Release, Sept 10, 2003, attached to Maduna declaration (the claim is "based on the general supposition that all of business actively supported apartheid.").

In the final analysis, it is not clear why inputs from economists such as Stiglitz would necessarily present greater difficulty than that of experts in other kinds of cases.[283]

6 THE ATS, SOVEREIGN EQUALITY AND WORLD ORDER

6.1 THE ATS AS JUDICIAL IMPERIALISM

The politicisation of the ATS engendered by uncritical deference to the views of the State Department threatens to reduce the ATS to a political tool. One need not be a cynic to suspect that the ATS's most notable successes – *Filartiga*, *Karadzic* and *Unocal* – owe something to the fact that, Paraguay, the Bosnian Serb Republic and Myanmar respectively had few friends in Washington.[284] The wording of the State Department's opposition to the *ExxonMobil* case illustrates how the ATS may be manipulated to serve a geo-political agenda. In lauding Indonesia's co-operation in the war on terrorism, Washington sends Jakarta an unmistakable message that, should such cooperation cease, the U.S. might reconsider its support for its struggle against the separatists.

All of this lends weight to the complaint of commentators like Michael Byers that provisions like the ATS threaten the principle of sovereign equality; only the powerful are in a position to subject other states to their jurisdiction.[285] The exercise by U.S.

---

[283] U.S. courts have become accustomed to considering conflicting views of, for example, medical epidemiologists in mass tort tobacco and asbestos cases. They routinely hear duelling experts in criminology, psychiatry, in matters of immense social and political and economic importance. In 2005, in *Kitzmiller v Dover Area School District*, 400 F. Supp. 2d 707 (M.D. Pa. 2005), a federal judge heard various experts in a case concerning the teaching of "intelligent design" in Pennsylvania schools. It is difficult to see why, if judges may consider expert testimony regarding evolutionary theory and cosmology, they should be deemed incapable of following experts in international relations theory and practice.

[284] See *Filartiga*, 577 F. Supp. at 862 (if Paraguayan government had felt that a U.S. court judgment would be offensive, it could have advised the court but had not done so.). The Clinton administration expressly declined to take a position on the *Karadic* litigation. See J. DELISLE, *Human Rights, Civil Wrongs And Foreign Relations: A "Sinical" Look At The Use Of U.S. Litigation To Address Human Rights Abuses Abroad*, 52 DePaul L. Rev. 473, 477-78. However, the Second Circuit has rejected an international comity argument where, although the foreign country concerned enjoys friendly relations with Washington, that country did not lodge an objection to the suit. See, e.g., *Bigio v. Coca-Cola Company*, 2006 WL 1236789 (2d Cir. May 9, 2006).

[285] *United States Hegemony & The Foundations of International Law (2005)* at 134. See also M. CHIBUNDU, 'Making Customary International Law Through Municipal Adjudication: A Structural Inquiry,' 39 *Va. J. Int'l L* 1069, 1073 (1999); J.B. FOWLES, 'Compounding The Countermajoritarian Difficulty Through "Plaintiff's Diplomacy": Can The International Criminal Court Provide A Solution?' B.Y.U. L. Rev. 1129 (2003), 1176; J. HARKER, 'Intervention Is Served: The US Federal Alien Torts Claims Act and the Irony of Ironies,' *Cambridge Review of International Affairs,* Volume 16, Number 1, 2003, 163 ("It is ironic that the one state so opposed to the rule of international law

courts of ATS jurisdiction has been likened to the judicial colonialism once exercised by the Privy Council.[286] Such criticisms were echoed by Judge Guillaume of the International Court of Justice, who warned against overly expansive exercises of jurisdiction that 'encourage the arbitrary for the benefit of the powerful, purportedly acting as agent for an ill-defined 'international community.''[287] Some might be tempted to dismiss this as akin to the anti-imperialist bluster too often used to excuse authoritarian government. Nevertheless, for a U.S. court unilaterally to assume the position, as Judge Weinstein put it, of a 'quasi international tribunal',[288] cannot but raise difficult legitimacy concerns. Suggestions that the ATS is a way of 'enforc[ing] international norms without having the American state place its treasure and blood at risk,'[289] likewise lends credence to suspicions that the ATS and forcible regime change are merely different points along a spectrum of intervention. The South African government's emphatic opposition to the apartheid suit may be disingenuous and cynical. But the broad sentiment underlying its objections (if not the particular rationales advanced by Pretoria), resonate with many around the world wary of U.S. unilateralism.

Of course, the doctrine of sovereign immunity limits the extent to which the ATS can directly offend state sovereignty. Nevertheless, the ATS permits a significant

---

though the proper functioning of the ICC should be the very place where the rule of law takes a form of coercive intervention with the prospect of providing for people other than its own citizens the rights they are meant to enjoy under international law").

286 KRISCH, 'International Law in Times of Hegemony: Unequal Power and the Shaping of the International Legal Order,' 16 *Eur. J. Int'l L.* 369, 402 (2005). Similar criticism is also to be heard from the right. Robert Bork (*Wall Street Journal*, June 17, 2003), writes that "Americans are rightly amused by Belgium's claim to universal jurisdiction," but that Americans "ought to consider that our courts are engaged in the same judicial imperialism," in the use of the ATS. Conservative antipathy to the ATS was reflected in Judge Sprizzo's comments in the hearing in *Apartheid Litigation*, when he remarked that "[t]he law of nations is nothing more than what the big powers of the world agree that it is in their self-interest to accede to so long as they think it's in their self-interest to accede to it." (Hearing Transcript, 72.) See also Id at 103-04 (at Nuremberg the victors "had the jurisdiction of a conqueror, we were the winners and it cost us a lot of time and money to defeat them and, therefore, without all these notions of international humanity and all of it we could have shot them anyway.").

287 *Case Concerning the Arrest Warrant of 11 April 2000 (Belgium v Congo)*, I.C.J. (*14 Feb. 2002)* (hereinafter *Arrest Warrant* case) (Separate Opinion of Judge Guillaume (para 15). Other judgments were more pungent. See Decision of Judge Rezek (asking "how certain European countries would react if a judge from Congo had indicted their officials for crimes supposedly committed on their orders in Africa."); Decision of Judge *ad hoc* Bula-Bula (para 81) (denouncing Belgium's attempt "to pose as prosecutor for all mankind . . [and to claim] the right to redeem human suffering across national borders and over generations.").

288 *Vietnam Ass'n for Victims of Agent Orange/Dioxin v Dow Chem.*, 373 F. Supp. 2d 7, 17 (E.D.N.Y. 2005). See also *First Nat'l City Bank v. Banco Nacional de Cuba*, 406 U.S. 759, 775 (1972) ("[u]ntil international tribunals command a wider constituency, the courts of various countries afford the best means for the development of a respected body of international law.") (Justice Powell).

289 H. RISHIKOF, 'Framing International Rights With A Janusism Edge – Foreign Policy And Class Actions-Legal Institutions As Soft Power,' 2003 *U. Chi. L.F.* 247 (2003), 265.

measure of indirect intrusion. First, as we have seen, acts in pursuance of 'unofficial' state policy may in certain circumstances not be immunised. The same goes for infractions against *jus cogens*, such as racial discrimination. Second, state officials may in certain circumstances not be eligible to claim sovereign immunity.[290] Third, a state's freedom of contract may be significantly constrained by the possibility of suit against private corporations to which it outsources functions.[291] Fourth, although this concern in the particular circumstances of the *Apartheid Litigation* seems fanciful, by discouraging TNC's from investing in regimes with poor human rights records, ATS suits might be said to impose *de facto* economic sanctions.[292]

The debate around the legitimacy of the ATS resonates with a familiar conundrum that afflicts international human rights law. On the one hand, national self-determination remains a founding premise. On the other, the spirit of the human rights revolution insists that abusers not be permitted to hide behind the cloak of national sovereignty. By the close of the 20th century, the former had been subordinated to the latter in mainstream human rights discourse. The very meaning of 'sovereignty' had evolved from the venerable Westphalian understanding to a broader conception of popular sovereignty – albeit still mediated, in the ordinary course, through a nation-state.[293] It might be said that the emergence for the first time in history of a global community made it necessary and, for the first time, possible, to vindicate a set of human rights that transcends national boundaries.[294]

---

290 *Enahoro v. Abubakar*, 408 F.3d 877, 892 (7th Cir. 2005).

291 Ironically, that is best illustrated by litigation against private contractors retained by the U.S. army alleged to have abused prisoners in Iraqi detention facilities. See *Saleh v. Titan*, No. 04 CV 1143 R (NLS) (S.D. Cal June 30, 2004). See also M.E. ROSEN, 'The Alien Tort Statute: An Emerging Threat to National Security,' 16 *St. Thomas L. Rev.* 627 (2004) at 628 (ATS "threatens the overseas activities of most U.S. companies, since the Department of Defense relies heavily on contractors for essential combat support."); *Jama v. United States INS*, 343 F. Supp. 2d 338 (D.C.N.J. 2004) (allegations of inhuman treatment by a private corporation to which the U.S. government had outsourced administration of immigration prison deemed actionable under ATS).

292 HUBER & EGG, 'Beyond the Nation-State: Privatization of Economic Sanctions,' *Middle East Policy* (Summer 2003).

293 I. SIMONOVIC, 'Relative Sovereignty of the Twenty First Century,' 25 *Hastings Int'l & Comp. L. Rev.* 371, 373 (2002) T.M. FRANCK, 'The Emerging Right to Democratic Governance,' 86 Am. *J. Int'l L.*. 46, 47 (1992).

294 See I. KANT, *Political Writings* 107-08 (Hans Reiss ed., H.B. Nisbet, trans., 2d ed. 1991), quoted in D. HARVEY, 'Cosmopolitanism and the Banality of Geographical Evils,' 12 *Public Culture* 2, 529, 532 (2000) ("The peoples of the earth have entered in varying degree into a universal community, and it has developed to the point where a violation of rights in one part of the world is felt everywhere.").

6.2 THE ATS AS PARADIGM OF A *NEW WORLD ORDER*

We have reviewed the institutional failures that, notwithstanding this triumph of universalist discourse, have frustrated the practical realisation of global justice. To be sure, there has been a degree of success in holding individuals accountable for gross abuses. But the international human rights system has afforded few effective responses to the novel challenges presented by the emergence of the transnational corporation as a powerful global player. The ATS, expansively interpreted, functions as a surrogate for other, arguably more appropriate, international mechanisms. But for some scholars, including notably Anne-Marie Slaughter, the ATS is not a second-best option. It presents rather a paradigm of human rights enforcement in the new world order.[295] Slaughter renounces the internationalist dream of shared sovereignty invested in (and ultimately subsumed by) international institutions. These bodies have proven too unwieldy and politically divided to do the job. She sees contemporary global concerns as best addressed by horizontal 'networks': loose, co-operative arrangements spanning national borders between and among homologous state agencies spun off by disaggregating nation-states.[296]

Slaughter points to a variety of legal networks that span the globe, ranging from the International Organisation of Securities Commissioners to transnational bankruptcy protocols.[297] In the aggregate, these institutions and arrangements constitute the framework for an international rule of law, enforced, in the first instance, not by the International Court of Justice nor the International Criminal Court, nor by other traditional transnational institutions, but by interconnected municipal institutions.[298] Links between municipal court systems are built from the ground up, in the form of mundane procedural mechanisms such as co-coordinated international discovery,[299] and the application of doctrines like comity and *forum non conveniens.*[300] Judges in municipal systems exchange their decisions with foreign judges on the internet and at judicial conferences. Increasingly, they cite each other's

295 'The Real New World Order' *Foreign Affairs*, Vol 76, No. 5, 183 (1997) 194.

296 *A New World Order* (P.U.P. 2004) 10 (hereinafter, "*NWO*"). Slaughter, draws upon the work of Robert Keohane and Joseph Nye, 'Transnational Relations and International Organizations,' *World Politics* 27 (1974), 43 (defining *transgovernmental relations* as "sets of direct interactions among sub-units of different governments that are not controlled or closely guided by the policies of the cabinets or chief executives of those governments.").

297 *NWO* 96.

298 *Ibid.* 19.

299 *Ibid.* 85.

300 *Ibid.* 86ff (referring to "positive" comity, in the form of active collaboration by judges self-consciously seeking collective solutions in international litigation). See also A. M. SLAUGHTER, 'A Liberal Theory of International Law', (2000) 94 *American Society of International Law Proceedings* 240.

judgments,[301] fostering 'constitutional cross-fertilization' and generating an 'emerging global jurisprudence.'[302] NGOs and activists are increasingly taking the lead in fighting global human rights abuses, and are more likely to develop transnational litigation strategies using domestic courts than to approach UN organs:

> "Individual groups in nondemocratic countries... 'borrow' government institutions of democratic states to achieve a measure of justice they cannot obtain in their own countries. The court or regulatory agency of one state may be able to perform judicial or regulatory functions for the people of another. Victims of human rights violations, for example, in countries such as Argentina, Ethiopia, Haiti and the Philippines have sued for redress in the courts of the United States. ... More generally, a nongovernmental organisation seeking to prevent human rights violations can often circumvent their own government's corrupt legislature and politicized court by publicizing the plight of victims abroad and mobilizing a foreign court, legislature, or executive to take action."[303]

On a descriptive level, Slaughter's key insight – the disaggregation of the nation state, the emergence of semi-autonomous units, each with a quasi-autonomous 'foreign policy', the evolution of horizontal networks linking these units, and the development of quasi-privatised international human rights enforcement via civil actions – is undeniably compelling. Yet her model offers no solution to the legitimacy crisis generated by the expansive use of the ATS that she celebrates and seeks to generalise. What standards will a U.S. federal judge apply in deciding that a particular foreign legislature is 'corrupt', or that a foreign judiciary is 'politicised'? More to the point, how can such a determination escape impeachment in a world where the U.S. itself is regarded by many as an aggressive hegemon and a serial violator of human rights? (It should be deeply troubling to ATS proponents that the objections of the South African government strike a chord even in some who are in other settings ardently committed to bringing TNCs to book).

Slaughter's vision seems starry-eyed in a world riven by deep disagreements about the very meaning of human rights. To be sure, one can point to co-operative institutions, protocols and practices that bind the globe more closely than ever. But Slaughter's success stories represent either arrangements between states that share a broadly similar political culture,[304] or international co-ordination in technical fields.

---

301 *NWO* 71 ff. To the extent they are active participants in the global constitutional dialogue, the South African Constitutional Court and the Canadian Supreme Court have, according to Slaughter, "been highly influential, apparently more so than the U.S. Supreme Court and other older and more established constitutional courts." (*Ibid.* 74).

302 *Ibid.* 78.

303 'The Real World Order,' *Foreign Affairs*, Vol. 76, No. 5, 183 (1997) 174. Slaughter echoes the comments of two labour lawyers, who have commented that, in their field, "the efficacy of the law seems inversely related to its international character." J. CRAIG & S. LYNK, *Globalisation and the Future of Labour Law* (CUP 2006), at 145-46.

304 Slaughter heavily relies on the European Union as an example of international collaboration (E.g. *NWO* 157-59). (But does also (at 134), acknowledge the commonality of its constituents).

This is undoubtedly important, but also relatively undemanding precisely because moral and political issues are not directly at stake.[305] Co-operative networks are relatively readily achieved, precisely because differences in this area relate more to means than ends. Much more difficult is collaboration in areas implicating the meaning, scope and reach of fundamental rights, reflecting fundamental conflicts of value systems, rooted in competing (and perhaps incompatible), interests.[306] Slaughter's model offers limited prospects for closing the ideological and cultural gaps that international human rights aspires to bridge.[307] She suggests that the legitimacy of judges involved in transnational adjudication remains ultimately rooted in municipal systems.[308] But that only displaces the legitimacy problem from the global level to the municipal – where it remains chronically unresolved, in the form of the countermajoritarian dilemma. The democratic deficit that vitiates the accountability of municipal judges to the voters of their own jurisdictions is aggravated in the attempt to anchor the accountability of municipal courts in a 'hypothetical global constituency.'[309] Some contend the 'domestic' deficit is mitigated by the appointment process.[310] Whatever the merits of that argument it would be difficult to defend the foreign impact of decisions of U.S. courts on that basis. Others argue that judicial review at the domestic level is not really inconsistent with representative democracy – because judicially enforced fundamental political rights foster the indispensable

---

305 An ostensibly value-neutral technical arena such as transnational co-operation between law enforcement agencies may raise fundamental rule of law issues. Slaughter cites as an instance of "positive comity" the active co-operation between the U.S. Department of Justice and foreign enforcement agencies. ('The Real New World Order,' 76 *Foreign Affairs* (1997) 183, 188. As Neil Boister ('Transnational Penal Norm Transfer: The Transfer of Civil Forfeiture from the United States to South Africa as a Case in Point,' 16 *SACJ* 271 (2003) 285 n. 47), observes, a less than salubrious example of transnational inter-agency collaboration is offered by the case of Khalfan Khalis Mohamed, who was convicted in a New York federal court for his role in the bombing of U.S. embassies in East Africa, having been secretly rendered to the FBI at a Cape Town airport by South African law enforcement officers, in what the South African Constitutional Court was later to condemn as a disguised extradition. See *Mohamed v. The President of the Republic of South Africa* 2001 (3) SA 893 CC). Boister (at 293), argues that "those who purport to export the virtues of good governance and the rule of law should themselves be democratically accountable."

306 A point candidly acknowledged by Slaughter. (*NWO* 226).

307 Slaughter suggests that differences between judicial systems narrow as judges meet face to face both in informal and formal settings, and at international judicial conferences, establish peer groups and develop shared reputational standing. (NWO, 96-99; *The Global Community of Courts, 44 Harv. J. Int'l L.* 191 (2003).) But critics have wondered whether this amounts to anything more than elite consensus among a group who, by reason of class and cultural commonality, enjoy high pre-existing levels of agreement. See, K. ANDERSON, 'Squaring The Circle? Reconciling Sovereignty And Global Governance Through Global Government Networks,' 118 *Harv. L. Rev.* 1255 (2005) 1272.

308 *NWO* 82. ("When a developing international rule, as promulgated by a supranational tribunal, moves too far out of line with a prevailing domestic democratic consensus, the national courts will not follow.").

309 *NWO* at 242.

310 See D.L. DONOHO, 'Democratic Legitimacy in Human Right: The Future of International Decision-making,' 21 *Wis. Int'l L.* J1 (2003), 53 (noting that Supreme Court Justices "have overwhelmingly voted with the general political orientation of the administration that promoted them to the bench.").

conditions for meaningful representation.[311] But, even aside from the fact that there exists no international representative body, it begs the question to apply that rationale at the transnational level; what is at issue at the global level is precisely competing conceptions of what *counts* as democracy in general, and the preconditions therefore in particular.[312]

7 SAVING THE ATS: A MODEST PROPOSAL

Slaughter fails to furnish a normative basis for the expansion of the reach of municipal courts that she advocates. But hers is an instructive failure, for it forces us to face the intractable normative problems that haunt attempts to use domestic tribunals to enforce human rights in foreign countries. Until we can find a way around the democratic deficit – or, more realistically, devise a way to reveal the question itself as misplaced – prospects for anchoring the legitimacy of the ATS in domestic institutions are not good.[313]

In the meantime, those anxious to retain the ATS as an indispensable means (albeit a wholly inadequate one), of challenging the global impunity of TNCs might consider settling for a more humble program. On the one hand, judges must understand that reflexive obedience to executive whims not only undermines the credibility of the ATS but also flies in the face of the very separation of powers doctrine in which theories of judicial deference are founded. On the other hand, ATS proponents must learn that the untrammelled expansion of the reach of the ATS poses no less of a threat to the fragile credibility of the ATS as does judicial pandering. From that perspective, the ATS is best safeguarded if located firmly within a structure that comes, at least to an extent, pre-legitimated. From the pragmatic perspective of those who opt to defer (perhaps permanently) the labour of devising a justificatory metanarrative, one could do worse than begin with international law, a system that enjoys at least the rhetorical support of every member of the United Nations, and articulates the professed aspirations of many of the most powerful global elites.[314] It is to the law of international

311 See J.H. ELY, *Democracy and Distrust* (1980), 73-183.

312 Compare O.M. FISS, 'The Autonomy of Law', 26 *Yale J. Int'l L.* 517, 525-26 (2001) ("the international tribunals recently established to protect human rights remain unaccountable to the citizens of the world organized according to democratic principles, and thus should be seen as a loss for democracy even though these tribunals further justice").

313 L.M. SEIDMAN, 'Ambivalence and Accountability', 61 *S. Cal. L. Rev.* 1571, 1571-73 (1988) (noting that generations of political theorists and academic lawyers have struggled, unsuccessfully, with the countermajoritarian dilemma).

314 See D.F. ORENTLICHER, 'Whose Justice? Reconciling Universal Jurisdiction with Democratic Principles', 92 *Geo. L.J.* (2004) 1057, 1129 ("bystander justice" can best be implemented in a manner "likely to enhance, rather than undermine, democratic values", through treaties "and by accepting established rules of customary international law.").

jurisdiction in particular that one might turn to develop a conception of the ATS that embeds it in a widely supported international system, preserves its practical utility, and at the same time protects it from the dilution and delegitimation with which it is threatened.

7.1 THE ATS AND UNIVERSAL JURISDICTION

Much as the traditional territorial approach to jurisdiction was displaced in the early 20th century by an approach based upon state contacts, the latter has given way to a conception that, while reflecting both developments in substantive human rights law and the imperatives of globalisation, also recognises that the nation state remains the principal actor in the international system.[315]

If it is true that, although the ATS represents a 'unilateral exercise of the function of guardian of international values', it has not 'attracted the approbation of States generally',[316] that is probably attributable to the fact that U.S. courts have interpreted the ATS within the parameters of the law of universal jurisdiction, as set forth below.

7.1.1 The necessity of 'minimum contacts'

Cassese writes:

> "[U]niversality may be asserted subject to the condition that the alleged offender be on the territory of the prosecuting state. It would seem contrary to the logic of current state relations to authorize any state of the world to institute criminal proceedings ... against any foreigner or foreign state official allegedly culpable of serious international crimes."[317]

---

315 See *Arrest Warrant* case Joint Separate Opinion of Judges Higgins, Kooijmans and Buergenthal, para 47 (noting "movement is towards bases of jurisdiction other than territoriality.") See P. BERMAN, 'The Globalisation of Jurisdiction,' *U. Pa. Rev.* 311 (2002) 322.

316 *Arrest Warrant* case, (Joint Separate Opinion), para 48. Compare International Law Association, *Final Report on the Exercise of Universal Jurisdiction in Respect of Gross Human Rights Offences* (2000) at 3 (noting that U.S. exercises universal jurisdiction under the ATS "with some success.")

317 A. CASSESE, 'Is The Bell Tolling For Universality? A Plea For A Sensible Notion Of Universal Jurisdiction,' 1 J. *Int'l Crim. Just.* 589 (2003), 592-93 (the "notion of universality, postulated or advocated by, among others, the scholars behind the Princeton Project and three distinguished judges of the ICJ. may perhaps be reserved for the future, if and when international relations become more geared to the realization of universal values."); see also *Regina v. Bow Street Metropolitan Stipendiary Magistrate, Ex Parte Pinochet Ugarte* (No. 3) (Lord Millett) ("the limiting factor that prevents the exercise of extra-territorial criminal jurisdiction from amounting to an unwarranted interference with the internal affairs of another [S]tate is that, for the trial to be fully effective, the accused must be present in the forum State."); *United States v. Yunis,* 681 F. Supp. 896, 900 (D.C. Cir. 1988) ("jurisdiction is conferred in any forum *that obtains physical custody* of the perpetuator of certain offenses considered particularly heinous and harmful to humanity") (emphasis added). But see *Arrest Warrant Case* 54-58 (Van den Wyngaert, J. ad hoc, dissenting) (concluding that international law does not prohibit universal jurisdiction in absentia). As a matter of practice, pure universal jurisdiction is a rarity; the storm provoked by Belgian's statute providing therefore, leading ultimately

The ATS is automatically subject to this limitation to the extent that it operates within the parameters of U.S. federal jurisdiction, which, as we have seen, demands 'minimum contacts' between the defendant and the United States. *In absentia* jurisdiction could therefore never be exercised under the ATS.[318] It is true that U.S. courts have been willing to find 'minimum contacts' in relatively attenuated links between foreign corporations and the U.S. But that does not seem inappropriate. First, this recognises the extraordinary global reach of the modern TNC. Second, corporations routinely factor into their decisions as to whether to do business in a foreign state the extent to which they will be subject to forms of liability particular to that jurisdiction. There is no reason a British bank that chooses to open a New York branch should not weigh potential ATS exposure as a cost of doing business in the world's biggest economy. Third, it is difficult to argue that such an exercise of ATS jurisdiction offends the sovereignty of any foreign state. Considerations of sovereignty weigh on the other side of the equation in cases where a foreign corporation conducts non-trivial business on U.S. territory, it being an incident of the U.S.'s own sovereignty that Congress regulate foreign conduct of such corporations as it sees fit. To be sure, the manner in which the ATS is used to enforce such regulation may be conditioned both by authentic human rights concerns or by a cynical calculation of U.S. interests. It is the role of federal judges to ensure that the former is not subordinated to the latter.

7.1.2 Delimiting the ATS: subject-matter jurisdiction

The *Sosa* decision, despite its unfortunate failure to define the limits of foreign policy deference, does have the virtue of effectually disciplining the ATS within the strictures of international jurisdiction in a fashion that, properly construed, stands to eviscerate the rationale for such political intervention. Although the constraints of the law of international jurisdiction were implicit in Justice Souter's opinion, it was Justice Breyer, writing in concurrence, who articulated those considerations when he suggested that courts pose the following question in determining whether a particular ATS matter is actionable:

> "[W]hether the exercise of jurisdiction under the ATS is consistent with those notions of comity that lead each nation to respect the sovereign rights of other nations by limiting the reach of its laws and their enforcement?"[319]

---

to its withdrawal, is well known. But see *Arrest Warrant*, para 45 (joint separate opinion) ("a state is not obliged to legislate up to the full scope of jurisdiction allowed by international law").

318 DONOVAN AND ROBERTS ('The Emerging Recognition of Universal Civil Jurisdiction,' 100 *Am. J. Int'l L.* 142 (2006) 146) cannot be literally correct in their statement that "many ATS cases have involved conduct and parties that have no connection to the United States." The writers elsewhere (n. 23), acknowledge that ATS cases "can proceed without any connection to the United States *other than the transitory presence of the defendant at the time of service.*" (Emphasis supplied).

319 *Sosa*, 42 U.S. 692 at 761 (2004).

International norms, Justice Breyer held, could properly be enforced through the ATS where international law reflected 'substantive agreement' as to certain universally condemned behaviour.[320] But that was not enough. There needed also to be 'procedural agreement' that universal jurisdiction exists to 'prosecute a subset of that behavior.'[321] Such agreement, he held, existed with regard to torture, genocide, crimes against humanity, and war crimes.[322]

It might be argued that, insofar as ATS jurisdiction is civil, it need not be subject to the limitations of international criminal jurisdiction, so long as there is no coercive international enforcement.[323] But that cannot be correct, given the realities of modern international relations and globalised commerce. As we have already seen, an ATS decision may well have a very significant extraterritorial impact, even absent enforcement. Moreover, there does not exist the international consensus permitting broad extraterritorial civil jurisdiction corresponding to that in regard to criminal jurisdiction. Justice Breyer properly acknowledged this when he held that international civil jurisdiction was not inconsistent with comity – provided it paralleled criminal jurisdiction in substance.[324]

The decision of the majority of the Supreme Court comports with the international law requirement that universal jurisdiction be reserved for only the most heinous of international crimes – those which, to adopt the *Filartiga* analysis, violate 'specific, universal and obligatory' international law norms.[325] It seems eminently sensible that

---

320 *Ibid.*

321 *Ibid.*

322 *Ibid.* ("Allowing every nation's courts to adjudicate foreign conduct involving foreign parties in such cases will not significantly threaten the practical harmony that comity principles seek to protect.").

323 *S.S. "Lotus" (Fr. v. Turk.)*, 1927 PCIJ (ser. A) No. 10, at 18-19 (Sept. 7), available at <*http://www.icj-cij.org*>. See M. AKEHURST, *1972-73 British Yearbook Inter. Law* 45, 177 (arguing that customary international law imposes no limits on civil jurisdiction); Restatement (Third) of the Foreign Relations Law of the United States, para 404 comment b ("In general, jurisdiction on the basis of universal interests has been exercised in the form of criminal law, but international law does not preclude the application of non-criminal law on this basis, for example, by providing a remedy in tort or restitution for victims of piracy.").

324 *Ibid.* ("[C]riminal courts of many nations combine civil and criminal proceedings, allowing those injured by criminal conduct to be represented, and to recover damages, in the criminal proceeding itself). See also N. NORBERG, 'The U.S. Supreme Court Affirms the Filártiga Paradigm' 4 *J. Int. Crim Justice* (2006), 387, 389 ("tort litigation is often used in the United States for public policy reasons in areas governed by criminal law in other countries."). All of that being said, inasmuch as civil suits are not constrained by prosecutorial discretion, it is probably desirable that courts carefully scrutinise ATS complaints to weed out bad faith litigation. See, e.g., *Zapata v. Quinn*, 707 F.2d 691 (2d Cir. 1983) (dismissing claim that payment of lottery winnings in annuity instead of a lump sum violated law of nations). See *Sosa*, 542 U.S. 692, 727 (2004) (noting concern over enforcement of ATS "without the check imposed by prosecutorial discretion"). Compare *Arrest Warrant* case, Joint Separate Opinion, para 50 (noting importance of role of prosecutor "who acts in full independence, without links to or control by the government of the State"); Steven R. Ratner, 'Belgium's War Crimes Statute: A Postmortem,' 97 *AJIL* 888, 896 (2003) (noting danger of allowing private parties to control lawsuits without facing costs).

325 *Filartiga*, 630 F.2d at 888.

domestic courts avoid vindicating rights violations, even those that are widely recognised, which cannot plausibly be said to be of indisputably universal concern. The facts of *Sosa* itself – involving a brief unlawful detention of an individual – provide a good example of a violation that cannot properly be addressed by the ATS. If plaintiffs were to succeed in such a case, that would, as Justice Souter noted, 'support a cause of action in federal court for any [unlawful] arrest, anywhere in the world.'[326]

Insisting that U.S. courts do not move out ahead of a very well-established international consensus answers at least some objections to judicial imperialism. (It has been recognised, for example, that U.S. environmental standards cannot be internationally imposed).[327] I would suggest several related but distinct respects in which U.S. courts should exercise particular caution in adjudicating ATS cases. Courts should eschew a definition of aiding and abetting liability that distributes responsibility so broadly that a corporation that merely sells, for example, ordinary consumer products into a country with an oppressive government, is exposed to the ATS. Moreover, U.S. courts enforcing the ATS should, to the extent practicable, apply international law procedural norms, rather than what might be seen by non-Americans as eccentric protocols.[328]

At the level of substance, courts should continue to exercise caution in defining the scope of conduct which may form the basis for an ATS complaint. For example, given the current state of relevant international norms, courts should resist demands that socio-economic rights be actionable. It has been argued that this would give to corporations a free pass in precisely the area in which they are most commonly delinquent.[329] Commentators suggest that the fact that Shell has built roads and hospitals to support its oil facilities in the Niger Delta demonstrates that it has the

---

326 *Sosa* at 736.

327 *Aguinda*, 142 F. Supp. 2d at 552 (citing *Beanal v. Freeport-McMoran, Inc.*, 197 F.3d 161, 167 (5th Cir. 1999)) (federal courts "should exercise extreme caution when adjudicating environmental claims under international law to ensure that environmental policies of the United States do not displace environmental policies of other governments.").

328 Compare D.F. DONOVAN, A. ROBERTS, 'The Emerging Recognition of Universal Civil Jurisdiction,' 100 *Am. J. Int'l L.* 142 (2006) 144-45 ("although the sanctionable conduct may be defined by international law, national law will inevitably influence enforcement. . . in the civil sphere, for example, by the application of national law procedures, such as class actions, and remedies, such as moral or punitive damages").

329 C. SCOTT, Multinational Enterprises and Emergent Jurisprudence on Violations of Economic, Social and Cultural Rights, in *Economic, Social and Cultural Rights* 563 (Asbjørn Eide et al. eds., 2d ed. 2001). See P. MACKLEM, 'Indigenous Rights and Multinational Corporations in International Law,' 24 *Hastings Int'l & Comp. L. Rev.* 475, 477 (2001).

capacity[330] to be subject to socio-economic duties in its foreign operations.[331] But the dilution and legitimacy effects we have already discussed apply also with respect to the attempt to enforce socio-economic rights under the ATS. Worse, such an extension of the ATS may expand the influence of TNCs in the developing world, in the process of justifying government's default. TNCs will inevitably claim powers corresponding to their increased responsibilities. As one writer puts it, 'a corporation's assumption of responsibility for the health care or education of a developing country's citizenry represents at least as much a perversion of the corporation's function as it does an abdication of responsibility by the state.'[332]

Finally, the ATS may be kept within proper bounds through the judicious use of the *forum non conveniens* doctrine, a limitation which shares the advantages of the exhaustion requirement, but is more flexible and context-sensitive in application.[333]

Over and above the legitimacy considerations we have been discussing, the repatriation of human rights cases has the potential to foster the development of judicial systems responsive to human rights in developing countries. All things considered, it is far more satisfactory that host country courts adjudicate a complaint against foreign corporations than that the matter be exported to distant tribunals, which are always subject to pressures that threaten to render such litigation both illegitimate and ineffectual. Just as, at its best, the FCPA complements the ATS, by protecting lines of accountability between governments and the people, the ATS finds its best justification if seen as an aspect of the U.S. federal court system's regulation of corporations that choose to do business in the U.S., so as to protect fundamental human rights, while at the same time promoting self-government and good governance around the world.

---

330 Compare A. CLAPHAM, *Human Rights Obligations of Non-State Actors* (OUP 2006), 71 (considering whether non-state entity has the requisite legal capacity "directly to acquire rights and obligations under international law," and "in what circumstances do these actors have the capacity to be a party to a claim (either as a claimant or as a defendant) at the international level.").

331 KINLEY, 'From Talk To Walk: The Emergence Of Human Rights Responsibilities For Corporations At International Law,' 44 *Va. J. Int'l L.* 931 (2004) n. 193 (citing N. HERTZ, *The Silent Takeover: Global Capitalism and the Death of Democracy* 220-21 (2001)); D.M. CHIRWA, 'The Right To Health In International Law: Its Implications for The Obligations of State and Non-State Actors In Ensuring Access to Essential Medicine' (2003) *SAJHR* 541, 563.).

332 Hon. Delissa A. Ridgeway & Mariya A. Talib, 'Globalization And Development – Free Trade, Foreign Aid, Investment And The Rule Of Law,' 33 *Cal. Western Int'l L.J.* 325, 332 (2003); L. CATÁ BACKER, 'Multinational Corporations, Transnational Law: The United Nations' Norms On The Responsibilities Of Transnational Corporations As A Harbinger Of Corporate Social Responsibility In International Law,' 37 *Colum. Hum. Rts. L. Rev.* 287, 371 (2006).

333 See Rome Statute of the ICC, Art 17(1) (embodying principle of complementarity). See D.F. ORENTLICHER, 'Whose Justice? Reconciling Universal Jurisdiction with Democratic Principles', 920 *Geo. L.J.* (2004) 1057, 1112-13 ("courts should respect the right of the 'home state' to prosecute if it is willing and able", and "should allow affected states to present their governments' views.") Of course, both of these measures are themselves potentially problematic. The first requires a court to evaluate the standard of justice in the home state, a judgment that will in itself be controversial. As for the second, difficulties associated with accomodating the views of foreign governments are exemplified in *Apartheid Litigation.*

Against that background, the limits upon the scope and reach of the ATS imposed in *Sosa* deserve to be applauded rather than deplored, by those who look to the statute as an important means of protecting human rights internationally. These judicially imposed constraints help preserve and legitimate the statute to do its vital work in cases where, as in the *Apartheid* litigation, systemic failure and politically inspired interventions by the U.S. and the South African governments threaten to immunise corporations from allegations that they actively supported a universally condemned system of oppression.

PART D: REPARATIONS CLAIMS PURSUED AT HOME

REDRESS FOR SLAVERY – THE AFRICAN-AMERICAN STRUGGLE

ROY L. BROOKS

1 INTRODUCTION

For almost two-and-one-half centuries, the US government (by which I mean not only the republic formed under the Constitution of 1787, but also its predecessor regimes) forced millions of black Africans and their descendants ('African Americans') into a brutal system of human bondage. Once captured in Africa, these innocent people were packed like sardines into ships for the hellish journey to what is now the US. Many died during the voyage, some by suffocation from being shackled in a coffin-size space for a long period of time and others by throwing themselves into the ocean. Mothers sometimes jumped with babies in arms. Those unlucky to survive the ordeal faced more hardships upon arriving in the US. The infamous auction block, for example, often broke up families as each member was sold to a different plantation owner. Plantation life for the vast majority of African Americans was sheer pain: backbreaking work, suffering, humiliation, and death from dawn to dusk. All this so that whites in the US could make a buck.[1]

This cruel attempt to bestialise human beings – what is generally referred to as 'chattel slavery'[2] – was quite different from prior practices of slavery dating back to Mesopotamia. Most significantly, American slavery, like slavery in other parts of the New World, injected the element of colour into the master-slave relationship. Colour became the social marker of slavery. As Alexis de Tocqueville noted: 'Among the ancients, the slave belonged to the same race as his master.'[3] Among the Africans as

---

1 See, e.g., Roy L. Brooks, "Slave Narratives," in *When Sorry Isn't Enough: The Controversy over Apologies and Reparations for Human Injustice*," Roy L. Brooks, ed. (New York: New York University Press, 1999), pp. 327-332 (sources cited therein); Franklin, John Hope, and Alfred A. Moss, Jr., *From Slavery to Freedom: A History of Negro Americans*. 6th ed. (New York: Alfred A. Knopf, 1988), pp. 1-180; Charles Johnson, *Middle Passage* (New York: Penguin Books, 1990).

2 See David Brion Davis, *In the Image of God: Religion, Moral Values, and Our Heritage of Slavery* (New Haven: Yale University Press, 2001), pp. 134-135. See Orlando Patterson, *Slavery and Social Death: A Comparative Study* (Cambridge: Harvard University Press, 1982), p. 96.

3 Alexis de Tocqueville, *Democracy in America*, Harvey C. Mansfield and Delba Winthrop, ed. and trans. (Chicago: University of Chicago Press, 2000), p. 327.

well, the slave belonged to the same race as his master. But in the Americas, the slave belonged to a *different* race from that of his master. When colour became the social marker of slavery, it destroyed the ancient prospect that a slave could one day become a respected teacher, an important statesman or even his master's master. Nathaniel Weyl summarises the social construction of slavery in ancient times:

> "[Roman] slaves provided, to a varying degree in different periods, much of the brain power of the Empire. Slaves brought Greek culture to the Roman *nouveaux riches*. Slaves and freedmen dominated most of the free professions. Those who gained their freedom served, especially during the reigns of Caligula, Claudius and Nero, as powerful elements in the managerial elite which ruled the Roman world. This bureaucracy of freedmen and slaves was depicted by Suetonius, Petronius and others as gross, uncouth, degenerate and money-mad, but those who drew the caricature were linked to the envious remnant of a dying aristocracy. . . . Enfranchisement was frequent and, in Cicero's opinion, a hard-working slave could buy his freedom in six years."[4]

With colour, or 'race,' as the social marker of slavery, pro-slavery Americans and their supporters had a visible way to justify slavery. This was no small matter, for even pro-slavery Americans knew they had to find a way to explain away a glaring contradiction – human bondage in a country founded on freedom (which is sometimes referred to as the 'peculiar institution'). The desire to strike it rich, which was the main motivation for slavery, lacked moral weight to justify the enslavement of human beings. So pro-slavery Americans drew upon the phenotypical differences between whites and African Americans as the basis for justifying the peculiar institution. They conjured up a race-specific ideology of condemnation, a theory that African Americans were by nature inferior to whites. The theory of racial inferiority was articulated by the US Supreme Court in *Dred Scott v. Sanford* (1857). In that case, the Court determined that African Americans were 'regarded as beings of an inferior order . . . unfit to associate with the white race' and, as such, 'they had no rights which the white man was bound to respect.'[5] Accordingly, the Court ruled, 'the negro might justly and lawfully be reduced to slavery for his benefit.'[6]

So resilient was this racist ideology that it has outlived slavery itself. The theory of African American inferiority today is articulated less as a biological imperative than as a cultural construct. In the US today, race still matters.[7]

Another very important aspect of American slavery that cannot be gainsaid or ignored is the heightened culpability of the founders of the US. The 'founding fathers' breathed new life into a morally moribund institution. 'By the eve of the American

4 Nathaniel, Weyl, *The Negro in American Civilization*. Washington, D.C.: Public Affairs Press, 1960), pp. 3-4, 5. See Ludwig Friedlaender, *Roman Life and Manners Under the Early Empire*, vol. I (London: Routledge, 1928), pp. 33-70.

5 *Dred Scott v. Sandford*, 60 U.S. (19 How.) 393, 408 (1857).

6 *Ibid.*

7 See, e.g., Cornel West, *Race Matters* (Boston: Beacon Press, 1993).

Revolution,' David Brion Davis observes, 'there was a remarkable convergence of culture and intellectual developments which at once undercut traditional rationalizations for slavery and offered new ways of identifying with its victims.'[8]

When slavery ended in the US in 1865 after a bloody civil war, it did not fold into a system of racial equality for African Americans. Instead, slavery took on a different look. After a ten-year period of Reconstruction, which brought tangible rights to African Americans, slavery was transformed into a regime of racially subordinating laws in the southern portion of the US, and racially restrictive social norms in the northern portion of the country. In his years of retirement, US President Ulysses Grant (the Union general who led the north to victory in the Civil War) wrote with uncommon candor about the true objectives of southern whites in particular in the aftermath of slavery. Southern whites 'by force and terror [intended] to . . . deprive colored citizens of the right to . . . a free ballot; to suppress schools in which colored children were taught, and to reduce the colored people to *a condition closely akin to that of slavery*.'[9] This system of racial hegemony (called 'Jim Crow') ended in 1972 with the passage of a federal law, the Equal Employment Opportunity Act of 1972, prohibiting racial discrimination and segregation in state and local employment markets.[10] This law capped a decade of federal civil rights legislation that expunged Jim Crow from the laws of the US.[11]

Thus, the atrocities of slavery and Jim Crow are not unrelated. Slavery created and Jim Crow sustained capital deficiencies within African-American society. These deficiencies include basic capital (meaning the denial of life, liberty, and human dignity), financial capital (consisting of labour, property, and investments), human capital (such as formal education, skills, and talent), and social capital (the way in which a group is viewed by other groups within the society and the ability to get things done).[12] As a result of these capital deficiencies, African Americans remain at the low end of the socioeconomic ladder in the US.

African Americans, then, continue to feel the effects of almost four centuries of racial oppression. Because of this, many Americans on both sides of the colour line believe the US government and others involved in the perpetration of these atrocities

---

8 Davis, *In the Image of God*, p. 133.

9 Philip B. Kunhardt, Jr., Philip B. Kunhardt, III, and Philip W. Kunhardt, *The American President* (New York: Riverhead Books, 1999), p. 28 (emphasis added).

10 See *Hazelwood School District v. United States*, 433 U.S. 299, 309 (1977); Roy L. Brooks, "Use of the Civil Rights Acts of 1866 and 1871 to Redress Employment Discrimination," *Cornell Law Review* 62 (1977): 258, 259, 283.

11 See generally Roy L. Brooks, Gilbert Paul Carrasco, and Michael Selmi, *Civil Rights Litigation: Cases and Perspectives* 3d edition (Durham: Carolina Academic Press, 2005).

12 See generally Glenn C. Loury, "A Dynamic Theory of Racial Income Differences," in *Women, Minorities and Employment Discrimination*, P.A. Wallace and A. Lamond, eds. (Lexington, Mass.: Lexington Books, 1977); Glenn C. Loury, *The Anatomy of Racial Inequality* (Cambridge: Harvard University Press, 2002).

should provide some form of redress to the current descendants of slaves. The concerted effort among Americans to seek redress for slavery and Jim Crow (hereinafter collectively referred to as 'slave redress') is known in the US as the 'Black Redress Movement' (or BRM). The BRM is not a movement of recent vintage. Claims for redress predate the Civil War and have been asserted by every succeeding generation of African Americans. But the claims asserted today have become more sophisticated and urgent.

After outlining the contours of the history of the BRM, I shall discuss the modern arguments made in support of redress. My main ambition here is to focus on the salient features of two rival perspectives on slave redress: the 'tort model' and the 'atonement model.' These models frame the modern African-American struggle for slave redress.

2 SHORT HISTORY OF BLACK REDRESS MOVEMENT

The first recorded effort to seek redress for slavery came at the time of the Revolutionary War. It came in the form of a request for repatriation to Africa. Some free blacks believed the government should free the slaves and repatriate both slaves and free blacks to their home land. One of the leading proponents of this view was Paul Cuffe, an African American born free in 1759 in Massachusetts. Cuffe viewed repatriation to Africa as a form of slave redress. He financed his own return to Africa in 1816, still committed to the belief in a government-financed program of repatriation. The federal government did in fact finance repatriation for a small group of free blacks in 1822 through the American Colonization Society. However, repatriation was not what most blacks wanted. Furthermore, the American Colonization Society did not have the best interest of blacks at heart.[13]

After the Civil War and prior to Reconstruction, former slaves were left penniless and defenceless. Redress legislation was viewed as a way to deal with such widespread economic privation. The claim for redress was based on a federal promise of 'forty

---

[13] See Robert Johnson, Jr., "Repatriation as Reparations for Slavery and Jim-Crowism," in *When Sorry Isn't Enough*, pp. 428-29. For a critical analysis of the repatriation movement from the nineteenth century through the end of the twentieth century, see Roy L. Brooks, *Integration or Separation? A Strategy for Racial Equality* (Cambridge: Harvard University Press, 1996), pp. 156-67. Although there were other efforts to seek redress for slavery during the antebellum period, most of the effort and energy of the anti-slavery forces were understandably directed toward manumission. James Grahame castigated the federal government and its citizens, both North and South, for not "redressing long and enormous injustice without any atoning sacrifice or reparatory expense, [for not] restoring and elevating . . . without any surrender of interest or convenience, the rights and the dignity of a numerous race of men whom they and their fathers have ruined and degraded." James Grahame, "Why the North and South Should Have Apologized," in *When Sorry Isn't Enough*, p. 349.

acres and a mule.' This unfulfilled promise originated in General Sherman's Special Field Order No. 15 issued near the end of the Civil War.[14] In a recent lawsuit, a federal district court judge, Paul L. Friedman, explained what happened:

> "As the Civil War drew to a close, the United States government promised to sell or lease to [black] farmers parcels of unoccupied land and land that had been confiscated by the Union during the war, and it promised the loan of a federal government mule to plow that land. Some African Americans took advantage of these programs and either bought or leased parcels of land. During Reconstruction, however, President Andrew Johnson rescinded the promise. Much of the promised land that had been leased to African American farmers was taken away and returned to Confederate loyalists. For most African Americans, the promise of forty acres and a mule was never kept."[15]

In 1890, an 'Ex-slave Pension and Bounty Bill' was introduced in Congress by Republicans. The Bill provided a maximum payment of $15 per month and a maximum bounty of $500 for each ex-slave. Unfortunately, the Bill was never enacted into law. Congress rejected the Bill on the ground that, *inter alia*, the pensions were too large a financial burden on taxpayers. Some members of Congress also believed that education was the only way to help the ex-slaves.[16]

Since the post-bellum period, each generation of African Americans has asserted the claim for redress. In most instances, the redress claim has been framed in the form of monetary redress. African American leaders as diverse as Marcus Garvey (who believed in racial separation) and Martin Luther King (who believed in racial integration) have called for reparations. And today, proponents of reparations include such diverse African Americans as Jesse Jackson, Louis Farakan, the NAACP (the oldest civil rights organisation in the USA), and former Secretary of State Colin Powell. What this tells us is that not only does the redress claim enjoy broad support among African Americans, but it also has historical pedigree – that is, it is not being raised for the first time some 140 years after slavery.

The year 1989 was a watershed year in the history of the BRM. In that year, Congressman John Conyers (Democrat, Michigan) introduced a slave redress Bill in Congress. Given the name H.R. 40 in recognition of the government's broken promise of 'forty acres and a mule,' this Bill calls for the creation of a commission to study the question of slave redress. It does not request any particular form of redress, but merely

---

14 See "Special Field Order No. 15," in *When Sorry Isn't Enough*, p. 365.

15 *Pigford v. Glickman*, 185 F. R. D. 82, 85 (D. C. D. C., 1999).

16 See David W. Blight, "If You Don't Tell it Like it Was, It Can Never Be As it Ought to Be," Keynote Talk, delivered at Conference on Yale and Slavery, September 27, 2002, available at http://www.yale.edu/glc/events/memory.htm., pp. 9-10. See also Deadria C. Farmer-Paellmann, "Excerpt from *Black Exodus: The Ex-Slave Pension Movement Reader*" in *Should America Pay? Slavery and the Raging Debate on Reparations* Raymond A. Winbush, ed. (New York: HarperCollins Publishers, 2003), p. 25.

asks that the commission study the redress issue. Despite these features, the Bill has never even been voted out of its congressional subcommittee. Consequently Congress, never having had the redress Bill brought before it for formal action, has never voted on it.[17]

HR 40 marks the beginning of the modern redress movement for slavery. The Bill was inspired by the Civil Liberties Act, which Congress enacted in 1988. This legislation reflects the growing global concern for human rights since the end of the Holocaust. Pursuant to that spirit, the Civil Liberties Act provides redress for Japanese Americans who were unjustly interned by their own government (the US) during World War II. The Act contains a US apology for internment and solidifies that apology by providing various forms of reparations, including $20,000 payable to each internee.[18]

Inspired by the Civil Liberties Act, African Americans have stepped up their longstanding claim for slave redress. Two interesting but contraposed perspectives or approaches to slave redress have emerged out of this activity. These redress models are discussed next.

3 REDRESS MODELS

There are two seemingly contraposed approaches to slave redress reflected in the US today. The first paradigm may be called the 'tort model,' and the second the 'atonement model.' Both models have distinct features, the contours of which are discussed in this section. A more extensive treatment of both approaches to slave redress is provided elsewhere.[19]

4 TORT MODEL

The tort model seeks to obtain slave redress without an apology from the perpetrator of the atrocities as a precondition for the tender of such redress. In this respect, the tort model is similar to a civil settlement wherein the defendant pays up without admitting to any liability. This approach to slave redress can operate within the legislative context, but it is pursued largely through litigation.

Some adjudicatory expressions of the tort model have asked for an apology in the pleadings. A true apology cannot, however, come at the end of the litigation gun.

---

17 H.R. 40, Section2 (b) (3) published in 143 Cong. Rec. E1548-E1549, 105th Cong., 1st Sess. (July 29, 1997).

18 For a discussion of the Japanese-American Redress Movement, see generally, *When Sorry Isn't Enough*, part 4 (sources cited therein).

19 I develop both models extensively in Roy L. Brooks, *Atonement and Forgiveness: A New Model for Black Reparations* (Berkeley: University of California Press, 2004).

Moreover, a genuine apology is more complicated than simply saying 'I'm sorry', as my discussion of the atonement model will show in due course. In addition, a genuine apology places the matter of forgiveness on the table. The question of forgiveness is conspicuously absent from the public discourse on the tort model in the US. Because it does not entertain the question of forgiveness, the tort model demonstrates an indisposition toward the larger question of racial reconciliation in the US.

Given the fact that litigation is the principal expression of the tort model, it may be useful to focus on that side of the model. Slave-redress lawsuits, the first of which was brought by African Americans in 1917, may be divided into two types of legal actions. The first may be called 'public actions' and the second 'private actions.' To date, none of these actions have survived pre-trial dismissal.

Public actions are brought against the government, typically the federal government, or a governmental agency. They are usually based upon *lex scripto*, the written law (statutory or constitutional law). *Cato v. United States*[20] is a somewhat typical public action.

In *Cato*, plaintiffs sought 'compensation of $100,000,000 for forced ancestral indoctrination into a foreign society; kidnapping of ancestors from Africa; forced labor; break-up of families; removal of traditional values; deprivations of freedom; and imposition of oppression, intimidation, miseducation, and lack of information about various aspects of their indigenous character.' Plaintiffs also requested that the court 'order an acknowledgment of the injustice of slavery in the United States and in the 13 American colonies between 1619 and 1865, as well as of the existence of discrimination against freed slaves and their descendants from the end of the Civil War to the present.' In addition, they sought 'an apology from the United States.'[21]

Both the trial court and the appellate court threw out the complaint. The former did so on the ground that plaintiffs' allegations did not translate into legally actionable harms or refer to any basis for the exercise of federal jurisdiction. On appeal, counsel for plaintiffs argued that the Thirteenth Amendment to the US Constitution provided a right of action against the US government for the harms enumerated in the complaint. Furthermore, the discrimination alleged in the complaint was fresh in that it was 'continuing.' Finally, counsel argued that sovereign immunity does not bar a Thirteenth-Amendment action against the federal government, 'otherwise, the Thirteenth Amendment's obligation is meaningless.'[22] The appellate court rejected each of these arguments on several grounds.

First, it ruled that the plaintiffs lacked standing to assert their constitutional claim, which the court read as a claim 'based on the stigmatizing injury to all African Americans caused by racial discrimination.' Under the doctrine of standing, the

---

20 70 F.3d 1103 (9th Cir. 1995).

21 *Ibid.* p. 1106.

22 *Ibid.* p. 1110.

plaintiff must have a tangible, personal injury traceable to the defendant's conduct. 'Without a concrete, personal injury that is not abstract and that is fairly traceable to the government conduct that she challenges as unconstitutional, Cato lacks standing,' the court ruled.[23] This claim was also defective, the court held, because it 'does not trace the presence of discrimination and its harm to the United States.'[24] Quite frankly, that was a silly ruling because slavery and the racial subordination and stigmatisation that followed in its wake would not have been possible without the federal government's complete complicity. The US Constitution created a 'slaveholding republic' prior to the Civil War and, thereafter, authorised a regime of racial apartheid under the separate-but-equal, or Jim Crow, doctrine. Federal law, in short, mandated and sanctioned '[racial] discrimination and its harms' in the United States.[25]

Next, the court raised the sovereign immunity question. It ruled that the Thirteenth Amendment itself is not a jurisdictional, or 'self-enforcing', provision. Unless a Thirteenth-Amendment claim can be asserted pursuant to a jurisdictional statute – the grant of jurisdiction carrying with it a waiver of sovereign immunity – the claim is without jurisdiction. The most likely jurisdictional statute for tort actions against the United States, the court noted, is the Federal Torts Claims Act (FTCA). The FTCA vests the Court of Claims with jurisdiction (and, hence, waives sovereign immunity) for tort claims against the federal government so long as those claims accrue on or after January 1, 1945 and are brought within two years after their occurrence.[26] Constitutional tort claims do not, however, fall within the FTCA, the court ruled.[27] But why not, then, use the Tucker Act, which applies to constitutional and statutory tort claims against the United States, but not to property claims? The court did not consider this question, but it did note another statute that waives sovereign immunity; namely the Administrative Procedures Act. This Act was, however, inapplicable, the court ruled, because it only applies to lawsuits seeking 'other than money damages' whereas plaintiffs were seeking damages.[28]

Finally, the court rejected plaintiffs' constitutional claim on nonjusticiability grounds. The appellate court, agreeing with the district court, ruled that the 'legisla-

---

23 *Ibid.* p. 1109.

24 *Ibid.*

25 See *Bolling v. Sharpe*, 347 U.S. 497 (1954) (dealing with federal law mandating school segregation in Washington, D.C.). For a discussion of the current historical perspective on the Constitution and the constitutional provisions that recognised the institution of slavery, see, e.g., Paul Finkelman, *Slavery and the Founders: Race and Liberty in the Age of Jefferson* 2d edition (Armonk, N.Y.: M.E. Sharpe, 1996.), pp. 3-36; Ira Berlin, "North of Slavery: Black People in a Slaveholding Republic," delivered at Conference on Yale, New Haven, and American Slavery (Yale University, September 27, 2002).

26 *Cato*, 70 F.3d at 1106 (citing 28 U.S.C. § § 1346(b) (FTCA) and 2401(b) (applicable statute of limitations)).

27 *Ibid.* pp. 1110-11.

28 *Ibid.* p. 1111 (*citing* 5 U.S.C. § 702).

ture, rather than the judiciary, is the appropriate forum for plaintiff's grievances.'[29] It is, however, difficult to take the court's nonjusticiability argument seriously given the fact that the federal courts have long been thrown into the political thicket by cases like *Brown v. Board of Education*.[30] The question of school desegregation in the era of Jim Crow, which *Brown* outlawed, was as much a political question as it was a legal or moral one.[31]

In contrast to public actions, private actions are brought not against the government but against wealthy white families or, more likely, large corporations that are successors-in-interest to slaveholding or slave-dealing corporations. Corporate defendants are alleged to have profited from slavery, such as by insuring slaveholders against the loss of slave property, by taking slaves as collateral for loans or by using slaves to manufacture their products. Private actions are based mainly on *lex non scripto*, the unwritten law, both domestic (such as quasi-contract or unjust enrichment) and international (such as the right to be free from torture, rape, and slave labour). Unlike public actions, which seek to spread the cost of slavery and Jim Crow among all Americans, private actions target the direct beneficiaries of slavery. Most private actions have been filed against corporations rather than against white families. Corporations named in these dozen or so private actions include commercial banks (such as Fleet Boston Financial Corporation), investment banks (such as J.P. Morgan Chase & Co., Lehman Brothers Holdings, Inc., and Brown Brothers Harriman), tobacco companies (such as R.J. Reynolds Tobacco Holdings, Inc., Brown & Williamson Tobacco Corp., and Liggett Group, which is now indirectly owned by Vector Group Ltd.), insurance companies (such as Aetna, Inc., Lloyds of London, and American International Group), railroads (such as CSX, Union Pacific, and Norfolk Southern Corp.), and textile companies (such as Westpoint Stevens, Inc.). Thus, private actions concentrate on many corporate sectors. Several of these cases were consolidated in one court under the title of *In re African-American Slave Descendants Litigation*.[32] These cases alleged that, 'Defendants, through their predecessors in interest, conspired and/or aided and abetted with slave traders, with each other and other entities and institutions . . . and other unnamed entities and/or financial institutions to commit and/or knowingly facilitate crimes against humanity, and to further illicitly profit from slave labor.'[33] These allegations gave rise to legal claims based primarily on customary international law and Anglo-American common law – *lex non scripto* (the unwritten law). Among the crimes against humanity under international human rights law alleged in the complaints were violations of the right

---

29 *Ibid.* p. 1105.

30 347 U.S. 483 (1954).

31 See Roy L. Brooks, *Integration or Separation? A Strategy for Racial Equality*10-16 (1996)..

32 See *In re* African-American Slave Descendants Litigation, 304 F. Supp. 2d 1027 (N.D. Ill. 2004). See further the chapter in this book by Diane Sammons at pages 315-358.

33 *Ibid.* pp 1041-42.

to be free of torture, rape, starvation, physical and mental abuse, summary execution, and forced labour. Common law claims included *quantum meruit*, conversion, and unjust enrichment. Thus, the essential claim was that even though slavery may have been legal as a matter of *lex scripto* (the written law), slavery, or some aspects of it, was illegal as a matter of *lex non scripto*, domestic as well as international law.[34]

The defendants in *In re African-American Slave Descendants Litigation* filed four motions, arguing that the complaint should be dismissed because: '(1) Plaintiffs' claims fall short of both constitutional and prudential standing requirements; (2) Plaintiffs' claims present a non-justiciable political question; (3) Plaintiffs' claims fail to state any cognizable claim; and (4) all of Plaintiffs' claims are time-barred.'[35] As to the first motion, the court ruled that plaintiffs lacked standing on constitutional grounds because although 'standing can be supported by a very slender reed of injury,'[36] that "slender reed' must still have its roots in the soil of an injury personal to the Plaintiffs, not a 'derivative harm' uprooted from the soil of another's injury.'[37] In addition, the court ruled that plaintiffs lacked standing based on prudential limitations placed on the exercise of federal jurisdiction, because 'plaintiffs impermissibly attempt[ed] to assert the legal rights of absent third parties'[38] – namely, the dead slaves – and because 'plaintiffs impermissibly attempt[ed] to litigate a generalized grievance which is best addressed in the representative branches.'[39] The court granted the remaining three motions on the basis of the political question doctrine, the complaint's failure to state a claim upon which relief could be granted, and the statute of limitations.[40] As of this date, no private action has survived a pre-trial challenge.

Whether public action or private action, slave redress cases present a normative challenge to the US legal system. They make the following argument collectively: If the slave descendants' claims are morally compelling, then they *must* be cognisable under US law, otherwise the extant law stands as the present incarnation of America's worst atrocity and the corrupt laws that made it possible. These cases, in other words, present a credibility check on US law no less important than the Supreme Court's landmark school desegregation case of *Brown v. Board of Education*.[41]

The tort model sits at the centre of the current discussion of slave redress in the US. It is, in fact, the dominant redress model in the BRM. Yet, the tort model may not provide the best approach to slave redress. An emerging model, which is more sophisticated than the tort model, is in fact challenging the latter's legitimacy.

---

34 See *Ibid.* pp. 1042-44..
35 *Ibid.* p. 1044.
36 *Ibid.* p. 1051 (citing 13 Charles Allen Wright, Arthur R. Miller & Edward H. Cooper, *Federal Practice and Procedure* § 3531.4 (2d ed. 1984)).
37 *Ibid.*
38 *Ibid.* p. 1052.
39 *Ibid.* p. 1053.
40 *Ibid.* pp. 1054-75.
41 347 U.S. 483 (1954).

5 ATONEMENT MODEL

Although less well known in the US than the tort model, the atonement model is the only approach to redress that has enjoyed a degree of success both in the US and in other countries. It has yet to be applied to slave redress, however. The atonement model offers a legislative approach to slave redress – a particular type of legislative action. First and foremost, the atonement model is centered around the perpetrator's atonement for the commission of an atrocity, whether recent or ancient, and the potential for reconciliation between the perpetrator and its victims that flows from such atonement.

More generally, the atonement model is crafted from a post-Holocaust spirit of heightened morality, identity between victim and perpetrator, egalitarianism, and restorative justice. Applied to slavery and Jim Crow, this redress model aligns the victims of these US atrocities with the victims of other historic acts of human injustice, including the victims of Nazi persecution, the 'Comfort Women' who suffered unspeakable sexual slavery, mutilation, and in many cases death at the hands of the Japanese Imperial Army during World War II, the victims of Apartheid in South Africa, and Japanese Americans to whom the US government atoned in 1988 for unjust internment during the Second World War.[42]

The atonement model has three components – apology, reparations, and forgiveness. Apology in response to an atrocity 'is more complex than 'contrition chic', or the canonization of sentimentality.'[43] Apology is a matrix of acknowledgment, redemption, and mourning that 'improves the national spirit and health.'[44] When the perpetrator of an atrocity apologises, he, she or it (1) confesses the deed, (2) admits that the deed constitutes an atrocity, (3) repents, and (4) asks for forgiveness. All four conditions are essential to taking personal responsibility.[45]

In furtherance of the apology, the atonement model requires the perpetrator to do something tangible. Just saying 'I'm sorry' is not enough. The perpetrator must solidify its apology with a redemptive act so as to make the apology believable – that is, more than just words. That redemptive act is, properly speaking, a 'reparation.' A reparation is the tangible act that transforms the rhetoric of apology into a meaningful, material reality. Thus, a reparation has a special social ontology. It can be defined as 'the revelation and realization of an apology.'[46]

---

42 See generally *When Sorry Isn't Enough.*

43 Brooks, "Age of Apology" in *When Sorry Isn't Enough*, p. 3.

44 *Ibid.*

45 See Brooks, *Atonement and Forgiveness*, p. 144. See also Roy L. Brooks, "The African American Redress Movement Post-Sept. 11, 2000," paper delivered at Clairmont Graduate University, 9 February 2002, p. 9 (mentioning three of the four conditions).

46 See Brooks, *Atonement and Forgiveness*, p. 155.

Reparations come in many forms. A basic distinction can be made between *compensatory* and *rehabilitative* reparations. A compensatory reparation is directed toward the individual victim or the victim's family. It is intended to be compensatory, but only in a symbolic sense, because nothing can truly return the victim to the *status quo ante*. In contrast, a rehabilitative reparation is directed toward the victim's community. It is designed to benefit the victim's group, to nurture the group's self-empowerment and, hence, aid in the nation's social and cultural transformation. At a minimum, a rehabilitative reparation can improve the conditions under which the victims live.[47]

Compensatory or rehabilitative reparations may further be divided into monetary or non-monetary forms of redress. Cash payments to the victims are the most basic form of monetary compensatory reparations.[48] Such payments may be unrestricted (e.g., a cheque with no strings attached) or restricted (e.g., a scholarship fund). A public commemoration in honour of the victim or the victim's family is an example of nonmonetary compensatory reparation. In contrast, an atonement trust fund or scholarship fund for members of the victims' community is a monetary rehabilitative reparation.[49] Nonmonetary rehabilitative reparations might include affirmative action

---

47 *Ibid.* p. 156.

48 There are several ways to determine the appropriate amount to be awarded. Boris Bittker suggests what might be called the earnings approach, in which each black would receive for a period of time an annual earnings boost equal to the gap between the average earnings for whites and blacks. See Boris I. Bittker, *The Case for Black Reparations* (New York: Random House, 1973), p. 131. Another approach, what might be called the capitalisation approach, takes the racial earnings gap calculated under the earnings approach and capitalises that value to determine the amount of investment required to generate the income necessary to close the gap. "For example, assume an average income gap of $5,000 a year and an average market rate of return of 10 percent. Under the capitalisation approach, it would take $50,000 of investment capital per eligible worker to close the gap (5,000 /.10 = 50,000)." Darrell L. Pugh, "Collective Rehabilitation," in *When Sorry Isn't Enough*, p. 372.

49 At a conference on reparations held in Copenhagen in 2001, I proposed an Atonement Trust Fund that worked as follows:

[T]he U.S. government should finance and administer a trust fund for every newborn African American child born within a particular period of time, say with a five- or ten-year period. The purpose of the trust fund is to give a core generation of African Americans one of the things slavery has denied them – family resources handed down generation to generation. At the age of 21, each African American within this group would receive the proceeds of the trust fund. He or she will now have the financial wherewithal to take a meaningful step toward a successful future. Money accumulated in the trust fund can only be used for certain purposes; namely, for education (e.g., to pay off undergraduate student loans or to attend graduate school); to start a new business, or as venture capital (business investment). These are the sorts of activities that build family resources that can be built upon from one generation to the next.

Roy L. Brooks, Address at the Danish Centre for Human Rights, Copenhagen, Denmark (27 April 2001). During that address, I made the following caveat which, in my judgment, should apply to all reparation proposals:

It is important to understand, however, that the Atonement Trust Fund is not intended to be a substitute for on-going civil rights reforms. The US government still has an obligation to do what governments are supposed to do – namely, resolve problems (including problems of racial discrimination) in education, housing, employment, and politics. The Atonement Trust Fund should be viewed as a special addendum to the struggle for racial justice in the United States.

programs implemented for members of the victims' community, a National Slave Memorial, and a National Museum of American Slavery.[50] Thus, whether for slavery or other atrocities, reparations need not be directed toward the victims themselves nor involve cash payments. Unlike the tort model, the atonement model is not primarily about the money.

The great variety in the forms of reparations underscores an important point about atonement. Atonement (meaning apology plus reparations) is not a punishment for guilt, but, rather, an *acknowledgment* of guilt. When the perpetrator of an atrocity apologises and solidifies that apology with a meaningful reparation, the perpetrator demonstrates a commitment to the victims. The perpetrator signifies publicly that he, she or it understands the moral enormity of the violation and the pain the perpetrator's action has caused and continues to cause the victims. Implicit in the atonement model's process of apology is the condition that the perpetrator set the historical record straight so that everyone fully understands why the apology is being made. In providing the factual foundation for the tender of the apology, clarification of the historical record results in a collective judgment regarding the extent of the perpetrator's responsibility in creating the atrocity as well as the magnitude of the injustice, including its lingering effects. Agreement on the factual predicate for the apology can, as Elazar Barkan suggests, 'fuse polarized antagonistic histories into a core of shared history to which both sides can subscribe.'[51] Such agreement helps a heterogeneous nation create what Jurgen Habermas calls 'discourse ethics,' a set of norms on which people with different experiences and interests can agree. Discourse ethics is demonstrated in Donald Shriver's description of 'a series of meetings between Polish and German teachers and historians for the purpose of revising school textbooks of the two countries so that the story of their twentieth-century relation would be interpreted to each other's young people in mutually acceptable accounts.'[52]

Clarification of the historical record regarding slavery in the US is desperately needed. White Americans know little about the actual facts of slavery or Jim Crow and, consequently, are complacent about the lingering effects of both atrocities. As I have written on another occasion:

> "When whites reject reparations on the ground that they had nothing to do with slavery, they fail to understand the centrality of slavery in the socioeconomic development of this great country from which they benefit. When whites reject reparations on the ground that there are plenty of successful African Americans today, including the oft-cited Oprah Winfrey, Tiger Woods, Michael

---

Ibid. For further discussion of the Atonement Trust Fund, see Brooks, *Atonement and Forgiveness*, pp. 159-163.

50 See Brooks, "The Age of Apology," in *When Sorry Isn't Enough*, p. 9.

51 Elazar Barkan, *The Guilt of Nations: Restitution and Negotiating Historical Injustices* (New York: Norton, 2000), p. xx n.

52 Donald W. Shriver, Jr., *An Ethic for Enemies: Forgiveness in Politics* (New York, Oxford University Press, 1995), p. 19.

> Jordan, and Colin Powell, they fail to see the millions of African Americans who have not been able to overcome the lethal legacy of slavery. When our government refuses to apologize for slavery, it reinforces white ignorance and complacency about slavery. When our government does not apologize, it makes it clear that, in the words of David Brion Davis, perhaps our leading historian on the institution of slavery, it fails to see '*racial slavery and its consequences as the basic reality, the grim and irrepressible theme governing both the settlement of the Western hemisphere and the emergence of a government and society in the United States that white people have regarded as "free".*'"[53]

Apology and reparations place the matter of forgiveness (the third element of the atonement model) on the table. While forgiveness is a conspicuous nonfactor under the tort model, it is an essential component of the atonement model. Forgiveness makes possible the atonement model's ultimate goal of reconciliation between the perpetrator and victims of an atrocity. In other words, once the perpetrator atones, the matter of forgiveness arrives on the victims' desk as a kind of civic subpoena. If the perpetrator's apology is complete and backed up by substantial reparations, the victims have a civic responsibility to forgive and thereby begin the process of repairing a broken relationship with the perpetrator. Forgiveness by African Americans makes national healing and racial reconciliation possible in the aftermath of two of America's greatest atrocities – slavery and Jim Crow.[54]

Although a relatively new idea in the BRM, the atonement model has been applied to slave redress in varying degrees in recent years. One of the first demonstrations of the model came in 2002. In January of that year, West Georgia College, which is a small college located in the state of Georgia, apologised for rejecting every African American applicant from the town's all-black high school in 1955 and 1956. To solidify that apology, the college established through an anonymous donor a scholarship fund for the descendants of the 60 or 70 students who were denied admissions some 50 years ago.[55]

Under the leadership of its president, Ruth Simmons, and its distinguished teacher and scholar, James Campbell, Brown University has undertaken an intensive two-year study of the slave-redress issue, including a self-examination of its involvement in slavery. Professor Campbell heads Brown University's Steering Committee on Slavery and Justice.[56] The Steering Committee's website articulates the Committee's mission as follows:

> "Welcome to the website of Brown University's Steering Committee on Slavery and Justice. The committee was appointed in 2003 by President Ruth Simmons and charged 'to organize academic

---

[53] Davis, *In the Image of God*, pp. 168-69 (emphasis added).

[54] On the question of forgiveness, see Brooks, *Atonement and Forgiveness*, pp. 163-69.

[55] See "Scholarship is Apology for Bias," San Diego Union-Tribune 18 January 2002, at A20.

[56] See, e.g., Brooke Donald, "Brown to Probe Past Links to Slave Owners," *San Diego Union-Tribune*, 22 March 2004, p. A3.

> events and activities that might help the nation and the Brown community think deeply, seriously, and rigorously about the questions raised' by the national debate over slavery and reparations. As an institution whose early benefactors included both slave traders and pioneering abolitionists, Brown has an intimate relationship to the history of American slavery. This history gives us, in the president's words, 'a special opportunity and a special obligation' to contribute to this ongoing debate.... Some of... [the programs sponsored by the committee] will focus specifically on Brown. Others will look at questions of slavery and reparations more generally. Still others will explore the history of movements for retrospective justice in other times and places. At the conclusion of its term, the committee will submit a report to the president and to the Brown community."[57]

Most of the atonements for slavery and Jim Crow have come not from colleges or universities but from corporations. On 11 January 2005, for example, J.P. Morgan Chase, the second largest bank in the country, apologised for its involvement in slavery. Two of its predecessor banks accepted thousands of African American slaves as collateral for business loans issued to slaveholders in Louisiana during the antebellum period. To demonstrate the sincerity of its remorse for contributing to what it called the 'brutal and unjust institution' of American slavery, the bank established a $5 million scholarship fund for blacks in Louisiana.[58]

Following on the heels of the J.P. Morgan Chase atonement, another major financial institution, Wachovia, atoned for its ties to slavery. In the fall of 2005, Wachovia issued a formal apology and backed it up with reparations. In explaining its actions, Wachovia issued the following statement:

> "Earlier this year, Wachovia contracted with The History Factory, a leading historical research firm, to conduct research on the predecessor institutions that, over many years, formed our company. The resulting research revealed that two of our predecessor institutions, the Georgia Railroad and Banking Company and the Bank of Charleston, owned slaves. Due to incomplete records, we cannot determine precisely how many slaves either the Georgia Railroad and Banking Company or the Bank of Charleston owned. Through specific transactional records, researchers determined that the Georgia Railroad and Banking Company owned at least 162 slaves, and the Bank of Charleston accepted at least 529 slaves as collateral on mortgaged properties or loans, and acquired an undetermined number of these individuals when customers defaulted on their loans. We are deeply saddened by these findings. We apologize to all Americans, and especially to African-Americans and people of African descent. While we can in no way atone for the past, we can learn from it, and we can continue to promote a better understanding of the African-American story, including the unique struggles, triumphs and contributions of African-Americans, and their important role in America's past and present. In this vein, Wachovia plans to partner with community organizations that are experts in furthering awareness and education of African-American history. Our aspiration is to preserve the African-American

---

57 http://www.brown.edu/Research/Slavery_Justice (available 2 October 2005).

58 See, e.g., Chris Sanders, "JP Morgan Says Predecessor Banks Owned Slaves," Reuters_News@reuters.com (available 12 January 2005); "J.P. Morgan Finds It Had Ties to Slavery," Chicago Tribune, Section 3 (Business), 21 January 2005, p. 3.

story and ensure that this important piece of our country's history is incorporated in educational forums. This is a natural fit with our company's strong focus on diversity, education and communities."[59]

Later in 2005, the Chairman of Bank of America, Kenneth Lewis, issued the following statement: 'The institution of slavery left an indelible and shameful mark on our nation's history, and we regret any actions our predecessors may have taken that supported or tolerated the institution of slavery in America.'[60] The bank pledged $5 million to 'institutions and programs involved in the preservation of African-American history.'[61]

Another institutional atonement that took place in 2005 came from the *Los Angeles Times*. When reminded by filmmaker Ken Burns of a racist editorial commentary regarding Jack Johnson, the first African-American heavyweight champion, that ran in the newspaper on July 6, 1910, the *Times*' editorial board 'wince[d] hard' and published an apology in its paper on 14 January 2005.[62] The publisher of the *Hartford Courant*, Connecticut's largest newspaper, made similar amends in 2000, the same year in which its Connecticut neighbour, Aetna, Inc., one of the largest insurance companies in the world, apologised and established a scholarship programme to atone for its support of slavery. Aetna traces its roots to 1853.[63]

Whether these institutional atonements constitute genuine atonement as defined earlier – apology and reparation – is a question I leave for another day.[64] For present purposes, it is sufficient to note that some institutional atonements are better than others and not all succeed. On the other hand, it cannot be gainsaid that institutions are taking the lead in atoning for slavery and Jim Crow. Curiously, the struggle for redress has been more successful in corporate America than in the halls of Congress or the presidency.

6 CONCLUSION

Claims for slave redress predate the Civil War (1861–1865) and, in fact, go as far back as the Revolutionary War (1775–1783). Hence, the BRM is as old as the republic itself. Yet, in recent years, the claim for redress has become more refined and highly

---

59 http://www.wachovia.com/misc/0,,877,00.html (available 2 October 2005).

60 Gary Washburn, "Bank of America Insists It Did Not Profit Off Slavery; It Will Give $5 million to Historical Groups," *Chicago Tribune*, Metro, 25 August 2005, p. 2.

61 *Ibid.*

62 See "Shame on Us," *Los Angeles Times*, 14 January 2005, p. B12.

63 See Brooks, *Atonement and Forgiveness*, p. 15.

64 If pressed, I would argue that Bank of America's statement does not constitute an atonement under the conditions set forth earlier in this chapter. The statement seems more like an attempt to mitigate culpability than an honest effort to accept responsibility.

theorised. The modern stage of the BRM, in fact, began with Congressman Conyer's 1989 Bill calling for a formal congressional study of the slave-redress issue. Taking the long view of the BRM, I am very much inclined to see the movement as a protracted expression of African-American pride. Whether pursued through the tort model or the atonement model, the struggle for slave redress is a gallant attempt by African Americans to take ourselves seriously enough to endeavour to hold accountable the perpetrators of what in my view is America's worst atrocity: slavery. The tort model endeavours to hold the perpetrators legally accountable, while the atonement model seeks moral accountability.

The distinction between the two models can be cut with even greater precision. When I look at the tort model, I see a backward-looking, victim-focused, and compensatory approach to slave redress. But when I look at the atonement model, I see almost the opposite, i.e., a forward-looking, perpetrator-focused, and racially conciliatory path to slave redress.

Which prescription is better?

In considering that question, one ought to note that the atonement model does more than offer a particular perspective on the question of how best to pursue redress for past atrocities. The atonement model also responds to the more basic question of why any society ought to or would want to dig up the past, especially where bad social memories are concerned. It holds that we bring up the past for at least two reasons: redemption and repair. That is, atonement in the first instance gives the perpetrator of an atrocity an opportunity to redeem its moral character in the aftermath of the atrocity. The perpetrator should be given this opportunity because it is the right thing to do. In the second instance, atonement gives the perpetrator and the victims an opportunity to repair their relationship, damaged by the atrocity. The atonement model imposes a civic obligation on the living victims of an atrocity to relinquish an attitude of resentment toward the perpetrator and to move forward with the perpetrator to establish or re-establish a healthy relationship, provided, of course, the perpetrator properly atones.

CORPORATE REPARATIONS FOR DESCENDANTS OF ENSLAVED AFRICAN-AMERICANS – PRACTICAL OBSTACLES

DIANE E. SAMMONS

1 INTRODUCTION

On March 26, 2002, in a United States federal court in Brooklyn, New York, a city transit worker,[1] a 72-year-old retired nurse,[2] and a law school graduate,[3] all descendants of enslaved African Americans, became the first to file corporate reparations lawsuits on behalf of themselves, their descendants and a putative class of approximately 21 million. Their targets: a bank, a railroad and an insurance company, all of which allegedly profited from the Transatlantic Slave Trade. Over the next year, in a coordinated, multi-state strategy, additional lawsuits were filed in federal courts in the cities of: Newark, Chicago, Austin, Los Angeles, and New Orleans. The list of corporate defendants grew to 17, including several banks, a textile company, a shipping company, finance houses and additional insurance and railroad companies. The lawsuits were consolidated for purposes of pre-trial procedures before a Federal District Court Judge, Charles R. Norgle, in the Northern District of Illinois.[4]

As the filings grew, so did the number of new representative plaintiffs, which came to include the aged children and grandchildren of slaves who could recount the stories of their enslaved parents and grandparents. The New Jersey plaintiff,[5] the son of a

1 André Carrington.
2 Mary Lacey Madison.
3 Deadria Farmer-Paellmann.
4 Parties can move to consolidate cases that involve essentially the same claims filed in different federal courts. These claims are consolidated for pretrial matters only and the cases then are returned to the filing court for trial. This application is heard by the Judicial Multidistrict Litigation Panel, which is comprised of federal circuit court judges who convene every several months in different federal circuits to rule on requests for consolidation. Each party can request a particular circuit court to hear the consolidated cases. In these cases, the defendants requested that the cases be heard in the District of Louisiana, while the plaintiffs requested the Eastern District of New York.
5 Richard E. Barber, Jr.

sharecropper and grandson of an enslaved master carpenter, vividly recalled the profound sadness of his Great-Aunt as she spoke of her emancipation at age 19. He shared his childhood memories of delivering newspapers and raking leaves for the white-occupants of stately homes built by his enslaved grandfather. Three California plaintiffs and one from Illinois are the children of Andrew Hurdle, who was born into slavery in 1845 and sired children well into his eighties. Ranging in age from 74 to 87, the children recalled the whipping scars on their father's back and his recounting of his devastating separation from his brother on the auction block.[6] In the summer of 2003, eight members of a family from Louisiana, claiming to have been enslaved in remote areas of the South up until the 1960s, joined the litigation. The hundred-year-old father, born in the early 1900s, and seven of his living children retraced their family history of being born enslaved on a rural farm in the Mississippi delta where a poor, white landholding family had kept successive generations of his family enslaved through physical abuse and terror.[7] One of the daughters remembered the family being fed nightly with dinner scraps discarded into a bucket and left outside the backdoor of the slaveholding family's house.[8] Her father described being flogged and tarred when he dared to challenge his slaveholders.[9]

The lawsuits hit a nerve. They were widely publicised in the national and international press. An opinion-editorial piece in the *New York Times* declared:

> "The goal of these historic investigations is to bring American society to a new reckoning with how our past effects the current conditions of African-Americans and to make America a better place by helping the disadvantaged."[10]

The article noted the crucial importance of the judicial system in righting the wrong of slavery:

> "The opportunity to use expert witnesses and conduct extensive discovery to get facts and documentation, makes the courtroom an ideal venue for this debate...reparations litigation will show what slavery meant, how it was profitable and how it continued to affect the opportunities of millions of black Americans."[11]

---

6 Yogi Cole, *The Real Story Behind the Movement for Reparations for African-Americans: A Movements' Ups and Downs*, DIVERSITYINC., June/July at 66-72; Tatsha Robinson, *Alive and Well*, THE CRISIS, May/June 2003 at 24-29.

7 Several of the plaintiffs' attorneys met with the Wall family in the summer of 2003 outside of New Orleans. Facts learned during this meeting became the basis of an Amended Consolidated Complaint adding the Wall family as plaintiffs to the lawsuit. Some of the Wall family's struggles were further recounted on December 3, 2003 in a television news show, Nightline by the American Broadcast Corporation ("ABC"). A transcript is available through ABC.

8 Meeting with counsel and members of the Wall family.

9 *Id.*

10 Charles J. Ogletree, Jr., *Litigating the Legacy of Slavery*, N.Y. TIMES, March 31, 2002 at 9.

11 *Id.*

Legal journalist Andrew Brownstein noted the cases were:

> "[T]he first wide-scale effort to bring the issue of slavery reparations from the college textbooks and T.V. talk shows into the courtroom."[12]

The Director of the National Urban League's Institute for Opportunity and Equality in Washington, spoke of the historical significance of the suits:

> "The suits ... open the door to a greater acknowledgement by the nation of the after effects of slavery and the discrimination that follows."[13]

On July 6, 2005, after a three-year battle in Court, Judge Norgle dismissed the lawsuit. In an 103-page opinion, the Judge outlined the history of slavery, the Civil War and the ongoing struggle for reparations from 1865 to the present, as he saw it. He ended with a detailed critique of every legal argument put forward by the plaintiffs.

As will be shown in this chapter, nascent efforts by the descendants of enslaved African Americans to secure legal victories can only be viewed as one component of a comprehensive, long-term strategy to obtain redress. The legal strategy must coincide with other efforts. Judges, scholars and the public need to be educated as to the historical and economic basis of slavery and its long-term legacy, racism. Early legal defeats must be anticipated. In the case of tobacco litigation, the first legal victories did not come until some 30 years after the early test cases. Similarly, the early cases brought by civil rights advocates to integrate public schools met with many defeats before the Supreme Court's landmark decision in *Brown v. The Board of Education.*[14] Also plausible is that slavery reparations may not be achieved in the courts, but through national, state and local legislative efforts. The struggle for reparations by the American survivors of Japanese internment succeeded only when the focus was shifted to a political campaign in Congress, following a five-year legal battle that went to the Supreme Court. Likewise, reparations for the survivors of the 1924 Rosewood race riots in Florida, where white lynch mobs killed six blacks and drove others from their homes destroying a prosperous black community, were secured as a result of 1994 legislation that provided $150,000 to each of the survivors and other monetary awards to 143 descendants of victims.

Even if various slavery suits eventually fail to secure legal relief for the plaintiffs, the actions have already sparked political initiatives that have resulted in several

---

12 Andrew Brownstein, *News & Trends, Suits Bring Debate Over Slavery Reparations Into the Courtroom* TRIAL: JOURNAL OF THE ASSOCIATION OF TRIAL LAWYERS OF AMERCIA, 38-dec, December 2002 at 68.

13 Tony Pugh, Maureen Fan and Ken Moritsugu, *Descendant of A Slave Sues Three Firms, Seeks Reparations*, PHILADEPHIA INQUIRER, March 27, 2002 at A03. (quoting Bill Spriggs).

14 347 U.S. 483, 495 (1954).

corporations admitting their role in slavery and taking the first steps to set up modest scholarship funds which benefit the descendants of slaves. Crucially, the lawsuits have helped transform the discourse on reparations from charity to one of legal rights and responsibilities. The legal discourse will continue to inform the progress and momentum of the efforts for reparations by the descendants of enslaved African Americans.

2 THE UNIQUE ROLE OF THE U.S. COURTS IN SHAPING POLICY

United States courts possess the power to influence fundamental political and social issues. A *New York Times* columnist who covered the United States Supreme Court in the 50s and 60s described the extraordinary power of this court as:

> "different from all other courts, past and present. It decides fundamental social and political questions that would never be put to judges in other countries---the boundaries between church and state the relations between the white and Negro races, the powers of the national legislature and executive, one could even forget it is a court at all.
>
> Its public image seems sometimes to be less that of a court than of an extraordinarily powerful demigod sitting on a remote throne and letting loose a constitutional thunderbolt whenever it sees a wrong crying for correction."[15]

Even though the jurisdiction of the federal courts is limited,[16] some courts offer solutions to large-scale social issues by ordering judicial relief or facilitating the settlement of legal claims involving hundreds, thousands or millions of litigants at a time including smokers; shareholders; human rights victims abroad and at home; veterans of war who were exposed to herbicides; multiple generations of women affected by the ingestion of a drug; environmentalists affected by the potential loss of a plant or animal species; consumers affected by deceptive trade practices; and groups of citizens within a given radius of a power plant affected by particulate emissions. As current Supreme Court Justice David D. Souter observed during his judicial

---

[15] Anthony Lewis, Gideon's Trumpet, 12 (1964) at 12; *See* Jack B. Weinstein and Eileen B. Hershenov, *The Effect of Mass Tort Law*, 1991 U. ILL. L. REV. 269 at 270 ("To many, particularly those in other countries, it may seem strange that in the United States we leave it to individual courts to provide ad hoc solutions for modern day disasters with their national and social repercussions.")

[16] Not every lawsuit can be brought in federal court, as the Constitution defines and limits the judicial power to "all Cases, in Law and Equity, arising under this Constitution, the Law of the United States and Treaties made...; to all Cases of Admiralty and Maritime Jurisdiction; to Controversies between two or more States... [and] between the Citizens of different States..." U.S.C.A. CONST. Art. III §2 cl. 1.

confirmation hearing before the United States Senate, 'if there is, in fact, a profound social problem...and if the other branches of Government do not deal with it, ultimately, it does and must land before the bench of the judiciary.'[17]

Despite the tremendous power that United States Courts have often exercised over policy, there remains one key factor that serves to moderate this tendency: an individual jurist's leanings as reflected in her views on: a) judicial restraint; b) rule of law and; c) collective justice.

2.1 JUDICIAL ACTIVISM VERSUS JUDICIAL RESTRAINT

The debate concerning the scope of the federal judicial authority in the United States formed part of the general debate between Supreme Court Justices Felix Frankfurter and Hugo L. Black that lasted from the 1930s to the 1960s. Justice Frankfurter counselled the philosophy of 'judicial self-restraint', which maintains that judges should defer to Congress and to the states, since an expansive judicial power weakens democracy in bypassing the political forum where unwise policies should be corrected. He argued that courts were often less equipped to deal with policies than expert administrators or politicians closer to the public will.[18] Justice Black, on the other hand, argued that undue deference by judges to other branches of government was tantamount to an abdication of their responsibilities.[19]

The philosophy of a given judge or collection of judges can weigh heavily in a judicial decision in which novel issues, such as the legal validity of claims for reparations are at stake. The individual legal philosophy of Judge Charles Norgle, who dismissed the claims of slave descendents, may be likened to Justice Frankfurter's philosophy of self-restraint. Certain answers given by him in his application to the Senate Judiciary Committee foreshadow his dismissal of the claims:

> "Power is of an encroaching nature and should be restrained from passing the limits assigned to it. In our free society, the people should decide and determine for themselves the course of their individual lives. Affirmative duties broadly imposed upon governments and society should not be the result of a Court order arising out of an individual lawsuit. It is essential to liberty that each department of government have a will and function on its own and that each department be accountable to the electorate."[20]

---

17 James Morone and Rogan Kersch, *Obesity, Courts, and the New Politics of Public Health*, 30 J. HEALTH POL. POL'Y&L 839, 861 (October 2005), citing David Souter, 1991 Testimony before Senate Judiciary Committee in Nomination for Associate Justice of Supreme Court of the United States, 101st Congress, 2nd Session (1990) Washington, D.C., Government Printing Office; Linda Greenhouse, *Filling in the Blanks*, NY TIMES, September 15, 1990 at 11.

18 Lewis, *supra* note 16 at 86.

19 *Id.*

20 Motion to Recuse, *In re African American Slave Descendants' Litigation* at ¶19 (filed 12/10/2003), Case No. 1:02-cv-07764, Document 124.

Judge Norgle's philosophy of judicial restraint also found its way into his 103-page opinion dismissing the suit. In urging that the issue of slave reparations should be resolved in the legislature, Norgle stated:

> "[P]rudential limitations prohibit the Court from deciding such broad questions of social importance...Ultimately, the legal obstacles prohibiting judicial resolution cannot be circumvented by the Courts...Moreover from the onset of the Civil War until the present, the historical record clearly shows that the President and Congress have the constitutional authority to determine the nature and scope of relief sought in this case, not the courts."[21]

The judicial restraint urged by Judge Norgle in the Northern District of Illinois regarding the *Slave Descendants' Litigation* may be contrasted with the judicial philosophy of Judge Jack Weinstein, a federal judge in New York, who presided over the *In re: Agent Orange Product Liability Litigation.*[22] This was one of the most complex, far-reaching judicial results to emerge during recent times, involving claims of injury to tens of thousands of Vietnam veterans resulting from exposure to herbicides in the Vietnam War, which were settled in a single class action:

> "The post war rule of the federal courts – particularly only when they were exercising their equitable jurisdiction – has been to protect the injured who come before them against those who have caused or whom are causing unjustified harm. *The judicial role is particularly important in the absence of any alternative remedies emanating from the executive or legislative branch.*"[23]

It was Weinstein's view that it was one the of the court's functions to 'jump start' the process of encouraging the government to accept its proper responsibility:

> "Overreaching the entire dispute is a feeling on both sides that whatever existing law and procedures may technically require, fairness, justice and equity in this unprecedented controversy demand that the government assume responsibility for the harm caused our soldiers and families by its use of Agent Orange in South East Asia...A class action is the best vehicle for achieving that end. A single class-wide determination on the issue of causation will focus the attention of Congress, the Executive branch and the Veteran's Administration on their responsibility, if any, in this case."[24]

A judge's philosophy on the issue of judicial involvement may determine the outcome of a case where large-scale social justice issues are at stake.[25]

---

21 *In re African-American Slave Descendants' Litig.*, 375 F. Supp 2d at 780.

22 597 F. Supp. 740 (E.D.N.Y. 1984), *aff'd*, 818 F.2d 1415 (2d Cir. 1997), *cert. denied*, *Pinkery v. Dow Chemical*, 484 U.S. 1004 (1988).

23 Weinstein & Hershenov, *supra* note 15 at 324, emphasis added.

24 *In re: Agent Orange Product Liability*, 100 F.R.D. 718, 721 (S.D.N.Y. 1983).

25 James Morone, Rogan Kersh, "*Obesity, Courts and the New Politics of the Public Health*" 30 J. HEALTH POL. POL'Y & L. 839, 861 (October 2005).

2.2 THE RULE OF LAW VERSUS EQUITY

Another element that may shape dramatically the legal landscape of reparations is an individual jurist's view on the 'rule of law'. The rule of law principle demands a strict adherence to statute and prior legal precedent necessary for reasons of predictability and certainty in ordering one's affairs. In contrast, the law of equity favours a more flexible approach, based on humanitarian democratic values which maintain that one cannot suffer a wrong without a remedy. The granting of equitable relief is an ancient principle, derived from English chancery law, finding its basis in implied obligations based in conscience, natural reason and grace.[26] Equity is a fundamental principle of the federal courts noted plainly in Article III of the Constitution and firmly embedded in federal common law.[27] Unless a statute specifically restricts a court's jurisdiction in equity, the full scope of the power may be recognised or applied.[28] Jurisdiction in chancery is inherent and original, comprehending every exigency of human disagreement for which there is not an adequate remedy of law.[29]

Just as a judge's philosophy concerning restraint versus activism may influence the direction and success of reparations litigation, so too may a judge's view of the proper role of the rule of law versus equity. For example, Judge Norgle's position on the issue of strictly enforcing the statutes of limitations, reflects his strong adherence to the principle of the rule of law:

> "The procedural requirements established by various legislatures for gaining access to the court are not to be disregarded out of vague sympathy for particular litigant. (Citations omitted) 'Statutory limitations are not arbitrary obstacles to the vindication of just claims, and therefore should not be given a grudging application.' (Citations omitted) Statutes of limitations are regulations set by the legislature, designed to set a time period in which to file an action. 'They protect important social interests in certainty, accuracy and repose.'" (Citations omitted)[30]

This may be contrasted with the judgment of a federal judge sitting in New York, who applied equitable principles to reach a contrary result, when he refused to dismiss a claim on statute of limitations grounds. This claim had been brought by a class of black policyholders, due to discriminatory pricing of insurance policies purchased over 30 years previously:

---

26 *Caparo v. Propati, et. al.*, 127 N.J.E. 419, 421-429 (1990).

27 U.S.C.A. CONST. Article III, §2, cl. 1 defines judicial power to include "all Cases in Law and Equity…".

28 *Porter v. Warner Holding Co.*, 328 U.S. 398 (1996).

29 *Williamson v. Berry*, 49 U.S. 495, 537 (1850).

30 375 F.Supp. 2d at 771.

> "... with most other rules there are exceptions...accrual may be postponed, until plaintiff has or with reasonable diligence should have discovered the critical fact of his injury and its cause". (Citation omitted).[31]

Claims for legal restitution for the wrongs of slavery depend primarily on principles associated with 'equity' law. It is the court's conscience and its ability to be flexible that is relied upon in helping the court to find a fair and reasonable solution to the enormous challenges of proof presented by plaintiffs in reparations cases. Plaintiffs rely on the court's power appropriately to acknowledge and embrace notions of flexibility and creativity in order to arrive at a just result. As will be described in greater detail in Section 3, below, the unique circumstances of slavery and its stubborn lingering effects provide the legal and moral justification for the application of the full breadth of a court's equitable powers.

2.3 INDIVIDUAL VERSUS COLLECTIVE JUSTICE

Another key to evaluating the prospects of success of future reparations claims, is an individual jurist's perspective on the issue of individual versus collective justice. Individuality and self-determination are often viewed as quintessential American traits. The law traditionally accepts the premise that lawsuits focus on the claims of an individual and the acts of a particular wrongdoer. In other words, Party A, being an individual victim, claims against Party B, the perpetrator of the wrongdoing. In this view, it is assumed that an individual is responsible for his own behaviour.[32] Traditionally this structure is favoured as the facts and circumstances of each person's case allows for justice to be fashioned around an individual's unique circumstances.

However, liberalising trends during the last fifty years in the areas of civil rights, mass tort, class action and most recently human rights, have had the effect of broadening the scope of litigation so as to allow claims of hundreds, thousands and even millions of litigants to be joined in one action. As some courts have expanded their vision of justice to include lawsuits that concern the rights of many parties, they have incorporated more collective approaches to justice. In this way the risks of unsafe, unhealthy or improper practices may be shared among the parties who are in the best position to remedy the harm.

---

31 *Thompson v. Metropolitan Life Insurance Co.*, 149 F.Supp. 38, 48 (S.D.N.Y. 2001).

32 *See e.g.*, Vincene Verdun, *If the Shoe Fits, Wear It: An Analysis Reparations to African Americans*, 67 TUL. L.REV. 597, 620 (1993)(citing Professor Mari Matsuda).

2.3.1 *Mass tort suits/class actions*

The rise of collective litigation occurred in the 1970s and 1980s, and may be traced to the rise of the mass tort suit. These suits involved consumers hurt by drugs, medical devices, or toxic substances, who brought suit against manufacturers for injuries associated with their products.[33] When courts were inundated with tens of thousands of cases at a time, they were forced to develop methods to adjudicate these cases efficiently without compromising the protection generally afforded to individual litigants. Creative federal judges turned to previously underutilised rules of federal procedure, specifically Federal Rule 23, to address these challenges.[34] The Rule allows courts to aggregate claims and issues rather than to require separate trials for each plaintiff and each defendant. Judges began to use the rule to address claims by multiple plaintiffs against multiple defendants in cases where plaintiffs were injured because of exposure to or use of Agent Orange, asbestos, tobacco, DES, Dalkon Shield and other products. The courts hearing these cases developed practical rules, which allowed claims to proceed which otherwise would have been defeated by the time delays and costs involved when thousands of plaintiffs have to proceed simultaneously with similar claims. Thus emerged the modern-day class action.

The number of class actions rose significantly in the 1990s. From 1988 to 1998, the number of class action filings against Fortune 500 companies, increased by 338% in federal courts. During the same period, the number of such filings increased by more than 1,000 per cent in state courts.[35]

There are, however, many legal scholars who believe the class action device is dying, due to the fact that courts in the mid-90s engaged in an ongoing process to decertify previously certified class action litigation. These cases included the decertification of a class of 120,000 haemophiliacs exposed to AIDS, who were suing defendant manufacturers of a blood-screening product. The judge in this case stated that the class action put undue pressure on the defendants to settle.[36] Another judge decertified one of the largest class actions ever (related to tobacco products) citing the violation of the rights of defendants in mass tort class actions.[37] This injured class had consisted of current, former and deceased smokers and their families. These two decisions were consistent with the 1996 decertifications of class actions involving injuries caused by

---

33 Myriam Giles, *Opting Out of Liability: The Forthcoming, Near-Total Demise of the Modern Class Action*, 104 MICH. L.REV. 373, 381 (December 2005), *citing*, Deborah R. Hensler, et. Al. RAND Institute for Civil Justice, Class action Dilemmas: Pursuing Public Goals for Private Gain 52-53 (2000).

34 Giles, *supra* at 381.

35 Steven. B Hantler, Mark A. Behrens and Leah Lorber, *Is the "Crisis" in the Civil Justice System Real or Imagined?* 38 LOY. L.A. L. REV. 1121, 1137 (Spring 2005).

36 *In re Rhone-Poulenc Rorer*, 51 F. 3d 1293, 1298 (7th Cir. 1995).

37 *Castano v. American Tobacco Co.*, 84 F. 3d 734, 747-750 (5th Cir. 1996).

penile inserts,[38] an epilepsy drug,[39] and asbestos.[40] Finally, the Supreme Court weighed in by rejecting a settlement in an asbestos class action that defendants agreed to certify for settlement purposes only.[41]

But the current cries proclaiming the demise of the class action, as a device for achieving collective justice, may be premature. In 2005, the Second Circuit allowed a putative class action to proceed on a claim for damages arising from the alleged deceptions of the fast food giant McDonald's, in failing to inform its customers of alleged health dangers inherent in eating its food.[42] In another recent case, a New York federal judge, William M. Skretny, oversaw a multimillion-dollar settlement in a lawsuit brought on behalf of the citizens of the entire State of New York against a number of power plants, for violations of the Clean Air Act and for medical harm caused by dangerous particulate emissions from the plants.[43]

Legal scholar Deborah Hensler remains optimistic about the future of collective social justice reform through a shift to a 'new litigation characterized by an emerging form of social policy torts that seek the kind of industry-wide change in corporate products and practices that advocates have pursued without much success in state and federal legislatures.'[44]

To succeed in litigation for corporate reparations, attorneys must be cognisant of the ever-changing developments in mass tort litigation and class action certifications. These developments reflect widely differing perspectives on the part of legal scholars and jurists towards the concept of collective justice. Attorneys should continue to file reparations claims in jurisdictions which have established a record which indicates that they are friendly towards the concept of collective justice.

---

38 *In re Am. Med. Sys.*, 75 F. 3d 1069, 1085-86 (6th Cir 1996).

39 *Valentino v. Carter-Wallace*, 97 F. 3d 1227, 1235 (9th Cir. 1996).

40 *Georgine v. Amchem Prods., Inc.*, 83 F.3d 610, 634 (3d. Cir. 1996), *aff'd*, 521 U.S. 591 (1997).

41 *Amchem Products, Inc. v. Windsor*, 521 U.S. 591 (1997).

42 *Pelmon v. McDonalds*, 396 F.3d. 508 (2d Cir. 2005).

43 *State of N.Y., et al. v. Niagara Mohawk Power Corp., et al.*, Civil No. 02-cv-0024 (W.D.N.Y. March 10, 2002) (Complaint, Document 10); *Governor and Attorney General Announce New York's Largest Coal Plants to Slash Polution Levels*, Press Release of N.Y. Governor and N.Y. Attorney General, January 11, 2005, (http://www.state.ny.us/governor/press/05/jan11_05.htm) (last viewed April 14, 2006) ("The agreement also requires the previous owner of the plants, Niagara Mohawk Power Corp. (NiMo) to pay a $3 million penalty and provide an additional $3 million to support several environmental benefit projects in Western New York, including weatherising low-income housing and adding pollution controls to school buses. NiMo also has agreed to convey 2,500 acres of environmentally sensitive land along the Salmon River to the state. The Oswego County parcel is valued at more than $2.5 million.").

44 Morone and Kersh *supra* note 17 at 855, citing, Deborah R. Hensler, *Revisiting the Monster: New Myths and Realities of Class Action and other Large Scale Litigation*, 11 DUKE J. COMP. & INTERN'L L. 179-213.

2.3.2 *Civil rights litigation*

A contemporary American novelist, Russell Banks, has noted that there are two differences between Americans and our European forbearers: race and space.[45] Traditionally the relationship between the races has been the subject of struggle between national authority and state's rights, often negotiated and resolved in the federal courts. From the decision of the Supreme Court in *Dred Scott* in 1856, to court-enforced integration of all public schools in *Brown v. The Board of Education*, the courts have exercised extraordinary powers over issues of race. Prior to emancipation, in *Dred Scott*,[46] the Supreme Court confirmed that the enslaved African-American was property and that African-Americans were not intended to be citizens under the Constitution, but were 'regarded as beings of inferior order...altogether unfit to associate with the white race, either in social or political relations; and so inferior, they had no rights that the white man was bound to respect…'.[47] Further it concluded that the 'right to traffic in [slaves], like an ordinary article of merchandise and property, was guaranteed to the citizens of the United States…'.[48] While emancipation in 1865 and the passage of the Thirteenth, Fourteenth, and Fifteenth Amendments, were designed to end servitude officially, states immediately took action to re-enslave Africans as they passed Black Codes – laws limiting the rights of African-Americans to own or rent property, permitting imprisonment for breach of employment contracts and severely limiting the right to vote.[49] Congress responded to the legal disabilities imposed on newly emancipated African-Americans at the end of the Civil War by establishing the Freemen's Bureau and by passing the Reconstruction Acts and the Civil Rights Acts. However, it was the Supreme Court which began to interpret Congressional legislation in such a way as to curtail sharply the substantive protections.[50] Thus, in the *Civil Rights Cases*,[51] the Court strangled the efforts of Congress to use its power to promote racial equality, by invalidating a section of the Civil Rights Act of 1875 that made it a crime to deny equal access to 'inns, public conveyances, theatres and other places of public amusement.'[52] A further devastating blow to the Civil Rights Amendments and the principle of equality came in *Plessy v. Ferguson*,[53] in which case the Supreme Court upheld a Louisiana law that required

---

45 http://www.wsws.org/articles/2002/feb2002/burn-d09.shtnl (last viewed March 2006).

46 *Dred Scott v. Sandford*, 19 How.393, 15 L.Ed. 691 (1857).

47 *Id.* at 404, cited in *Bakke v. Regents of the University of California*, 438 U.S. 265, 389 (1978) (Marshall J., concurring).

48 *Id* at 451, cited in *Bakke*, 438 U.S. at 390 (Marshall J., concurring).

49 *Bakke* at 390-391. (Marshall J., concurring).

50 *See* e.g. *Slaughter-House Cases*, 16 Wall. 36, 70, 21 L.Ed 394 (1873); *U.S. v. Cruikshank*, 92 U.S. 542 (1876); *U.S. v. Reese*, 42 U.S. 214 (1876).

51 109 U.S. 3 (1883).

52 *Id.* at 24-25.

53 163 U.S. 537 (1996).

railway companies to provide 'equal but separate accommodations for whites and blacks, as the Court concluded that the Fourteenth Amendment was not intended to abolish distinctions based upon color, or to enforce social as distinguished from political equality or a commingling of the two races on terms unsatisfactory to either.'[54] The *Plessy* court remarked:

> "We consider the underlying fallacy of the plaintiff's argument to consist in the assumption that the enforced separation of the two races stamps the colored race with a badge of inferiority. If this be so, it is not by reason of anything found in the act, but solely because the colored race chooses to put that construction upon it."[55]

As late as 1908, in *Berea College*, the Court enforced a state criminal conviction against a private college for teaching blacks together with whites.[56] It was not until almost fifty years later, with the decisions leading up to *Brown v. Board of Education,* that the Court re-examined its view of the collective disabilities visited upon African-Americans by the institution of slavery and its aftermath.[57] Even then, these decisions did not end the legacy of slavery as the 'years of second class citizenship in the wake of emancipation could not be so easily eliminated'.[58] During the 1950s and 1960s, the federal courts exercised greater authority in aggressively quashing states' resistance to integration and equal rights through school desegregation, voting rights, and integration of public facilities. The procedure was taken one step further in *Bakke* in which case the Court endorsed an expansive view of the need to remedy past discrimination by allowing remedial race-based programs designed to redress past inequitable treatment.[59]

However, there has been a significant retreat from court-enforced, race-based remedial measures as the ever-changing Supreme Court has systematically reversed this trend through a growing emphasis on the right of individuals, by adopting a 'colour-blind' interpretation of the Constitution, an approach that refuses to look to general societal discrimination or institutional discrimination.[60] Notably, in *Richmond v. J.A. Crosen,*[61] the Court rejected a minority set-aside program put in place by the City of Richmond, which required that thirty percent of municipal contracts be

---

54 *Id.* at 544, cited in *Bakke* 438 at 392. (Marshall J. concurring).

55 *Id.* at 551, cited in *Bakke*, 438 U.S. at 392 (Marshall J. concurring).

56 *Berea College v. Kentucky*, 211 U.S. 45 (1908).

57 347 U.S. 373 (1954) *See* e.g., *Morgan v. Virginia*, 328 U.S. 373 (1946); *Sweatt v. Painter*, 339 U.S. 629 (1950); *McLaurin v. Oklahoma State Regents*, 339 U.S. 637 (1950).

58 *Bakke*, 438 U.S. at 394 (Marshall J. concurring).

59 *Bakke v. Regents of the University of California*, 438 U.S. 265, 362 (1978).

60 *Adarand Construction, Inc. v. Pena*, 515 U.S. 200, 227 (1995). The Supreme Court interpreted the Constitution as "protect[ing] persons, not groups... [and] governmental action based on race – a *group* classification long recognized in most circumstances irrelevant and therefore prohibited, (citations omitted) should be subjected to detailed judicial inquiry to ensure that the *personal* right to equal protection of the laws has not been infringed."

61 488 U.S. 469 (1989).

awarded to minority contractors. The Court ruled that any racial classification was considered suspect, whether it was remedial or not. The City of Richmond was required to show that it had been individually injured and that the proposed remedy was narrowly drawn to address this specific injury.

Hence, the Supreme Court's retreat from its role as protector of the collective rights of its minority citizens will be a key factor which could severely jeopardise the success of future reparations actions.

2.3.3 Human rights litigation

At the same time that attorneys were testing the limits of collective justice in mass tort actions, there arose a similar trend in human rights litigation. In 1988, there was an early defeat for human rights lawyers in a five-year litigation battle brought by 19 representative plaintiffs on behalf of a class of 120,000 Japanese-American internees and their descendants against the U.S. government for illegal detention.[62] Shortly after, however, there were some victories. In the mid-90s, a class action suit brought on behalf of 10,000 victims of torture and abuse against the Marcos family in the Philippines, was successful in securing a judgment of close to two billion dollars, in a trifurcated jury trial that took place over several years.[63] While the case presented enormous administrative challenges and problems of proof due to the sheer number of victims, Judge Manuel L. Real of the federal court in Hawaii allowed the plaintiffs to employ an inferential statistical engineer to arrive at an average damage figure, based on a limited sampling of plaintiffs, thus precluding the need for one-on-one trials for each plaintiff.[64] The Judge concluded that the sampling procedure did not violate the defendant's due process rights where it was likely that individual trials would result in a higher sum of damages being awarded; could take over 10 years to complete; would require enormous judicial resources; and would unconscionably 'deny relief to persons who suffered significant damages simply based on the number of persons [hurt by] a single tortfeaser'.[65] In 2000 there were successful settlements arising out of New York putative class action litigation brought by holocaust survivors and their descendants against Swiss banks which unjustly retained survivor assets.[66] Likewise, a year later, in 2001, a 40 million dollar settlement was approved in a similar reparations suit filed in New York against Austrian and German banks.[67] In 2002, a

---

62 *U.S. v. Honhri*, 586 F. Supp. 769 (D.D.C. 1984), *aff'd in part revs'd in part*, 782 F.2d 227 (D.C. Cir. 1986), *vacated and remanded*, 482 U.S. 69 (1987), *remand affirming initial dismissal*, 847 F.2d 779 (Fed. Cir. 1988), *cert. denied*, 488 U.S. 925 (1988).

63 *Hilao v. Estate of Marcos*, 103 F.3d 767 (9th Cir. 1996).

64 *Estate of Marcos Human Rights Litig.*, 910 F. Supp. 1460, 1468 (D. Hawaii 1995), *aff'd*, 103 F. 3d 767 (9th Cir. 1996).

65 *Id.*

66 *In re Holocaust Victim Assets Cases*, 105 F. Supp. 2d 139 (E.D.N.Y. 2000) (approving settlement).

67 *D'Amato v. Deutsche Bank*, 80 F.Supp. 2d 169 (E.D.N.Y. 2000), *aff'd*, 236 F. 2d 78 (2d Cir. 2001).

New York case survived initial motions to dismiss the claims of Nigerian victims of gross human rights abuses, brought against the Royal Dutch Petroleum Co., which allegedly assisted the Nigerian police and military in brutal acts to stifle opposition to an oil excavation plan.[68] A similar claim brought in 2000 by Burmese victims against an oil company operating in Myanmar resulted in a final settlement in March 2005.[69] Finally, in 2003, the claims of thousands of Sudanese who alleged gross human rights violations on the part of a Canadian oil company, survived initial dismissal motions in the Southern District of New York.[70] Yet, in a surprising subsequent decision in 2005, the court refused to grant class certification, a harbinger of its possible defeat as the plaintiffs now face the difficult task of having to proceed by means of individual trials. Distinguishing the facts of the case from other civil rights, human rights and mass tort claims in which class actions were certified, Judge Denise Cote concluded that a collective approach could prejudice defendants by 'lifting the description of the claims to a level of generality that tears them from their substantively required moorings to actual causation and discrete injury', and further suggested that in such a 'scenario, the jury trial would become but a precursor to a capacious administrative morass where the majority of substantive issues of causality would be resolved on a piecemeal basis.'[71] Moreover, the success of some of the human rights cases referred to above must be tempered by the 2004 Supreme Court decision of *Sosa*,[72] a case involving the kidnapping of a Mexican doctor who was suspected of participating in the murder of a U.S. drug enforcement agent. The doctor was acquitted in a criminal trial and then brought an action of his own, arguing that his kidnapping constituted a violation of the law of nations. Justice Souter, writing for the majority of the court, directed lower courts to be cautious in recognising new causes of actions under the primary statute utilised by most human rights attorneys in bringing their claims before U.S. courts. Souter, signalling a more narrow interpretation of cognisable claims, stated that the 'door was still ajar subject to vigilant doorkeeping.'[73] While the *Sosa* Court was faced with an individual claim and not a collective one, the Court's words send a chilling message to attorneys considering the expansion of human rights claims based upon violations of international law.

To conclude, it is the confluence of mass tort law, human rights law and the unique role that the courts have played in resolving issues of race that has shaped the initial course of the latest wave of reparations litigation. The philosophies of jurists

---

68 *Wiwa v. Royal Dutch Petroleum Co.*, 2002 WL 319887 (S.D.N.Y. Feb. 28, 2002).

69 *Doe I v. Unocal Corp.*, 110 F. Supp. 2d. 1294, 1310 (C.D. Cal. 2000), *aff'd in part, revs'd in part*, 395 F.3d 932 (9th Cir. 2002) *op. vac.* 403 F.3d 708 (9th Cir. 2005); EarthRights International, *Final Settlement Reached in Doe v. Unocal*, http://earthrighs.org/content/view/113/41/ (last viewed April 4, 2006).

70 *Presbyterian Church of Sudan v Talisman Energy, Inc.*, 244 F.Supp. 3d 289 (S.D.N.Y. 2003).

71 *Presbyterian Church of Sudan v Talisman Energy, Inc.*, 226 F.R.D. 456, 484-485 (S.D.N.Y. 2005).

72 *Sosa v Alvarez-Machain*, 542 U.S. 692 (2004).

73 *Id.* at 729.

on questions of judicial restraint, the rule of law, and individual justice, will ultimately dictate the likelihood of future success in reparations litigation.

3 LEGAL THEORIES

3.1 INTRODUCTION

Legal actions are classified as either criminal or civil. Criminal suits punish wrongdoers for the commission of intentional or extremely reckless acts and deter others from committing such acts. A nation, state or political sub-division prosecutes an individual on behalf of the whole society. The remedy provided is to the victim and the society as a whole: the incarceration of the wrongdoer. Civil litigation, on the other hand, involves claims brought by private individuals or entities for harm to their property or person. The remedy generally sought is monetary recompense. Civil litigation is further broken down into a number of subcategories. Contract claims regulate the commercial rights between parties, including buyers and sellers, landlords and tenants, employers and employees, debtors and creditors or any other individuals or entities who have established a legally cognisable agreement. Tort actions deal with recompense for harm to the property or person of another and are further broken into two categories: intentional torts and negligence. Intentional torts concern intentional or willful acts that cause harm to another, such as assault and/or battery, defamation or invasion of privacy. The tort of negligence applies when there is a duty owing by one party to another, and that party violates the duty by failing to use ordinary care, which results in harm that was foreseeable.

In the realm of human right's litigation, which mostly involves claims for civil damages, the legal tests and theories are often based upon criminal paradigms including theories providing for secondary liability, involving accessories or co-conspirators who are alleged to be liable for the acts of others.

The unique nature of slavery as an institution provides a wealth of possible legal avenues to secure relief. As slaves were considered property and their work arose in a semi-contractual way, claims may be grounded in multiple property theories. Likewise, if one asserts that slavery was illegal at its inception and ought never to have been legally sanctioned, then a possible claim exists for physical and emotional harm arising as a consequence of the institution. The knowing participation of corporations in the maintenance of such a system will form the basis for claims against them. As slavery has been deemed a crime against humanity, claims may also be brought in terms of human rights laws.

Essentially, the major themes in US reparations litigation are linked to five distinct legal concepts: a) the law of slavery; b) property; c) harm against the person; d) human rights law; and e) modern-day, statutory consumer protection violations.

3.2 SLAVERY AS VIOLATION OF NATURAL LAW

States abolished the slave trade before the federal government did. Both state and federal courts created a body of common law finding slavery to be a violation of the natural law of man. As early as 1781, in one of the famous Quork Walker cases, *Commonwealth v. Jennison,*[74] Chief Justice William Cushing of the Supreme Judicial Court of Massachusetts charged his jury as to the natural law against slavery:

> "[W]hatever usages formally prevailed or slid in upon as by the examples of others on the subject, they can no longer exist... *[S]entiments more favorable to the natural rights of mankind, and to that innate desire for liberty which heaven, without regard to complexion or shape, has planted in the human breast – have prevailed since the glorious struggle for our rights [the Revolution] began... [S]lavery is in my judgment as effectively abolished as it can be by the granting of rights and privileges wholly incompatible and repugnant to its existence.*"[75]

Several years later in 1789 in a First Circuit case, Justice Joseph Story in the *La Jeune Eugenie* case, concluded that the international slave trade violated the natural law of man in that it was:

> "repugnant to the great principles of Christian duty, the dictates of natural religion, the obligation of good faith and morality, and the eternal maxims of social justice [and]... was inconsistent with any system of law that purports to rest on the authority of reason or revelation. And it is sufficient to stamp any trade as interdicted by public law, when it can be justly affirmed that it is repugnant to the general principles of justice and humanity."[76]

Moreover, in 1847 in *Anderson v. Poindexter*, the Ohio Supreme Court held that a slave coming into a free jurisdiction (with the consent of the master) for a temporary sojourn was automatically freed because slavery was repugnant to reason and the principles of natural law.[77]

In fact, current-day legal scholars in the United States continue to write extensively about slavery always having been contrary to fundamental laws of the nation and of the world. In 1987, prior to his elevation to Supreme Court Justice, Clarence Thomas wrote about a 'higher law' that condemns inequality and hence slavery. Thomas argued that the 'original intent' of the United States Constitution must follow the ideals of the Declaration of Independence, which should be read as hostile to slavery in order to conform with the 'higher' principles of the nation that rest on natural law:

---

74 William M. Wiecek, *Somerset: Lord Mansfield and the Legitimacy of Slavery in the Anglo-American World*, 42 U. CHI. L. REV. 86, 124-125 (1974), citing from the unreported decision.

75 *Id.* (emphasis added).

76 *Id.* at 130, citing, United States v. *La Jeune Eugenie*, 26 F.Cas. 832, 846 (no. 15,551) (C.C.D. Mass. 1822).

77 6 Ohio St. 623 (1857); *see also the similar holding, Lemmon v. The People*, 20 N.Y. 562 (1860).

> "Paine captured well the revolutionary meaning of basing a particular nation on a universal truth, the truth of human equality. Edwin S. Corwin described this many years ago as the 'higher law background' of the Constitution. And Martin Luther King, Jr. brought out the contemporary significance of 'higher law' well in his famous letter from a Birmingham Jail. Paraphrasing St. Thomas Aquinas, King declared, 'A just law is a man-made code that squares with the moral law or the law of God ...An unjust law is a human law that is not rooted in eternal law and natural law.'"[78]

Like Justice Thomas' argument that slavery has to be interpreted legally as against the specific intent of the Founding Fathers, in 2003 Professor Keith Hylton asserted that slavery cannot be viewed as an institution sanctioned by law, but rather, as a corruption or displacement of law:

> "We have to reject the notion that anything we would wish to call law would ever sanction such an institution. For the institution is founded on the absence of law...
> Law and slavery are, in essence, 'universal complements,' in the sense that one can exist in the space where the other is absent. Hence, the only morally consistent position that a state can take with respect to slavery is that it never cohabited with the institution."[79]

When the actual institution of slavery was formally ended in the United States, the entrenched racial inequalities and cultural psychic scars[80] caused by the institution left a huge number of slaves and their descendants injured and without legal remedy. Further, it left Americans with ingrained beliefs about the superiority of the Caucasian population. This has ensured that inequality continues through to the present day in the form of racism.[81]

This connection between a past rooted in slavery, and lingering racism today, is aptly described by Hylton as follows:

> "American slavery, unlike Roman slavery, contributed greatly to the spread and resilience of racism. Slavery gave racist attitudes an economic function that would otherwise not have existed. First, the propagation of racist beliefs served the dominant slaveholding class by reducing likelihood that bonds would form between poor whites and slaves, whose economic interests were in many respects perfectly aligned. Second, racism served an economic function by reducing the payoff to slaves from gaining freedom ... The third reason slavery gave racism an economic

---

78 Clarence Thomas, *Toward a "Plain Reading" of the Constitution – The Declaration of Independence in Constitutional Interpretation*; 30 HOW. L.J. 983, 989 (1987).

79 Keith M. Hylton, *Slavery and Tort Law*, Boston University School of Law, Working Paper Series, Public Law & Legal Theory, Working Paper No. 03-02 (2003) at 30-34 (http://www.bu.edu/law/faculty/papers).

80 Numerous authors document the "spiritual injuries" arising out of slavery. *See e.g,*, Verdun, *supra* note 32 at 633-635, n.37.

81 Ethan Watters, *Claude Steele Has Scores to Settle*, N.Y. TIMES, September 17, 1995 at 45. (Steele revealed in testing that lower scores by African Americans in standardised aptitude tests were due to a sense of inferiority with which African-Americans go into testing situations). *Id.*

> function is the need to deter slave insurrections. This need... justified the use of oppressive force ... Like a resilient virus, racism has a tendency to replicate itself in successive generations. The racist belief structure promoted in order to justify the oppression of slavery replicates itself over time and is to some extent self-confirming."[82]

Hylton further details the manner in which the past begets successive replications of racism over generations:

> "It replicates itself over time because the first generation within an agency such as a police force will tend to screen for applicants that hold the same views. They will do this because of the tendency to train according to the methods that have been used in the past, and in order to avoid dissension within the agency. Thus racism once imbedded in an institution is likely to remain for several generations until it works itself out."[83]

Evidence of the insidious effects of a past rooted in slavery is borne out in statistics. A 1998 census report shows that 26 percent of African-Americans in the United States live in poverty compared to 8 percent of whites;[84] 14.7 percent of African-Americans have four-year college degrees, compared with 25 percent of whites.[85] That same year, African-American infant mortality rates were more than twice as high as those among the white population.[86] Federal figures also show that a black man born in 1996 can expect to live, on average, 6.6 fewer years than a white man born the same year.[87]

African-Americans are more likely than whites to go to jail, to be there longer, and if their crime is eligible, to receive the death penalty. They lag behind whites according to every social yardstick: literacy, life expectancy, income and education. They are more likely to be murdered and less likely to have a father at home.[88]

The economic deprivation resulting from slavery may be gleaned from discrepancies in earnings between whites and blacks. According to a 1993 report, black families earn only $580 for every $1,000 earned by white families. Only 3.4% of all black men earned $50,000 or more compared to 12.1% of white men. Additionally,

---

82 Hylton, *supra* note 79 at 30-40.

83 *Id.*

84 Joseph Dalakar, *Poverty in the United States, Current Population Report 1998* (September 1999) (www.census.gov/hhes/www/poverty/prevcps/p60-20f.pdf).

85 Complaint and Jury Demand, *Farmer-Paellmann v. FleetBoston Fin. Corp.*, Civil Action No. 02-cv-1862 (E.D.N.Y. filed March 26, 2002) at 18.

86 T.J. Matthews, Sally Curtin and Marian F. MacDermon, *Mortality Statistics from the 1998 Period Linked Birth National Infant Death Data Set,* Vital Statistics Report, Centers for Disease Control and Prevention Vol, 48, No. 12 July 20, 2000 (www.nber.org/perinatal/1998/docs/nvs48_12.pdf).

87 National Center for Health Statistics. Health United States, 1998 With 5000 Census Statistics and Health Chartbooks. Hyattsville, Ma. 1998 (www.cdc.gov/nchs/data/hus/hus98.pdf).

88 Farmer-Paellmann Complaint, *supra* note 85 at 19.

44.8% of black children live below the poverty line, compared to 15.9% of white children.[89]

Documented discrepancies in net worth are a direct result of slavery and the lost inheritance from slave ancestors to their descendents. A comparison of income, net worth and net financial assets for black and white middle-class families shows that, although blacks in the sample earned 70-85% of the income that whites earned, their net worth was only 16-18% of whites' net worth, and their net financial assets were zero.[90] Another study showed that a typical white family enjoys a net worth that is more than eight times that of its black counterpart.[91] This inequity is partly a result of the head start whites enjoy in accumulating and passing on assets. Some economists estimate that 80% of lifetime wealth accumulation results from gifts passed on by earlier generations.[92]

It was precisely these types of disparities between African-Americans and Caucasians that provided the rationale for allowing race-based remedial measures in admissions procedures employed by educational facilities, for example as permitted by the Supreme Court's decision in the case of *Bakke.*[93] As the above statistics attest, the realities for African-Americans have not changed dramatically since the 1978 decision in *Bakke*, where Justice Marshall confirmed the reality of continuing disparities among the races:

---

89 Rhonda V. Magee, *The Masters Tools From the Bottom Up: Responses to African-American Reparations Theory on Mainstream and Outsiders Remedies Discourse,* 79 VA. L. REV. 863, 873 (1993).

90 Tuneen E. Chisolm, *Sweep Around Your Own Front Door: Examining the Argument For Legislative African-American Reparations,* 147 U. PA. L. REV. 677, 690 (1999).

91 Dalton Conley, *The Cost of Slavery*, NY TIMES, February 15, 2003 at 25.

92 *Id.*

93 *Bakke v. Regents of the University of California*, 438 U.S. 265,371 (1978). (Brennan, White, Marshall and Blackmun J., concurring in part and dissenting in part: "From the inception of our national life, Negroes have been subjected to unique legal disabilities impairing access to equal educational opportunity. Under slavery, penal sanctions were imposed upon anyone attempting to educate Negroes. After enactment of the Fourteenth Amendment the States continued to deny Negroes equal educational opportunity, enforcing a strict policy of segregation that itself stamped Negroes as inferior, that relegated minorities to inferior educational institutions, and that denied them intercourse in the mainstream of professional life necessary to advancement (citations omitted). Segregation was not limited to public facilities, moreover, but was enforced by criminal penalties against private action as well. Thus, as late as 1908, this court enforced a state criminal conviction against a private college for teaching Negroes together with whites. *Berea College v. Kentucky*, 211 U.S. 45 (1908)... [T]he habit of discrimination and the cultural tradition of race prejudice cultivated by centuries of legal slavery and segregation were not immediately dissipated when *Brown I, supra,* announced the constitutional principle that equal educational opportunity and participation in all aspects of American life could not be denied on the basis of race. Rather, massive official and private resistance prevented, and to a lesser extent still prevents attainment of equal opportunity in education at all levels and in the professions.").

> "The position of the Negro today in America is the tragic but inevitable consequence of centuries of unequal treatment. Measured by any benchmark of comfort or achievement, meaningful equality remains a distant dream for the Negro.
>
> A Negro child today has a life expectancy which is shorter by more than five years that of a white child. The Negro child's mother is over three times more likely to die of complications in childbirth, and the infant mortality rate for Negroes is nearly twice that for whites. The median income of the Negro family is only 60% of that of the median of a white family and the percentage of Negroes who live in families with income below the poverty line is nearly four times greater than that of whites. The relationship between those figures and the history of unequal treatment afforded to the Negro cannot be denied. At every point from birth to death the impact of the past is reflected in the still disfavored position of the Negro. In light of the sorry history of discrimination and its devastating impact on the lives of Negroes, bringing the Negro into the mainstream of American life should be a state interest of the highest order. To fail to do so is to ensure that American will forever remain a divided society."[94]

Despite the decisions in *Bakke* and *Brown v. the Board of Education*, the reality of the current disparities between African-Americans and whites reflects that the work of emancipation is still incomplete. Lingering consequences are still apparent in the economic, educational, psychological and physical disparities evident between African-Americans and their white counterparts. It is the overriding responsibility of the US Courts to interpret the laws in such a way as to accomplish the aim of complete emancipation. To this goal, slavery must be viewed as a displacement of law: it can never be reconciled with any acceptable code of human behaviour. It must be regarded as void, *ab initio*. Likewise, all available law must be interpreted broadly to accomplish the aims of the Thirteenth, Fourteenth and Fifteenth Amendments. Courts must continually be reminded that the work of emancipation is not complete.

3.3 PROPERTY CLAIMS

Building on the legal notion of slavery as a derogation of law, as well as the factual evidence of its harmful generational effects, there are three possible property claims that may be considered by reparations plaintiffs: accounting, unjust enrichment and conversion.

3.3.1 Accounting

A claim for equitable accounting is a remedy of restitution requiring a fiduciary defendant who has taken undue advantage of a plaintiff, to disgorge the gains he has

94 *Bakke*, 438 U.S. at 395 (Marshall J. concurring) (emphasis added).

received from his improper use of plaintiff's property or entitlements.[95] The right to an accounting typically arises when defendant possesses money or property which, because of some particular relationship between himself and the plaintiff, he is obligated to surrender.[96] In the *Slave Descendants' Litigation,* each of the named corporate defendants benefited or profited from the slave trade. The goal of the litigation is to compel these defendants to account to the descendants of slaves for the profits they derived from the practice of slavery. The corporations have claimed that, for the plaintiffs to succeed on this theory, there must be a direct fiduciary relationship between the plaintiffs and defendants. However, the flexibility of equity allows the court to 'imply' an obligation between the parties. Hence, a court could find an implied duty between a beneficiary of the profits of the slave trade and the plaintiffs, as equitable owners of the unpaid labour of their ancestors.

3.3.2 Unjust enrichment

The legal claim for unjust enrichment is generally applied between parties who lack a contract yet one party has unjustly retained a benefit to another's detriment. Where that retention of the benefit violates the fundamental principles of justice, equity, and conscience,[97] one should disgorge the benefit. The beneficiary is obligated to relinquish the benefit where he has procured the benefit through some type of wrongful conduct, or even merely where the party bringing the suit had a better claim to the benefit than the defendant. The disgorgement is not barred merely because the benefit has not proceeded directly from one to another.[98]

This equitable claim arising out of unjust enrichment has it roots in the earliest jurisprudence of the United States. Hence, as early as 1886 the US Supreme Court embraced the concept that a wrongdoer who holds the fruits of another's labour is deemed to be holding the profits as a constructive trust, and has an obligation to preserve these funds in favour of those who are equitably entitled to them.[99]

---

95 *Government Guarantee Fund of Republic of Finland v. Hyatt Corp.*, 955 F.Supp. 441, 466 (D.C.V.I. 1997) citing 1 DAN B. DOBBS, *LAW OF REMEDIES* § 4.3(5), at 610 (2d ed.1993).

96 *In re Midway Airlines, Inc.*, 221 B.R. 411, 456 (Bkrtcy. N.D. Ill. 1998) (citing, 1A C.J.S. *Accounting* § 15 at 13 (1985)).

97 *HPI Health Care Services, Inc. v. Mt. Vernon Hospital, Inc.*, 545 N.E.2d 672, 679 (Ill. 1989)(citing *Drury v. County of McLean*, 433 N.E.2d 666 (Ill. 1982).

98 *Id.* at 679; *accord National American Ins. Co. v. Indiana Lumbermen's Mutual Ins. Co.*, 221 F.3d 1339 2000 WL 975176 (7th Cir. July 11, 2000) (unpublished opinion); *see generally* 4 G. Palmer, *The Law of Restitution* §§21.2, 21.4, 21.5 at 292-93, 298-99, 316-18 (1978).

99 *Moore v. Crawford*, 130 U.S. 122, 128 (1889) (quoting 2 J. Pomeroy, Equity Jurisprudence §1053, at 628-629 (1886). "Whenever the legal title to property is obtained though means or circumstance 'which render it unconscientious for the holder of the legal title to retain and enjoy the beneficial interest, equity impresses a constructive trust in the property thus acquired in favor of the one who is truly and equitably entitled to same, although he may never, perhaps, have had any legal estate therein; and a court of equity has jurisdiction to reach the property either in the hands of the original

Notably, even if the courts do not find the defendants' behaviour to have been wrongful, reparations plaintiffs still have a claim, as 'unjust enrichment does not require fault or illegality on the part of the defendant; rather, the essence of the cause of action is that one party is enriched and it would be unjust for that party to retain the enrichment.'[100]

3.3.3 Conversion

Another property claim made in the *Slave Descendants' Litigation* is based on conversion, meaning the wrongful taking of chattel, which is generally an object or personal property that is tangible. The defendant corporations have claimed that where there are no allegations of a wrongful taking of 'an object,' but where plaintiffs seek the return of tangible money, there can be no return of the object. However, when property is converted, the owner may sue for return of the specific article *or for the market value* thereof, 'or, if sold, treat [the] conversioner as a constructive trustee and sue for the proceeds.'[101] A wrongful taking does not change the title to the object, and title may be recovered if its identity is perceptible to the sense though changed in form and enhanced in value by the taker's labour.[102] Here it is axiomatic that the enslaved were viewed as property. Hence, as early as 1677, Justices of the Kings Bench in England ruled that an action for trover (conversion) was permitted for the taking of one hundred Negro slaves.[103] A more recent legal scholar has posited that the enslaved had a property interest in their person – a property right of self-ownership. Kaimipono David Wenger describes this right as follows:

> "Self-ownership can be viewed as simple ownership of one's physical body and bodily integrity. Legal scholars widely accept this minimum definition of self-ownership. A more expansive definition would view self-ownership as ownership in one's liberty---less about direct ownership of one's body, and more about ownership of the ability to make choices. In that sense, the right of self ownership can be seen as related to the constitutional rights of privacy and of familial integrity. Under either a limited or an expanded right of self-ownership, slaves were the owners of that right."[104]

---

wrong-doer, or in the hands of any subsequent holder, until a purchaser of it in good faith and without notice acquires a higher right and takes the property relieved from the trust'".) *Id.*

100 *Firemen's Annuity & Benefit Fund of the City of Chicago v. Municipal Employees', Officers', and & Official's Annuity & Benefit Fund of Chicago*, 579 N.E.2d 1003, 1007 (Ill. App. Ct. 1991) (citing, *Partipilo v. Hallman*, 156 Ill. App. 3d 806, 810 (Ill. App. 1st Dist. 1987).

101 *Kelly v. R-F Finance Corporation*, 60 S.W. 2d 1067 (Tex. Civ. App. 1933).

102 *Rip v. Les*, 118 S.W. 1084 (Tex. App. 1909).

103 *Butts v. Penney*, 2 Lex. 201, 83 Eng. Rep. 518 (K.B. 1677).

104 Kaimipono David Wenger, "Slavery as a Takings Clause Violation" 53 AM. U. L. REV. 191(October 2003).

3.4 TORT LIABILITY CLAIMS

Reparations plaintiffs allege claims arising in tort by alleging intentional infliction of emotional distress. While traditional tort law generally requires the existence of a duty between the wrongdoer and the victim, as well as proximate cause between the harm caused and the defendants' acts and damages (as discussed in greater detail at page 347 below), US courts have found ways to ease the burden of strict causation when it is equitable to do so.

3.5 CRIMES AGAINST HUMANITY[105]

International law recognises certain peremptory norms that are so basic that no country may deviate or derogate from them. *Jus cogens* principles bind all nations regardless of consent.[106] The prohibition against slavery is such a peremptory norm.[107] Slavery constitutes a *per se* violation of international law, and is regarded as a crime against humanity.[108] After World War Two, private citizens and corporate entities were tried criminally before an international military tribunal at Nuremberg for utilising slave labourers.[109]

---

105 The support for the law in this section is derived primarily from the work of Jon M. Van Dyke, *Reparations for the Descendants of American Slaves Under International Law*, in SHOULD AMERICA PAY? – *SLAVERY AND THE RAGING DEBATE ON REPARATIONS* 57 (Raymond A. Winbush ed. 2003).

106 *Siderman de Blake v. Republic of Argentina*, 965 F. 2d 699, 715 (9th Cir. 1992). *See also* Vienna Convention on the Law of Treaties, Articles 53, 64, May 23, 1969, U.N. Doc A/CONF. 39/27, 1155 U.N.T.S. 331, 8 I.L.M. 6799 (treaty provisions in violation of the *jus cogens* norms are void); *The Schooner Amistead*, 40 U.S. (15 Pet.) 518, 553, 595-96 (1841) (treaty with Spain cannot be applied to the return of purported slaves since it could not be interpreted to deprive the protection given to them via the law of nations.); *United States v. Matta-Ballesteros*, 71 F.3d 754, 764 n.5 (9th Cir 1995), *cert. denied*, 519 U.S. 1118 (1995) (*jus cogens* rules are peremptory, enjoy the highest status within customary international law, are binding on all nations); *Committee of U.S. Citizens Living in Nicaragua v. Regan*, 859 F.2d 929, 935 (D.D.C. 1988).

107 *Siderman*, 965 at 715-16 (citing Restatement (Third) of the Foreign Relations Law of the United States §§ 702 cmt. (1987)).

108 *The Nuremberg Trial*, 6 F.R.D. 69, 130 (Int'l Military Tribunal 1946), See Report of the International Law Commission, 5 U.N. GAOR Supp. (No 12) at 11-14, U.N.Doc A/1316 (1950); *Mehinovic v. Vuckovic*, 198 F. Supp.2d 1322, 1352 (N.D. Ga. 2002).

109 *See United States of America v. Alfred Felix Alwyn Drupp von Bohlen und Halbach*, IX Trials of War Council Law No. 10 (1950) (finding criminal liability despite government compulsion to meet quotas because the company was a private-profit-making institution and defendants independently sought to improve their profit margin by increasing production with slave labour); *United States v. Friedrich Flick*, VI Trials of War Criminals Before The Nuremberg Military Tribunals Under Control Council No. 10 (1952) (finding criminal culpability for two defendants who took the initiative to increase the company's production of freight cars and attempted to further use slave labour to accomplish this end); *United States of America v. Carl Krauch*, VIII Trials of War Criminals Before the Nuremberg Military Tribunals Under Control Council Law No. 10, 1179 (1952) (finding criminal liability for

Civil liability in U.S. courts for the use of slave labour is established by showing that a private party 'participated [or cooperated] in the forced labor practices.'[110]

Furthermore, principles of aiding and abetting in crimes against humanity have been recognised in United States law.[111]

Blackstone recognised that those who aided and abetted piracy were themselves liable as pirates.[112]

The US Supreme Court held in 1795 that a French citizen who had aided and abetted a U.S. citizen in unlawfully capturing a Dutch ship acted in contravention of the law of nations and was liable for the value of the captured assets.[113] Even in domestic tort law, aiding and abetting is commonplace.[114]

Therefore, United States courts have significant precedent to utilise human rights law in recognising a claim by the descendants of enslaved Africans against corporations who aided and abetted the slave trade, for their participation in crimes against humanity.

3.6 CONSUMER PROTECTION STATUTES

State consumer protection statutes are another source to be utilised in grounding claims by the descendants of slaves. In essence, at the time of the first filings certain corporations made statements to the newspapers that their predecessor entities did not profit from nor utilise slave labour. Some of these same corporations later changed their positions and admitted the involvement of their predecessor entities. Many states possess statutes that protect consumers from misleading practices or statements by

---

members of chemical and pharmaceutical company for their actions in constructing a synthetic rubber plant adjacent to Auschwitz; an act demonstrating their "embrac[ing] the opportunity to take full advantage of the slave-labor program."). *See also* Matthew Lippman, *War Crimes Trials Of German Industrialists: The "Other Schindler,"* 9 TEMP. INT'L & COMP. L.J. 173 (1995).

110 *Doe v. Unocal Corp.*, 110 F. Supp. 2d 1294, 1310 (D.D. Cal 2000), *aff'd in part, revs'd in part, Doe (1) v. Unocal Corp.*, 395 F.3d. 932 (9th Cir. 2002), *op. vacated*, 403 F.3d 708 (9th Cir. 2005). While the *Unocal* decision was ultimately vacated and therefore lacks formal precedential value, in light of the settlement of the case, it has significant moral weight.

111 *Presbyterian Church*, 244 F. Supp. 2d. at 321 (S.D.N.Y. 2003) (federal courts have almost unanimously permitted actions premised on a theory of aiding and abetting under the Alien Torts Claims Statute), *Presbyterian Church*, 374 F. Supp. 2d 331 (S.D.N.Y 2005) (aiding and abetting reaffirmed subsequent to the Supreme Court decision of *Sosa*), *Cabello v. Fernandez-Larios*, 402 F. 3d. 1148 (11th Cir. 2005) (conspiracy and accomplice liability accepted under international law and common law).

112 William Blackstone, Commentaries on the Law of England, Book IV, Chap. 5 (1769).

113 *Talbot v. Janson*, 3 U.S. (3 Dall.) 133 (1975).

114 Restatement (Second) of Torts §876(b); William L. Prosser, Handbook of the Law of Torts § 46 (4th ed. 1971) 1 Thomas M. Cooley, A Treatise on the Law of Torts, 244 (3d ed. 1906); *see* note 112. See also *Haberstan v. Welch*, 705 F. 2d. 472, 478 (D.C. Cir. 1983) (test for aiding and abetting focuses on whether defendant 'knowingly gave assistance' to someone who performed wrongful conduct).

sellers. Hence, in the case of *Nike,*[115] advocacy groups claimed that Nike, an athletic shoe and clothing manufacturer, made shoes in third world sweat shops. Nike launched a public relations campaign to counteract the bad publicity and was sued by a California consumer, Marc Kasky on behalf of the public, claiming violations of state consumer protection statutes. The California Supreme Court upheld plaintiffs' right to apply the law to Nike's misrepresentations. Nike's conduct is parallel to that alleged of certain defendants in the *Slave Descendants' Litigation* claims who, after the filing of the plaintiffs' lawsuits, made public statements misrepresenting their involvement in or benefit from the Transatlantic Slave Trade. The alleged misrepresentations by certain defendants served intentionally to deceive consumers. If these corporations had told the truth, consumers would not have purchased their product or service.

The advantage of these present-day state consumer protection claims is that they do not rely on past corporate actions dating back to the era of slavery, nor do they rely on accessory or derivative liability. These claims are based on the actions of the corporations today, and hence, provide less fodder for critics who seek to discount the claims arising from the past as too speculative.

To conclude, the plaintiffs' legal claims for reparations rest in traditional legal concepts of natural law, equity, property and tort. Additional possibilities arise in the expanding areas of human rights law, consumer protection and concepts of collective liability.

4 LEGAL STUMBLING BLOCKS

Given the straightforward character of the reparation claims, and the growing acceptance of collective justice claims and human rights theories by US courts, why has the suit brought before Judge Norgle been summarily dismissed without **any** of the theories being considered sufficient to allow a trial on the merits to proceed?

The Judge has justified the dismissal in the language of the courts, but when pieced together, the legal rationale for the dismissal may be attributed in part to the conservative judicial philosophy of the judge, as well as a continuing gap in knowledge regarding the history of slavery and its continuing legacy, racism.

The court expressed three reasons for the dismissal of the suit: standing, statute of limitations and the political question doctrine. A brief exploration of each of these legal concepts reveals that they are not as inflexible as the lower court and some critics have argued. This further raises the posssibility that the court's failure to allow the cases to proceed has little to do with bedrock principles of law and more to do with political

---

115 *Nike v. Kasky*, 27 Cal. 4th 939, 969-970, 45 P. 3d. 243, 262 119 Cal. Rptr. 296, 319 (Cal. 2002), *petition for writ of cert. granted*, 537 U.S. 1099 (2003), *dismissed as improvidently granted*, 539 U.S. 654 (2003).

conservatism and a reluctance to accept, or understand the continuing legacy of slavery.

4.1 STANDING

As the federal courts are created by the US Constitution, they are considered courts of limited jurisdiction and may only hear a matter that presents a case or controversy. The standing inquiry is a simple one that looks at whether a case presents a hypothetical question as opposed to a concrete one between adverse parties: '[A] justiciable controversy is thus distinguished from a difference or dispute of a hypothetical or abstract character, from one that is academic or moot, it must be definite and concrete, touching the legal relations of parties having adverse legal interests.'[116] Standing, however, need not be a wall that plaintiffs must scale to get into federal court.[117] Standing requires three elements: 'First, the plaintiff must have suffered an 'injury in fact' – an invasion of a legally protected interest which is (a) concrete and particularised…; and (b) 'actual or imminent', and not 'conjectural' or 'hypothetical'. Second, there must be a causal connection between the injury and the conduct complained of – the injury has to be fairly traceable to the challenged action of the defendant, and not…th[e] result [of] the independent action of some third party not before the court. Third, it must be 'likely,' as opposed to merely 'speculative', that the injury will be 'redressed by a favorable decision.''[118]

Judge Norgle interpreted this standard to require proof in the initial pleading that the defendants were *directly* involved in causing the injury to specific plaintiffs.[119] The Judge further asserted that plaintiffs could not meet this burden as plaintiffs' harm arose from the institution of slavery and not from the acts of the corporate defendants. The reasoning by the Court is the equivalent of suggesting that soldiers injured by the exposure to Agent Orange could not have their lawsuits heard because it was the substance, not the defendants' production of it, that caused the harm. While it is certainly true that no plaintiffs, save one,[120] claim that their ancestor was enslaved by a specific corporate defendant, the mere absence of a direct claim is not a proper basis for a dismissal of the suit on grounds of lack of standing.

---

116 *Aetna Life Ins. Co. v. Haworth*, 300 U.S. 227, 241 (1937).

117 Wright & Miller, 13 Fed. Prac. & Proc. Jurisdiction 2d §3531.4 (amended 2003).

118 *Lujan v. Defenders of Wildlife*, 504 U.S. 555, 560-561 (1992); *In re African American Slave Descendants' Litig.* 375 F. Supp. at 745-747.

119 *Id.* at 752.

120 In court papers filed subsequent to the complaints, plaintiff Farmer-Paellmann now claims she may be able to trace the enslavement of one of her ancestors to a predecessor company of one of the corporate defendants.

The court failed to address plaintiffs' contention that, in many other cases, courts have allowed standing to plaintiffs under causal chains more attenuated than those suggested by the plaintiffs in this case. The Court ignored the Supreme Court's proscription that, to grant standing, any level of injury is sufficient, even 'an identifiable trifle.'[121] The Judge further disregarded the wealth of case law that supports the precise harms the plaintiffs alleged: acts that cause segregation;[122] acts that affect one's aesthetic sensibilities;[123] stigmatic injury;[124] lost opportunity;[125] a recognised property right (even a derivative one);[126] or even where an award

---

121 *U.S. v. SCRAP*, 412 U.S. 669, 689 n. 14 (1973) (Standing was accorded to plaintiffs who alleged that a rail freight surcharge would discourage use of recyclable goods, encourage greater use of virgin materials, and thus impair the pleasures of outdoor activities).

122 *City of Chicago v. Matchmaker Real Estate Sales Center*, 982 F.2d 1086, 1095 (7th Cir. 1992) (A city had standing to challenge racial steering practices by realtors. Racial steering can lead to resegregation, destabilisation of the community, increased burdens in the form of crime and erosion of the tax base, and devotion of scarce city resources to ensure compliance with the fair-housing laws.), *Southside Fair Housing Committee v. City of New York*, 928 F. 2d 1336, 1341-1343 (2d Cir. 1991) (Latino and African-American residents of a nineteen-block urban renewal area had standing to challenge conveyance of one block to a Hasidic Congregation for development of a synagogue, yeshiva and faculty residence apartment. They adequately pleaded injury in claiming that the project would contribute to an increased displacement of racial and ethnic minorities from a neighbourhood that had been racially and religiously mixed. An order undoing the sale might reverse the trend.)

123 *Cantrell v. City of Long Beach*, 241 F.3d 674, 679-682 (9th Cir. 2001) (birdwatchers were accorded standing to challenge compliance with National Environmental Policy Act requirements in the process of developing plans to reuse a closed navy base. The court concluded that there was a legally protected, concrete aesthetic interest arising from the effect on the plaintiffs' viewing of birds on the base from places accessible to the public. The Court held that the the fact that the litigant's interest must be greater than that of the public at large does not imply that the interest must be a substantive right sounding in property or contract. Nor did it matter that there was no showing the birds themselves had been harmed, actual environmental injury is not required, only injury to the plaintiffs' enjoyment of the environment).

124 *Smith v. City of Cleveland Heights*, 760 F.2d 720, 722-23 (6th Cir. 1985), *cert. denied*, 474 U.S. 1056 (1985). Here a black resident had standing to challenge a racial steering practice adopted by the city population on the basis that in terms of the practice "a badge or a label of inferiority [was imposed] on him based purely on race".

125 *Regents of the University of California v. Bakke*, 438 U.S. 265 (1978). An unsuccessful non-minority applicant to medical school was accorded standing to challenge a preferential minority admissions program, without showing that he would have been admitted, but for the preference extended to minority applicants. Injury was found "in the University's decision not to permit Bakke to compete for all 100 places in the class simply because of his race". Hence, loss of an opportunity may constitute injury, even though it is not certain that any benefit would have been realised if the opportunity had been accorded. The irony is not lost that the beneficiaries of the *Bakke* decision were primarily white males who were protected by the equal protection clause of the Constitution that was designed to address the historic and legal injustices that African-Americans had suffered in slavery and its aftermath.

126 *U.S. v. 5 S 351 Tuthill Road*, 233 F.3d 1017, 1021-1024 (7th Cir. 2000) (The beneficiary of 'an unorthodox land trust' had standing to contest, as 'innocent owner', civil forfeiture of real property used in connection with drug offences. Here the claimant had a right to receive whatever proceeds might be realised on the sale of the property. On forfeiture, he would lose that right. " We think this is more than enough to give him an actual stake in the outcome…"); *Sanders v. City of San Diego*,

or distribution to one diminishes the amount available for others.[127] Nor need the harm plaintiffs suffer be direct to suffice for the purpose of standing.[128] On their face, plaintiffs' claims are replete with allegations of individualised harm stemming from the participation of the defendants' predecessors in the slave trade. But plaintiffs' claims go even further. Plaintiffs allege modern day harm as a result of actions arising out of defendants' present conduct: 1) defendants' intentional acts to minimise, distort and hide their predecessor companies' involvement in the Transatlantic Slave Trade (State Consumer Protection claims) and; 2) defendants' refusal to provide records regarding their connections to the slave trade (Demand for Accounting). It is submitted that plaintiffs sufficiently pleaded that some of this harm was *fairly* traceable to the defendants' predecessors who profited and/or participated or aided and abetted in the Transatlantic Slave Trade.

4.2 STATUTE OF LIMITATIONS

Generally, all claims are subject to statutes of limitations, to encourage certainty and to discourage stale claims. Courts are urged to enforce these limitations strictly, apart from certain well-defined exceptions. Critics have long-posited that claims brought by the descendants of African-American slaves arose some 250 years ago and are subject to be dismissed in terms of relevant statutes of limitations. Despite the practical necessity of barring old claims, courts have developed notable theories to toll limitations in recognition of extraordinary factual circumstances that make the strict application of limitations severely unjust. Specifically, where a plaintiff would reasonably have had difficulty discerning the fact or cause of injury at the time it was inflicted, the so-called 'diligence-discovery rule of accrual' applies.[129] In these

93 F. 3d 1423, 1426-1427 (9th Cir. 1996) (a pawnbroker had standing to complain of the warrantless seizure of pawned property where as pledgee, he had a legitimate possessory interest against the rest of the world, except for the person having title).

127 *Consolidated Edison Co. v. Richardson*, 233 F.3d 1376, 1383 (D. Col. 2000) (Standing found where any award to one person necessarily diminishes the amount available for distribution to the others. Oil purchasers who had claims on overcharge funds collected by the Department of Energy under the Emergency Petroleum Allocation Act for distribution to oil purchasers had standing to challenge an award to another purchaser).

128 *Warth v. Seldin*, 422 U.S. 490, 504-505 (1975); *Duke Power Co. v. Carolina Environmental Study Group, Inc.*, 438 U.S. 59, 72-81 (the Court found such indirect causation when plaintiffs, a group of neighbours living near a nuclear power plant, sued the NRC in an effort to invalidate a statutory limitation on nuclear liability); *Roe v. Wade*, 410 U.S. 113 (1975) (a "third party" was given standing because of harm that arose from a prohibition or restriction imposed on someone else. Thus, a pregnant woman had standing to challenge a statute that prohibited a doctor from performing an abortion); *United States v. SCRAP*, 412 U.S. at 688.

129 See *Kronisch v. United States*, 150 F. 3d 112, 121 (2d Cir. 1998), *cert. denied*, 531 U.S. 1078 (2001), *see also*, *Singleton v. City of New York*, 632 F. 2d 185, 191 (2d Cir. 1980), *cert denied*, 450 U.S. 920 (1981) (holding that the time of accrual is the "point in time when the plaintiff knows or has reason

circumstances, 'accrual may be postponed until the plaintiff has or, with reasonable diligence, should have discovered the critical facts of his injury and its cause.'[130]

Thus, courts have postponed the accrual of statute of limitations periods in a lawsuit by descendants of Jewish customers of a French bank for deposits made some 60 years earlier, when the banks failed to reveal records that would have allowed the survivors to learn facts that connected them to the assets being withheld.[131] Likewise, the courts postponed accrual of the statute of limitations on a claim brought by Holocaust survivors against the US government, which involved stolen assets of a Hungarian gold train which had been seized, and the Government was the sole possessor of relevant information and continued to deny culpability while refusing requests for information.[132] In *Thompson*,[133] the court refused to bar the claims of African-Americans who had been taken advantage of by a corporation which sold discriminatory insurance polices in the 1920s and 30s after the plaintiffs argued successfully that the corporations had affirmatively concealed their actions or that the actions were of a self-concealing nature. More recently in the 2005 decision of *Cabello*,[134] a human rights claim against a Chilean military official for the death of a citizen, the Court tolled the ten year statute of limitations until the surviving family members had uncovered the circumstances surrounding the death, since there had been concealment of the facts by the perpetrators.

Importantly, the facts of slavery present a textbook rationale for postponing accrual of claims. The conditions of slavery left most enslaved and newly emancipated slaves simply unable to make a claim for restitution. Moreover, state codes and Jim Crow prohibitions subsequently left most locked in semi-servitude. Moreover, even now, most defendants have refused steadfastly to provide records detailing their past connection to slavery, making it impossible for most even to know which corporations enslaved or profited from the labour of their ancestors. Hence, equitable postponement of accrual provides a viable mechanism for plaintiffs to secure justice.

There are two additional relevant theories for avoiding a statue of limitations bar. First, it is the view of the international community that statutes of limitations should not bar claims based upon crimes against humanity.[135] A California federal court has

---

to know of the injury which is the basis of his action... A claim does not accrue when a person has a mere hunch, hint or suspicion, or rumor of a claim").

130 *Corcoran v. New York Power Authority*, 202 F.3d 530, 544 (2nd Cir. 1999), *cert. denied*, 529 U.S. 1109 (2000) (citing *Kronisch* at 121) ("...claim will accrue when the plaintiff knows, or should know, enough of the critical facts of the injury and causation to protect himself by seeking legal advice.").

131 *Boder v. Baque Paribas*, 114 F. Supp. 2d 117, 135 (E.D.N.Y. 2000) citing *Long v. Abbott Mortgage Corp.*, 459 F. Supp. 108, 113 (D. Conn. 1978).

132 *Rosner v. U.S.*, 231 F. Supp. 2d 1202, 1209 (S.D. Fla. 2002).

133 *Thompson v. Metropolitan Life Insurance Co.*, 149 F. Supp.2d 38, 54 (S.D.N.Y. 2001).

134 *Cabello v. Fernandez-Larios*, 402 F. 3d 1148, 1155 (11th Cir. 2005).

135 Convention on the Non-Applicability of Statute of Limitations to War Crimes and Crimes Against Humanity, November 26, 1968.

noted that tolling limitations may be appropriate in suits for crimes against humanity based upon a 'wide variety of considerations' including the 'disruptions of war to the difficulty of obtaining authenticated documents located in confidential government files.'[136] Needless to say, plaintiffs have been unable largely to access corporate documents that could reveal connections between their ancestors and individual corporate defendants.

The second theory for avoiding limitations is that a court considering equity is not bound by limitations. In the US Supreme Court decision of *Holmberg*,[137] the Court concluded that statutes of limitations do not control measures in equity. Because the essence of plaintiffs' claim is that defendants were unjustly enriched by the labour of plaintiffs' ancestors, these claims are equitable in nature.[138] Rather than plaintiffs requesting an equitable tolling of their claims, it would be the burden of the defendants to prove the equitable defence of 'laches'. This equitable defence precludes plaintiffs from sleeping on their rights. To bar a claim on the ground of laches, a defendant must show: (1) the plaintiffs' knowledge of the defendants' misconduct; (2) plaintiffs' inexcusable delay; and (3) prejudice to the defendants.[139] In the *Slave Descendants' Litigation*, the application of this principle would allow the plaintiffs' claim to proceed unless the defendants could prove these three elements to establish a defence. Given that the corporate connections to slavery have only been discovered in recent years, defendants would have difficulty in meeting their burden.

Accordingly, a wealth of viable legal theories exist which undermine any argument that the time to bring reparations claims has expired.

4.3 THE POLITICAL QUESTION DOCTRINE

Another legal obstacle often cited is the political question doctrine. It reflects the reality of the division of responsibilities among the three branches of government as imposed by the Constitution. It allows courts to refuse to entertain a case where it could involve an issue more appropriately decided by another branch. In *Baker v. Carr*[140] the U.S. Supreme Court set forth the following list of relevant factors to be considered by a court when deciding a political question:

---

136 *Handel v. Artukovic*, 601 F. Supp. 1421,1431, n.4 (C.D. Cal. 1985).

137 *See Holmberg v. Ambrecht*, 327 U.S. 392, 396 (1946) ("Traditionally and for good reasons, statutes of limitations are not controlling measures of equitable relief.").

138 *See e.g., SEC v. Common-Wealth Chemical Sec., Inc.*, 574 F.2d 90, 95 (2d Cir.1978) (disgorgement of ill-gotten profits and restitution are equitable remedies).

139 *See Ikelionwu v. United States*, 150 F.3d 233, 238 (2d Cir.1998).

140 369 U.S. 186, 210-11 (1962).

"[1] a textually demonstrable constitutional commitment of the issue to a coordinate political department; or [2] a lack of judicially discoverable and manageable standards for resolving it; or [3] the impossibility of deciding without an initial policy determination of kind clearly for non-judicial discretion; or [4] the impossibility of a court's undertaking independent resolution without expressing lack of the respect due coordinate branches of government; or [5] an unusual need for unquestioning adherence to a political decision already made; or [6] the potentiality of embarrassment from multifarious pronouncements by various departments on one question."[141]

Generally, all of these relevant factors may be summarised in two general concerns: 1) will a judicial ruling interfere with the proper functioning of the executive or legislative branch; and 2) is the suit impractical or unmanageable for a court?

4.3.1 Courts not precluded from hearing reparation claims

From the time of the Civil War forward, neither the Executive nor Legislative branch meant to preclude judicial claims for restitution against corporations for the profits derived from slavery. Merely because a claim might be considered political by some, does not mean that a lawsuit is barred.[142] In fact, courts have warned against dismissal on political question grounds stating that 'judges should not reflexively invoke these doctrines to avoid difficult and somewhat sensitive decisions'[143] and that 'proper regard for the complex nature of our constitutional structure requires...that the Judicial Branch [not] shrink from confrontation with the other two coequal branches of the Federal Government'.[144]

4.3.2 Textual constitutional commitment to other branches

In order to succeed in barring a suit on political question grounds, the defendants must show that there was a commitment on the face of the Constitution for the political branches or executive branch to handle exclusively all aspects of financial recompense to those enslaved. There is a logical error in such an argument, as it assumes that because Congress or the Executive branch could do something, the other branches could not. This is a *non sequitur*. Merely because Congress could, for example, enact public or private legislation compensating individuals for tortuous acts through the instrumentalities of the federal government, does not mean that the judiciary is automatically disabled from hearing all claims. Reconstruction scholars agree that had the Framers chosen to make the power of Congress exclusive to itself, they could have

141 *Id.* at 217.

142 *Japan Whaling Ass's v. American Cetacean Soc.*, 478 U.S. 221, 230 (1986).

143 *Kadic v. Kadzic*, 70 F.3d 232, 249 (2d Cir. 1995).

144 *Valley Forge Christian College v. American United for Separation of Church and State, Inc.*, 434 U.S. 464, 473 (1981).

done so, but instead, they repeatedly demonstrated their intent to rely on the judiciary as a coordinate partner in the enforcement of Reconstruction policy.[145] While Judge Norgle in his dismissal of the *Slave Descendants' Litigation* argued that Reconstruction and the subsequent Civil Rights Acts were political efforts solely, the Court notably ignored the wealth of post-Civil War cases in which the Supreme Court chose to exert extraordinary powers to strangle early efforts of Congress to end the disabilities of African-Americans.[146]

Similarly, to suggest that Congress actually considered and rejected a compensation plan for the repayment of slaves for the work they performed during the Reconstruction is unthinkable, except by a small group of visionary Republicans. At the time the issue of reparations was so far from mainstream thought that it was never seriously discussed.[147]

4.3.3 Lack of manageable standards

The challenge of judicial manageability has not hindered the judiciary in other areas involving equal or greater challenge. Hence, courts have handled and continue to handle questions of school desegregation, massive human rights claims, as well as the exposure of thousands to chemical agents (as discussed above at pp. 323-324).

4.3.4 Embarrassment or contradictory prior statements of the administration or other constituent branches of government

To suggest that a court's management of a suit brought by private individuals against private entities for disgorgement of profits from the slave trade would cause embarrassment to the executive or legislative branch gains little traction when neither the legislature nor executive has taken any position either in support of or against the limited notion of corporate disgorgement. Hence, it does not invoke the same types of considerations as invoked in the Holocaust slave labour cases where some US courts refused to allow the cases to proceed under 'political question' defences. There, the cases invoked the consideration of treaties that were entered into after the war by the executive branch which covered specific arguments on reparations to be paid and

---

145 Stanley I Kutler, Judicial Power and Reconstruction Politics, 69-160 (University of Chicago Press 1968), Harold M Hyman and William Wiecek, Equal Justice under Law 355-385, 415-418 (Harper & Rowe, 1982); Harold M. Hyman, A More Perfect Union, 224-244, 263-271 (Knopf 1973), William M. Wiecek, The Reconstruction of Federal Judicial Power, *1863-1876*, 13 AM. J. LEGAL HISTORY, 339-359 (1969).

146 See cases described *supra* at n. 46-56.

147 Eric Foner, Reconstruction: America's Unfinished Revolution, *1863-1877*, 228-230. (Harper & Row 1988).

could, in some way, be argued to involve the power of the President to wage war and to make peace. There is no such executive power that can be invoked here.

In fact, recent statements made by the executive branch in openly acknowledging that slavery is a crime against humanity[148] and further acknowledging that lingering questions of race contributed to the slow response by the federal government to hurricane victims in New Orleans, suggest that these lawsuits are politically consistent with the sentiments of the executive branch.[149]

4.4 CAUSATION

Finally, some critics have suggested that perhaps the largest stumbling block to the successful prosecution of these reparation claims in US courts, is the challenge of establishing a causal chain between a specific slave descendant and a specific successor corporation. It is the absence of this causal link that has troubled many in terms of being able to hold present-day corporations accountable. For plaintiffs' claims arising under the quasi-contract theory of unjust enrichment, a direct causal claim is unnecessary as plaintiffs need only show that they have a better-positioned right in the disgorged funds than the corporations. Traditionally, a basic element of a tort claim is to establish that the acts of a specific tortfeasor caused the harm to a specific plaintiff. Traditionalists claim that this requires a 'but for' test, meaning that absent the tortfeasor's conduct the harm would not have occurred. It is plain that enforcing this type of causal test in respect of the slave descendants' litigation would, in all probability, doom all further litigation, except for the narrow group of claims arising under current-day consumer protection statutes.

However, as with many traditional tests once applied by courts in torts, judges have fashioned numerous theories to restrict a rigid interpretation of this test where it tends to thwart justice. Hence, as early as the 1800s, the courts developed the concept known as *res ipsa loquitur* – the thing speaks for itself. The most common application of this doctrine is when a patient goes into surgery and is given an anaesthetic and comes out to find that a sponge or other instrument has been left inside of him or her.[150] In that

---

148 On July 8, 2003, President Bush, in a major policy speech given on Goree Island in Senegal, declared slavery to be "one of the greatest crimes in history" and to have been a crime even in "John Adam[s']" time. (http://www.whitehouse.gov/news/releases/2003/07/20030708-1.html).

149 In the wake of the devastation wrought by Hurricane Katrina, President Bush in his speech to the nation on September 16, 2005, noted: " … poverty has roots in a history of racial discrimination, which cut off generations from the opportunity of America…We have a duty to confront this poverty with bold action." Nedra Pickler and Terrence Hunt, *Washington will pick up the majority of the $200B tab*, STAR LEDGER, (New Jersey), September 16, 2005 at 8.

150 The doctrine of *res ipsa loquitur* ("the thing speaks for itself") provides that, in some circumstances, the mere fact that an accident occurred raises an inference of negligence. Black's Law Dictionary 1336 (8th ed. 2004). The earliest reported case in which the doctrine was applied is *Byrne v. Boadle*, 159

situation, the law allows the patient to sue all those in the operating room, requiring that they disprove their involvement. Another unique fact pattern provides a basis for further flexibility from a traditional casual analysis: two hunters shoot at the same person, both mistaking that person for a deer. One hunter's bullet wounds the victim, yet it cannot be determined which bullet is the one that caused the harm. In the case of *Summers v. Tice*,[151] the court allowed the prosecution of both hunters, and shifted the burden onto the hunters to disprove their involvement, since 'practical justice' so required. The theory has been termed 'alternate liability' and has been applied in different factual situations.[152] The *Summers* principle was expanded to apply to an industry in *Hall v. E.I. Du Pont De Nemours*,[153] where thirteen children were injured in twelve unrelated accidents by unmarked blasting caps. The plaintiffs could not identify the particular manufacturers and sued almost the entire industry and its trade associations. The court permitted plaintiffs to establish liability and shift the burden of causation where there was a joint control of risk based upon evidence of 'explicit or implicit safety standards, codes and practices which are widely adhered to in an entire industry.'[154]

Another relaxation of the traditional causation model is the theory of 'concert of action'. It derives from the criminal concept of aiding and abetting.[155] It allocates responsibility among parties who 'in pursuance of a common plan or design to commit a tortuous act, actively take part in it, or further it by cooperation or request, or . . . lend aid and encouragement to the wrongdoers or ratify and adopt the wrongdoer's acts done for their benefit…'.[156] The application of market share theories in product liability claims provides another example of relaxation of causal standards when justice

Eng. Rep. 299, 300 (Ex. 1863). There the plaintiff was struck and injured by a barrel of flour that fell out of the defendant's shop window, and the court concluded that the barrel could not have rolled out of the window without negligence. For the doctrine to apply, the plaintiff must establish three criteria: (1) that the injury-producing occurrence is not the kind that ordinarily happens without someone's negligence; (2) that the injury was caused by some agent or instrumentality under the exclusive control of the defendant; and (3) the injury-producing occurrence is not due to any action by the plaintiff.

151 33 Cal. 2d 80, 86-88 (1984).

152 Restatement (Second) of Torts § 433B(3) (1965) ("Where the conduct of two or more actors is tortuous, and it is proved that harm has been caused to the plaintiff by only one of them, but there is uncertainty as to which one has caused it, the burden is upon each such actor to prove that he has not caused the harm"). The comment to this subsection urges modification of the rule where all actors cannot be joined: "…It is possible that cases may arise in which some modification of the rule stated may be necessary because of complications arising from the fact that one of the actors involved is not or cannot be joined as a defendant…or because of substantial difference in the character of the conduct of the actors or the risks which they have created".

153 345 *F.Supp*. 353 (E.D.N.Y. 1972).

154 *Id.* at 373-374.

155 *Ryan v. Eli Lilly & Co.*, 514 F.Supp. 1004, 1015 (D.S.C. 1981).

156 *Shackil v. Lederle Laboratories*, 116 N.J. 155, 162-63 (1989), citing, W. Keeton, D. Dobbs, R. Keeton & D. Owen, Prosser & Keeton on The Law of Torts § 46 at 323 (5th ed. 1984).

so requires. In the 1970s women discovered that the drug diethylstilbestrol (DES) that they took in the 1950s to prevent miscarriages sometimes had detrimental effects on the reproductive systems of their children and grandchildren. Problems of proof existed in that pharmaceutical and doctors' records were destroyed, memories had faded, and many of the doctors who prescribed the drug could not be located. As a result, most women could not identify the manufacturer of the drug their mothers or grandmothers took. Despite this failure of traditional proof, some courts allowed the cases to proceed by fashioning theories to hold the defendants responsible for the injuries to these women. Thus, the court in *Sindell v. Abbott*[157] held DES manufacturers liable to the plaintiff daughters unless the manufacturers could show that they did not cause the harm. Since multiple actors contributed to the injury, and causation could not be traced individually, the court held all manufacturers liable up to their proportionate market share in respect of the drug at the time. The court reasoned that as 'between an innocent plaintiff and negligent defendants, the latter should bear the cost.'[158] Importantly, some courts allowed claims in respect of injury to the granddaughters of the women who had originally ingested the drug.[159] The courts' extension of claims to the third generation and the act of burden shifting to the wrongdoer provides a crucial and viable theory for sustaining slave descendants' claims. If: 1) the institution of slavery is properly recognised as the displacement of law; and 2) any corporation who participated or benefited from the trade is found to be a wrongdoer; and 3) if we view descendants as the equivalent of the third generation descendants of the DES women who are unable through no fault of their own to trace the specific offenders, then these corporate defendants should be responsible for their own unjust enrichment unless they are able to disprove their specific involvement. The application of a modified causal proof standard would be even less burdensome to the court than in the DES cases, since the slave descendants are seeking disgorgement of benefits into a common benefit fund, thus precluding the need for individual trials for each plaintiff.

Currently courts are allowing modified causal theories in other toxic tort cases. In asbestos exposure cases, where it is impossible for plaintiff to prove medical causation as to a specific defendant's product because of exposure to multiple products of multiple defendants over an extended period of time, courts have adopted a test merely requiring proof of an exposure of sufficient frequency, with a regularity of contact, and with the product in close proximity to the plaintiff, to establish causation.

---

157 26 Cal.3d 588, *cert denied*, 449 U.S. 912 (1980).

158 *Id.* at 610-611; *in accord*, *Bichler v. Eli Lilly*, 79 A.D. 2d 317, 324-325 (N.Y. App. Div. 1981).

159 *DiMeo v. Schmidt*, No. 625, 1989 Phila.Cty. Rptr. LEXIS 73 at *1 (C.P. Philadelphia County Dec. 28, 1989); *McMahon v. Eli Lilly & Co.*, 774, F. 2d 830 (7th Cir. 1985); *see generally*, Kaimipano Wenger, *Causation and Attenuation in the Slavery Reparation Debate*, EXPRESSO PRE-PRINT SERIES (2004) at 50-51. (http://law.bepress.com/expresso/eps/778).

This eliminates the need for proof of direct contact.[160] Likewise, in toxic cases where the plaintiffs cannot prove that a particular disease, for instance, a type of cancer, was caused by exposure to defendant's chemical, courts have relaxed the traditional tort model, allowing proof of a quantifiable increased risk through epidemiological tests, animal studies, and *in vitro* studies, to suffice as cause-in-fact.[161]

As the Supreme Court of New Jersey has opined: 'The torts process, like the law itself, is a human institution designed to accomplish certain social objectives.'[162] One of the primary objectives is to ensure 'that innocent victims have avenues of legal redress, absent a contrary, overriding public policy.'[163] If the purposes of a judicial system are to compensate and deter, and this cannot be accomplished because traditional proof requirements are too strict due to circumstances beyond the control of the plaintiffs, courts should exercise their equitable power in easing traditional proof requirements. Ultimately, courts should aim to strike a balance between providing a viable forum to harmed individuals, while ensuring that tortfeasors are not saddled unreasonably with a disproportionate share of liability in respect of uncertain and unpredictable risk.

5 THE REAL STUMBLING BLOCKS

While there are viable legal arguments that may support the successful prosecution of the claims under discussion, there remain multiple practical obstacles.

5.1 GAPS IN HISTORICAL KNOWLEDGE

Evidence as to the complicity of corporations in the institution of slavery did not become available to attorneys until developments in 2000. One of the key plaintiffs in the *Slave Descendants' Litigation*, Deadria Farmer-Paellmann, a law school graduate,

160 *James v. Bessemer Processing Co*, 155 N.J. 279, 301-302 (1998) (Court described "frequency, regularity and proximity" test being applied in asbestos cases in the states of Michigan, Massachusetts, New Jersey, Illinois, Pennsylvania, Maryland, Nebraska, Oklahoma, and all Circuits except the District of Columbia, First, Second, and Fifth).

161 *Elam v. Alcolac, Inc.*, 765 S.W.2d 42, 188, n.63, 208 (Mo. 1998) ("A recovery for increased risk of cancer, however – whatever the theory adopted – involves proof of a quantified risk. One theory treated the cause of action for increased risk of cancer as a present injury with future consequences. It allows recovery if the toxic exposure has induced some biological manifestation from which the anticipated cancer is reasonably certain to occur…The other theory treats increased risk of cancer as a present invasion of a legally protected interest, and hence actionable even absent any manifestation of injury. The increased risk, as quantified by expert testimony as a percentage of probability, measures the recovery.").

162 *People Express Airlines, Inc. v. Consolidated Rail Corp.*, 100 N.J. 246, 254 (1985).

163 *Id.* at 245-55.

was able to uncover scores of corporate connections to slavery.[164] Her initial research into Aetna's ties to slavery resulted in March 2000 in an admission and apology by Aetna for writing slave insurance policies in the 1850s.[165] Some four months later, the *Hartford Courant*, a Connecticut newspaper, ran an article admitting its complicity in running advertisements for the sale of slaves.[166] In February 2002, a *USA Today* journalist, Jim Cox, wrote a series of articles connecting eighteen corporations in various industries to profits from the Transatlantic Slave Trade.[167]

The knowledge of the connection between corporations and slavery has improved dramatically since the filing of the case in 2002. As described in greater detail below, the passage of numerous slavery disclosure laws requiring corporations to report their slavery connections have added to the pool of available information. Certain historians, motivated by the initial progress of disclosures, continue to contribute to the growing pool of information about corporate involvement in slavery.[168]

5.2 LIMITED RESOURCES

The financial expense of bringing a class action suit or multiple suits of a similar magnitude is extraordinary. The cost of prosecuting the current claims, drawn entirely from the resources of the attorneys themselves, has exceeded a million dollars. Large law firms which are best positioned to bring the claims often have corporate clients and such a controversial claim could create conflicts of interest, or could upset their corporate client base. Often small law firms are not equipped to bear the financial risk that these suits entail. The continued successful prosecution of these claims requires a consistent, ongoing and concerted strategy to obtain sufficient funding for additional research, experts and lawyers to pursue the claims.

---

164 Jim Cox, *Farmer-Paellmann Not Afraid of Huge Corporations*, USA TODAY, February 21, 2002 (Farmer-Paellmann claimed to have uncovered slavery ties to 60 corporations).

165 Tamar Lewin, *Calls for Slavery Restitution Getting Louder*, NY TIMES, June 4, 2001.

166 *Id.*

167 *See e.g.*, Jim Cox, *Rail Networks Own Lines Built with Slave Labor; Firms Own Dailies That Were Vital to Slavery; Fleetboston Traced to Slave Trading Merchant; Brown Bros.: Loans Gave Planters Cash to Buy Slaves; Lehman Bros: One Brother Owned Seven Slaves in 1860; Textile Companies Linked to 'Negro Cloth' For Slaves; Insurance Firms Issued Slave Policies*, USA TODAY, January 21, 2002.

168 Anne Farrow, Joel Lang, Jennifer Frank, *How the North Promoted, Prolonged and Profited from Slavery: Complicity at Preface*, xvii-xix. (Ballentine Books 2005) (Some of the authors were the reporters who had participated in the Hartford *Courant's* original revelations about its own connections to slavery and had further participated in a lengthy supplement further exploring the complicity of the Connecticut people, institutions and businesses in the institution of slavery. The book grew out of additional research spurred by the revelations arising out of the *Slave Descendants' Litigation*).

5.3 TRADITIONAL CIVIL RIGHTS ORGANISATIONS AT ODDS WITH GRASSROOTS ACTIVISTS

The *African-American Slave Descendants' Litigation* also presents challenges relating to the issue of who has a 'legitimate claim' to supervise, coordinate and prosecute a reparations strategy. While one might expect non-profit, civil rights organisations to take the lead in reparations litigation strategy, they have remained primarily on the sidelines. Instead, reparations litigation has been advocated primarily by nationalist organisations.[169] Similarly, even the initiation of the lawsuit by private attorneys not associated with either mainstream civil rights organisations, or with nationalist organisations, has resulted in challenges in coordination of strategies among non-traditional bedfellows.

5.4 POLITICAL EFFORTS

Although Congressman John Conyers, Jr. of Michigan has fought since 1989 to get national legislation passed that would provide for the effects of slavery and possible remedies to be studied, the legislation has failed even to make it out of the committee stage.[170] Some members of the Congressional Black Caucus (a recognised association of African-American Congressional representatives) have been reluctant to fight for reparations legislation because they are unwilling to spend their political capital when they regard such legislation as 'doomed' from the start. It is far easier to support a bill that elevates Rosa Parks to the status of a national hero, than to face the prospect of supporting a bill that may continue failing to secure passage into law.

The most promising developments in the ongoing legal strategy to secure reparations are the continuing efforts to pass slavery disclosure laws at a city and state level. These disclosure statutes force companies doing business in certain locales to report their ties to the Transatlantic Slave Trade, or face sanctions if they fail to do so fully, or if they wrongfully withhold information. At the time of this printing, the state of California[171] and the cities of Richmond, California;[172] Chicago,

---

169 *See generally*, Adjoa A. Aiyetora, *Mounting the Challenges and Claiming the Victory* (http://www.ncobra.org.resources1.htm#challenge) (last visited, April 11, 2006) (Leader of Grassroots Organisation involved in movement for reparations describes the ongoing struggle for reparations and cautions against divisiveness).

170 *See* H.R. 375, 101st Cong. (1989); H.R. 1684, 102nd Cong. (1991); H.R. 40, 103d Cong. (1993); H.R. 891, 104th Cong. (1995); H.R. 40, 105th Cong. (1997); H.R. 40, 106th Cong. (1999); H.R. 40, 107th Cong. (2001); H.R. 40, 108th Cong. (2003).

171 CA INS. § 13813 *et. al.*; California Code of Regulations, Title 10, §§ 2393-2398.

172 Katie Benner, *Wachovia apologies for slavery ties,* CNN MONEY, June 2, 2005 (References ordinances in Chicago, Richmond, Philadelphia and Los Angeles).

Illinois;[173] Philadelphia, Pennsylvania;[174] Detroit, Michigan;[175] and Los Angeles, California,[176] have all passed slavery disclosure bills that require companies to report their connections to slavery in the past.[177] To date the effect of these laws has been dramatic. They have led numerous corporations to hire historical archivists to engage in comprehensive searches of the corporation's past. This in turn has resulted in significant admissions by major defendant corporations. In 2002, defendant Lehman Brothers, a financial service giant, admitted that the three Lehman brothers, who in 1850 founded the firm's predecessor, bought a female slave named Martha.[178] In January 2005, JP Morgan Chase[179] announced that a predecessor Louisiana entity had owned slaves and further described its commitment to a $5 million scholarship fund. In June 2005 this was followed by the admission of Wachovia bank that two previously acquired entities had owned hundreds of slaves, accepted hundreds of slaves as collateral on loans, and one of the predecessor entities had owned an 'undetermined' number of slaves when debtors had defaulted on their loans.[180] Wachovia spokesman Scott Silvestri said the company was talking to the NAACP, the Urban League and other civil rights groups about how to proceed: 'We didn't want to have a donation or gift right out of a gate', he said. 'We wanted to think about what's the best way to address that.'[181]

Also, in the summer of 2005, defendant Bank of America (formerly known as Fleet Bank) disclosed its slavery links and pledged $5 million to be used by institutions to preserve African American history.[182] The bank was required to report its slavery

173 Cynthia Greenlee-Donnell, *Reparations for slavery still big debate*, THE HERALD-SUN (North Carolina), June 18, 2005. (References ordinances in California, Philadelphia, Chicago and others pending); *See* Municipal Code City of Chicago, 2-92-585.

174 Benner *supra* at n.172.

175 Darryl Fears, *Seeking More Than Apologies for Slavery: Activists Hope Firms' Disclosure of Ties Will Lead to Reparations*, WASH. POST, June 20, 2005 at A01 (http://www.washingtonpost.com/wp-dyn/content/article/2005/06/19/AR2005061900694_pf.html).

176 Article 15, Chapter 1, Los Angeles Administrative Code, Ordinance No. 175346. Regulations Regarding Participation or Profit Derived from Slavery By Any Corporation Doing Business with the City (June 30, 2003).

177 Greenlee-Donnell, *Reparations for Slavery Still Big Debate*, *supra*, note 174; Fears, *Seeking More Than Apologies*, *supra*, note 173.

178 Fran Spielman, *Company Admits to Slave History*, CHICAGO SUN TIMES, September 13, 2005 (http://findarticles.com/p/articles/mi_qn4155/is_20050913/ai_n15668468).

179 *Benner*, *supra* at n 172. (In January 2005, J.P. Morgan Chase revealed that a predecessor institution in Louisiana had used slaves. They simultaneously announced a 5 million dollar scholarship fund for students in Louisiana. This disclosure by J.P. Morgan Chase was followed by a similar disclosure in June 2005 by banking giant Wachovia. Wachovia revealed that two of its acquired entities, Georgia Railroad and Banking Company and the Bank of Charleston owned slaves. Georgia Railroad and Banking Co. owned 162 slaves and accepted 529 slaves as collateral while the Bank of Charleston acquired an undetermined number of slaves when debtors defaulted on loans).

180 *Id.*

181 Fears *supra* at n. 175.

182 Spielman, *Companies Admit Slavery History*, *supra* at n. 178.

connections in accordance with the Chicago ordinance and was forced to fight accusations at Chicago City Hall that it did not disclose its ties to slavery in a sworn affidavit. The city reviewed evidence showing slave ownership by John Brown – a former director of Providence Bank. Providence Bank was a predecessor entity to defendant Fleet-Boston, a bank later acquired by Bank of America.[183] The City of Chicago could have sanctioned Bank of America if it found that it had misrepresented its connections to slavery in its disclosure to the City. Later, in Fall 2005, Lehman Brothers, which had previously disclosed its founders' ownership of one slave, acknowledged that the company had owned numerous slaves and, in all likelihood, profited significantly from slavery.[184] Notably, this revised response came only after the entity sought to underwrite a $15 billion bond issue[185] for the City.

Attorneys in the *Slave Descendants' Litigation* have sought to use these admissions to their advantage by securing an order from the Court taking judicial notice of certain disclosures, as a means to bolster their claims of misrepresentation and violations of state consumer protection laws by certain corporate defendants.[186]

These ordinances could lead to additional legal requirements being imposed by states and local governments on corporations, obliging such corporations to provide more sophisticated plans, which may include defined corporate commitments to urban redevelopment, education, health care, and employment opportunities, to name a few possibilities.[187] Experience shows that once corporations are required to present financial reparations plans, they will in turn pressure the government and other public institutions to bear some of the costs for the injuries and lost opportunities suffered by the descendants of enslaved African-Americans.

5.5 EFFORTS BY CIVIL SOCIETY

Other institutions are beginning to study and examine the feasibility of reparations plans. For instance, Brown University appointed a task force to look at the question

---

[183] *Id.*

[184] *Id.*

[185] *Id.*

[186] Judge Norgle's Order of Judicial Notice, *In re African American Slave Descendants' Litigation* (filed February 17, 2005), Case No. 1:02-cv-07764, Document 172.

[187] Angela Couloumbis, *Goode Expected to Declare Banks' Slavery Disclosure*, PHILADELPHIA INQUIRER, June 9, 2005) (www.philly.com) (In addition to an ordinance requiring disclosure of slavery financial ties which had been previously passed, this proposed legislation would go one step further and would require banks with ties to produce a financial plan including how the bank planned to introduce products or services designed to "address racial disparities in its lending or investment activities").

of its role in facilitating the Transatlantic Slave Trade.[188] The National Methodist Convention USA, a protestant religious grouping with 14.5 million adherents,[189] passed a resolution calling for the study of reparations.[190] The Presiding Bishop of the Episcopal Church USA,[191] with over 3.4 million adherents,[192] has stated publicly that:

> "I don't think we have addressed the wounds that still exist over [slavery] ... [Addressing it properly] should involve the acknowledgement that we were perpetrators and that pushes us in a direction that will be costly."[193]

In June 2006, at their triennial National Convention, the Episcopalians passed resolutions acknowledging their past involvement in slavery, supporting a study of the monetary and non-monetary recompense to descendants of the victims of slavery and urging Congress to begin dialogue on the history of slavery and entertain proposals for possible resolution.[194] In the same month, the Moravian Church apologised for slavery and promised amends for racism.[195] Likewise, a North Carolina commission urged the state to repay the descendants of victims of an 1898 campaign in which 60 blacks died and thousands were driven from their homes in an effort violently to strip blacks of power in Wilmington, North Carolina.[196]

The New York City Historical Society recently presented its first exhibition on slavery in New York with a significant emphasis on the economic benefit of slavery to the pre-Civil War economy.[197] In 2007 the U.S. National Slave Museum is due to

---

188 *Brown University Committee Examines Historical Ties to Slavery* BLACK ISSUES IN HIGHER EDUCATION (March 25, 2004) (http://www.findarticles.com/p/articles/mi_m0DXK/is_3_21/ai_n5998813).

189 http://www.adherents.com/rel_USA.html#2004total

190 Linda Green, *United Methodist Church Supports Reparations for African Americans*, GENERAL CONFERENCE NEWS. UNITED METHODIST CHURCH (March 6, 2004) (http://archives.umc.org/interior-asp?.ptd=178&mid=4711) (The resolution 1) supports the passage of Rep John Conyers proposed legislation H.R. 40 calling for a study on the feasibility of reparations; 2) petitions the President, Vice-President and the U.S. House of Representatives to support the signing of the passage of H.R. 40; 3) mandates the development of a strategy and interpretation of the church resolution by a subcommittee of the church; 4) requires that resources be made available for the study of slavery and the role of theology in validating and supporting the institution and abolition of slavery).

191 Most Rev. Frank T. Griswold.

192 *Supra.* at n.191.

193 Steve Waring, *Apology For Slavery Sought* THE LIVING CHURCH (November 6, 2005) at 9.

194 Jim DeLa, *From Columbus: Church acknowledges role in slavery, plans reparations study* EPISCOPAL NEWS SERVICE (June 21, 2006) (http://www.episcopalchurch.org./3577_76321_ENG_HTM.htm).

195 Erin Texeira, Trend grows to make amends for slavery THE STAR LEDGER (July 10, 2006) at 22.

196 Id.

197 http://www.nyhistory.org/exhibits.html (last visited March 28, 2006) (The official web site of the Society describes the exhibit as the first to tell "the full story of slavery in New York – from its early 17th century roots, through the aftermath of the Civil War" while further stating that the "unprecedented exploration into slavery and its impact on the people, landscape, institutions, and economy of New York City, State, and the nation, attracted record crowds, generated favorable

open in Fredericksburg, Virginia, with a price tag of $200 million.[198] In 2012 the National Museum of African American History and Culture is scheduled to open in Washington DC. It is to be a part of the prestigious Smithsonian Museum and will be located near the National Monument. Its estimated price tag is approximately $500 million.[199]

These examples evidence a growing awareness of and continued study into the financial, psychological and spiritual harm that the institution of slavery wrought on successive generations of African-Americans.

5.6 CONSERVATIVE JUDICIARY

It appears plain that in the future the US faces a more conservative federal judiciary that may reverse progress in civil rights, mass torts and collective justice as a whole. The recent addition of Supreme Court Justices John Roberts, Jr. and Samuel Alito, Jr. will no doubt move the Supreme Court in a more conservative direction. This may have trickle-down effects in federal courts throughout the country and could adversely affect the outcome of future reparations litigation.

5.7 EFFECTIVE GRASS ROOTS SUPPORT

Cases such as these are part of a growing trend that have their roots in politics, as much as law. These cases may be strengthened significantly by sophisticated and coordinated efforts to mobilise grass-roots support. While the cases received positive coverage in the press, efforts to mobilise boycotts and form effective coalitions, such as those mobilised and formed around the divesture campaign in opposition to South Africa under apartheid, have met with limited success. In 2002 a march in Washington for reparations was attended primarily by core supporters.[200]

---

reviews in the media and, very importantly, visits from tens of thousands of teachers and students." Due to the unprecedented number of people who wanted to see the exhibition, the viewing dates were extended for three weeks through March 26, 2006 and the Society created a version of this exhibition for permanent display).

198 Margaret Moffet Banks, *Eyes on the Prize*, NEWS RECORD OBSERVER (North Carolina), March 21, 2006. (http://www.news-record.com/apps/pbcs.dll/article?AID=/20060321/NEWSREC0101/603210306/1001/NEWSREC0201).

199 *Id.*

200 Charles Ogletree, E.R. Shipp. *Does America Owe Us: A Harvard Law Professor and a Pulitzer-prize Winning Journalist Discuss the Pros and Cons*, ESSENCE (February 2003) (http://www.findarticles.com/p/articles/mi_m1264/is_10_33/ai_97117973).

Some political action groups have gained extraordinary clout from successful internet fund raising and mobilisation strategies.[201] Reparations activists could also benefit through the employment of consultants, who could provide the necessary tools for maximising grass roots support both domestically and internationally.

6 THE ROAD FORWARD

The road forward in litigating slavery reparations cases is to acknowledge first that such litigation is in its infancy and that success can only be judged over an extended period of time. Since these cases touch on large-scale political and social problems, they will continue to be constrained by the vicissitudes of jurists' views on issues of judicial restraint, rule of law, and collective justice.

Second, proponents must convince judges, attorneys and scholars that one of the judiciary's most historic and fundamental obligations is to employ equity where a combination of circumstances would: 1) leave viable plaintiffs without a meaningful legal remedy; 2) benefit society as a whole and; 3) not unduly prejudice defendants or unduly interfere with other branches of government. Judicial examples of courts recognising this inherent power and concomitant duty abound. The fundamental point thus far unassimilated into legal discourse is that the institution of slavery, by its very nature, constitutes the absence of law, therefore, it can never be sanctioned by any past, current or future law. It is this premise that has led the international legal community to accept the prohibition against slavery as *jus cogens* law, not requiring the consent of a nation to be binding. Claims related to slavery, whenever they arise or are discovered, must be investigated, prosecuted and remedied. Civil liability for modern day violations of aiding and abetting in cases of slavery is well established in the common law jurisprudence of the United States. Extending these holdings to historical violations should be unproblematic, especially since no statutes of limitations exist for crimes against humanity. Alternatively, Judges should consider slavery and its violent and virulent racist aftermath as a textbook example for the tolling of limitations *per se*. A refusal to acknowledge so basic a historical disability is tantamount to an unconscionable abdication of judicial responsibility.

Third, education must continue as to the fundamental and recurring harm caused by slavery to the descendants of enslaved African-Americans as well as in respect of the unjust benefit retained by those who still continue to gain from its legacy.

Fourth, attorneys need closely to coordinate their efforts with those of political interest groups, including civil rights organisations, youth organisations, church

201 *See* Montague Kern. *Web and Mass Media Campaigns by Political Candidates, MoveOn.org and the Democratic Party in the 2003-2004 Democratic Primaries: Struggling for Votes and Unity in a Year of Web Innovation* (April 19, 2004)(http://sherpa.bl.uk/2/01/PMKern.pdf) (unpublished).

groups, labour groups, environmental groups and international human rights groups. A broad-based, powerful coalition is essential to efforts going forward.

Fifth, attorneys should be ready imaginatively and tenaciously to deploy the full panoply of legal procedures and claims to succeed in reparations litigation.

What we all gain from a thorough look at our past involvement in slavery is an ability to pursue a more united and fully human future. By studying the debt owed due to slavery in the past, by acknowledging it and making recompense, we strengthen the very heart and vitality of our judicial system.

REPARATIONS FOR RESIDENTIAL SCHOOL ABUSE IN CANADA: LITIGATION, ADR AND POLITICS

KEN COOPER-STEPHENSON[1]

1 INTRODUCTION AND BACKGROUND

The long-overdue movement to provide redress to those who suffered abuse in Canada's Residential Schools is on the threshold of achieving effective resolution, arguably a historical success in relative terms by comparison with reparations claims in other countries. The processes employed for claims by Residential School survivors – for psychological abuse, physical abuse, sexual abuse, and cultural genocide – have included litigation, alternative dispute resolution (ADR) and political negotiation. This chapter will review recent developments with respect to these resolution processes, in which the leading Native Indian non-governmental organisation in Canada, the Assembly of First Nations (AFN),[2] has played a major role.[3] The chapter will also begin to explore questions of justice and legal theory raised by the processes.[4]

---

1 I am indebted to Ms. Amanda Doucette, student at the College of Law, for her research and editing work in connection with this chapter.

2 See particularly the *Assembly of First Nations Report on Canada's Dispute Resolution Plan to Compensate for Abuses in Indian Residential Schools* (November 2004) online: Assembly of first Nations <www.afn.ca/cmslib/general/Indian-Residential-Schools-Report.pdf> [AFN Report].

3 This chapter draws in part on three conference presentations: Ken Cooper-Stephenson, "Reparations for State Wrongs: Tort Law's Political and Theoretical Role" (Paper presented at a conference, "The Residential Schools Legacy: Is Reconciliation Possible?" Calgary Alberta, March 2004) [Cooper-Stephenson, "Reparations for State Wrongs"]; Ken Cooper-Stephenson, "Rights, Reparations, Dispute Resolution and Politics: Reflections on Justice and Theory in Residential School Abuse Claims" (Paper presented to a human rights conference, University of Saskatchewan, September 2005) [Cooper-Stephenson, "Reflections on Justice"]; and Ken Cooper-Stephenson & Michaela Keet, "Conceptual and Computation issues in Damages for Sexual Assault" (2005). Paper presented to Saskatchewan Trial Lawyers Association Seminar, November 2005 [Cooper-Stephenson, "Sexual Assault Damages"].

4 Some of the theoretical questions emerge from collaborative work with Professors Marjorie Benson and Michaela Keet at the University of Saskatchewan. For consideration of the jurisprudential theory which lies behind reparations claims generally, see Ken Cooper-Stephenson, "Theoretical Underpinnings for Reparations: A Constitutional Tort Perspective" (2003) 22 Windsor Y.B. Access

1.1 POLITICAL AWARENESS: *RESTORING DIGNITY*

The 1996 Royal Commission on Aboriginal Peoples, *Looking Forward, Looking Back,*[5] recommended that there be a public inquiry to examine the origins and effects of government policies with respect to Residential Schools and the abuses which took place in that context. This task was handed to the Law Commission of Canada. In 1998, the government also made a *Statement of Reconciliation* which acknowledged and expressed regret for the harms caused. After a series of dialogues between government representatives, church representatives, and school survivors, a number of pilot ADR projects were undertaken. Recommendations were then made with respect to the design of any future resolution processes. In 2000 the government released the Law Commission Report, *Restoring Dignity: Responding to Child Abuse in Canadian Institutions,*[6] which set out principles for a compensation plan and called for a public inquiry into the problem.

The *Restoring Dignity* Report identified the 'needs' of survivors of abuse in the Residential Schools from their own perspective. The Report resolved to keep the interests of these children (who are now adults) at the forefront of any further resolution. *Restoring Dignity* revealed two overarching 'values' that were reflected in the way survivors themselves had expressed their needs. These were:[7]

(a) Respect and engagement; and
(b) Information and support.

As for the 'needs of survivors', *Restoring Dignity* recognised them in the following way:[8]

> "Each person who was abused as a child experienced it differently, coped with it differently and suffered different consequences. The effects of childhood abuse depend not only on the duration of the abuse, but also on its nature, its intensity, the institutional context within which it occurred, the particular psychological make-up of the child and the subsequent support that child received, among other factors. It follows that the needs of survivors are as unique and varied as are the survivors themselves."

Just. 3 [Cooper-Stephenson, "Theoretical Underpinnings"]. For scholarly writing addressing reparations claims worldwide, see generally the articles in (2003) 22 Windsor Y.B. Access Just.

5 *Report of the Royal Commission on Aboriginal Peoples* (1996) online: <www.ainc-inac.gc.ca/ch/rcap/sg/sg1_e.html>.

6 Law Commission of Canada, 2000 ["Restoring Dignity"]. For the history of Residential Schools, see the University of Saskatchewan author, J.R Miller, *Shingwauk's Vision: A History of Native Residential Schools* (Toronto: University of Toronto Press, 1996), and J.R. Miller, "Troubled Legacy: A History of Native Residential Schools" (2003) 66 Sask. L. Rev. 357.

7 "Restoring Dignity", *ibid.*, at 71-73.

8 *Ibid.*, at 74.

The Report then described what the Commission viewed as '... the primary areas of needs identified by survivors...':

(a) Establishing an historical record; remembrance;
(b) Acknowledgement;
(c) Apology;
(d) Accountability;
(e) Access to therapy or counselling;
(f) Access to education or training;
(g) Financial compensation; and
(h) Prevention and public awareness.

It was noted that most of these needs were 'felt not only by individuals but also by families and communities'. The list was therefore a 'starting point' and was perhaps 'a springboard for imagining how these needs can be fulfilled in ways specifically suited to certain individuals or groups'. It was also hoped that the list 'may assist in identifying further needs of survivors'.

When *Restoring Dignity* came to analyse 'financial compensation', it suggested that there was no need for survivors to 'downplay the importance of financial compensation' which, the Report pointed out, they were entitled to 'just like all other victims of a crime or a civil wrong'. As well, it was noted that such compensation can go towards fulfilling the other needs voiced by survivors. From a theoretical standpoint it is interesting that *Restoring Dignity* defends the award of compensation on grounds which are constructive and forward-looking rather than merely backward-looking, compensatory, and reflective of what was lost. However, it is clear that survivors viewed tort compensation as a mere component of a larger conception of 'justice'.

1.2 RESIDENTIAL SCHOOL LITIGATION

Litigation with respect to abuse in Residential Schools began before the Commission delivered its *Restoring Dignity* Report. By March 2003, there were approximately 18,000 tort claims,[9] and several class actions, including the Ontario *Baxter Cloud* action,[10] claiming loss of language and culture for $76 billion. By that time some 1,150 claimants had reached a settlement with the government; and as of May, 2004, 17 court judgments had been issued. The most prominent of these were the British Columbia

---

9 Treasury Board Secretariat *Indian Residential Schools Resolution Canada Performance Report for the Period ending March 31, 2003.* (Ottawa: Supply and Services Canada). ["Treasury Board Report"].

10 Certified in Ontario, see www.thomsonrogers.com/class_ action_pressreleasesandnotices.htm .

Court of Appeal's decision in *Blackwater v. Plint*,[11] and the Saskatchewan Court of Appeal's decision in *H.L. v. Canada (Attorney General)*.[12] In *Blackwater*, the court held that the government was the sole employer of church officials in the Residential School context, thereby letting the church off the hook with respect to vicarious liability. In *H.L.*, a large trial award for a Residential School survivor was drastically reduced. Another relevant case was the Supreme Court of Canada's decision in *John Doe v. Bennett*,[13] which clarified the position of the Catholic Church and its officials with respect to institutional and vicarious responsibility.

More recently, however, the Supreme Court of Canada allowed the appeals in both *Blackwater*[14] and *H.L.*[15] In *Blackwater* the Court held that vicarious liability could be shared between employers, thereby rendering the church jointly and severally liable with the government for the tort of an employee at a Residential School. And in *H.L.*, by a bare majority, the Supreme Court restored the trial judge's award of $376,464.09,[16] and clarified numerous tort doctrines as they applied to the measure of damages in sexual assault cases.[17] However, the Supreme Court's decision in *E.B. v. Order of the Oblates of Mary Immaculate in the Province of British Columbia*[18] cut in the opposite direction. In *E.B.*, another Residential School case, the Court construed narrowly the degree of connection which must be shown between the employer and the act of abuse by the employee (*E.B.*). This resulted in a refusal to impose vicarious liability on the defendant for the abusive conduct of a lay employee who lived on the school premises.[19]

---

11 (2003), 235 D.L.R. (4th) 60, [2004] 3 W.W.R. 217 (B.C.C.A.), reversed on the issue of joint vicarious liability 2005 SCC 58, 258 D.L.R. (4th) 275 [*Blackwater*].

12 *Sub nom. L. (H.) v. Canada (Attorney General)* (2003), 230 D.L.R (4th) 135, 19 C.C.L.T. (3d) 226 (Sask. C.A.), reversed on numerous issues 2005 S.C.C. 25 [*H.L.*].

13 [2004] 1 S.C.R.436, 236 D.L.R. (4th) 577 [*John Doe*]. This was not a Residential School case, but it involved sexual abuse by a Catholic priest, and the status of the bishop of a Catholic diocese, and of the diocese itself. (The Catholic Church is incorporated in Canada separately in each diocese, whilst other churches are incorporated as national entities).

14 *Supra* note 10.

15 *Supra* note 11.

16 *L. (H.) v. Canada (Attorney General)* (2001), 5 C.C.L.T. (3d) 186, [2001] 7 W.W.R. 722 (Sask. Q.B.). Klebec J. reviewed almost all the previous reported Residential School abuse claims in his judgment. The Supreme Court reduced the pecuniary damages for loss of past earnings to reflect the time the plaintiff had spent in prison and the social assistance he had received.

17 See Zoe Oxaal, "Removing that which was Indian from the Plaintiff': Tort Recovery for Loss of Language and Culture in Residential Schools Litigation" (2005) 68 Sask L. Rev. 367 [Oxaal, "Tort Recovery for Language and Culture"]. See also Ken Cooper-Stephenson, "Reparations for State Wrongs", *supra* note 2. The Supreme Court of Canada decision in *H.L.* is, however, largely concerned with the appropriate standard of review by appeal courts.

18 2005 SCC 60, 258 D.L.R. (4th) 385 [*E.B.*].

19 The recent Supreme Court of Canada decisions are considered below in more detail.

1.3 THE DR MODEL

In November, 2003, the federal government introduced its much criticised *Indian Residential School Alternative Dispute Resolution Process* [the 'DR Model'].[20] The DR Model had the character of a settlement process rather than an ADR process. Broader interests, such as loss of culture and the interests of significant others and the Native communities affected by abuse of their members, were specifically excluded from the program. Furthermore, the method of assessment of compensation for victims, by a geographically-discriminatory, ill-informed and starkly insensitive 'grid' system,[21] was thought unacceptable and inadequate. It is clear that the Canadian government's primary motivation in devising the DR Model was simply to resolve out of court the huge number of legal claims already launched. Absent an alternative method of resolving these legal actions, the caseload was estimated to take another 53 years to conclude, at a cost of $2.3 billion in 2002 dollars (not including the value of the actual damages awards themselves).[22] The figures with respect to potential claimants are startling, although time has depleted the number of survivors still living.[23] In 1991, Statistics Canada estimated that there were approximately 105,300 former residential school children survivors, and by early 2004 that number had dropped to approximately 87,500. Of the original 13,044 claims, in 2004:

- The average age of claimants was 57 years old.
- 11,315 former students had unresolved claims against the Government of Canada.
- This means that approximately 76,185 claims had not been filed.
- 1,729 settlements had been reached with individual claimants.

Within the last category:

- 1052 claimants settled before going to trial;
- 198 claimants settled in pilot projects;
- 15 were resolved in court decisions;
- 3 were resolved through the Dispute Resolution process;
- 461 were dismissed or discontinued.

$74.8 million had been spent on the claims process.

---

20 See *Indian Residential Schools Resolution Canada: Guide for Alternative Dispute Resolution Process*, online: <http://www.irsr-rqpi.gc.ca/english/pdf/Application-Guide.pdf> ["The DR Guide"].

21 *Ibid.*, at 43-49.

22 "Treasury Board Report", *supra* note 8.

23 Figures taken from the AFN "Fact Sheet", online: Assembly of first Nations <http://www.afn.ca/article.asp?id=766>.

The Residential School survivors and Native communities were understandably sceptical of the DR Model, which was devised without any significant consultation with Native peoples. In particular, the refusal of the government to address cultural harm was almost prohibitive of any meaningful participation by the survivors. Hence, by November 2004, fewer than 750 applications had been filed and were waiting for a hearing and/or adjudication. Five hundred of these claims were for sexual abuse and/or serious physical abuse (Model A claims), the remainder being for lesser physical abuse (Model B claims).[24] Only nineteen claims had been settled by that time.[25]

2 THE ASSEMBLY OF FIRST NATIONS REPORT

2.1 BACKGROUND TO THE REPORT

Following a national conference in Calgary, Alberta in March 2004, the AFN assembled a group of experts. The activity in the ensuing months is described in the AFN Report as follows:[26]

> "An extensive review of the relevant case law, historical literature, government documents, reports, and estimates was undertaken as well as a review of many legislated and non-legislated compensation schemes for damages caused by mass torts and mass human rights violations in Canada and internationally. A careful review of application forms under various compensation schemes was undertaken as well as numerous discussions held with experts in human rights, child abuse, survivor groups, litigators, church representatives, judges, academics, psychiatrists, psychologists and counsellors. Relevant case law was examined from Canada, Ireland and the United Kingdom. A fact-finding mission to Ireland and England was undertaken by two members of the expert group.... Throughout the period between March and September, the Task Force compiled its views, distilled its findings and research, and drafted recommendations...".

The culmination of this work was the *Assembly of First Nations Report on Canada's Dispute Resolution Plan to Compensate for Abuses in Indian Residential Schools*, made public in November 2004.[27]

---

24 Indian Residential Schools Resolution Canada "Statistics to Sept.1, 2004", online: IRSRC <http://www.irsr-rqpi.gc.ca/english/statistics.asp>.

25 Much of the information given in this part of the paper is derived from the AFN Report, *supra* note 1.

26 *Ibid.*, at 11-12.

27 *Ibid.*

2.2 CRITIQUE OF THE DR MODEL

The response of Native communities and survivors to the original DR model was summarised in the AFN Report as follows:[28]

> "Notwithstanding the positive elements of the DR model, it has not been well received in First Nation communities across the country or by a large number of residential school survivors. In addition to the criticisms cited above [which included critique of the method of calculating losses, the manner of determining vicarious liability, and overall that the compensation package was 'based on tort law principles, narrowly interpreted'], survivors have forcefully indicated that the current model under-values or ignores their personal injuries and does not take into account the context of residential schools. They say in order to be just, fair, and reasonable, the compensation plan must consider and account for their personal losses more accurately and comprehensively as well as compensate for group-based systematic abuse and the consequences that flowed from that abuse."

The Report identified the following as 'the most common criticisms expressed by survivors of the current DR model' (these are in addition to those indicated in the above summary):[29]

- The current model does not address emotional abuse, neglect, slave labour, loss of family life and parental guidance and their consequences.
- The present measure of compensation does not consider the injuries and consequences associated with racism, assimilation, and cultural genocide.
- The provisions for compensating survivors from abuse by other students are too limited.
- Survivors, regardless of health or age status, cannot access interim awards.
- The application form is complicated, confusing, and intimidating.
- The process takes too long.
- The model does not take into account the healing needs of survivors, their families, and their communities.
- The model does not take gender differences into account, neither for the gender-specific injuries inflicted nor for the gender-specific consequences of the injuries.
- The model judges punishment by the standards of the time it was administered.
- The model does not address the need for truth telling, public education, or awareness of the Canadian public about residential schools.

The Report indicated that many if not all of the criticisms could be resolved. The recommendations built 'on the time, resources, and expertise already invested by

[28] *Ibid.*, at 16-17.

[29] *Ibid.*, at 17

Canada by working from the positive elements in the current model'. The recommendations sought to extend the positive elements of the DR Model 'to cover the unique harms caused by the residential school experience in a more contextual, sensitive manner, and by including a healing component'.

2.3 COMPENSATION RECOMMENDATIONS

The AFN Report then proposed a compensation scheme which had slightly different goals from those generally recognised by tort law:[30]

> "[W]e are not seeking full tort law damages in an alternative dispute process. However, our recommendations do support fair and just redress for the full range of injuries suffered and we encourage the federal government to restore the dignity of survivors by responding with generosity, compassion and speed. The amount of compensation should recognize that people were harmed, provide solace for their injuries, assist in repairing the emotional, physical and psychological damage caused by residential schools, and provide funds for the reconstruction of the survivors' (sic) lives."

Most notably, for the purposes of a comparison with the goals and principles of tort litigation, the recommendations included the following:[31]

> "1. To ensure that the full range of harms are redressed, we recommend that a lump sum award be granted to any person who attended an Indian residential school, irrespective of whether they also suffered the separate harms generated by sexual, physical or severe emotional abuse...
>
> 10. In the interests of fair compensation, healing, reconciliation, and accepting full responsibility for past wrongs, we recommend that Canada expressly acknowledge its responsibility and accept fault for both the physical and sexual abuses of First Nations students and Canada's assimilation policy...
>
> 25. In the interests of reconciliation and in recognition of the on-going harms of residential schools to survivors and their families, we recommend that the Agreement Towards Reconciliation [i.e. the claims release] include a commitment by Canada to recognize and deal with the on-going needs of survivors and their communities arising from the harms caused by residential schools...".

In order to facilitate fair treatment and the move away from a 'settlement' process to a true ADR process, the Report made recommendations with respect to the appointment and expertise of adjudicators, including the following:[32]

30 *Ibid.*, at 17-18.
31 *Ibid.*, at 18, 24, 32.
32 *Ibid.*, at 22, 33, 34.

"6. To achieve a more accurate and fair assessment of the consequences of the physical, sexual and severe emotional abuses experienced by survivors, we recommend that medical or therapeutic professionals sit as one of two adjudicators on each claim…

27. In the interests of fairness and for the appearance of fairness in the adjudicative process we recommend that the qualifications for adjudicators be re-visited to place greater emphasis on ADR skills, medical/therapeutic experience and education, Aboriginality, gender, and knowledge and familiarity with equality jurisprudence, child abuse, native studies and human rights standards.

28. In light of their past history of negative experiences First Nations citizens have had within the Canadian justice system and in the interests of achieving fair and unbiased decision-making in this process, we recommend that the training of adjudicators and other participants in the ADR process be much more context-specific to residential schools".

2.4 TRUTH-TELLING AND RECONCILIATION

Part II of the AFN Report concluded in addition that:[33]

"1. …a truth-telling and reconciliation process be a component in this national, holistic mechanism complementary to the DR process and survivor participation should be voluntary".

The Report considered that 'it is a fundamental principle that the harms done be addressed in a holistic manner', and that this truth-telling, healing, and reconciliation process should 'be in tandem with the refinement of the DR model'. It 'could be connected to community-based processes but the design of the truth telling process would ultimately be that of the survivors and their communities'. The purpose was said to be as follows:[34]

1. To create a space for the survivors to tell their stories and have them understood.
2. To create public awareness and a public record of what happened and the consequences.
3. To create a plan or recommendations for the future, for restoration and healing of relationships.
4. To ensure that another state-committed atrocity does not take place again.
5. To acknowledge and support the need for the healing of relationships between families and communities, survivors and their families and communities, and all other people who were adversely affected by residential schools.

---

33 *Ibid.*, at 37.

34 *Ibid.*, at 36.

These extracts from the AFN Report do not address the suggested reformulation and restructuring of tort claims for physical and sexual abuse *per se*. The extracts are selected to indicate how, as in a true ADR Model, interests and parties other than those likely to be addressed by a rights-based tort claim can be introduced and become prominent. Indeed, the inclusion in the AFN Report of the claim for 'cultural loss', a claim which may be difficult, though not impossible, to sustain in law,[35] is considered by the AFN and by survivors as a necessary prerequisite of the claims process. The failure to include in the DR process this claim for cultural loss – viewed rightly as the systemic underlying cause of the more discreet physical and sexual abuses – was the primary impediment to the signing up of survivors for the DR Model.

3 POLITICAL AND LEGAL PROGRESS

3.1 THE POLITICAL ACCORD

The upshot of the AFN Report and of the energy of the parties involved was the historical Political Accord signed by National Chief Fontaine on behalf of the AFN with the federal government. In this document, dated May 1st, 2005, the Parties agreed as follows:[36]

1. Canada recognises the need to continue to involve the Assembly of First Nations in a key and central way for the purpose of achieving a lasting resolution of the IRS [Indian Residential School] legacy, and commits to do so. The Government of Canada and the Assembly of First Nations firmly believe that reconciliation will only be achieved if they continue to work together;
2. That they are committed to achieving a just and fair resolution of the Indian Residential School legacy;
3. That the main element of a broad reconciliation package will be a payment to former students along the lines referred to in the AFN Report;
4. That the proportion of any settlement allocated for legal fees will be restricted;
5. That the Federal Representative will have the flexibility to explore collective and programmatic elements to a broad reconciliation package as recommended by the AFN;
6. That the Federal Representative will ensure that the sick and elderly receive their payment as soon as possible; and
7. That the Federal Representative will work and consult with the AFN to ensure the acceptability of the comprehensive resolution, to develop truth and reconciliation

35 Oxaal, "Tort Recovery for Language and Culture", *supra* note 16.

36 Online: Assembly of First Nations <http://www.afn.ca/article.asp?id=1185> ["The Political Accord"].

processes, commemoration and healing elements and to look at improvements to the Alternative Dispute Resolution process.

Former Supreme Court of Canada Justice Iacobucci was simultaneously appointed as the negotiator for the government.

3.2 THE AFN CLASS ACTION

Little more than three months after the Political Accord, on August 3rd, 2005, the AFN decided to file a Class Action against the Attorney General of Canada, naming Chief Fontaine, himself a survivor of Residential School maltreatment, as one of the representative plaintiffs.[37] The Statement of Claim sought, *inter alia*, an Order for certification as a Class Proceeding, and the appointment of plaintiffs for four sub-classes: (1) a 'Survivor Sub-Class'; (2) a 'Deceased Sub-Class'; (3) a 'Family Sub-Class'; and (4) an 'Aboriginal Sub-Class'. It also sought a series of Declarations with respect to the role of the Crown in relation to the Residential Schools, and included actions in negligence, breach of fiduciary duty and breach of statutory duties pursuant to the *Indian Act*. The action requested an Order requiring the Crown to establish a fund 'to mitigate the Cultural, Linguistic and Social Damage caused by the Crown's Residential Schools Policy'. The claims for compensation total $40 billion, composed of $12 billion for non-pecuniary damages, $12 billion for pecuniary losses, $12 billion for aggravated, exemplary and punitive damages, and $4 billion for the family sub-class pursuant to Ontario's *Family Law Act*[38] and equivalent statutes in other provinces.

The legal action might initially have been thought of as somewhat disingenuous in light of the movement toward legal and political compromise and settlement. However, the very much warranted purpose of the action was indicated in a statement by Chief Fontaine:[39]

> "Because of our lack of formal legal status, we have only been participating in a consulting capacity in [the negotiations]. However, this matter is far too important for us not to have a full seat at the table that will ensure not only that our voices are heard on an equal basis with all other parties, but that our consent will be required for any agreement that is reached.
>
> We will continue to work with the federal representative, Mr. Justice Frank Iacobucci, on this important matter and we have the full confidence he is operating in good faith…".

---

37 Class Action, online <http://www.afn.ca/article.asp?id=1632> ["Class Action"].

38 R.S.O. 1960, c. F.3, S. 61 as amended.

39 *Supra* note 36.

It is obvious that the tort claims which grounded the initial court litigation have changed their jurisprudential character into something quite different from 'ordinary' tort claims. Nevertheless, the discrete tort wrongs are still at the heart of the process.

3.3 RECONCILIATION AND COMPENSATION AGREEMENT

Most recently, on November 20th, 2005, an historic reconciliation and compensation agreement[40] was reached between the Government of Canada,[41] the Plaintiffs,[42] the Assembly of First Nations, and the Churches.[43] This included an agreement to implement the earlier Political Accord, as well as a reformulated and restructured settlement process for the Residential School abuse claims,[44] and the allocation of sufficient resources to bring this chapter of Canadian history to an acceptable close. The AFN noted that the agreement met 'the overall standard that the AFN has been seeking – that it be demonstrably fair and just to the survivors, and that it would lead and contribute to reconciliation, respect, and recognition.'[45] As stated by National Chief Fontaine:[46]

> "This is the largest and most comprehensive settlement package in Canadian history. Today marks the first step towards closure on a terrible, tragic legacy for the thousands of First Nations individuals who suffered physical, sexual, or psychological abuse."

The settlement was heavily based on the critique of the earlier Dispute Resolution Model in the AFN Report.[47] The settlement included (1) a national apology; (2) an improved compensation process for victims of sexual and physical abuse in the Residential Schools; (3) a lump sum payment for former students; (4) an expedited process to resolve the claims of the elderly; and (5) a Truth and Reconciliation Commission with both national and regional processes. As well, the Aboriginal Healing Foundation[48] is to receive additional funding for another five years.

---

40 Assembly of First Nations, News Release, online: <http://www.afn.ca/article.asp?id=1935> ["Major Victory"]. Full text of the "Agreement in Principle" can be viewed at http://www.thomsonrogers.com/Agreement(OCR)andTOC.pdf.

41 The Agreement in Principle was approved by Cabinet on November 21st, *ibid.*

42 Represented by a National Consortium, a leading Saskatchewan law firm (whose clients numbered in the thousands), and other legal counsel.

43 The General Synod of the Anglican Church of Canada, the Presbyterian Church in Canada, The United Church of Canada, and Roman Catholic Entities.

44 "Agreement in Principle", *supra* note 39 at Schedule B.

45 "Major Victory" *supra* note 39.

46 *Ibid.*

47 *Supra*, text at note 27, "Critique of the DR Model".

48 Online: Aboriginal Healing Foundation <http://www.ahf.ca/e_Announcements.aspx>.

With respect to any existing causes of action, survivors currently involved in individual or class action lawsuits qualify for all of the benefits of the new settlement package, including compensation. In addition, the lawyers involved in court actions were rewarded with substantial payments of up to $4,000 plus reasonable disbursements per claim. Somewhat controversially, both the National Consortium (which was handling the *Baxter* class action) and a Saskatchewan law firm that had signed up large numbers of survivors, are each to receive $40 million.

As for the legal processes involved in the Canada-wide settlement, it is intended that a common-form class action will be drafted, and that certification of classes of claimants will be sought in each Canadian province (tort law being a matter of provincial jurisdiction). This will give the opportunity for the settlement to embrace the vast majority of survivors. However, if a significant number of survivors 'opt out' of the class actions within a one-year time period after the actions are certified, then the government has the option of refusing to continue with the agreement. Another potential frustration may come if the new Progressive Conservative minority government, elected on January 23rd, 2006, decides not to honour the agreement, which was negotiated by the outgoing Liberal government.

4 RECENT SUPREME COURT OF CANADA RULINGS

Lying in the background of the political and alternative dispute resolution processes are the rights and entitlements which Residential School survivors have or may have under the common law of torts. Although a claimant's path to legal redress might be hampered procedurally – by such things as limitation periods, and the questionable substantive grounds of some of the claims[49] – the political and ADR processes have largely operated in the 'shadow of the law', and are significantly influenced by mainstream legal entitlement. Notably, the removal by provincial legislation of limitation periods for sexual assault cases[50] gave life to some of the most serious cases. Furthermore, the very fact that the conduct of the churches and government may have been in some manner open to legal sanction at the time of its occurrence has had an influence on the political progress. In any event, it is now possible to make a moral, quasi-legal argument that a present obligation exists to compensate for conduct which, *ex post*, can be viewed as morally reprehensible.[51]

49 See Oxaal, "Tort Recovery for Language and Culture", *supra* note 16.
50 See, e.g. *Limitations Act*, R.S.S. c. L-16.1, s. 16.
51 Considered below, Cooper-Stephenson, "Theoretical Underpinnings", *supra* note 3 at 12-13.

This chapter earlier noted the very recent decisions of the Supreme Court of Canada in the Residential School abuse cases of *H.L.*,[52] *Blackwater*,[53] and *E.B.*,[54] and also the Court's decision in *John Doe*.[55] Although the issues addressed in these cases engage a wide range of concepts in the fields of tort law and damages assessment, they give particular focus to questions of vicarious liability and factual causation. These concepts are significant not merely in the narrow legal context of tort compensation, but also as an influence on the revised DR Model and for political assessment of Residential Schools claims.

4.1 VICARIOUS LIABILITY

Two decisions of the Supreme Court of Canada in 1999, *Bazley v. Curry*[56] and *Jacobi v. Griffiths*,[57] expanded the scope of vicarious liability for intentional torts committed by employees. Vicarious liability attaches liability to an employer where the tort committed by an employee is in some manner associated with the employment context.[58] A critical requirement laid down in both *Bazley*[59] and *Jacobi*[60] is the need for a 'strong connection' between the enhanced risk created by the employment situation and the tort committed by the employee.[61] In its decision in *H.L.*,[62] the Supreme Court of Canada did not disturb a plaintiff-friendly application of *Bazley* and *Jacobi*. The employee in question was actually functioning in an extra-curricular recreational program outside his regular employment duties at the time he committed the sexual assaults, and the child who was assaulted only visited the school for the purposes of this program. Nevertheless, when Klebuc J. and the Saskatchewan Court

52 *Supra* note 11.
53 *Supra* note 10.
54 *Supra* note 17.
55 *Supra* note 12. (A sexual assault case, but not in the context of a Residential School).
56 [1999] 2 S.C.R. 534 (1999), 46 C.C.L.T. (2d) 1 [*Bazley*].
57 [1999] 2 S.C.R. 570 (1999), 46 C.C.L.T. (2d) 49 [*Jacobi*].
58 The underpinning of vicarious liability is not based on the fault of the employer, but on the perceived distributive fairness of making the employer internalise the cost of the general activity involved.
59 *Supra* note 55.
60 *Supra* note 56.
61 *Supra* note 55 at para. 41. The relevant factors showing sufficiency of the connection between the employer's creation or enhancement of the risk and the wrong complained of "may include, but are not limited to, the following": (a) the opportunity that the enterprise afforded the employee to abuse his or her power; (b) the extent to which the wrongful act may have furthered the employer's aims (and hence be more likely to have been committed by the employee); (c) the extent to which the wrongful act was related to friction, confrontation or intimacy inherent in the employer's enterprise; (d) the extent of power conferred on the employee in relation to the victim; (e) the vulnerability of potential victims to wrongful exercise of the employee's power.
62 *Supra* note 11.

of Appeal applied the five *indicia* of 'close connection', they found a sufficiently close relationship to support vicarious liability.[63]

In contrast, the arguably narrow view of the scope of the close connection test exhibited by the bare majority in *Jacobi*[64] was reaffirmed by an overwhelming majority of the Supreme Court of Canada in the very recent case of *E.B.*.[65] In *E.B.* the plaintiff had attended a Residential School run by the defendant Order, and had suffered sexual abuse by a lay employee (also of First Nations origin) who worked in the school bakery and operated the school motorboat. The majority held that the nature of the employment had created only a 'mere opportunity' and that the employee's work 'did not involve any degree of intimacy.'[66] It was therefore held that there was no liability unless negligence could be established on the part of the defendants.

In vicarious liability cases, prior to an examination of the requisite close connection between employer and employee, it must be established that the abuser was indeed (a) working for the defendant, and (b) working as an employee rather than as an independent contractor. It was these issues, along with the identification of the status of the office of 'Bishop' in the Catholic Church hierarchy, which engaged the Supreme Court's attention in the case of *John Doe.*[67] The Court concluded that there was 'direct liability' resulting from the Bishop's failure to properly direct and discipline the priest once the abuse was known, and that this made the Church corporation itself liable because the office of bishop or archbishop was 'legally synonymous' with the corporation. Lastly, the defendants were held vicariously liable since the evidence overwhelmingly satisfied the close connection test: (1) The defendants had created an enhanced risk of abuse by providing the priest with the opportunity to abuse his power; (2) the priest's acts were strongly related to the psychological intimacy inherent in his role as priest; and (3) the Bishop had conferred an enormous degree of power on the priest in relation to his victims. Furthermore, the Court left open the question whether the Roman Catholic Church as a whole, which incorporates its units by diocese, might be liable as a global institution.[68]

The third important Residential School's case from the Supreme Court is *Blackwater*,[69] where the question was raised as to who were the employers of the abusers – the church or the government, or both? The Canadian government and the United Church of Canada had operated a Residential School in British Columbia. At trial, the first holding was that the Canadian Government was liable on the basis of

63 *Supra* notes 11, 15.

64 *Supra* note 55.

65 *Supra* note 17.

66 The strong dissent of Abella J., who likened the Residential School situation to a prison camp where all employees would have an almost unchallengeable power over inmates, and where the vulnerability of inmates is extreme, is worthy of note.

67 *Supra* note 12.

68 *Supra* note 12 at paras. 35-36.

69 *Supra* note 10.

a breach of non-delegable statutory duty for the sexual assaults of a dormitory supervisor. The Canadian Government and the Church were also found jointly and vicariously liable for wrongs committed at the school. Liability was apportioned at 75 percent to the Government and 25 percent to the Church. In contrast, the British Columbia Court of Appeal[70] had applied a notion of charitable immunity to exempt the Church,[71] and had therefore placed all liability on the government on the basis of its sole vicarious liability, despite evidence that the employees were paid by the Church, and that those employees had considered Church officials to be their 'boss'. On further appeal, however, the Supreme Court of Canada restored the trial judgment on this issue.[72] The Church was held to have exerted sufficient control over the operations at the school such that it might be construed as an employer of those working in the school. The Court stated that it was wrong to think that the presence of the government somehow guaranteed the safety of children, particularly where the non-profit organisation had management of the day-to-day functioning of the institution. Furthermore, it was held that co-employers should be jointly and severally liable, based on their respective degree of control.[73]

4.2 FACTUAL CAUSATION OF DAMAGES

The Residential Schools cases highlight the point that in a tort action it is necessary to show factual causation not only between the defendant's act and the initial injury, but also, and often more importantly, between the initial injury and the resulting loss. The so-called 'but-for' test is the proper test of factual causation in the vast majority of situations. However, the 'but for' test is not applicable where there are two wrongs, each of which was sufficient by itself to cause the harm.[74] Such a circumstance arises frequently in sexual abuse cases, perhaps more often than in any other type of case. Furthermore, a different standard of proof, 'simple probability', is applied to much of the causal chain involved in the assessment of damages. Causation is evaluated according to the degree of probability that events would have happened, or will happen in the future; and damages are awarded reflecting that degree of probability, whether it be more or less than even.[75]

70 (2003) 21 B.C.L.R. (4th) 1, 20 C.C.L.T. (3d) 207 (B.C.C.A.).

71 Seemingly on a complete misinterpretation of a few sentences in *Bazely*, *supra* note 55.

72 Although it denied responsibility on the basis of a non-delegable statutory duty.

73 *Supra* note 10 at 68-69.

74 Ken Cooper-Stephenson, *Personal Injury Damages in Canada*, 2nd ed. (Toronto: Carswell, 1996) at 786 [*Personal Injury Damages*].

75 *Ibid.*, at 67.

H.L.[76] is illustrative of the question of proof of a causal connection between the abuse and the resulting life circumstances of the plaintiff. A significant portion of the damages claimed was denied by the Saskatchewan Court of Appeal[77] on the ground that a causal connection had not been established between the abuse at a Residential School and the victim's subsequent alcoholism and criminal behaviour. However, these damages were for the most part restored by the Supreme Court of Canada. As well, the case showed that factual causation with respect to the post-injury scenario may involve the 'thin skull' and 'crumbling skull' rules, which are simply applications of the 'but for test' in atypical circumstances. The plaintiff in *H.L.* was more susceptible – because of his social situation – to extensive psychological harm from the assaults. But his situation was such that it could be argued (and was argued) that much of the harm would have happened anyway from other causes. However, the trial judge's ruling that the assaults were a 'necessary cause' of the eventual harm was restored by the Supreme Court of Canada. The Court permitted the inference from expert opinion and other testimony that the plaintiff's alcoholism was caused by the sexual abuse, and that it resulted in a loss of self-esteem and self-confidence which, in turn, affected his employability or 'work ethic'.[78]

The incredible complexity of multiple factual causation was also evident in the cases of *Blackwater*[79] and *E.D.G. v. Hammer.*[80] In *Blackwater* the plaintiff had suffered sexual abuse prior to his attendance at a Residential School, where he was again abused. He also later, or concurrently, suffered trauma from non-sexual abusive treatment at the school, an action for which, if it was tortious, was statute-barred. The court (perhaps mistakenly) used the 'but for' test to determine causation. But the same result might have been reached if it had been held that there were multiple sufficient *wrongful* causes.[81] On such an analysis the so-called 'devaluation theory' might be applied, whereby the plaintiff is considered already harmed when the second independently sufficient cause occurs.[82] In another relatively recent Supreme Court of Canada case, *E.D.G.*,[83] it was held that most of the damage the victim suffered was 'indivisible' and was caused both by the abuse of a school janitor and by subsequent persons. The court did not explain whether this meant that each was sufficient on its own to cause all the harm, or whether the two harms were each a necessary cause of the total harm. The court refused to overturn the trial judge's findings on the causation issue, absent overriding error.

76 *Supra* note 11.
77 *Ibid.*
78 *Supra* note 11 at paras. 122-133.
79 *Supra* note 10.
80 [2003] 2 S.C.R. 459, 230 D.L.R. (4th) 554 [*E.D.G.*].
81 Which would preclude use of the 'but for' test. See *Personal Injury Damages*, *supra* note 73.
82 *Ibid.*, at 797.
83 *Supra* note 79.

These complex causal determinations reproduce themselves on a systemic level for Residential School maltreatment in the context of politically-generated reparations claims for the widespread cultural loss or 'cultural genocide'.

5 JUSTICE AND ALTERNATIVE DISPUTE RESOLUTION

5.1 THEORETICAL QUESTIONS

Most of the literature which considers the justification for ADR has focused on contrasting ADR's practical and theoretical dimensions with those of rights-based processes, such as adversarial litigation. Very little has been written on the effect of integrating the processes.[84] Still less has been written on the underlying 'justice' factors involved in ADR, including its jurisprudential justification. The well-accepted rationalisations for ADR are essentially pragmatic, involving the economic and time constraints of traditional litigation, and the enhanced psychological benefits and comfort-level of the parties where ADR processes are employed.

Accepting that interest-based negotiation, mediation and adjudication must almost by definition have different ('alternative') theoretical underpinnings than adversarial rights-attainment legal approaches, it seems important to generate thought about some aspects of the jurisprudential relationship between 'rights discourse' and 'interest-based discourse' in the legal system. This might include the following questions:[85]

(a) Whether a system of legal rights is a necessary background and pre-requisite to ADR interest-based dispute resolution.
(b) Whether, and if so to what extent, the processes of ADR affect the actual content of substantive legal rights.
(c) What theoretical basis exists for the consideration in ADR of interests and third party concerns that are not directly protected by conventional legal norms.
(d) The extent to which ADR ignores interests, such as social or community morality, which are taken into account by legal rights determination.
(e) The extent to which in ADR more than in rights discourse, considerations of justice are trumped, compromised or minimised by pragmatic concerns.
(f) Whether the role of power and politics in ADR determinations exceeds their prevalence in the mainstream legal process – whether ADR reflects the insights

[84] But see now, Michaela Keet, "The Evolution of Lawyers' Roles in Mandatory Mediation: A Condition of Systemic Transformation" (2005) 68 Sask. L. Rev. 313 [Keet, "The Evolution of Lawyers' Roles"].

[85] These were generated through collaboration with Professors Marjorie Benson and Michaela Keet at the University of Saskatchewan, both acknowledged experts in the field of ADR.

of the Critical Legal Studies (CLS) scholars to a greater degree than does traditional rights-based adjudication.

(g) Whether considerations of distributive justice are integrated with those of corrective justice and/or retributive justice in ADR to a greater extent than is the case in a court-based system of rights entitlement.

(h) Whether the underpinnings of ADR involve to a greater extent the goal of subjective personal or community 'harmony' by comparison with the underpinnings of mainstream rights entitlement; and in turn, the extent to which the goal of 'harmony' is recognised in the court-based adversarial system.

A tentative conclusion of this chapter is that the cumulative answers to these questions reveal that ADR, in whatever form, converts legal entitlements into something of a very different character than they are understood in the context of traditional adjudicative processes. In a sense, the underpinning of discrete ADR processes exemplifies 'Critical Legal Studies writ small'. The cumulative, diverse and systemic employment of alternative processes in the context of redress for Residential School abuse serves to amplify this insight. These processes bring to light the intellectual deficiency of pure 'rights discourse', and are testimony to the theoretical complexity of law, and to its political and ideological nature as emphasised by CLS scholars. A concluding question raised by this chapter – one which may have intense practical significance – is the extent to which ADR processes and resolutions, in that they exhibit such practical and political characteristics, can be said to be 'legal'. To what extent can they be said to be part of 'law', or do they in some manner stand outside it?

5.2 THE RIGHTS-ENTITLEMENT BACKCLOTH

Addressing the first of the questions posed above, it should be noted that the government's DR Model was instigated primarily as a settlement mechanism for much-delayed traditional-style tort claims. The theoretical bases of claims resolved through this process might therefore begin as a mirror of those of ordinary tort law (at least insofar as settlement processes within mainstream litigation retain the theoretical character of the rights dispute they seek to resolve). Insofar as the claims are tort claims, the core of those claims involves: (1) the commission of a legally-recognised 'wrong'; (2) compensation, which is intended in large part to provide restitution for the economic losses consequent on that wrong; and (3) solace for the non-economic losses.[86] Although this is said by some to exemplify the dictates of

[86] The tort doctrines particularly implicated in Residential School Claims are reviewed in Cooper-Stephenson, "Reparations for State Wrongs", *supra* note 2. They include (1) The torts of battery and assault; (2) The intentional indirect infliction of physical and mental suffering; (3) The tort of

'corrective justice',[87] the predominant view is that there are widespread distributive implications of tort law generated in part by insurance and another loss-spreading mechanisms. Tort law therefore combines notions of 'corrective' and 'distributive' justice in a scheme of 'moral distribution'.[88]

The underpinnings of Residential School tort claims for physical and sexual abuse may thus remain largely those of mainstream tort litigation. However, the 'corrective' character of such tort claims is clearly modified because: (1) they have a cultural and community context; (2) they are against government and large-scale private religious institutions; (3) they are sometimes in the form of class actions; and (4) they involve or integrate with large-scale future-oriented wealth distribution. Nevertheless, the Residential Schools cases show that for many, if not most ADR procedures, 'legal rights' are prominent as a background and driving force for choices by the parties and decisions of adjudicators. Indeed, the launch by the AFN of a class action for Residential School claims[89] serves to keep those involved in implementing the current DR Model aware of the potential 'rights' of the survivors, and to thereby influence those who are charged with restructuring, rethinking and implementing the DR Model.

Although rights-entitlement lies in the forefront of traditional-style tort claims, the Residential School claims show us that the law does not simply apply itself. This runs counter to the perceptions of those who champion legalistic 'mechanical jurisprudence' (the so-called 'model of rules') as a satisfactory explanation of law. Residential Schools claims do not involve a straightforward application of 'close-textured' specific and detailed obligations to easily ascertainable facts.[90] However, if this is so for those claims litigated in court, what does one make of the theoretical position where: (a) a completely different quasi-legal ADR adjudicative process is employed using non-legally-trained personnel; (b) there are claims for 'cultural loss', and loss by third persons and communities as a result of the individual abuses; and (c) the ultimate solution of claims, far from being imposed by a court, results from the acceptance of claims by survivors and communities following political pressure exerted on both sides at a national level? The resolution of these claims cannot easily be fitted into *any* of the other traditional jurisprudential constructs, not even those which contemplate a more 'open-textured' style of reasoning, where the adjudicator, although constrained by rules, is understood to legitimately accept *some* influence of moral, social, economic and political factors.

---

negligence; (4) The concept of vicarious liability; (5) The tort-like action for breach of fiduciary duty; (6) Requirements of factual causation; (7) Limitations imposed by remoteness of damage; (8) Principles of measure of damages.

87 See particularly E. J. Weinrib, *The Idea of Private Law* (Cambridge: Harvard University Press, 1995).

88 For my early conclusions, see K. Cooper-Stephenson, "Corrective Justice, Substantive Equality and Tort Law" in K. Cooper-Stephenson & E. Gibson eds. *Tort Theory* (North York: Captus, 1993), at 48. For further discussion see below, "Corrective and Distributive Justice".

89 *Supra* note 36.

90 It likely fails to provide an accurate explanation of "law" *anywhere* in the legal system.

Instead, these claims are in significant part the product of political power – the relative power of Canada's First Nations, of the Canadian government, and of the churches who administered the Residential Schools. Furthermore, each individual's *present* life situation – including, in cases involving aging survivors, the pressing need for *some* recompense for wrongs committed – plays an important role in the amount of compensation he or she will be willing to accept. These claims have the form of context-specific, highly pressurised bargains, with traditional-style tort 'justice' featuring only in the relatively distant background, rather than as an ever-present dominant force. This is, indeed, the form of many traditional settlements of rights-based legal disputes, but in the Residential School context it is dramatically emphasised. Nevertheless, the legal rights backcloth is *always* there in some form – almost by definition in *all* legally-related dispute resolution. At a minimum, the parties' and the adjudicator/mediator's *perceptions* of the rights entitlement involved are there.[91]

5.3 JUSTICE, ADR AND CRITICAL LEGAL STUDIES

Progressing the issue of theoretical underpinnings one step further, it is useful to reiterate that a discussion of the practical, economic and psychological advantages of ADR procedures is more prominent in the literature than is a consideration of ADR's theoretical justifications. ADR is essentially *de facto*, while legal rights are *de jure*. But it is important not to ignore the *de facto/de jure* interplay, or to overlook the backcloth of rights entitlement bearing down on *de facto* agreements or determinations (and, conversely, the effect of *de facto* agreements on *de jure* 'rights'). Surely, then, there is a need to ask why, *from a justice point of view*, a person would be held bound by an agreement which sells that person short in terms of full rights-enforcement (if, indeed, ADR and negotiation results in what might be considered something less than 'full' justice)? Or, from the opposite standpoint, why is it that a strategically more powerful person or institution is permitted to enforce an agreement, or to choose an ADR process, which enables that person or institution to come away conceding something less than 'justice' to the other party? The answer may be that such questions are wholly misguided because they presuppose that there is indeed a fixed, unambiguous and fully understandable, utopian, rights-based 'justice' which *might* theoretically (hypothetically) have been attained or imposed had ADR not intervened to somehow avoid it. We therefore need a jurisprudential theorising which justifies ADR's practices and processes. We need a justification which the legal practitioner can understand, relate to, and use, and which we might consider as ultimately 'just' in this highly active,

91 Since law shapes our culture and thought processes, rights entitlement is in any event ever-present in our lives.

practical, functional, somewhat unwieldy, historically-contextual world. Our notions of 'justice' and the so-called 'rule of law' must surely be intimately contextual and politically contingent, and must take into account much more than utopian ideals and intellectual aspiration.[92]

A wider sense of *practical* and contextual 'justice' might then explain why the AFN has agreed in both its Report and in the historical Accord to an improved DR Model for Residential School claims. Although this new process might *appear to be* a compromise or makeshift one at some points, it is more expansive and comprehensively 'just' at others. The newly-proposed model provides compensation for losses which arguably might not be successfully claimed under the traditional tort system, and embraces considerations stretching far beyond those which would be recognised by the legal system, including assurances from the Government of Canada to address First Nations' poverty by 2010.

It is likely true that ADR processes *always* in some way affect legal rights *in their implementation*. This is, indeed, exemplified by the revisions to the DR Model proposed in the AFN Report. The simple fact is that in almost every ADR determination, the individual power position of the parties, or the collective power position of the groups of which the parties are a member, will have a greater play than in a law-centred, power-minimised, traditional adjudicative environment.[93] Furthermore, the play of that power may lead to a greater 'justice' than the 'legal justice' provided by traditional law, because the power of the parties can bring into consideration factors absent from the legal rules. Conversely, power can also result in a solution which falls far short of what would be described as 'justice' *by any jurisprudential standpoint or moral code*. Perhaps an increased sense of the underpinnings of ADR will minimise the prospect of the latter, and will ensure that inappropriate 'external' considerations do not easily come into consideration such that the overplay of power leads to injustice.

5.4 THE 'JUSTICE' OF NEGOTIATED RIGHTS

Another set of observations concern 'agreed-to solutions' – where parties have opted for ADR over traditional legal remedies, or have simply agreed to settle their legal dispute on their own, with or without the assistance of lawyers. This happens because contracts can almost always change pre-existing 'default' rights, although there is an

---

92 As the Critical Legal Studies scholars have been at pains to point out to us for some 25 years, and as the legal realists argued long before that time.

93 One question which this paper will *not* address is the extent to which ADR directly or indirectly influences the substantive content of "legal rights" (actually changes "the law"). See Keet, "The Evolution of Lawyers' Roles", *supra* note 83.

increasing number of restrictions and requirements. I have summarised this theoretical position in relation to tort as follows:[94]

> "[The] rights and entitlements [of tort law] can often be found outside the domain of tort law. In some respects they are preliminary to tort law and in others are integrated with it... Hence a system of backcloths: (1) A distributive entitlement backcloth from other areas of law ...; (2) tort law's default-mode distributive scheme of fault-based correction for relatively localized denial of entitlements; and (3) contract law's potential for market-based alteration of the *prima facie* entitlements established in the two-layered backcloth of (1) and (2)."

However, once contracts have reached the stage of agreement and are enforceable, the entitlements established by those contracts immediately become part of (1) – the distributive entitlement backcloth. And so the cycle continues.

There is very little which circumscribes what parties can agree upon. However, the legal system will not permit settlement without judicial approval in some situations, including settlements on behalf of those below the age of majority or those who are incompetent. Furthermore, there is a growing contracts jurisprudence which disturbs agreements if there has been duress, undue influence or unconscionability. Rules governing the law of 'mistake' and 'illegality' may also overturn bargains. And in certain circumstances, if agreements were preceded by fraudulent or negligent representation, the effects of the bargain may be nullified by tort compensation. Nevertheless, considerations and remedies far removed from those embraced by 'the law' can be included in an ADR-generated solution. It is then important to ask, what is the nature of a 'justice' which allows and would enforce a solution falling far short of rights-based compensation?

At first glance, the theoretical answer might appear quite simple: contract will usually be permitted to trump rights-based tort law by a pre- or post-tort agreement. However, it is surely not always sufficient simply to espouse the virtues of individualism, contractual freedom and the free market. It may be a mistake to acclaim as necessarily 'just' the results of an unfettered 'right' of any person at any given time to choose his or her route to a desired life plan. This would ignore a whole series of potential inequities, including:[95] (1) the effect in a bargaining situation of one party's altruistic concern for the other; (2) *de facto* oppression of one party; (3) incapacity, such as that of children; (4) unequal and insufficient information; (5) the socialisation and manipulation of preferences; (6) wealth effects; (7) the effect of aggregation of claims; (8) inability to financially underscore preferences; (9) the lack of representation for third persons and unborn future persons; and (10) a very real difficulty in choosing an acceptable moment in time at which to assess the justness of a solution, since

94 Ken Cooper-Stephenson, "Economic Analysis, Substantive Equality and Tort Law", in *Tort Theory supra* note 87, 131 at 158.

95 *Ibid.*

morality and justice are always historically contingent. One is also provoked to ask *some* justice-related questions about themes of feminist jurisprudence which advocate conciliation, concern and compromise, where the personal, the particular and the subjective are emphasised, but where, as a result, there may be the infusion of an uneven power dynamic.[96]

The justice of ADR's negotiation and compromise processes is particularly troublesome if considerably lower compensation is accepted *because the processes of obtaining 'justice' are so cumbersome, costly and slow.* This raises the question of how far legal theory can continue to ignore the ubiquitous reality that 'justice' as it is understood by rights theorists is very rarely if ever accomplished by the institutions of justice – such that the lack of justice ('injustice'?) is daily endorsed by the legal ('justice') system? The deepest jurisprudential theory must surely take account of the humanness and practicality of justice and its procedures – of its *de facto* reality in a fast moving, fast growing and imperfect world.[97] If the theorists are merely speaking to a utopian ideal, they should be open about that, and concede the impracticality of their understandings and goals. Both CLS[98] and feminist[99] scholars emphasise this in their theorising, and 'action theory' concerns itself in part with theorising which allows parties to resolve disputes efficiently and effectively, and thereby return to the pursuit of their life goals.[100]

5.5 CORRECTIVE AND DISTRIBUTIVE JUSTICE

As previously indicated,[101] according to some theorists, at the heart of tort law is the Aristotelian notion of 'corrective justice' (i.e. the justice of the state's correcting

[96] One area to which ADR might increasingly turn to correct some of the free market imbalances is the area of consent to medical treatment, where the law imposes stringent requirements of informed consent.

[97] The imperfection of legalism and rights-talk also stretches to the granting of remedies for the most egregious human wrongs, particularly with respect to injunctions, where all manner of qualifications and external considerations are taken into account as potentially denying the specific remedy which would instate the legally-protected rights of plaintiffs. See *e.g.* Ken Cooper-Stephenson, "Principle and Pragmatism in the Law of Remedies" in Jeff Berryman, ed., *Remedies: Issues and Perspectives* (Toronto: Carswell, 1991) at 31-40. This was perhaps most evident in the United States desegregation cases, where the Supreme Court amended its original order in *Brown* to the effect that the changes to school systems must be made at "all deliberate speed" rather than instantly. See also P. Gewirtz, "Remedies and Resistance" (1983), 92 Yale L. Rev. 585.

[98] Pragmatism is a consistent theme of CLS writings: the infusion of the "real" with the "ideal". For an introductory survey of CLS themes see K. Cooper-Stephenson, "Gender Harassment in Universities: The Perspective of Critical Legal Studies" in F. McArdle ed. *The Cambridge Lectures 1991* (1994).

[99] Empiricism and reference to sociological and scientific data are emphasised by feminist analysis: "reasoning from the ground up".

[100] See, e.g., J.C. Smith, "Action Theory and Legal Reasoning", in *Tort Theory*, *supra* note 87 at 104.

[101] Text at note 86.

discrete individual and institutional 'wrongs'). If that were so, the discrete tort claims involved in the Residential School litigation would of course exhibit that 'form' of justice. However, an alternative view now espoused by many leading theorists is a more coherent and expansive view of tort law that exhibits also characteristics of 'distributive justice' (the fair allocation by the state of entitlements generally in society on the ground of merit and need). So, as I have argued elsewhere,[102] tort actions, and particularly tort actions against governments or large-scale organisations, such as the churches, 'draw on *both* these forms of justice in some interesting and important way – if, indeed, it is possible at the present day to make any sharp distinction between these two forms of justice?' This theoretical underpinning reveals itself most powerfully when government is held liable in tort for its failure to act – for *omission* – which may simply involve the inadequate allocation of resources and energy to a threatened sector of the population.[103]

Leaving aside this argument about the underpinnings of tort claims, one question for ADR theory is whether or not under alternative resolution processes a claim ever retains a predominantly 'corrective', rights-based character, or whether, instead, distributive considerations often begin to influence dispute resolution so potently that 'correction' is minimised as a jurisprudential explanation of the resolution's legal character? And, as indicated previously, the answer is surely that fair distribution becomes increasingly significant through ADR. Even where ADR is concerned with disputes which centre on a legal 'wrong' or perceived wrong, the relative wealth of the parties or of the groups to which the parties belong will not only begin to determine the nature and extent of the remedy, but may play a very important part in our perception of the morality and 'justice' of that remedy.

I have explored elsewhere the role of distributive justice with respect to reparations claims, where the legal 'rights' basis can be tenuous at best.[104] Such claims tend for the most part to be diverted from mainstream legal adjudication to political or other alternative dispute locales. This is so even though the traditional legal route may lie in waiting to assist in providing political pressure. Such pressure is overtly one goal of the AFN in its launching of its class action for Residential School abuse. In all of this – and it may be true of many ADR determinations – the role of the distributive concept of 'unjust enrichment' cannot be ignored. If there is a distributional disadvantage suffered by the claimant group, resolution of claims may begin to focus on the extent to which past conduct contributed to such disadvantage and enriched the dominant group, giving greater moral force to both discrete and systemic present day claims.

---

102 Cooper-Stephenson, "Theoretical Underpinnings", *supra* note 3 at 5.

103 Cooper-Stephenson, "Reparations for State Wrongs", *supra* note 2.

104 Cooper-Stephenson, 'Theoretical Underpinnings', *supra* note 3 at 8-18.

5.6 THE RISKS OF QUASI-LEGALITY

It is no-doubt troubling for ADR theorists to examine the 'justice' factors which might be *absent* or *lost* in ADR determinations. These, it would seem, need to be openly articulated; their exposure may well generate a defensive response from ADR practitioners. However, if ADR processes are to gain full acceptance, and to be further incorporated into mainstream legal processes, the relative justice-related downside of such processes, insofar as there are any, should be examined.

5.7 HARMONY AND HOLISM

It may be questioned whether 'the harmony promised by ADR' might mean simply 'preservation of the status quo with ADR a coercive mechanism of pacification'[105] – a healthy 'bedside manner' which encourages acceptance of an unsatisfactory rights regime and disease-like outcomes. In contrast, 'the truth and reality of ADR' might mean, *inter alia*, that:[106]

> "... alternative images of disputing that more accurately mirror people's diverse experiences, that overcome barriers to bringing disputes forward, that reduce dependence on professionals, that empower those who traditionally have been excluded from having their important struggles aired, and that take a holistic view of the dispute?"

The ADR processes employed in the context of Residential School abuse in Canada appear to exemplify this latter conception. It has more accurately mirrored the diverse experiences of the survivors of the schools. It is in the process of reducing dependence on lawyers. It has empowered Canada's First Nations Peoples and permitted them to air their vitally important struggle for compensation and reconciliation. And, without question, it has enabled adjudicators to take a more holistic view of the dispute than is possible in the context of traditional court procedures. The harmonising notion of 'restorative justice' has played a prominent role, which is an approach that has been carefully examined by Jennifer Llewellyn in an intense scholarly treatment.[107] Furthermore, 'truth-sharing, healing and reconciliation' were given focus in the final recommendations in the AFN Report.[108]

---

105 Andrew J. Pirie, *Alternative Dispute Resolution: Skills, Science and the Law* (Toronto: Irwin Law, 2000) at 31: 'Is ADR displacing the state in dispute resolution and substituting a private, market-driven model for those who can afford it?'

106 *Ibid.*

107 Jennifer J. Llewellyn, "Dealing with the Legacy of Native Residential School Abuse in Canada: Litigation, ADR, and Restorative Justice" (2002) 59 U.T.L.J. 253.

108 *Supra* note 1 at 36. For quotations, see above, text at note 32.

6 POLITICS, RIGHTS AND COMPROMISE

There are some unique theoretical problems which emerge where claims are pursued on many fronts, through diverse processes, and in different adjudicative settings.[109] In particular, these problems arise where a single person – in this context, First Nations Grand Chief Phil Fontaine – is: (a) the lead plaintiff in a traditional-style class action lawsuit; (b) a major player in working towards the development of an alternative adjudication process for his own and other actions; and (c) the representative political figure for the wholesale welfare of Canada's First Nations peoples and communities, having comparable status in negotiations to a Premier of one of the Canadian provinces. But even if this unique situation was not present, the parallel assertion of the legal/political/moral right to compensation or reparation for past wrongs raises some telling questions as to the theoretical nature of what is being asserted.

6.1 FRICTIONS AND DICHOTOMIES

There appear to be at least four dichotomies or frictions which present themselves for consideration in the context of the Residential Schools legacy and its legal and political aftermath, some of which have been adverted to in the discussion of ADR processes.

(1) *Law or Politics*. This dichotomy asks whether 'law' should be viewed as constituting a set of rigid norms which mechanically realise individual rights, or, alternatively, viewed as a mere rights-statement backcloth for political practice. There were clearly points of discussion in the processes leading to the historic Accord between First Nations Peoples and the Canadian government when it was pertinent to ask the government to make up its mind whether it was 'doing law' or 'doing politics'. It is equally difficult to characterise some aspects of the AFN Class Action, which seeks damages for 'cultural genocide', the inception of which lay in the middle of the 19th Century, and which was conducted pursuant to legislative mandate, and for which a 'legal' right of redress would be difficult to sustain at the present day.

(2) *Individual or Collective*: This asks whether justice should focus on the rights of individuals, or on the interests of communities and the collective welfare. The decisions of the AFN to encourage litigants to divert their traditional legal actions to an ADR model, and (with respect to some aspects of those claims) to concede to political resolution, may in some cases mean that survivors will give up components of their claims for the collective good of the First Nations Communities in years to come. In

109 For earlier discussion, see Cooper-Stephenson, "Reparations for State Wrongs", *supra* note 2. This part of the present chapter reproduces, in amended form, some portions of that paper.

part, this will concede the rewards of the legal and political efforts of some survivors to their children and grandchildren, which may in turn be as meaningful as anything else for those survivors as an important form of comfort and consolation. Nevertheless, the result may fall short of what might have been expected individually for them, given the harms they and their predecessors suffered.

(3) *Retrospective or Prospective*: This questions whether the focus of 'law' should be backward-looking and corrective, or forward-looking and constructive. There is an on-going question whether at the *remedy stage* of rights-based law, there should be a focus on restorative measures, or simply a backward-looking reflection of what has been lost. Various components of the law of remedies are now beginning to reflect a more forward-looking focus, including restorative justice within the criminal justice system, and the tort law measure of non-pecuniary damages by what is needed for 'solace' of the injured person. The response to the Residential School abuse claims has sought to balance and integrate retrospective-focused justice with prospective-focused justice.

(4) *Fixed or Contingent*: The last dichotomy asks whether law and morality should be viewed as fixed and immutable, or instead as fluid and historically contingent. This speaks not merely to the gradual shift of law to respond to new social realities, but also encompasses the very difficult moral/political question of whether and to what extent the planet's current population should provide redress not only to the current survivors of Residential School abuse but also to the descendants of those who were abused in the distant past. The question is deeper if and insofar as the past 'maltreatment' was conducted at a time when the conduct was done under legal sanction and with moral acclaim.

Why is it that the moral claim for reparations seems strong even where the original legal claim is time-barred, and where the original conduct was at the time considered justified? How would one formulate a moral/legal argument for the right to reparations in these circumstances, and avoid present day legal arguments by governments who can assert the force of historical, but now stale-dated legal defences which are supported by equally stale-dated moral justifications? I have previously suggested that the present day claim may be founded on the following ground, *viz.* that:[110]

(1) There was (by the relevant taking of property, imprisonment, systemic abuse or cultural genocide) either:
   (a) A disturbance of existing rights which as a matter of corrective justice *ought to have been corrected* by tort-style litigation in its relatively immediate aftermath, but which was not so corrected; *or* an allocation

[110] Cooper-Stephenson, "Theoretical Underpinnings", *supra* note 3 at 12-13.

or taking away of entitlements by the state which was distributively wrongful at the time and which as a mater of distributive justice *ought to have been redistributed* at the time of its occurrence, but which was not so redistributed; ***or***

(b) An event or disturbance of rights which *in retrospect is now considered as wrongful and deserving of correction or readjustment*, but which was not necessarily perceived as such at the time;

and, as a result of one of the above,

(2) There is a present-day harm or maldistribution of rights, which, *as a matter of current distributive justice* ought to be rectified by the state, because the current state authorities are now the constitutional managers of present-day distributive entitlements, which ought to be made fair.

The role of a present day inherited enrichment (an 'unjust' enrichment) by the successors of those who perpetrated the original 'wrong', seems part of the moral imperative that requires that the situation be realigned such that the wronged party has the opportunity to be equally enriched. This involves a present-day distributive justice founded on a past wrong which ought to have been corrected in the aftermath of its occurrence.[111]

These four dichotomies – 'law or politics', 'individual or collective', 'retrospective or prospective', 'fixed or contingent' – manifest themselves, perhaps more clearly than anywhere else, in the struggle for satisfactory resolution of the individual, social, and cultural problems in reparations claims such as those concerning the Residential Schools legacy.

6.2 INSIDE OR OUTSIDE LAW

One very real question, related to the law/politics dichotomy, which arguably pervades a discussion of ADR theory and its application to the Residential Schools legacy, is whether and if so in what circumstances, ADR processes and its resolutions are 'inside' or 'outside' law. If they are 'inside law', then it seems even more necessary to explore their jurisprudential underpinning. If they are 'outside law', although their justification may lie primarily in the area of moral or political theory, the jurisprudential understandings of legal theory cannot ignore them. Legal theorising ought surely not simply to proceed on the basis that conflict situations resolved outside the domain of mainstream legal institutions are irrelevant. Such theorising would then truly lie in the realm of aspiration rather than explanation. In any event, so-called 'alternative'

111 Legal analogy can be made to the tort liability of those who "continue" or "adopt" a nuisance, where the present land-enriched defendant is held liable for the conduct of the "creator" of the nuisance.

dispute resolution mechanisms are now being co-opted by mainstream law, and in some cases mandated as part of traditional law.

My previous, tentative observations on this dilemma were as follows:[112]

> "[T]he justification for some reparations claims may lie beyond the reach of traditional doctrine ... and [i]t may therefore be necessary to look ... to the jurisprudential and philosophical perspectives which ground [legal] principles, including the politics of law. The extent to which such enquiries can be incorporated in legal argument is very unclear, although their incidence as a component of judicial reasoning is on the increase. The enquiries into "rights" are also likely a necessary precursor to the pursuit of therapy and harmony; and it may be that therapy and harmony symbiotically and pervasively provide the ultimate justification for rights. It is simply not clear whether the psycho-political dimension lies "inside" or "outside" law – or, for that matter, whether *anything* lies completely inside or outside law."

My final conjecture following these comments was to the effect that: 'One would suspect that, for reparations claims, everything counts.' It would seem that almost everything has counted in the struggle for reparations for the survivors of abuse perpetrated in Canada's Residential Schools. And it may well be that the potential success, albeit long-overdue success, of the movement to bring this chapter of Canada's history to a relatively satisfactory close, and to begin to energise a healthy renewal of the First Nations communities which were subject to historical maltreatment, is due in large part to the fact that legal rights were viewed as a mere component of 'overall' justice, rather than being located in a separate and isolated normative domain with identifiable theoretical boundaries.

[112] Cooper-Stephenson, 'Theoretical Underpinnings', *supra* note 3 at 40.

A 'DIMINISHED NATION' – AUSTRALIA'S RESPONSE TO CLAIMS FOR REPARATIONS BY THE 'STOLEN GENERATIONS'

MARK HARRIS

1 INTRODUCTION

There are numerous examples that may be drawn from around the globe that attest to the desirability, indeed the necessity, for nations to take responsibility for injustices which form part of their history. Although Thompson affirms that 'historical obligations and entitlements do exist and are of considerable moral importance',[1] there continues to be ambiguity and uncertainty as to why certain past actions are deemed to be worthy of reparations while others are not. Within Australia, the issue which has been aligned most consistently with the international move towards reparations, is that of the 'stolen generations'. The phrase itself was first coined by historian Peter Read in 1970 and is used to describe those Indigenous children who were removed from their families throughout Australia in the period between 1910 and 1970, in terms of government policies. During this time the various State legislatures were implementing a policy of assimilation, that was intended to remove any trace of the Indigenous Australian population. While there were explicit legislative provisions that allowed government authorities to exercise control over Aboriginal children, Chesterman makes the point that the policy was implemented also through the application of existing child welfare provisions that were not explicitly racially based.[2]

Without in any way diminishing the enduring horror of these government policies for Indigenous Australians, it is important to reflect that this is but one example of many historical injustices perpetrated against Indigenous Australians following white settlement. While the impact of this particular atrocity upon somewhere in the vicinity of 50 000 individuals and their extended families was profound, it is only part of a

---

1 J. Thompson, *Taking Responsibility for the Past*, (Blackwell, Oxford, 2002), 149.

2 J. Chesterman, *Civil Rights: How Indigenous Australians Won Formal Equality*, (UQP, St Lucia, 2005), 5.

broader story of dispossession and appropriation. Despite limited ameliorative measures such as the *Native Title Act 1993* (Cth), that followed the *Mabo* judgment,[3] there has not been any comprehensive redress for the injustices that followed the dispossession of traditional lands from Indigenous Australians.[4] The destruction of aspects of Indigenous culture that commenced in the colonial period and continues to this day, has similarly remained unaddressed, with only limited protection afforded to Aboriginal cultural property, sites and objects.[5] While these claims are no less valid, it has been the removal of the 'stolen generations' that has assumed particular significance. This atrocity has become the embodiment of the dispossession and abuse suffered by Indigenous Australians. The extent of this harm was acknowledged by Sir Ronald Wilson, who conducted an inquiry into the Stolen Generations and observed that:

> "Indigenous families and communities have endured gross violations of their human rights. These violations continue to affect Indigenous peoples' daily lives. They were an act of genocide, aimed at wiping out Indigenous families, communities and cultures, vital to the precious and inalienable heritage of Australia."[6]

2 HISTORICAL BACKGROUND TO THE STOLEN GENERATIONS

Any understanding of the manner in which government policies gave rise to the forcible removal of Indigenous children from their families must take account of the various legislative provisions that defined Aboriginality, invariably in reference to a measure of blood quantum. The Government regulations in many of the States prevented any contact between those Aboriginal people who resided on reserves, with their family members who had been removed or excluded from the reserves. Based upon the arbitrary assignation of 'caste', the controlling bodies could determine where Aboriginal 'full bloods' and 'half-castes' were entitled to reside.

Over a period of time many of the reserves that originally were controlled by the different missionary orders, were taken under the control of the State governments. The treatment of the Aboriginal people on those reserves was often brutal and some

---

3 *Mabo v Queensland* (1992) 75 CLR 1.

4 As at 3 July 2006 there had been 60 determinations that native title exists either wholly or in part in a claimed area. Such determinations do *not* necessarily guarantee the native title holders exclusivity of possession against all other parties.

5 Note for example the Commonwealth legislation; *Aboriginal and Torres Strait Islander Heritage Protection Act 1984 (Cth)* and similar legislative measures enacted in a number of the different States and Territories.

6 HREOC, *Bringing Them Home: A guide to the findings and recommendations of the National Inquiry into the Separation of ATSI children from their families*, (HREOC, Sydney, 1993), 33.

commentators have referred to them as being akin to 'concentration camps'.[7] Aboriginal people on the reserves were housed in basic, sub-standard huts, were given limited rations, and were frequently subjected to punishment by the white manager. On occasion this included lashing with a whip.[8] Apart from the oppressive conditions which the Aboriginal people endured on the government reserves and missions, there was also the unrelenting message that they were an inferior people. For example, Jimmie Barker recalled of his experience at the Brewarrina mission that:

> "...I learnt that as I was black, or partly coloured, there was no place in Australia for me. I learnt that anyone of my colour would always be an outcast and different from a white person. It gave me the firm idea that an Aboriginal, even if he was slightly coloured, was mentally and physically inferior to all others."[9]

Those Aboriginal people who were not on the reserves lived in fear of the arrival of government officials, who would come and take their children away to be placed either in missions or apprenticeships. Agnes Palmer, who was taken from her family and placed at the Santa Teresa Catholic Mission near Alice Springs, recounts the lengths to which the families went to try to hide the lighter-skinned children in order to prevent them from being removed. She recalls how her grandmother sought to conceal the children, taking the lighter skinned ones to hide in the hills when they heard the approach of the government officials. Since the welfare officials were most interested in the lighter-skinned Aboriginal children, the adults attempted to make their skin darker by daubing them with charcoal. Palmer recalls:

> "They would put charcoal on them to make them look dark and this man would walk and look at them like they were some prized horse or something. He would look them over and as soon as he saw someone with a light skin he would just grab that person, the little girl or the little boy, just grab them, and the mother would be sitting there crying her heart out and the kids would all get put on these trucks and just taken."[10]

Over a period of time it became clear that the Aboriginal race was not going to die out and concern was expressed at the growth of the number of Aboriginal 'half-castes'. The 1937 Commonwealth and State Native Welfare Conference resolved, for example, that 'this conference believes that the destiny of the natives of aboriginal origin, but not of the full blood, lies in their ultimate absorption by the people of the Common-

---

7 N. Parbury (1986) *Survival: A History of Aboriginal Life in New South Wales*, (Ministry of Aboriginal Affairs NSW, Sydney), 85.

8 J. Mathews, *The two worlds of Jimmie Barker*, (Australian Institute of Aboriginal Studies, Canberra, 1990), 54.

9 *Ibid.*, 56.

10 S. Rintoul, *Wailing: A National Black Oral History*, (William Heinemann, Melbourne, 1993) 129-130.

wealth.'[11] The conference also determined that 'children of mixed aboriginal blood' should be educated and trained 'with a view to their taking their place in the white community.' The clear imperative was that the children who were sufficiently white would attain all the attributes and benefits of Australian white society and would cease to identify to any degree as Aboriginal. One of the strongest advocates of this policy was A O Neville, the Director of Native Affairs in Western Australia from 1915 to 1940. It was Neville who detailed a plan which would safeguard against the white population being 'swamped' by the increasing numbers of half-caste Aborigines.[12] Neville outlined his plans to facilitate the breeding out of the Aboriginal race in his book *Australia's Coloured Minority*, which was published in 1947 and included a number of photographs demonstrating the different genetic 'crosses'. The book advocated the minimisation of inter-marriage between 'half-breed' Aboriginal people. Neville wrote:

> "It seems apparent with these people of European-Aboriginal origin that like breeds like – two half-breeds will produce children of similar blood and not of quarter blood as many think – and therefore it requires the admixture of further white blood to alter the ratio and produce the quadroon."[13]

Neville believed that it was only through such a program of selective breeding that the danger presented by a race of half-caste Aborigines (who were regarded by Neville and his cohorts as indolent, lawless and immoral) could be averted. The removal of the 'half-caste' Aboriginal children during the 1930s took place during a time when racist attitudes towards Aborigines were prevalent and ideas of scientific racism were increasingly popular.[14] The missions and stations were to become the last refuge of those Aborigines deemed 'too black' to be assimilated into white society. Those children considered 'white' enough were dispersed into white society as house-servants or apprentices. Throughout Australia a range of legislative measures allowed for the removal of Aboriginal children from their families. Termed the 'assimilation' policy, its intention was effectively to ensure that Aboriginal people ceased to exist as a distinct minority within the Australian population. Under the policy, children who were deemed to be sufficiently 'white' were taken into care and placed in apprenticeships or sent to homes, while the 'dark' children were confined to the missions and government reserves. It is impossible to calculate the number of Aboriginal children who were removed from their families, because not all removals were documented and many records were lost, damaged, or destroyed over the years. It is suggested in the *Bringing Them Home* report that between one in three and one in ten Indigenous

---

11 R. Wilson, *Bringing Them Home*, (HREOC, Canberra, 1997), 32.

12 Q. Beresford & P. Omaji, *Our State of Mind – racial planning and the stolen generations,* (Fremantle Arts Centre Press, Fremantle, 1998), 48.

13 A. Neville, *Australia's Coloured Minority,* (Currawong Publishing, Sydney, 1947), 61.

14 Q. Beresford & P. Omaji, *Our State of Mind*, (Fremantle Arts Centre Press, Fremantle, 1998), 40.

children were forcibly removed from their families during the period between 1910 and 1970.[15] In his assessment of the impact of this policy Peter Read argues that the figure could be as high 50 000.[16] While the exact numbers of those who were removed from their families remains unclear, it is undeniable that the policy had a disastrous impact upon the families and the communities from which the children were removed. In the course of giving evidence to the Royal Commission into Aboriginal Deaths in Custody,[17] the Secretariat for National Aboriginal and Islander Child Care (SNAICC) made the observation that 'there is no Aboriginal family that is untouched by this policy.'[18]

The impact upon the individuals who were removed and grew up without any connection to their family and culture was even more catastrophic. This was demonstrated clearly between 1989 and 1991 during the course of the collection of evidence for the Royal Commission into Aboriginal Deaths in Custody. Of the 99 Aboriginal deaths in custody that were investigated ultimately by the Commission, it was found that 43 had experienced separation from their families through government, mission or institutional intervention. In the States of New South Wales and Western Australia more than half of the Indigenous deaths that were investigated involved a person who had been removed from their family as a child. Among the consequences of this policy that were discussed by the Royal Commission, was the major disruption to the transmission of Aboriginal culture. Being removed from the support and care of family, as well as the extended Aboriginal community, resulted in the institutionalisation of Aboriginal youths, which left many of them, according to a submission by the National Aboriginal Islander Legal Service Secretariat (NAILSS) 'struggling against the odds to live normal lives in a world that is permanently disordered from the inside out.' As a consequence, they concluded, 'an indeterminate number find themselves in a revolving door relationship with police, hospitals, prisons and various debilitating dependencies.'[19]

3 THE STOLEN GENERATIONS INQUIRY

In May 1995 the Federal Government directed the Human Rights and Equal Opportunity Commission (HREOC) to conduct an inquiry into the separation of

15 R. Wilson, *Bringing Them Home*, (HREOC, Canberra, 1997), 37.

16 P. Read, *A rape of the soul so profound*, (Allen & Unwin, Sydney 1999) 26.

17 The Royal Commission into Aboriginal Deaths in Custody was established in 1987 following widespread concern over the number of Aboriginal people who were dying in custody. It considered all deaths of Indigenous Australians in all forms of custody (prisons, police cells, and while under arrest) in the period between1980 and 1989.

18 E. Johnston, *Final Report of the Royal Commission into Aboriginal Deaths in Custody*, (AGPS, Canberra, 1991) Vol. 2. para 11.7.7.

19 *Ibid.*, para. 11.7.18.

Aboriginal children from their families. The terms of reference of the Inquiry called upon the HREOC to consider both past and current laws and policies relating to the separation of Aboriginal children from their families. Also, the review was required to consider whether there was a need to change any current laws and to examine the possibility of compensation being made to those people affected by the separations. The Inquiry travelled throughout Australia, to most regions including every state and territory capital, and took evidence in both public and private sittings. The Inquiry received evidence from 535 Indigenous people, as well as submissions from a further 242 individuals, including representatives from government agencies, churches, academics, law enforcement officials, health professionals and persons who had fostered or adopted the children who had been removed.

Based upon the testimony received, the inquiry observed that there were certain consistent aspects to the lives of those Aboriginal children who had been forcibly removed. Apart from their exploitation as a source of cheap labour and the fact that the education provided at institutions where the children were sent was of a very basic nature, the inquiry determined that there were recurring accounts of physical and sexual abuse; that the authorities in charge had failed in their duty of care to those children placed in their care; and that the children placed in institutions were dissuaded from having any family contact and were taught to reject Aborigines and Aboriginality. In considering the impact of removal upon the children who were removed, the inquiry also commented on the manner in which the effect of removal manifested itself, both upon the child removed and upon the community from which the child was taken. The inquiry observed, for example, that the removal of children had a profound impact upon those who had been left behind, often evidenced in self-destructive behaviour and self-harm. The cycle of neglect that was initiated by removing the children at a crucial point from the primary care giver was also, it was observed, manifested in a range of symptoms that included depression and suicide, alcohol and substance abuse, and a lack of self-esteem.

The *Bringing Them Home* final report made 54 recommendations to the Australian government. These included making reparations to all persons affected by forcible removal, including the payment of monetary compensation to those who were affected in a variety of ways, including abuse (either physical, sexual or emotional), pain and suffering, racial discrimination, labour exploitation and loss of cultural rights and fulfilment. In particular, the Report considered the applicability of the Van Boven principles regarding the nature of reparations for gross violations of human rights and fundamental freedoms.[20] Drawing from Van Boven's principles, the *Bringing Them Home* report recommended that compensation should be equated with reparation

20 T. Van Boven, (Special Rapporteur of the United Nations). Study concerning the right to restitution, compensation and rehabilitation for victims of gross violations of human rights and fundamental freedoms: Final Report, UN Doc. E/CN. 4/Sub.2/1993/8, 2 July 1993, 7.

to the stolen generations and that this should comprise the following: acknowledgement and apology, guarantees against repetition, measures of restitution, measures of rehabilitation and monetary compensation.[21] The Report also recommended that reparations should be extended to include those individuals forcibly removed as children, as well as their direct families. Also, it was recommended that the reparations should be extended to the communities from which the stolen generations had been removed, which had suffered 'cultural and community disintegration' as a consequence of their removal, and to include the descendants of those who were removed. In respect of the descendants of those who were removed, it was argued that this group of people would encompass those persons who had been deprived of links to their traditional communities, lands, culture and language.[22]

Other recommendations related to the provision of services to assist members of the stolen generation to trace their families, and the provision of appropriate specialist treatment for those who had experienced trauma as a consequence of their forced removal. The recommendations also called upon the various agencies which had been involved in the removal of children to take responsibility for and to acknowledge their part in the policy, and to apologise. Significantly, this recommendation pointed to the churches, police forces and the Australian Parliaments. It was the recommendation that the Australian Parliaments should apologise that was to become particularly contentious in the years that followed. Perhaps even more controversial than the demand for an apology from the various levels of government, the *Bringing Them Home* Report concluded that the child placement policies could be deemed to be genocidal, consistent with the definition of genocide under international law:

> "...any of the following acts committed with intent to destroy, in whole or in part, a national, ethnical, racial or religious group, as such:
>
> a. killing members of the group;
> b. causing serious bodily or mental harm;
> c. deliberately inflicting on the group conditions of life calculated to bring about its physical destruction in whole or in part;
> d. imposing measures intended to prevent births within the group;
> e. forcibly transferring children of the group to another group."[23]

In considering whether the forcible removal of Indigenous children to non-Indigenous families and institutions could be deemed to be genocidal, the Wilson inquiry addressed a number of key issues. As to whether the forcible transfer of children could

---

21 R. Wilson *Bringing Them Home*, (HREOC, Canberra, 1997), Recommendation 3.

22 R. Wilson, *Bringing Them Home*, (HREOC, Canberra, 1997), Recommendation 4.

23 Article 2 of the Convention on the Prevention and Punishment of the Crime of Genocide. Approved and proposed for signature and ratification or accession by General Assembly resolution 260 A (III) of 9 December 1948. Entry into force 12 January 1951, in accordance with article XIII.

be genocidal, the HREOC inquiry determined, drawing from the work of Lemkin, that 'genocide does not necessarily mean the immediate physical destruction of a group or nation.'[24] On the question of whether partial destruction of a group may amount to genocide, it found that a conspiracy to commit genocide constitutes a crime irrespective of whether any 'actual destruction' occurred.[25] The assimilative purpose of the policy was genocidal because its objective was to destroy the 'cultural unit' of Indigenous peoples, which includes cultural, linguistic, social and religious dimensions.[26] The HREOC inquiry also considered whether the existence of 'mixed motives' (such as benevolent intentions) might demonstrate the *lack* of an intention to commit genocide. On this question the *Bringing Them Home Report*, citing the debates that preceded the drafting of the *Genocide Convention,* determined unequivocally that 'an act or policy is still genocide when it is motivated by a number of objectives.'[27] Importantly, the report concluded that the planned extermination of a group need not be motivated solely by hatred or animosity. The final question considered by the inquiry was how early in time the policies and practices of the various Australian governments could be said to have been in breach of international law. On this point the inquiry determined that the forcible removal of Indigenous Australian children could 'properly be labeled 'genocidal'' from at least 11 December 1946.[28] In conclusion, the report stated that the policies were not only contrary to the legal principles of received British law, but also constituted, from 1946 onwards, a crime against humanity.

Reflecting on the historical extent of the injustice, the Report noted further that the 'continuation into the 1970s and 1980s of the practice of preferring non-Indigenous foster and adoptive families for Indigenous children was also arguably genocidal.'[29] Significantly this same issue was considered some six years earlier by Commissioner Elliott Johnston QC in the course of the Royal Commission into Aboriginal Deaths in Custody, who found that the child removal policies were adopted 'not for the purpose of exterminating a people, but for their preservation.'[30] The report by Sir Ronald Wilson rejected the view of Johnston, however, and argued instead that:

> "...the predominant aim of Indigenous child removals was the absorption or assimilation of the children into the wider, non-Indigenous, community so that their unique cultural values and ethnic identities would disappear."[31]

---

24 R. Wilson, *Bringing Them Home,* (HREOC, Canberra, 1997), 271.

25 *Ibid.*, 272.

26 *Ibid.*, 273.

27 *Ibid.*, 274.

28 *Ibid.*, 275.

29 *Ibid.*, 274.

30 E. Johnston. *Royal Commission into Aboriginal Deaths in Custody*, Vol. 5, (AGPS, Canberra, 1991), para 36.3.7.

31 R. Wilson, *Bringing Them Home*, (HREOC, Canberra, 1997), 272-3.

The final report relating to the stolen generation inquiry was released in 1997 and it provided a comprehensive and graphic account of the experiences of the children who were forcibly removed from their families. Among certain sectors of the community, there was disbelief and amazement at the revelations and the fact that the events had taken place so recently in the history of the nation. As Robert Manne so aptly put it: 'This story had the power to change forever the way they saw their country's history.'[32] Unfortunately the release of the *Bringing Them Home* Report also prompted a concerted program of denial and opposition amongst right-wing commentators and, more notably, the Howard Federal Government. While the State Parliaments of Western Australia, South Australia, Victoria, Tasmania, the Australian Capital Territory and New South Wales adopted resolutions supporting a formal apology to the stolen generations, the Federal Government steadfastly refused to entertain the possibility of such an action. While expressing personal regret at the plight of those people who had suffered, the Prime Minister steadfastly refused to countenance any form of apology to the stolen generations. Initially this reluctance was attributed to the fear of the Federal government that it would be tantamount to an admission of guilt, which would expose the government to legal actions for compensation. As time passed, however, it became clear that the reluctance to acknowledge the suffering of the stolen generations was grounded in more than a simple pragmatic economic analysis of the events. The tenor of the government's response to the *Bringing Them Home* Report was clear in the assertion made in April 2000 by the then Federal Minister for Aboriginal Affairs, John Herron, who maintained that the number of Aboriginal children removed was insufficient to warrant their being called a 'generation'.

In November 1999 the Senate called upon the Legal and Constitutional References Committee to consider the extent and effectiveness of the Federal Government's response to the *Bringing Them Home* Report. In addition the Committee was asked to determine an appropriate model for alternative dispute resolution which might circumvent the limitations of remedies based upon litigation. After taking submissions from 147 interested parties the Committee made a number of recommendations, including that there should be provision for individual monetary compensation to members of the stolen generations; that a motion of national apology and reconciliation should be passed by the Australian Federal Parliament; and that a reparations tribunal should be created, similar to those that had been created in New Zealand, South Africa and Canada. It was argued that this form of tribunal would avoid divisive litigation and could implement the main recommendations of the *Bringing Them Home* Report. The advantages of such a tribunal would be that it would be less costly than going through the courts and that, taking into account the relaxing of rules of

32 R. Manne, "In Denial: The Stolen Generations and the Right", (2001) 186, *The Australian Quarterly Essay,* 104.

evidence and procedure, it would not be as adversarial in nature and would be less distressing for those people who had been forcibly removed. Of course the adoption of any such reparations tribunal would have to address substantial procedural and administrative hurdles. Not least amongst these would be to resolve the question of who would be eligible for reparations and the manner in which 'forcible removal' should be interpreted. Such a tribunal would also need to consider the nature of compensation and how the appropriate defendants in the cases should be identified. Importantly, given the difficulties that have emerged in respect of obtaining sufficient evidence, either in the form of witnesses or relevant documents, such a tribunal would need to decide whether or not the proceedings would depart from the usual standards adopted in legal cases.[33] Despite strong support for the establishment of such a tribunal, both in the *Bringing Them Home* Report and a subsequent report prepared for the Public Interest Advocacy Centre (PIAC), the Australian government has shown no inclination to embrace the concept.

In the Commonwealth Government submission to the Committee a challenge was advanced to the use of the term 'stolen'. It was insisted that children ought to be described as 'separated'. The government response also argued that the methodology used in the HREOC inquiry was flawed. The government further argued that the percentage of separated Aboriginal children was no more than 10 per cent, and that this was inclusive of children who were removed under legitimate child-placement policies. Most tellingly, the Commonwealth Government contended that: 'There was never a 'generation' of stolen children.' In reference to past policies the Commonwealth Government maintained that the treatment of the children was 'essentially lawful and benign in intent' and that it 'is impossible to evaluate by contemporary standards decisions that were taken in the past.' This point was put most clearly in a letter from the then Minister for Aboriginal Affairs, Senator John Herron, who stated that:

> "The government does not support an official national apology. Such an apology could imply that present generations are in some way responsible and accountable for the actions of earlier generations, actions that were sanctioned by the laws of the time, and that were believed to be in the best interests of the children concerned."[34]

Lest it be thought that the resistance to the concept of an apology and reparations has emanated solely from Prime Minister Howard, it must be noted that there has been strident opposition from a group of right-wing commentators. In 1998, for example, anthropologist Ron Brunton attacked the credibility of the *Bringing Them Home*

---

33 C. Cunneen & J. Grix, *The Limits of Limitation in the Stolen Generation Cases*, (Institute of Criminology, Sydney, 2003), 61.

34 Quoted in R. Manne, "In Denial: The Stolen Generations and the Right", (2001) 186 *The Australian Quarterly Essay*, 75.

Report in a paper titled 'Betraying the Victims'. Specifically, Brunton took issue with the failure to distinguish between those children who may have been 'unjustly separated', from those who had been willingly placed into care by their parents or were in danger of abuse. On the claims that the assimilation policies constituted a form of genocide, Brunton argued that such a charge was based on scant evidence and that the government's eugenic program could not be viewed as genocidal. Consistent with Prime Minister Howard's scathing criticism of the 'black arm-band view of history', Brunton railed against the Wilson report, arguing that: 'On page after page, *Bringing Them Home* selectively stacks the deck against Australia.'[35]

4 STOLEN GENERATIONS LITIGATION

While the Howard Government has failed to act upon the most important recommendations of the *Bringing Them Home* Report, the avenue of litigation has also provided little in the way of redress for the children who were forcibly removed. To date there have been three main cases that have argued that the Commonwealth or State Governments or Administrative Agencies should be accountable for the harm suffered by the stolen generations. The first case decided by the courts was that of *Kruger v The Commonwealth*,[36] in which two Aboriginal plaintiffs brought an action against the government based upon their removal from their families in the Northern Territory at the direction of the Chief Protector of Aborigines under the *Aboriginals Ordinance 1918 (NT)*. The relevant provisions of the Ordinance stated that:

> "7. (1.) The Chief Protector shall be the legal guardian of every aboriginal and of every half-caste child, notwithstanding that the child has a parent or other relative living, until the child attains the age of eighteen years, except while the child is a State child within the meaning of the Act of the State of South Australia in force in the Northern Territory entitled *The State Children Act* 1895, or any Act of that state or Ordinance amending or substituted for that Act."

Essentially, the basis of the claim in *Kruger* was that the Ordinance was unconstitutional and damages were sought for the breach of the plaintiffs' constitutional rights. The Court held, however, that the Ordinance was valid and could not be struck down by any implied rights (including freedom of movement and association and due process). Whilst there was some judicial comment as to the ill-advised nature of the policy to which the Ordinance gave effect, this was not seen to impact upon its validity.

The next case was brought by Joy Williams, who was removed from her mother within hours of her birth in September 1942 and placed in Bombaderry Children's Home as a ward of the New South Wales Aborigines Welfare Board. Due to the

---

35 R. Brunton, "The stolen reputation", *The Age* 4 April 2001.

36 *Kruger v Commonwealth* (1997) 146 ALR 126.

overcrowding at the home and the perception that Williams' fair skin would allow her to pass as white, she was shifted subsequently to the Lutanda Children's Home in the Blue Mountains. The conditions at the home were harsh and Williams absconded on a number of occasions. Upon reaching the age of eighteen, Williams was removed from the home. In the ensuing years she was homeless and developed alcohol and drug addictions. She was imprisoned and was admitted on eight occasions to psychiatric hospitals. Her first child was also removed from her and adopted out. Williams ultimately made contact with her birth mother in the early 1980s through the *Link Up* organisation. In 1991 Williams was examined by an expert in childhood and adolescent psychiatry who diagnosed her as having a serious psychiatric condition which was caused probably by her treatment while in the children's home. In the same year Williams commenced legal proceedings in the New South Wales Supreme Court alleging negligence, breach of fiduciary duty and wrongful imprisonment. In the first instance the plaintiff had to apply for an extension to the time in which she could bring her case under the *Limitation Act* 1969. Although Justice Stoddert had the discretion to extend the limitation period within three years of the plaintiff becoming aware of the nature and extent of the personal injury, he declined to give the extension. In making this decision Stoddert J enunciated grounds that were to arise in subsequent stolen generations litigation. He held that the Board was merely applying what he termed the 'inappropriate and erroneous' social policies of the day and that there was no evidence of an alternative location to which Williams could have been sent. Further, Stoddert J held that the lengthy delay meant that it was likely that many relevant documents would either have been lost or destroyed, and that the persons who might be called upon to give evidence as to the conditions in the home either would be deceased or elderly. On appeal to the Court of Appeal, the decision of Justice Stoddert was overturned and it was held that the Statute of Limitations should be waived to allow Williams' case to be heard. Perhaps the most significant aspect of the decision to allow the Williams case to proceed was that made by President Kirby, who noted that 'if she can make good her contentions, she has suffered a grievous wrong at the hands of the agencies of the State.' He went on to state:

> "The law which has often been an instrument of injustice to Aboriginal Australians can also, in proper cases, be an instrument of justice in the vindication of their legal rights. It is not just and reasonable in this case to close the doors of the Court in Ms Williams' face."[37]

When the matter was heard before Justice Abadee however, he ruled that the plaintiff had failed to establish a duty of care or breach of duty of care and that there was no negligence on the part of defendant. Whilst the court did not rule on the existence of a fiduciary duty, it found that there was no evidence that could support the existence

[37] *Williams v Minister, Aboriginal Land Rights Act 1983* (1994) 35 NSWLR 497 at 515.

of such a relationship. In conclusion, Justice Abadee rejected the claim for damages or equitable compensation. This judgment was subsequently upheld on appeal to the NSW Supreme Court, which held that Justice Abadee had not erred in his findings. Significantly the grounds of the matter that were argued before the Court of Appeal differed from the earlier action in that it was no longer asserted that Ms Williams had suffered mistreatment by virtue of her Aboriginality. The claim that she was a member of the stolen generations was also abandoned.[38] The change to Ms Williams' pleadings did not affect the outcome of the case. It is clear, however, that her lawyers had resolved that the issues related to the stolen generations did not give rise to a recognisable ground for action before the courts. The case was re-presented in a form that was cognisable to the legal system. Instead of claims based upon her difference, her Aboriginality, it was presented as a case in which she experienced subsequent mental distress due to a lack of maternal care. The plaintiff's statement of claim also shifted, according to Heydon JA, from denunciation of the effects of the assimilation policy to an argument that the same assimilation policy had demanded a duty of care that had been breached.[39]

To date the most notable of the three 'stolen generations' cases has been that of *Cubillo v The Commonwealth*,[40] which was an action brought by two Aboriginal people from the Northern Territory against the Commonwealth Government, claiming that they had been wrongfully imprisoned, that the Commonwealth Government had failed in its duty of care to them and had breached its fiduciary duty. The two Aboriginal parties in the case were Lorna Cubillo and Peter Gunner. Lorna Cubillo (or Napanangka as she was then) was nine years old when she was taken on 14 July 1947 from the Aboriginal depot in Phillip Creek in the Northern Territory. She was placed in the Retta Dixon hostel in Darwin where she resided for the next ten years. As Manne puts it:

> "Retta Dixon was a place where she was starved of all physical and emotional affection, where her language was beaten out of her, where a regime of joyless, puritanical religiosity prevailed and where the beliefs of people like her mother and grandmother were said to condemn the soul to hell."[41]

The other claimant in the *Cubillo* case was Peter Gunner, who was only seven years old when he was removed in 1956 from a 'native camp' in central Australia. Gunner was taken to the St Mary Hostel in Alice Springs where the children endured shocking

---

38 *Williams v The Minister Aboriginal Land Rights Act 1983 and The State of New South Wales* [2000] NSWCA 255.

39 *Williams v The Minister Aboriginal Land Rights Act* [2000] NSWCA 255 at paragraph 24.

40 *Cubillo v The Commonwealth* [2000] FCA 1084.

41 R. Manne, "In Denial: The Stolen Generations and the Right", (2001) 186 *The Australian Quarterly Essay*, 19.

conditions and facilities and were subjected to physical and sexual abuse. At the age of fourteen, Peter Gunner left the hostel to go and work on a cattle station. The statement setting out the claims of Lorna Cubillo and Peter Gunner alleged that:

> "By the actions of the Commonwealth, Lorna Cubillo and Peter Gunner were removed as young children from their families and communities. They were taken hundreds of kilometers from the countries of their birth. They were prevented from returning. They were made to live among strangers, in a strange place, in institutions which bore no resemblance to a home. They lost, by the actions of the Commonwealth, the chance to grow among the warmth of their own people, speaking their people's languages and learning about their country. They suffered lasting psychiatric injury. They were treated as orphans when they were not orphans. They lost the culture and traditions of their families. Decades later, the Commonwealth of Australia says in this case that it did them no wrong at all."[42]

In fact the Commonwealth went even further than simply to deny that it had done any wrong to the claimants and the stolen generations in general. What emerged during the course of the case was a harrowing example of the manner in which the Commonwealth lawyers not only disputed that the assimilation policies were harmful, but also challenged the truth of the accounts given by the two Aboriginals and maintained that the child removal policy had benefited them. In the case of Peter Gunner, the lawyer for the government went so far as to suggest that, as a half-caste baby, he would have been killed and that the act of removal actually saved his life.

In handing down the judgment in the *Cubillo* case Justice O'Loughlin ruled that the claims by the two applicants were not made out. In the case of Peter Gunner the judge accepted that he had been the victim of a sexual assault whilst at St Marys, but noted that there was no evidence that he had been removed from his mother against her will. In the case of Lorna Cubillo Justice O'Loughlin also accepted her claims that she had been viciously assaulted by a missionary at the Retta Dixon home and that she had been very unhappy there, but observed that there were too many documents that were missing to be able to establish that the Director of Native Affairs at the time, Frank Moy, had not acted in her best interests. Significantly, Justice O'Loughlin commented in his judgment that there was nothing in the evidence that was presented to the court that supported an assertion that the stolen generations did not exist. He went on to comment that the importance of an apology to the stolen generations had never been raised by either of the applicants in the case. Ultimately Justice O'Loughlin found that the 'state of the law as it existed at the time when Mrs Cubillo and Mr Gunner were removed from their families' meant that the Director of Native Affairs could remove children from their families even when it was 'against the express wishes of the child's family.'

42 *Cubillo v The Commonwealth* [2000] FCA 1084 at paragraph 2.

Though the judgment takes a sympathetic stance in relation to the claims of Gunner and Cubillo, the legality of the legislation and the lack of corroborating evidence was deemed to be fatal to the plaintiffs' case. Interestingly Marchetti and Ransley, drawing on critical race theory, present an argument that Justice O'Loughlin's application of legal rules and doctrine reflected an 'element of unconscious racism.'[43] According to the authors, this 'unconscious racism' was manifested in a number of ways, but in particular the representation of the testimony of the plaintiffs as unreliable, and a privileging of the testimony of government officials and missionaries, in the determination of the facts.[44] Marchetti and Ransley argue that the meanings that are subsequently read into the judgment of O'Loughlin ('the cultural meaning') by the general populace, are confirmation of the racialised nature of the decision. Whilst ostensibly presented as a sympathetic and fair adjudication, the statements made by the judge confirm the unreliability of the plaintiffs.[45]

While to this stage the stolen generation's cases have been unsuccessful, it should be emphasised that this does not mean the claims made of physical, emotional and sexual abuse have been disproved or found to be false. Rather it is an indication that the courts believe that the passage of time has meant that much of the relevant evidence is no longer available, as witnesses or persons involved have died and the relevant documents have been destroyed or are lost. Also, the courts have ruled that the Commonwealth is not the right defendant in some cases, which makes it difficult for the stolen generations to bring an action against persons who are no longer alive. Furthermore, the courts have accepted that the legislation under which the children were taken was legal, even though it would be condemned as inhumane today.[46] A substantial body of commentary upon the litigation on behalf of the stolen generation attests to the procedural difficulties encountered in successfully establishing a claim.

Most importantly, however, the decision by the Government to respond to the stolen generation's cases as discrete and separate matters is further evidence of a refusal to accept the general discriminatory application of protection and welfare laws. More particularly, as Cunneen and Grix observe: 'The reality of entrenched racial discrimination which these laws embodied has been obscured.'[47] By concentrating upon the (contested) legal claims of individuals, the Government has attempted to void the cases of any broader significance for Indigenous Australians. It is worth noting that the response of the Federal Government to the stolen generation's litigation is consistent

---

43 E. Marchetti & J. Ransley, "Unconscious Racism: Scrutinizing Judicial Reasoning in 'Stolen Generation' Cases, (2005) 14 (4) *Social & Legal Studies*, 533 at 545.

44 *Ibid.*, 545-6.

45 *Ibid.*, 547.

46 C. Cunneen and J. Grix, *The Limitations of Litigation in Stolen Generations cases*, p 56. See also J. Clarke, (2000) 'Case Note – Commonwealth not liable: Cubillo and Gunner v Commonwealth', 5(2) *Indigenous Law Bulletin* 11.

47 C. Cunneen & J. Grix, *The Limitations of Litigation in Stolen Generations cases*, p 59.

with what Freeman has termed the 'perpetrator principle'. In analysing the deficiencies of United States anti-discrimination measures Freeman defined the perpetrator perspective as presupposing:

> "…a world composed of atomistic individuals whose actions are outside and apart from the social fabric and without historical continuity. From this perspective, the law views racial discrimination not as a social phenomenon but merely the misguided conduct of particular actors."[48]

In a similar vein it may be argued that the effect of litigating each individual claim of the stolen generations lends credence to the position that the forcible removals were not part of a policy over a lengthy period of time that was directed at a specific racial group. The government is exonerated from any of the harm that might have been suffered by the children who were removed, and there is no simple attribution of blame to 'particular actors', save for the fact that their actions may be retrospectively labelled as 'misguided conduct'. The broader issues of reparations and apology are negated by the Federal Government's insistence upon treating the plaintiffs as atomistic individuals who remain 'outside and apart from the social fabric'.

Consistent with the Federal Government's desire not to treat the stolen generations claims as a 'social phenomenon' was its assertion that the cases needed to be determined according to legal principles. To this end the government's barrister, Mr Meagher QC, reminded the court:

> "You're here to determine the facts and apply the law, you're not charged with determining the correct historical view or social science view of what went before. Nor are you here to pass judgment on those societies or their politics, rather you're here to determine a very narrow issue, namely, whether on facts capable of being established by reliable evidence, there is liability in law, and nothing else."[49]

While Mr Meagher's courtroom address focused upon the legality of the removal of the stolen generations, the manner in which the Crown so strenuously opposed every aspect of the stolen generation's claims suggests that it was not solely about determining liability in law. Judith Bessant goes so far as to question whether the government's conduct could be seen to constitute a breach of its own model litigant principles.[50] The assertion by Mr Meagher QC that the court should not be concerned with 'determining the correct historical view…of what went before' is made problematic by the fact that his own father had been involved in the administration of Aboriginal Affairs in Victoria as the Chairman of the Aborigines Welfare Board. The extent of Meagher's

48 A. Freeman, "Legitimizing Racial Discrimination through Antidiscrimination Law" in K. Crenshaw et al. (eds.), *Critical Race Theory*, (The New Press, New York, 1995), 30.

49 The Law Report, "Radio National Transcripts" ABC radio, broadcast March 9 1999.

50 J. Bessant "Procedural Justice, Conflict of Interest and the Stolen Generation's Cases", (2004) 63(1) *Australian Journal of Public Administration*, 80.

personal investment in the outcome of the *Cubillo* case can be seen in the article which he penned for the *Quadrant* magazine, following his involvement in the *Cubillo* case.[51] Significantly Meagher castigated Sir Ronald Wilson, the head of the *Bringing Them Home* inquiry for creating false expectations as to financial compensation amongst the members of the stolen generations. Meagher also went so far as to argue that it was the publication of the *Bringing Them Home* Report that acted as a catalyst for the commencement of proceedings in the *Cubillo* case. In addition he charged that the characters and reputations of those who worked with Indigenous Australians had been 'attacked and destroyed' such that it constituted a 'bleak and dismal chapter in Australia's history.'[52]

In the period since the ruling was handed down in the *Cubillo* case there have been a number of developments that suggest that there may be an avenue for legal redress open to members of the stolen generation, notwithstanding the substantial legal hurdles discussed above. The option remains available for members of the stolen generation who have suffered harm as a result of violent crimes (such as physical or sexual assault) to seek compensation that is available in many jurisdictions for the victims of crime. Cornwall notes, for example, that those members of the stolen generations who sought compensation in Victoria received payments in the range of $4000 each.[53] Similarly, a case brought in New South Wales by Valerie Linow in February 2001, claimed damages for the psychological harm she had suffered as a consequence of being sexually assaulted in 1958. The claims were made pursuant to section 5(1)(c) of the *Victims Support and Rehabilitation Act 1996 (NSW)*, and was resolved ultimately on appeal to the Victim's Compensation Tribunal, with the Chairperson of the Victim's Compensation Tribunal finding that there was a connection between her diagnosed disorders and the sexual assaults she had suffered, and awarding her compensation of $35 000.[54] Whilst Valerie Linow saw the damages as a victory for justice, it should be noted that such an action does not address the broader issue of governmental or societal responsibility for the injustices perpetrated against the stolen generations. The avenue of victim's compensation allows the children who were forcibly removed to have their matter heard and provides for compensation; however it also serves to de-racialise the issue of the stolen generations and to absolve the broader community of any responsibility for past actions.

---

[51] D. Meagher "Not Guilty" (2000) XLIV, *Quadrant* XLIV.

[52] *Ibid.*, 34.

[53] A. Cornwall, *Restoring Identity Final Report*, (Public Interest Advocacy Centre, Sydney, 2002) 47.

[54] C. Cunneen & J. Grix, *The Limitations of Litigation in Stolen Generation's cases*, 33.

5 WRITING A NATION'S HISTORY

Reflecting on the reasons for the incapacity (or unwillingness) of the current Australian government to respond to the profound inequality that is the lot of Indigenous Australians, it becomes clear that one of the major areas of conflict is not just how the history of past injustices should be told, but whether there were indeed any past actions that might be characterised as injustice. The divergent nature of the two accounts of the past treatment of Indigenous children, between government officials and agencies on the one hand and Indigenous communities on the other, suggests that there is little prospect of reconciling the differing views. In a paper delivered at the Sorbonne in 1882 the French historian Louis Renan commented that a nation is 'a soul, a spiritual principle.' This spiritual principle, he argued, was constituted by two elements: one of which is located in the past and one in the future. He further elaborated as follows:

> "One is the possession in common of a rich legacy of memories; the other is present-day consent, the desire to live together, the will to perpetuate the value of the heritage that has been received in an undivided form."[55]

The validity of the nation, according to Renan, therefore depends upon the melding of a heritage that is 'received in an undivided form.' The nature of Australia's settlement and the violent dispossession of the Indigenous population is patently at odds with this homogenised, celebratory remembering. In elaborating upon how a nation might reconcile itself to the foundational violence that almost inevitably accompanies the passage to nationhood, Renan comments that a capacity for forgetting is crucial in the creation of a nation. It follows, therefore, that the progress of historical studies 'often constitutes a danger for [the principle of] nationality.'[56]

The stance of the Howard government, whilst ostensibly based upon the legal necessity of avoiding any liability that might arise from acknowledgment for past government policies, appears more concerned with the articulation of what was for them an acceptable and, importantly, valid narrative of Australian history. As early as 1988 the Liberal Party had stated in its Aboriginal Affairs Policy that: 'The Coalition rejects the notion that this generation of mainly European Australians should feel a sense of guilt concerning the actions of mainly European Australians against the Aboriginal people. Guilt is not hereditary.' In the Liberal Party's *Future Visions* document that was released in the same year it was further argued that the existence of such divisive visions of the past would threaten the future of the nation. Howard's vision therefore did not – could not – admit to the possibility of past atrocities and

---

[55] L. Renan, "What is a Nation?" in H. BHABHA, *Nation and Narration*, (Routledge, New York, 1990), 19.

[56] *Ibid.*, 11.

horrors, for it would mean the fragmentation of the Australian nation. Importantly, Howard articulated a vision of one Australia, rather than an 'Australia of individual groups.'[57] This 'one Australia' that Howard envisaged was clearly grounded in the restoration of the British roots of the nation, a fact borne out in the accompanying images in the *Future Directions* document that showed 'one Australia' proud of its heritage – 'not an Australia of individual groups'. Significantly this denunciation of the idea that the dispossession of Indigenous Australians should give rise to any claim against the current population was made during the year that Australia celebrated the bi-centenary of the founding of the nation. Even as much of Australia celebrated the achievements of two centuries of non-Indigenous presence there were widespread protests amongst some sections of the Indigenous community and renewed calls for the negotiation of some form of treaty or compact to address historical injustices. Conversely, there is a clear sense from the Howard government that there can be no attribution of blame for past events.

This contrasts strongly with the position adopted during the tenure of former Labor Prime Minister, Paul Keating, who made a powerful statement in 1992 acknowledging the past injustices suffered by Indigenous Australians. Speaking at a park at Redfern, in inner-city Sydney, Prime Minister Keating declared:

> "It begins, I think, with the act of recognition. Recognition that it was we who did the dispossessing. We took the traditional lands and smashed the traditional way of life. We brought the disasters. The alcohol. We committed the murders. We took the children from their mothers. We practised discrimination and exclusion.
>
> It was our ignorance and our prejudice. And our failure to imagine these things being done to us. With some noble exceptions, we failed to make the most basic human response and enter into their hearts and minds. We failed to ask – how would I feel if this were done to me?
>
> As a consequence, we failed to see that what we were doing degraded all of us."[58]

Explicit within the Keating Redfern speech is an acknowledgment of responsibility for the manner in which Indigenous lands were taken and the traditional way of life was 'smashed'. Importantly Keating's speech draws a connection between the violence perpetrated, the children taken from their mothers, and a diminution of the spirit and essence of each individual and, consequently, the entire Australian nation. The vision of Prime Minister Keating gave rise to a number of initiatives that sought to address the issue of Indigenous disadvantage. In 1991 a Council for Reconciliation was established by the *Council for Reconciliation Act 1991* which was to undertake a process of consultation around the nation with a view to negotiating a process of reconciliation

---

57 "Future Directions" Liberal Party policy statement quoted in A. Markus, *Race: John Howard and the Remaking of Australia*, (Allen & Unwin, Sydney, 2000), 83.

58 P. Keating, "Redfern Park Speech" in M. GRATTAN (ed.) *Essays on Australia Reconciliation*, Melbourne, Bookman Press, 2000.

between Indigenous and non-Indigenous Australians. This process of consultation was being undertaken during the course of the Stolen Generations Inquiry and at the time the unsuccessful court cases were argued. The Council, which ceased to exist in 2002, produced two documents that set out a process and made recommendations as to the manner in which reconciliation could be achieved in Australia. The documents were handed to State and Federal government representatives at an event in Sydney in 2001. The ceremony, called Corroboree 2001, was also marked by the People's Walk for Reconciliation on 28 May 2000 when more than 250 000 people walked across the Sydney Harbour Bridge. Despite this dramatic display of public support for reconciliation the Howard government has chosen not to implement the recommendations produced by the Council for Aboriginal Reconciliation. Barkan has emphasised the important link between the successful restitution cases and the acknowledgment of the role of guilt, mourning and atonement in effectively transforming a 'traumatic national experience into a constructive political situation [that] ... facilitates changes in national identities.'[59] The Howard government's refusal to engage with or acknowledge what he has dubbed the 'black arm-band view of history', suggests that reparations for the stolen generations will continue to be ignored so long as the nature of the Australian national identity and history remain contested.

Consistent across the global responses to historical wrongdoings Thompson suggests that it is possible to distinguish two main discourses.[60] The first is the legalistic response that is couched in terms of rights, restoration and compensation, what might be called reparation as restoration. The second approach is what Thompson terms a 'theological response', which is characterised by a concern with aspects such as apology, reconciliation and atonement.[61] Thompson further clarifies that the two can be termed, respectively, as 'backward looking' and 'forward looking' forms of reparation. Significantly the Howard government fails to embrace either of these possibilities for discourse. It disavows the possibility for 'backward-looking' reparations, based upon a legalistic conception of rights, by refusing to accept that its predecessors may have been responsible for the suffering of the Indigenous Australians. Even more telling, however, is the fact that the government repudiates the very existence of the 'stolen generations', which in itself negates any prospect for future resolution of the claims of Indigenous Australians.

---

59 E. Barkan, *The Guilt of Nations*, (Norton & Co, London, 2000) 345.

60 J. Thompson, *Taking Responsibility for the Past*, (Blackwell, Oxford, 2002), 47-9.

61 *Ibid.*, 47.

6 CONCLUSION

In November 2005 it was announced that the Canadian government had agreed to pay more than two billion dollars Canadian as compensation to First Nations children who were abused while staying at government-controlled residential schools.[62] The agreement, which is conditional upon endorsement being received from the courts, would resolve the existing claims of 15 000 individuals. In response to the action by the Canadian government Brian Butler, the National Sorry Day Aboriginal co-chairperson, called upon the Australian government to follow the example of its Canadian counterpart, commenting that it 'should prompt all Australians to push for positive action by the Government.'[63] The office of John Howard, the Australian Prime Minister, rejected such calls, however, asserting that the Canadian developments were a reflection of the unique circumstances in that country and had no bearing upon the Australian situation. It served as a clear reminder of the Federal Government's intransigence on the issue of either issuing an apology to the stolen generations or sanctioning any form of reparation or compensation to them. As a consequence the issue of the stolen generations remains a divisive and contested subject. Clearly the failure to achieve any resolution of the clams of the stolen generations is indicative of the general incapacity of the Australian nation to resolve and heal its relationship with the original Indigenous owners of this land. Put simply, the issue goes to the heart of the legitimacy of the Australian nation, a point made clear by the former Australian Governor-General, Sir William Deane, in the inaugural Lingiari lecture, where he expressed his fervent belief that:

> "I am convinced that until true reconciliation with its indigenous peoples is reached, Australia is a diminished nation. I am also convinced that such reconciliation is possible... One hundred years from now, when we are approaching the second century of our nation, the dreamings of the Aboriginal peoples will record whether we Australians had the determination, tolerance and goodwill to convert short-term possibility into a reality that is timeless."[64]

---

62 The term 'First Nations' was used in Canada to refer to Indigenous or Aboriginal peoples from the 1980s onwards, although the Canadian government continues to use the term 'registered Indians' for those who have entitlements under the *Indian Act of Canada 1876*. See also the chapter by Ken Cooper-Stephenson in this book at pages 359-388.

63 K. Liddle, "Canada to pay stolen victims" *Koori Mail* 30 November 2005, 5.

64 W. Deane, *Some signs from Dagaragu – the Inaugural Lingiari Lecture* 22 August 1996.

PART E:
REPARATIONS CLAIMS PURSUED AGAINST FOREIGN STATES

'I WILL BE FORGOTTEN': LEGAL REDRESS FOR KOREAN COMFORT WOMEN

BO JUNG KWON

1 INTRODUCTION

'Comfort women' were young women of various ethnic and national backgrounds who became sex slaves for the Japanese Imperial Army before and during World War II. Over a fifteen-year period, the comfort system implemented the rape and sexual enslavement of women from Japanese colonies and occupied territories.[1] Although the exact number of comfort women is unknown, most scholars agree that between 80,000 and 200,000 women were kidnapped, forcibly drafted, or deceived into sexual slavery. A recent study estimates that as many as 400,000 women might have been victimised.[2] Of these women, about 80% were Korean. As part of the overall Japanese war effort, the comfort system was administered by the Japanese military, as well as by Japan's Home Ministry and other Ministries.

Toward the end of the war, Japanese troops sought to expunge traces of the comfort system by slaughtering the women. Soldiers rounded up most of the women and shot them indiscriminately, or drove them into trenches and bombed the sites. Sometimes they used the women as bullet shields or abandoned them to fend for themselves.[3] Only 30% of the women survived.[4] Those who did survive the war suffered years of isolation: many remained unmarried and did not go back to their families due to feelings of guilt and shame. A 1998 survey indicates that '90 percent of surviving comfort women are

1 Soh, Chunghee Sarah. 2000. "From Imperial Gifts to Sex Slaves: Theorizing Symbolic Representations of the 'Comfort Women.'" *Social Science Japan Journal*. Vol. 3, No. 1. 59-76.

2 "Estimated Number of Japanese Sex Slaves during World War II Doubles." 2002. *Contemporary Sexuality*. Vol. 36, No. 1. 8. The new estimate was presented at the "Japanese Crimes Against Humanity: Sexual Slavery and Forced Labor" conference in Los Angeles in November of 2002. I have not been able to verify it in other sources.

3 Askin, Kelly D. 2001. "Comfort women – Shifting shame and stigma from victims to victimizers." *International Criminal Law Review*. Vol.1. 5-32. 21.

4 Soh, 124.

not married, live in poverty, and suffer from physical and psychological diseases.'[5] Most significantly, former comfort women did not speak of their experiences, even with friends and families. While the victims kept silent, both the Korean and Japanese governments suffered from a collective amnesia. Neither party broached the issue during their frequent diplomatic interactions following the war.

In 1991, Kim Hak Sun, a former comfort woman who had served in a comfort station in China, finally broke the silence that spanned half a century by bringing a lawsuit against the Japanese government to claim compensation for her sufferings. Although the Japanese government initially denied any involvement in the comfort system, Professor Yoshimi Yoshiaki's fortuitous discovery of relevant documents at the National Institute for Defense compelled the administration officially to recant its denial. In an attempt to appease the international community, the Japanese government initiated a *private* fund to provide financial assistance to former comfort women. The establishment of the Asian Women's Fund in 1995 received harsh criticism from both victims and their governments, as being an attempt to evade official responsibility. It 'created more animosity than reconciliation and has aggravated the internal Japanese debate.'[6]

Most victims have refused to accept money from the Asian Women's Fund and have sought instead reparations through legal actions. Such a tendency reflects the women's desire for justice, rather than monetary compensation. Unfortunately, the Japanese government has not prosecuted a single war criminal since the Tokyo Trial and remains unsympathetic to the women's claims. Consequently, Korean comfort women have sought legal redress elsewhere: in addition to pursuing litigation in Japan, they have turned to the United States district courts, as well as an unofficial international tribunal organised by a coalition of women's rights groups in Asia.

In this chapter, I examine various attempts by former Korean comfort women to obtain compensation for and recognition of their ordeal, and evaluate the accomplishments and shortfalls of each of these attempts. I begin by discussing the challenges involved in the prosecution of sexual violence committed in wartime, illustrated by the case of comfort women. I examine litigation in Japan and the United States, followed by a discussion of the 2000 International Women's Tribunal. I then consider the need for legal redress in the case of comfort women, maintaining that despite its inadequacies, the courtroom is the most appropriate forum in which to address the women's demands. By understanding and appreciating the arduous legal battles that former comfort women have waged, we may acquire a greater insight into the issues

[5] Kakuchi, Suverndrini. "Comfort Women Battle on Despite Legal Blow." *Interpress Service*, 12 Oct, 1998. This seems to be the only survey conducted on the status of former comfort women. In *all* of the personal accounts I have come across, the women are chronically ill and live alone; most of them have never married, and those who have are now separated from their spouses.

[6] Barkan, Elazar. 2000. *The Guilt of Nations: Restitution and Negotiating Historical Injustices.* New York: W.W. Norton & Company. 47.

involved in prosecuting crimes of sexual slavery that occur in the context of current armed conflicts.

2 CHALLENGES IN PROSECUTING SEXUAL VIOLENCE IN WAR

Taking legal action against crimes involving sexual violence under U.S. domestic law presents formidable obstacles to both the victims and the prosecutors. In addition to an existing tendency to ignore gender and sex based offences, the crimes themselves are 'intensely personal' in nature, involving 'injuries [which are] often less visible' than those resulting from other types of physical violence, and the 'details [of which] provoke discomfort and aversion.'[7] Court procedures further accentuate such difficulties. Judges treat victims with scepticism and do not protect them from inappropriate and humiliating questioning that may force them to relive the incident and suffer further trauma. In many instances, perpetrators are sentenced to a few months in jail, while public opinion and the media chastise victims for improper conduct.

As for sexual violence committed during wartime, international treaties, as well as war crimes tribunals, historically have failed to take such crimes into account. For instance, after World War II, the International Military Tribunals in Nuremberg (IMT) and Tokyo (IMTFE) focused mainly on the 'supreme crime,' i.e. crimes against peace. Consequently, sexual violence remained at the periphery of the legal process. Even in the post-World War II trials held in Tokyo, where the indictment did include gender-related crimes, it merely characterised rape as 'mistreatment' and 'inhumane treatment,' and prosecuted it under the Conventional War Crimes provision in the Charter.[8] More significantly, no one raised the issue of comfort women, for reasons I explore below.

A significant advance in the prosecution of sexual violence committed during armed conflict came about in 2002 at the International Criminal Tribunal for the Former Yugoslavia (ICTY), where rape was prosecuted as a crime against humanity. Several members of the Serbian military and paramilitary forces who took part in the enslavement and systematic rape of Muslim women in the town of Foca were indicted, successfully prosecuted, and convicted.[9] Despite the landmark victory, however, the Foca case also revealed a number of weaknesses in the treatment of sexual violence

---

7 Askin, Kelly D. 2003. "Stefan A. Riesenfeld Symposium 2002: Prosecuting Wartime Rape and Other Gender-Related Crimes under International Law: Extraordinary Advances, Enduring Obstacles." *Berkeley Journal of International Law*. 288-349. 346.

8 *Ibid.*, 300-301.

9 ICTY November 2002, Case IT-96-23 and IT-96-23/1.

within the sphere of international law. In particular, the longstanding problem of definitions re-emerged. Although the ICTY statute listed both rape and enslavement as crimes against humanity, neither fully captured the experience of the women in Foca. Some scholars have argued that the judgment explicitly should have used the term 'sexual slavery' to describe what had happened to the victims. The perpetrators kept the women in a number of designated locations, such as a school building and a sports centre, and repeatedly raped them over a significant period of time. Thus, instead of treating rape 'as merely one of the number of things that indicated that enslavement occurred,' the judges should have maintained that 'the sole reason for the enslavement was to effectuate continuous rape.'[10]

The question of categories and definitions resides at the heart of the legal debate surrounding the issue of Korean comfort women. Soon after the stories of former comfort women emerged, limitations in the legal vocabulary, which was unable to characterise the egregious nature of the comfort system, became evident. Was the comfort system a war crime, a crime against humanity, a commercial enterprise, or simply a violation of personal integrity? The issue lent itself to multiple definitions, which then complicated the search for appropriate remedies and accountability.[11] For instance, many scholars and legal experts long considered the comfort system to be a form of forced prostitution. As such, comfort women could not be treated as victims of a crime against humanity.[12] On the other hand, the Japanese government maintained that it was a commercial enterprise consisting of professional prostitutes, thereby denying responsibility for forcibly recruiting and enslaving the women. It was not until 1996, when the United Nations took it upon itself to define comfort women as sexual slaves, that the comfort system, as a form of slavery, was unequivocally recognised as constituting a violation of a *jus cogens* norm.[13]

The difficulties in seeking legal redress for former comfort women extend beyond contested definitions. At the heart of the issue lies the silence that shrouded the women's experiences for more than fifty years. Former comfort women remained voiceless and isolated from others largely because of fear of stigmatisation.[14] Moon

10 Barkan, Joanne. 2002. "As Old as War Itself: Rape in Foca." *Dissent.* Winter: 60-66. 66.

11 Shin, Susan. 2003. "Justice Delayed: Accountability in the 'Comfort Women' Case." *Accountability for Atrocities: National and International Responses*, edited by Jane E. Stromseth. New York: Transnational Publishers. 425.

12 Prior to the creation of the Rome Statute, forced prostitution was not generally considered a crime against humanity, which was defined as " murder, extermination, enslavement, deportation, and other inhumane acts committed against any civilian population, before or during the war," based on the precedent set by the International Military Tribunals in Nuremberg.

13 Coomaraswamy, Radhika. 1996. *E/CN.4/1996/53/Add.1.* UN Economic and Social Council Committee on Human Rights. I.8.

14 Dolgopol, Ustinia. 1995. "Women's Voices, Women's Pain." *Human Rights Quarterly* 17.1. 127-154. 147.

Pil-gi, who was deceived into becoming a comfort woman at the age of 18, came home after the war, only to leave a year later:

> "My mother wanted me to get married, but I didn't want to. How could I? I didn't tell her that I had been a comfort woman during the war... I was miserable at home, my heart was so tormented. I couldn't stay."[15]

Neither the Korean nor the Japanese government raised the issue of comfort women during their post-war diplomatic meetings.[16] In fact, public discourse on the issue of 'military comfort women' did not surface until the late 1980s in Korea, when feminist political activism emerged as a salient force in Korean society.[17]

When the first Korean comfort woman spoke out in 1991, the Japanese government was quick to deny any connection to the comfort system. When the overwhelming evidence confirming government involvement made denial untenable, Japan resorted to post-war treaties to evade responsibility. The Japanese government maintained that the question of liability for crimes and atrocities committed by its troops during World War II was settled in accordance with the provisions of the San Francisco Peace Treaty of 1945 and the Japan/Korea Peace Treaty of 1965. This was despite the fact that these treaties only addressed economic concerns and did not mention the issue of human rights. Furthermore, the Japanese government has refused to release surviving documents pertaining to the establishment and maintenance of comfort stations.

International law has proven inadequate in addressing the grievances of the victims. The International Criminal Court (ICC), hailed by some as one of the most significant achievements in the legal sphere during the past century, does not have the right to prosecute those responsible for the comfort system, since crimes committed before the Rome Statute came to force in 2002 cannot be prosecuted. As of 2005, Japan remains, along with the United States and China, one of the few nations that have not yet ratified the Statute. Nonetheless, scholars and prosecutors continue to hope for a legal solution to the demands of former comfort women for justice. Their optimism is based primarily on the hope of successfully prosecuting the perpetrators for violating a *jus cogens* norm. A *jus cogens* norm is a peremptory norm that is 'accepted and

---

15 Moon, Pil-gi. *Testimony of the Survivors.* The Korean Council for the Women Drafted for Military Slavery by Japan. Article retrieved on November 20, 2005, from http://www.womenandwar.net/. My translation.

16 The Korean government's attitude toward comfort women remains ambiguous. It only began to condemn the Japanese government after the women started to speak out. Until the early 1990s, the Korean government did not take any action to either compensate the women for their suffering or confront the Japanese government for its crimes. One may speculate that diplomatic and economic interests prevented the Korean government from taking an active stand. At present, there are few written sources dealing with this issue.

17 Soh, Chunghee Sarah. 1996. "The Korean 'Comfort Women': Movement for Redress." *Asian Survey*. 36.12. 1226-1240. 1232.

recognised by the international community of states as a whole as a norm from which no derogation is permitted and which can be modified only by a subsequent norm of general international law having the same character.'[18] Such a norm is binding on all states, without statute of limitations. The comfort system, as a form of sexual slavery, constitutes a violation of a *jus cogens* norm against slavery. Therefore, the optimists contend that an international court of law remains a viable venue to address the demands of former comfort women for recognition and justice.

Scholars have suggested three possible avenues for prosecuting human rights violations and war crimes: trials within a state jurisdiction according to its laws, trials in a third-party state, and trials by the international community in a court such as the ICC. Interestingly, former comfort women have sought to use each of these avenues in order to obtain legal remedies. In subsequent sections, I shall discuss each attempt and evaluate its effectiveness in exposing and rectifying the heinous evils inflicted on the victims of the comfort system.

3 LITIGATION IN JAPAN

According to some legal experts, trials within the jurisdiction of the perpetrator's state provide the 'most convenient and most fitting forum,' to address human rights violations, 'in terms of witness availability, local knowledge, and language, and the desirability of confronting and understanding the past.'[19] Up to the present, there have been two ground-breaking cases involving Korean comfort women in the Japanese courts: one case put an end to years of silence surrounding the issue and awakened public consciousness, and the other resulted in a limited form of compensation. In both cases, plaintiffs appealed to the Japanese constitutional law for redress. In addition, they argued that the comfort system as a form of slavery was a violation of norms which existed at the time the crimes were committed, as defined in numerous international accords to which Japan was a signatory. The Japanese government had signed the Hague Convention of 1907, which prohibited rape and forced prostitution during armed conflict, and had also signed the Conventions for the Suppression of the White Slave Traffic (1910) and the Suppression of the Traffic in Women and Children (1921).[20]

The first comfort women case was brought to court in Japan in 1991. On December 6, 1991, a day before the fortieth commemoration of the attack on Pearl Harbor, Kim Hak Sun filed a lawsuit in Tokyo against the Japanese government for the sufferings

18 Arakawa, Maki. 2001. "A New Forum for Comfort Women: *Fighting Japan in United States Federal Court.*" *Berkeley Women's Law Journal.* 172-200. 185.

19 Robertson, Jeffrey.1999. *Crimes Against Humanity.* New York: Penguin Press. 230.

20 Arakawa, 186.

she endured as a comfort woman during World War II. In initiating a legal action against the Japanese government, Kim Hak Sun became the first Korean comfort woman to speak out about her experience. Two anonymous plaintiffs (named Plaintiffs A and B) later joined Kim. Six other former comfort women and thirty-five ex-military and paramilitary plaintiffs also filed claims. Described as the Asia-Pacific War Korean Victims Compensation Claim Case, the class action lawsuit marked the first time that former comfort women shared their stories with the public. Most of the plaintiffs were nearing death; the shame and guilt that had haunted them throughout their lives had subsided as their family members and friends passed away, while their anger and desire for justice had deepened.

For almost seven years, the Tokyo District Court did not respond to the women's claims. When it did finally issue a statement on October 9, 1998, the court dismissed the women's claims based on the ground that international law does not provide for individual claims for compensation against a former occupying country, as well as on the familiar ground that post-war treaties between Japan and Korea have ineradicably settled all claims for compensation.[21] Tragically, several women passed away while awaiting the court's decision, including Kim Hak Sun, who died in 1997 due to chronic problems stemming from years of sexual slavery.[22]

The dismissal by the Tokyo District Court was all the more devastating due to the fact that symbolically it overturned a favourable decision issued to another group of former comfort women by the Shimonoseki Branch of the Yamaguchi District Court on April 17, 1998. The latter case was launched on December 25, 1992, when ten South Korean women, including three former comfort women and seven former members of 'Female Labor Volunteer Corps'[23] filed a suit in Shimonoseki,[24] which had served as a regular port for shipping goods and labourers to the Korean port of Pusan during Japanese colonial rule.[25] The Yamaguchi District Court subsequently ordered the Japanese government to pay 300,000 yen ($2,272) to three South Korean comfort women.

The 'Kan-Pu Trial,' as the Yamaguchi District Court case came to be known, served several important functions in setting a precedent for the comfort women litigation. To begin with, it established judicial recognition of the comfort system as a gross violation of human rights, and confirmed the participation of the Japanese government in its creation and expansion. In his ruling, Judge Chikashita Hideaki maintained that

21 Kakuchi.

22 Hicks, George. 1999. "The Comfort Women Redress Movement." *When Sorry Isn't Enough: the Controversy over Apologies and Reparations for Human Injustice*, edited by Roy L. Brooks. New York: New York University. 113-150. 119.

23 "Female Labor Volunteer Corp" is an euphemism for forced labour organizations; while former comfort women received compensation, the claims of former forced labourers were dismissed.

24 Shimonoseki is a city at the western extremity of the island of Honshu.

25 Arakawa, 182.

the comfort system violated the International Convention for the Suppression of the Traffic in Women and Children (1921) and the Convention Concerning Forced Labor (1930), two pre-World War II conventions that Japan had signed. He stated of the crimes that:

> "These ugly acts are clearly anti-humanitarian even as reflected by the civilised standards of the middle of the 20th century… Imperial Japan, not only its former military but also the government itself, participated in this scheme thus creating a grave invasion of human rights and human damage."[26]

Furthermore, the judge acknowledged the women's suffering as victims of unimaginable violence and humiliation: 'Even now, 50 years after the enactment of the Japanese Constitution, they are in never ending agony.'[27] The suit thus provided an occasion to restore the women's dignity and affirm their status as victims of grave human rights abuses.

The court awarded monetary compensations to the plaintiffs based on the concept of legislative nonfeasance. Judge Hideaki opined that the Diet should have initiated legislation to address the women's suffering after it admitted in 1993 that it had been involved in the comfort system. Since the government did not fulfil its obligation to offer assistance to the plaintiffs, it had violated the State Compensation Law.[28]

Despite such positive pronouncements, the ruling was incomplete and disappointing in many respects. Most significantly, the court rejected the women's demand for an official apology from the government. The court held that since the Constitution contains no provision requiring direct apology and compensation for victims of war and colonisation, the Japanese government has no obligation to undertake such actions. Consequently, the court asserted that: 'The propriety of such a claim is still questionable, and its necessity cannot be recognised at the present time.'[29] Since apology, rather than money, was the primary motivation behind the suit, the Yamaguchi District Court failed to meet the most essential part of the women's demands. Former comfort women have made it clear that the damage done by the Japanese government is not measurable in material terms. Hwang Keum-ju, who was deceived into becoming a comfort woman at the age of thirteen, said the following in an interview:

---

26 Kim, Chin; Kim, Stanley S. 1998. "Delayed Justice: the Case of the Japanese Imperial Military Sex Slaves." *UCLA Pacific Basic Law Journal.* Spring, 263-280. 276. Please note that I have relied extensively on this article for the English translation of the judgment.

27 *Ibid.*, 267.

28 *Ibid.*, 264.

29 *Ibid.*, 267.

> "What I want to say is that it would not be enough even if they gave me half of Japan to make up for what they did to me. There is no use telling them to give me back my youth. The only thing I want now is that Japan show true repentance and act accordingly."[30]

Although one may argue that apology without compensation is meaningless, it is evident that, in the case of comfort women, an admission of guilt by the Japanese government is more valuable than any payment offered in its place.

Not surprisingly, the Japanese government immediately appealed the decision. In 2001, the Hiroshima High Court overturned the district court's decision. The Supreme Court affirmed the High Court's ruling later in the same year.[31] Thus, the small victory the plaintiffs had won was quickly reversed. Since the 'Kan-Pu Trial,' no other claims on behalf of former comfort women have come close to obtaining a formal hearing, let alone a favourable verdict. It is an illuminating example of the limited prospects of success for victims who pursue redress within the Japanese judicial system.

4 TAKING THE CASE TO U.S. COURTS

On September 18, 2000, a group of Korean comfort women filed a class action lawsuit against the Japanese government in the United States District Court for the District of Columbia under the Alien Torts Claims Act (ATCA). They decided on this course of action after witnessing the failure of several attempts to obtain justice on Japanese soil. The ATCA gives the United States district courts original jurisdiction over 'any civil action by an alien for a tort only, committed in violation of the law of nations or a treaty of the United States,'[32] even if neither the plaintiff nor the defendant resides in the United States. Although the U.S. Supreme Court is yet to judge cases filed under the ATCA, foreign victims of human rights violations may sue their perpetrators in the United States district courts in the Second and Ninth Circuits,[33] as long as the alleged behaviour meets the above criteria.[34] Since its reinstitution in 1976,[35] the ATCA has resulted in several successful suits brought against perpetrators of human rights

30 Hwang, Keum-ju. 2000. *Comfort Women Speak: Testimony by Sex Slaves of the Japanese Military*, edited by Sangmie Choi Schellstede. Holmes & Meier Publishers, New York. 8-9.

31 Shin, 429.

32 Arakawa, 176. Please note that I have relied primarily on the article for the statements of the plaintiffs and the court.

33 The U.S. Federal Circuit Courts constitute regional and special courts of the federal judicial system in the United States. Second Circuit includes Connecticut, New York, and Vermont; the Ninth Circuit includes Alaska, Arizona, California, Guam, Hawaii, Idaho, Montana, Nevada, Northern Mariana Islands, Oregon, and Washington.

34 Arakawa, 192.

35 The ATCA was originally part of the Judiciary Act of 1789 and lay dormant as an obscure statute until 1979 in *Filartiga v. Pena-Irala*, a case in which a citizen of the Republic of Paraguay charged a government official with torture. *Ibid.*, 192.

abuses, including two cases finding Bosnian-Serb leader Radovan Karadzic guilty of genocide, torture, forced prostitution, and rape.[36] In view of such precedents, it appeared plausible that former comfort women would finally receive a fair hearing of their case in the seemingly neutral U.S. court.

In order for the court to act under jurisdiction, however, the women first had to overcome the obstacle of sovereign immunity. Under the Foreign Sovereign Immunities Act (FSIA) of 1976, sovereign states enjoy immunity from a broad range of crimes. The plaintiffs expected that the Japanese government would convince the court to drop the case by appealing to the FSIA. Moreover, the District of Columbia Circuit had already favoured a strict interpretation of the FSIA, thus setting a discouraging precedent for the women's case. In *Princz v. Germany* (1995), for example, the court refused to grant jurisdiction to a victim of Holocaust slave labour camps, due to the principle of sovereign immunity.

The comfort women plaintiffs contended that the FSIA did not apply to their case, because the 'waiver exception' in Section 1605 (a)(1) and 'commercial activity exception' in Section 1605 (a)(2) precluded the Japanese government from exercising sovereign immunity. According to Section 1605 (a)(1) of the FSIA, countries do not retain their traditional sovereign immunity from suit if they have explicitly waived it. The women asserted that by signing the Potsdam Declaration, which demanded unconditional surrender, Japan unambiguously waived its sovereign immunity. Furthermore, the women argued that under Section 1605 (a)(2), 'the planning, establishing, and operation of a network of 'comfort houses' is a commercial activity that is not subject to sovereign immunity.'[37] Finally, they asserted that sexual slavery is a *jus cogens* violation and consequently free from the constraints of the FSIA.

Thus, to secure jurisdiction, the plaintiffs presented two conflicting arguments on the structure of the comfort system. In order to establish the commercial activity exception, they portrayed the comfort system as similar to a privately managed brothel; at the same time, they maintained it was a form of sexual slavery. In the first case, the plaintiffs painted a false picture of the comfort system and thereby conceded to the argument put forth by the Japanese government that comfort women were voluntary military prostitutes who received monetary compensation for their services. Therefore, from the outset, the plaintiffs were obliged to make certain concessions to bring their case before a U.S. court.

On October 4, 2001, the District Court for the District of Columbia issued an official dismissal of the suit on the grounds of the FSIA. The court stated that although the comfort system constitutes a *jus cogens* violation, such a violation merely *implies* waiver and does not meet the norm of explicit waiver. The court further rejected the claim that the comfort stations were commercial enterprises: the comfort system was

---

36 *Kadic v. Radovan Karadzic*, 70 F.3d 232, 239 (2d Cir. 1995).

37 Arakawa, 194.

a premeditated government policy and thus differed significantly from private brothels.[38] Ironically, the court's reason for dismissing the former comfort women's case stemmed from the very fact that their suffering was the result of organised violence and slavery by the Japanese state.

In addition to the anticipated legal technicalities, it seems that diplomacy and political interests may have influenced the court's decision to dismiss the lawsuit. In May, 2001, the Bush Administration requested the Department of Justice to file an *amicus curiae* brief, in order to convince the District Court to drop the case. In the brief, the U.S. government expressed full support for Japan's motion to dismiss the suit, warning that if the District Court granted jurisdiction, it might damage relations between the United States and Japan.[39] It is likely that the U.S. government was reluctant to prosecute Japanese war crimes for political reasons. As the nation responsible for the bombing of Hiroshima and Nagasaki, the United States may feel that any judgment by a U.S. court on war crimes committed by the Japanese government will appear hypocritical and inappropriate.

The Bush Administration's opposition to the suit has historical roots in the role played by the United States as an occupying power in post-war Korea and Japan. The U.S. played a part in deliberately ignoring the comfort system after World War II, although it is clear that the American government was aware of the existence of the system. Reports such as *Amenities in the Japanese Armed Forces*, prepared in February of 1945 by the Allied Translator and Interpreter Service (ATIS), explain in detail how comfort stations were organised and managed. The *Japanese Prisoner of War Interrogation Report, No. 49* by the Psychological Warfare Team of the U.S. Army contains interviews with 20 Korean comfort women who had been attached to the 114th Infantry Division of the Japanese Imperial Army in Burma.[40] Although such reports confirmed the forced recruitment and enslavement of comfort women, the U.S. government took no action against the Japanese government and did not raise the issue during the Tokyo Military Tribunal.

Yuki Tanaka, a Japanese scholar who has carried out research on the topic of comfort women, has suggested that racism, misogyny, and complicity led the U.S. government to ignore the comfort women issue. Since the majority of victims were Asian and 'neither white women nor civilians of the Allied nations,'[41] they felt no responsibility to address the women's suffering. Even when the Dutch forces conducted an investigation of the comfort stations in Indonesia, they focused only on the Dutch

---

38 "Federal district court in District of Columbia dismisses actions by Korean 'comfort women' against Japan on grounds of sovereign immunity." 2001. *International Law Update*. Vol. 7. 156-157.

39 Park, Byoungwook. 2002. "Comfort Women during World War II: Are U.S. Courts a Final Resort for Justice?" *American University International Law Review*. 403-458. 405-6.

40 Tanaka, Yuki. 2002. *Japan's Comfort Women: Sexual Slavery and Prostitution during World War II and the US Occupation*. New York: Routledge. 84.

41 Tanaka, 87.

victims and completely neglected the Indonesian comfort women. Tanaka has argued further that misogyny, inherent in armed forces across cultures, led many American soldiers to believe that providing 'amenities' to soldiers, even enemy soldiers, did not constitute a criminal act.[42] Certain American soldiers appear to have been recipients of services rendered by comfort women, albeit unknowingly, since they themselves frequented comfort stations as members of the occupation troops in Japan. Korean comfort women who had been shipped to Okinawa during the latter half of the war were forced to service the American troops after the war officially ended and before the Japanese government set up a new network of professional prostitutes.[43]

Given the history of the U.S. involvement in the comfort system, as well as the discouraging dismissal of the former comfort women's claims, it is unlikely that a U.S. court will provide a welcoming forum for redress. Even the option of civil proceedings under the ATCA – directing a claim against individual perpetrators rather than the state – is unsatisfactory, because such an action would permit the Japanese government to avoid official acknowledgement of responsibility. As in the Yamaguchi case, any monetary compensation the victims may receive will be meaningless without an open assumption of guilt. Therefore, in these circumstances, civil actions are 'second best.'[44]

5 WOMEN'S INTERNATIONAL WAR CRIMES TRIBUNAL ON JAPAN'S MILITARY SEXUAL SLAVERY

As noted before, Korean comfort women unsuccessfully sought redress in the judicial sphere for almost a decade. Domestic legal constraints and diplomatic concerns prevented the victims from fully articulating their rights. Although international law provided the most forceful and suitable vocabulary to validate the women's claims, they were not successful on the international level.

To put an end to the passivity of the international community and deliver justice that is long overdue, members of VAWW-NET Japan (Violence Against Women in War Network, Japan) proposed the creation of an international tribunal during the Asian Women's Solidarity Conference in April 1998. Feminist grassroots organisers from the victimised countries, including North and South Korea, China, the Philippines, Indonesia, Taiwan, Malaysia, East Timor, and the Netherlands, quickly

42 *Ibid.*, 86.

43 *Ibid.*, 86-87. It is not clear when the comfort stations officially closed. It is also unclear what became of thousands of Korean comfort women in Okinawa after the war. After WW II, the Japanese government set up "entertainment centers" for the occupation troops, which consisted mainly of professional Japanese prostitutes.

44 Robertson, 237.

embraced the proposal and began recruiting legal experts, historians, politicians, and donors. They also sought victims and perpetrators who might be willing to testify at the tribunal. After two years of preparation, the Women's International War Crimes Tribunal on Japan's Military Slavery ('Women's Tribunal') convened on December 8, 2000 in Tokyo and lasted for four days.

Each participating country formed a prosecution team consisting of lawyers, historians, and researchers and drafted its own country indictment. Two chief prosecutors, Patricia Viseur-Sellers and Ustina Dolgopol, wrote the common indictment. Although the Japanese government was asked to participate in the tribunal, it did not respond to the invitation. The tribunal consequently appointed Japanese law firms Isomi, Suzuki, Koga and Partners, and Imamura Tsuguo as *amicus curiae* to present Japan's arguments in support of its denial of responsibility.[45] More than sixty survivors testified through written, oral, and video testimonies, and three former members of the Japanese military in China shared their experiences as perpetrators. Each day, more than 1,000 people attended the hearings.

At its inception, the Women's Tribunal followed the tradition of Bertrand Russell's Vietnam War Crimes Tribunal and the Permanent People's Tribunal in Italy.[46] The architects of these tribunals were 'private citizens of high moral authority' who overcame national and cultural barriers in pursuit of justice and human dignity.[47] These citizens created the tribunals outside of both domestic and international legal systems in order to address crimes that courts had overlooked. The Women's Tribunal likewise stressed its 'moral authority' to '[bring] out truths and to establish the legal responsibility of states and individuals involved in...the sexual slavery of 'comfort women...'' and to demand 'wide acceptance and enforcement by the international community and national governments...'.[48] At the same time, it went beyond what the previous tribunals had accomplished. The organisers of the Women's Tribunals came from Japan and its former colonies with the sole aim of rectifying a grave injustice. Such a task required a transcendence of differences in the personal and historical experiences of the women involved. Women came together solely as women,

45 Chinkin, Christine. "Toward the Tokyo Tribunal 2000." *Women's Initiatives for Gender Justice.* Retrieved on October 24, 2004 from www.iccwomen.org/tokyo/ chinkin.htm. 4.

46 In 1967, the first international People's Tribunal, organized by Bertrand Russell and other European intellectuals, including Jean-Paul Sartre and Simone de Beauvoir, convened in Stockholm and Roskilde, Denmark, to investigate cases of American and South Vietnamese war crimes in Vietnam. Historically linked to Russell's war crimes tribunal, the Permanent Peoples' Tribunal was formed in 1979, based on the "law for the rights of peoples" whose norms are established not by states, but by "the requirements and exigencies of peoples." (Lelio Basso International Foundation for the Rights and Liberation of Peoples. *Permanent People's Tribunal.* Retrieved on January 7, 2006 from http://www.grisnet.it/filb/.)

47 Chinkin, 4.

48 Women's International War Crimes Tribunal on Japan's Military Sexual Slavery. 2001. *Charter of The Women's International War Crimes Tribunal on Japan's Military Sexual Slavery.* Retrieved on October 24, 2004 from http://www1.jca.apc.org/vaww-net-japan/english/. 2.

not as women of a particular nationality, nor as women of formerly colonising or colonised states. Through this transnational movement, they were able to renounce the hatred and mistrust they had felt for one another. A history of conflict and opposition was put aside, as women from Japan and Korea held hands and shed tears, and as the two Koreas came together to draft a joint indictment.

The primary purpose of the tribunal was to empower the victims through listening to their testimonies. Its goal was to 'enable and encourage surviving victims to speak out, to tell the truth of their lives in front of judges and witnesses *who believed them* (emphasis added).'[49] The tribunal became a willing listener that did not contest the truthfulness of the evidence. The main task of the tribunal was to provide a sympathetic environment for sharing the victims' stories. Dignity, which is not always treated as an established legal category, served as the key principle throughout the litigation. When one distraught survivor struggled to continue her testimony, Chief Justice Gabrielle Kirk MacDonald turned to her and said:

> "If you'd like some water, if you'd like to be excused, if you'd like to take a moment, please, we're all here to listen to you."[50]

To validate the women's experiences and their right to speak, the tribunal renounced traditional modes of listening employed in courtrooms (characterised by scrutiny, questioning, and doubt) and instead accepted the testimonies at face value. These protective mechanisms distinguished the Women's Tribunal from official courts that are required to adhere to a strict methodology. The Women's Tribunal differed significantly not only from the courts in which the former comfort women had testified, but also from the ICTY, where victims of rape had to endure aggressive and insensitive questioning from the prosecutors and defence attorneys alike.[51]

The tribunal also defied the limitations of international law described previously. The results of the tribunal's radical shift in methodology were evident in its judgment. The tribunal found Emperor Hirohito 'guilty' of individual and superior responsibility for crimes against humanity in the form of sexual slavery and rape, and forcefully

---

49 Dudden, Alex. 2001. "'We Came to Tell the Truth': Reflections on the Tokyo Women's Tribunal." *Critical Asian Studies*. 33:4, 591-602. 592.

50 Dudden, 593.

51 Although the victims' identities were protected during the ICTY trials, the integrity of their experiences was constantly put to test. See transcripts of the trials, notably sessions held in March, 2000. http://www.un.org/icty/transe23.

rejected the claim that he was a mere figurehead who did not participate in decision-making.[52] The judges stated that:

> "The scale of the 'comfort system' was so enormous, the conditions so inhumane, and the operations of the stations so consistent, that no other conclusion can be reached but that the highest level political and military officials must have known of the criminal nature of the system".[53]

The Emperor, as the supreme commander of the Japanese Imperial Army and Navy, 'exercised the ultimate decision-making authority,'[54] and consequently must have been aware of the existence of the comfort system. Furthermore, the tribunal established state responsibility, contending that:

> "The evidence has established that private individuals recruiting 'comfort' women were selected, monitored, assisted, and...directly accompanied by the Japanese military... As such, the civilian recruiters were...clearly agents of the Japanese military."[55]

The tribunal also reprimanded the Japanese government for its failure to make a valid apology to the victims, stating that the official statements of regret had been 'deficient in content, process and the language of apology chosen.'[56]

By using the language of international law to its full potential, the tribunal was able to expose the evils of the comfort system and demand accountability in a resolute manner. However, there were significant shortfalls in attempting to draw attention to the plight of former comfort women by setting up such a tribunal. To begin with, the tribunal had no effective means of enforcement because it had no official standing. The best it could do was to recommend that the United Nations adopt its decisions and urge the international community to recognise its self-proclaimed legitimacy. Furthermore, since the Japanese government refused to acknowledge the tribunal, it did not accept any of the tribunal's judgments. To the cynics, the Women's Tribunal thus remains nothing more than a well-constructed and highly sophisticated mock court. Finally, in focusing on validating the victims and their stories, the tribunal wilfully ignored other parts of history that are equally significant: the North-South Korean prosecution team, for instance, devoted much of its presentation to the illegal colonisation of Korea by Japan, while completely neglecting the complicity of Korean

52 Women's International War Crimes Tribunal on Japan's Military Sexual Slavery. 2000. *Transcript of Oral Judgement.* Retrieved on October 24, 2004 from http://www1.jca.apc.org/vaww-net-japan/english/. 13.

53 *Ibid.*, 14.

54 *Ibid.*, 16.

55 *Ibid.*, 20.

56 *Ibid.*, 21.

civilians in recruiting comfort women.[57] Thus, in order to counteract Japan's denial of its responsibility for creating and promoting the comfort system, the tribunal at times adopted a somewhat one-sided viewpoint.

The Women's Tribunal indeed had its limitations, but it was by no means inconsequential. The tribunal granted victims the freedom to tell their stories without constraint and enabled them to receive recognition for their suffering. It also offered them an opportunity to seek healing and achieve closure, and it promoted moral clarity in relation to the events of the time. In concluding her judgment, Justice MacDonald wrote:

> "While the names inscribed in history's page are often those of the men that commit the crimes, rather than the women that suffer them, this Judgment bears the name of the survivors that took the stage to tell their stories, and thereby, for four days at least, put wrong on the scaffold and truth on the throne."[58]

The tribunal demonstrated how powerful international law can be, when applied without certain political or technical restrictions that often curtail its force. The tribunal's sensitivity toward the victims' voices and desires suggested the need to increase the victim's space in a traditional court. In this sense, the Women's Tribunal bears a greater significance that goes beyond the parameters of the comfort women issue and extends to the application of international law itself.

6 TO LITIGATE OR NOT TO LITIGATE: MERITS OF LEGAL REDRESS FOR KOREAN COMFORT WOMEN

In the first section, we discussed the challenges involved in prosecuting cases of sexual violence, particularly in relation to the crimes committed against comfort women. Aside from procedural difficulties and the lack of legal precedents, however, one may argue that seeking redress in courtrooms may be undesirable in the case of former comfort women. Nonetheless, as I explain below, the courtroom remains a unique forum within which to seek redress for the women's grievances.

Those who oppose seeking legal redress argue that victims of the comfort system do not possess a substantial legal arsenal with which to fight matters in courts, despite the fact that the victims are the primary witnesses to the crimes and can testify against the perpetrators. Such opponents agree with critics of international law, who maintain that international law lacks both the legitimacy and the power of enforcement to bring

---

57 Dudden, 598.

58 *Transcript of Oral Judgement*, 26.

justice to victims of gross human rights violations. Professor Jovan Bavic of the University of Belgrade wrote in his acerbic criticism of international law that:

> "It appears to me that international law is not, and cannot be, law in the fundamental sense of the word. International law lacks the institutional structure...and instead appeals to the moral...sentiments of those...powerful enough to take their moral feelings at face value and transform their moral judgments into legal ones."[59]

To Bavic, the 'moral authority' of the Women's Tribunal, grounded largely in the principles of international law, may appear as no more than pompous and self-righteous. As we have seen in the dismissal of the class action lawsuit in the U.S. district court, international law often fails to overcome the barrier of national sovereignty. Even the ICC exercises jurisdiction only over those nations that have ratified the Rome Statute. Sovereignty, as 'a nearly absolute value,'[60] dictates the limits of legal authority and diminishes the scope of effective litigation.

In addition, scholars raise serious questions regarding the appropriateness of the courtroom as a forum for victims of grave human rights abuses. In particular, they maintain that the litigation process hinders reconciliation between victims and perpetrators, who must undergo 'a prolonged dredging of the past.'[61] As new allegations and revelations arise, resentments may increase and chances of reconciliation may dwindle. Moreover, focusing on punishment and individual perpetrators may 'represent an incomplete and superficial step toward reconciliation,'[62] unless a fundamental change in values and conduct takes place outside of the courtroom by the society as a whole.

Recently, a political as opposed to a judicial solution has been proposed in order to resolve the comfort women issue. There is an overwhelming sentiment both in and outside the legal field that redress for former comfort women is first and foremost a political issue, to be resolved through political means. This sentiment may explain the hesitancy of courts to address the issue. In its ruling, the Yamaguchi District Court stated:

> "[T]he plaintiff comfort women seek an official apology. As to the form of the apology, the matter should be decided by the judgement and discretion of the political department, and the judicial court system cannot participate in this."[63]

---

59 Babic, Jovan. 2001. "War Crimes: Moral, Legal, or Simply Political?" *War Crimes and Collective Wrongdoing: A Reader*, edited by Aleksandar Jokic. Oxford: Blackwell Publishers Ltd. 62-63.

60 Wilkins, Burleigh T. 2001."Whose Trials? Whose Reconciliation?" *War Crimes and Collective Wrongdoing: A Reader*, edited by Aleksandar Jokic. Oxford: Blackwell Publishers Ltd. 88.

61 *Ibid.*, 94.

62 *Ibid.*, 93.

63 Kim, 267.

Similarly, the District Court of the District of Columbia declared:

> "There is no question that this court is not the appropriate forum in which plaintiffs may seek to reopen those discussions nearly half a century later...[T]he current claims of the 'comfort women' [should] be addressed directly between governments..."[64]

Yet, given the fact that the comfort system was a form of sexual slavery and therefore entails a legal responsibility to punish those who committed the crime, it is difficult to explain why the courts have relinquished their right (and duty) to deal with the issue. One possibility is that the courts, facing the formidable obstacle of national sovereignty, have come to terms with the limits of their own capabilities. One may also question the wisdom of seeking legal resolution through the Japanese courts since the Japanese Diet, rather than the judiciary, 'remains in control for answering and correcting the historical record of [Japan's] past.'[65] However, the prospects for redress in the political sphere are just as doubtful, if not more so. The Japanese Diet, which oversees all political processes in Japan, not only has many members who are former officers of the Imperial Army, but also has members who have openly expressed prejudice against Korean residents in Japan.[66] Furthermore, the economic and political inequality between the governments of Korea and Japan may force the Korean government to accept a limited form of compensation in return for significant financial concessions.[67] Consequently, a political solution on its own is unlikely to be effective.

Another alternative to the legal approach is the formation of a Truth and Reconciliation Commission (TRC). The Women's Tribunal, in its ruling, recommended a TRC as a means to achieve 'acknowledgement, catharsis, and vindication, all without the harsh strictures of a prosecuting courtroom.'[68] It is unclear, however, whether a TRC is a suitable mechanism to handle human rights violations in general or the comfort system in particular. In South Africa, for instance, opponents of the TRC criticised it as an attempt to 'dress up political expediency as justice,'[69] where torturers and assassins were allowed to walk free without having to feel remorse for their actions. One anti-apartheid activist who lost his family in a bombing asked: "Are we going to have a situation where people can qualify for indemnity just by saying, as if they were reeling off a grocery list, 'I killed this one and poisoned that one and

64 "Federal district court in District of Columbia dismisses..." 157.
65 Shin, 435.
66 *Ibid.*, 436.
67 Thus far, the Korean government has encouraged the victims to refuse monetary compensation from the Asian Women's Fund. However, if the Japanese government offers an appealing aid package or promises a large-scale economic cooperation program, it is likely that the Korean government will accept such an offer in return for a conciliatory resolution in relation to the comfort women issue.
68 Shin, 445.
69 Robertson, 255.

beat the shit out of the third one.'?"[70] The TRC process may have the effect of circumventing an *erga omnes* obligation to prosecute and punish the perpetrators of crimes against humanity. While one may contend that obtaining the truth is more important than punishing the perpetrators, former comfort women have repeatedly stated that no closure is possible without punishment, without an official acknowledgment of the crime as such. Song Shin Do, who is the only former Korean comfort women residing in Japan to have filed a suit against the Japanese government, states:

> "I want to do the right thing. I must have the Japanese government punished for its wrongdoing."[71]

Victims of the comfort system rarely mention the need for reconciliation, speaking instead of the enduring anger and resentment that drives their battle for reparations. Yi Bok-nyo, who was forcibly drafted by military police, states:

> "Even today, thinking of such tortures and such inhumane treatment, my rage has not subsided... When I recall the painful past, I still feel uncontrollable bursts of anger, resentment, and hatred toward them."[72]

Such anger, which remains raw and powerful even after fifty years, suggests that justice in the form of proper punishment, rather than reconciliation, is the ultimate aim of the victims' demands. As the main goal of a TRC is to facilitate the rebuilding of a society by healing internal political divisions, the merits of utilising such a commission to deal with the issue of comfort women are uncertain.

Ultimately, determining the most appropriate forum for redress comes down to understanding what the victims seek to attain through the process. Only by meeting the victims' demands will a particular movement for redress have proven itself to be successful. Of course, I do not mean to suggest that *any* demand made by the victims must be fulfilled. I am speaking of those that have been specifically articulated through previous legal and political movements for reparations. In the case of former comfort women, the alternatives to legal redress are unlikely to meet the women's demands, considering the women's ardent desire to see the perpetrators receive punishment for their crimes. The personal accounts of former comfort women reveal that the women desire an official apology from the Japanese government, punishment for the perpetrators, as well as an affirmation that such an atrocity will not happen again. Despite the shortfalls of the current legal system, the courtroom remains a viable

70 *Ibid.*, 255.

71 "Interview with Miss Song Shin Do." 1999. *The People's Korea*. Retrieved on November 1, 2005, from http://210.145.168.243/pk/116th_issue/99101002.htm.

72 *Ibid.*, 92-93.

forum to address the comfort women issue, because it is the only setting in which all these demands may be met.

The courtroom is the place where judgment and punishment coincide. For victims of human rights violations '[t]he judgment is important.'[73] Especially for former comfort women who have suffered isolation and stigmatization throughout their lives, it is imperative to 'right the wrong by affirming that behavior which violates agreed standards of international conduct is wrong and warrants response and condemnation…'.[74] Such an affirmation may produce enough pressure from the international community and public opinion to induce an official apology from the Japanese government. An expression of remorse may also constitute part of the punishment itself.

The judgments of courts are aimed at deterrence and prevention of further crime. The legal system operates under the principle of precedent. Setting a precedent creates a lasting reminder of a crime, which may prevent such evil from recurring in the future. Former comfort women have continually expressed concern that the horrors of their experience may be repeated in the future. 'I worry now,' says Kim Yoon-shim, who was kidnapped at the age of thirteen into sexual slavery, 'what if a war breaks out in the future, how do we know that they will not repeat such atrocities again?'[75] When the ICTY successfully prosecuted rape as a war crime and a crime against humanity, it established a precedent in favour of punishing perpetrators guilty of rape during wartime. Unless the comfort women case is brought to court and prosecuted successfully, sexual slavery may persist in future conflicts and continue the legacy of impunity.

Lastly, legal procedures themselves, as constraining and disagreeable as they may sometimes be, play an important role in establishing the truth of an event. One scholar noted that 'rape generally leaves its stain on the historical record only if it comes to trial.'[76] The investigation of the issues and the testimony of witnesses, inherent in the legal process, helps to establish an accurate record of what took place. Trials disclose and publicise facts that may otherwise remain buried. They compel governments to release relevant documents and encourage scholars and journalists to further probe the issue. Testimonies also provide victims with a chance to speak of their experiences and finally put an end to years of solitary suffering. Susan J. Brison, a philosopher and a victim of sexual assault, once described her frustration when her relatives did not

---

73 Bergofeen, Debra. 2003. "Toward a Politics of the Vulnerable Body." *Hypatia – a Journal of Feminist Philosophy*. 18(1).

74 Stromseth, Jane E. 2003. "Introduction: Goals and Challenges in the Pursuit of Accountability." *Accountability for Atrocities: National and International Responses*, edited by Jane E. Stromseth. New York: Transnational Publishers. 7.

75 *Comfort Women Speak*, 47.

76 Askin, Kelly D. 1997. *War Crimes Against Women: Prosecution in International War Crimes Tribunals*. Cambridge: Martinus Nijhoff Publishers. 378.

call or write to her after the attack. The relatives thought it would be best for her to forget about the experience and move on. Brison, angry and deeply hurt, railed at her parents, saying: 'Didn't they realize that I thought about the attack every minute of every day and that their inability to respond made me feel as though I had, in fact, died and no one had bothered to come to the funeral?'[77] Former comfort women have been effectively dead for the past fifty years. No one mourned or even knew of their deaths. To be given the opportunity to speak on the witness stand and to have their voices recorded as part of history, will be an empowering experience that will rejuvenate the women's lives.

As for reconciliation, its place remains largely ambivalent in the legal sphere, although a number of courts, such as the South African Constitutional Court, have demonstrated a keen awareness of its significance in the judicial process. Some argue that the responsibility of courts does not lie in achieving an amicable resolution between parties. In the case of rape, for instance, seeking reconciliation in court may be 'totally inappropriate' since: 'What rape demands is *prevention*...and that is the only thing that is realistic to expect the criminal law to do to any significant extent.'[78] Since the primary duty of the court is to deliver judgment and punishment, it is not surprising that reconciliation stands at the periphery of its duties. However, the fact that legal redress holds little hope for reconciliation does not mean that the courtroom is an unsuitable place to seek reparations for Korean comfort women. As we have seen from the women's narratives, the desire for reconciliation is weak, although not altogether absent.

Given the nature of the victims' demands and the shortcomings of other forums, we must not discount the possibility of redress within the legal sphere. Admittedly, up to this point the courts have not shown themselves to be a favourable place for former comfort women to seek redress. However, taken at face value, the legal system is capable of punishing the wrongdoers, offering healing and closure through listening, and establishing historical veracity to prevent further crimes. Instead of regarding past failures as illustrations of insurmountable limitations within the system, we must find ways of continuing to support the victims' struggle within the domain of international law.

---

77 Brison, Susan J. 1998. "Surviving Sexual Violence: A Philosophical Perspective." *Violence Against Women: Philosophical Perspectives*, edited by Stanley G. French, Wanda Teays, Laura M. Purdy. Ithaca: Cornell University Press. 20.

78 Ellis, Anthony. 2001. "What Should We Do with War Criminals?" *War Crimes and Collective Wrongdoing: A Reader*, edited by Aleksandar Jokic. Oxford: Blackwell Publishers Ltd. 107.

7 CONCLUSION

In public testimony shortly before her death, Kim Hak Sun said:

> "Why couldn't I lead a normal life like everyone else? When I look at other elderly women, I say to myself, 'They are not like me' and feel ashamed. A part of me wants to murder the man who took my virginity. But there is nothing that can relieve this pain I feel. I want to stop digging into my memory. The [Japanese and Korean] governments wouldn't give a damn about the suffering of a worthless woman like me once I am dead. I will be forgotten."[79]

Her words are those of a defeated victim: they betray shame, misery, hatred, loss of trust, and a fear of being forgotten. Toward the end of her life, Kim resigned herself to the idea that no redress, whether political or legal, is possible. While waiting in vain for a response from the Tokyo District Court, Kim dug deeper and deeper into her memory and relived the horrors as she had done since the day the first soldier violated her at the age of seventeen.[80]

Kim and other Korean comfort women failed to attain justice. Their quest for legal redress was also a quest for restoration of their faith in the world, in the belief that universal norms and values exist to uphold and affirm our shared humanity. In the courtroom, the women discovered that the world is governed not only by values but also by interests, and that the victim's space in the legal sphere is often small and ill-defined. Former comfort women, like so many victims of war crimes before them, appeared 'as the truly incorrigible, irreconcilable ones, as the antihistorical reactionaries in the exact sense of the word…',[81] whose relevance to today's society seemed uncertain.

Nonetheless, the women's endeavours have had an extraordinary impact in reawakening and preserving the historical memory of the comfort system. Kim Hak Sun, eight years after her death, is not forgotten. She is an inspiration to activists, survivors, and scholars, and remains at the forefront of the ongoing struggle for justice. The lawsuits accelerated a massive effort to archive the narratives of former comfort women. The world now wants to listen, wants to know. From being part of a 'community of those without community,' an 'inoperative…unavowable community,'[82] the victims now belong to an international community that recognises their presence in history.

---

79 Kim, Hak Sun. *Testimony of the Survivors*. The Korean Council for the Women Drafted for Military Slavery by Japan. Article retrieved on November 10, 2005, from http://www.womenandwar.net/. My translation.

80 *Ibid.*

81 Amery, Jean. 1980. *At the Mind's Limits: Contemplations by a Survivor on Auschwitz and Its Realities*, translated by Sidney. Rosenfeld and Stella P. Rosenfeld. Bloomington: Indiana University Press. 80.

82 Derrida, Jacques. 1997. *Politics of Friendship*, trans. George Collins. New York: Verso Press. 42.

If remembrance is the starting point for redress, efforts to achieve legal reparation for former comfort women are likely to continue into the future, with greater vigour and ingenuity. One possible strategy for successful legal action is to combine international pressure with international law. Scholars have suggested that the application of *jus cogens* norms will be more successful if the international community explicitly expresses its support for the lawsuits and condemns Japan for its unwillingness to accept responsibility.[83] The Japanese government is more likely to respond favourably to the suits once they have won the endorsement and recognition of the United Nations.

Sexual slavery during war is not an issue which may be ignored as a problem that occurred in the past. In various conflicts around the globe, in nations such as Sierra Leone and Democratic Republic of Congo, young girls and women are forced into sexual slavery and 'marriages.' Fortunately, increasing awareness on the part of the international community in relation to wartime sexual violence, as well as developments in international law, have led to extensive documentation of such crimes by human rights organisations as well as the United Nations.

The creation of the International Criminal Court (ICC) is an example of continuing progress in the realm of international law. Although it cannot prosecute crimes committed prior to its inception, its establishment has significant implications in relation to the crimes committed in current armed conflicts, as well as those that may arise in the future. The ICC has jurisdiction over the crimes of genocide, war crimes, and crimes against humanity, including rape and sexual slavery. Even though it is complementary to national criminal jurisdictions, it may step in for national courts when they are unwilling or unable to prosecute the perpetrators.[84] With the ICC in place, it is unlikely that egregious crimes of sexual violence taking place in current conflicts will go unpunished. Of course, victims of recent sexual violence may face similar difficulties in the ICC as those faced by former comfort women. For instance, just as the Japanese government maintained that comfort women were professional prostitutes, perpetrators of forced marriages may argue that the marriages are legitimate and took place with the women's consent. It may be equally difficult to establish command and state responsibility in the case of nations that remain disorganised at governmental level. Most significantly, the barrier of national sovereignty may remain insurmountable, especially if the perpetrators belong to states that have not ratified the Rome Statute. Nonetheless, the very existence of an institution devoted to eradicating impunity and upholding justice promises that the

83 Boling, David. 1995. *Mass Rape, Enforced Prostitution, and the Japanese Imperial Army: Japan Eschews International Legal Responsibility?*. Baltimore: University of Maryland School of Law. 55.

84 Dormann, Knut. 2002. *Elements of War Crimes Under the Rome Statute of the International Criminal Court*. Cambridge: Cambridge University Press. 2.

age of silence has come to an end, and that a new era of international cooperation and global concern on the issue of sexual violence has begun.

THE HERERO DEMAND FOR REPARATIONS FROM GERMANY: THE HUNDRED YEAR OLD LEGACY OF A COLONIAL WAR IN THE POLITICS OF MODERN NAMIBIA

SIDNEY L. HARRING

Reparations claims have many forms, depending on the historical and political context in which they arose. Southern African claims often turn on specific land dispossessions. The Herero, a Namibian tribe of about 120,000 have persisted in a reparations claim against Germany that dates back at least to 1946, when Paramount Chief Frederick Maharero tried to place claims against Germany before the newly formed United Nations.[1] The legal basis of this action, as well as its timing, was tied directly to the widespread genocides committed by Germany against various peoples during World War Two.[2] German genocide against their people in the Herero War of 1904-1905 opened the twentieth century's wave of genocides. The idea that Germany could occupy land, in Africa or Europe, forcibly relocate vast populations in doing so, justify these actions on racial grounds, and kill whole populations whether they resisted or not, was not simply the result of Nazi ideology.[3] This kind of thinking had a precursor in German South West Africa, now Namibia, just after the turn of the century.[4] If the

1 "Herero Legal Claims Against Germany in SW Africa," at www.marcusgarveylibrary.org.uk/hererofarmlands.htm, last visited December 28, 2005.

2 This is a strategy by the Herero to distinguish their reparations claims from those of other African peoples.

3 The reasons for the genocides committed by Germany in World War Two have produced a vast literature, and cannot be said to be a settled issue. Isabel V. Hull, *Absolute Destruction: Military Culture and the Practices of War in Imperial Germany* (Ithaca: Cornell University Press, 2005) demonstrates that the German military tactics in Namibia were rooted in tactics used in Europe in both the Franco-Prussian War and World War One. Deborah Dwork and Robert Jan Van Pelt, *Auschwitz* (New York: Norton, 1996) argues that at least some of the motivation for the Holocaust in eastern Europe was to clear the vast steppes of Jewish farmers and villagers in order to make way for German farmers and their families, seen as critical for building the Germanic race.

4 Some of the thinking behind Germany's experiments with eugenics was rooted in South West Africa. See Henry Friedlander, *The Origins of Nazi Genocide: From Euthanasia to the Final Solution* (Chapel Hill: University of North Carolina Press, 1995), at 11.

Herero were not at present rigorously pursuing reparations claims against Germany, the Herero War would be relegated to the status of an obscure historical footnote, with 60,000 nameless dead. Instead, the legacy of this war follows modern Germany with a clear message: genocide is never forgotten. The purpose of reparations is symbolic as well as financial. It matters both that Germany acknowledges these past wrongs, as well as compensates its victims.

1 GERMAN COLONISATION OF NAMIBIA AND THE HERERO WAR

The conquest of Africa, Asia, and Latin America by European nations gives rise to a wide range of demands for reparations. These conquests, spanning more than four hundred years, took a variety of forms, but all were bloody in one form or another. Millions of indigenous people died, were enslaved, or forcibly removed from their lands. Whole European societies were planted in different parts of the world, including the modern nations of Canada, the United States, Australia, and New Zealand. Other European colonies were returned to the political control of indigenous populations, including Namibia, South Africa, Angola, and Zimbabwe.

Germany came late to the business of colonisation, only arriving in Africa in the 1880s. This late start put Germany, a nation with grand ambition, 'behind' other European countries, a factor that may have increased the violence of colonial warfare in German South West Africa. Bolstered by its victory in the Franco-Prussian War, domestic prosperity, and an Emperor with great visions of Germany's place in the world, Germany turned a small trading treaty negotiated by a German businessman at Luderitz, into a full scale agricultural and mining colony within twenty years.[5] German cities were built, railroad lines connected them with the coast, Lutheran churches sprang up over much of the country and, by 1890, German farmers had been granted land for large scale farming and cattle raising operations.[6] Indeed, modern Namibia still proudly reflects this German colonial heritage.

German South West Africa was, at the time of colonisation, inhabited by a number of distinct peoples. To the north, a number of Ovambo nations lived on both sides of the still un-demarcated Angolan border. In the centre of the country, on a high plain, lived Herero, Nama, Damara, and Baster peoples. San moved freely across most of these lands.[7] All of these peoples came into conflict with the Germans, but it was

---

5 Helmut Bley, *South West Africa Under German Rule, 1894-1915*, (Evanston, Ill, Northwestern University Press, 1981).

6 *Ibid.*

7 There is not complete agreement on the exact occupation of lands in late nineteenth century Namibia, but it approximates the current distribution of Native peoples, with the exception of some removed San populations. A map of the current distribution of peoples of Namibia can be found in John

in the heart of the Herero country that the Germans settled, the most temperate lands and therefore the most suited to European settlement.

Herero lands were taken through a wide variety of devices, essentially the full gamut of colonial land expropriation practices. There were some treaties negotiated with Herero chiefs, ceding some of their lands. Other lands were 'purchased' directly from individual Herero chiefs, often under various ruses, or under the influence of alcohol. Other lands were, apparently, simply occupied by Germans under various colonial government pretensions. Within only a few years, by the late 1890s, the Herero people were divided, fragmented, land poor, and impoverished. Cattle herds, direct indicators of the wealth of the Herero, were greatly reduced, and rinderpest, a new disease, further decimated these herds. German colonial authorities had routinely interfered in internal Herero politics, executing Herero kings who did not defer to German authority and promoting chiefs who would.[8]

None of these actions are unfamiliar to students of imperialism and colonialism. These are the tactics that European nations used to gain control of the lands of indigenous peoples. Similarly, the exact cause of the Herero uprising is irrelevant: indigenous peoples around the world rose up against their colonial oppressors – and so did the Herero. Samuel Maharero, a chief who owed allegiance to the Germans, was apparently pushed to his limit by continuing German demands for Herero lands. He ordered a surprise attack on the Germans, specifically ordering his warriors not to kill women, children, or clergymen. Several hundred German farmers were killed in the initial attacks aimed at remote and unprotected farms.[9]

German colonial authorities believed that the several hundred well trained German troops stationed in the country would be able to put down the uprising swiftly, but fast moving Herero horsemen led the German army on a series of futile chases, stalemating the war and inflicting serious casualties on German troops. This led the German Imperial Government to take over direct control of the war from the colonial authorities, sending in General Luther von Trotha with an army of ten thousand to win the war. Von Trotha escalated the war in every area and, after a series of battles, engaged the Herero at Waterburg, in north central Namibia. In the process, he brought the Nama in the south into the war, dividing his troops and prolonging the war.

A series of battles were fought near Waterburg and, in the end, the Herero were driven into the Kalahari Desert, to the East. Von Trotha issued the following now infamous proclamation:

Mendelsohn, Alice Jarvice, Carole Roberts and Tony Robertson, *Atlas of Namibia*, (Cape Town, David Phillip, 2003), 164, 165. Particularly, Nama and Herero lands were contested by active warfare.

8 Jan-Bart Gewald, *Herero Heroes* (Athens: Ohio University Press, 1999).

9 Jan-Bart Gewald, *Herero Heroes* (Athens: Ohio University Press, 1999); Horst Drechsler, *Let Us Die Fighting: The Struggle of the Herero and Nama Against German Imperialism (1885-1915)*, (London: Zed Press, 1980); Jon Bridgeman, *The Revolt of the Hereros* (Berkeley: University of California Press, 1981).

> "I the great General of the German troops send this letter to the Herero people. The Herero are no longer German subjects....The Herero people must however leave the land. If the populace does not do this I will force them with the Groot Rohn (cannon). Within the German borders every Herero, with or without a gun, with or without cattle, will be shot. I will no longer accept women and children, I will drive them back to their people, or I will let them be shot at. These are my words to the Herero."[10]

The proclamation was read in front of prisoners who were to be hanged. Then, copies of the proclamation already printed in the Herero language, were distributed. Herero men, women, and children were driven out into the Kalahari Desert. German troops blocked routes back, poisoned waterholes, and fought the final resisters. Thousands of Herero died in captivity, in large camps in Windhoek, Swakopmund, and Shark Island, near Luderitz. By mid 1905 the war was over.

A German law of 1907 deprived all Herero of the right to own land or cattle. The immediate result of the war was that the Herero were forcibly removed from all their lands in Namibia, and all Herero land and cattle were put in the hands of German farmers.[11]

The exact number of Herero who were killed in the war or who died of thirst or starvation after being driven into the desert, cannot be known. The census of 1911 counted 15,130 Herero in the country, down from about 80,000 before the war.[12] A few thousand Herero made their way across the desert to Bechuanaland, now Botswana, a British Protectorate. Others made their way to Angola, or to the remote northwest corner of Namibia, beyond the reach of the German army. Assuming that 20,000 survived, it would mean that 75% of the Herero people died in the war. There were other colonial wars that were similarly devastating to native populations, but the war against the Herero is distinguished by the fact that the action announced in the proclamation of von Trotha is held, by most authorities, to have signalled the intent to destroy the entire Herero population, making the war an act of genocide.[13] The loss

---

10 Quoted in Jan-Bart Gewald, *Herero Heroes*, (1999) 172-173. Gewald has dismissed the view that Von Trotha's proclamation has been interpreted "out of context," concluding instead that the proclamation meant what it threatened, a policy of genocide. The fact that it was printed in the Herero language and distributed to women and children about to be driven out into the desert demonstrates that there was a clear intention underlying the proclamation.

11 Jan-Bart Gewald, *Ibid.*

12 John Bridgeman, *Revolt of the Hereros* (1981), 164.

13 The Convention on the Prevention and Punishment of the Crime of Genocide, adopted by the United Nations on 9 December 1948 defines genocide as "any of the following acts committed with intent to destroy, in whole or it part, a national, ethnical, racial or religious group, as such:
(a) killing members of the group;
(b) causing serious bodily or mental harm to members of the group;
(c) deliberately inflicting on the group conditions of life calculated to bring about its physical destruction in whole or in part;
(d) imposing measures intended to prevent births within the group;
(e) forcibly transferring children of the group to another group."

of all Herero land would also support a claim for reparation, but such a claim would not be substantially different from the claims of money by other dispossessed indigenous peoples.

It is the charge of a twentieth century genocide that gives the Herero claim for reparations its weight and credibility in the international arena. In the context of post World War Two reparations paid by Germany to Israel, as well as to individual Jews, arising from acts of genocide, the claim of the Hereros raises issues of equity and of racism in the application of international law.[14] When compared to the hundreds of 'ordinary' colonial wars, in relation to which the idea of reparations may seem somewhat abstract and remote, the Herero War is a twentieth century war, waged by Germany, during what may be regarded as an early stage of a virulently racist and nationalist campaign against many peoples of the world, that culminated in the Second World War. The Herero have insisted on analysing the war and its result in this way.[15]

2 THE HERERO DEMAND FOR REPARATIONS

After the end of German rule in South West Africa in 1915 the Herero people reconstituted themselves in remarkable ways. By the 1920s, many returned from Bechuanaland, moving back to their lands north and east of Windhoek. They began farming and raising cattle, entering into a range of legal and illegal relationships with local white farmers, sometimes squatting on government owned land, sometimes working as labourers, sometimes buying land. They were hard workers and by the 1950s had rebuilt substantially their herds together with a substantial dairy industry. Good relations with local white farmers and with the Namibian government led to several reserves being created for the purpose of returning land to the Herero people. Hereroland changed boundaries several times after the first reserves were created in the early 1920s, but it was a sizable tract of land, holding nearly a million cattle, representing great wealth.[16]

The Herero also experienced a cultural revival. Among the events that galvanised the nation was the repatriation of Samuel Maharero's body and his burial near the

It is the "intent" to commit these acts, as evidenced in Von Trotha's proclamation, that sets Germany's actions in the Herero War apart from similar actions in other colonial wars.

14 Sidney L. Harring, "German Reparations to the Herero Nation: An Assertion of Herero Nationhood in the Path of Namibian Development" 104 *West Virginia Law Review* 393 (2002) at 402-409.

15 "Hereros Seek Compensation on Same Basis as Nazi Slaves," SouthScan, Sept. 9, 2000, Internet at AllAfrica.com.

16 The history of these reserves is mapped in John Mendelsohn and Selma el Obeid, *The Communal Lands in Eastern Namibia*, (2002) at 6-7. South African administrators consolidated these reserves and added more land to create Hereroland, a homeland (created in Namibia by the Odendaal Commission) which extended South Africa's homeland policy into Namibia.

graves of other chiefs at Okahandja in 1925. The date is still celebrated as 'Herero Day', when thousands of Herero return to Okahandja, to speak to their departed chiefs, to feast, to march, and engage in competitions, all in celebration of their heritage.[17] The experience of the war and removal is not far from the heart of this event, a sense of never forgetting, and of preserving their identity.

Similarly, the Herero lands themselves are also remembered in this way. The Herero have returned to Waterburg, and the land there holds great meaning to the people. There are stories and songs that record their history.[18] The cattle are still central to Herero culture and Herero cattle farms spread across hundreds of miles of their traditional lands.

For obvious reasons, there was no open talk of the reparations issue during the period that the South African regime was in control of Namibia. Black Namibians, like Black South Africans, engaged in a bitter war of resistance. The war of liberation was a popular movement, primarily involving the Ovambo, but supported by many Herero. Namibia's independence in 1990 presented the opportunity to raise the reparations issue again, and the Herero did so. Initially, Germany ignored the Herero, but the tribe was not to be dismissed easily.

This history is important in that it structures the logic of Herero reparations. The underlying issue is the forcible deprivation of their lands which, in turn, meant that there was no place to graze Herero cattle, the centre of their culture.[19] But, no direct reparation for land is likely. In few places in the world have indigenous lands been returned once taken by European settler societies. Furthermore, the Government of Namibia does not support such action. Therefore, while the Herero often talk about reparations for the land they were dispossessed of, the actual demand for economic reparations is based on genocide, on the intentional and systematic killing and starvation of the Herero during the 1904/05 war.[20] This claim is grounded in the logic of reparations for Jews and other peoples victimised by the Germans before and during World War Two. An analogy is drawn between the Herero War and the German genocide against the Jews, rather than linking the claim to other African and Asian colonial wars.

It is the linking of the Herero claim for reparations with Holocaust reparations that is the most unique and controversial element of the former claim. This both distances the Herero claim from other African reparations claims, but also links it to

---

17 Wolfgang Werner, *No One Will Become Rich: Economy and Society in the Herero Reserves in Namibia, 1915-1946*, (Basel, Switzerland: P. Schlettwein Publishing, 1998), at 116, 209 and 221.

18 Larissa Forster: "Land and Landscape in Herero Oral Culture: Cultural and Social Aspects of the Land Question in Namibia" *Namibia Institute for Democracy, Analysis and Views*, 1,1 (2005).

19 J.S. Malan, *Peoples of Namibia*, (1995) 67-84; C.H.L. Hahn, H. Vedder, and L. Fourie, *The Native Tribes of South West Africa* (London: Frank Cass and Co., Ltd, 1928), 153-208. It is impossible to overstate the symbolic importance of cattle in Herero culture.

20 John Grobler, "The Tribe Germany Wants to Forget," Mail and Guardian, March 13, 1998.

the law and theory of what are perceived to be the most successful reparations claims to have been brought to date.[21] This link must not be emphasized too much, since an invidious comparison of genocides must be resisted. Nothing that the Herero say in any way dismisses or diminishes the unique crimes that Germany committed against Jews and other social minorities. That being said, genocide is genocide.[22]

Discussion of reparations is often dominated by extensive reference to Jewish claims for reparations against Germany and other countries.[23] But these do not represent the legal boundaries of reparations claims. Even in the context of World War Two, reparations have been paid to others, including $1.2 billion to Americans of Japanese descent for their imprisonment and loss of their lands;[24] a parallel settlement to Japanese Canadians,[25] and claims have been made against the Japanese for reparations for Korean 'comfort women', who were forced into prostitution by the Japanese army.[26] Other European claims raised by various groups subjected to mass extermination in concentration camps, including those of the Romani people, have failed.[27] None of these claims for reparations compare to those in respect of the Jewish Holocaust, but they nevertheless represent important advances in human rights law.

The Herero are very aware of these legally recognised reparations claims, and base their claim accordingly. Mburumba Kerina, a Herero leader, commented on the forced sexual slavery of Herero women carried out by Germans. Comparing this to the case of the Japanese 'comfort women', Kerina explained: 'Hey, that's my grandmother –

---

21 This statement does not mean to dismiss the importance of that discussion, or of seeking a better understanding of the meaning of genocide in human actions. Rather, it is grounded in the futility of rank ordering of various categories of "genocide" for various legal purposes. There is a substantial literature on genocide, in all its aspects. See for instance Frank Chalk and Kurt Jonassohn, *The History and Sociology of Genocide* (New Haven: Yale University Press, 1990).

22 Scholarly efforts to better understand genocide by a comparative approach are few, but the comparative method does offer insight. See Vahakn N. Dadrian, "The Historical and Legal Interconnections between the Armenian genocide and the Jewish Holocaust: from Impunity to Retributive Justice, 23 *Yale Journal of International Law* 503 (1998).

23 Christian Pross, Belinda Cooper, and Erich H. Loewy, *Paying for the Past: The Struggle over Reparations for Surviving Victims of the Nazi Terror*, (Baltimore: The Johns Hopkins University Press, 1998).

24 Mitchell T. Maki, Harry H. Kitano, and Megan S. Berthold, *Achieving the Impossible Dream: How Japanese Americans Obtained Redress*, (Champaign: University of Illinois Press, 1999); Roger Daniels, Sandra Taylor, and Harry Kitano, *Japanese Americans: From Relocation to Redress*, (Seattle: University of Washington Press, 1986); Eric K. Yamamoto, "Racial Reparations: Japanese American Redress and African American Claims," XL *Boston College Law Review* 477 (1998).

25 Roy M. Kobayashi, *Justice in Our Time: The Japanese Canadian Redress Settlement*, (General Distribution Press, 1994).

26 Tong Yu, "Reparations for Former Comfort Women of World War II" 36 *Harvard International Law Journal* 528 (1995).

27 Barry A. Fisher, "No Roads Lead to Rome: The Fate of the Romani People Under the Nazis and in Post-War Restitution", 20 *Whittier Law Review* 513 (1999).

a comfort woman... If the Japanese could pay for that, the Germans could.'[28] This careful attention to the existing international examples of reparations claims is an important strategy adopted by the Herero to support their claim for reparations.

Chancellor Helmut Kohl made a state visit to Namibia in September 1995. Germany is the largest contributor of foreign aid to Namibia and Kohl doubtlessly expected to be well received. He must have been surprised when Chief Kuaima Riruako and three hundred members of the Herero tribe marched on the Germany embassy to submit a petition demanding $600 million in reparations, as well as a meeting with Kohl. Kohl hurriedly left town for the resort city of Swakopmund.

The Herero demonstrations were quite colourful, including 'truppenspeiler', bands dressed in old carefully maintained German uniforms. These bands, part of the Herero revitalisation movement, are deeply rooted in Herero culture, supposedly originating in Herero troops that been trained and uniformed by the Germans, but who thereafter deserted and joined the uprising in 1904. According to one story, these warriors drew German troops into an ambush by calling out to them in flawless German, learned as farm workers and at mission schools. Thus Kohl was, in a sense, ambushed in the same way, during his state visit to the former colony, 'captured' by the Herero and their demand for reparations.[29] Since this event, the reparations issue emerges whenever high-level German officials visit Namibia. It is clearly a source of embarrassment to the German government.

Germany has consistently denied the Herero claim, officially taking the position that it supported and continues to support foreign aid to the country as a whole. Germany is careful never to admit that any form of genocide occurred, but its position may be changing.[30] In August 2004 Germany did issue an apology for its actions during the Herero War at the 100-year commemoration of the war at Waterburg, but the apology was expressed in very general language. Minister of Economic Cooperation and Development Heidemarie Wieczorek-Zeul, representing the German Government stated: 'And so, in the words of the Lord's prayer that we share, I ask you to forgive our trespass.' She went on to say that 'atrocities committed at the time would today be termed genocide and a General von Trotha would be prosecuted and convicted.'[31]

---

[28] Donald G. McNeil, Jr., "Its Past on Its Sleeve, Tribe Seeks Bonn's Apology", New York Times, May 31, 1998, 1, 3. Kerina is apparently making a political point about the comparison between the Herero situation and the Japanese lawsuit. There is a legal distinction. Many "comfort women" are alive and are personally seeking from the Japanese government reparations for their injuries. None of the Herero women forced into sexual slavery is alive.

[29] Reuters News Service, "Namibian Tribe Protests Against German Massacre", Sept. 15, 1995. The Truppenspieler (literally "troop players") appear at Herero occasions. Wolfgang Werner, "Playing Soldiers": The Truppenspieler Movement among the Herero of Namibia, 1915-1945" *Journal of Southern African Studies* 16, 3 (Sept. 1990), 485-502. The movement is unique to Namibia.

[30] Donald G. McNeil, Jr, "Its Past on Its Sleeve, Tribe Seeks Bonn's Apology", New York Times, May 31, 1998, 3; John Grobler, "The Tribe Germany Wants to Forget", Mail and Guardian, March 13, 1998; "Reparations not on the Table", Namibian, Aug. 31, 2000.

[31] "Forgive Us, Says Germany", Namibia, Aug. 16, 2004.

Herero, on the same podium, were caught off guard, but recognised the significance of this carefully worded statement. Former deputy foreign minister Kaire Mbuende commented: 'Apology and then what?...It is hanging in the air. How is Germany going to own up to it?'[32]

Not making sufficient progress with the German government, the Herero Traditional Authority, led by Chief Riruako, filed a lawsuit in the United States against two German companies – Deutsche Bank and Woermann Line (now known as SAF Marine) that had done business in colonial South West Africa – and the German Government, demanding $2 billion in damages for loss of life, land, and cattle in the Herero war.[33] While the action against the German government has been stayed at the request of the United States Department of State, at the time of writing the suit against the two German companies is still active.[34] There have been rumours that the German government entered into secret negotiations to settle the claim, but these have been officially denied by Germany.[35]

Reparations, while they are certainly a legal matter, are also deeply political in nature. Indeed, the primary impact of the lawsuit has been political. The Herero have stated a clear position on their demand for reparations that can no longer be ignored.

For Germany, the mere existence of the Herero demand for reparations forces the government to confront the consequences of its colonial wars in Namibia, in the same way it has confronted the consequences of its actions in European wars. Germany should not be allowed to distinguish the two kinds of wars when it comes to reparations. In acknowledging guilt and paying reparations in Europe, Germany should do the same in Africa. The distinction is ultimately one that goes to the underlying issue of racism: is it somehow less culpable to kill Africans? Or is genocide in Africa different to genocide in Europe? Germany has, in fact, weakened its own position by arguing that under international law, the colonial wars are not actionable as acts of genocide, while European wars are. In 1998 on a visit to Namibia, German President Roman Herzog proclaimed that there was no international law at the time of the Herero War that would form the basis for the payment of reparations.[36] When Herero activist Mberumba Kerina responded by arguing that the Hague Convention of 1899 outlawed 'reprisals against civilians on the losing side', Herzog responded that

32 *Ibid.*

33 "Hereros to Pursue Another Avenue on Reparations" Namibian, Oct. 13, 2003; "Germany Mulls Remedy other than Reparations" Aug. 6, 2004; Herero Lawsuit Still Standing" www.grnnet.gov.na/News/Archive/2004/February/week3/herero.htm.

34 *Ibid.* Chief Riruako states, "we will never withdraw the case because we know that we have a legitimate right to demand for reparation."

35 "Germany Mulls Remedy other than Reparations", Namibian, Aug. 6, 2004; "Germany Denies Herero Negotiations", Namibian, Dec. 9, 2004.

36 John Grobbler, "The Tribe Germany Wants to Forget" Electronic Mail and Guardian, March 13, 1998.

too much time had passed – and blamed his translator for mistranslating his earlier statements.[37]

3 THE HERERO AND THEIR REPARATIONS CLAIM IN NAMIBIAN POLITICS

While there is no question that the Herero intend the main object of their reparations claim to be Germany, the claim has struck a complex chord in Namibian politics that is intended by the Herero. Namibia is a multi-ethnic nation, brought together by a lengthy war for independence. The Ovambo, a group of northern tribes, constitute over 50% of the population of the entire country, and dominate the government and the political process. Sam Nujoma, First President of Namibia, is an Ovambo, as is the current President, Hifikepunye Pohamba.

The Namibian government strongly takes the position that Namibia is one nation whose peoples suffered together under colonialism. Accordingly, in the view of the government there should be no individual restitution schemes for particular people or tribes. In the area of land reform this view manifests itself as the idea that there can be no restitution of particular lands to particular people. In the area of reparations, the government takes the view that Germany should make its aid available to the entire nation, through the government, and not make any effort to pay reparations to any particular group or tribe.[38]

The Government's longstanding opposition to reparations claims seemed to shift suddenly in early December 2005 during a meeting in Germany. At that meeting President Pohamba unexpectedly announced that Namibia would sign an agreement with Germany for $20 million Euros for reparations to the Herero, Nama, Damara, and all of the communities who suffered under German rule, and that this money would be used for economic development. Immediately, there was a protest that these tribes had not been consulted about this agreement and further negotiations were put on hold pending those discussions.[39] The Herero Genocide Committee immediately 'lambasted' the Government for proposing the agreement without consultations with the affected people.[40] Whatever the Government's intentions may be, its support may well make it more likely that the Herero reparations claim will be settled in due course.

---

37 *Ibid.*

38 "Hereros Seek Compensation on Same Basis as Nazi Slaves", SouthScan, Sept. 9, 2002, at http://allafrica.com/stories/200009090019.html.

39 IRINnews.org/report.asp?ReportID=50480.

40 *Ibid.*

While this position might make political sense, especially from the standpoint of a national government that would be strengthened by German aid, it runs the risk of playing down the fact that tribal groups other than the Herero also suffered greatly in the past. The Herero may have born the brunt of German power in the Herero war, but up to half of the Nama in the country were also killed, and some of their lands lost. The Ovambo lived north of the German 'police line', the effective line of control, so their cattle and lands were not lost to the Germans. But the Ovambo did fight the Germans on several occasions. During more recent times the Ovambo who live near the northern border of Namibia were hardest hit in the national war of liberation in the 1980s. This means that other tribal groups resent the Herero claim for reparations and consider it both divisive, and evidence that the Herero have a tribal identity that is put above the Namibian state.

The Herero insistence on promoting their demand for reparations takes place within this difficult social context. It is a claim of Herero nationalism within Namibia, asserted against national policy and over the will of other tribes. Thus, while the claim may unify the Herero and build internal Herero cohesion, its effects are divisive within the rest of Namibia.

The Namibian government has not stood idly by, but has used its considerable power to undermine the Herero claim. Its most basic weapon is through its power to appoint chiefs, through the Traditional Authorities Act. The government has refused to confirm Chief Riruako, meaning that it does not recognise legally that he is, in fact, a Herero chief. At the same time, the government has confirmed other Herero chiefs that – officially at least – do not support the reparations claim. Forty-one Herero chiefs sued the government for recognition and the Namibian High Court ruled in favour of the chiefs on procedural grounds, but sent the process back to the government for reconsideration.[41]

This division also reflects political divisions within Namibia. Chief Riruako is a long time leader of the DTA Party, the main opposition party to the ruling SWAPO.[42] Many of the newly confirmed Herero chiefs are members of SWAPO, which uses its extensive political clout to reward its followers and discipline its opponents. While it may be assumed that Chief Riruako is a traditional chief of long standing and that the majority of Herero are, like Riruako, supporters of the DTA, there is a division within the country over this reparations claim that is also creeping into internal Herero politics. The extent of this is difficult to measure within the complex arena of Namibian politics.[43]

---

41 "Hereros, Himba Challenge Government in Court", Namibian March 2, 2001; "Hereros to March As Legal Challenge Starts", Namibian, March 1, 2001.

42 "DTA Slams Government over Recognition of Herero Chiefs", Namibian, Aug. 20, 2004.

43 Namibian Human Rights On-Line Journal, 2004, at 1-3, www.hrdc.unam.na/journal/Events.htm.

In turn, the traditional Herero chiefs who support the reparations claim both intend to promote Herero tribal interests as well as to demonstrate that the SWAPO government, dominated by members of the Ovamo tribe, has not done enough to redress past wrongs, not only the wrongs inflicted by Germany, but the wrongs of apartheid under South African rule. The Herero claim is not dependant on the SWAPO government. Moreover, it undermines the Government's political goal of pursuing close relations with Germany, and unsettles the accepted perception that Germany is Namibia's largest aid donor for reasons of generosity and the cultural links which exist between the two countries.

Finally, underlying the whole claim is the issue that started the Herero War: land and cattle. The Namibian government, while always committed to a program of land reform, has not achieved much in this respect in the years since independence. Only in 2005 did the government begin to expropriate farms, having relied on a slow and expensive process of 'willing buyer, willing seller'.[44]

Because there is no policy of restitution of individual lands taken by the Germans or South Africans, there is no real prospect that the Herero are going to regain much of their land under the SWAPO government's program of land reform. With adequate compensation, however, the tribe could initiate a wide variety of its own social programs, including the restoration of hundreds of formerly Herero farms.

The pressure for land reform is primarily in the north of Namibia. The land in this area is occupied by approximately 800,000 Ovambo and is seriously overcrowded and the people impoverished.[45] Herero lands are much less densely occupied, and are located in the central part of the country.[46] There is not likely to be substantial land reform in this area. Moreover, the land reform that will occur will take place without regard to tribe. This is consistent with the SWAPO government's policy against individual land restoration. This means that it is not necessarily the Herero who will gain land in former Herero areas. The communal lands of Eastern Namibia – the former Herero homeland – are currently the home of only about 32,000 Herero, out of a total population of about 112,000. This reality lies just below the surface of Namibian politics and raises extremely difficult social and political issues.

SWAPO, with its main power base to be found among the Ovambo, as the current Namibian government, has also played a mean and petty politics of domination against other Namibian peoples. The Himba, another Herero tribe, have been shabbily treated

---

44 Sidney Harring and Willem Odendaal, *One Day We Will All Be Equal* (2002) at 35-36.

45 John Mendelsohn, Selma el Obeid and Carole Roberts, *A Profile of North Central Namibia* (Windhoek: Gamsberg Macmillan Publishers, 2000) is an atlas that reveals the overcrowding and poverty of Ovambo lands.

46 John Mendelsohn and Selma el Obeid, *The Communal Lands in Eastern Namibia* (Windhoek: Namibian Nature Foundation, 2002) is an atlas of the Herero and San areas of Namibia, showing lower population densities than in Ovambo areas.

in the context of a proposed hydro-power scheme.[47] The Basters have lost many of their land rights in a long-standing dispute with the government.[48] The Fwe in Caprivi raised a small insurrection in 1999.[49] One hundred Herero traditional leaders, including Paramount Chief Riruako, marched on the Namibian government in 1998 to protest the lack of legal recognition of their status.[50] All this demonstrates a complex pattern of Ovambo domination over smaller tribes – and all tribes in Namibia are much smaller than the Ovambo.

Already substantial numbers of Ovambo have taken lands in areas that were formerly occupied by other groups. The Rehoboth Basters, a mixed race people occupying farmland south of Windhoek have lost much of their land to Ovambo in the recent past.[51] Similarly, the former San homeland 'Bushmanland' has been divided among several thousand occupants, mostly Ovambo and Kavango, at the expense of the San.[52] The Herero tribe's claim of reparations stakes out its own development scheme, independent of the SWAPO government, and potentially protects the Herero land base.

4 CONCLUSION

The Herero claim for reparations is one of many arising from colonial killings, enslavement, and loss of land in Africa over the past four hundred years. It is unique

47 Sidney L. Harring, "'God Gave Us This Land': The OvaHimba, the Proposed Epupa Dam, the Independent Namibian State, and Law and Development in Africa", XIV *Georgetown Journal of International Environmental Law* 35 (2001).

48 Y.J.D. Peeters, "On the Discrimination of the Rehoboth Basters: An Indigenous People in the Republic of Namibia", paper submitted to the Working Group on Indigenous Populations" Geneva, July-August, 1993; Rudolf G. Britz et al, *A Concise History of the Rehoboth Basters until 1990*, (Windhoek: Klaus Hess Publishers, 1999). *The Rehoboth Bastergemeente v. The Government of the Republic of Namibia*, Case No. SA5/05, delivered May 14, 1996.

49 "Playing Politics in West Caprivi", Namibian June 20, 1997; "More than 1000 Have Fled Namibia", Mail and Guardian (on line), Nov. 17. 1998 It is not entirely clear what occurred on August 2, 1999 and there is some evidence that the government of Namibia has exaggerated the nature of the "insurrection." Maria Fisch *The Secessionist Movement in the Caprivi: A Historical Perspective* (Windhoek: Namibian Scientific Society, 1999).

50 "Herero Chiefs March on Government," Electronic Mail and Guardian, April 24, 1998. Under the Traditional Authorities Act, traditional chiefs have local governmental powers and are paid a salary by the Namibian state.

51 Y.J.D. Peeters, "On the Discrimination of the Rehoboth Basters: An Indigenous People in the Republic of Namibia" paper submitted to the Working Group on Indigenous Populations Geneva, July-August, 1993; Rudolf G. Britz et al, *A Concise History of the Rehoboth Basters until 1990*, (Windhoek: Klaus Hess Publishers, 1999). The Baster community unsuccessfully sued the Government of Namibia over their land title which then opened the way for the resettlement of non-Basters on their former lands. *The Rehoboth Bastergemeente v. The Government of the Republic of Namibia*, Case No. SA5/05, delivered May 14, 1996.

52 John Mendelsohn and Selma el Obeid, *The Communal Lands in Eastern Namibia* (2002), 6-7.

in that the Herero have chosen to frame it in the context of European genocide in World War Two. This sets this reparations claim apart from other African reparations claims. Because the claim is against Germany, alleging genocide for German military actions in a twentieth century war, the Herero have seized on an obvious historical connection, which has given their reparations claims international publicity and increased currency. Even the remoteness of Namibia works to the advantage of the Herero claim. While other nations such as the United States, Britain, France, and South Africa are able to defend such claims by arguing that it is historically 'impossible' to identify victims and make reparations, this is not true of the Herero claim. Germany could settle the claim for a fraction of its World War Two reparations payments and, in doing so, would set little precedent for other African claims.

This is both a strength and a weakness in the Herero claim. The Herero have constructed their claim for reparations in the form most likely to put political pressure on Germany and the Namibian government. It has certainly done so. Every people has the right to determine their own struggle to regain their lost land, dignity, and culture. It is not for others to judge the Herero claim. Rather, it is for each people to engage fully the distinct models of reparations claims used in the past in order to determine which model might work best for them. Each claim is socially and historically specific, even though the injuries suffered are often similar from people to people. Every possible model must be considered by victims seeking to make a claim for reparations. It is hoped that, in this way, the number of successful models will grow over the coming years.

In the current context, for the Herero, reference to Germany and the Holocaust makes political sense. The persistence of this reparations claim, in a world in which few claims of other tribes are taken seriously, validates that legal and political judgment. It would be a great advance in the wider movement toward reparations if the Herero were to successfully claim reparations from Germany in any form.

NOTE ON THE AUTHORS

Roy L. Brooks

Professor Roy L. Brooks is Warren Distinguished Professor of Law at the University of San Diego School of Law. He received his JD in 1975 from Yale University where he served as a senior editor of the Yale Law Journal. He has taught at the University of San Diego since 1979 where he teaches and writes in the areas of civil procedure, civil rights, employment discrimination, jurisprudence, critical theory, and reparations. He is the author of more than 20 books and supplements, including *Rethinking the American Race Problem* (University of California Press) and *Integration or Separation? A Strategy for Racial Equality* (Harvard University Press), both of which received the Gustavus Meyers Outstanding Book Award for civil rights. His writings on reparations include *When Sorry Isn't Enough: The Controversy over Apologies and Reparations for Human Injustice* (New York University Press, 1999) and *Atonement and Forgiveness: A New Model for Black Reparations* (University of California Press, 2004). Prof. Brooks has also written more than 100 articles and book chapters and presented more than 100 papers. He is a member of the American Law Institute.

Ken Cooper-Stephenson

LLB (London), LLM (Cambridge), LLD (London) 2000. Professor Cooper-Stephenson has been a member of the Faculty of Law, University of Saskatchewan, since 1971. He was previously a founding faculty member at the University of Leicester, England (1966-71). He has acted as Assistant Dean at Saskatchewan, and is currently Faculty Supervisor of the Saskatchewan Law Review. He has also taught in Australia at Bond University and James Cook University of Northern Queensland. His publications include *Personal Injury Damages in Canada* (1981, 1996); *Charter Damages Claims* (1990); and (co-editor), *Tort Theory* (1993), as well as articles and book chapters on tort law, damages, legal theory, constitutional law and reparations. In 2000 he was committee Chair for the statutory review of Saskatchewan's no-fault auto-accident insurance plan. Most recently he was consultant for the Assembly of First Nations' Report on Abuse in Residential Schools.

Max du Plessis

B Iuris (SA) LLB (Natal) LLM (Cambridge). Max du Plessis is an Associate Professor in the Faculty of Law, University of KwaZulu-Natal, Howard College Campus, Durban, South Africa. He is an Advocate of the High Court of South Africa and an Associate Member of the KwaZulu-Natal Bar. He is a Research Associate at Matrix Chambers,

London. He specialises in international law and human rights and has published a number of articles in this field.

Michael Freeman

BA, LLB, PhD. Professor Freeman is a Research Professor, Department of Government, University of Essex, United Kingdom. His research interests are in human rights theory, especially transitional justice, reparations, the right to health, and, generally, interdisciplinary approaches to human rights. He was formerly Deputy Director of the Human Rights Centre, University of Essex, and Chairperson of Amnesty International's British Section. In 2006 he was Torgny Segerstedt Visiting Professor, Institute for the Study of Human Rights, Gothenburg University, Sweden.

Sid Harring

Sid Harring holds a law degree and a PhD in sociology from the Univesity of Wisconsin and has taught at the City University of New York School of Law since 1983. He taught at the University of Namibia Law Faculty in 1995 and has been working on indigenous and communal land rights in Namibia for ten years.

Mark Harris

BA (Hons), LLB (University of Melbourne); Dip Ed (MCAE); MA (Monash University); PhD (Latrobe University). Dr Harris is a Barrister and Solicitor of the Supreme Court of Victoria and the High Court of Australia, and a Senior Lecturer, School of Law, La Trobe University, Bundoora, Australia. His research interests include Indigenous Peoples' Rights, Environmental Law, Water Law, Human Rights Law, and Race and the Law.

Catherine Jenkins

MA (Oxon), LLM, DESU. Catherine Jenkins is Chair of the Centre for Law & Conflict at SOAS, University of London, where she lectures in transitional justice and human rights law. She was a close observer of the South African Truth and Reconciliation Commission and has published a number of articles reflecting on its work and addressing issues of reparation, reconciliation and reconstruction in South Africa and other post-conflict societies. Her forthcoming monograph is an examination of the use of amnesty in conflict resolution and peace-building, with particular reference to the South African experience. She is currently editing (with Max du Plessis and Karthy Govender) a collection of essays on 'Law, Nationbuilding & Transformation: The South African Experience in Perspective'.

Bo Jung Kwon

Ms Kwon received her BA in political science, *magna cum laude*, from Yale University in 2005. She currently works at Soros Fund Management LLC in New York City.

Regula Ludi

Dr. Ludi is a historian and research fellow at the Karman Center for Advanced Studies in the Humanities, University of Berne. She is working on a book on Reparations for Nazi Victims in France, Germany and Switzerland. She worked as a staff historian for the Independent Commission of Experts Switzerland – Second World War (1997-2000) and was a research fellow at the Minda de Gunzburg Center for European Studies, Harvard University, the Center for Eurasian Studies, UCLA, and the Center for Advanced Holocaust Studies, Washington DC. Among her recent publications are: 'The Vectors of Postwar Victim Reparations: Relief, Redress and Memory Politics,' Journal of Contemporary History 41:3 (2006), 421-450; 'What Is So Special about Switzerland? Wartime Memory as a National Ideology in the Cold War Era,' in Richard Ned Lebow, Wulf Kansteiner and Claudio Fogu (eds), The Politics of Memory in Postwar Europe (Durham, London: Duke University Press, 2006), 210-248.

Mahmood Mamdani

Professor Mamdani is from Kampala, Uganda. He received his PhD in Government from Harvard University. He is currently Herbert Lehman Professor of Government in the Departments of Anthropology, Political Science and International and Public Affairs at Columbia University, where he was also director of the Institute of African Studies from 1999 to 2004. He has taught at the University of Dar-es-Salaam (1973-79), Makerere University (1980-93), and the University of Cape Town (1996-99) and was the founding director of the Centre for Basic Research in Kampala, Uganda (1987-96). Professor Mamdani is the author of *Good Muslim, Bad Muslim: America, the Cold War and the Origins of Terror* (Pantheon, 2004), *When Victims Become Killers: Colonialism, Nativism and Genocide in Rwanda* (Princeton, 2001) and *Citizen and Subject: Contemporary Africa and the Legacy of Late Colonialism* (Princeton, 1996), as well as ten other books. *Citizen and Subject* was recognised as '*one of Africa's 100 best books of the 20th century*' in Cape Town in 2003 and was also awarded the Herskovitz Prize of the African Studies Association of USA for '*the best book on Africa published in the English language in 1996.*' Mahmood Mamdani was President of CODESRIA (Council for the Development of Social Research in Africa) from 1999 to 2002. In 2001, he was invited to present one of nine papers at the Nobel Peace Prize Centennial Symposium in Oslo. In 2004, he presented one of nine papers at the African Union-organised Global Meeting of Intellectuals from Africa and the African Diaspora in Dakar.

Michael Osborne

BA, LLB (Wits) LLM (Notre Dame). Michael Osborne has lectured at the University of Chicago Law School, at the New School for Social Research, and at the law schools of the Universities of Cape Town and the Witwatersrand. He practiced law at Davis Polk and Wardwell in New York City, and is a member of the New York Bar and of the Cape Bar. He practices International, Constitutional and Administrative law in Cape Town., and is representing plaintiffs seeking reparations for apartheid under the Alien Torts Statute in Federal Court in New York City.

Andreas O'Shea

An honorary professor at the University of KwaZulu-Natal, Andreas O'Shea completed his PhD thesis at the University of the Witwatersrand. Professor O'Shea completed the Licence Special (International and European Law)(distinction) at the University of Louvain La Neuve, University of Liege, and in 1992 was called to the Bar of England and Wales (member of Lincoln's Inn). He has published substantially in the field of international criminal law. Professor O'Shea is currently practising before the International Criminal Tribunals for Rwanda and the former Yugoslavia and the Special Court for Sierra Leone. He is a Door Tenant at the Chambers of Mr Rock Tansey QC, 25 Bedford Row, London.

Stephen Peté

BA LLB (Natal) LLM (Cape Town) M Phil (Criminology) (Cambridge). Stephen Peté is an Associate Professor in the Faculty of Law, University of KwaZulu-Natal, Howard College Campus, Durban, South Africa. He practiced as an Attorney of the High Court of South Africa in both the public and private sectors for many years. He has authored and co-authored a number of articles and textbooks in the fields of civil procedure, jurisprudence, criminology and human rights.

Diane E. Sammons

Diane E. Sammons is a partner with the law firm of Nagel Rice & Mazie, in New Jersey. She received her undergraduate degree in Government from the College of William & Mary in Williamsburg, Virginia and her law degree from Seton Hall University. A portion of her legal practice is devoted to human rights law including efforts on behalf of non-governmental entities in Austria and the Czech Republic to secure documentation through the Freedom of Information Act, as well as being appointed co-lead counsel in the first-ever class-action U.S. slavery reparations case against corporations who benefited from the profits of slavery. These efforts were followed by the filing of a class-action suit against U.S. and European companies seeking reparations on behalf of victims of apartheid. She is completing a three-year appointment as Chancellor (legal advisor) to the Episcopal Church of the Diocese of Newark where she oversees all legal matters for the 113-church Diocese and has recently been appointed by the Presiding Bishop of the Episcopal Church of the United States to serve on its Constitution and Canons Committee. She has appeared as a guest on major national and international news programs and has spoken extensively on human rights law and on canon law.

Jeremy Sarkin

BA LLB (Natal) LLM (Harvard) LLD (UWC). Jeremy Sarkin is a Senior Professor of Law at the University of the Western Cape in Cape Town South Africa and Visiting Professor of International Human Rights at the Fletcher School of Law and Diplomacy at Tufts University in Boston. He is admitted to practice as an attorney in the United States of America and South Africa. Some of his present areas of research, which fall broadly within the constitutional and human rights fields, are on the role and functioning of national human rights institutions, transitional justice, reparations for historical human rights violations, developing a human rights culture and the role of the courts. He has worked on constitutional and transitional issues in various countries, including Rwanda, the Democratic Republic of the Congo, Sierra Leone, Ethiopia, Angola, Namibia and Burma, and has assisted various truth commissions in their work. His recent books in the field of transitional justice are *Carrots and Sticks: The TRC and the South African Amnesty Process* (Intersentia 2004) and *Reconciliation in Divided Societies: Finding Common Ground* (University of Pennsylvania Press 2006).

Yasmin L. Sooka

Yasmin Louise Sooka is Executive Director of the Foundation for Human Rights in South Africa. She is Council and Senate member of the University of Witwatersrand in South Africa and a former Commissioner of the Truth and Reconciliation Commission for Sierra Leone (2002-April 2004), and a former Truth Commissioner on the South African Truth and Reconciliation Commission (1995-2002). While working for the South Africa TRC she was Chairperson of the Human Rights Violations Committee of the Commission (as well as the Chair of the Legal Sub-Committee). She is a former Executive Director of the Panel of Religious Leaders for Electoral Justice.